H. P. BLAVATSKY
COLLECTED WRITINGS

FROM THE CAVES AND JUNGLES
OF HINDOSTAN

H. P. BLAVATSKY

COLLECTED WRITINGS

FROM THE CAVES AND JUNGLES
OF HINDOSTAN

By

RADDA-BAI
(H. P. BLAVATSKY)

Translated from the Russian

1883-1886

THE THEOSOPHICAL PUBLISHING HOUSE
WHEATON, ILL., U.S.A.
MADRAS, INDIA / LONDON, ENGLAND

© Copyright The Theosophical Publishing House, 1975

*The Theosophical Publishing House, Wheaton, Illinois,
is a department of The Theosophical Society in America*

First edition, 1975
Second printing, 1983
Third printing, 1993

Blavatsky, Helene Petrovna Hahn-Hahn, 1831-1891.
  From the caves and jungles of Hindostan, 1883-1886.

  (Her Collected writings)
  1. India—Description and travel—1859-1900.
2. India—Religion.   3. Tibet—Description and travel.
4. Tibet—Religion.   5. Blavatsky, Helene Petrovna
Hahn-Hahn, 1831-1891.   I. Title.   II. Series.
BP561.A1 1950, suppl [DS413] 212'.52s [915.4'04'35]
ISBN 0-8356-0219-2   74-26605

Printed in the United States of America

PREFACE

[This Preface applies to the entire Edition of H. P. Blavatsky's *Collected Writings*, and not to the present volume only. Together with the Acknowledgments which follow, it was published for the first time in Volume V of the present Series, issued in 1950.]

I

The writings of H. P. Blavatsky, the chief Founder of the modern Theosophical Movement, are becoming with every day more widely known.

They constitute in their totality one of the most astounding products of the creative human mind. Considering their unequalled erudition, their prophetic nature, and their spiritual depth, they must be classed, by friend and foe alike, as being among the inexplicable phenomena of the age. Even a cursory survey of these writings discloses their monumental character.

The best known among them are of course those which appeared in book form and have gone through several editions: *Isis Unveiled* (New York, 1877), *The Secret Doctrine* (London and New York, 1888), *The Key to Theosophy* (London, 1889), *The Voice of the Silence* (London and New York, 1889), *Transactions of the Blavatsky Lodge* (London and New York, 1890 and 1891), *Gems from the East* (London, 1890), and the posthumously published *Theosophical Glossary* (London and New York, 1892), *Nightmare Tales* (London and New York, 1892) and *From the Caves and Jungles of Hindustan* (London, New York and Madras, 1892).

Yet the general public, as well as a great many later theosophical students, are hardly aware of the fact that from 1874 to the end of her life, H. P. Blavatsky wrote incessantly, for a wide range of journals and magazines, and that the combined bulk of these scattered writings exceeds even her voluminous output in book form.

The first articles written by H. P. B. were polemical in nature and trenchant in style. They were published in the best known Spiritualistic journals of the day, such as the *Banner of Light* (Boston, Mass.), the *Spiritual Scientist* (Boston, Mass.), the *Religio-Philosophical Journal* (Chicago, Ill.), *The Spiritualist* (London), *La Revue Spirite* (Paris). Simultaneously, she wrote fascinating occult stories for some of the leading American newspapers, including *The World, The Sun* and *The Daily Graphic,* all of New York.

After she went to India, in 1879, she contributed to *The Indian Spectator, The Deccan Star, The Bombay Gazette, The Pioneer, The Amrita Bazaar Pâtrika,* and other newspapers.

For over seven years, namely during the period of 1879-newspaper, *Moskovskiya Vedomosty* (Moscow), and the celebrated periodical, *Russkiy Vestnik* (Moscow), as well as for lesser newspapers, such as *Pravda* (Odessa), *Tiflisskiy Vestnik* (Tiflis), *Rebus* (St. Petersburg), and others.

After founding her first theosophical magazine, *The Theosophist* (Bombay and Madras), in October, 1879, she poured into its pages an enormous amount of invaluable teaching, which she continued to give forth at a later date in the pages of her London magazine, *Lucifer,* the short-lived *Revue Théosophique* of Paris, and *The Path* of New York.

While carrying on this tremendous literary output, she found time to engage in polemical discussions with a number of writers and scholars in the pages of other periodicals, especially the *Bulletin Mensuel* of the Société d'Études Psychologiques of Paris, and *Le Lotus* (Paris). In addition to all this, she wrote a number of small pamphlets and Open Letters, which were published separately, on various occasions.

In this general survey no more than mere mention can be made of her voluminous correspondence, many portions 1886, she wrote serial stories for the well-known Russian

of which contain valuable teachings, and of her private *Instructions* which she issued after 1888 to the members of the Esoteric Section.

After 25 years of unremitting research, the individual articles written by H. P. B. in English, French, Russian and Italian, may be estimated at close to *one thousand.* Of special interest to readers is the fact that a considerable number of her French and Russian essays, containing in some cases teachings not stated anywhere else, and never before fully translated into any other language, are now for the first time made available in English.

II

For many years students of the Esoteric Philosophy have been looking forward to the ultimate publication of the writings of H. P. Blavatsky in a collected and convenient form. It is now hoped that this desire may be realized in the publication of the present series of volumes. They constitute a uniform edition of the entire literary output of the Great Theosophist, as far as can be ascertained after years of painstaking research all over the world. These writings are arranged in strictly chronological order according to the date of their original publication in the various magazines, journals, newspapers and other periodicals, or their appearance in book or pamphlet form. Students are thus in a position to trace the progressive unfoldment of H. P. B.'s mission, and to see the method which she used in the gradual presentation of the teachings of the Ancient Wisdom, beginning with her first article in 1874. In a very few instances an article or two appears out of chronological sequence, because there exists convincing evidence that it was written at a much earlier date, and must have been held unprinted for a rather long time. Such articles belong to an earlier date than the date of their actual publication, and have been placed accordingly.

Unless otherwise stated, all writings have been copied *verbatim et literatim* direct from the original sources. In a very few cases, when such source was either unknown, or, if known, was entirely unprocurable, articles have been copied from other publications where they had been reprinted, apparently from original sources, many years ago.

There has been no editing whatsoever of H. P. B.'s literary style, grammar or spelling. Obvious typographical errors, however, have been corrected throughout. Her own spelling of Sanskrit technical terms and proper names has been preserved. No attempt has been made to introduce any uniformity or consistency in these particulars. However, the correct systemic spelling of all Oriental technical terms and proper names, according to present-day scholastic standards, is used in the English translations of original French and Russian material, as well as in the Index wherein it appears within square brackets immediately following such terms or names.*

A systematic effort has been made to verify the many quotations introduced by H. P. B. from various works, and all references have been carefully checked. In every case original sources have been consulted for this verification, and if any departures from the original text were found, these were corrected. Many of the writings quoted could be consulted only in such large Institutions as the British Museum of London, the Bibliothèque Nationale of Paris, the Library of Congress, Washington, D. C., and the Lenin State Library of Moscow. In some cases works quoted remained untraceable. No attempt was made to check quotations from current newspapers, as the transitory nature of the material used did not seem to justify the effort.

Throughout the text, there are to be found many footnotes signed "Ed.," "Editor," "Ed., *Theos.*," or "Editor, *The Theosophist*"; also footnotes which are unsigned. It should be distinctly remembered that all these footnotes are H. P. B.'s own, and are *not* by the Compiler of the present volumes.

All material added by the Compiler—either as footnotes

---

*See explanatory Note on page 662.

or as explanatory comments appended to certain articles—
is enclosed within square brackets and signed "Compiler."
Obvious editorial explanations or summaries preceding
articles or introducing H. P. B.'s comments are merely
placed within square brackets.

Occasionally brief sentences appear which are within
square brackets, even in the main body of the text or in
H. P. B.'s own footnotes. These bracketed remarks are
evidently by H. P. B. herself, although the reason for such
usage is not readily apparent.

In a very few instances, which are self-evident, the
Compiler has added within square brackets an obviously
missing word or digit, to complete the meaning of the
sentence.

H. P. B.'s text is followed by an Appendix which consists
of three sections:

(a) Bibliography of Oriental Works which provides
concise information regarding the best known editions of
the Sacred Scriptures and other Oriental writings quoted
from or referred to by H. P. B.

(b) General Bibliography wherein can be found, apart
from the customary particulars regarding all works quoted
or referred to, succinct biographical data concerning the
less known writers, scholars, and public figures mentioned
by H. P. B. in the text, or from whose writings she quotes.
It has been thought of value to the student to have this
collected information which is not otherwise easily obtain-
able.

(c) Index of subject matter.

Following the Preface, a brief historical survey will be
found in the form of a Chronological Table embodying
fully documented data regarding the whereabouts of H. P. B.
and Col. Henry S. Olcott, as well as the chief events in
the history of the Theosophical Movement, within the
period covered by the material contained in any one volume
of the Series.

III

The majority of articles written by H. P. Blavatsky, for both magazines and newspapers, are signed by her, either with her own name or with one of her rather infrequent pseudonyms, such as Hadji Mora, Râddha-Bai, Sañjñâ, "Adversary," and others.

There are however, a great many unsigned articles, both in Theosophical journals and elsewhere. Some of these have been included because a most careful study by a number of students thoroughly familiar with H. P. B.'s characteristic literary style, her well-known idiosyncrasies of expression, and her frequent usage of foreign idiom, has shown them to be from H. P. B.'s pen, even though no *irrefutable* proof of this can be advanced. Other unsigned articles are mentioned in early Theosophical books, memoirs and pamphlets, as having been written by H. P. B. In still other cases, clippings of such articles were pasted by H. P. B. in her many *Scrapbooks* (now in the Adyar Archives), with pen-and-ink notations establishing her authorship. Several articles are known to have been produced by other writers, yet were almost certainly corrected by H. P. B. or added to by her, or possibly written by them under her own more or less direct inspiration. These have been included with appropriate comments.

A perplexing problem presents itself in connection with H. P. B.'s writings of which the casual reader is probably unaware. It is the fact that H. P. B. often acted as an amanuensis for her own Superiors in the Occult Hierarchy. At times whole passages were dictated to her by her own Teacher or other Adepts and advanced Chelas. These passages are nevertheless tinged throughout with the very obvious peculiarities of her own inimitable style, and are sometimes interspersed with remarks definitely emanating from her own mind. This entire subject involves rather recondite mysteries connected with the transmission of occult communications from Teacher to disciple.

At the time of his first contact with the Masters, through the intermediation of H. P. B., A. P. Sinnett sought for an explanation of the process mentioned above and elicited the following reply from Master K. H.:

". . . Besides, bear in mind that these my letters are not written, but *impressed*, or precipitated, and then all mistakes corrected. . . .

". . . I have to think it over, to photograph every word and sentence carefully in my brain, before it can be repeated by precipitation. As the fixing on chemically prepared surfaces of the images formed by the camera requires a previous arrangement within the focus of the object to be represented, for otherwise—as often found in bad photographs—the legs of the sitter might appear out of all proportion with the head, and so on—so we have to first arrange our sentences and impress every letter to appear on paper in our minds before it becomes fit to be read. For the present it is *all* I can tell you. When science will have learned more about the mystery of the lithophyl (or litho-biblion), and how the impress of leaves comes originally to take place on stones, then I will be able to make you better understand the process. But you must know and remember one thing—we but follow and servilely copy Nature in her works."*

In an article entitled "Precipitation", H. P. B., referring directly to the passage quoted above, writes as follows:

"Since the above was written, the Masters have been pleased to permit the veil to be drawn aside a little more, and the *modus operandi* can thus be explained now more fully to the outsider . . .

". . . The work of writing the letters in question is carried on by a sort of psychological telegraphy; the Mahatmas very rarely write their letters in the ordinary way. An electro-magnetic connection, so to say, exists on the psychological plane between a Mahatma and his chelas, one of whom acts as his amanuensis. When the Master wants a letter to be written in this way, he draws the attention of the chela, whom he selects for the task, by causing an astral bell (heard by so many of our Fellows and others) to be rung near him just as the despatching telegraph office signals to the receiving office before wiring the message. The thoughts arising in the mind of the Mahatma are then clothed in words, pronounced mentally, and forced along the astral currents he sends towards the pupil to impinge on the brain of the latter. Thence they are borne by the nerve-currents to the palms of his

---

*A. P. Sinnett. *The Occult World* (orig. ed. London: Trübner and Co., 1881), pp. 143-44. Also *Mah. Ltrs.*, No VI, with small variations.

hand and the tips of his fingers which rest on a piece of magnetical-
ly prepared paper. As the thought-waves are thus impressed on
the tissue, materials are drawn to it from the ocean of *âkas*
(permeating every atom of the sensuous universe), by an occult
process, out of place here to describe, and permanent marks
are left.

"From this it is abundantly clear that the success of such
writings as above described depends chiefly upon these things:—
(1) The force and the clearness with which the thoughts are
propelled, and (2) the freedom of the receiving brain from disturbance of every description. The case with the ordinary electric
telegraph is exactly the same. If, for some reason or other the
battery supplying the electric power falls below the requisite
strength on any telegraph line or there is some derangement in
the receiving apparatus, the message transmitted becomes either
mutilated or otherwise imperfectly legible. . . . Such inaccuracies,
in fact, do very often arise as may be gathered from what the
Mahatma says in the above extract. 'Bear in mind,' says He,
'that these my letters are not written, but *impressed*, or precipitated, and *then all mistakes corrected*.' To turn to the sources
of error in the precipitation. Remembering the circumstances
under which blunders arise in telegrams, we see that if a Mahatma
somehow becomes exhausted or allows his thoughts to wander off
during the process or fails to command the requisite intensity in
the astral currents along which his thoughts are projected, or the
distracted attention of the pupil produces disturbances in his brain
and nerve-centres, the success of the process is very much inter-
fered with."*

To this excerpt may be added H. P. B.'s words which
occur in her unique article entitled "My Books," published
in *Lucifer* the very month of her passing.

". . . Space and distance do not exist for thought; and if two
persons are in perfect mutual psycho-magnetic *rapport*, and of
these two, one is a great Adept in Occult Sciences, then thought-
transference and dictation of whole pages become as easy and as
comprehensible at the distance of ten thousand miles as the
transference of two words across a room."†

It is of course self-evident that if such dictated passages,
long or short, were to be excluded from her *Collected
Writings*, it would be necessary to exclude also very large

---

*The Theosophist, Vol. V, Nos. 3-4 (51-52), Dec.-Jan., 1883-84, p. 64.
†*Lucifer*, London, Vol. VIII, No. 45, May 15, 1891, pp. 241-247.

portions of both *The Secret Doctrine* and *Isis Unveiled,* as being either the result of direct dictation to H. P. B. by one or more Adepts, or even actual material precipitated by occult means for her to use, if she chose to do so. Such an attitude towards H. P. B.'s writings would hardly be consistent with either common sense or her own view of things, as she most certainly did not hesitate to append her name to most of the material which had been dictated to her by various high Occultists.

IV

A historical survey of the various steps in the compiling of H. P. B.'s voluminous writings should now be given.

Soon after H. P. B.'s death, an early attempt was made to gather and to publish at least some of her scattered writings. In 1891, resolutions were passed by all the Sections of The Theosophical Society that an "H. P. B. Memorial Fund" be instituted for the purpose of publishing such writings from her pen as would promote "that intimate union between the life and thought of the Orient and the Occident to the bringing about of which her life was devoted."

In 1895, there appeared in print Volume I of "The H. P. B. Memorial Fund Series," under the title of *A Modern Panarion: A Collection of Fugitive Fragments from the pen of H. P. Blavatsky* (London, New York and Madras, 1895, 504 pp.), containing a selection from H. P. B.'s articles in the Spiritualistic journals and a number of her early contributions to *The Theosophist*. It was printed on the H. P. B. Press, 42 Henry Street, Regent's Park, London, N.W., Printers to The Theosophical Society. No further volumes are known to have been published, although it would appear that other volumes in this series were contemplated.

The compiling of material for a uniform edition of H. P. Blavatsky's writings was begun by the undersigned in 1924,

while residing at the Headquarters of the Point Loma
Theosophical Society, during the administration of Kath-
erine Tingley. For about six years it remained a private
project of the Compiler. Some 1,500 pages of typewritten
material were collected, copied, and tentatively classified.

Many foreign sources of information were consulted for
correct data, and a great deal of preliminary work was
done.

It was soon discovered in the formative stage of the plan
that an analytical study of the early years of the modern
Theosophical Movement was essential, not only as a means
of discovering what publications had actually published
articles from the pen of H.P.B., but also as providing data
for running down every available clue as to dates of publication which often had been wrongly quoted.

It was at this particular time that a far-flung inter-
national correspondence was started with individuals and
Institutions in the hope of eliciting the necessary information. By the end of the summer of 1929, most of this work
had been completed in so far as it concerned the initial
period of 1874-79.

In August, 1929, Dr. Gottfried de Purucker, then Head
of the Point Loma Theosophical Society, was approached
regarding the plan of publishing a uniform edition of
H. P. B.'s writings. This idea was immediately accepted,
and a small Committee was formed to help with the
preparation of the material. It was intended from the
outset to start publication in 1931, as a tribute to H. P. B.
on the Centennial Anniversary of her birth, provided a
suitable publisher could be found.

After several possible publishers had been considered,
it was suggested by the late Dr. Henry T. Edge—a personal
pupil of H. P. Blavatsky from the London days—to approach
Rider and Co., in London.

On February 27, 1930, A. Trevor Barker, of London,
Transcriber and Compiler of *The Mahatma Letters to
A. P. Sinnett,* wrote to Dr. G. de Purucker and among

other things advised that he and his friend, Ronald A. V. Morris, had been for some time past working upon a plan of collecting H. P. B.'s magazine articles for a possible series of volumes to be published in the near future. Close contact was immediately established between these gentlemen and the Committee at Point Loma. They first sent a complete list of their material, and in July, 1930, the collected material itself, which consisted mainly of articles from *The Theosophist* and *Lucifer*. While duplicating to a very great extent what had already been collected from these journals, their material contained also a number of valuable items from other sources. In May, 1930, A. Trevor Barker also suggested Rider and Co., of London, as a possible publisher.

In the meantime, namely, on April 1, 1930, the suggestion had been made by the Compiler that this entire work become an Inter-Organizational Theosophical project in which all Theosophical Societies would collaborate. Since this idea dovetailed with the Fraternization Movement inaugurated by Dr. G. de Purucker at the time, it was accepted at once and steps were taken to secure the cooperation of other Theosophical Societies.

On April 24, 1930, a letter was written to Dr. Annie Besant, President, The Theosophical Society (Adyar), asking for collaboration in the compilation of the forthcoming Series. Her endorsement was secured, through the intermediation of Lars Eek, at the Theosophical Convention held in Geneva, Switzerland, June 28—July 1, 1930, at which she presided.

After a period of preliminary correspondence, constructive and fruitful literary teamwork was established with the officials at the Adyar Headquarters. The gracious permission of Dr. Annie Besant to utilize material in the Archives of The Theosophical Society at Adyar, and the wholehearted collaboration of C. Jinarâjadâsa, A. J. Hamerster, Mary K. Neff, N. Sri Ram, and others, extending over a number of years, have been factors of primary importance in the success of this entire effort.

The help of a number of other individuals in different parts of the world was accepted and the work of the compilation took on the more permanent form of an Inter-Organizational Theosophical project, in which many people of various nationalities and Theosophical affiliations co-operated.

While work proceeded on various portions of the mass of material already available, the main effort was directed towards completing Volume I of the Series, which was to cover the period of 1874-1879. This volume proved, in some respects, to be the most difficult to produce, owing to the fact that material for it was scattered over several continents and often in almost unprocurable periodicals and newspapers of that era.

Volume I was ready for the printer in the summer of 1931, and was then sent to Rider and Co., of London, with whom a contract had been signed. Owing to various delays over which the Compiler had no control, it did not go to press until August, 1932, and was finally published in the early part of 1933, under the title of *The Complete Works of H. P. Blavatsky.*

A stipulation was made by the publisher that the name of A. Trevor Barker should appear on the title page of the Volume, as the responsible Editor, owing to his reputation as the Editor of *The Mahatma Letters to A. P. Sinnett* and *The Letters of H. P. Blavatsky to A. P. Sinnett.* This stipulation was agreed to as a technical point intended for business purposes only.

Volume II of the Series was also published in 1933; Volume III appeared in 1935, and Volume IV in 1936. The same year Rider and Co. published a facsimile edition of *Isis Unveiled,* with both volumes under one cover, and uniform with the preceding first four volumes of the *Complete Works.*

Further unexpected delays occurred in 1937, and then came the world crisis resulting in World War II which stopped the continuation of the Series. During the London "blitz," the Offices of Rider and Co. and other Publishing

Houses in Paternoster Row, were destroyed. The plates of
the four volumes already published were ruined (as were
also the plates of *The Mahatma Letters to A. P. Sinnett*
and other works), and, as the edition was only a small one,
these volumes were no longer available and have remained
so for the last fourteen years.

During the World War period, research work and preparation of material for future publication went on uninter-
ruptedly however, and much new material was discovered.
Very rare articles written by H. P. B. in French were unexpectedly found and promptly translated. A complete
survey was made of all known writings in her native Russian,
and new items were brought to light. This Russian literary
output was secured in its entirety, direct from the original
sources, the most rare articles being furnished free of charge
by the Lenin State Library of Moscow.

The hardships of the economic situation in England,
both during and after World War II, made it impossible
for Rider and Co. to resume work on the original Series.
In the meantime the demand for the writings of H. P.
Blavatsky has been steadily growing, and an ever increasing
number of people have been looking forward to the publication of an American Edition of her Collected Works. To
satisfy this growing demand, the present edition is being
launched. Its publication in the seventy-fifth year of the
modern Theosophical Movement fills a long-felt need on the
American Continent, where the cornerstone of the original
Theosophical Society was laid in 1875.

The writings of H. P. Blavatsky are unique. They speak
louder than any human commentary, and the ultimate proof
of the teachings they contain rests with the disciple himself—when his heart is attuned to the cosmic harmony they
unveil before his mind's eye. Like all mystic writings
throughout the ages, they conceal vastly more than they
reveal, and the intuitive student discovers in them just what
he is able to grasp—neither more nor less.

Unchanged by time, unmoved by the phantasmagoria of
the world's pageant, unhurt by scathing criticism, unsoiled

by the vituperations of trivial and dogmatic minds, these writings stand today, as they did on the day of their first appearance, like a majestic rock amidst the foaming crests of an unruly sea. Their clarion call resounds as of yore, and thousands of heart-hungry, confused and disillusioned men and women, seekers after truth and knowledge, find the entrance to a greater life in the enduring principles of thought contained in H. P. B.'s literary heritage.

She flung down the gauntlet to the religious sectarianism of her day, with its gaudy ritualism and the dead letter of orthodox worship. She challenged entrenched scientific dogmas evolved from minds which saw in Nature but a fortuitous aggregate of lifeless atoms driven by mere chance. The regenerative power of her Message broke the constricting shell of a moribund theology, swept away the empty wranglings of phrase-weavers, and checkmated the progress of scientific fallacies.

Today this Message, like the Spring flood of some mighty river, is spreading far and wide over the earth. The greatest thinkers of the day are voicing at times genuine theosophical ideas, often couched in the very language used by H. P. B. herself, and we witness daily the turning of men's minds towards those treasure chambers of the Trans-Himâlayan Esoteric Knowledge which she unlocked for us.

We commend her writings to the weary pilgrim, and to the seeker of enduring spiritual realities. They contain the answer to many a perplexing problem. They open wide portals undreamt of before, revealing vistas of cosmic splendor and lasting inspiration. They bring new hope and courage to the fainthearted but sincere student. They are a comfort and a staff, as well as a Guide and Teacher, to those who are already travelling along the age-old Path. As for those few who are in the vanguard of mankind, valiantly scaling the solitary passes leading to the Gates of Gold, these writings give the clue to the secret knowledge enabling one to lift the heavy bar that must be raised before the Gates admit the pilgrim into the land of Eternal Dawn.

ACKNOWLEDGMENTS

In the course of this literary undertaking, a great deal of volunteer help has been received from many individuals and several distinguished Institutions. Contacts established with them have been the cause of many pleasant associations and friendships of a lasting nature. The Compiler wishes to express his indebtedness to each and every one of them. In particular, a debt of gratitude is due to the following friends and associates:

Gottfried de Purucker, late Leader of the Point Loma Theosophical Society, for his constant encouragement, his invaluable hints concerning H. P. B.'s writings, and the opportunity to share his profound learning on subjects pertaining to Occultism; Henry T. Edge and Charles J. Ryan, for assistance in determining the authorship of many unsigned articles; Bertram Keightley, who, in the closing years of his life, provided valuable information regarding certain articles in the volumes of *Lucifer*, on whose editorial staff he served in H. P. B.'s time; E. T. Sturdy, member of H. P. B.'s Inner Group, for suggestive data and information; C. Jinarâjadâsa, President of The Theosophical Society (Adyar), for his many years of collaboration and his moral and material support; A. J. Hamerster and Mary K. Neff, for their meticulous care in the transcription of material from the Adyar Archives; Marjorie M. Tyberg, whose trained editorial abilities were an important factor in the production of the earlier volumes; Joseph H. Fussell, Sec'y-Gen. of the Point Loma Theosophical Society, for his co-operation in connection with the Society's Archives; A. Trevor Barker and Virginia Barker, London, and Ronald A. V. Morris, Hove, Sussex, for editorial work on portions of the MSS and their role in the business transactions with Rider and Co.; Sven Eek, onetime Manager of the Publications Department, Point Loma, Calif., for valuable assistance in the sale of earlier volumes; Judith Tyberg, for helpful suggestions in connection with Sanskrit technical terms; Helen Morris Koerting, New York; Ernest Cunningham, Philadelphia; Philip Malpas, London; Margaret Guild Conger, Washington, D. C.; Charles E. Ball, London; J. Hugo Tatsch, President, McCoy Publishing Company, New York; J. Emory Clapp, Boston; Ture Dahlin, Paris; T. W. Willans, Australia; W. Emmett Small, Geoffrey Barborka, Mrs. Grace Knoche, Miss Grace Frances Knoche, Solomon Hecht, Eunice M. Ingraham, and others, for research work, checking of references, copying of the MSS and assistance with various technical points connected with the earlier volumes; Mary L. Stanley, London, for painstaking and most able research work at the British Museum; Alexander Petrovich Leino, Helsingfors, Finland, for invaluable assistance in securing original Russian material at the Helsingfors University

Library; William L. Biersach, Jr., and Walter A. Carrithers, Jr., whose thorough knowledge of the historical documents connected with the Theosophical Movement has been of very great assistance; and Mrs. Mary V. Langford, whose most careful and intelligent translation of Russian material provided a major contribution to the entire Series.

The Compiler is also indebted to the following Institutions, and their officials who have contributed information essential to the production of this Series: Stanford University, and the Hoover Institute, Palo Alto, Calif.; British Museum, London; The American-Russian Institute, New York; Avraham Yarmolinsky, Chief of the Slavonic Division and Paul North Rice, Chief of the Reference Department, New York Public Library; University of California at Los Angeles, Los Angeles, Calif.; Library of Congress, Washington, D. C.; Mary E. Holmes, Librarian, Franklin Library, Franklin, Mass.; Foster M. Palmer, Reference Librarian, Harvard College Library, Cambridge, Mass.; University of Pennsylvania Library, Philadelphia, Pa.; Bibliothèque Nationale, Paris; Lenin State Library, Moscow, U.S.S.R.; Kungliga Biblioteket, Stockholm; Universitetsbiblioteket, Upsala; Boston Public Library; Columbia University Library, New York; Yale University Library, New Haven, Conn.; Grand Lodge Library and Museum, London; American Antiquarian Society, Worcester, Mass.; Public Library, Colombo, Ceylon; The Commonwealth of Massachusetts State Library, Boston, Mass.; The Boston Athenaeum; Imperial Library, Calcutta, India; London Spiritualist Alliance; Massachusetts State Association of Spiritualists, Boston, Mass.; California State Library, Sacramento, Calif.; Library of the Philosophical Research Society, Inc., Los Angeles, Calif.

Other individuals from time to time have contributed in various ways to the success of this literary work. To all of these a debt of appreciation is due, even if their names are not individually mentioned.

BORIS DE ZIRKOFF.
Compiler.

LOS ANGELES, CALIFORNIA, U.S.A.
September 8th, 1950.

FOREWORD

The Translator and Compiler wishes to express his gratitude to all those who have helped in the preparation of this Volume.

The continued interest and helpful assistance of our collaborators and friends has been of inestimable value.

Special mention should be made of Irene R. Ponsonby, Lina Psaltis and Dara Eklund who have read the proofs in various stages of production; and of Joy Arnevig who typed the greater part of the manuscript.

Acknowledgment is also due to Stockton Trade Press in Santa Fe Springs, California, for their sustained interest and collaboration in solving many technical problems connected with the production of this Volume.

BORIS DE ZIRKOFF
Translator and Compiler.

LOS ANGELES, CALIFORNIA, U.S.A.
JANUARY 15, 1975.

THE WRITINGS OF H. P. BLAVATSKY IN RUSSIAN

As far as can be ascertained, after long and extensive search, the earliest known writings of H.P.B. in Russian date from 1877, and therefore belong to the period of her residence in New York.

There are on file seventeen articles, all published between the summer of 1877 and December, 1878. Sixteen of them are pasted in H.P.B.'s *Scrapbook,* Vol. VI (1878), now in the Adyar Archives.

Eight of these articles appeared in *Pravda* (Truth), a daily newspaper then only recently started, and edited and published at Odessa, from the summer of 1877 to 1880, by General Joseph Florovich Dolivo-Dobrovolsky and K. E. Rosen.

H.P.B.'s cousin, Alexander Yulievich de Witte was much interested in this new Daily. He and his brother, Serguey Yulievich (the future Prime Minister of Russia), urged H.P.B. to become the New York correspondent of this paper and to write articles for it on various aspects of American life. *Pravda* was started under very favorable auspices and acquired prominent contributors both in Russia and abroad. General Dolivo-Dobrovolsky was himself a relative of H.P.B. by marriage, his sister being married to the renowned Senator Yevgeniy Feodorovich von Hahn (1807-74), first cousin of H.P.B.'s father. The Editors were willing to pay H.P.B. from 8 to 10 kopecks per line, which was a very good price for that day.*

---

* *Vide* letter written to H.P.B. by Nadyezhda A. de Fadeyev, her aunt, under date of Oct. 20 (old style), 1877, now in the Adyar Archives.

H.P.B. accepted the proposal and sent one or more articles in care of her aunt at Odessa. These, however, were lost in the mail. Urged by her aunt, H.P.B. tried again and mailed to her another article or two. These were again lost, and suspicion fell on the Austrian authorities through whom mails were apparently transmitted.* Undismayed, H.P.B. wrote once more, and this time her article reached its destination and was forthwith taken to the editorial offices of *Pravda*.

One series published in *Pravda* consisted of four articles and was entitled "From Across the Sea, from Beyond the Blue Ocean." The first installment of this was published Feb. 23/March 7, 1878, and was dated 1/13 Jan. [1878].† The second installment was dated New York, 18/30 April [1878], but the actual date of publication does not appear on the clipping pasted in H.P.B.'s *Scrapbook*. The third article of the Series is dated New York 1/13 October [1878] and was published Oct. 24/Nov. 5, 1878. The fourth is dated New York 2/14 November [1878] and appeared in print on the 3/15 December, 1878.

Another series, entitled "Letters from America," seems to have consisted of four installments, but the first of these must have been lost in the mails. The second installment, marked II, was dated New York, 1/13 February [1878],

---

* In Col. Olcott's *Diaries* there is the following entry in H.P.B.'s handwriting, under date of February 7, 1878: "2 Letters from N. A. Fadeew, Odessa. H.P.B. 4 feuilletons definitely lost. Asks to write more . . ."

Reference is here to Nadyezhda A. de Fadeyev's two letters dated December 8/20 and 10/22, 1877, respectively, now in the Adyar Archives, which deplore the loss of articles sent in by H.P.B. for *Pravda*.

†The two dates divided by a slanting line refer to the Gregorian Calendar or New Style (now in general use), and the Julian Calendar or Old Style, which was current in Russia at the time, and is even now used by the Greek Orthodox Church. The difference between the two modes of reckoning was 10 days from 1582 to 1700; 11 days from 1700 to 1800; 12 days from 1800 to 1900, and 13 days since 1900. It is important to bear this in mind, because many of H.P.B.'s dates are in terms of the old Julian Calendar. The difference of 12 days is applicable to all dates within her lifetime.

and the date of its publication, namely, March 19, 1878, is written on the clipping in H.P.B's own handwriting. The third installment, dated New York, 14/26 February [1878], appeared March 25/April 6, 1878. The fourth is dated New York, April 22/May 4 [1878], but the actual date of its publication is not noted on the clipping.

H.P.B. definitely wrote more articles for *Pravda* than those which were published by that paper. It is also possible that we do not have on file another article which actually appeared in print. In a letter which H.P.B. wrote to her aunt, N. A. de Fadeyev, on July 3, 1878, she says: "I have sent to Dobrovolsky seven articles in all on the last two occasions. He returned three of them, he published two, and the last two he also rejected. It means I lost five articles, more than 200 rubles; he had asked for two each month and was ready to pay 50 r. per month. Even for the two which he published he has not paid. What a pig! I shall not write any more for him."

It is very probable that *Pravda* began eventually to have financial troubles and was unable to live up to its former promises.

Nine articles from H.P.B.'s pen appeared in the *Tiflisskiy Vestnik* (Tiflis Messenger), a politico-literary journal published at Tiflis, Caucasus, by Prince K. A. Bebutov during the years 1873-1880. Its editors were Prince Bebutov, D. Eristov, I. E. Pitoyev and Prince G. Chikoani. Eight of these articles form a series entitled "A Voice from the Other World" (*Golos s togo svyeta*) and bear the signature of "Golos" (Voice). The first is marked "I" in H.P.B.'s handwriting, bears no date of any kind and seems to have been published after the start of the Russo-Turkish War which occurred on the 12/24 April, 1877. The second is neither marked nor dated, but can be identified as the second by means of its context. The third installment, marked thus by H.P.B., was published (as has been ascertained from library files) May 17/29, 1878. The fourth appeared Sept. 13/25, 1878; the fifth Sept. 16/28, 1878; the sixth bears no date whatever in the *Scrapbook;* the seventh was published Sept. 23/Oct. 5, 1878, and the eighth and last on Sept. 29/Oct. 11, 1878.

In addition to the above series, H.P.B. wrote a letter to the editor of the *Tiflisskiy Vestnik* which was published June 7/19, 1878, and may be found in Vol. I of the *Collected Writings*.

Madame Vera Petrovna de Zhelihovsky, H.P.B.'s sister, says in her biographical sketch of H.P.B.'s life* that "as soon as the Turkish War began, H. P. Blavatsky started a correspondence from New York with the *Tiflisskiy Vestnik,* and donated her entire remuneration to the Red Cross and the homes for the wounded. Her articles, extremely entertaining and witty, were signed with the pseudonym 'The Voice,' and entitled 'Voice from Beyond the Ocean'." She is in error, however, as to the title of this Series.†

After H.P.B. and Col. H. S. Olcott had settled at Bombay, India, H.P.B. began writing her famous Russian Series entitled "From the Caves and Jungles of Hindostan." Its sub-title was "Letters to the Fatherland." This Series began appearing in an old and very well-known Russian daily newspaper, the *Moskovskiya Vedomosty* (Moscow Chronicle, or Moscow Gazette), then under the editorship of the renowned publicist and literary figure, Mihail Nikiforovich Katkov.

Katkov was born in Moscow, November 1/13, 1818, and lost his father in infancy. Together with his younger brother, he was educated under the immediate supervision of his mother who was of Georgian descent. In 1834, he entered the University of Moscow in the department of literature,

---

* *Russkoye Obozreniye* (Russian Review), Vol. VI, November, 1891, p. 262. A similar statement by her occurs in the *Rebus* (Riddle), No. 48, 1883, p. 439.

† It is somewhat doubtful, however, whether H.P.B. began writing her Russian articles "as soon as the Turkish War began." This may be only a generalization. Although we do not have the dates of her first two articles for the *Tiflisskiy Vestnik,* collateral evidence seems to point to the later part of 1877 as being the period when she sent her initial contributions to that paper.

It is also known from H.P.B.'s letter to her aunt, dated July 3, 1878, that she had made arrangements to have payments for some of her articles — probably those published at the time in the Caucasus — go to Vera P. de Zhelihovsky, her sister, who was in need of help.

graduating with distinction four years later. His literary career began even before graduation, and many of his essays, published in some of the best journals of the day, gave expression to a mystical attitude towards life, and the intimate unity between man and nature. His philosophical views were strongly influenced by Schelling and Hegel. After three years abroad, where he lived in several European countries and became a close friend of Schelling in Berlin, he returned home to find himself in very difficult financial circumstances and without any of his former friends, who did not share his current views. He earned his livelihood by tutoring, and devoted himself to the study of philology, history and classical antiquity. In 1845, he successfully presented his Master's thesis on Slavonian-Russian philology and became an assistant professor at the Moscow University where he taught logic and psychology for about five years, supporting both his mother and younger brother. In 1850, he suddenly lost his position, due to the fact that the teaching of philosophy in the universities was handed over to priests who were professors of theology.

After another short period of struggle, Katkov was very suddenly offered the position of editor of the famous *Moskovskiya Vedomosty* (Moscow Chronicle) which he assumed in March, 1851. On a salary of two thousand rubles, with a 25 kopeks' commission on every new subscriber and free lodging, Katkov considered himself secure; this led to his marrying Princess Sophie Sergeyevna Shalikov, the daughter of a well-known literary man.

Under Katkov's leadership, the number of subscribers to his newspaper rose from seven to fifteen thousand, and the quality of the paper was greatly enhanced through the participation of new literary talent. To this period of his literary activity belongs Katkov's basic work entitled *Outline of the most ancient Period of Greek Philosophy* (1854) which interprets the teachings of Heraclitus, Pythagoras and others in a symbolic manner, as expressing various abstract truths.

Various governmental restrictions, especially along political lines, and the lack of freedom which Katkov experienced

in the conduct of his paper, which actually was the property
of the Moscow University, made him decide to seek permission from the authorities to publish his own independent
organ. After some tribulations and delays, he was allowed
to publish, a couple of times a month, a small journal under
the name of *Russkiy Vestnik* (Russian Messenger) which
began to appear in 1856. Katkov resigned from the editorship of the *Moscow Chronicle*.

The new Journal soon acquired considerable reputation,
and some of the finest literary talents in Russia wrote for
its pages, such as Tolstoy, Turgenyev, Goncharov and others.
The number of subscribers rose steadily. Dissatisfied with
the way his political department was being conducted, he
took charge of it himself, even though he was conscious of
not being well versed along these lines. His chief characteristics in that field were his passionate patriotism, so warmly
commended by H.P.B. herself on several occasions, his deep
religious feeling, and his devotion to the Throne. Some of
these attitudes have been gravely misunderstood by later,
post-revolutionary writers, who have permitted themselves
to classify Katkov among the reactionaries, owing to their
own narrow outlook and fanatical adherence to new-fangled
ideas. Such an appraisal of Katkov's figure is historically
unsound.

Katkov was in favor of far-reaching reforms in the
structure of the State, and was inclined at the time towards
the English form of government. He was the proponent of a
relatively free press and some of his editorials, as well as his
defense of other peoples' contributions, repeatedly provoked
the ire of the censors. Katkov fought back, and with considerable success. He soon realized that he needed a daily
paper. At this time, the University of Moscow decided to
lease out its paper, the *Moscow Chronicle*. Katkov offered
for it the sum of 74,000 rubles and the paper passed into
his hands for a second time, and began to be issued under
his editorship on January 1, 1863. His battle was against
the existing bureaucracy. At one time his *Chronicle* was
suspended for a period of two months, but resumed publication. In May, 1866, he obtained an interview with Emperor Alexander II who was visiting Moscow, and was

received with much kindness and assured of the Emperor's special protection.

In 1868, Katkov and his close friend Leontyev opened a new educational establishment, a Lyceum to be run on lines of classical education which had always been a deep-seated conviction of Katkov's. A special department was devoted to the free education and upkeep of especially promising boys from among the people, and from all parts of Russia, who were to be trained as future teachers.

Katkov was greatly interested in the future of all Slavonic nations, then under the yoke of both Austria and Turkey, and he became the proponent of Slavophilism. His enthusiasm for reforms, however, was gradually undermined by the growing abuses of various liberally-minded people, and his opposition against the violent radical element became a real power after the assassination of the Emperor on March 1/13, 1881. The *Moscow Chronicle* acquired a position of importance such as no other paper in Russia ever had before. In its pages were discussed the most important problems of the day, and from these discussions matured in time various moves of both internal and foreign policy. Katkov's own life was completely submerged in, and dedicated to, this activity of public and national service which he looked upon as a perpetual crusade in the interests of the State. He worked day and night, allowing himself no rest of any kind, and finally undermined his health beyond the point where it could be restored. He died at his estate of Znamenskoye, in the Province of Moscow, July 20/August 1, 1887, and was buried in the Alexeyev Monastery in Moscow.

Such was the personality and the background of the man whom H.P.B. considered to be one of the great patriots of her native country, and who opened the pages of his publications to her pen.

———————

Letter No. I of H.P.B.'s "Caves and Jungles," depicting the arrival of the Founders at Bombay, was published Nov. 30th (old style), 1879. In his *Diaries,* now in the Adyar

Archives, Col. H. S. Olcott has the following entry for January 15, 1880: "Mail today brings news that Latchkey's first article in the Moscow magazine creates a stir in Russia." "Latchkey" was Olcott's nickname for H.P.B.

The series appeared in 39 issues of the *Moscow Chronicle* from November 30 (o.s.), 1879, to January, 1882. Curiously enough, there are only twenty-three numbered Letters, with some of the installments bearing no numbr at all and others definitely wrongly numbered. Only Letter No. I has a definite title, namely, "Arrival at Bombay."

The series obviously was never finished as it broke off rather suddenly.

In January, 1883, however, in Vol. 163, the *Russkiy Vestnik* (Russian Messenger), founded by Katkov, began republishing the same series in monthly installments in a special *Supplement* consecutively paged throughout. In Vol. 166, July, 1883, the *Supplement* reached page 411, closing Part I of the "Caves." In its August, 1883, issue, the *Russian Messenger* published 32 pages of Part II. The text breaks off in the middle of a sentence: ". . . Only we did not sleep, and Nârâyaṇa was still"— ending without any punctuation. There are twenty-nine chapters in all in this reprint, but two chapters are marked XVIII, chapter XXIII is not numbered, and chapter XXIX is marked XXIII. The contents, however, are consecutive, in spite of wrong numeration.

The reason for this sudden break is not clear, although an editorial note of December, 1884, states that the articles terminated because H.P.B. went to the Nîlgiri Hills and then to Europe. This really does not explain a break so abrupt as to end in the middle of a sentence.*

---

* The partial and rather faulty English translation of the "Caves and Jungles," which was published in 1892, ends at approximately the middle of Chapter XXII (which should have been called XXIII), on page 283 of the consecutively paged *Supplement* to the *Russian Messenger*. This translation, made by Vera Johnston, H.P.B.'s niece who was married to Charles Johnston, the Orientalist, cannot be considered an authentic text. It is rather in the nature of excerpts. Some of the footnotes of the original have been placed in the main body of the text; many descriptions have been abbreviated and all paragraphs and

This reprint in the *Russian Messenger* appears to be identical with the text in the *Moscow Gazette,* but has a few additions; a few footnotes have been added here and there by the author, and a rather lengthy description of Âgra has been incorporated into Chapter XXVIII.

In November, 1885, in its Vol. No. 180, the *Russian Messenger* resumed publication of the "Caves and Jungles" series. It started by reprinting verbatim the 32 pages of text from its issue of August, 1883, and continued from there on, explaining that new text had been received from the author. The continuation of Part II appeared in the February, March and August, 1886, issues of the Journal; it ran through seven chapters in all. Chapter Seven ends on page 718 with the closing of a paragraph, after which, in addition to the signature "Radda-Bai," there is also the statement "to be continued." No continuation, however, has ever been found.

It has been suggested that H.P.B.'s serial story was discontinued because of Katkov's death. But this is most unlikely, because he died July 20/August 1, 1887, a year after the last installment of H.P.B.'s story appeared in print. However, writing to A. P. Sinnett under date of March 3, 1886, H.P.B. speaks, among other things, of Vsevolod S. Solovyov, who from friend had turned enemy and was attempting to hurt her. She says: "Now in Russia as everywhere else *hating* is synonymous with slandering. Solovyoff, moreover, will not forgive me for rejecting *his propositions*

---

footnotes containing some of H.P.B.'s witty and sometimes sarcastic remarks about Englishmen and the British Administration in India have been invariably left out. This may be explained by the fact that Charles Johnston was for a time in the service of the Anglo-Indian Government.

Another edition of this partial translation was published in 1908 by The Theosophical Publishing Society of London.

Available information indicates that this translation was rendered into French under the title of *Dans les cavernes and jungles de l'Hindoustan* (Paris, 1934, 8vo., viii, 272 pp.) ; into German as *In den Höhlen und Dschungeln Hindostans* (Leipzig, Wilhelm Friedrich, 1899) ; and into Spanish as *Por las grutas y selvas del Indostán,* translated by Mario Roso de Luna, with Preface and Commentaries (Vida de Pueyo, 1918, 4to., xxxix, 533 pp.).

— that you know. He knows Katkov; he is a writer; and I expect to lose through his kind offices my position on the *Russian Vyestnik* and as a consequence a few thousand rubles a year."* It is quite possible that H.P.B.'s premonitions actually took effect, although we have no definite information about it.

While "Caves and Jungles" contains many descriptions of actual circumstances and events in H.P.B.'s and Col. Olcott's travels in India, this serial story should not be considered a regular Travelogue, *i.e.*, a consecutive account of a specific journey. It is a story woven out of events and occurrences that had taken place during several journeys, some of them long prior to the beginning of H.P.B.'s public mission, at a time when she wandered by herself in far-off lands. Some of the characters of this story and some of the adventures are, no doubt, entirely fictitious, but are obviously brought in to point out an occult fact or explain some of Nature's mysteries. Writing in the *Bombay Gazette,* on March 5, 1881, in refutation of some unfriendly criticism of her "intense hostility to the British Government," H.P.B. points out that ". . . The hostility must be passed to the account of *Thornton's Gazetteer of India* and sundry 'Guide Books' which, as can most easily be proved, supply their author with all the needed political information, except perhaps, occasional clippings from the London and English Indian papers, required as *historical* ballast to her purely fictitious tales. 'Radda-Bai' does not pretend to write either history or political news. So long as her geographical, ethnological, and psychological facts are correct, she has a perfect right to evolve heroes and heroines out of her fancy as does

---

* A. P. Sinnett, *The Letters of H. P. Blavatsky to A. P. Sinnett,* Letter No. LXXX, p. 193

Vsevolod Sergueyevich Solovyov (1849-1903) was a romantic writer and poet, the eldest son of the famous historian, Serguey Mihailovich Solovyov (1820-79). His brother, sometimes ignorantly confused with him, was Vladimir Sergueyevich Solovyov (1853-1900), one of the greatest philosophers of Russia. See Vol. VII, pp. 332-34, footnote, of the *Collected Writings,* for further data about Vsevolod S. Solovyov and his relation to H.P.B.

MIHAIL NIKIFOROVICH KATKOV
1818-1887

FACSIMILES OF PAGES WRITTEN BY H.P.B. IN RUSSIAN

any other author. They are no more than gilt upholstery nails to hold her descriptive tapestry together . . ." *

The same paragraph contains the unexpected information that her story is being translated into English by the author and will be issued in due time by an American publisher simultaneously with a London edition. No further information on this score has ever come to light.

Sometime in the early part of 1886, she wrote on the same subject to Sinnett, referring to her *"Russian Letters from India:"* ". . . where while describing a fictitious journey or tour through India with *Thornton's Gazetteer* as my guide, I yet give there true *facts* and true personages only bringing in together within three of four months time, facts and events scattered all throughout years as some of Master's phenomena. Is it a crime that? . . . Why, if having been in Calcutta and Allahabad I have to write upon their antiquities — *which I have seen myself* — why shouldn't I resort to *Asiatic Researches* and even *Thornton's Gazetteer* for historical facts and details I could never remember myself. Is it considered a literary theft to refer to encyclopaedias and guide books? I do not copy or plagiarize, I simply take them as my guides, *safer than my memory.*" †

These lively sketches from H.P.B.'s pen were never intended to be taken *au pied de la lettre;* they are wonderfully graphic, mingling grave and gay, fact and fancy, with a deftness that none but her travelling companions could easily detect.

Reviewing the partial English translation of the "Caves and Jungles" which was published in 1892, Col. H. S. Olcott, writing in *The Theosophist* (Vol. XIV, January, 1893, pp. 245-46), says:

"If it were possible to think that a great spirit like H.P.B.'s could be interested in what the world she so scorned, while living, would say about her talents when dead, it would be a grim satisfaction to it to know that the people and papers,

---

* *Collected Writings*, Vol. II, "A Berlin Mare's Nest."

† A. P. Sinnett, *Letters of H. P. Blavatsky to A. P. Sinnett*, Letter LXI, p. 153.

which spoke naught but ill of her aforetime, are now lavishing their praises upon one of her books and declaring her
to have been a genius. She is beyond their reach, but this
beginning of a change of public verdict is sweet to her family
and friends, who knew her greatness and loveableness all
along, and who felt that a bright star had passed into eclipse
when she died. And this is but the beginning of what will be
seen as time and Karma work out their changes, and the
fullness of this woman's power, knowledge and sufferings
becomes revealed. The book under notice is unlike her "Isis"
and "Secret Doctrine" in every respect, save in their mystical
undertone and their flashes of literary brilliance. The brightness in them glints upon pages and paragraphs, here and
there, amid a murk of heavy narrative and argument and a
confusion of metaphysics; while here it shines in every page,
and the reader feels the fascination of her style and the gor-
geousness of her imagination from the beginning to the end.
Unsympathetic journals, like the *Times* and its bigoted
namesake, the *Methodist Times,* which would begrudge
a word of praise for her more serious books, have been captivated by her 'Caves and Jungles' and betrayed into admiring criticism by her 'Nightmare Tales.' For the reason,
doubtless, that they fit their mental calibre while the others
require a larger bore.

"When we first came to Bombay, H.P.B. employed her
leisure time in writing for the *Russkiy Vestnik,* a series of
sketchy letters descriptive of the landscapes, peoples, feelings
and traditions of India and the Indian; spicing and immensely increasing the interest of her narrative by weaving
into it the story of a long journey by a select party of us, in
the company of an Adept whose wisdom instructed and
psychical powers astounded us. She carries us to Kârlî Caves,
to mystery-hiding jungles near Nâsik, to a Witch's Den
where horrors cluster around one, to a city of the Dead in
the Vindhya Mountains, to the Caves of Bâgh in Mâlwâ,
to an Isle of Mystery in Noman's Land, and to Jubbulpore,
where the sight of the Marble Rocks leads to a dissertation
upon the Thugs and Yoga. Having accompanied her in all
the wanderings that suggested the idea of her mystical
journey, and shared all the incidents which provoked her

magnificent romances of travel, I can detect the substantial basis of every one of her tales save a certain few which relate to and are souvenirs of a former journey of hers, from Southern India to Tibet, when she was really in the company and under the protection of the Adept whom she personifies under the sobriquet of Gulâb-Lal-Singh — a real name of a real Adept, by the way, with whom I have had to do. I am not going to dampen the pleasure of the readers of this splendid book, while the first charm of its influence is being felt, by uncovering the hard soil from which these flowers of fancy have sprung. But I will say this, that, knowing the facts she had to deal with, and now reading her book, I am amazed at this latest, and to me, most surprising proof of her literary power and exhuberance of imagination.

"In the best sense of the word, H.P.B. was versatile to an extent that I doubt if any contemporary author has surpassed. One could hardly believe that the same hand had written her various works unless, like some of us, he had passed years, or at least months, in her company, listened to her conversations and, perhaps, edited her manuscripts. The 'Caves and Jungles of Hindostan' is a revelation, even to her closest friends, of mental resources in the department of creative imagination, hitherto unsuspected . . ."

For the benefit of readers unfamiliar with Russian, it should be stated that the original text of the "Caves and Jungles" in H.P.B.'s native tongue is of high literary value and contains many passages of a descriptive nature which in elegance of style, richness of imagination, and poetic elevation of thought, equal the finest productions of well-known Russian writers. When considered purely from the standpoint of style, apart from any ideas expressed therein, H.P.B.'s stories were fit material to be sought after by Katkov or any other editor of the time, and aroused the admiration and interest of the reading public in her native land.

Part I of the Russian text of the "Caves and Jungles" was published by the University Printing House at Moscow in 1883, as a separate volume. The text does not seem to have been reset or in any way altered, as is evident by comparison of lines. The pages, however, were "leaded," and the text therefore was considerably stretched out, so that it covers 508 pages. The Russian title is: *Iz peshcher i debrey Indostana. Pis'ma na rodinu* (From the Caves and Jungles of Hindostan. Letters to the Fatherland).*

Another edition, profusely illustrated, was published in 1912 at St. Petersburg by A. S. Suvorin, the editor of the *Novoye Vremya.* It contains 438 pages, and is very scarce.

Before Part I of the "Caves and Jungles" began to appear as a serial *Supplement* in the *Russian Messenger,* namely, in May, June and July, 1881, H.P.B. published in that Journal (Vols. 153-154) her story entitled "The Durbâr at Lahore," which remained untranslated and practically unknown until the middle of the present century, when our definitive translation was finally published in *The Theosophist,* Vol. 81, August-December, 1960; January-March, 1961.

It was in November, 1880, that H.P.B. and Col. Olcott went to Lahore to organize a local Branch of The Theosophical Society and discuss various metaphysical subjects with several distinguished scholars. The Viceregal Durbâr, held by the Marquess of Ripon, fell on November 15th, and was described by H.P.B. in her inimitable style for the

---

* *Hindostan* (written in Russian *Indostan*) is a Persian word, and is pronounced *Hindûstân* in modern Persian. It means the country of the Hindûs. In mediaeval Persian, the word was *Hindôstân*, with an *ô*, but in later periods the distinctions between *ê* and *î*, and between *ô* and *û* have been lost. Indian languages borrowed Persian words in their mediaeval form. The word *Hindu* is in mediaeval Persian *Hindô*, representing the ancient *Avesta* word *hendava* (Skt. *saindhava*), a dweller on the *Sindhu* or Indus. The word *Hindu* is now well established in modern English and is often written without any accent. *Hindostan* with *o* is much more common both in English and in Indian languages, although *Hindustan* is also used. The spellings of *Indostan* and *Hindoostan* occur also in some English texts. The word is not an Indian one, and both pronunciations, with *ô* and with *û*, are current in India at present, but that with *ô* is definitely the one demanded by the history of the word and of the form which other Persian words take on Indian soil.

The word *Hindî* has another derivation, however, being formed from the Persian *Hind*, India (*hindu* in the *Avesta*; Skt. *sindhu*, a river, the Indus). *Hindî* means "of or belonging to India," while *Hindu* now means "a person of the Hindu religion."

benefit of the Russian reading public. Col. Olcott, himself, gives a brief description of these festivities in the Second Series of his *Old Diary Leaves,* pp. 259-65. Not being versed in the Russian language, he could not read the Russian version of this event, unless H.P.B. translated for him passages from her story. Our final English translation is based on a rough manuscript-translation made many years ago by Miss Inga Sjöstedt. It has been compared word for word with the original Russian text, worked over by the Compiler of the *Collected Writings,* and thoroughly gone over by Irene R. Ponsonby. Every effort has been made to preserve, as much as possible, the flowing style of H.P.B.'s Russian original, her witticisms, and the many characteristic expressions with which her writings abound.

During the period from December, 1884, to April, 1885, inclusive, and before a continuation of the "Caves and Jungles" was published in the *Russian Messenger,* H.P.B., having lived for some time in the Nîlgiri Hills, published in that Journal in five monthly installments her series called "The Enigmatical Tribes of the Blue Hills of India."

The only clue we have as to the remuneration which H.P.B. received for her serial stories appears in connection with the "Enigmatical Tribes," and the information is contained in a letter which she wrote to Vsevolod S. Solovyov from Torre del Greco, Italy, May 23, 1885. She speaks of "seven rubles or six and two-thirds or three-quarters per page (the devil himself could not make out their accounts) . . ." She also asks Solovyov whether she could ask Katkov for ten rubles per printed page (160 per sheet), instead of 6 r. 71 kop. (100 per sheet). In the same letter, she says that in America she is getting twenty-five dollars for a single column of her "Letters from India." * It is not known what she actually meant by this, because no article or series of articles under that title have ever been found in any American publication. The only time H.P.B. used

---

* See V. S. Solovyov, *A Modern Priestess of Isis,* St. Petersburg, N. F. Mertz, 1904, p. 175; Engl. transl. by Walter Leaf, London, 1895, p. 123.

such a title was in connection with an article she wrote for the *Russian Messenger* in May, 1880, and which may be found in its English translation in Vol. II of the *Collected Writings*. That article forms no part of any Series and stands entirely by itself. H.P.B. may have meant, however, that she *would* get $25 for a single column if she wrote these letters for American publication.

The Russian text of the "Enigmatical Tribes" together with "The Durbâr at Lahore" were both published in book form by Gubinsky at St. Petersburg in 1898. Madame Vera P. de Zhelihovsky, H.P.B.'s sister, contributed to this edition a biographical sketch of the author. It contains, as frontispiece, a little known portrait of H.P.B. This edition was republished by Olga Dyakova & Co. at Berlin in 1925.

A rather faulty and incomplete English translation of the "Enigmatical Tribes" appeared in *The Theosophist* (April, 1909 — November, 1910) under the title of "Mysterious Tribes." It is supposed to have been a translation from a German version published by Arthur Weber at Leipzig in 1908. It was published in book form by The Theosophical Press, Wheaton, Ill., in 1930, under the title of *The People of the Blue Mountains*.

A better, but still somewhat faulty, translation by Vera Johnston, entitled *The Magicians of the Blue Hills*, exists in the form of page-proofs; it bears the date of New York, 1897, but does not seem to have actually appeared in print.

A French translation by Mark Semenoff entitled *Au Pays des Montagnes Bleues* (255 pages), was published at Paris in 1926 by the Editions du Monde Moderne. There is some indication that this French rendering was re-translated into English at a later date.

A German translation by Arthur Weber entitled *Rätselhafte Volkstämme* appeared at Leipzig in 1908. A new edition of it was published by J. J. Couvreur at The Hague, Holland, 1970 (xii, 255 pp.).

A few items written by H.P.B. in her native Russian appeared also in the pages of *Rebus* (meaning Riddle or Charade). This weekly Sunday Journal was started at St. Petersburg in 1881 as a mere sheet of riddles, but became later the organ of Spiritualism and Mediumism in Russia. Its editor, Victor Pribitkov, was very friendly to H.P.B. and her work. The early volumes of the *Rebus* contained numerous articles by such prominent scientists and writers as A. M. Butlerov, N. P. Wagner, A. N. Aksakov, N. Strahov and others. Only three items from H.P.B.'s pen are known to have appeared in the pages of *Rebus*: a Letter to the Editor from which a mere excerpt was published December 9, 1883, p. 447, and which may be found in Vol. VI, p. 73, of the *Collected Writings;* another Letter to the editor published in September, 1885, and which speaks of her reasons for leaving India in 1885 (*ibid.,* VI, pp. 406-11); and a Russian version (undoubtedly written by her) of her English story entitled "The Cave of the Echoes," originally published in *The Banner of Light* (Boston, Mass.), Vol. XLIII, March 30, 1878 (also printed in *The Theosophist,* Vol. IV, April, 1883). The Russian version was entitled "The Cave of the Ozerky," this being the name of an estate, and appeared serially in the *Rebus,* Vol. V, January 5, 12 and 19, 1886. The story is signed "Radda-Bai" and is dedicated to her aunt, Nadyezhda A. de Fadeyev; the introductory portion differs markedly from the earlier English versions, but the story continues later more or less in the same way. The original English version may be found in Vol. I of the *Collected Writings.*

Another periodical which needs to be mentioned in connection with H.P.B.'s writings in Russian, is the *Novoye Vremya,* the very well-known daily newspaper established at St. Petersburg in 1876 and edited by A. S. Suvorin. H.P.B.'s article entitled "Chinese Shadows" was published therein February 10/22, 1888, and may be found in its English translation in Vol. IX of the *Collected Writings,* pp. 25-29. Writing to her relatives in Russia, H.P.B. informed them that she had written from Simla an article for the *Novoye Vremya* entitled "The Truth about the Nephew of Nâna-Sâhib." This was Prince Ramchandra, a "self-proclaimed and false ally of Russia," as she says, whose biography, most unreliable, had appeared in the June, 1889, issue of the *Russian Messenger.* This article, however, was rejected as "evidently written under the pressure of the Anglo-Indian officials," and no copy of H.P.B.'s manuscript has been preserved.*

During the winter of 1887-88, the *Novoye Vremya* informed the Russian public that H. P. Blavatsky, a compatriot of theirs, had settled in London with the intention of demolishing Christianity and spreading Buddhism, to further which she had already built a pagoda with Buddha's idol in it. H. P. B. wrote a letter on the subject to the office of this newspaper, in a very good-natured and humorous tone, but it never was printed.† No copy of this letter has been preserved.

There was another very well-known journal in Russia called *Russkoye Obozreniye* (Russian Review), a monthly founded in Moscow in 1890 and edited at first by Prince D. N. Tserteleff. H.P.B. under her pseudonym of "Radda-Bai" is mentioned on the back cover of this journal as one of those "closely associated" with it. A comprehensive inspection of the volumes of this periodical failed, however, to show anything whatever from the pen of H.P.B.

Mention should also be made of a Russian story which H.P.B. was apparently writing in the last months of her life. It was to be entitled: "The Theosophical Society — A True Story of the Nineteenth Century." Its sub-title states: "Materials for a future History of Psychism in the Epoch of Darwin. Dedicated to the Skeptics of my Fatherland." It is an unfinished story which exists in H.P.B.'s handwriting in the Adyar Archives. It was published for the first time in the Russian Journal *Alba* (No. 8, 1962), a valuable and historically interesting periodical issued at irregular times at Boston, Mass., U.S.A. by two of the finest and most devoted Russian Theosophists in exile, a brother and sister, Nicholas Pavlovich and Dagmar Pavlovna von Reincke. This fragment from H.P.B.'s pen was translated into English by Zoltán de Âlgya-Pap and published in *The Theosophist* Vol. 82, September, 1961. This translation will appear in the *Collected Writings* among other material posthumously published.

---

* *The Path*, New York, Vol. IX, March, 1895, p. 414. Also *Collected Writings*, Vol. II, "A Berlin Mare's Nest."

† *The Path*, New York, Vol. X, November, 1895, p. 236.

While H.P.B.'s output in her native Russian is rather voluminous as it is, it could have been a great deal larger had she accepted an offer made to her by Katkov. Writing to Sinnett on August 19, 1885, from Würzburg, Germany, she refers to a contract with Katkov to write exclusively for his journal and paper, a contract "that would put yearly 40,000 francs at least in my pocket." But the Master "would not permit me to sign such a contract last year in Paris when proposed, and does not sanction it now for — He says — my time 'shall have to be occupied otherwise'." *

In another letter to Sinnet, undated but presumably written in the early part of 1886, she speaks of a letter which she received from Moscow, "offering me if I leave the *Antichrist* (!!) T.S. one thousand rubles *in gold* (5,000 francs) monthly and a contract for several years to write exclusively for two papers. I wish they may get it." †

Most of H.P.B.'s contributions to Russian periodicals were signed by the pseudonym of "Radda-Bai." We have left this signature in its exact transliteration from the Russian. It is uncertain whether H.P.B. meant the first word to be *Râdhâ*, "prosperity," or "success," the name of a celebrated cowherdess or Gopî, beloved by Kṛishṇa, and a principal personage in the poem *Gîtagovinda*, who was later worshipped as a goddess and regarded as an Avatâra of Lakshmî, as Kṛishṇa was of Vishṇu; or whether the Russian form was meant for *râddha*, which means "accomplished, prepared, ready," and even "perfect in magical power" or "initiated." *Bâi* is a Marâthî term and means *Lady* or *Madame;* it is used as a respectful way of addressing an elderly woman.

In preparing the present edition, the Russian text of H.P.B.'s serial stories was first literally but roughly translated. It was then checked, corrected and improved. At that stage, the translation was given to Mrs. Irene R. Ponsonby who critically went over every page and line of it, eliminating awkward expressions, non-English idioms and structures, smoothing the translation and substituting, whenever re-

---

* A. P. Sinnett, *The Letters of H. P. Blavatsky to A. P. Sinnett,* Letter LXVI, p. 112.
† *Ibid.,* Letter LXX, p. 173.

quired, more suitable words. Without her consummate knowledge of English and her vast background of reading, as well as her familiarity with H.P.B.'s way of expressing herself, the translation of these writings would have left much to be desired. Her unfailing patience and remarkable skill made it possible to have this translation rendered into good English without losing any of the typically "H.P.B.-esque" style and atmosphere.

H.P.B.'s Russian writings abound in various technical terms, expressions, and proper names from the Sanskrit and the vernaculars of India, such as Hindî, Bengalî, Tamil, Urdu, Marâthî, and others. To establish the correct English transliteration of many of these words presented considerable difficulty, and adequate scholarly advice from experts was obtained whenever the Translator and Compiler was unable to solve the problem himself. In connection with this aspect of the work, the willing and efficient help of Mrs. Radha Burnier, and Mrs. Seetha Neelakantan, both of the Adyar Library and Research Center, should be acknowledged with much gratitude. Their extensive and many-sided scholarship and careful handling of the problems involved have been of inestimable value.

Generally speaking, all Sanskrit terms are spelled according to Sir M. Monier-Williams' *Sanskrit-English Dictionary,* with only minor variations. Terms belonging to the vernaculars of India have been in many cases checked by individuals speaking them, and their suggestions followed.

In regard to proper names — most of which are those of Hindu and Moslem kings and rulers, names of ancient cities, historical sites, and famous figures in Oriental history — we have adhered on the whole to the spelling adopted in the *Cambridge History of India.* This was done because some well-known and established standard in the English language had to be adhered to, in the midst of a great variety of spellings encountered from one author to another.

It should be remembered that H.P.B. transliterated Oriental terms and names into Russian *as they were pronounced.* Her handwriting was not always legible to the editor who handled the stories. The proofreading, while excellent on the whole, left much to be desired in regard to technical terms and proper names unfamiliar in Russia. The result was anything but satisfactory. To re-transliterate these terms and names from the Russian script into English would have rendered some of them unrecognizable, even in the Orient. Hence they had to be first identified in English published works and reference sets, an effort which has consumed much time. With the exception of a very few, most of these terms and names have been identified and checked by the best scholarly standards available.

Boris de Zirkoff,
Translator and Compiler.

TABLE OF CONTENTS

— PART I —

— I —

PAGES

ARRIVAL AT BOMBAY — GHÂRÂPURI OR ELEPHANTA — MALABAR HILL TEMPLE OF VÂLUKEŚVARA — HARBOR OF BOMBAY — SUSPICIONS OF THE ENGLISH — DRUNKEN CROWS. 1

— II —

UNIQUE CHARACTER OF INDIA — ATHANASIUS NIKITIN, THE TRAVELLER — DAYÂNANDA SARASVATÎ SVÂMI, HIS CHARACTER AND WORK — BADRINÂTH AND ITS MYSTERY — FORMATION OF THE THEOSOPHICAL SOCIETY — ALLIANCE WITH THE ÂRYA-SAMÂJA — EVENTUAL BREAK WITH DAYÂNANDA — THE PÂRSÎ TOWER OF SILENCE — PÂRSÎ BURIAL RITES — JAINAS AND THEIR BELIEFS — THE PÂÑJRÂPOL. 16

— III —

THE FAIRY-DRAMA OF SÎTÂ-RÂMA — ITS ANCIENT MYTHOLOGICAL SYMBOLISM — GHEBERS AND THEIR WANDERINGS — VARIEGATED TYPES AND COSTUMES OF THE CROWD. 38

— IV —

CATHOLIC CONVERTS — MÂTHERÂN — THÂKUR GULÂB-LAL-SINGH — BHÂO-MALLIN — INSOLENCE OF ENGLISHMEN — MATERIALISM OF YOUNG HINDUS — ARDHANÂRÎ AND VEDÂNTIC PANTHEISM — MATAPHYSICS OF INDIA — THE FOUR-FACED ŚIVA. 47

—V—

— XII —

— XIII —

— XIV —

— XV —

— XVI —

— XVII —

— XVIII —

—XIX—

—XX—

—XXI—

—XXII—

—XXIII—

—XXIX—

—PART II—

—I—

—II—

—III—

—IV—

— V —

— VI —

— VII —

ILLUSTRATIONS

FROM THE CAVES AND JUNGLES OF
HINDOSTAN

PART I*

—I—

Late in the evening of February 16, 1879, after a rough passage of thirty-two days out of Liverpool, joyful exclamations were heard from the passenger deck: "The Lighthouse! The Bombay Lighthouse! . . . ." And everyone, whatever they were doing, laid down their cards, books and music, and rushed on deck. The moon had not yet risen, and in spite of the starlit tropical sky, it was dark on the upper deck. The stars were shining so brightly that, at first, it seemed hardly possible to distinguish a point of light on earth below them. Like so many huge and protruding eyes, the stars winked at us out of the black sky, at one end of which serenely shone the Southern Cross . . . . . Finally, however, still lower on the distant horizon, we caught a glimpse of the shining lighthouse, a tiny fiery point bobbing up and down on the phosphorescent waves. The welcome given by the harassed passengers to this long-expected event was warm indeed. Everyone was happy . . . .

We did not get a chance, however, to observe the lighthouse for any length of time. The bell rang, and all lights went out in the main cabin. It was ten o'clock and everyone, filled with pleasant thoughts about tomorrow, retired

---

*These letters from the pen of our compatriot appeared at various times in the *Moskovskiya Vedomosti* (Moscow Gazette) over the signature of "Radda-Bai" and will be continued in the *Russkiy Vestnik* (Russian Messenger). [Note by the Editor of the *Russkiy Vestnik*.]

1

to his respective cabin. Hardly anyone, however, slept that night. They were all busy packing, and preparing to bid farewell as early as possible next morning to our washtub, full of holes, taking in water, yet dignified by the name of "ocean steamer" by the Liverpool Company, and to take leave of its drunken and rude captain who, by the way, nearly drowned us, and on Sundays forbade the passengers to play cards or chess, or even to occupy themselves with some music.

By about four o'clock in the morning, all the passengers were on deck, even the ladies. Such an early appearance of the fair sex had not been taken into account by a group of Anglo-Indian officers and embarrassed them greatly. One party of brave warriors, with the help of sailors, dowsed themselves with water from the deck-pumps, while their comrades, awaiting their turn, walked about in the national dress of the Hindus—none. But the bashful ladies were *returning*—this was not their first voyage to India. Seemingly already accustomed to this sort of changing circumstances, they remained cool-headed, the more so as in this case the only difference was that of color, and moreover dawn was just beginning . . . . . .

And what a dawn! . . . . . The ship was not rolling any more . . . . Under the skillful steering of a native pilot, who had just arrived dressed in the costume of Hercules, and whose bronze silhouette was sharply defined against the pale sky, our steamer, puffing heavily due to its damaged engine, was quietly slipping over the calm and translucent waters of the Indian Ocean straight towards the harbor. We were nearing the Gulf, and only a few miles separated us from Bombay. To those of us who, only four weeks earlier, had shivered in the penetrating cold of a snow storm which caught us at the entrance to the Gulf of Biscay— often glorified by the poets, and oftener yet cursed by the sailors—our surroundings seemed like a magical dream! . . . After the tropical nights of the Red Sea, and the incredibly scorching days which had tortured us since Aden, something strange and bewitching cast its spell over us Northerners, in this wonderfully soft freshness of the pre-dawn air. Not a cloud could be seen in the sky, still thickly strewn

with stars about to be extinguished . . . . . The fading
light of the moon, that had up to that moment spread
its silvery veil over the sky, began to vanish little by
little; and while before us over a distant island in the
East appeared the first rosiness of dawn, the last radiance of the moon centered itself more and more in the
West, showering golden sparks upon the dark watery wake
our ship was leaving—as if the light of the West were bidding us, people from America, good-bye, while the light from
the East greeted the newcomers from far-off lands. Brighter
and bluer became the sky, swiftly absorbing one after the
other the remaining dimly-twinkling stars, and there was
something touching in the sweet dignity with which the
Queen of Night resigned her sovereign rights to the powerful usurper. At last, she quietly merged with the waves and
disappeared. Suddenly, almost without break between darkness and light, the fiery-red globe, emerging from behind
the cape on the opposite side, rested its golden chin for a
few moments on the lower rocks of the island and seemed to
pause awhile, as if examining us . . . Then, with one powerful thrust, the day-star rose high over the sea, and triumphantly sailed on its upward path, dispelling darkness
and enveloping in its fiery embrace the blue waters of the
bay, the homes on the shore, and the islands with their
rocks and their cocoanut groves . . . . Nor did the
golden rays fail to warm a crowd of devoted worshippers,
of Pârsî-Ghebers, who stood on the shore with their arms
raised towards the mighty "Eye of Ormazd." The sight was
so impressive that everyone on deck became silent for a
moment; even the red-nosed old sailor near us, who was
busy with the cable, stopped working and, clearing his
throat, nodded approvingly at the sun.

Moving slowly and cautiously through the charming but
equally treacherous bay, we had plenty of time to admire
the neighbouring surroundings. On our right was a group
of islands, headed by *Ghârâpuri* or "Elephanta," with its
very ancient temple. "Ghârâpuri" translated means "the
town of caves," according to the Orientalists, and "the town
of purification," if we are to believe the native Sanskrit
scholars. This temple, cut by an unknown hand out of the

very heart of a rock resembling porphyry, has been for a
long time an apple of discord among the archaeologists,
none of whom can, so far, make even an approximate estimate of its antiquity. Elephanta raises its rocky brow,
thickly overgrown with centuries-old cactus, while right
below it, at the foot of the rock, are hollowed out the chief
temple and the two lateral ones . . . Like the Serpent-
Gorinich,* it seems to open wide its black mouth, as if to
swallow the daring mortal who comes to fathom the secret
mystery of the Titan. It shows, as it were, its two remaining eye teeth, dark with time—the two huge pillars which
at the very entrance sustain the palate of the monster . . . . .

How many generations of Hindus, how many races, have
prostrated themselves in the dust before the *Trimûrti,* thy
three-fold deity, O Elephanta! . . . How many centuries
were spent by weak man in carving from thy porphyry
bosom this whole city of cave-temples and marble pagodas
and in modeling thy gigantic idols? Who can tell? Many
years have gone by since we last saw each other, ancient
and mysterious temple. Yet the same restless thoughts, the
same recurrent questions vex me now as of yore, and still
remain unanswered . . . . . In a few days we shall see each
other again. Once more shall I gaze upon thy stern image,
upon thy three-fold granite face nineteen feet high, and
feel as hopeless as ever of piercing the mystery of thy being!
. . . . . . This mystery fell into safe hands three centuries
before ours. It is not in vain that the old Portuguese historian Don Diogo do Couto † boasts that:

---

* (In the Russian fairy tale.)

† [Diogo do Couto was a Portuguese historian, who was born at
Lisbon in 1542, and who died at Goa in 1616. After some years of
education along very liberal lines, specializing in philosophy, he embarked for India, and eventually settled at Goa where he married. His
research expeditions earned for him the position of chief historiographer
of Spanish possessions in India. His voluminous work, *Da Asia,* etc.,
is a continuation of the so-called *Decadas* of João de Barros (1496-
1570) who was called the Portuguese Livy. Couto's work appeared in
a number of installments which are rather scarce today. The best modern edition of the entire work is the one published at Lisbon from
1778 to 1788, in 14 volumes.—*Compiler.*]

. . . . . the big square stone fastened over the arch of the pagoda, with a large and distinct inscription on it, having been torn out and sent to King Don Juan III, subsequently *mysteriously* disappeared . . . . .

and adds further:

. . . . close to this large pagoda there stood another . . . and even a third one . . . . the most amazing edifice on the island, both on account of its beauty, and its incredibly large proportions and richness of material. All these pagodas and caves were built by the kings of *Kannaḍa,* the most important of whom was Bâṇâsura, and these structures of Satan our Portuguese soldiers attacked with such vehemence that in a few years not one stone was left upon another.*

Still worse, no inscriptions that might have given a clue to many things were left. Thanks to the fanaticism of these Portuguese vandals, the chronology of the Indian cave-temples must remain forever an enigma to the archaeological world, beginning with the Brâhmaṇas who assure the tourist that Elephanta is 374,000 years old, and ending with Fergusson, who tries to prove that this temple was carved in the tenth century of our era.† Wherever one may turn in their history, there is nothing but hypotheses and darkness. And yet Ghârâpuri is mentioned in the epic poem *Mahâbhârata,* written, according to Colebrooke and Wilson, a considerable time before the reign of Cyrus. In another ancient legend, it is said that the temple of Trimûrti was built on Elephanta by the sons of *Pâṇḍu* who were expelled by the triumphant race of the Sun, at the end of the war described in the *Mahâbhârata,* the war between the dynasties of the Sun and the Moon. The Râjputs (descendants of the former) to this day sing their victory over the enemies, but even in their popular songs there is nothing positive. Centuries have gone by and will continue to go by, but the archaic secret will die in the rocky bosom of the cave.

---

*[Don Diogo do Couto, *Da Asia,* Decada VII, Book III, pp. 259-61; Lisbon, 1778-88, in 14 vols.]

†James Fergusson, *Illustrations of the Rock-cut Temples of India,* 1845, Text Volume, p. 52.

On the left side of the bay, exactly opposite Elephanta, as if in contrast to all this antiquity and greatness, spreads the Malabar Hill, the residential section of present day Europeans and rich natives. Their brightly painted bungalows are bathed in the greenery of banyans, Indian fig, and various other trees, while the tall, straight trunks of coconut palms cover with the fringe of their leaves the whole ridge of the hilly headland. Over there, on the southwestern end of the rock, surrounded on three sides by the ocean, one can see the lace-like, almost transparent, edifice of Government House. This is the coolest and most comfortable part of Bombay, fanned from three different directions by sea breezes. This is the residence of Sir Richard Temple, the governor and ruler of the Bombay Presidency.*
The flag waving from the tall mast notifies both the loyal and the unfaithful ones that His Excellency is "at home." This is a location as beautiful as it is suitable for the esteemed baronet who is suffering, by the way, from an overheated imagination. Only the fresh air saves him from a constantly threatening stroke, as a result of a painful monomania, the central features of which are "Russian spies" and the insidious "Russian intrigue."

The island of Bombay, called "Mumbâï" by the natives, received its name from the goddess "Mumbâ"—in Marâthî, Mâhîm and Ambâ, "Mahâ" and "Ammâ," according to the dialect—a word meaning literally the "Great Mother." Hardly one hundred years ago, on the site of the modern esplanade, there stood a temple consecrated to "Mumbâ-Devî." With incredible difficulty and expense it was moved nearer to the shore, close to the Fort, and erected opposite the temple of Bâlêśvara, *Lord of the Innocents* — one of the names of the god Śiva. Bombay is one of the consider-

---

*Alas! A few months later, this severe ruler of the Marâthâs, whose conscience is burdened with the death of a million and a half souls who, owing to his stupidity, perished during the last famine, was fired with the desire to become a member of Parliament. Throwing aside his governorship, he hurried to England for the election, and received there his rightful retribution. At the first opportunity, the electorate threw rotten eggs at him and caused him to take flight.

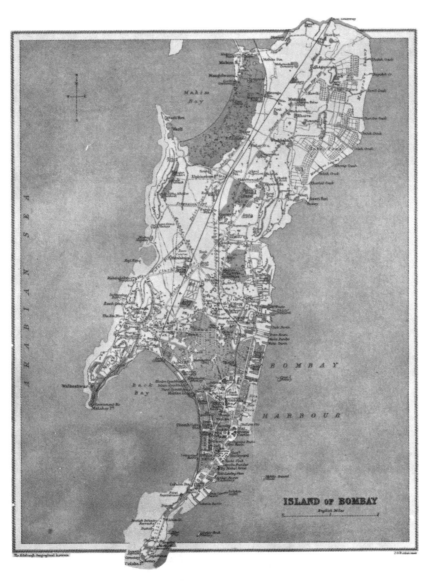

MAP OF THE ISLAND OF BOMBAY

ENTRANCE TO THE CAVE OF ELEPHANTA

ably large group of islands; the most remarkable of them, due to their antiquity, are: Sâlsette, joined to Bombay by a mall; Elephanta, so named by the Portuguese because of a huge rock cut in the shape of an elephant, thirteen feet long; and Trombay, whose lonely rock rises 900 feet above the sea.

Bombay, appearing like a large crayfish on the map, is at the head of the rest of the islands. Spreading its two claws far out into the sea, it stands like a permanent guardian watching over his younger and less protected brothers . . . . Between it and the continent there is a narrow arm of a river which gets gradually wider and then narrows again, deeply indenting the curved sides of both shores, and thus forming a harbor that has no equal in the world. Not without reason have the Portuguese, who were expelled by the English, called it "Buon Bahia," or excellent bay.

In a fit of tourist exaltation, some travellers have compared the Bay of Bombay to that of Naples. As a matter of fact, the one is as much like the other, as a *lazzaroni* is like a *coolie*—the only likeness between these is in the color of the skin; as for the respective harbors, both have water in them. In Bombay, as well as in its harbor, everything is original and unlike anything else, and in no way reminds one of Southern Europe. Look at those coasting vessels and fisherman's boats: both are built in the likeness of a bird, and had for a model the sea-bird "sat," which is somewhat like the kingfisher. Such a boat, especially when in motion, is the very personification of grace, with its long, bird-like prow and blunt, rounded poop. It looks as if it were gliding backwards, and its strangely shaped, slanting triangular sail (lateen) is fastened to a long pole, with its narrow angle up, like the two wings of a bird. When the wind fills these two wings, such a native boat careens so as almost to touch the surface of the water, and sails with astonishing swiftness, especially when the wind is right. Unlike our own boats, they do not cut through the waves, but glide over them like a sea gull, exactly like a kingfisher in appearance.

The surroundings of the bay transported us that morning to some fairy land of the *Arabian Nights*. The range of the Western Ghâts, cut through here and there by separating hills almost as high as the range itself, stretched all along the eastern shore. From their base to their fantastic rocky summit, they are overgrown with impassable forests and *jungles* inhabited by wild animals, and every rock has been endowed by popular imagination with its own special legend. All the slopes are strewn with pagodas, minarets and temples of numberless sects. Here and there, bathed in the early morning sun, emerges an old fortress, once awesome and inaccessible, but now half-ruined and covered with impenetrable cactus. There is a holy spot at every step. Here—a "vihâra," the cave-cell of a Buddhist *bhikshu,* deep inside the mountain; there — a rock protected by the symbol of the god Śiva; further on—a Jaina temple; a holy *tank*—a pond all covered with slime and filled with water blessed by a Brâhmaṇa and therefore capable of purifying every sin—an indispensable attribute of all pagodas.

The whole surrounding country is strewn with symbols of gods and goddesses. Each of the thirty-three million deities of the Hindu Pantheon is represented by some object consecrated to it—a stone, a flower, a tree, or a bird. On the west side of the Malabar Hill peeps out Vâlukêś-vara, the temple of the *Lord of Sand*. A long file of Hindus, clad in bright turbans and snow-white raiments, with foreheads freshly painted with sacred sect marks of red, yellow and white, moves towards this celebrated temple. The men and women wear golden rings on their feet and hands, and bracelets from the wrist to the elbow and from the ankle to the calf of the leg which make them shine in the sun. The legend says that Râma spent a night here on his way from *Ayôdhyâ* (Oudh) to Lankâ (Ceylon) to fetch his wife Sîtâ who had been stolen by the wicked King Râvana. Râma's brother Lakshmaṇa, whose duty it was to furnish him every evening with a new *linga* from Benares, was one day late in doing so. Losing patience, Râma erected for himself a *linga* of sand. When, at last, the symbol arrived from Benares, it was placed in a temple, and the *liṅga* erected by Râma was left on the shore. There it stayed during long centuries, but upon the arrival of the Portuguese, the "Lord of Sand" felt so disgusted with the *feringhee* (foreigners)* that he jumped into the sea and was seen no more.

A little farther on there is a charming pond (tank) called *Bânatîrtha,* or the "Pond of the Arrow." Here Râma (the beloved and deified hero of the Hindus) felt thirsty and, not finding any water, shot an arrow into the earth. Immediately there appeared a pond. Its crystal waters were then surrounded by a high wall, steps were built leading down to it, and a circle of white marble pagodas and dwellings for the *dvija* (twice-born) Brâhmaṇas was erected.

India is the land of legends and of mysterious nooks. There is not a ruin, not a monument, not a thicket, that has no story associated with it. Yet, however entangled these may be in the cobweb of popular imagination, which becomes thicker and thicker with every generation, it would be difficult to point to a single story that is not founded on some historical fact. With patience, and especially with the help of the learned Brâhmaṇas, once you have secured their trust and friendship, you can always arrive at the truth. Naturally the English, with their haughtiness and contempt openly shown towards the "conquered *race,*" cannot expect this. That is why there is as much difference between *officially* explored India and (what we may be permitted to call) *underground* India, as there is between

---

* [*Feringhee* is a term for European, especially Indian-born Portuguese; also for a Eurasian, especially of Portuguese-Indian blood. A *Dictionary of Anglo-Indian Colloquial Words and Phrases* by Col. Henry Yule and A. C. Burnell lists the word under *Firinghee* and says: "Pers. *Farangî, Firingî;* Ar. *Al-Faranj, Ifranji, Firanji, i.e.,* a Frank. This term for a European is very old in Asia, but when now employed by natives in India is either applied (especially in the South) specifically to the Indian-born Portuguese, or, when used more generally, for 'European', implies something of hostility or disparagement . . ."—*Compiler.*]

the Russia of the novels of Dumas-père and the real *Russian* Russia.

A little further along the same road stands a temple of the Pârsî fire-worshippers. On its altar burns an inextinguishable flame which daily consumes hundredweights of sandalwood and aromatic herbs. Lighted three hundred years ago, the sacred fire has never been allowed to go out, in spite of disorders, sectarian discords, and even wars. The Pârsîs are very proud of this temple of *Zarathusht,* as they call Zoroaster. By comparison to it, the Hindu pagodas look like brightly painted Easter eggs. Generally they are places of worship consecrated to Hanuman, the monkey-god and faithful ally of Râma, or to some other deity as, for instance, the elephant-headed Gaṇêśa (the god of occult wisdom) or one of the Devas. Such temples are to be found on every street. In front of each of them there is a row of centuries-old pîpals (*ficus religiosa*), which no temple can dispense with, because these trees are the favorite abode of elemental spirits and of sinful souls. All these commingle and suddenly appear before your eyes, like a dream picture—tangled and scattered helter-skelter.

Thirty centuries have left their mark on these islands. Long before the invasion of the Europeans, the innate laziness of the Hindus and their inherent conservatism preserved, even from the ruinous vengeance of the fanatics, these monuments of Buddhists and other sects hostile to the Brâhmaṇas. The Hindus are not naturally given to senseless vandalism, and a phrenologist would vainly look for a bump of destructiveness on their skulls. If one finds so many monuments of antiquity which, having been spared by time, are today disfigured, spoiled or destroyed, they were laid low by either the Moslems or the Portuguese under the guidance of the Jesuits.

The beauty of the Bay of Bombay does not compensate for the shortcomings of its harbor, from the strategic point of view. Its weakness, which none but a specialist would notice, is, curiously enough, pointed out by the English themselves. They talk about it to foreigners, discuss it in the newspapers, and even complain of it in their "guides." For instance, in Captain E. B. Eastwick's *Handbook for*

Travellers in India (1859),* the author enters into a long discussion concerning the danger threatening England in case of an enemy invasion of Bombay from the sea. This defect, long since noticed by the jealous rulers of the land, renders them sleepless. Is it possible that what happened to the Portuguese at the hands of the Mogul admiral Yakub Khân Sîdî, who in 1690 took the fortress of Bombay in a few hours, could be repeated in 1880? Can this great, *unconquerable* nation, with more than a thousand cannons on the Admiralty bastion, on the Mândavî-Bandar and other batteries, fear an invasion? To judge by the avowal of its own sons, and by their methods, they are not only sorrowful, but constantly afraid of something. "Whatever ails you—*that* you speak of." One is led to assume that this splinter is deeply lodged and aches badly in the hip of the British lion. We were hardly a hundred miles out of Liverpool before being initiated at the common dinner table into all the weaknesses of the Bombay harbor. Listen to what they are saying! "Our fort may be strong enough from the side of the continent," the captain was telling us, "but on the side of the sea it isn't so good. It would be hard to imagine anything more vulnerable . . . . Moreover, it is the narrow part of the bay that is apt to be uncomfortable to the enemy's fleet, rather than its outlet. As to the castle of *Fort St. George,* built by the Portuguese, it reminds one of the flat, one-wall castles of an opera stage; it hasn't even a decent parapet. The fortress itself (the commercial part of town) is not even protected by a wall. On the other hand, it is hemmed in to the very shore with old, half-rotten factories and shops, and a lot of poorly built warehouses and private dwellings . . . . At the first cannon shot

---

*[Edward Backhouse Eastwick (1814-1883) was educated at Charterhouse and Merton College, Oxford; having gone to India in 1836, he devoted himself to Oriental languages and served in the political department in Kattiawar and Sind. Returning to Europe, he held a number of political offices connected with the administration of India and translated several Oriental works, visiting India several times. He also prepared Murray's *Handbooks for Travellers in India* which began to be published in 1859, and are currently available in new and revised editions.—*Compiler.*]

our renowned fort will tumble like a house of cards," and so forth.

And now, let us look into the *Handbook* and see what Eastwick, who dedicates the work to his brother, a captain of the Bombay army, has to say. He writes:

> If our unlucky fortress were to pretend sometime to defend itself, the enemy would not have to pay any attention to it. All he would have to do would be to round the island, without entering the harbor, and to land troops from the northern and completely unprotected side. It is only during the *monsoon* (rainy season) that the Back-Bay is dangerous on account of its storms, and especially owing to the underwater reefs which are strewn thickly around the Prong lighthouse. During the other eight months ships can drop anchor outside the bay in no danger whatsoever.

Very frank, isn't it? For this reason, the malevolent remark of a well-known Anglo-Indian writer reminding us that in case of war or invasion, "Back-Bay would be *as attractive a temptation as it would be dangerous and crafty*," loses all its meaning. This danger exists only during the four-months-long *monsoon*, as the *Handbook* declares, and the rest of the year—everyone is welcome!

And yet, while describing with so much detail their weak points, the Anglo-Indians see in every innocent tourist from other lands — a spy. A Russian artist, the pianist Miss Olga Duboin, was here some two years ago, and decided to make a tour of India; twenty agents of the secret police shadowed her everywhere she went. A German painter (Horace van Ruith),* born in St. Petersburg, but speaking hardly any Russian, came here to study the national types of Hindostan. The spies dressed appropriately and offered themselves to him as models. A party arrived, made up of an American Colonel, a genuine Yankee, two Englishmen from London—rabid patriots, but liberals—and an American citizen, though *Russian* by birth, and see how the nationality of the latter alerts the entire police-force! It would be use-

---

* [Horace van Ruith was a painter of portraits and landscapes who resided in Italy, 1874-89, and in London 1892-1915; he also travelled in British India, and exhibited in the Royal Academy of London from 1888.—*Compiler.*]

less to try and show that these tourists are occupied solely with metaphysical speculation about unknown worlds, and that not only are they not interested in the politics of this earthly abode, but their Russian travelling companion does not know the first thing about it. "The wiliness of Russia has long become proverbial," she is told. "We have cut off Russia's route over the Himâlayas by means of the Afghânistân war, so, naturally, she is trying another angle . . . . They made friends with the Chinese, and now they urge them to move on India through Rangoon. That's why we simply have to take possession of Burma."* They are afraid of the Chinese, with their earthen pots of evil-smelling liquid. Well, let them rule to their heart's content, if nobody interferes! At least there is an excuse for it. But why on earth tell such fibs about Russia?

This national characteristic of the English to shout: "Help, they are killing us!" when nobody even thinks of touching them, is disgusting. It has developed especially during the premiership of Beaconsfield. But if this trait is notable even in England, how much more so is it in India? Here suspicion has become a monomania. Anglo-Indians see Russian spies even in their own shoes, and this drives them to madness.

"Tell me," asks an American colonel of the chief police inspector in one of the North-West Provinces, "do you think a repetition of the Sepoy mutiny of 1857 possible? Are the Hindus pacified?"

"Pshaw! . . . . To fear such a mutiny would be as reasonable as to fear the moon will fall on our heads," is the haughty answer.

And yet, the same captain tells you at lunch about the superiority of the police organization in his province; not

---

*That's why the Burmese Ambassador, sent this summer (1882) to Simla for discussions and the signing of a new treaty, went away empty-handed. All the newspapers rose up in arms against the "impudent" demands of Burma, that impudence consisting in the fact that Burma demanded the right to deal directly with the English Cabinet, instead of through the Calcutta government, and the curtailing of the rights of Anglo-Indian officials to treat the King of Burma, the subject of the Queen, as a mere coolie. [*Later Note by the Author.*]

a Hindu comes for an hour into town from a village but the fact is known to the secret police. They watch every new arrival from one province to another, even should he be an Englishman. People have been deprived not only of every weapon, but of all knives and axes. The peasant can hardly chop his wood, or protect himself from a tiger. But the English are still afraid. It is true that here there are but 60,000 of them, while the native population numbers 245 million. And their system, which they took over from successful animal-tamers, is good only until the animal senses his tamer is fearful in his turn . . . .Then his hour has come! At all events, such a manifestation of chronic fear merely admits a recognition of one's own weakness.

At last we were anchored, and, in a moment, were besieged, ourselves and our baggage, by numbers of naked, skeleton-like Hindus, Moguls, Pârsîs and various other tribes. All this crowd emerged as if from the bottom of the sea and began to shout, chatter and yell, as only the tribes of Asia can. To rid ourselves of this Babel-like confusion of tongues which threatened to deafen us permanently, we took refuge in the first bunder-boat and made for the shore.

Once settled in the bungalow prepared for us ahead of time, the first thing that struck us in Bombay was the millions of crows and vultures. The first are, so to speak, the garbage collectors of the city, and to kill them is not only forbidden by the police, but would in fact be very dangerous, as it would arouse the vengeance of Hindus, who are always ready to offer their own lives in exchange for a crow's. The souls of their sinful forefathers transmigrate into crows; to kill the bird is to interfere with the law of retribution, and to doom the soul to something still worse. Such is the firm belief, not only of the Hindus, but of the superstitious Pârsîs (even the most enlightened among them). The strange behavior of the Indian crows (noticed later) explains to a certain extent this superstition. On the other hand, the vultures, the constant grave-diggers of the Pârsîs, are under the direct protection of *Farvardin,* the angel of death, who soars over the Tower of Silence, directing the occupation of the feathered workmen. The terrible cawing of the crows, which does not cease even at night, strikes the newcomer as uncanny, but it can be very simply explained after a while. Every tree of the numerous coconut forests surrounding Bombay is leased from the government; a hollow pumpkin is tied to it, the sap of the tree runs into the pumpkin and, after fermenting, becomes a strong intoxicating beverage, known here as "toddy."* Completely naked *toddy-wâlâs* (usually Portuguese),† modestly adorned with a coral necklace, fetch this beverage twice a day, climbing the hundred and fifty feet high trunks like squirrels. The crows build their nests in these trees and incessantly drink out of the open pumpkins. The result is the chronic intoxication of these noisy birds. Immediately when we went into the garden of our future abode, flocks of crows flew down from every tree, cawing noisily. The birds surrounded us, jumping on one leg. There seemed to be something positively *human* in the position of the slyly bent heads of the *drunken birds,* and a fiendish expression shone in their cunning eyes, as they examined us from head to foot . . .

---

*["Toddy" is a corruption of the Marâthî word *tâdi* which is derived from *tâd*, the *Marâthî* form of the Hindî *târ* and the Sanskrit *tâla*, the name for the palmyra or fan-palm (*Borassus flabelliformis*), sometimes applied to the corypha and other palms. The juice extracted from the palmyra, the date or the coco-palm, when first drawn, is sweet and not intoxicating, but after fermentation becomes a strong spirituous liquor.—*Compiler.*]

†[*Wâlâ* is a word of very common use in the vernaculars of India; it may be affixed to almost any noun or verb, and the word so formed then denotes a person connected in some way with the thing expressed by the first word, for instance: *gâri-wâlâ*, cartman; *jâdu-wâlâ*, sorcerer; *tonga-wâlâ*, one who draws a tonga, etc. This word is often spelled *wallah* in English.—*Compiler.*]

—II—

We occupied three small bungalows, lost, like nests, in
the greenery of the garden, their roofs literally smothered
in roses blooming on bushes fifteen feet high, and their
windows covered only with muslin, instead of the usual
panes of glass. The bungalows were situated in the native
part of the town, thus we were transported all at once to
the real India. We were living *in* India, unlike the English
who are merely *surrounded* by India at a proper distance.
We were enabled to study her character and customs, her
religion, superstitions and rites, to become acquainted with
her traditions, in fact, to live among Hindus—an enchanted
circle, inaccessible to the English because of both the centuries-old native prejudice, and the innate haughtiness of
the Anglo-Saxon race.

Everything in India—the land of the elephant and the
poisonous cobra, of the tiger and the unsuccessful English
missionary—is unique and strange. Everything strikes one
as unusual and unexpected, even if one has travelled in
Turkey, Egypt, Damascus and Palestine. In these tropical
regions, the conditions of nature are so varied, that the
reason why all the forms of life in the animal and vegetable

16

kingdom must differ from those we are accustomed to in Europe becomes clear. Look, for instance, at those women on their way to the well through a garden which, though private, is open to all, and where someone else's cows graze. Who has not met women, seen cows, and admired a garden? It would seem these are among the commonest things. But a single attentive glance will suffice to show you the enormous difference that exists between the same objects in Europe and in India.

Nowhere does a human being feel his insignificance and weakness more, than when facing the magnificence of tropical nature. The trunks of the coconut palms, straight as an arrow, reach sometimes 200 feet in height. These "princes of the vegetable kingdom," as Lindley* called them, crowned with a tuft of long branches, are the nurses and benefactors of the poor; they furnish him with food, clothing and a roof. Our highest trees would look dwarfed, compared to the banyans and especially the coconut and other palms. A European cow mistaking, at first sight, her Indian sister for a calf, would very soon deny any kinship between them, as neither the mouse-colored hide, nor the straight, goat-like horns, nor the humped back of the latter (reminding one of the American buffalo, but without its mane), would permit her to make such a mistake. As to the women, while any one of them would arouse an artist's enthusiasm over the gracefulness of her movements and her raiment, yet no rosy-cheeked and rotund Anna Ivanovna would condescend to greet or show kindness to these beauties of Hindostan. "Such a shame, God forgive me, the woman is completely naked!" The opinion of our Russian woman of 1879 would be but an echo of the views of the renowned Russian traveller of the fifteenth century,

---

*[John Lindley (1799-1865) was an English botanist and horticulturist, and the first professor of botany in the University of London (afterwards University College). He was prominently connected with the Horticultural Society and the famous Kew Gardens, and was the author of a large number of works and monographs on the botanical science, many of them profusely illustrated by himself and others. In 1828, he was elected a Fellow of the Royal Society, receiving later its royal medal.—*Compiler*.]

"the sinful slave of God, Athanasius, son of Nikita, from Tver." Having made his "sinful voyage" over three seas— the Sea of Derbent, the Sea of India and the Black Sea— Athanasius Nikitin arrived at Chaul * (*Chevil*, as he calls it) in 1470, and describes India as follows:

This is an Indian country. People go about naked, with their heads uncovered and bare breasts; the hair tressed into one tail, and thick bellies. They bring forth children every year and the children are many; and men and women are black. When I go out many people follow me, and stare at the white man.

Their *kniaz* [prince] wears a *fata* [large silken garment] on the head; and another on the loins; the *boyars* [noblemen] wear it on the shoulders and on the loins; the *kniagini* [princesses] wear it also round the shoulders and the loins. The servants of the kniaz and of the boyars attach the fata round the loins, carrying in the hand a shield and a sword, or a scimitar, or knives, or a sabre, or a bow and arrows— but all naked and barefooted. Women walk about with their heads uncovered and their breasts bare. Boys and girls go naked till seven years, and do not hide their shame . . . . . .†

---

*Thirty miles out of Bombay, Chaul was a rich and prospering city in Portuguese days.

†Lacking the original, the above is from the English translation of Count Wielhorsky, in *India in the Fifteenth Century*. Edited by R. H. Major, London, 1857, Part III, pp. 8-9.

[Athanasius Nikitin—called Mikitin in old-Russian—was a merchant from the town of Tver' who undertook several voyages to the South and the East, one of which took him as far as India. This was in the years between 1468 and 1472. His interesting account entitled *Hozhdeniye za tri morya*, meaning *Travel* (or Travelog) *Beyond the Three Seas*, was published in its entirety in the *Sofiyskiy Vremennik* (Sophian Chronicle), edited by Paul Stroyev, Moscow, 1820-21. This work contains a number of distinct Chronicles, written down by various monks between 862 and 1534, and kept in the college of the Cathedral Church of St. Sophia at Novgorod. It is in the second volume of this work, pp. 145-164, that Nikitin's journey to India was originally laid before the public *in extenso*. A less defective manuscript of Nikitin's journey was found in the archives of the Troitse-Sergiev monastery, near Moscow. It is this latter manuscript that was used by Count Wielhorsky, Secretary to the Russian Legation at the Court of St. James, for his English translation.

The original text of Nikitin's narrative may be found in the monumental work entitled *Polnoye sobraniye russkih lyetopisey* (Complete Collection of Russian Chronicles), published by the Archeographical

This description is quite correct, but with regard to the *nakedness* of the people, our Athanasius, son of Nikita, is not accurate; his description can refer merely to the lowest and poorest castes. These walk about covered with a mere veil, which often enough is so poor that it is no better than a ribbon. In the case of women, it consists of a piece of material sometimes as long as ten yards. One end is used like a pair of wide breeches, while the other covers the head and breasts when out on the street, though the faces are always uncovered. The hairdo reminds one of a Greek chignon. The legs up to the knees, the arms up to the shoulders and the waist are always uncovered. No respectable woman here would consider putting on a pair of shoes; shoes are the prerogative and attribute of "disreputable" women. In southern India, on the contrary, shoes are permitted only to the wives and daughters of Brâhmaṇas. When, some time ago, the wife of the Madras governor, under the influence of the missionaries, conceived the idea of promoting the passing of a law that would require native women to cover their breasts, it almost created a revolution. Not a woman agreed to this, because an upper garment is worn here only by public dancers. To the great consternation of the missionaries and the noble ladies, the project fell through. The Government soon realized the foolishness of antagonising the women (who upon occasion are more dangerous than their husbands and brothers) by an attack upon a custom prescribed by the *Laws of Manu,* and sanctified by an antiquity of three thousand years.

Commission, St. Petersburg (pr. by Eduard Pratz), 1843, etc.; it appears in Volume VI of this Series.

Nikitin's journey took place 25 years prior to the epoch-making voyage of Vasco de Gama, at a time when very little was known about India. He died approximately in 1475, before he reached Smolensk, on his return trip from a third journey, this time to Persia and Turkey.

In his narrative, Athanasius Nikitin uses the Russian words: *kniaz',* *kniaginya* (plural *kniagini*) and *boyar,* to designate their equivalents in India. Many terms and words to be found in the original old-Russian text are almost untranslatable, and present difficulties even to a Russian whose current language has departed to a very considerable extent from the language spoken in those days.—*Compiler.*]

For over two years before we left America, we were in constant correspondence with a certain learned Brâhmaṇa, known in Europe, whose reputation is at present [1879] high all over India. This Brâhmaṇa is Pandit Dayânanda Saraswatî Svâmi;* we came to study under his guidance the ancient country of the Âryans, the *Vedas*, and the difficult language. He is considered the greatest Sanskritist of contemporary India, and is a complete enigma to everyone. He appeared in the arena of reform only five years ago; until then, he lived as a hermit in the jungle, like the ancient "Gymnosophists" mentioned by Greek and Roman writers. Later, with the help of mystics and anchorites,† he studied the chief philosophical systems of "Âryâvarta" and the occult meaning of the *Vedas*. From the very day of his appearance, the impression he produced was remarkable and he acquired the surname "Luther of India." Wandering from one town to another, today in the south, tomorrow in the north, and travelling from one end of the country to the other with incredible swiftness, he has covered the whole peninsula from Cape Comorin to the Himâlayas, and from Calcutta to Bombay, preaching the *One Deity,* and showing—*Vedas* in hand—that in these ancient writings no word existed that could be interpreted in any sense as polytheism. Thundering against idol worship, the great orator fights with all his might against caste, infant marriages and superstition. Chastising all the evils grafted on India by centuries of casuistry and misinterpretation of the *Vedas*, he squarely and fearlessly blames the Brâhmaṇas for them, declaring them, in the hearing of the masses,

---

*[Svâmi is the title of learned anchorites, initiated into the mysteries of their religion which are unattainable by common mortals; they are monks who never marry, but are quite different from other mendicant brotherhoods, such as the *Gosâin* and the *Sannyâsin*.

†There is an old and deep-rooted belief among the Hindus that on the Badrînâth Mountains (22,000 feet above sea-level) there exist spacious underground dwellings inhabited for thousands of years by these anchorites. Badrînâth (in Northern India, on the right shore of the river Bishaṇgaṅgâ) is famous for its temple of Vishṇu, built right in the center of town. Inside the temple there are hot mineral springs, visited yearly by some 50,000 pilgrims who come to be purified of their sins by them.

guilty of the humiliation of their country, once great and independent, now fallen and enslaved. And yet Great Britain has in him rather an ally than an enemy. Not only does he not urge the people to revolt, but, on the contrary, he says openly: "If you expel the English, then, the very next day, you and I, and everyone who rises against the idol-worship of the Brâhmaṇas, and the evils of Moslem despotism, will have our throats cut like mere sheep. The Moslems are stronger than the idol-worshippers, but these last are stronger than we are . . . . ." And yet the English have so little recognition of their own advantage that two years ago, when the people at Poona were divided into two parties—the reformers and the idol-worshipping conservatives—and when the former presented their orator triumphantly riding on an elephant, while the latter threw stones and mud at him, the English, instead of defending Dayânanda, sent him out of the town, forbidding him henceforth to return.

The Pandit held many a warm argument with the Brâhmaṇas, those treacherous enemies of the people, and invariably was victorious. In Benares, secret assassins were sent to slay him, but the attempt did not succeed. In a small town of Bengal, when he attacked fetishism with special severity, some fanatic deftly threw a huge cobra-de-capello on his bare feet, the bite of which causes death within three minutes, and against which medicine at present knows no antidote. "Let the god *Vâsuki* himself show which one of us is right!"* exclaimed the worshipper of Śiva, feeling sure that the snake, trained purposely for the mysteries of the pagoda, would at once end the offender's life. "Very well," quietly replied Dayânanda, shaking off, with a single vigorous movement, the cobra twirling round his leg, "but

---

*"Vâsuki" is the snake twirling around the neck of Śiva on his idols, and is deified by Brâhmanical mythology, just as is the snake "Ananta," upon which reposes the god Vishṇu. At the end of July, when the festival of *Nâgas* or snakes is celebrated, vessels with milk are placed in all the squares and streets, and hundreds of snakes are brought by professional conjurers to various towns and villages. On that day, India feeds its reptile "gods," and Europeans are afraid to leave their houses.

your god is too slow; it is I who decide the issue . . ."
With one quick and mighty blow of his heel, he then
crushed the head of the snake. "Now go," he added, addressing the crowd, "and tell everyone how easily perish
the false gods!"

Thanks to his excellent knowledge of Sanskrit, the Pandit
performs a great service, not only to the masses by dispelling their ignorance concerning the monotheism of the
Vedas, but also to science, showing exactly who are the
Brâhmaṇas, the only caste in India which, for centuries,
had the right to study Sanskrit literature and to interpret
the *Vedas*, and which used this right solely for its own advantage. Long before the time of such learned Orientalists
as Burnouf, Colebrooke and Max Müller, there has been in
India many a native reformer who tried to prove the pure
monotheism of the Vedic doctrine. There have even appeared founders of new religions who denied the revelation
of these Scriptures, such as Râjâ Ram Mohun Roy, and
after him, Bâbû Keshub Chunder Sen, both Calcutta Bengalîs.* But neither of them had any definite success, and
merely added new sects to the numberless sects in India.
Ram Mohun Roy died in England, having achieved very
little, and his successor, Keshub Chunder Sen, having
founded the Church of the "Brahmo-Samâja" — which
professes a religion extracted from the depths of the Bâbû's
own imagination—plunged himself into the most abstruse
mysticism, and is now "a berry from the same field"† as
the Spiritualists, who consider him a medium and declare
him to be a Calcutta Swedenborg.

Thus, all the attempts to re-establish the pure primitive
monotheism of Âryan India have remained so far more or
less futile. They broke like waves upon the rock of Brâh-

---

*At present, the latter appears to have lost his mind, and become
a kind of dancing dervish. He sits in a dirty tank, singing praises to
Chaitanya, the *Qur'ân* and Buddha, and calling himself a prophet; he
performs a mystic dance with his followers, dressed in woman's attire
as a tribute to a "woman-goddess," whom he calls his "mother, father
and elder brother."

† [Russian proverb.]

manism and of prejudices deeply rooted for centuries. But lo! there appeared unexpectedly Pandit Dayânanda. None even among his closest disciples know who he is or whence he came. He himself openly confesses to the crowds that even the name under which he is known is not his, but was given to him at his initiation as a Yogin.* One thing, however, is certain: India has never witnessed a more learned Sanskrit scholar, a deeper metaphysician, a more wonderful orator, and a more fearless denunciator of every evil, than Dayânanda, since the time of Śamkarâchâra, the famous founder of the *Vedânta* philosophy—the most metaphysical of Indian systems, and the crown of pantheistic teaching. Even his outer appearance is remarkable: he is immensely tall, his complexion, though swarthy, is pale (rather European than Indian), his eyes are large and full of fire, and his greying hair is long.† His voice is clear and sonorous, able to give expression to every shade of feeling, ranging from a sweet, almost feminine whisper or admonition, to thundering wrath against the evil doings and falsehoods of the contemptible priestcraft. Altogether this produces an irresistible effect on the impressionable, meditative Hindu.

Wherever Dayânanda appears, crowds prostrate themselves in the dust of his footprints. Unlike Bâbû Keshub Chunder Sen, he does not teach a new religion and does

---

*Patañjali, the founder of one of the six principal philosophical systems of ancient India, established a mystical school known as that of Yoga. It is supposed that the Neo-Platonists of the second and third Alexandrian Schools were the followers of Indian *yogins*, especially of their theurgy which, according to tradition, was brought from India by Pythagoras. There still exist in India hundreds of yogins who strenuously follow the system of Patañjali and, if we are to believe them, are in communion with *Brahman*. However, most of them are do-nothings, and though "mendicants" by profession, are nevertheless frauds, owing to the insatiable passion of the natives for the miraculous. *Real yogins,* on the other hand, do not appear in public, but spend their entire life in complete seclusion and study, except when, as in Dayânanda's case, they emerge in time of need to "save their country."

†Yogins and Dîkshitas ("initiated") wear their hair long, and never cut either beard or moustache.

not proclaim new dogmas. He merely asks them to go back to their well-nigh forgotten Sanskrit language; and, having compared the doctrines of their forefathers, those of Âryan India, with the teachings of Hindu Brâhmaṇas, to return to the pure conceptions of deity held by the primitive Ṛishis —Agni, Vâyu, Aditya and Aṅgiras.* Nor does he teach, as others do, that the *Vedas* were received as a "revelation from on high"; he teaches that "every word of the *Vedas* belongs to the highest type of divine inspiration *possible* for man on this earth—an inspiration which in the history of mankind has been repeated, when necessary, to other nations as well . . ."

During the last five years, Svâmi Dayânanda gained some two million proselytes, chiefly among the higher castes. Judging by appearances, they are all ready to sacrifice their lives and souls and even their earthly possessions— which are often more precious to the Hindus than their lives—to him. But Dayânanda, like a genuine *yogin,* never touches money, despises pecuniary affairs, and is content with a few handfuls of rice a day. The life of this remarkable Hindu seems to be a charmed one, so heedlessly does he play with the worst of human passions, arousing in his enemies that vicious wrath, so dangerous in India. A marble statue could not be less disturbed in moments of terrible danger. We saw him once at work. He sent all his faithful followers away, forbade them to protect or to defend him, and stood alone before the infuriated crowd, calmly facing the monster ready to spring upon him and tear him to pieces . . . . . Two years ago, he began to translate the *Vedas,* with his own, entirely new commentaries, from the Sanskrit into *Hindî,* the most widespread dialect here. His *Veda-Brâshya*† is an inexaustible source for the scholar-

---

*According to tradition, the four books of the *Vedas* were given to mankind by these four patriarchs.

†It is edited and published monthly at Bombay, and its subscription funds go to the support of schools and libraries of the *Ârya-Samâja* of Bombay, which literally means "society" or rather "brotherhood of Âryans." Pandit Dayânanda has now organized more than 60 such schools and libraries throughout India; they are all maintained at their own expense, and Sanskrit is obligatory in them.

ship of Max Müller, in the translations of this German Sanskritist, who is in constant correspondence and consultation with Dayânanda. Monier-Williams, an Oxford professor and another bright luminary in Orientalism, owes a great deal to Dayânanda also, having become acquainted with him, and with his disciples, while in India.*

At this point, a brief digression seems necessary.

A few years ago a Society of educated, energetic and determined people was formed in New York. A certain keen-witted savant surnamed them *La Société des Malcontents du Spiritisme.* The founders of this association were people who, believing in the phenomena of Spiritualism as much as in the possibility of any other phenomena in Nature, nevertheless denied the theory of the "spirits." They also considered modern psychology to be a science—but in the very early stages of its development, being in total ignorance concerning the nature of the "spiritual man," and through the mouthpiece of many of its representatives denying all it cannot immediately explain to suit itself to its own satisfaction.

From the earliest days of the foundation of this Society (The Theosophical Society), some of the most learned men in America joined it. Its members differed on many points regarding their views and opinions, much as do the members of any geographical or archaeological body, who can argue for years about the sources of the Nile or the hieroglyphs of Egypt. But just as the latter unanimously agreed that, since the waters of the Nile and the pyramids do exist, therefore there must exist somewhere the source of these waters and the key to the hieroglyphs, the same must be true with regard to the phenomena of *spiritism*

---

*During his two-year stay in India, Monier-Williams sought a helper in his translations from the Sanskrit. Finally he was able to secure the best of Dayânanda's disciples, the young Pandit Shamji Krishnavarma. This young Hindu has recently gone to Oxford to win laurels for the learned English Sanskritist, and has now become an Oxford celebrity. In two years he has mastered Latin and Greek, and passed a most exacting examination, leaving far behind the young lords. English newspapers mention him constantly.

and *magnetism.* These phenomena were merely awaiting their Champollion—and the Rosetta stone was to be sought neither in America nor in Europe, but in the lands where they still believe in magic, where "miracles" (in which the Society did not believe) were performed by the native priesthood, and where the cold materialism of science had not yet reached — in one word, the Orient. The Lama-Buddhists, for instance — as the Council of the Society thought—do not believe in God, and deny the personal individuality of the human soul, yet they are celebrated for their phenomena; and "mesmerism" was known and practised in China for many thousands of years, under the name of yin and yang. In India, they fear and hate the spirits so venerated by the spiritists, yet many a simple and ignorant fakir can perform "wonders" calculated to nonplus the more learned investigators and to be the despair of the most renowned European jugglers. Many of the members of The Theosophical Society had visited India, many were born there and had themselves witnessed the "magic" of the Brâhmaṇas.

The founders of the association, observing the prevailing ignorance concerning the spiritual side of man, thought that some day Cuvier's method of comparative anatomy would surely be applied to metaphysics, and would pass from the *physical* to the *psychological* realm of science, and upon the same deductive and inductive foundations as in the first case; otherwise, psychiatry would not advance one step forward, and might even obstruct the progress of every other branch of natural science. Already we see how physiology—claiming little by little rights which do not belong to it—is hunting upon the preserves of purely metaphysical, abstract sciences, all the time feigning no interest in the latter, and, having bound them upon the unyielding Procrustean bed of natural philosophy, seeks to class psychology among the sciences.

Within a short time, The Theosophical Society counted its members not by hundreds, but by thousands. All the "malcontents" of American Spiritualism (there are an estimated twelve million Spiritualists) joined the Society.

Meanwhile, collateral branches were formed in London, Corfu, Australia, Spain, Cuba, California, etc.* Experiments were performed, and the conviction became more firmly established that *it is not "spirits" alone who are the causes of the phenomena.*

In due course of time branches of The Theosophical Society were formed in India and Ceylon.† The Buddist and Brâhmanical members became more numerous than the European. An alliance was formed, and to the name of the Society was added the subtitle, "The Brotherhood of Humanity." After an animated correspondence with the leaders of the *Ârya-Samâja* (the Society of Âryans), the religious and reformatory party founded by Swâmi Dayânanda, an alliance was arranged between them and The Theosophical Society. Then the Chief Council of the New York Society decided to send a special delegation to India, for the purpose of studying on the spot, and under the guidance of Sanskritists, the ancient language of the *Vedas,* the manuscripts, and the "wonders" of *yogism.* For this they chose the president of the New York Society, two secretaries and two councilors. On the 17th of December, 1878, this delegation sailed from New York to Bombay, via London, and arrived at their destination in February, 1879.

It is evident that the members of this delegation were far better able to study the country and to make careful research under such favorable circumstances, than might have been the case with others who did not belong to the Society. They are looked upon as "brothers" and are being helped by some of the most influential natives. Counted

---

*In The Theosophical Society of London, there are at least seven Fellows of the Royal Society, among hundreds of other individuals well known in the realm of science and literature. To their F. R. S. (Fellow Royal Society), they add their F. T. S. (Fellow Theosophical Society). The president of the London Society is the son of a notable member of Parliament, while the president of the "*Eclectic* Theosophical Society" at Simla, is the late Secretary for India, A. O. Hume.

†Now, in 1882, there are thirty-six Theosophical Branches in India, and 8 in Ceylon, founded by our American Society. [*Later Note by the Author.*]

among the members of the Society are pandits from Benares and Calcutta, Buddhist high-priests from Ceylon *vihâras*— among them the learned Sumaṅgala, head of the pagoda on Adams Peak, mentioned by Minayeff * in his travel-descriptions—Lamas from Tibet, pandits in Burma, Travancore, and elsewhere. The members of the delegation are admitted to sanctuaries where, so far, no European has set foot. Consequently they may hope to render more than one service to humanity and science in spite of the unwillingness to listen and the ill will which the representatives of *exact* science bear to those who are believers.

As soon as we landed in Bombay, a telegram was dispatched to Dayânanda, as we were anxious to make his personal acquaintance. In reply, he said he was obliged to go to Hardvâr, where hundreds of thousands of pilgrims were expected to assemble that year. He asked us not to go to Hardvâr, since cholera was sure to break out, and designated a certain spot, at the foot of the Himâlayas, in the Pañjâb, where we were to meet in a month's time.†

---

*[Ivan Pavlovich Minayev (1840-1890) was an outstanding Russian scholar of Buddhism and allied subjects. He acquired thorough knowledge of both Sanskrit and Pâli and worked for awhile in the British Museum and the Bibliothèque Nationale of Paris cataloguing Pâli manuscripts. He made three trips to India and Ceylon, publishing several accounts regarding his journeys. From 1883, he was Professor of Sanskrit at the Oriental Department of the University of St. Petersburg. His chief work is *Buddhism: Researches and Materials,* St. Petersburg, 1887. He wrote a large number of works and articles in various Russian scientific journals.—*Compiler.*]

†Alas! This was written in 1879, and much water has flowed under the bridge since. The attitude of Swâmi Dayânanda has changed, and from an ally and friend, he became a declared enemy of The Theosophical Society and its two founders—Colonel Olcott and the author of these letters. It appeared that, on entering into an offensive and defensive alliance with The Theosophical Society, the Swâmi nourished the hope that *all* its members, Christian, Brâhmanical and Buddhist, would acknowledge him as supreme leader and teacher, and become members of the Ârya-Samâja. Needless to say, this was impossible.

The Theosophical Society rests on the principle of strictest *non-interference* in the religious beliefs of its Fellows. The highest degree of tolerance exists, inasmuch as the Society embraces purely philosophical objectives, preaching the *brotherhood* of all mankind, without

Thus we had plenty of time to examine all the remarkable sights of Bombay and its neighbourhood.

We decided to take a quick look around, and then to strike out for Dekkan and attend the great temple festival at *Kârlî*,* according to some, an ancient cave-temple of the Buddhists, according to others, one that belonged to the Brâhmaṇas. Afterwards, having visited Thâṇâ, on Sâlsette Island, and the temple of Kânheri, we planned to go to Chaul, so glorified by our Athanasius, son of Nikita.

In the meantime, let us ascend to the summit of the Malabar Hill, to the "Tower of Silence," which is the last earthly abode of all the sons of Zoroaster. It is, in fact, a Pârsî cemetery. Here the bodies of their rich and poor, *nawâb* or *cooli*, men, women and children, are laid out in rows, and *in a few minutes* nothing remains of them but bare skeletons . . . The foreigner receives a strange, dismal

---

regard to caste, faith or colour (*i.e.*, nationality), and has nought to do with personal religious views. This did not suit the Swâmi. He wanted *all the members*, either to become subservient to him, or to be expelled from the Society. It was quite clear that neither the president nor the Council could assent to such a demand. Englishmen, whether Christians, Freethinkers, Buddhists and especially Brâhmaṇas, revolted against this and insisted that the alliance be dissolved. The Swâmi then, seeing that power was slipping between his fingers, declared The Theosophical Society *anathema*, and his agents started abusing it at every street corner. The result of this was that all the *intelligenzia* of the Ârya-Samâja joined The Theosophical Society and severed all relations with the Swâmi-fanatic, who calls the Society the "faithless *Feringhees*." [*Later Note by the Author.*]

[The relation of Svâmi Dayânanda Sarasvatî to The Theosophical Society in the early days of the Movement is explained by Col. Henry S. Olcott in his *Old Diary Leaves*, Series I, Chapter XXV.—*Compiler.*]

*These religious gatherings (*melâs*) are organized in various places of India in sequence and usually in towns whose history is connected with some specially sacred tradition. At Hardvâr, such a *melâ* is held every 12 years. It is a sort of religious *fair* which attracts representatives of various sects; they read learned dissertations in defence of their special sects, and debate their views in public. This year the *Sannyâsins* — mendicant hermits — alone numbered 35,000. Cholera actually broke out.

impression from these "towers," where absolute silence
has actually reigned for centuries. These buildings are to be
found wherever Pârsîs live and die, especially in Surat. Of
the six towers in Bombay, the largest was built 250 years
ago, and the next in size but a short time ago. They are
round, or sometimes square, buildings without roof, windows
or doors, from 20 to 40 feet high, with but a single opening
to the east, which consists of a heavy iron gate covered by
shrubbery. The first corpse brought to a new *dakhma*
(which is the name of these towers) must be the body of
the innocent child of a "mobed" or priest. These towers
stand by themselves on a hill or in a secluded garden, and
no one, not even the supervisor of the guards, is allowed to
approach to within less than thirty paces of them. Alone
the *nasasâlârs* * (corpse-carriers)—whose trade is hereditary, and who are strictly forbidden by law to talk to, to
touch, or even to approach the living — can enter and leave
the "Tower of Silence." Entering it with the corpse covered,
whether that of a rich or a poor man, with old white rags,
they undress it and place it, in silence, in one or another of
three circles; then, still in perfect silence, they withdraw,
shut the gate until next time, and burn the rags, then and
there.

Amongst the fire-worshippers, death is divested of all its
majesty, and the corpse is to them a mere object of disgust.
As soon as the last hour of a sick person approaches, everyone leaves him, as much to avoid impeding the departure
of the soul from the body, as to shun the risk of polluting
the living by contact with the dead. The *mobed* alone remains for awhile, and having whispered into the ear of
the dying man the *Zend-Avesta* parting precepts, "Ashem-

---

*The life of these unfortunate people is more wretched than that
of our executioners. They live entirely apart from the rest of the world,
in whose eyes they are the acme of defilement, and do not communicate with anyone. Being forbidden to enter the market, they must get
their food as they may. They are born, marry and die, perfect strangers
to all except their own kind, passing through the streets only to fetch
the dead and to carry them to the tower.

Vohu" and "Yathâ ahû vairyo," leaves the room while the man is still alive.* Then a dog is brought in and made to look straight into the face of the dying. This ceremony is called *sag-dîd* (dog's stare). The dog is supposed to be the only living creature whose glance frightens the *drug-nasu* (evil demon), watching for a chance to obtain possession of the body ... It is important that no one's shadow falls between the dying man and the dog, otherwise the full power of the dog's gaze will be lost, and the demon will profit by the favorable occasion. When a Pârsî dies, his body remains wherever it is until the *nasasâlârs* appear, their arms hidden to the shoulders under old bags. Having placed the corpse in an iron coffin — the one used for everyone — they carry it to the *dakhma*. If the one being carried there should regain consciousness, which often happens, he can not return to the world in such a case; the *nasasâlârs* will kill him. Anyone who has been polluted by contact with a dead body and has been to the "tower" cannot be allowed to return to the living, because he would then contaminate

---

* [These are two of the three most important mantras or invocations of the Zoroastrians. The second of those mentioned in the text is often spoken of as *Ahûna-Vairyo* (*Ahûnavêr* in Pahlavi, and *Honover* in Pârsî), and runs as follows:

"*Yathâ ahû Vairyô athâ ratush ashât chit hachâ Vangheush dazdâ manangho shyaothnanam angheush Mazdâi Khshathremchâ Ahurâi â Yim dregubiô dadât Vâstârem.*"

One of the most devoted workers in H.P.B.'s time in India, Judge Navroji Dorabji Khandalavala, in his Essay on the "Primitive Mazdayasnyan Teachings," in *The Theosophist* (Vol. VII, November and December, 1885), gives the following rendering of this mantra:

"As is the Will (or Law) of the Eternal Existence so (its) Energy solely through the Harmony (*ashâ*) of the Perfect Mind is the producer (*dazdâ*) of the manifestations of the universe and (is) to Ahura Mazda (the Living Wise One) the Power which gives sustenance to the revolving systems."

His rendering of the *Ashem-Vohu* formula is as follows:

"Purity is the best good, a blessing it is, a blessing to him who (practises) purity for the sake of the Highest Purity."—*Compiler*.]

the whole community.* The relatives follow the bier at some distance and stop about 90 feet from the "tower." After a last prayer at the gate, pronounced from afar by the *mobed,* and repeated in chorus by the carriers, the dog ceremony is repeated. In Bombay, there is a dog trained for this purpose and kept on a chain at the entrance to the tower. Finally, the *nasasâlârs* take the body inside and, removing it from the coffin, place it on one of the spots designated according to its sex and age.

We have twice been present at the ceremony of "dying," and once at a "burial," if it be permitted to use such an incongruous term. In this regard, the Pârsîs are much more tolerant than the Hindus, who look upon the presence of a European as a desecration of their religious rites. It was the burial of a rich woman, and our acquaintance, N. Bayranji, chief official of the tower, invited us to be present at his home. Thus we witnessed all the rites at a distance of about 40 feet from the tower, while sitting on the verandah of our obliging host's bungalow. He, himself, while serving for many years at the "tower," had never entered it and did not even approach it. While the dog was staring into the dead woman's face, we were gazing as intently, but with a secret feeling of disgust, we must confess, at the huge flock of vultures flying above the *dakhma.* They entered it and flew out again with pieces of bloody human flesh in their beaks . . . These birds which have built their nests by the hundreds round the "Tower of Silence," have been purposely imported from Persia. Indian vultures proved to be too weak, and not sufficiently bloodthirsty, to take care of the stiff corpses with the speed laid down by the law of Zoroaster. We were told that the entire process of denuding the bones occupies no more than a few minutes . . .

---

*As a result of several such cases, the Pârsîs are trying to have a new law passed which would permit the resuscitated one to return to the land of the living, and that would compel the *nasasâlârs* to leave the only gate of the tower unlocked, so as to allow the ex-corpse to escape. It is curious that vultures, which devour the corpses at once, will never touch those who are only seemingly dead, but fly away with loud shrieks.

As soon as the ceremony was over, we were led into another building where a wooden model of the *dakhma* stood on a small table, complete with all its interior arrangement. We could very easily picture to ourselves now what was going on inside the tower. Imagine a square smokestack standing erect upon the earth, and you will have an idea of the empty "tower." On the granite floor, in the very center of the tower, there is a deep waterless well, covered with an iron grating like the opening of a drain. Around it are three broad circles gradually sloping downwards from the walls; in each one of them are coffin-like receptacles for the bodies, separated from each other by a thin partition a couple of inches high. There are 365 such places. The first and smallest circle (2 feet in width) near the well is destined for children; the second (4 feet) for women; and the third (5 feet in width), next to the wall, for men. This threefold circle is symbolical of the three cardinal Zoroastrian virtues: "pure thoughts, kind words, and good actions."

Thus the first circle belongs to the men and the last one to the children. Thanks to the flocks of hungry vultures, the bones are laid bare in less than an hour, and, in two or three weeks, the tropical sun scorches them into such a state of fragility, that at the slightest touch they are reduced to powder and dumped into the well. No smell is left behind, and there is no cause for plague or other epidemics. This method may be even preferable to burning, which leaves in the air about the *Ghât* * a faint but unpleasant odor. Instead of feeding humid "mother earth" with carrion, the Pârsîs give *Aramaiti* (the earth)† nothing but completely purified dust. The worship of the Earth, admonished by Zoroaster, is so great among them, that they take all possible precautions against polluting the "cow wet nurse" that gives them "a hundred golden grains for every single grain." In the monsoon season when, during four months, the rain pours down in torrents and washes

---

*The *Ghât* is a place by the sea, or river shore, where Hindus burn their dead.

†*Aramaiti* literally means "cow wet nurse." Zoroaster teaches that the cultivation of land is the noblest of all occupations in the eyes of God. See *Yasna* (hymns).

into the well all the refuse left by the vultures, the water thus absorbed by the earth is filtered, for the bottom of the well, the walls of which are covered with plates of granite, is strewn with sand and charcoal, especially for this purpose.

The sight of the Pâñjrâpol is less mournful and much more curious. It is the Bombay "Hospital for Aged Animals," an institution which exists, by the way, in every town where Jainas dwell, concerning whom something might be said here. This sect is doubtless one of the most ancient here; it is also one of the most interesting. Jainism is much older than Buddhism, which began its rise about 543-477 B.C. Jainas boast that Buddhism is nothing but a heresy of Jainism, as Gautama, the Founder of Buddhism, had been a disciple and follower of one of their chief *gurus* and holy men. The customs, rites, and philosophical conceptions of Jainas place them midway between the Brâhmanists and the Buddhists; in their social customs, they more closely resemble the former, but in their religion they incline towards the latter. Like the Brâhmanists, they observe caste, never eat meat, and do not worship the relics of saints; on the other hand, like Buddhists, they deny the Hindu gods and the authority of the *Vedas;* instead, they revere their twenty-four *Tîrthamkaras,* or *Jinas,* who belong to the host of the "Blessed." Again like Buddhists, their priests never marry and live in secluded *vihâras,* choosing their successors from amongst the members of any social class. According to them, *Pâli* (as in Ceylon) is the only sacred language and is used in their sacred literature. They have the same traditional chronology as do the Buddhists. They do not eat after sunset and carefully dust any spot before sitting upon it, that they may not crush even the tiniest of creatures. Both systems, or rather both schools of philosophy, follow the ancient atomistic school of Kaṇâda and defend the theory of the eternity of the atoms or elements and the indestructibility of matter. They assert that the universe never had a beginning and never will have an end. "The world and everything in it is an illusion, a *mâyâ,*" say the Vedântins, the Buddhists and the Jainas. But while the followers of Śaṃkarâchârya preach *Parabrahman* (a deity devoid of will, understanding and action)* and *Îśvara* emanating from it, the Jainas and the Buddhists deny a creator of the universe and teach merely the existence of *Svabhavat,* a plastic, eternal and self-created principle in Nature. They firmly believe, as do all the other sects in India, in the transmigration of souls. Their fear that in killing an animal or an insect, they may perchance destroy the life of an ancestor, causes them to go to unbelievable extremes in their love and care for every living creature. Not only is there a hospital for old and maimed animals in every town and village, but their priests go about with a muslin "muzzle" (may they forgive me this disrespectful expression) covering their noses and mouths, lest by breathing they destroy the smallest animalcule. For this same reason, they drink only filtered water. There are a few million Jainas, scattered in Gujarât, Bombay, Konkan and some other places.

The Bombay *Pânjrâpol* occupies a whole quarter of the town and is separated into yards, squares, meadows and groves, with ponds, cages for beasts of prey, and enclosures for tame animals. This institution could well serve as a model for Noah's Ark. In the first yard, however, we saw no animals, but, instead, a few hundred living human skeletons — old men, women and children. These were the surviving inhabitants of the so-called famine districts, who had crawled into Bombay to beg for bread. The fatherly government, having driven them out of their hovels for defaulting on their taxes, which are collected during a year of famine as well as of abundance,† made perfect its Christ-like guardianship of the heathens, by finding room for them in a hospital for beasts. In the meantime, while a few veterinarians, constantly in attendance at this curious hospital, were busily bandaging the broken paws of jackals, pouring ointment on the backs of mangy dogs, and fitting wooden crutches to lame storks — a few steps away in another yard,

---

*Brahma is without understanding, mind or will, "for Brahma is itself *absolute understanding, mind and will,*" according to the *Vedânta.*

†Some years ago taxes from peasants were collected in kind, but now they must pay them in cash, irrespective of conditions.

old men, women and children were dying of starvation. Fortunately, there were at that time fewer hungry animals than
usual, and so the famine-stricken were fed at the expense of
the beast benefactors. No doubt many of these wretched
sufferers would have gladly consented to transmigrate forthwith into the bodies of any of the animals, who were ending
their earthly sojourn so snugly in this hospital.

But even the *Pâñjrâpol* roses are not without thorns. The
herbivorous "subjects," of course, could not wish for anything better; but I doubt very much whether the carnivorous ones, such as tigers, hyenas, jackals and wolves, were
entirely satisfied with the rules, and the forcibly prescribed
diet. Jainas themselves do not eat flesh and turn away in
disgust even from eggs and fish; in consequence, all the
animals in their care are obliged to fast also. We were
present at the feeding of an old tiger wounded by an English
bullet. Having sniffed at a kind of rice soup offered him, he
lashed his tail, snarled, showing his yellow teeth, and with
a dull roar turned away from the unusual food, casting a
look askance upon his keeper, who was meekly trying to
persuade him to taste his dinner. Only the strong bars of
the cage saved the Jaina from a vigorous protest on the part
of this veteran of the forest. A hyena, with a bleeding and
bandaged head, and an ear half torn off, began by sitting
in the trough filled with this Spartan sauce, and then upset-
ing it without any further ceremony, as if to show its utter
contempt for the mess. The wolves and the dogs then raised
such a deafening howl that they attracted the attention of
two inseparable friends, an old elephant with a wooden
front leg and an emaciated ox with a green shade over his
sore eyes, the veritable Castor and Pollux of the institution.
In accordance with his noble nature, the elephant thought
only of his friend; he wound his trunk round the neck of
the ox, and both, raising their heads, moaned dismally.
Parrots, storks, pigeons, flamingos and wrens — the whole
feathered tribe — revelled over their breakfast, singing at
the top of their voices. Monkeys were enjoying it also, being
the first to answer the call. We were also shown a *holy* man
who, sitting in a corner, was feeding insects with his own
blood. Entirely naked, he lay motionless and with his eyes

closed, in the full blaze of the sun. He was literally covered with flies, mosquitoes, ants and bugs. "All these are our brothers," touchingly observed the keeper of the institution, pointing to the hundreds of animals and insects. "How can you Europeans kill and even devour them?"

"What would you do," I asked, "if this snake over here were to crawl up to you and try to bite you? Is it possible you would not kill it, if you had to do so?"

"Not for all the world! I would cautiously catch it, carry it to some deserted place outside the town, and there set it free."

"And what if it bit you just the same?"

"I should then recite a *mantra*,* and if that did not help, I would take it for a decree of Fate and quietly leave this body to enter into another."

These were the words of a man who was educated to some extent, and very well-read. When we pointed out that no gift of nature was aimless, and that if the arrangement of the human teeth were carnivorous, man must have been **destined by Fate** itself to feed on meat, he replied by quoting almost entire chapters from Darwin's *On the Origin of Species by Means of Natural Selection*. "It is not true," argued he, "that the first men were born with canine teeth. It was only in the course of time, with the degradation of humanity, and when it developed an appetite for flesh food, that the jaws began gradually to change under the influence of necessity, until finally their original shape was entirely altered."

Just think: «*Où la science va-t-elle se fourrer?*»

---

*Mantra is a prayer in verses and also an exorcism against any evil. In India, everyone has a strong belief in the power of mantras.

--III--

[THE FAIRY DRAMA OF SÎTÂ-RÂMA. — ITS ANCIENT MYTHOLOGICAL
SYMBOLISM. — GHEBERS AND THEIR WANDERINGS. — VARIEGATED TYPES
AND COSTUMES OF THE CROWD.]

That same evening, an unusual performance was given in
Elphinstone's Theatre in honor of the "American Mission," as we are styled here. Native actors presented in
Gujarâtî the ancient fairy drama of *Sîtâ-Râma,* adapted
from the *Râmâyana,* the celebrated epic poem of Vâlmíki.
The drama consisted of fourteen acts and innumerable
tableaux and transformation scenes. All the women's parts,
as is the custom, were acted by young boys, and the actors,
true to the historical and national dress, were bare-footed
and half-naked. Still, the great variety of the costumes, such
as there were, and the stage adornments and transformations, were truly amazing. For instance, it would have been
difficult even on the stages of large metropolitan theatres to
give a better and more faithful representation of the army
or Râma's allies, who are monkeys under the leadership of
Hanuman — the soldier, statesman, god, poet and dramatist,
so celebrated in history (that of India, if you please).

The oldest and best of all Sanskrit dramas, *Hanuman-
Nâṭaka* (drama), is ascribed to this talented *forefather* of
ours . . . Alas! Gone are the days when, proud of our white
skin — perchance *après tout* merely the result of *fading* under the northern sky — we looked down upon the Hindus
and other dark people with a feeling of contempt well-suited
to our own magnificence. The soft heart of Sir William
Jones must have ached when translating from Sanskrit sen

38

THE TRIMÛRTI IN THE ELEPHANTA CAVE

THE CAVES OF KARLÍ

tences humiliating to European self-love, such as *"Hanuman was our forefather."* If legend is to be believed, Râma, hero and demi-god, in recognition of the services rendered by the brave army of monkeys, married every bachelor of his army to one of the daughters of the giants of the island of Lankâ (Ceylon), the Râkshasas, and gave as dowry to these "Dravidian" beauties all the *Western* lands . . . Then, after the greatest marriage celebration ever seen, the monkey-soldiers made a bridge of their tails and swinging it from Lankâ to Europe, safely landed with their spouses on the other shore, where they lived happily and bred a host of children. Those children are we Europeans. Dravidian words found in the languages of Western Europe (such as Basque, for instance) brought delight to the Brâhmanas. In gratitude for this important finding, so unexpectedly confirming their ancient legend, they very nearly promote philologists to the rank of the gods. Darwin climaxed this whole subject. With the spread of western education and scientific literature in India, the people became more than ever convinced that we are the descendants of their Hanuman, and that, if one took the trouble of examining carefully, the European would be found to have a *tail*. The narrow trousers and long skirts of arrivals from the West greatly contribute toward the firm establishment of this, to us, rather uncomplimentary idea . . . Well! Once that science, in the person of Darwin, supports the wisdom of the Âryans, there is nothing left for us to do but to submit. And, surely, it is better to have Hanuman, the poet, the hero and the god, for a forefather, than some other monkey, even though it be a tailless one . . .

Sîtâ-Râma, being presented that evening, belongs to the category of mythological mystery-dramas, similar to those of Aeschylus. Witnessing this classical production of remotest antiquity, the spectator is involuntarily carried back to the time when the gods, descending upon earth, took an active part in the everyday life of mortals; there is nothing to remind one of a modern drama, though the exterior form is similar. "From the sublime to the ridiculous there is but one step," and *vice versa*. The goat, chosen for a sacrifice to Bacchus, has presented the world with

tragedy (τράγος ῳδή). The bleatings and buttings preceding
the death of the four-footed victim of antiquity have been
polished by the hands of time and civilization. As a result,
we get the dying whisper of Rachel in the part of Adrienne
Lecouvreur, and the fearfully realistic "kicking" of the
modern Croisette in the poisoning scene in *The Sphinx* . . .*
But, whereas the descendants of Themistocles gladly received, during the long years of both captivity and freedom,
all the changes and "improvements," considered as such by
western standards, accepting them as a revised and enlarged
edition of the genius of Aeschylus, the Hindus, fortunately

---

*[Adrienne Lecouvreur was a French actress, born at Damery
(Marne), April 5, 1692, the daughter of a hatter, Robert Couvreur.
After a long apprenticeship, she made her début in 1717, as Électre,
in Crébillon's tragedy of that name, and as Angélique in Molière's
Georges Dandin. She was immediately received in the Comédie Française and for thirteen years was the queen of tragedy there, attaining
a popularity never before accorded an actress. She was able to change
the stage traditions of generations, and her *salon* was frequented by
Voltaire and other famous men. Naturally enough, she aroused jealousy
and enmity among many, and when she died, March 30, 1730, she was
denied the last rites of the Church, and her remains were refused
burial in consecrated ground, a fact which inspired Voltaire to write
a poem expressing his indignation at this barbarous treatment of a
woman for whom he felt the greatest admiration.

The life of this remarkable actress inspired Eugène Scribe and
Ernest Legouvé to write a tragedy entitled *Adrienne Lecouvreur* (1849),
which was written expressly for another famous French actress Rachel,
whose real name was Elisa Félix (1821-1858), and who played the
leading part in it. She was the daughter of poor Jewish peddlars and
was born at Mumpf (Aargau), Switzerland; after a rather meteoric
career in Paris, she died of consumption near Nice.

As to Sophie-Alexandrine Croisette, she was born at St. Petersburg,
Russia, March 19, 1847, the daughter of Louise Croisette and a
member of the Russian aristocracy, and was raised in France. After
a brilliant period of studies, she made her début at the Comédie
Française in 1870, and was recognized as a first class actress. She
was especially acclaimed in *The Sphinx,* which is a fragment of a
"lost play" by Aeschylus, telling of Oedipus' solution of the Sphinx's
riddle. After further successes in London, she left the stage at the
height of her career in 1883. Subsequent to her marriage to Jacques-
S.-A. Stern, an American banker, she experienced a great change;
deprived of the stage, she aged very rapidly, lost both her husband and
her son, and died March 19, 1901—*Compiler.*]

for archaeologists and lovers of antiquity, preserved them, just as they were, most likely, in the days of our unforgettable forefather, Hanuman.

We awaited the performance of *Sîtâ-Râma* with the liveliest curiosity. Except for ourselves and the theatre building, everything was strictly indigenous, and nothing reminded us of the West. There was no trace of an orchestra. Music was to be heard only from the stage itself or from behind it. Finally the curtain rose . . . The silence which was very noticeable before the play, considering the large crowd of spectators of both sexes, now became even more pronounced. It was obvious that in the eyes of the public — mostly worshippers of Vishnu,* the spectacle was not an ordinary play, but a religious mystery representing the life and adventures of their favorite and most revered gods.

The prologue was laid in the *epoch before the creation of the world* (no dramatist has ever attempted to choose an earlier one), or rather before its latest manifestation, at a time when the *Pralaya* is coming to an end.† Parabrahman awakens and with this awakening, the whole universe that rested in deity — having been withdrawn without leaving a trace into the subjective essence of it, at the latest destruction of the world — emanates again from the divine principle and becomes visible. All the gods who died, together with the universe, begin slowly to return to life. The "Invisible" Spirit alone, "eternal, unmanifested," for it is the unconditional, self-existent life, soars, surrounded by shoreless chaos. The holy "Presence" is not visible. It manifests itself only in the regular, periodic pulsation of chaos, represented by a dark mass of waters spread over the whole scene. These waters are not yet separated from dry land, for Brahmâ, the creative spirit of Nârâyana, has not yet

---

*Râma is one of the incarnations of Vishnu.

†All the philosophical systems of India, except that of the Moslems, agree that the universe has always existed. The Hindus divide its periodical appearances and disappearances into *days* and *nights* of Brahmâ. The nights or withdrawals of the objective universe are called *Pralayas*, and the epochs of new awakening into life and light, *Manvantaras*, *Yugas*, or "centuries of the gods." These periods are also called, respectively, the "inbreathings" and "outbreathings" of Brahmâ.

separated from the Ever-Present. But lo! mighty motion stirs the waters, and they begin to acquire transparency.

From the golden egg that lies beneath them, rays come forth. Fructified by the spirit of Nârâyana, the egg bursts, and the awakened Brahmâ rises to the surface of the waters in the shape of a huge lotus. Light clouds appear, at first white and transparent like a spider's web. They gradually become condensed and transform themselves into "Prajâpatis" — the ten personified creative powers of Brahmâ, the lord of all creatures, and sing a hymn of praise to the creator. Something naïvely-poetical, to our unaccustomed ear, breathed in this strange melody sung in unison, unaccompanied by any orchestra.

The hour of general awakening had struck. *Pralaya* is at an end. Everything rejoices, returning to life. In the sky, now separated from the waters, appear the *Asuras* and *Gandharvas*.* Then come Indra, Yama, Varuna and Kubera — the spirits presiding over the four cardinal points. From the four elements, water, fire, air and earth, spring forth atoms which engender the serpent *Ananta*. The monster rises to the surface of the waters and, bending its swanlike neck, forms the couch on which Vishnu reclines, while his wife, Lakshmî, Goddess of Beauty, sits at his feet. "Svâhâ, Svâhâ, Svâhâ!" † exclaim the heavenly choristers, hailing the deity. In one of his future incarnations (*avatâras*), Vishnu will be Râma, the son of a great king, and Lakshmî will become Sîtâ. The subject of the whole *Râmâyana* poem is sung in a few words by the celestial choir. *Kâma*, the god of love, overshadows the divine couple, and from this flame suddenly awakened in their hearts, the entire universe is engendered and multiplies . . .‡

---

*Heavenly musicians and choristers—the cherubim.

†[H.P.B. gives here in a footnote the Slavonic equivalent of this Sanskrit exclamation: *Svyat, Svyat, Svyat!* — meaning "holy, holy, holy!"—*Compiler*.]

‡Vishnu is one of the three hypostases of the *Trimûrti* (literally three faces, as *mûrti* means a sacred image or idol), the Hindu Trinity, the *sustainer* of all that lives, while Brahmâ is the *creator*, and Śiva, the *destroyer*.

Then come the fourteen acts of the well-known poem, in which several hundred people take part. At the end of the *prologue,* the whole assembly of the gods appear, as was the case with the actors of ancient dramas, and briefly acquaint the audience with the contents and the denouement of the coming performance, asking the public not to be too exacting. It is as though all the familiar deities, made of painted granite and marble, had left their temple-niches and had come to remind mortals of

"Deeds of long forgotten days,
Traditions of a distant era . . ." *

The hall was packed with natives. We four were the only Europeans. Like a huge flower-bed, a crowd of women seated in armchairs displayed the bright colors of their wraps. Here and there, among handsome, bronze-like heads, appeared the pretty, often dull-white faces of Pârsî women, whose beauty reminds one of the Georgians. The front rows were occupied by women only. While the fire-worshippers among them could be noted by their clear faces, and their hair covered with a white kerchief under a bright veil, their Hindu sisters were marked by uncovered heads, their sumptuous, shining black braids twisted at the back of the neck into a kind of Greek chignon, painted markings on their forehead and rings in the nostril.† And this is the only difference in their costume.‡ Both passionately love bright

---

* [A. S. Pushkin, *Ruslan and Ludmila.*]

†It is quite easy in India to ascertain a person's religion, sect and caste, and even whether a woman is married, single or widowed, from the marks painted on the foreheads of the various sectarians of both sexes.

‡Since the time when Alexander the Great destroyed the Sacred Books of the Ghebers, they have constantly been oppressed by the idol-worshippers. King Ardashir I Pâpakhân restored fire-worship in the years 229-243 A.D. Since then they have been persecuted again up to the reign of one of the three Shahpur kings, II, IX or XI, of the Sassanid dynasty, but exactly which one is not known. One of them, it is said, was a great protector of Zarathusht's doctrines. After the fall of Yazdegerd III, the fire-worshippers emigrated to the island of Ormuz, and some fifteen years later, having found an ancient book of Zoroastrian prophecies, lost for many a century, they set out for Hindostan, in obedience to one of the prophetic utterances. After

but uniform fabrics, cover their bare arms with bracelets
up to the elbow and wear identical *sârî*. Behind the women,
a whole sea of most wonderful turbans was waving in the
parterre — turbans that can be found nowhere but in India.
There were long-haired Râjputs with regular, pure Grecian
features, their beards parted in the middle, with ends
fastened behind the ears, their heads covered with *pagrîs*,
a turban of some twenty yards of this muslin, wound thread-
like around the head, wearing earrings and necklaces; there
were Marâṭhâ Brâhmaṇas, their heads shaved clean, leaving only one long central lock, wearing an enormous flat
turban of blinding red, decorated in front with a sort of
golden horn of plenty; then *Baniyas,* wearing three-cornered
golden helmets, with a kind of red cockscomb on the top;
Kâchis in headgear like Roman helmets; *Bhîls,* from the
borders of Râjasthân, in white pyramidal turbans, whose
ends are wrapped three times around their chins, so that the
innocent tourist thinks that they constantly suffer from toothache; *Bengalîs* and *Calcutta Bâbûs,* bareheaded all the year
round, at home and outside, wearing their hair as ancient
Athenians did on their statues and in their pictures, their
bodies proudly clothed in a white garment in no wise different from the Roman senatorial *togas; Pârsîs,* in their
black mitres, like archbishops; *Sikhs,* the followers of Nânak,
monotheists and mystics, whose white turbans are very like
those of the Bhîls, and who wear long hair down to their
waists; and hundreds of other tribes.

Attempting to count how many different headgear are to
be seen in Bombay alone, we had to acknowledge ourselves
beaten in less than a fortnight; it is easier to count the
stars in heaven. Every caste, every trade, guild and sect,

---

many wanderings, they appeared, about 1000 to 1200 years ago, in
the territory of Mahârânâ Jayadeva, a vassal prince of the Râjput
King of Châmpânîr, who allowed them to settle on his lands, but on
condition that they laid down their arms, abandoned their Persian
language for *Hindi,* that their women put off their national dress and
change to the garment of Hindu women, and that they conformed to
the customs of the land. He allowed them, however, to wear shoes, as
this is strictly prescribed by Zoroaster. Since then some changes have
occurred, though they are very insignificant.

every one of the thousand subdivisions of the social hierarchy, has its own distinguishing turban, often sparkling
with gold-lace and regal purple, which is laid aside only
in case of mourning. Yet everyone, even the rich councillors
of the municipality, merchants, Brâhmaṇas, Râo-Bahâdurs
and those created baronets by the Government, all to a man,
go barefooted, with legs uncovered up to their knees, and
wearing snow-white garments, a sort of semi-shirt or semi-
coat which cannot be compared with anything else. Upon
occasion you can see some minister of state or a râjâ seated
on an elephant,* chewing *pân-supârî* (betel leaves) — we
have seen them even on a giraffe from the stables of the
Gaekwar of Baroda,† on some festive occasion. His head
droops under the weight of the precious stones on his turban,
and his fingers, toes and legs are adorned with rings and
bracelets. That evening, however, there were neither elephants nor giraffes in the hall, though there were both
râjâs and ministers.

We had with us the handsome ambassador and late tutor
of the Mahârâṇâ of Udaipur, who was himself a râjâ and
a pandit, by the name of Mohunlal Vishṇulal Pândia. He
wore a small light-pink turban with diamonds, a pair of
pink barège trousers, and a white gauze coat. His raven
black hair fell on his amber-colored neck, adorned with a
necklace that might have driven any Parisian woman frantic
with envy. The poor Râjput was awfully sleepy, but heroi-
cally stuck to his duties and, thoughtfully pulling his beard,
led us through the endless labyrinth of the metaphysical
entanglements of the *Râmâyaṇa*. During the intermission
we were offered coffee, sherbet and cigarettes, which we
smoked even during the performance, sitting in front of the
stage in the first row. We were covered, like idols, with long
garlands of jasmin, and the manager, a stout Hindu, his
swarthy body clad in white transparent muslin and with a
crimson turban shaped like a horn, sprinkled us several
times with rose-water.

---

*In Bombay, under the pretext that they frighten the horses of
Englishmen, elephants are now forbidden, but they are very numerous
in all the other provincial towns.

†*Gaekwar* is the general title of the ruling Princes of Baroda.

The performance began at eight, and at half-past two in the morning had only reached the ninth act. In spite of a *pankhâ-wallah* at each of our backs, the heat was unbearable. Having reached the limits of our endurance, we tried to excuse ourselves. This led to a general disturbance, on the stage as well as in the hall. The airy chariot, on which the wicked king Râvana was carrying Sîtâ away, stuck in mid-air above the cliffs; the king of the Nâgas (serpents) ceased breathing flames; the monkey-warriors hung motionless on the branches, just where they happened to be; and the god Râma himself, clad in light blue raiments and with a miniature printed pagoda on his head, came to the front and made a speech in pure English in which he thanked us for the honor of our presence. Then fresh bouquets, *pân-supârîs,* and rose-water, and, finally, we got home about four A.M. Next morning we learned that the performance had ended at half-past six.

—IV—

It is an early morning near the end of March. The sky is bright and cloudless. A light breeze caresses with its velvety hand the sleepy faces of the pilgrims, and the intoxicating perfume of tuberose and jasmin in full bloom mingle with the pungent odors of the bazaar. Crowds of barefooted Brâhmaṇa women, stately and haughty, clad in colorful *sârî*, direct their steps, like the Biblical Rachel, toward the well, with copper *loṭâs* (water jugs) shining like gold upon their heads. Numerous sacred *tanks* (ponds) can be seen here and there, filled with stagnant water, in which Hindus of both sexes perform their prescribed morning ablutions. Under a hedge at the foot of the Malabar hill, somebody's tame *mongoose,* the size of a marmot, is devouring the head of a *cobra* he has just caught; the headless body of the snake convulsively, but harmlessly, winds itself around, and beats against, the thin flanks of the little animal, which views these futile efforts with evident delight. Near this animal group you can see a human figure: a naked mâlî (gardener) offering betel and salt to an ugly stone idol of Śiva to pacify the wrath of the "Destroyer" over the killing of the dangerous cobra, one of its subservient gods.

Just before reaching the railway station, we meet a modest Catholic procession consisting of a few newly converted

pariahs and some native Portuguese. Under a *baldachin*
is a litter on which swings to and fro a dusky Madonna
dressed as a native goddess, with a ring in her nose (*sic*).
In her arms is a babe clad in yellow pajamas and a red
Brâhmanical turban. "Hari, Hari, Devakî!" (Glory, glory
to the Virgin goddess!) exclaim the new converts, unconscious of any difference between the *Devakî*, mother of
Krishna, and the Catholic Madonna. All they know is that,
excluded from the pagodas by the Brâhmanas owing to
their low caste, or rather to the fact of not belonging to
any caste whatever, they are now occasionally admitted into
the Christian pagoda, thanks to the *padris*.* It should also
be stated that in order to please some newly-converted
Brâhmana (converted into Catholicism or Protestantism, but
never into Christianity), both Catholic and Protestant missionaries quite often do not admit converted *pariahs* into
the church, "so as not to offend unnecessarily the *caste* prejudices of the high-born Brâhmanas." †

At last our *gharris* ‡ — native two-wheeled vehicles drawn
by a pair of strong bullocks with long straight horns —
arrive at the station. The eyes of the English employees
pop in amazement at the sight of Europeans going about in
native gilded chariots. But we are Americans, and we have
come here to study India, not Europe and its products on
native soil.

If the tourist casts a glance at the shore opposite to the
harbor of Bombay, he will see a dark blue mass rising like
a wall between himself and the horizon. This is Prabal, a
flat-topped mountain, 2,250 feet high. Its right slope firmly
leans on two sharp rocks covered to their very top with
woods. The highest of them is *Mâtherân*, the object of our
trip. From Bombay to Neral, a station situated at the foot
of this mountain, it takes four hours by train, though, as
the crow flies — from the harbor to Mâtherân itself — the

---

*This term is applied here indiscriminately to any missionary, prob-
ably as a result of the early Portuguese Catholic missionaries being
called *padre*.

†This is the reply of a Madras missionary, published in the *New
York Herald*.

‡[Corruption from the Hindî *gâṛi*.—*Compiler*.]

distance is not more than 12 miles. The railroad track wanders round the foot of charming hills, crosses hundreds of little lakes, and pierces with more than twenty tunnels the very heart of the rocky *Ghâts*.

We were accompanied by three Hindu friends. Two of them once belonged to a high caste, but were expelled from it and "severed" from their pagoda for association and contact with us, benighted foreigners. At the station we were joined by two more natives, with whom we had been in correspondence for many years from America. All were members of our Society, reformers of young India, enemies of Brâhmaṇas, castes and prejudices, and had decided to keep us company on a visit to the annual fair at the temple festival in the caves of Kârlî, stopping on our way at Mâtherân and Khaṇḍâlâ. One of them was a Brâhmaṇa from Poona, the second a *mudaliyâr*,* a landowner from Madras, the third a Singhalese from Kegalla, the fourth a *zamindâr*,† a landholder from Bengal, and the fifth a tall Râjput, an independent *Ṭhâkur* from the province of Râjasthân,‡ whom we had known for a long time by the name of Gulâb-Lal-Singh, and had called simply Gulâb-Singh. I am speaking of him at some length, because some strange and varied tales were abroad about him. It was asserted that he belonged to the sect of *râja-yogins,* initiated into the mysteries of magic, alchemy, and various other occult sciences of India. He was rich and independent, and rumor did not dare to suspect him of deception, the more so because, even if he actually delved into these sciences, he carefully concealed his knowledge from all but his closer friends.

Ṭhâkurs are, in almost all cases, descendants of *Sûrya* (the sun), and are accordingly called *Sûryavaṅśa,* and have

---

*[Name of a caste of Tamil non-Brâhmaṇas in the South of India, from the Tamil *mudal*, chief.—*Compiler.*]

†[Hindustânî word, from the Persian *zamin*, land, and *dâr*, who has or possesses. Under the Moslem administration, this term meant a collector of land revenues in a specified district for the Government. Later meaning a kind of feudatory recognized as an actual proprietor so long as he paid the Government a fixed revenue.—*Compiler.*]

‡This name means "abode or the land of kings," and is derived from two words: *râjan*, king or prince, and *sthân*, land, abode or domain.

more pride than other people. As one of their proverbs puts it: "The mud of the earth cannot stick to the rays of the sun," *i.e.*, the Râjputs. They do not despise any caste except the Brâhmaṇas and honor only the bards who sing the valor of their warriors of which they are so justly proud.* Englishmen fear them greatly and do not dare to disarm them, as they did the rest of the Indian nations. Gulâb-Singh came accompanied by servants and shield-bearers.

Possessing an inexhaustible store of legends, and being evidently well-acquainted with the antiquities of his country, Gulâb-Singh proved to be the most interesting of our companions.

"There, against the azure sky," said Gulâb-Lal-Singh, "rises the majestic *Bhâo-Mallin.*† It was once the abode of a holy hermit and is now yearly visited by crowds of pilgrims. According to deep-seated popular belief (he added with a smile), all sorts of wonders happen there . . . On the top of the mountain, 2,000 feet high, is the platform of the fortress. Behind it rises another rock two hundred and seventy feet high, and at the summit of this sharp-pointed

---

*Speaking of the ignorance of Europe in regard to India, Col. Tod writes among other things as follows:

". . . . The splendour of the Râjpoot courts, however, at an early period of the history of that country, making every allowance for the exaggeration of the bards, must have been great. Northern India was rich from the earliest times; that portion of it, situated on either side the Indus, formed the richest satrapy of Darius. It abounded in the more striking events which constitute the materials for history: there is not a petty state in Râjasthân that has not had its Thermopylae, and scarcely a city that has not produced its Leonidas. But the mantle of ages has shrouded from view what the magic pen of the historian might have consecrated to endless admiration: Somnâth might have rivalled Delphos; the spoils of Hind might have vied with the wealth of the Lybian king; and compared with the array of the Pandus, the army of Xerxes would have dwindled into insignificance. But the Hindus either never had, or have unfortunately lost, their Herodotus and Xenophon." (*Annals and Antiquities of Râjasthân*, etc., Vol. I, Introduction, p. xii.)

† [This mountain range, some ten miles long, is also known as Bâwâ Malang or Malangad, and runs Northwest to the Southeast above Neral.—*Compiler.*]

peak are to be found the ruins of a still more ancient fortress, which for seventy-five years served as a shelter for the hermit. Whence he obtained his food will forever remain a mystery; some think it was the roots of plants, but these are conspicuous by their absence. The only mode of ascending this perpendicular rock is by means of a guide-rope and placing a toe in recesses cut in the rock. One would think that only acrobats and monkeys would be tempted to climb it! It would seem that fanaticism provides the Hindus with wings, for no accident has ever happened to them.

"About forty years ago, a party of Englishmen unfortunately conceived the idea of climbing to explore the ruins. A strong gust of wind rose and carried them into the precipice. After this, General John Dickinson gave orders for the destruction of all means of access to the upper fortress. As for the lower fortress (the siege of which cost the Bombay Army, in the early days of the invasion, great bloodshed and losses), it is now entirely deserted, and serves merely as a shelter for tigers and eagles . . ."

In the meantime, an Englishman with a long reddish moustache, and evidently in a very heated condition, came tumbling into our compartment, spreading all around him an odor of whiskey. He sniffed the air, looked us over with a scrutinizing and somewhat contemptuous glance, paused a moment in thought, and left the compartment.

"Hey, conductor!" he exclaimed in a hoarse voice, standing on the steps of the car. "Hey, isn't there another coach where I could be alone, without all these 'blacks'?"

And the drunk representative of the "superior race," proud but uncertain of his feet, proceeded to another car.

"Drunken pig," was the trenchant remark of the American.

Englishmen congratulate themselves on, and are proud of, the culture supposedly brought by them to this land, and of the education offered to "Young India." But in reality, they have arranged things in such a way that neither the one nor the other is of much good to India. A Hindu, for instance, were he of superior intelligence and of the highest caste, would not dare to buy a first-class ticket on the railway. The Englishman reserves to himself the right to turn out unceremoniously any native he does not like, who might be seated even in a second-class coach, and the railway administration keeps the second-class fare while the passenger rides third-class. Not so long ago, an officer wishing to go to sleep ordered a richly dressed native to leave the second-class coach. The Hindu — a judge in one of the high courts — courteously refused, showing his ticket and remarking that he had a perfect right to his seat. The officer called in the conductor, and the Hindu judge was turned out. He lodged a complaint, but it was sidetracked. Two weeks ago, a similar case took place. The editor of one of the Calcutta newspapers was turned out of a coach in a similar manner. *Might is right* has become a proverb here. "Kali-Yuga," * exclaim old conservative Hindus, with grim despair. "Who can strive against Kali-Yuga (the black age)?" Thus, this deep-rooted fatalism, the firm belief that no good can be expected throughout the duration of this age, and that even the powerful god Śiva himself can neither appear nor help them until the end of Kali-Yuga, in their eyes justify even the most bloody outrage.

As for the younger generation of Hindus, receiving their education as they do in universities and the best establishments of higher education and memorizing their Herbert Spencer, John Stuart Mill and Darwin, with all the German philosophers thrown in as a bargain, they entirely lose all respect, not only for their own but for all other religions.

---

*The Hindu system consists of a Kalpa, or great age, of 4,320,000,000 years, which is subdivided into four smaller *yugas* apportioned as follows:

1st—Satya-yuga consisting of	1,728,000 years
2nd—Tretâ-yuga consisting of	1,296,000 years
3rd—Dvâpara-yuga consisting of	864,000 years
4th—Kali-yuga consisting of	432,000 years
Total	4,320,000 years

The total makes one Divine Year—*Mahâ-yuga.*

[Intentionally or otherwise, there is a very definite confusion in these numbers. It may be one of those cases when H.P.B., in the early stages of her work, tried to conceal more than she revealed. The number 4,320,000 is correctly stated to be the length of the *Mahâyuga.* A *Kalpa* or Day of Brahmâ, however, is equal to one thousand Mahâ-yugas, namely 4,320,000,000 years—*Compiler.*]

Young "educated" Hindus are materialists almost without exception, often falling into the most radical atheism. They are quite convinced that, in spite of all their intelligence and higher education, they will seldom become anything more than "chief assistant to a junior clerk." As a result, they either become sycophants, engaging in disgusting toadism at the feet of their rulers, or (which is still worse, and sillier), begin to edit a liberal newspaper, which gradually develops into a revolutionary organ, until the editor of it finds himself in jail, happy if he does not end his career there . . .

But all this is merely "by the way." Compared with the mysterious and majestic past of India, the ancient Âryâ-varta, her *present* is a natural India ink shading; a somber shadow against the light background of the picture, the inevitable evil in the cycle of every nation. India has become decrepit and has collapsed, like some huge monument of antiquity shattered into a thousand pieces. But the most insignificant of these fragments will forever remain a treasure for the archaeologist and the artist and, in the course of time, may even afford the philosopher and the psychologist a clue. "Ancient Hindus built like giants and finished their work like goldsmiths," Archbishop Heber * exclaims in delight, describing his travels in India. In his description of the "Tâj-Mahal" at Âgra,† that veritable eighth wonder of the world, he calls it "a poem in marble." He might have added that it is difficult to find in India a ruin, whatever its state of preservation, that cannot speak more eloquently than whole volumes of India's past, her religious aspirations, her beliefs and hopes.

---

* [Reginald Heber (1783-1826). English bishop and hymn writer; studied at Brasenose College, Oxford; admitted to holy orders, 1807. Became prebendary of St. Asaph, 1812, preacher at Lincoln's Inn, 1822, and bishop of Calcutta, 1823. Wrote a fascinating *Narrative of a Journey through the Upper Provinces of India, from Calcutta to Bombay, 1824-1825*, London, 1828.—*Compiler.*]

†The Tâj-Mahal is an enormous monument-mausoleum erected by Emperor Akbar over the tomb of his favorite wife. His body lies next to hers, at Âgra, on the right bank of the river Jumnâ. This edifice, which I will describe later, is renowned for its beauty and has no competitor in all the world.

There is no country of antiquity, not even excluding Egypt
of the Pharaohs, where the transition from subjective ideal
to an objective symbol has been expressed more graphically, more skillfully and yet artistically, than in India. The
whole pantheism of the Vedânta is contained in the symbol
of the bisexual deity *Ardhanârî*. This symbol is surrounded
by a double triangle known in India as the "sign of Vishṇu."
At its sides lie a lion, a bull and an eagle, and in the deity's
hands rests a full moon, reflected in the waters at its feet.
The Vedânta has taught for thousands of years what some
of the German philosophers began to preach last century
and still do in the present one, namely, that everything
objective in the world, as well as the world itself, is no
more than an illusion, a *mâyâ,* a phantom created by our
imagination, as unreal as the reflection of the moon in the
water. The phenomenal world, as well as the subjectivity
of our conception concerning our *ego,* are but a dream. The
true sage will never submit to the temptations of illusion.
He knows that man will attain to self-knowledge, and become a real *Ego,* only after the final merging of the personal fragment with the All, thus becoming the immutable,
eternal and universal *Brahman;* therefore, the entire cycle
of birth, life, old age and death, is in his eyes but a phan-
tasm of the imagination . . .

Generally speaking, Indian philosophy, split as it is into
a multitude of metaphysical teachings, possesses in connection with its ontological doctrines such a highly developed logic, such a wonderfully refined psychology, that it
holds its own well against all the ancient and modern schools
of both idealists and positivists, and bests them one by one.
The positivism of Lewes, which makes every hair on the
heads of Oxford theologians stand on end, is no more than
a ridiculous plaything compared with the atomistic school
of Vaiśeshika, with its world divided, like a chessboard,
into six categories of everlasting atoms, nine substances,
twenty-four qualities, and five motions. However difficult
and even well-nigh impossible may seem the correct representation of all these abstract ideas, which are idealistic,
pantheistic, and even purely materialistic, into the condensed shape of allegorical symbols, India, nevertheless, has

been able to express all these teachings more or less success-fully. She has immortalized them in her grotesque, four-headed idols, in the geometrical and ingenious forms of her temples and monuments, and even in the complex lines and signs on the foreheads of her sectarians.

We were discussing this and other topics with our Hindu travelling companions, when a Catholic *padri,* a teacher in the Jesuit College of St. Xavier in Bombay, entered at one of the stations. Soon he could no longer contain himself and joined in our conversation. Smiling and rubbing his hands, he said he was curious to know on the strength of what sophistry our companions could find anything re-sembling a philosophical explanation, for instance, "in the fundamental idea of the four faces of the ugly Śiva, crowned with snakes, which sticks out there at the entrance to the pagoda," and he pointed to it with his finger.

"Very simple," answered the Bengali *Bâbû.* "You see, its four faces are turned towards the four cardinal points, north, south, east and west, but the faces are on one body and belong to one and the same God."

"Would you mind explaining to us first the philosophical idea of the four faces and the eight hands of your Siva?" remarked the *padri.*

"With great pleasure . . . Thinking of our great Rudra * as *omnipresent,* we represent him with his face turned simultaneously in all directions. The eight hands indicate his omnipotence, and his single body serves to remind us that he is One, though he is everywhere, and nobody can escape his all-seeing eye or his chastising hand."

The *padri* was about to say something, but the train stopped. We had arrived at Neral.

---

*The name of this God as used in the *Vedas.*

—V—

Hardly twenty-five years have elapsed, since a white man set foot for the first time on Mâtherân, a huge mass of various kinds of igneous rock, for the most part crystalline in form. Though at the very elbow of Bombay, and only a few miles from Khandâlâ (the summer residence of the Europeans), the formidable heights of this giant were long considered to be entirely inaccessible. On the north, its smooth, almost perpendicular face rises 2,450 feet over the valley of the river Pen; numerous separate rocks rise even higher, almost to the clouds, their lower slopes covered with thick forests and divided by valleys and precipices. In 1854, the railway tunnelled through one of the sides of Mâtherân, and now has reached the foot of the last mountain, stopping at Neral, a deep basin where, not so long ago, there was nothing but a precipice. From there to the upper plateau is about eight miles, and the tourist, according to his taste, has to choose as a means of conveyance between a pony or an open or closed palanquin.

Considering that we arrived at Neral about six in the evening, the latter method offered certain inconveniences: civilization has conquered soulless nature but, despite all the despotism of its rulers, has not been able to conquer either tigers or snakes. Even if the former have retired into still

56

more impassable jungles, snakes of all kinds, especially cobras and *coralillos,* by preference inhabiting trees, have full sway in the forest of Mâtherân as in days of old and wage a regular guerrilla warfare against any invader. Woe to the pedestrian, or even a horseman, if he happens to pass under a tree which harbors such a snake! Cobras and other reptiles seldom attack man and will generally flee and hide unless accidentally trodden upon, but these guerrillas of the forest, the *tree serpents,* the snakes of the shrubs, lie in wait for their victims. As soon as the head of a man comes under the branch which shelters this "enemy of mankind," the snake, coiling its tail around the branch, dives full length into space and strikes the man on his *forehead.* This curious fact was long considered to be a legend, but it has now been verified and belongs to the natural history of India. In these cases, the natives see in the snake the envoy of death, the fulfiller of the will of the bloodthirsty Kâlî, the spouse of Śiva.

But the evening, after the scorching day, was so enchanting, and the forest held out to us from afar such a promise of coolness, that we decided to risk our fate. In the heart of this wondrous nature, one longs to shake off earthly chains, to unite oneself with her boundless life, so that death itself has its *attractions* in India.

Besides, the full moon would rise at eight in the evening, and we had ahead of us a three hours' ascent of the mountain on one of those moonlit tropical nights for which tourists are ready to sacrifice almost anything, and which only genuine, outstanding artists are able to portray. Public opinion begins to speak of our own V. V. Vereshchagin, as one of those rare artists who is able to catch upon canvas the subtle charm of a moonlit night in India . . .*

---

*[Vassiliy Vassilyevich Vereshchagin (1824-1904) was a Russian painter and traveller born at Tcherepovetz, in the Government of Novgorod. His father was a landowner of noble birth, while his mother was of Tatar descent. He graduated from the St. Petersburg naval school, but left the service almost immediately to study drawing, which he did under Gérôme in Paris. In 1867, he accompanied General Kauffmann's expedition to Turkestan, and later travelled extensively in the Himâlayas, India and Tibet. In 1874, he exhibited at St. Peters-

After dining somewhat hurriedly in the dâk-bungalow (postal station), we asked for our sedan-chair and, drawing our *topis* with their wide, roof-like rims — protecting the eyes and the nape of the neck — low on our foreheads, we started on our way about eight p.m. Eight coolies clad, as usual, in rags no larger than "vine-leaves," took up each chair and hurried up the mountain, uttering shrieks and yells which are the unavoidable travelling companions of Hindus. Each chair was accompanied by eight relief-men besides, so that, without counting the Hindus with their mounted servants, we were 64 men all told — an army sufficient to frighten any stray leopard or tiger from the jungle, in fact *any* animal, except our fearless "cousins" on the side of our great-grandfather Hanuman. As soon as we turned into a thicket at the foot of the mountain, several dozen of these kinsmen joined our procession. Thanks to the merits of Râma's ally, monkeys are sacred, almost inviolable in India. The Government, emulating the earlier wisdom of the East India Company, forbids anyone to molest them or to drive them away from the city-gardens, let alone from the forests which, in all justice, belong to them. Leaping from one branch to another, chattering like magpies, and making the most awful grimaces, they followed us almost all the way, like so many spooks. Flooded by the light of the full moon, they hung on trees like forest nymphs

---

burg; among his paintings were two which were suppressed for a time; these were "The Apotheosis of War"—a pyramid of skulls dedicated "to all conquerors, past, present and to come," now in the Tretyakov Gallery at Moscow; and "Left Behind," the picture of a dying soldier deserted by his fellows.

Vereshchagin was with the Russian army during the Turkish campaign of 1877 and was severely wounded, while his brother was killed. He later acted as secretary to General Skobelev at San Stefano. After the war he settled at München producing a number of controversial paintings, such as those of a Roman execution (portraying the Crucifixion), of sepoys blown from guns in India, and of the execution of Nihilists at St. Petersburg. He finally settled in Moscow. Later he was in the Far East during the Chino-Japanese War, with the American troops in the Philippines, and with the Russian troops in Manchuria. He perished in the sinking of the flagship *Petropavlovsk* on the 13th of April, 1904.—*Compiler.*]

and, running ahead of us, awaited our arrival at the turns of the road, as if showing us the way. One baby-monkey alighted on my knee, right in my palanquin. In a flash, the parent-monkey, jumping unceremoniously over the coolies' shoulders, came to the rescue, clutched him to her chest and, after making the most ungodly face at me . . . was off.

"The presence of *bandars* (monkeys) always brings luck," remarked one of the Hindus, as if to console me for my crumpled *topi*. "Besides," he added, "seeing them here at night we may be sure there isn't a tiger for ten miles around."

Higher and higher we ascended on the steep, winding path, and the forest grew thicker, more somber, and more impenetrable. Some of the thickets were as dark as a grave. Passing under centuries-old banyans, it was hard to distinguish one's own finger at a distance of two inches. In some places, it seemed to me that it would be impossible to advance without feeling one's way, but the *coolies* never made a false step, and even proceeded faster. Not one of us uttered a word, as if we had agreed to remain silent at such moments. In the midst of the heavy pall of darkness which enwrapped us, one heard but the short, periodic breathing of the porters and the cadence of their quick, nervous footsteps upon the stony soil of the path. One felt sick at heart and ashamed for the human race, or rather for that part of it which makes of others mere beasts of burden. These poor wretches are paid four *annas* a day for their work all the year round: four annas for going eight miles up and eight miles down not less than twice a day — altogether thirty-two miles up and down, a mountain 1,500 feet high, carrying a burden of two hundredweight! . . . However, in India, a country congealed in centuries-old customs, where everything has been long established, four annas a day is the usual pay for any kind of work. Call in a skilled jeweller working by the day; he will squat on the floor and, without any tools but a pair of pliers and a tiny iron stove, fashion for you, from your own gold and according to your own design, an ornament worthy of a workshop in fairyland. And for this, a ten-hour working day, he will ask four annas . . .

Gradually open spaces and glades became more frequent, and the light grew as bright as day. Millions of grasshoppers were shrilling in the forest, filling the air with a metallic sound reminding one of a small mouth organ; owls were hooting, and flocks of frightened parrots rushed from tree to tree. Sometimes the thundering, prolonged roar of tigers rose from the foot of the thickly covered virgin forest precipice — a roar which, according to the *śikârîs* (hunters) can be heard for miles on a quiet night. The panorama, as if lit by Bengal fires, changed at every turn. Rivers, fields, forests and rocks, spread at our feet over vast distances, shimmered and trembled, irridescent, in the silvery moonlight, like the flowing waves of a mirage.

The fantastic nature of this picture made us hold our breath. We became dizzy if we glanced into the depths by the uncertain light of the moon, and the precipice, 2,000 feet deep, seemed to draw you . . . One of our American travelling companions, who was at first on horseback, had to dismount, afraid of being unable to resist the temptation to dive headlong into the abyss. Several times we met lonely pedestrians, men and even young women, coming down Mâtherân on their way home after a day's work. But it often happens that a man, having left home the day before, never returns, disappearing without a trace. The police cold-bloodedly decide that the missing man has been carried off by a tiger or killed by a snake, and his disappearance is promptly forgotten. One person less, out of the 240 millions inhabiting India, cannot matter very much! But there exists a very strange superstition among the tribes of Dekkan, centered about this mysterious and still only partially explored mountain. The natives assert that, in spite of the considerable number of people who perish on the mountain, *no single skeleton* has ever been found! They maintain that the corpse, whether intact or mangled by tigers, is immediately taken possession of by the monkeys who, in the latter case, gather the bones and bury them so skillfully in deep holes that no trace ever remains. Englishmen laugh at this superstition, but the police do not deny the fact of the traceless disappearance of the bodies. When the sides of the mountain were excavated, during the construction of the railway, several skeletons were found at a remarkable depth, with bracelets and silver adornments on the arms, legs and neck, which were broken and smashed by animals' teeth. These adornments were a proof that their owners had not been buried by men, because neither the religion of the Hindus, nor their greed, would allow them to do thus. Is it possible, then, that as amongst men, one hand washed the other — even in the animal kingdom?

Having spent the night in a Portuguese inn, woven like an eagle's nest out of bamboos and clinging to the almost perpendicular side of the rock, we rose at daybreak and, after visiting all the scenic points famed for their beauty, made our preparations for the return trip. By daylight the panorama was still more splendid, and volumes would not suffice to describe it. Had it not been that on three sides the horizon was shut out by rugged ridges of mountains, the whole of the Dekkan plateau would have appeared before our eyes: Bombay seemed quite near at hand, and the estuary that separates the town from Sâlsette shone like a tiny silvery streak. It wound its coils like a snake on its way to the harbour, surrounded Khânderi and other islands —scattered like green peas on the white cloth of its waters— and, finally, joined the unbearably bright line of the Indian Ocean on the far horizon. On the other side is the northern Koṅkaṇ, terminated by the range of Tal-Ghâts, the needle-like summits of the Jano-Naoli rocks, and, lastly, the jagged ridge of Funnel, whose bold silhouette stands out in strong relief against the distant bluish haze of the sky, like the castle of some fairy tale giant. Further on looms Prabal, whose flat top, in the days of old, was the seat of the gods whence, according to tradition, Vishṇu communicated with the mortals. And then below, where the defile widens into a valley studded with huge separate pointed rocks, each abounding with historical and mythological legends, you may perceive another range of mountains, still loftier and more oddly shaped. That is Khaṇḍâlâ, overhung by a huge stone block known as the "Duke's Nose." On the opposite side, under the very summit of the mountain, is "Kârlî" or *Kurlî,* which, according to the opinion of the archaeologists, is the most ancient and best preserved of the Indian cave-temples.

One who has many times crossed the passes of the Caucasus, and beheld from the top of the Cross Mountain a display of thunderstorms and lightning below; who has seen the Alps and ascended the Rigi; who is acquainted with the Andes and the Cordilleras, and knows every corner of the Catskills in the United States, may be allowed, I hope, the expression of a humble opinion. It may well be that the Caucasian Mountains are more majestic than the *Ghâts* of India, and their splendor favorably compares with these; but that splendor is classical, if I may use this expression. It inspires delight, and arouses fear at the same time. Man feels himself a mere pigmy before these Titans of nature. But in India, with the exception of the Himâlayas, the feeling aroused by the sight of mountains is entirely different. The highest summits of the Dekkan plateau, as well as of the triangular ridge that fringes northern Hindostan, and even those of the Eastern Ghâts, do not exceed 3,000 feet. Only in the Western Ghâts stretching along the entire Malabar coast, from Cape Comorin to the Surat River, are there heights of 7,000 feet above sea level. So that no comparison can possibly be drawn between the mountains of Hindostan and the snow-capped patriarch Elbruz, or Kazbek, rising 15,000-16,000 feet.

The chief and completely unique charm of Indian mountains consists in their amazingly capricious shapes. Sometimes these mountains or, rather, separate volcanic peaks, standing close to each other, form chains; but more often they are scattered, to the great perplexity of geologists, without any obvious reason, in places where the geological formation seems quite unsuitable. Spacious valleys are frequent, surrounded by high walls of rock, over the very ridge of which runs the railway. Look below, and it will seem to you as if you are gazing upon the studio of some whimsical Titanic sculptor, filled with half-finished groups of statues and monuments, all strewn about . . . Here is a dreamland bird, seated upon the head of a monster six hundred feet high, spreading its wings, and its dragon's mouth gaping widely; by its side is the bust of a man, surmounted by a helmet, crenelated like the walls of a feudal castle; again there are legendary beasts devouring each other, statues with broken limbs, disorderly heaps of huge balls, lonely walls with loopholes, ruined towers and bridges. These are all scattered around in confusion, and constantly change their shape as we move along, like phantom-visions of a delirium . . . The chief thing here is that nothing is artificial: it is all a pure sport of nature which, upon occasion, has been turned to account by ancient builders. The art of man in India is to be sought rather *inside* the earth than *on its surface*. Ancient Hindus seldom built their temples otherwise than in the bosom of the earth, as though ashamed, or considering it a sin, to compete with the sculptures of nature. Having chosen, for instance, a sharp pyramidal rock, or a cupola-shaped hillock like Elephanta, or Kârlî, they hollowed them out for centuries, according to the *Purânas,* planning on so grand a scale that no modern architecture has been able to conceive anything to equal it. Fables (?) about the Cyclops seem even truer in Hindostan than in Egypt.

The railroad route from Neral to Khandâlâ reminds one of a similar line from Genoa up the Apennines, in its amazing construction. One may be said to travel in the air, instead of on land. The railroad winds 1,400 feet above Konkan, and in some places, while one rail is laid on the sharp edge of the rock, the other is supported on vaults and arches. The Malî Khindî viaduct is 163 feet high. For two hours we soared between sky and earth, with abysses on both sides, thickly covered with flowering mango trees and bananas. It must be acknowledged that English engineers are wonderful builders.

The pass over Bhor-Ghât is safely crossed and we are now in Khandâlâ. Our bungalow here is built on the very edge of a precipice, whose depth nature carefully concealed under a cover of most luxuriant vegetation. Everything is in bloom, and a botanist would find in this unfathomed recess enough to occupy him for a lifetime. Palms have disappeared, as they grow for the most part near the sea. They have been replaced by banyans, mango trees, pîpals (*ficus religiosa*), fig trees, and thousands of other trees and shrubs, unknown to such laymen as ourselves. The Indian flora has often been slandered; it has been said to have gorgeous flowers but no scent. At some seasons this may be true enough, but as long as jasmine, various balsams, white tuberoses and golden *champac* — in size a king among flowering trees — are in bloom, this statement is entirely false. The aroma of *champac* alone is so powerful as to make one almost giddy; the tree grows, as a rule, in mountainous regions and flowers, like the aloe, once in a hundred years. This year hundreds of them were in bloom on Mâtherân and in Khandâlâ.

We sat on the verandah of the hotel that evening, high above the precipice, and enjoyed the surrounding view until well-nigh midnight. An Englishman who sat near us, an elderly retired captain, noticed that we made no distinction between him and the Hindus, and were not burning any incense to him as representative of the *"higher* race." And so he greeted us and went away. Everything slept around us, and we were all alone with our travelling companions, who spoke English as well as any Oxford professor.

Khandâlâ is nothing but a big village, situated on the flat even top of one of the mountains of the Sahyadra range, about 2,200 feet above sea level, and is surrounded by isolated peaks, as strange in shape as any we have seen. One of them in front of us, on the opposite side of the abyss, looked exactly like a long, one-storied building, with a flat roof and a crenelated parapet. Hindus swear that somewhere in the neighborhood of this hill there exists a secret entrance leading into vast underground halls, in fact a whole subterranean palace, and that there still exist people who possess the secret of the interior abode. A holy hermit, yogin and magician, who has "inhabited this underground for many a century," imparted its secret to Śivâjî, the famous leader of the Marâthâ armies. Like Tannhäuser in Wagner's opera, the unconquerable hero spent seven years of his youth in this mysterious abode. It was there that he acquired his extraordinary strength and courage.

Śivâjî — a kind of seventeenth century Ilya Murometz *

---

* [A giant warrior and knight in Russian folklore.—*Compiler.*]

— from the Dekkan, was leader and king of the Marâthâs, and founder of their rather short-lived empire. It is to him that India owes the weakening, if not the entire destruction, of the Moslem yoke. No taller than an ordinary woman, and with the hand of a child, he was, nevertheless, possessed of unusual strength, which his compatriots ascribe of course to magic. His sword is still preserved in a museum, and everyone wonders at its size and weight, and the hilt through which only a ten year old child could put his hand. The basis of this hero's fame is the fact that he, the son of a poor officer in the service of a Mogul emperor, like another David, slew the Moslem Goliath — Afzal-Khân. It was not, however, with a sling that he killed him, but with the formidable Marâthâ weapon known as *wâghnâkh,* consisting of five long steel nails as sharp as needles and shaped like claws.* This weapon is worn by public combatants on the fingers of their right hand and is used by them to tear each other to pieces like wild beasts.

The Dekkan is full of legends about Sivâjî, and even the English historians mention him with great esteem. Just as in the legend concerning Charlemagne, one of the local traditions asserts that Sivâjî is not dead, but lives secreted for the time being in one of the underground dwellings of the Sahyadra range. When the hour of liberation strikes (and according to the astrologers it is not far off), he will appear again, and will bring freedom once more to his beloved country.

The learned and artful Brâhmanas, those Jesuits of India, profit by these deeply-rooted traditions among the masses by extorting money from them, and often the last cow — the only food-giver of a large family. There is a curious example of this which occurred a couple of months ago. At the end of July, 1879, the following mysterious document went the rounds in Bombay: I translate it literally from the Marâthâ original:†

"Srî!" (an untranslatable greeting).

---

* [From the Marâthî *wâgh,* tiger, and *nâkh,* claw.—*Compiler.*]
† It was translated into all the dialects of India, of which there are 273!!

"Let it be known to everyone that this epistle, originally traced in golden letters, came down from Indra-loka [the heaven of Indra], in the presence of holy Brâhmaṇas, to the altar of the Viśvêśvara temple, which is in the sacred city of Benares.

"Harken and understand, O nations of Hindostan, Râja-sthân, Pañjâb, etc., etc. On Saturday, the second day of the first half of the month of *Magha*,* in the year 1809 of the Sâlivâhana era [*i.e.*, 1887], in exactly eight years, during the *Aśvinî Nakshatra*,† when the sun enters the sign of Capricorn, and the hour of the day will be nearing the constellation of Pisces, that is to say, exactly one hour and thirty-six minutes after sunrise, the hour of the end of Kali-Yuga will strike, and the much desired Satya-Yuga will recur.‡ This time Satya-Yuga will last 1,000 years. During all this time a man's life-span will be 128 years. The days will become longer and will consist of 20 hours and 48 minutes, and the nights of thirteen hours and 12 minutes, that is to say 34 hours and 1 minute all told. The first day of Satya-Yuga, an important day for us, four hours and 24 minutes after sunrise, there will appear a new king with white face and golden hair, who will come from the Far North. He will become the autocratic ruler of India. The *Mâyâ* (illusion) of human unbelief, with all the heresies over which it presides, will be cast into *Patâla*,§ and the *Mâyâ* of the righteous and pious will abide with them, and will help them to enjoy life in *Mṛityu-loka*.‖ Let it also be known to everyone that the disseminator of every copy of this divine document will be rewarded by the forgiveness of as many sins as are generally forgiven when a pious man sacrifices to the Brâhmaṇas one hundred cows. As for the disbelievers

---

*Magha—the eleventh month, according to the Sâlivâhana era.

†*Aśvini Nakshatra*—the first of the 27 constellations on the moon's path.

‡In other words, the end of the Mahâ-Yuga will have arrived, the great cycle comprising all the four yugas.

§*Patâla* means both hell and the antipodes.

‖*Mṛid* is our earth [soil]; "Mṛityu-loka" means the locality of our earth.

and those who do not help us, they will be sent to *Naraka* (hell).

"Copied out and transmitted by the slave of Vishnu, Madlau Śrîram, in the temple of Viśvêśvara, at Benares, on Saturday, the 7th day of the first half of Śrâvana,* 1801, of Sâlivâhana era . . ." (*i.e.*, July 26th, 1879).

The fate of this ignorant and cunning epistle is not known to me. Whether the police put a stop to its distribution concerns the wise administrators. But it splendidly illustrates both the credulity of the populace, drowned in fanaticism, and the unscrupulousness of the Brâhmanas exploiting their flock.

Concerning the word *Patâla,* which literally means the "nether regions," a recent discovery by a Sanskrit scholar (Svâmi Dayânanda Sarasvatî, about whom I wrote in my second letter) is of interest, especially if it is supported by philologists, as the facts seem to promise. Dayânanda tries to show that the ancient Âryans knew, and even visited America, which in ancient MSS. is called Patâla — the land "down under," which term in the course of time was transformed by popular fancy into hell or something similar to the Greek Hadês (Ἅδης). He supports his contention by means of numerous quotations from the oldest scriptures, especially from the legends about Krishna and his favorite disciple Arjuna. In the history of the latter it is said that Arjuna, one of the five *Pândavas,* descendants of the Lunar Dynasty, visited Patâla on his travels, and there married the widowed daughter of King Nagual, called *Illupl.* Comparing the names of father and daughter, we reach the following conclusions, which speak strongly in favour of Svâmi Dayânanda's supposition.

1) *Nagual* is the name by which the Mexican Indian magicians, natives of America, are still designated. Like the Assyrian and Chaldean Nargals, chiefs of the Magi, the Mexican *Nagual* unites in his person the functions of priest and magician, having at his service a demon in the shape of some animal, generally a snake or a crocodile. He is considered to be the descendant of *Nagual,* king of the

---

*Śrâvana is the fifth month of the Hindu year.

snakes. The Abbé Brasseur de Bourbourg * devotes a considerable amount of space to them in his work about Mexico, and says that the *Naguals* are servants of the evil one,
who, in his turn, serves them for the time being. In Sanskrit,
likewise, a snake is called *Nâga,* and the "King of Nâgas"
plays an important part in the history of Buddha and in
the *Purânas.* According to tradition, it was Arjuna himself
who introduced snake worship into Patâla. The converging
circumstances, and the identity of names are so striking,
especially when found on the opposite sides of the earth,
that our scientists should really pay some attention to it.

2) The name of Arjuna's wife, *Ulûpî,* is purely old-
Mexican, and if we reject the hypothesis of the Svâmi, it
will be quite impossible to account for the actual existence
of such a name in Sanskrit manuscripts long before the
Christian era. Of all the ancient languages and dialects, it
is only in those of the American natives that one constantly
meets with such combinations of consonants as *tl, pl,* etc.
They are especially abundant in the language of the Toltecs
(or Nahuatl), but can never be found either in Sanskrit or
in ancient Greek. The words "Atlas" and "Atlantis" find
no etymological equivalent in any European languages.
Wherever Plato may have found them, it was not he who
invented the name of Atlantis. In the Toltec language we
find the root *atl,* meaning water and war, and soon after
the discovery of America by Columbus a town called *Atlan*
was found at the entrance of the gulf of Urabá.† Only in

---

*[Charles Étienne Brasseur de Bourbourg (1814-74). Belgian ethno-
grapher and writer. From 1848 to 1863, travelled as a missionary in
Mexico and Central America. Published in 1857-59 a history of
Aztec civilization, and from 1861-64 edited a collection of documents
in the indigenous languages. Translated into French the *Popol-Vuh*
(1861), the sacred book of the Quiché Indians, and wrote a Quiché
grammar. His *Monuments anciens du Méxique et du Yucatan* was
published by the French government in 1866.—*Compiler.*]

†It is now a poor fisherman's village called Acla. See also *Le
Mexique,* by Brasseur de Bourbourg, and John D. Baldwin, *Prehistoric
Nations,* pp. 397-98.

[Ref. is to the Abbé Brasseur de Bourbourg's work entitled: *Monuments anciens du Mexique et du Yucatan,* etc., Paris, 1866, where the
subject is discussed on pp. 33-40.—*Compiler.*]

America do we meet with such names as Itzcohuatl, Zempo-altecatl, Popocatépetl. To attempt to explain such coincidences by the theory of blind chance would be too much. Consequently, until science shall have successfully overthrown the contention, which it is yet unable to do, we consider Svâmi Dayânanda's hypothesis as the most reasonable, be it only in order to follow the axiom that "one hypothesis is as good as another." Among other things, Dayânanda points out that Siberia and the Bering Straits may have been the route that led Arjuna to America 5,000 years ago.

We would have lingered past midnight listening to these and similar legends, if the innkeeper had not sent a servant to warn us of the dangers that threatened us on the verandah at night, especially a *moonlit* night. The list of these dangers was divided into three sections: 1) snakes; 2) wild beasts; 3) *dacoits*. Besides the cobra and the "rock snake," the surrounding mountains are full of a kind of very small mountain snake, called *fursâ,* the most dangerous of all; their bite kills a man with the swiftness of lightning. The moonlight attracts them, and whole parties of these uninvited guests crawl up on the verandahs of houses, in order to "warm" themselves, as they find it warmer there than on the ground. The flowering and perfumed abyss below our verandah happened to be the favorite stamping ground for tigers and leopards, who come there to quench their thirst at the wide brook which runs along the bottom, and then wander until daybreak under the windows of the bungalow. Lastly, there are the insane *dacoits,* whose dens are scattered in these mountains inaccessible to the police, and who often shoot Europeans simply for the pleasure of sending *ad patres* one of the hateful *bellatis* (foreigners).*

---

* [*Vilâyat* in Hindî means "a foreign country" and *vilâyatî* "a foreigner"; it also means a "native country," and is derived from the Arabic *wilâyat.* In some North Indian vernaculars "v" is pronounced as "b." *Bellati* is apparently a corruption of *bilâyatî,* commonly used among Anglo-Indians. Among Arabs, Pathâns and Sidis, those who had lately come from their native land are called *vilâyatî,* as distinguished from the descendants of old settlers in India. The word, especially in its corrupted form, has come to be used especially of the Englishmen's native country.—*Compiler.*]

Three days before our arrival, the wife of a Brâhmaṇa was
carried off by a tiger into the abyss, and two favorite dogs
of the commandant were killed by snakes. Without waiting
for further explanations, we hurried to our respective rooms.
At daybreak we were to start for Kârlî, six miles away.

———

VESTIBULE OF THE CHAITYA AT KÂRLÎ

ROCK-CUT TEMPLE OF KÂRLÎ

—VI—

At five o'clock in the morning, we arrived in our bullock-cart at the foot of the mountain, and at the end of not only a drivable road, but of even a bridle path. The last half mile was only a rough sea of stones, and we had no alternative but to climb on all fours up an almost perpendicular slope some 900 feet high. Nearly at our wit's end, we gazed at the historical mass before us, not knowing what course to take next. Almost at the summit of the mountain, under the overhanging rocks, were a dozen black apertures. Hundreds of pilgrims were crawling upward, looking, in their holiday dresses, like so many multicolored ants. Now, however, our faithful Hindu friends came to our rescue. One of them, putting the palm of his hand to his mouth, produced a strident sound, something between a shriek and a whistle. This call was immediately answered from above. In a minute, several half-naked Brâhmaṇas, hereditary watchmen of the temple, began jumping from rock to rock as swiftly and skillfully as wild cats on their way down. Five minutes later they were with us and, fastening leather straps round our bodies, dragged rather than led us upwards. Half an hour later, exhausted but perfectly safe, we stood before the porch of the chief temple, until then hidden from us by giant linden trees and cacti.

This majestic entrance, resting on four massive pillars

which form a quadrangle, is 52 feet wide and covered with ancient moss and carvings. In front of it stands the "lion column," so called from the four lions carved in natural size, and seated back to back on the four sides of the capital. Over the principal entrance, its sides covered with colossal male and female figures, there is a huge arch, in front of which three gigantic elephants are sculptured in relief, with heads and trunks that project far out from the wall. The temple itself is oval in shape, 124 feet and 3 inches in total length, and 45 feet and 6 inches in width. The nave is separated from the side aisles by 15 columns on each side, which sustain the cupola-shaped roof. Beyond, there is an altar dividing the first dome from a second, which rises over a small secret holy of holies, formerly used by the ancient Âryan high priests as an inner altar. Two side-passages leading towards it do not actually reach it and come to a sudden termination, which suggests that, once upon a time, either doors or walls, which exist no longer, were there. Each of the columns has a high base, an octagonal shaft, and a capital of magnificent sculptured work, representing two kneeling elephants surmounted by a god and goddess, "of the most exquisite workmanship," in the words of Fergusson.

According to him, this temple or *chaitya* is older and better preserved than any other, and may be assigned to a period about 200 B.C., because Prinsep,* who has deciphered the inscription on the Siṇhastambha, asserts † that

_____

*[James Prinsep (1799-1840) was both an architect and an Orien-- talist. Having gone as assistant assay-master to the Calcutta mint, his chief was the famous Dr. Horace Hayman Wilson, for many years librarian at the India House. Prinsep succeeded him in later years as assay-master to the mint Committee. He returned to England in 1838 in very poor health due to overwork. He reformed the weights and measures of India and introduced a uniform coinage in 1835. He laid the foundations for the *Journal* of the Asiatic Society of Bengal, of which he became secretary in succession to Wilson. His Oriental studies were mainly devoted to the decipherment of inscriptions in the Pâli language on pillars erected by Aśoka, and to the science of numismatics. He became a Fellow of the Royal Society.—*Compiler.*]

†*Journal of the Bombay Branch of the Royal Asiatic Society*, Vol. VI, as quoted by E. Eastwick, *A Handbook for India*, Vol. II, p. 321.

the *lion* pillar was a gift to the temple from Ajmitra Ukass, son of Saha Ravisabhoti, and that another inscription shows that the temple was visited by Datthama Hara (otherwise Dattagamini), king of Ceylon, in the twentieth year of his reign, *i.e.,* 163 years before our era. For some reason or other, Dr. J. Stevenson * insists on seventy years B.C. as the date, asserting that *Kârlên* (Kârlî) was built by the Emperor Devabhûti, under the supervision of Xenocrates (Dhanukâkatâ or Dhenukâkati). But how can this be maintained in view of the above-mentioned, and proven, perfectly authentic inscription? Even Fergusson, that celebrated defender of Egyptian antiquities and hostile critic of those of India,† definitely proves that Kârlî belongs to the structures of the third century B.C., adding that "the disposition of parts is exactly the same as those of the choir of a Gothic round, or polygonal apse cathedral." ‡

Above the main entrance, across the façade, there is a gallery, which reminds one very much of the rood-loft in Catholic churches, where the organ is placed. Off the porch, in addition to the chief entrance, there are two lateral ones, leading to the side aisles, and over the gallery there is a single window in the shape of a horseshoe across the entire

---

* *Journal of the Bombay Branch of the Asiatic Society,* Vol. V, p. 322.

[Rev. John Stevenson, D.D. (1798-1858) was a Scottish divine, sent out by the Scottish Missionary Society, 1823, to their Bombay Mission, the first Scottish Mission established in India. In addition to being a zealous missionary, he was a distinguished Sanskrit scholar, one of the pioneer editors and translators of Vedic literature, a founder of the *Bombay Gazette,* and a student of native dialects. He became President of the Royal Asiatic Society of Bombay and published several scholarly works and translations of Vedic texts.—*Compiler.*]

† [James Fergusson (1808-1886) was educated at Edinburgh and Hounslow and resolved to devote himself to archaeological studies. He spent a number of years in India but settled in London for the remainder of his life. A skilled draughtsman, he made lengthy tours while in India (1835-42 and 1845), exhibiting an unusual power for laborious research. The results of his explorations are embodied in a vast number of works, one of the most important ones being his *Illustrations of the Rock-Cut Temples of India,* 1845.—*Compiler.*]

‡ [J. Fergusson, *Illustrations of the Rock-cut Temples of India.* Text Volume, p. 32.]

middle space. Thus all the light falls on the *dâghoba* (altar)* entirely from above, leaving the aisles, sheltered by the columns, in semi-obscurity, which increases as one approaches the far end of the building. To the eyes of a spectator standing at the entrance, the *dâghoba* must have thus appeared surrounded with radiance, behind which was impenetrable darkness, where the profane was not permitted to enter. The figure of the *dâghoba*, from the summit of which "râjâ-priests" used to pronounce verdicts upon the people, is called "Dharma-Râjan," the Hindu Minos.

Above the main temple are two other tiers of caves, in each of which are wide, open galleries formed of thick carved columns; from these galleries an opening leads to roomy cells and corridors, sometimes very long, but quite useless now, as they come to an abrupt termination at what appears to be solid walls. The guardians and custodians of the temple have either themselves lost the secret of any entrances that may lead farther, or jealously conceal it from the Europeans. The old Brâhmaṇa and his two sons complained bitterly that the Government was giving them a subsidy of merely 600 rupees for the expenses of two temple festivals of Śiva, while the East India Company gave them 2,000. Much as we sympathized with them, we could not help being surprised at such *generosity* — Christian rulers giving subsidies for pagan festivals and idol-worship! A rare characteristic! But then, in any case, why spend millions on the missionary work, instead of converting to Christianity the numerous *unbelievers* at home? . . .

Besides the main *vihâras,* or temple-monasteries, there are many smaller ones scattered over the slope of the mountain, which, according to the opinion of archaeologists, are much older. To what particular century or epoch they actually belong is not known except to a few Brâhmaṇas, who remain silent. Generally speaking, the position of

---

*[Also *dâgoba,* from the Singhalese *dâgaba, dâ* meaning relics, and *gaba,* container or receptacle. It is derived from the Pâli *dhâtugabbha,* and the Sanskrit *dhâtugarbha.* It is usually a solid dome-shaped structure built over relics of the Buddha or a saint.—*Compiler.*]

archaeologists in India is a sad one. The masses, immersed in ignorance, are utterly unable to be of any use to them, while the learned Brâhmaṇas, initiated into all the mysteries of the secret libraries in the pagodas, remain silent and do all they can to prevent archaeological research. However, after all that has occurred, it would be unjust to find fault with the conduct of the Brâhamaṇas in these matters. The bitter experience of many centuries has taught them that their only salvation was in distrust and caution, without which their national history and their most sacred treasures would have been irrevocably lost. Political upheavals and Moslem invasions which have for so many centuries torn India and shaken that country to its very foundations, the all-destructive fanaticism of the Moslem vandals, and the Catholic padris, capable of any cunning scheme to secure manuscripts and destroy them — all these more than justify the Brâhmaṇas.

However, in spite of these destructions occurring through the centuries, there exist in many places in India vast libraries, access to which would shed a bright light not only on the ancient history of India itself, but also on the darkest problems of universal history. Some of these libraries, filled with priceless manuscripts, are in the possession of native princes and of the pagoda priests subservient to them, but the greater part is in the hands of the Jainas (the oldest sect) and of the Râjputâna Thâkurs,* whose ancient hereditary castles are scattered all over Râjasthân, like so many

---

*The Ṭhâkurs occupy in India a position similar to that held by European feudal barons of the middle ages. Nominally they are dependent on their native ruling princes or on the British Government; but de facto they are entirely independent. Their castles are built on inaccessible rocks, and in addition to the obvious difficulty of reaching them other than in single file, they claim another advantage, namely, that of being interconnected by underground passages, the secret of which is inherited from father to son. We have visited two such underground halls, one of which was big enough to contain a whole village. Only yogins and initiated adepts (apart from their owners) are allowed free access to them. It is well known that no torture would ever induce any of them to reveal the secret, especially when one bears in mind the fact that they daily inflict torture upon themselves.

eagle's aeries on the summits of rocks. The existence of the celebrated collections at Jaisalmer and Pathâna are known to the Government, but they remain wholly beyond its reach. The manuscripts are written in an ancient and long forgotten language, intelligible only to the high priest and his initiated librarians. One thick folio is considered so sacred and inviolable that it is fastened to a heavy golden chain in the center of the temple of Chintâmani in Jaisalmer (the capital of the Râjputâna desert), and is taken out to be dusted and rebound only at the advent of each new pontiff. This is the work of Somaditya Saurâchârya, a great high priest, well-known in history, who lived prior to the Moslem invasion. His mantle is still preserved in the temple, and every new high priest dons it at his initiation. Col. James Tod,* who spent so many years in India and gained the love of the people as well as of the Brâhmanas — which no other Englishman ever had or will have — a man who became attached to these people with all the strings of his soul, and who wrote the only true history of India,† never was permitted to touch this folio. Rumor says an offer was made to take him into this sect, with the promise that he would be initiated then into all the mysteries. Being a passionate archaeologist, he almost resolved to accept but, forced to go

---

* [Colonel James Tod was an Indian diplomatist, born at Islington, March 20, 1782, and who died November 17, 1835. His rather short life was filled with scholarly achievements. He went to India in 1799, and did not return to England until 1823. During this long period, he held various responsible positions among which was that of political agent in the Râjput States, where he became eminently successful in restoring peace and confidence, earning the respect of both the chiefs and the people. Bishop Heber testifies to the love which ordinary people bestowed upon Col. Tod. In his travels, he was constantly engaged in surveying or collecting topographical information. After returning to England, he was for a time librarian to the Royal Asiatic Society. Apart from various detailed Journals he kept and which concern his many travels in India, Col. Tod is the author of a very important two volume work entitled: *Annals and Antiquities of Râjasthân, etc.,* London, 1829-32, in which a very considerable amount of information is given concerning the customs and ancient legends of Râjasthân. —*Compiler.*]

† *Annals and Antiquities of Râjasthân,* etc., London, 1829-32.

to England on account of his health, he died before he could return to his second fatherland. Thus the mystery of this new Sibylline Book remains unsolved.

A similar story is told concerning Kârlî and its libraries and underground passages. And yet, archaeologists are unable even to determine whether this ancient temple was built by Buddhists or Brâhmaṇas. Over the huge *dâghoba,* resembling a low minaret with a cupola, that hides the holy of holies from the eyes of the worshippers, a mushroom-shaped roof extends; archaeologists call such roofs "umbrellas," and they usually go with statues of the Buddha and of Chinese sages. But the worshippers of Śiva, who are nowadays in posession of the temple, assert that this low building, somewhat like a drum with a cupola, is merely a *liṅga* of Śiva. Moreover, the sculptures and carvings of gods and goddesses cut out of the rock preclude one from thinking that the temple is the production of Buddhists.

Fergusson writes:

It is to this cave, more especially, that the remark applies that I made [p. 6], that the Chaitya caves seem at once to have sprung to perfection; for whether we adopt the *Mahâvanśa* for our guide, or Aśoka's inscriptions, it is evident, that this country, under the name of Maharatthan in the former, and Pitenika in the other, is one of the unconverted countries to which missionaries were sent in the tenth year of Aśoka's reign; and if, therefore, we assume the above date to be at all near the truth, a century had scarcely elapsed between the conversion of the country and the execution of this splendid monument. There is nothing in the Viharas here or elsewhere which I have placed about the same date, that might not have been elaborated from a natural cavern in that period, but there is a complication of design in this that quite forbids the supposition; and it must either be brought down to much more modern epoch, or it must be admitted to be a copy of a structural building; and even then but half the difficulty is got over. Was that structural building a temple of the Brahmans or Buddhists? Was it designed or invented since the death of Sakya Sinha? Or did it belong to a former religion? And lastly, if we are correct in supposing cave digging to have commenced only subsequent to Aśoka's reign,* why, while the Viharas were still so small, and so insignificant [with the exception, by the way, of dozens of others, such as Elephanta, Ajanta, Kânheri, etc., which Fergusson is trying to

---

*He died in 222 B.C. [H.P.B.]

place as close as possible to our own times], was so great a work undertaken in the rock?*

That is the question. If Fergusson, forced by the factual
evidence of inscriptions to acknowledge the antiquity of
Kârlî, still persists in asserting that Elephanta is of more
recent date, he will scarcely be able to extricate himself from
this dilemma, because the two architectural styles are the
same, and the carvings of the latter are grander yet. To
ascribe the temples of Elephanta and Kânheri to the Buddhists, and to place their construction in the fourth and
fifth centuries A.D. in the first case; the tenth in the second,
is to impose upon history a very strange and unfounded
anachronism. After the first century A.D., not a single influential Buddhist was left in India. Scattered and persecuted by the Brâhmaṇas, they fled by the thousands to
Ceylon and beyond the Himâlayas. After the death of King
Aśoka, Buddhism speedily lost its hold, and was entirely
displaced in India by theocratic Brâhmaṇism. Fergusson's
hypothesis that the followers of Śâkyasiṇha, driven from the
continent, probably sought refuge on the islands surrounding Bombay, would hardly sustain critical analysis. Elephanta and Sâlsette, so near to Bombay (a distance of two
and five miles respectively) are full of ancient Hindu
temples.

Is it possible to imagine that the Brâhmaṇas, more powerful than ever just before the Moslem invasion, fanatical as
they were, and mortal enemies of the Buddhists at the time,
would have allowed these hated heretics to build Buddhist
pagodas not merely within their possessions in general, but
on "Ghârâpuri" in particular, on the island of their sacred
"city of cave-temples"? It is not necessary to be either a
specialist in architecture or an eminent archaeologist to be
convinced at first glance that such temples as Elephanta
are the work of Cyclops, requiring centuries and not years
for their construction. Whereas at Kârlî everything is built
and carved after a carefully thought out plan, at Elephanta

---

*James Fergusson, *Illustrations of the Rock-cut Temples of India.*
Text Volume, London, 1845, pp. 30-31.]

it seems as if thousands of different hands had wrought at various times, each following its own idea and fashioning after its own plan. All the three caves, for instance—the central temple as well as the two side ones — are dug out of hard porphyry rock. The first temple is practically a square (130½ feet long by 130 feet wide) and contains 26 thick pillars and 16 pilasters. Between some of them there is a distance of twelve and sixteen feet, between others 15 feet 5 inches, 13 feet 3½ inches, and so forth. The same variation is found in the bases of the columns, whose finish and neatness of style constantly vary. Why, then, should we not consider the explanations of the Brâhmanas? They say that the temple was conceived and begun by the sons of Pându after "the great war," *Mahâbhârata,* and that they charged all the believers to continue the work after their death, according to the discretion of the latter. Thereafter, the building of the temple continued for three centuries. Anyone who wished to redeem his sins would bring his chisel and set to work. Many were members of royal families, and even kings themselves, who personally took part in these labors . . .* If the temple gradually became neglected, it was because people of both past and present generations became unworthy of visiting such a sacred place.

As for Kânheri and many other cave-temples, there is not the slightest doubt that they were erected by Buddhists. In many of them were found inscriptions in a perfect state of preservation, and their style does not remind one in the least of the symbolical buildings of the Brâhmanas. Archbishop Heber thinks the Kânheri caves were built in the first or second centuries B.C. But Elephanta is much older and must

---

*On the right-hand side of the temple, there is a cylindrical stone, called "liṅga" (the emblem of Śiva in his character of fructifying force in nature), which rests in the middle of a small square chapel with four doors. Round this chapel are many huge human figures; according to the Brâhmanas, these are portrait-statues of the sculptors themselves, Hindus of the highest caste, portrayed as doorkeepers of the holy of holies. Each of the larger figures leans upon a dwarf representative of the lower castes, which have been promoted by popular fancy into "demons" (*piśâchas*). The temple is full of carvings by unskilled hands.

be classed among prehistoric monuments, dating from the epoch immediately following the "great war," *Mahâbhâ-rata,* an event which the eminent and learned Dr. Martin Haug * relegates almost to antediluvian times, but which the equally celebrated and learned Max Müller transfers practically to the first century of our era.

----

* [Martin Haug (1827-76). German Orientalist; studied Oriental languages, especially Sanskrit, at Tübingen and Göttingen. Assisted Bunsen in his literary work at Heidelberg. Left for India, 1859, and became superintendant of Sanskrit studies and professor of Sanskrit at Poona. Having returned to his native land, 1866, was called to Munich as professor of Sanskrit and comparative philology. His chief work is: *Essays on the Sacred Languages, Writings, and Religion of the Parsees,* Bombay, 1862 (2nd & 3rd ed., 1878). He translated the *Aitareya-Brâhmaṇa of the Ṛigveda,* Bombay, 1863, 2 vols.—*Compiler.*]

—VII—

The fair was at its height when, having visited and climbed over all the levels of the caves, and having examined the famous "hall of wrestlers," we descended, not by the way of the stairs, because there were none, but after the fashion of buckets being lowered into a well, namely, by means of ropes. A crowd of about three thousand people from the neighboring villages and towns had assembled. Women were adorned to the waist in brilliant-hued *sârîs,* with rings in their noses, ears, lips, and wherever else they could be hooked; their raven-black hair with bluish glint, smoothly combed back and shining with coconut oil, was ornamented with crimson flowers, sacred to Śiva and Bhavânî, the feminine aspect of that God. In front of the temple there were rows of small shops and tents, where all the requisites for the usual sacrifices — incense, aromatic herbs, sandalwood, rice, *gulâb,* and the red powder with which the pilgrim sprinkles first the idol and then his own face — were sold. The entire body of the mendicant brotherhood — fakirs, bairâgins, gosâîns — wandered among the crowd. Wreathed in chaplets, with long uncombed hair twisted at the top of the head into a veritable feminine chignon, with their faces and bodies smeared with bluish soot, and their bearded appearance, they presented an amusing likeness to naked monkeys. Some of them were covered with wounds, due to mortification of the flesh. There were also some *gunîs,* snake-charmers, with dozens of cobras, fursâs and other snakes around their waists, necks, arms and legs — models worthy of the brush of a painter intent on depicting a male Fury. One *jâdûgar* (sorcerer) among them was especially remarkable. His head was crowned with a turban of cobras. Expanding their hoods and raising their dark green leaf-like heads, these cobras hissed without let up, reminding

81

one of a dying man's heavy breathing, which could be heard
a hundred paces away. Their sharp tongues* quivered like
lightning, and their small eyes glittered with anger at every
passer-by . . . And here, by the way, is what took place;
I relate the event just as it happened, without indulging in
explanation or hypotheses of any kind, and leave the solution of the enigma to a student of natural science.

Undoubtedly anticipating a tip, the cobra-turbaned *guṇî*
by means of a messenger boy offered to exhibit his powers
of snake-charming. Since we did not wish to lose any opportunity, we accepted, but on condition that between us
and his nurslings there should be what Mr. Disraeli would
call a "scientific frontier." For this reason we placed ourselves from the very outset at about fifteen feet from the
"magical circle." I will not dwell on all the tricks and
wonders that we saw, but will proceed at once to the main
fact. With the help of a *vaguḍâ*, a kind of musical pipe of
bamboo, the *guṇî* caused all the snakes to fall into a sort
of cataleptic sleep. The melody that he played, quiet, slow
and original to the last degree, nearly sent us to sleep, too;
at least we suddenly grew extremely sleepy, and without
any apparent cause.

We were aroused from this semi-lethargy by our friend
Gulâb-Singh who gathered a handful of a species of grass,
with which he advised us to rub our temples and eyelids.
Then the *guṇî* produced from a dirty bag a round stone,
no bigger than a ten kopek piece, resembling the eye of
a fish, or a black onyx with a white spot in the center. He
declared that anyone who bought the stone would be able
to "charm" any cobra, paralyzing it at once and causing it

---

*The expression "the sting of a snake," found in several languages,
is exceedingly inaccurate to describe the process of *biting*. The sting
(or tongue) of a snake is perfectly harmless. To introduce the poison
into the blood of a man or of an animal, the snake must pierce the
flesh with its fangs, not prick with its sting, which no snake ever
does. The needle-like eye teeth of a cobra communicate with a little
bag—the poison gland situated under the palate. If this gland is cut
out the cobra will not live more than two or three days. Thus the
assertion made by some skeptics that the *guṇîs* cut this gland from their
snakes is quite unfounded.

to fall asleep (no other kind of snake would be affected by the stone). Moreover, according to him, it is the only remedy for the bite of a cobra. One has merely to place this talisman on the wound, where it sticks so firmly that it cannot be torn away until all the poison has been absorbed, when it will fall off by itself, and all danger will be over ...

Being aware that the Government had offered a large premium for the discovery of such a remedy, we showed a not unreasonable enthusiasm at the sight of such a wonderful talisman. Meanwhile, the *guṇî* began to annoy his snakes. Choosing a huge cobra eight feet long, he teased it until it became enraged. Twisting its tail around a tree, the cobra rose and hissed terribly.* At last it bit one of the fingers of the *guṇî*, on which several drops of blood soon appeared. A unanimous cry of horror arose in the crowd. But the *guṇî*, without any hurry, stuck the little stone onto his finger, let it adhere like a leech, and proceeded with his performance. "The poison gland has been cut out of the snake," remarked our New York Colonel, "this is a mere farce." As if in answer to this remark, the *guṇî*, after a brief contest in skill, caught the cobra by the neck with one hand, and with the other introduced into its mouth a broken match, placing it perpendicularly between the jaws, so that they remained wide open. He then brought the snake over and showed it to each one of us separately, pointing to the death-dealing glands in its mouth. But our Colonel would not give up. "The gland is there all right, but the poison may not be there. How are we to know?" Then a live hen was brought and, with its legs tied together, was placed beside the snake. But the latter turned away from the would-be victim and went on hissing furiously at the *guṇî*. Then placing a stick between the tied legs of the hen, the *guṇî* started to tease the cobra again, until it bit the unfortunate hen. The victim attempted to cacle, shuddered once or twice, and became still. Death was instantaneous ...

---

*"Hissing" is also a wrong expression. A snake (at least a cobra) does not hiss, but rather "rattles"; the heavy loud breathing expands its entire body like the chest of a man.

Then something happened that was so strange that I know my account will rouse all the anti-spiritists and critics of St. Petersburg and Moscow against me. But *facts* remain facts, and do not become fiction, the most murderous criticism notwithstanding. Little by little, the cobra grew so infuriated that it became evident the *jâdûgar* himself found it too dangerous to approach. As if glued to the trunk of the tree by its tail, the upper part of the snake's body darted in all directions trying to bite anything within reach. Somebody's dog happened to wander a few steps away from us, and it seemed to attract the full attention of the *gunî.* Sitting on his haunches, at a reasonable distance from the infuriated cobra, he stared at the dog with motionless glassy eyes, and then began to hum a song at low breath. The dog immediately showed signs of restlessness. Putting its tail between its legs, it turned halfway round to run away, but remained as if fastened to the ground. After a few seconds, the dog started crawling on its stomach towards the *gunî,* nearer and nearer, whining and unable to tear its gaze from him, as if charmed. I understood the thought of the magician and felt awfully sorry for the dog; I wished to put an end to this influence and somehow or other to save the dog. But, to my horror, I suddenly found that my tongue would not move, and that it was impossible for me either to stand or even to raise my finger. Happily this fiendish scene did not last long. Crawling slowly, the dog was by now but a couple of feet from the cobra. The next moment, the snake darted at it with a frightful hiss and bit it in the head . . . The poor animal fell on its back with a plaintive squeal, made a few convulsive movements with its legs, and died almost at once.

It was impossible any longer to doubt there was poison in the gland. In the meantime, the little stone had dropped from the *gunî's* wound, and the magician showed everyone his healed finger on which could be seen the mark of the prick, a red spot no bigger than the head of an ordinary pin. Next he made all his snakes rise on their tails and, holding the little stone between his first finger and thumb, he proceeded to demonstrate the influence of his talisman on them. The nearer his hand approached to the head of

the snakes, the more their bodies recoiled. Looking steadfastly at the stone, they shivered, bent lower and lower,
and finally dropped on the ground as if in a trance . . . the
gunî then offered to permit the skeptical Colonel to try
the experiment himself. In spite of our protests, he accepted
at once and chose a very large cobra for his initial effort.
Armed with the stone, the Colonel bravely approached the
snake and placed it near its head. At first, inflating its hood,
the cobra made an attempt to strike at him, but suddenly
stopped and, bending its head backward, stared at the
stone, which the Colonel slowly moved back and forth,
drawing nearer and nearer to its forehead, and forcing the
cobra to twist on its tail. We did not dare to move, from
sheer fright. When the stone and the Colonel's finger had
come to within half an inch of the snake's head, it staggered
as if intoxicated, its hissing grew weak, its hood dropped
helplessly on both sides of its neck, and its eyes closed.
Drooping lower and lower, the snake fell at last on the
ground like a broken stick and fell asleep . . .

Only then did we breathe freely. Taking the magician
aside we expressed our desire to buy his stone, to which he
at once assented, to our astonishment, and asked two rupees
for it. The talisman became my property and is at the present moment in my keeping. The *gunî* asserts (and our
Hindu friend corroborates it) that it is not a stone but an
excrescence. It is found in the mouth of one cobra in a
hundred, between the bone of the upper jaw and the skin of
the palate. The "stone" is not fastened to the skull, but
hangs on a tendon and can be taken out by simply cutting
open the skin; as the result of this operation, however, the
cobra dies. If we are to believe Bishnu-Nâth (the name of
our magician), this excrescence makes of the cobra possessing it something of a king among the rest of its kind. "Such
a cobra," said the *gunî*, "is like a Brâhmana among Sûdras;*
other cobras obey it. This excrescence is sometimes to be
found in one of the poisonous species of toads, but its effect

---

*Sûdras are the lowest of the four castes: 1) Brâhmanas; 2) Ksha-
triyas (warriors); 3) Vaisyas (merchants); and 4) Sûdras (tillers
of the soil, servants). These four castes are subdivided into numberless
other divisions.

is much weaker. To destroy the effect of a cobra's poison, one should apply the toad's stone not later than *two minutes* after the bite; but the stone of a cobra is effectual to the last minute; it will save one as long as the heart has not ceased beating."

In confirmation of his words, the *guṇî* offered to catch another dog; this he did, the snake bit it, and he placed the stone over the bite. The dog seemed not to notice anything as long as the stone was in place. Bidding us good-bye, the *guṇî* advised us to keep the "talisman" in a dry place and to be sure not to leave it in the vicinity of a dead body, also to hide it from light during an eclipse of the sun or of the moon, lest it lose its power. In case we were bitten by a mad dog, we were to put the "stone" into a glass of water and leave it there overnight: the next morning the sufferer was to drink the water, and thus be healed.

"He is a regular devil and not a man," exclaimed our Colonel, when the *guṇî* had departed in the direction of the temple of Śiva, where, by the way, we were not admitted.

"Just the same kind of mortal as you or I," remarked the *Râjput* with a smile, "and a very ignorant one at that. Like almost all these snake-charmers, he has been brought up in a temple of Śiva, the great patron of snakes; they teach them there all sorts of 'mesmeric tricks,' in practice, without explaining anything to them; so they believe that all of it is done by Śiva, who naturally gets all the honor for their *miracles*."

"For some time the Government has been offering a premium of several thousand rupees for an antidote against the bite of a cobra. Why then do they not claim it, rather than let thousands of people die every year?" *

"The Brâhmaṇas would never let them do so. If the Government took the trouble to examine the statistics of deaths caused by snakebites more carefully, they would find that no *Hindu of the Shaiva sect has ever died from the bite*

---

*Every year from *two* to *three thousand* people die in India from snakebite. Last year some 15,000 persons perished on account of tigers and snakes.

of a cobra. People of other sects die, while those of their own are saved."

"But did he not disclose his secret to us, total strangers to him, and foreigners to boot? Why should the English not take advantage of this also?"

"Because the secret is completely useless to Europeans. The Hindus do not try to conceal the antidote, they know full well that without their aid no one can use it. The 'stone' retains its power only if it has been taken from a *live* cobra. In order to catch the snake alive, it is necessary first to cast it into a lethargic sleep or, as it is said, to 'charm' it. Who is there among the foreigners who is able to do that? Even among the Hindus themselves, you will hardly find an individual in India who possesses this ancient secret, unless he be a disciple of the Shaiva Brâhmaṇas. Only these possess the monopoly of this secret, and not even all of them, but only those who belong to the pseudo-Patañjali School, the *bhûta* (demon)-ascetics so-called. Throughout this land, there are but half-a-dozen such pagoda-schools now, scattered here and there over India, and their inmates would rather part with their lives than with their secret."

"We paid two rupees for the stone which, in the hands of the Colonel, proved to be as potent as in the hands of the *gunî*. Is it then so difficult to procure a supply of these stones?"

Our friend laughed.

"In a few days the talisman will lose all its healing power in your inexperienced hands. That is why he let it go at such a low price, and probably, at this very moment he is making an offering of his skillful cheating on the altar of his deity. I guarantee you a week's healing value for your purchase, after which you might as well throw it out the window."

Actually we soon learned the truth of these words. On the following day we came across a little girl, bitten by a green scorpion; she seemed to be in her last convulsion. No sooner had we applied the stone to the wound, than the child seemed relieved, and, in an hour, she was playing gaily, whereas, even in the case of the sting of a common black scorpion, the patient would suffer for a couple of weeks. But when, some *ten days* later, we intended to test the potency of the "stone" upon a poor coolie of Allâhâbâd, just bitten by a cobra (which was killed then and there), our *talisman* would not even stick to the wound, and the poor wretch died within the hour. I do not attempt to offer either a defense or an explanation of the virtues of the "stone." I simply state the facts and leave them to fate and the mercy of the skeptics. Yet I can readily find a great many living witnesses in India to bear me out. When Dr. Joseph Fayrer,* who lately published his *Thanatophidia* (a book on the snakes of India, a work well known throughout Europe), categorically stated his disbelief in the alleged means of the "wonderworkers" of India, the following incident took place. A fortnight or so after the appearance of his book among Anglo-Indians, a cobra bit his cook. A *gunî*, who happened to pass by, offered to save the man's life. The celebrated scholar was about to order the *gunî* thrown out, when Major Kelly and other officers begged him to "try" the experiment. Declaring, sneeringly, that in spite of it his cook would be no more in less than an hour, the doctor gave his consent. In less than one hour the cook was preparing dinner in the kitchen for the esteemed scholar and his guests, and the professor very nearly tossed his book into the fire . . .

The day grew dreadfully hot; the sun had heated the rocks to such an extent that they burned our feet even through our thick-soled shoes. Also the general curiosity aroused by our presence, and the troublesome pursuit of the crowd, were becoming annoying. We resolved to go home, that is to say, to return to the cool cave, some six hundred feet from the great temple, where we were to spend the evening and to sleep. Without waiting for our Hindu companions, who had gone to see the fair, we started off by ourselves.

---

*[Sir Joseph Fayrer, Bart. (1824-1907). English physician; was a member of the Indian medical service, and on his return to England acted as president of the medical board of the India Office, 1874-95. Especially known for his studies on the poisonous snakes of India and on the physiological effects produced by their virus. His *Thanatophidia of India* (1872) is the standard work on the subject and is illustrated by plates drawn from life by members of the Calcutta School of Art. —*Compiler.*]

—VIII—

Entering the portico of the main entrance, we were
struck by the appearance of a young man, who stood apart
from the crowd and was of a classic beauty. He was a member of the *Sâdhu* sect, a "candidate for saintship," to use the
expression of one of our party.

The *sâdhus* differ greatly from all other sects. They do
not go about naked, do not cover their bodies with damp
ashes, wear no painted signs on their faces or foreheads, and
do not worship idols. Belonging to the strict Advaita sect of
the Vedânta School, they believe only in Parabrahman
(the great Spirit). The *sâdhu* was dressed in a fairly good
light yellow muslin shirt without sleeves; he wore his long
hair loose and stood with uncovered head, his elbow resting on the back of a cow, which had a "fifth leg" growing
out of her hump. This extraordinary freak of nature waved
its fifth leg as if it were a hand and arm, scratching its head
with the hoof and killing flies with it. At first we thought
it was a trick and looked with some distrust both at the
animal and at its handsome owner; but upon drawing
nearer, we became convinced that here was a playful freak
of nature and not the cunning of man. We learned from the
young man that this animal had been presented to him by
the Mahârâja Holkar, and that its milk has been his only
food for the last two years.

Sâdhus are followers of *Râja-Yoga* and, as said above, usually belong to the Vedânta School; they are disciples of initiated mystics who have entirely renounced the world and lead a life of monastic chastity. They are not distinguished by any special dress, other than a white turban and long hair. Between *sâdhus* and *guṇîs* (disciples of Śiva) there exists a mortal enmity, which manifests itself in silent contempt on the one side, and on the other, an unsuccessful attempt on the part of the *guṇîs* to sweep the *sâdhus* off the face of the earth. This antipathy reminds one of the conflict of light and darkness, something like the dualism of Ahura-Mazda and Ahriman among the followers of Zoroaster. The masses look upon the former as Magi, sons of the sun and of the Divine Principle, while the latter are considered to be dangerous sorcerers. Having heard of the reputation of the former and their abilities as "wonder-workers," and burning with curiosity to see some of the *miracles* ascribed to them by some people (even many Englishmen), we invited the *sâdhu* to visit our vihâra in the evening. But the handsome ascetic curtly refused, under the pretext that we were staying within the temple of idol worshippers, the very atmosphere of which would prove hostile to him. Seeing his inflexibility, we tried to offer him money, but he resolutely refused it, and so we went our way.

A path, or rather a ledge cut into the well-nigh perpendicular face of a rocky mass 900 feet high, led from the chief cave-temple to our vihâra. A man needs good eyes, sure feet and a very strong head to avoid sliding down the precipice at the first false step. Help would be practically useless, for the ledge being only two feet wide does not allow walking side by side. We had to walk single file, depending for aid on whatever presence of mind we had, and the latter, in the case of some of us, had taken an unlimited furlough. The predicament of our American colonel was especially unfortunate, for he was rather stout, very shortsighted, and hence subject to vertigo. As slight encouragement, we indulged in a choral performance of the duet from *Norma*,* "moriamo

---

* [Title and heroine of an opera (1831) by Bellini.—*Compiler.*]

insieme . . .", all the while firmly holding each other's hands to assure being spared by Death, or all four of us "dying together." But the Colonel succeeded in frightening us nearly out of our wits.

We were half way up, when he made a false step, staggered, suddenly lost hold of my hand, and rolled over the edge. We three, having to clutch the bushes and rocks with one hand, had no chance of helping him with the other. A unanimous cry of horror escaped us, but died away the very next moment as we perceived, looking down into the abyss, that he had succeeded in clinging with both hands and feet to the trunk of a small tree which he had encountered some six feet below us down the slope. Fortunately, we knew him to be good at athletics, and remarkably cool-headed. Still the moment was a critical one. The slender stem of the tree might give way any minute and our Colonel fall into the abyss. We were just about to shout for help, when suddenly there appeared before us, as if sprung from the heart of the rock, the mysterious *sâdhu* with his cow . . .

They were both walking some twenty feet below us, on such hardly visible projections of the rock that it seemed a child's foot could have barely found room to rest; and they were going as confidently, and even carelessly, as if they were travelling on a wide highway instead of a vertical rock. Lifting his head, the *sâdhu* called to the Colonel to hold on as firmly as he could, and for us to keep quiet. Patting the "five-legged" cow kindly on her neck, he untied the rope with which he was leading her, all the while quietly chanting some sort of "mantra"; then, taking hold of her head with both hands, turned it in our direction, and, making a snapping sound with his tongue, calmly said to her: "Chal!" (go). With a few wild goat-like bounds up the cliff, the cow found herself on our path and stood motionless a few steps in front of us. As to the *sâdhu* himself, he started climbing towards the tree, with equal agility; tying the rope around the Colonel's body and putting him on his legs again, he then, climbing higher up the path, with a single effort of his strong arm, pulled the Colonel up — rather pale and minus his *pince-nez,* but not his presence of mind.

An adventure that had threatened to become a tragedy ended comically.

"What is to be done now?" was our unanimous inquiry. "We cannot let you go further alone."

The sun was dipping towards the western horizon, and it was getting very risky to tarry any longer. "In a few moments it will be dark, and then we shall all perish," remarked the Colonel's secretary, Mr. Edward W—. In the meanwhile, the *sâdhu,* evidently not understanding a word of English, having refastened the rope on his cow's neck, stood motionless at the turn of the path. His tall, slender figure seemed suspended in air above the precipice. Only his long, black hair, blowing in the breeze, showed that in him we beheld a living being and not some wondrous statue cast in bronze. Forgetting our recent danger and our present awkward predicament, Miss B., a born artist and a passionate admirer of all that was artistic, loudly exclaimed: "Just look at his majestic, purely Greek profile! . . . Observe the poise of the man! . . . How he stands out against the golden and azure sky! A Greek Adonis, truly, and not a Hindu! . . ." But the "Adonis" put a sudden stop to her ecstasy. He slowly turned towards us, glanced briefly with half-kindly, half-mocking, laughing eyes, at Miss B— who was staring at him, and said in his quiet ringing voice in Hindî:

"Mahâ-Sâhib (Great Sir) cannot go any further without the help of someone else's eyes. Sâhib's eyes are his enemies. Let the Sâhib ride on my cow. She cannot stumble . . ."

"I? Ride on a cow, and a five-legged one at that? Never!" exclaimed the poor Colonel, with such a disconcerted look that we all burst out laughing.

"It would be better for the Sâhib to sit on a cow than to lie on a *chitâ,*"* remarked the *sâdhu* with kindly seriousness. "Why call forth the hour which has not yet struck?"

There was nothing else to be done, and we succeeded in persuading the Colonel to ride. Carefully mounting him on the cow's back, and telling him to hold firmly to the fifth leg, the Hindu led the way, and we all followed behind.

---

* [The pyre on which dead bodies are burned.]

A few minutes later we were on the verandah of our vihâra, which was deeply hewn from the rock, and found our Hindu friends, who had arrived by another path. We eagerly related our adventures and then looked for the *sâdhu,* but found he had already disappeared with his cow.

"No use looking for him; he has taken a road known only to himself," casually remarked Gulâb-Singh. "He is well aware of your gratitude, and would not take any money. He is a *sâdhu,* and not a *guni,*" he added, proudly.

We remembered that our proud friend himself belonged to the *sâdhu* sect.*

"Who can tell," whispered the Colonel in my ear. "Maybe what is being said about him is true!"

In the main hall of the vihâra, a life-size statue of Bhavânî, the feminine aspect of Śiva, was cut in the rock, and twelve doorways led into as many smaller cells. From the bosom of the "Devakî" gushed the pure cool water of a mountain spring, which fell into a reservoir at her feet. Piles of sacrificial flowers, rice, betel leaves and incense surrounded it. It was so damp there, that we preferred to spend the night in the open air; we remained on the verandah, hanging, as it were, between sky and earth, and lit from below by numerous blazing fires kept burning by Gulâb-Singh's servants to scare away wild beasts, and from above, by the light of the full moon. A supper arranged after the eastern style, on carpets spread upon the floor, with thick banana leaves for plates; the noiselessly gliding steps of the barefooted servants, as silent as ghosts, in their white muslins and red turbans; the limitless depth of space before us, lost in the waves of moonlight, and behind, the dark vaults of ancient caves, dug by an unknown race, in unknown times, and in honor of an equally unknown prehistoric religion — all these circumstances transported us into a strange world and to distant epochs very different from our own . . . Right

---

*Sâdhu-Nânak must not be confounded with the sect of the Sikhs, followers of Guru-Nânak. The former are Advaita-Vedântists; the latter monotheists. The Advaitas believe only in an *impersonal* deity—Parabrahman.

there with us sat the representatives of five different peoples, five entirely different types, and in five costumes wholly different, one from the other. All five are known to ethnographers under the generic name of *Hindus,* similar to the fact that eagles, condors, hawks, vultures and owls are known to ornithologists as "birds of prey," though differing from each other just as much. Each of these five companions, a Râjput, a Bengalî, a Madrasî, a Singhalese and a Marâthâ, is a descendant of a race the origin of which European scientists have argued about over half a century without coming to an agreement.* Irrespective of all this the tradi-

---

Râjputs, for instance, are called "Hindus" and are classified as Âryans, while they call themselves *Sûryavaṇśa, i.e.,* descendants of *Sûrya* (sun). Brâhmaṇas derive their origin from *Indu* (moon) and are called *Induvaṇśa* (*Indu, Soma,* or *Chandra,* meaning moon in Sanskrit). If the first Âryans to appear in the prologue of universal history, *i.e.,* the people who, according to Max Müller, having crossed the Himâlayas, conquered the country of the "five rivers," are Brâhmaṇas, then the Râjputs are not Âryans; and if they are Âryans, then they are not Brâhmaṇas, as all their genealogies and sacred *Purâṇas* show that they are much older than the Brâhmaṇas; in such a case, Âryan tribes have existed in other countries of our globe, as well as in the renowned district of the *Oxus,* the cradle of the *Germanic race, the ancestors of the Âryans and the Hindus,* in the imagination of the above-named scholar and his German school. The "lunar" line begins with Purûravas (according to the genealogy prepared by Col. Tod from *Purâṇa* MSS. in the Udaipur archives), *i.e.,* more than 2200 years B.C., and much later than Ikshvâku, the forefather of the Sûryavaṇśas. The fourth son of Purûravas, Raya, heads the line of the Lunar Race, and it is only in the fifteenth generation after him that appears Hârîta, who founded the Kauśika-gotra or the *"Brâhmana-tribe."* The Râjputs can hardly tolerate them. They say: "the children of the *Sun* and of *Rama* have nothing in common with the children of the *Moon* and of Krishna." As for the Bengalîs, according to their traditions and history, they are aborigines. The Madrasîs and the Singhalese are Dravidians; these in turn have been said to belong to the Semites, the Hamites and the Âryans; and finally, they have been left to the will of God, with the conclusion drawn that the Singhalese, at all events, must be Mongolians of Turanian origin. The Marâthâs are aborigines of the west of India, as the Bengalîs are of the east; but to what group of tribes these two nationalities belong, no ethnographer can actually vouch, save perhaps a German.

[Cf. Col. Tod, *Annals and Antiquities of Râjasthân* (1880), Vol. I, pp. 24-25.]

tions of the people themselves are generally denied, mainly because they are not in harmony with preconceived notions. The meaning of their ancient manuscripts is distorted, and facts are sacrificed to fiction, if only the latter proceeds from the mouth of some favorite oracle.

Ignorant masses are often accused of superstition just because they create for themselves fanciful idols in the spiritual world. And yet the educated world, the world that is athirst for knowledge, the enlightened world, acts even more foolishly than they when dealing with its own favored authorities. Permitting half a dozen laurel-crowned scholastic heads to draw their own conclusions, according to their own liking, it stones anyone who dares to question the decisions of these quasi-infallible specialists and brands him an ignorant fool. Let us remember the case of Louis Jacolliot, who spent twenty years in India, had studied the language and the country thoroughly, and who, nevertheless, was rolled in mud by Max Müller, whose foot never touched Indian soil.

The oldest people of Europe are mere babes, hardly out of swaddling clothes, compared with the tribes of Asia, and especially of India. How poor and pitiful, indeed, appear the genealogies of the oldest European families, when compared with those of some Râjputs! In the opinion of Col. Tod, who for over twenty years studied these genealogies on the spot — in Râjasthân itself, theirs are the most complete and most trustworthy of all similar records of the peoples of antiquity. They date from 1000 to 2200 years B.C., and are in many instances upheld by Greek writers. After long and careful research and comparison with the *Purânas* and various inscriptions on monuments, Col. Tod came to the conclusion that in the Udaipur archives (now inaccessible), not to mention others, may be found the key, not only to the history of India, but to ancient universal history in general. Here is what he says on this subject:

In order to discover this key, we should not follow the example of many credulous archaeologists unacquainted with India and who therefore imagine the stories of Râma, the *Mahâbhârata*, of Krishna and the five Pandavas brothers, to be nothing but "allegories." He who would seek seriously to fathom these legends will very soon become convinced that these so-called "fables" are from first to last founded on historical facts, the proof of which is to be found in the descendants of these heroes, their tribes, their ancient cities, and coins which exist even today. Let us first decipher the inscriptions on the pillars of *Indraprastha, Purâga* and *Mewâr,* on the cliffs of *Junâgarh* in Bijolia, on the *Arâvali* and in the ancient Jaina temples scattered all over India. Where we find so many inscriptions in a language so far unknown to us, a language in comparison with which even hieroglyphics are child's play—and only then shall we have the right to express our final opinion.

And yet, Professor Max Müller, who, as already mentioned, never got a glimpse of India, sits as a judge and establishes chronological tables for it, according to his own ideas; while Europe, taking his words for those of an oracle, endorses his decisions. *Et c'est ainsi que s'écrit l'histoire . . .* Talking about the chronology of the esteemed German Sanskritist, I cannot resist the desire to show (be it only to Russia) on how fragile a basis all his scientific allegations are founded, and how little he is to be trusted in his pronouncements upon the antiquity of this or that manuscript. It may be that what I am about to say will seem irrelevant in this superficial description of India which makes no pretence to learning: but it must be remembered that in Russia, as elsewhere in Europe, people judge the value of this philological luminary merely by the acclaims and plaudits lavished upon him by his servile followers. As to the *Veda-Bhâshya,** for instance, of Svâmi Dayânanda, no one ever reads it, and possibly has never even heard of it, which is fortunate for Professor Max Müller. I shall try to state the essential points of the case as briefly as possible.

Stating in his *Sâhitya-Grantha* that the Âryan tribe in India acquired the notion of God step by step and exceedingly slowly, Professor Max Müller wishes to prove thereby that the *Vedas* are far from being old as is supposed by some of his colleagues. Later, having presented some more or less weighty evidence in support of this new theory, he

---

*A translation of the *Vedas* into Hindî, with commentaries and explanations. It is the first complete translation.

concludes with a fact, which, in his opinion, is indisputable. He points to the word *hiranya-garbha* in the *mantra*-section, which he translates as "gold," and adds that, as the section of the *Vedas* called *chhandas* appeared 3,100 years ago,* the *mantra*-section could not have been written earlier than 2,900 years ago. Moreover, he divides the *mantra*-section ("Agniḥ pûrvebhiḥ," etc.) † philologically and chronologically, and, finding in it the word *hiranya-garbha,* he triumphantly denounces it as an anachronism. "The ancients," he says, "had no knowledge of gold, and, therefore, if gold is mentioned in the *mantra*, it means that the *mantra* was composed at a comparatively modern epoch," and so forth.

But the eminent Sanskritist is very much mistaken in this. Svâmi Dâyananda and other pandits, even those now antagonistic to him, prove and confirm that Max Müller has completely misunderstood the meaning of the term "*hiranya*." Originally it did not, and, when united with the word *garbha*, even now does not, mean "gold," a word of more recent origin which does not exist in the ancient Sanskrit of the *Vedas*. Thus all the Professor's brilliant demonstrations are so much labor lost. The word *hiranya* in this *mantra* should be translated "divine light," a symbol of knowledge in the mystical sense, just as with the alchemists "light" was called *sublimated gold,* from whose rays they hoped to obtain the objective metal. In combination with the second word—*hiranya-garbha* (literally, radiant womb), it designates in the *Vedas* the primeval principle, in whose womb (like gold in the womb of earth) rests the light of divine knowledge and truth, the essence of the soul liberated from the sins of the world.‡

---

*The *Vedas* are divided into two parts: *chhandas*—ślokas, verses, etc.; and *mantras*—prayers, rhythmical hymns, which are, at the same time, incantations used in white magic.

† [*Agniḥ pûrvebhiḥ* are the first two words from the second verse of the Hymn to Agni, *Ṛigveda*, I, 1.—*Compiler.*]

‡ [The same subject is treated of in *The Secret Doctrine*, Vol. I, p. 360, where H.P.B. refers to the "unpublished polemics" of Dayânanda Sarasvatî with Prof. F. Max Müller. The source of such "polemics" has not been traced.—*Compiler.*]

In the *mantras,* as in the *chhandas,* one should always look for a double meaning: 1) a purely metaphysical and abstract one, and 2) the purely physical, as everything that is earthly or that exists on earth is closely bound to the spiritual world, from which it proceeds and into which it is reabsorbed. For instance, *Indra,* the god of thunder, *Sûrya,* the sun-god, *Vâyu,* the god of the wind, and *Agni,* the god of fire, all four, depending upon this primeval divine principle, issue, according to the *mantra,* from the womb of *hiranya-garbha.* In this case, they — the gods — are spirits or personifications of the forces of Nature, subordinate to the One Principle. But the initiated Adepts of India understand very clearly that the god *Indra,* for instance, is nothing else but sound generated by the collision of electrical forces, or, more correctly, electricity itself; *Sûrya* is not the god of the sun, but the center of fire in our system — the essence of that whence issue fire, heat, light, etc., hence the very thing which none even among our greatest scientists, sailing an even course between Tyndall and C. Schöpffer,* has as yet defined . . . This concealed meaning has totally eluded Professor Max Müller's research, as a result of which he makes bold assertions, clinging to the dead letter alone. How, then, can he claim to establish the antiquity of the *Vedas,* according to his own deductions and conclusions, when his understanding of the language of this ancient scripture is so imperfect? . . .

Such is the gist of the Svâmi's reply, and to him we shall refer the Sanskritists, if they care to consult his *Ṛigvedâdi-Bhâshya-Bhûmika* (Bk. IV, p. 76).†

That night, all the travellers slept soundly, except me. They were all curled up around the slowly dying fires and paid no attention at all either to the distant drone of the

---

*[Reference is to Professor C. Schöpffer who delivered in Berlin a lecture entitled *Die Erde steht fest* (5th ed., 1854), in which he attempted to show that the Earth does not rotate on its axis and does not revolve around the sun. H.P.B. mentions it in *Isis Unveiled,* Vol. I, pp. 621-23.—*Compiler.*]

†This periodical monthly publication may be available in Russia, at the St. Petersburg Academy.

thousand voices which reached us from the fair, or the prolonged dull roar of the tigers, rising like a distant thunder from the valley, or even to the loud prayers of the pilgrims who passed to and fro all night long along the narrow ledge of the cliff from which we very nearly fell during the daylight. They came in parties of twos and threes, and sometimes there appeared a lonely woman. As they could not reach the vihâra because we occupied its verandah, they entered, after some little grumbling, a small lateral cell, something like a chapel, with a statue of Devakî-Mâtâ (mother-goddess) in it, and a *tank* full of water. Approaching the entrance, each pilgrim postrated himself, then placed his offering at the feet of the goddess and bathed in the "holy waters of purification," or, at least, drawing water, sprinkled some of it over his forehead, cheeks and breast; he then prostrated himself again, retreated backward towards the entrance, prostrated himself once more, and vanished into the outer darkness with a final invocation: *"Mâtâ, mahâ-mâtâ!"*—Mother, great mother! Two of Gulâb-Singh's servants, with traditional spears and shields of rhinoceros skin, who had been ordered to protect us from wild beasts until sunrise, sat on the steps of the verandah, at the edge of the precipice. Unable to fall asleep, I watched with increasing curiosity all that went on. The Ṭhâkur was also sleepless. Every time I half-opened my eyelids, heavy with fatigue, there appeared before me the gigantic figure of our mysterious friend . . .

Having seated himself after the Eastern fashion, with his feet drawn up and his arms round his knees, he sat motionless on a bench cut in the rock at the very end of the verandah, gazing intently into the silvery distance. Our Râjput sat so close to the edge that the least incautious movement, it seemed, would have thrown him into the yawning abyss at his feet. But the granite goddess Bhâvanî herself, a few steps away from him, was hardly more immovable. The light of the moon, in which everything in front of him was bathed, was so strong that the black shadow under the rock sheltering him was quite impenetrable, shrouding his face in absolute darkness. From time to time, the flames of the sinking fires leaping up cast their warm reflection of his dark-bronze face, enabling one to distinguish its sphinx-like features and his shining eyes, glowing like bright embers, yet as motionless as the rest of him.

What am I to think? Does he sleep or is he entranced? Entranced as are the initiated *râja-yogins* about whom he was telling us this morning? Oh, if I could only go to sleep! . . . Suddenly a loud, prolonged hissing sound erupted close to my ear, as if from under the hay on which we were curled, and made me jump with vague reminiscences about a "cobra." Then it struck: one, two . . . It was our American travelling alarm clock, which somehow or other happened to get under the hay. I felt ashamed and amused at this involuntary fright.

Yet neither the hissing sound, nor the loud striking of the clock, nor my sudden movement — which made Miss B— raise her sleepy head — awakened Gulâb-Singh, who was hovering, as before, above the precipice. Another half-hour went by. In spite of the distant hum of the festival, all was quiet and motionless; but sleep eluded me more and more. A fresh and rather strong wind rose just before dawn, at first rustling the leaves, then moving the tips of the trees that grew from the abyss before us. My whole attention was now centered upon the three Râjputs before me — the two shield-bearers and their master. I cannot tell why, but I was especially attracted at this moment by the sight of the long hair of the servants, which was waiving in the wind, though they sat on the more sheltered side of the verandah than their *Sâhib*. As I turned by eyes toward the latter, I felt as though my blood had congealed in my veins. The muslin veil of someone's *ṭopi*, which hung beside him, tied to a pillar, was whirling in the wind, while the hair of the *Sâhib* himself lay as still as if it had been glued to his shoulders; not a single hair moved, not the slightest movement could be noticed in the light folds of his white muslin garment. No statue could have been more motionless . . .

What is this? A delirium, a hallucination, or an amazing and inexplicable reality? Shutting my eyes tightly, I decided not to look any longer. At that very moment something produced a crackling sound but a few feet from the steps, and the long, dark silhouette of some animal — either a dog or a wild cat — became clearly outlined against the brightening sky. The animal stood in profile on the edge of the precipice, its long tail lashing to and fro. Both Râjputs rose swiftly and noiselessly and turned their heads towards Gulâb-Singh, as if asking for orders. But where was Gulâb-Singh? On the spot where he sat so motionless but a minute earlier, there was no one to be seen; only the *topi* lay there, torn down by the wind. Suddenly an awful roar, deafening and prolonged, made me jump; penetrating into the vihâra, it awakened the silent echoes and resounded along the edge of the precipice like the dull rumbling of thunder. Good heavens! A tiger! Before this thought had time to shape itself clearly in my mind, there came the sound of crashing branches, and of something heavy sliding down into the abyss. Everyone sprang up, and all the men seized their guns and revolvers. The alarm was general.

"What's the matter now?" said the calm voice of Gulâb-Singh, seated again on the bench as if nothing had happened. "What has caused you this fright?"

"A tiger! Was it not a tiger?" came in rapid questioning remarks from Europeans and Hindus alike. Miss B— trembled like one stricken with fever.

"Tiger or not matters very little to us now. Whatever it was, it is by now at the bottom of the abyss," answered the Râjput, yawning. "You seem to be especially disturbed," he added with a slight irony in his voice, addressing the English lady who was hysterically crying, undecided whether to swoon or not.

"Why doesn't our Government destroy all these terrible beasts?" sobbed our Miss B—, who evidently believed firmly in the omnipresence of her government.

"Probably because our rulers save their powder for us, giving us the honor of being considered more dangerous than the tigers," said the courtly Gulâb-Singh.

There was a ring of something both threatening and derisive in the way our Râjput used that word "rulers."

"But how did you get rid of the 'striped one'?" insisted the Colonel. "Has anyone fired a shot?"

"It is but with Europeans that firearms are considered the *only,* or at least the *very best way* to overcome wild beasts. We savages have other means, even more dangerous," explained *Bâbû* Norendro-Das-Sen. "When you visit us in Bengal, you will have a splendid opportunity of becoming acquainted with tigers; they come to us uninvited both day and night, even in towns ..."

It was getting light, and Gulâb-Singh proposed that we descend and examine the rest of the caves and the ruins of the fortress before the seasonal heat; in a few moments everything was ready for breakfast, and at half past three we started by another and less steep road down into the valley, having no special adventures on our way. The Marâthâ, however, lagged behind and vanished, without saying a word to us.

———

BUDDHIST VIHÂRA AT KÂNHERI CAVES

FRONT VIEW OF PĀṆḌULENA CAVE AT NĀSIK

—IX—

[LOHOGARH. — WADGAON. — CONFLICT BETWEEN THE ENGLISH AND THE MARÂṬHÂS. — THE DEAD TIGER. — CAVES OF BIRSA AND BHÂJÂ. — CHINCHVAD AND THE INCARNATIONS OF GAṆAPATI. — RETURN TO BOMBAY.]

We went through Lohogarh, a fortress which was captured by Śivâjî from the Moguls in 1670, and the ruined chambers where the widow of Nânâ Farnavîs,* under the pretext of an English protectorate and a yearly pension of 12,000 rupees, became *de facto* the captive of General R. C. Wellesley in 1804.† We started for the village of Wadgaon,

---

*Nânâ Farnavîs was the first minister of the peshwa, the young Mahâdeo Râo; the latter was held in such a firm grip by the former, that after having been subjected to a public rebuke, he committed suicide on the morning of October 25, 1795, by jumping off the terrace of his castle at Poona.

†[Richard Colley Wesley Wellesley (1760-1842), son of an Irish peer, was the brother of the famous duke of Wellington. Educated at Eton and Christ Church, Oxford. After a period in the English House of Commons, was appointed a lord of the treasury by Pitt. Became in 1793 a member of the board of control over Indian affairs, and in 1797 accepted the office of governor-general of India. The rivalry with France made Wellesley's rule in India an epoch of enormous and rapid expansion of English power. His attempts to remove some of the restrictions on the trade between England and India brought him into hostility with the East India Company, and he resigned in 1805. Became ambassador to Spain, 1809; foreign secretary in Perceval's cabinet from which he resigned in 1812. Identified himself with the claims of the Irish Catholics for justice. Appointed lord-lieutenant of Ireland, 1821, and had the satisfaction of seeing the Catholic claims settled for a while.—*Compiler*.]

once fortified and still very rich. We were to spend the hottest hours of the day there (from 9 a.m. to 4 p.m.), and then proceed to the historically famous caves of Birsa * and Bhâjâ, about three miles from Kârlî.

Wadgaon is famous because of two shameful events in English history. On January 12 and 13, 1779, a considerable military force was defeated by a mere handful of Marâthâs. Then William Hornby, the governor of Bombay, after consultation with the former peshwa, Râghunâth Râo, appointed him regent at Poona, with four thousand armed men, six hundred of whom were English, and called upon John Carnac, the President of the Council, to carry out this agreement. In so doing, Carnac brought shame upon his country and the honor of the East India Company, thus becoming a traitor to his regent and his government.[†] Frightened by the small Marâthâ army under the command of Nânâ Farnavîs, Sindhia and Tukoji Râo Holkar, he ordered a retreat and later entered into a shameful bargain with the triumphant Marâthâs, an act of treason to his peshwa, planning even then to double-cross his new allies. Surrounded by the enemy, he threw cannon and ammunition into the lake and ordered his men to *save* themselves even before the battle, leaving his rear guard to the mercy of the attacking Marâthâs. Fifteen English officers were killed that day. Colonel James Cockburn, seeing that the battle was lost and his forces at the mercy of the enemy, was the first

---

* [These caves are also known under the names of Beira and Bêdsâ.—*Compiler.*]

† [John Carnac (1716-1800) was a colonel who began his military service in the 39th foot ("Primus in Indis"); admitted, 1758, into the East India Company's service. Succeeded, 1760, Col. John Caillaud in command of the army at Patna; the following year won a victory over the troops of the Emperor of Delhi and a French contingent. Appointed brigadier-general, 1764; after a brief stay in England, returned to India, rendering effective aid to Lord Clive. While member of council at Bombay, was appointed, 1778, as one of the civil committee with the army who the following year executed the unfortunate convention of Wadgaon. Was subsequently dismissed from the company's service. Remained in India until his death. (*Nat. Cyclop. of Biography.*)—*Compiler.*]

to recommend surrender to Carnac. Carnac then sent an officer to arrange for the capitulation and, in the words of James Grant Duff, "did not consider it too shameful to send a letter to the governor of Bombay, wherein he consoled him by saying that all the promises and concessions given that day to the Marâthâs were given *with the tacit understanding among the English not to carry them out.*"* Accordingly, no sooner had the valiant committee of diplomats crossed the mountains and were out of danger, than all the promises, which the Marâthâs accepted without hesitation, were thrown to the winds. The auxiliary army, which had been temporarily held back, was recalled from Bengal; Sindhia received not a penny of the sum promised him, and many of the hostages were killed. The people of the "chosen superior race" proved once more the superiority of their civilized ideas of honor, over the prejudices of the brown "savages."†

---

*A History of the Mahrathas, Vol. II, p. 363.

[James Grant Duff (1789-1858) was a Scottish historian. Having sailed to India as a cadet, he attracted the attention of Mountstuart Elphinstone and became his assistant and devoted friend. He became prominently involved in the struggle with the Marâthâs and was eventually appointed Resident of Sattara, the center of the Marâthâ confederacy. He was particularly successful in understanding the native character and proved himself to be a peace-maker. After returning to Scotland, he completed his *History of the Mahrattas*, the material for which he collected under favorable circumstances from state papers and temple archives, as well as his personal acquaintance with the Marâtha chiefs.—*Compiler.*]

†One of the latest of these politico-diplomatic tricks, and one of the ugliest and most Judas-like, was played by our friends the English, in 1857, during the mutiny. Of all the independent and to them dangerous princes, the Mahârâja Sindhia remained the most faithful and true to the English. To safeguard themselves from the sepoys of Sindhia, forcefully restrained by the Mahârâja, they found themselves in need of a fortress, recognized for its strength and inaccessibility, situated on a mountain above the Mahârâja's palace. The English had neither time to take this fortress nor did they attempt to do so. Making use of Sindhia's good will and his sincere desire to help his *allies*, they took possession of the fortress *for a time*, giving their *word of honor* to withdraw as soon as the mutiny was crushed. Sindhia, a true Marâthâ, was cruel and inexorable with his enemies, but ready to sacrifice his

At about two p.m., when, in spite of the huge *pankhâs* stretched across the full length of the room and waving to and fro, we were grumbling at the heat, there suddenly appeared our friend the Marâṭhâ Brâhmaṇa, who had disappeared on the journey. Accompanied by half a dozen Dakhinîs (inhabitants of the Dekkan plateau) he rode slowly, seated practically on the ears of his horse, which snorted and seemed unwilling to move. When he reached the verandah and dismounted, we saw what was the matter: across the saddle a huge tiger was tied, its tail dragging in the dust, and some black congealed blood protruding from its half-open mouth. It was taken off the horse and laid by the doorstep.

"Was it our visitor of the night before?" was the thought that flashed through my mind. I looked at Gulâb-Singh. He lay on a rug in a corner, resting his head on his hand and reading. He knitted his brows slightly, but did not say a word. The Brâhmaṇa who had brought the tiger was silent also, quietly giving directions, as if making ready for some solemn rite. We soon learned that, according to the superstitions of the people, it was to be a solemn rite indeed.

A tuft of fur off a tiger that has been killed, neither by a bullet, nor any other weapon, but by a *word,* is considered the best of all talismans against an attack by one of its kind. "Such cases are exceedingly rare," the Marâṭhâ told us, "as one very seldom meets a man who possesses this *word.* Hermit *yogins* and *sâdhus* do not kill them, thinking it sinful to destroy even a tiger or a cobra, so they simply turn the animals away. There exists only one brother-

---

own life in order to carry out a promise given a friend and ally. He consented. The English took possession of the well-known fortress, into which they were led by the Mahârâja himself. The mutiny was crushed, and a year later he asked the Government to return to him his fortress. However now, 22 years later, the English, using all sorts of excuses, have not yet given up the premises whence they can with ease keep an eye on their amiable *allies.* Moreover, as is well-known, they now plan to disband the army of Sindhia.

[Reference is here to Mahârâja Jaijî Râo Sindhia of Gwalior.]

hood in India whose members possess all the secrets, and for whom there are no mysteries in nature . . . . . . And the fact that the tiger was not killed as a result of a fall (they never lose their footing), or by a bullet or some other weapon, but simply by the *word* of Gulâb-Lal-Singh, was evidenced by the body of the animal itself. I found it very easily," continued the Brâhmaṇa, "in the bushes, where it lay exactly under our vihâra, at the foot of the rock over which the tiger had rolled, already dead . . . Gulâb-Lal-Singh, thou art a râja-yogin, and I salute thee! . . ." added the proud Brâhmaṇa, putting his words into practice and prostrating himself before the Ṭhâkur.

"Use not vain words, Kṛishṇa Râo!" interrupted Gulâb-Singh. "Get up and do not play the part of a Śûdra . . . The tiger only fell off the cliff and broke its neck. Otherwise we might have had to use weapons instead of *words.*"

"I obey you, Sâhib, but forgive me for still believing as I do . . . No *râja-yogin* ever yet acknowledged his connection with the *brotherhood*, since the time Mount Abu came into existence."

He began distributing bits of fur torn off the dead animal. No one spoke. I gazed with a strange feeling of curiosity at my travelling companions. The Colonel (president of our Society) sat with downcast eyes, very pale; his secretary, Mr. W——, lay on his back, smoking a cigar and staring at the ceiling, with no expression on his face. He silently accepted the tuft of hair and put it in his purse. The Hindus stood around the tiger, and the Singhalese traced some Kabbalistic sign on its forehead. Gulâb-Singh alone continued quietly reading in his corner. Miss B—— calmly propounded to me the question: "Does *our* government know of the existence of this *brotherhood*, and are the *râja-yogins* kindly disposed towards the English?"

"Oh, most kindly!" earnestly replied the Râjput, before I had time to open my mouth; "that is, if they exist. They are the only ones who up to now have not allowed the Hindus to cut the throat of everyone of your countrymen; they hold them off with a . . . word."

The English woman did not understand.

Apparently, our psychological investigation in India had

made a good beginning, promising as abundant a harvest for our Society as the archaeological one.

The Birsa cave, about six miles southwest from Wadgaon, is excavated on the same plan as Kârlî. The vault-like ceiling of the temple rests upon twenty-six pillars, ten feet high, and the portico on four pillars, twenty-five feet high, surmounted by carved groups of horses, bulls and elephants, of the most exquisite beauty. The hall of "Initiation" is a huge oval room with pillars, and eleven cells cut deep into the rock.

The Bhâjâ caves are older and more beautiful. Inscriptions may still be seen there showing that all these temples were built by Buddhists, or rather by Jainas. Modern Buddhists, as is well known, believe in *one* Buddha only — Gautama, prince of Kapilavastu (sixth century B.C.), whereas the Jainas recognize as Buddhas all their twenty-four divine teachers (*Tîrthamkaras*), the last of whom was the teacher (*guru*) of Gautama. This disagreement is a serious handicap to the accurate determination of the antiquity of certain vihâras or *chaityas*. The Jaina sect is of unknown and very remote antiquity; hence the name of *Buddha,* mentioned in the inscriptions and the tablets, may refer as easily to the last as to the first Buddha who lived (according to the genealogy outlined by Tod) much earlier, 2200 years B.C. One of the inscriptions in the Beira cave, for instance, written in cuneiform characters, says:

"From an ascetic in Nâsik, assimilated to the *holy* [Buddha], purified from sins, primeval, heavenly and great."

This led to the conclusion that the cave was dug by Buddhists.

Another inscription in the same cave, but over another cell, contains the following:

"A righteous offering of a small gift to the moving power [*life*], to the mind-principle [soul], the well-beloved material body, offspring of Manu, priceless treasure, the supreme heavenly, present here."

From this it would appear that the edifice does not belong to Buddhists, but to Brâhmanas, who recognize Manu.

Here are two more inscriptions, this time from the Bhâjâ cave:

1) "A righteous gift of a symbol and chariot [vehicle] of Śâka-Śâka, purified of all sin."

2) "Gift of a vehicle of Râdhâ [wife of Krishṇa, symbol of perfection] to Sugata who is gone forever."

Sugata is also one of the names of Buddha. A new contradiction!*

It was somewhere here, in the neighborhood of Wadgaon, that the Marâthâ seized Captain Vaughan and his brother and hung them, after the battle of Khirkî.

Next morning, we drove to Chinchor or, as it is called here, Chinchvaḍ. This place is celebrated in the annals of the Dekkan. Here one meets with a repetition in miniature of what takes place on a larger scale at Lhasa in Tibet.

---

*[The text of the inscriptions has been carefully translated from the Russian rendering given by H.P.B. However, when traced to the periodical where they first appeared in print, a somewhat modified form was encountered. These inscriptions occur in a letter from N. L. Westergaard to James Bird, in the May, 1844, issue of the *Journal of the Bombay Branch of the Royal Asiatic Society* (Bombay, Vol. I, July, 1841 to July, 1844). We subjoin below the Pâli text and the English translation from the *Journal.*

1) The first inscription, from the Beira Cave, executed over the door of a small cell, reads:

Nâsikâ tapâsino sâ sathapûtâsa puvânâka mâha.

"By an ascetic of Nâsika resembling the purified Saint [Buddha], the primeval heavenly great one."

2) The second inscription over a well is:

Mahatya pâlakaiyya manuvaya mahâratanayya sâmadhinakaiyya dayâdhamâ upâda manâkâsa vâtya kaiyya.

"A righteous gift of a small offering to the moving power, the intellectual principle, the cherishing material body, the offspring of Manu, the precious jewel, the supreme heavenly one here."

3) The third inscription is from the Bhâjâ Cave, over a well, and reads:

Mahâratha śâkaśâkapûtasâ tânamdâtasa dayyâdamâpâda.

"The righteous gift of a symbol and vehicle of the purified Śâka, the resting place of the giver."

4) The fourth inscription is not too clear as to its meaning, but "it may, perhaps, be read thus:"

Raddhasavahanya satasattamsugata dânam.

"A gift to the vehicle of the Râddha [the perfect one] the Sugata [Buddha] eternally gone."

—*Compiler.*]

As Buddha incarnates in every new Talay-Lama, so, here,
Śiva allows his own *Gaṇapati* (the god of wisdom, with the
elephant's head and trunk) to incarnate in the eldest son
of one or another family of Brâhmaṇas. There is a richly
adorned temple erected in his honor, where the *avatâras*
(incarnations) of Gaṇapati have lived and received adoration for over two hundred years. This is how it happened:

About 250 years ago, a poor Brâhmaṇa couple while sleeping were promised by the god of wisdom that he would
incarnate in their eldest son. The boy was named Maroba
(one of the god's titles) in honor of the deity. Maroba grew
up, married, and begot several sons, after which he was
commanded by the god to relinquish the world and take
abode in the desert. There, during twenty-two years, according to the legend, Maroba wrought miracles, and his
fame grew day by day. He lived in an impenetrable jungle,
in a corner of the thick forest that covered Chinchvaḍ in
those days. *Gaṇapati* appeared to him once more and promised to incarnate himself in his descendants for seven
generations. There was no limit to Maroba's miracles, so
that finally he was deified, and the people built a splendid
temple for him. At last Maroba ordered that he be buried
alive, in a sitting posture, with a book in his hand, and that
his grave never be opened under penalty of a terrible curse
upon those who would do so. After the burial of Maroba,
Gaṇapati incarnated in his first-born, who began a magician's career in his turn. Thus Maroba-Deo I was replaced by Chintâman-Deo I. This latter God had eight
wives and eight sons. The eldest of these, Nârâyan-Deo, was
so full of wonders that his fame reached the ears of Emperor
'Âlamgîr. In order to test the extent of his "deification,"
'Âlamgîr sent him as a gift a piece of a cow's tail (for a
Hindu, an object most sinful to the touch) wrapped in rich
material. When the latter was unwrapped, Nârâyan-Deo
sprinkled water on it, and instead of the objectionable tail,
there was found in the parcel a nosegay of jasmine. This
transformation so pleased the emperor that he presented
the god with eight villages, as an income in perpetuity for
his upkeep. The successor to Nârâyan was Chintâman-
Deo II, followed by Dharmadhar and then by Nârâyan II.

The latter drew down upon himself the curse of *Gaṇapati*, by violating the grave of Maroba. That is why his son, the last of the gods, is now dying without issue . . . We saw him as an old man of about ninety, seated on a raised platform; his head was shaking, and his eyes stared at us blankly, without seeing us, the result of his constant use of opium. On his neck, ears and toes, shone precious stones, and all around were heaped all kinds of offerings. We had to remove our shoes before being allowed to approach this disintegrating relic.

On the evening of the same day, we returned to Bombay. Two days later we were to start on our long journey to the North-West Provinces, and our route promised to be very attractive. We were to see Nâsik, one of the few towns mentioned by Greek historians, its caves, and the tower of Râma; to visit Âllâhâbâd, the ancient Prayâga, the prehistoric capital of the Lunar Dynasty, built at the confluence of the sacred Ganges and the Jumnâ; Benares, the city of five thousand temples and of as many monkeys; Cawnpore, notorious for the bloody revenge of Nânâ-Sâhib, and the ruins of the City of the Sun, destroyed, according to Colebrooke, six thousand years ago; Âgra and Delhi; and then, having covered Râjasthân with its thousands of fortified castles and fortresses belonging to the Ṭhâkurs, its ruined towns and legends, we were planning to go to Lahore, the capital of the Pañjâb, and finally to stay at Amritsar. There, in the *Golden Temple,* built in the center of the Lake of "Immortality," was to be held the first meeting of the members of our Society, Brâhmaṇas, Buddhists, Sikhs—in other words, the representatives of the one thousand and one sects belonging to the two hundred and forty-five million of India—who all sympathized, more or less, with our Theosophical Society and its idea of a *Brotherhood of Humanity.*

—X—

Benares, Prayâga (now Allâhâbâd), Nâsik, Hardvâr,
Badrînâth, Mathurâ — these were the most sacred places
of ancient prehistoric India which we were to visit one
after the other; to visit them, however, not after the usual
manner of tourists, *à vol d'oiseau,* with a cheap guidebook
in our pockets, and a cicerone to confuse our minds and
wear out our feet. We were well aware that all these ancient
places are shrouded in tradition and overgrown by the weeds
of popular fancy, like ruins of ancient castles smothered with
ivy; that the original shape of the buildings has been destroyed by the cold embrace of these parasitic plants, and
that it is as difficult for the archaeologists to form an idea of
the architecture of the once complete edifice, judging only
from the heap of disfigured rubbish littering the countryside, as for us to select from the mass of legends the wheat
from the chaff. No guidebooks and no cicerone can be of
any use. They can merely point out to us places where once
stood a fortress, a castle, a temple, a sacred grove, or a
celebrated town, and repeat traditions which only lately,
under the Moslem rule, came into existence. As to the actual
truth, the original history of every interesting spot, we should
have to search for these ourselves, following our conjectures.
Modern India does not present even a pale shadow of

112

the India of olden days, prior to the Christian era, or even of Hindostan under the rule of Aurangzîb, Akbar and Shâh-Jahân. The neighborhood of every town shattered by many a war, of every ruined hamlet, is strewn with round reddish pebbles, as if with so many petrified tears of blood. And in order to approach the high iron gate of some ancient fortified towns, you will have to walk, not over natural pebbles, not over gravel which hurts your feet, but over the broken fragments of some older granite remains, under which frequently rest the ruins of a third town, still more ancient than the last. Modern names have been given to them by Moslems, who generally built their towns upon the ashes of those they had razed or taken by assault. The names of the latter are sometimes mentioned in traditions, but the names of their predecessors have disappeared from the memory of the people even before the Moslem invasion. Who will ever succeed in penetrating into these centuries-old secrets? . . .

Knowing all this beforehand, we resolved not to lose patience, and even, if circumstances warranted it, to devote whole years to frequent explorations of the same places, until we had obtained more reliable historical information, and facts less distorted than those of our predecessors. These had to be contented with a choice collection of wild phantasies, drawn with difficulty from the mouth of some frightened savage, unwilling to answer questions, or of a Brâhmaṇa, in his enmity often deliberately distorting the truth. On the other hand, we are assisted by a whole society of educated Hindus interested in the same problems as ourselves; we already have been promised at least some of the secrets held by their custodians, the *mahantas*, and to hear, instead of mere tradition, the accurate translation of ancient chronicles and city records that had been preserved intact as if by miracle.

The history of India has long since faded from the memory of her sons, and is entirely unknown to her conquerors. Yet it does exist, without the slightest doubt, though perchance only in torn scraps, and in manuscripts jealously concealed from European eyes. On rare occasions of friendly expansiveness, some Brâhmaṇas did open up on the subject, and for good reasons. Thus, Colonel Tod, whom I have already mentioned several times, is said to have been told by an old *mahanta* (father-superior) of an ancient temple-monastery: "Sâhib, do not lose time in vain research; the *bellati* India [the India of foreigners, of Englishmen] is before you; but the *gupta* India [secret India] you will never see; we, custodians of its mysteries, would rather cut out each other's tongues, than permit you to know."

Yet, Tod succeeded in learning a good deal. It is true that no Englishman has ever been as well-loved as this old and courageous friend of the Mahârâṇâ of Udaipur. He, in turn, loved the natives and never showed contempt even for the humblest of them. He wrote before ethnology had reached its present state of development, yet his book is still authoritative on everything concerning Râjasthân. Though, according to the author's own modest appraisal of his source, it is but "a conscientious collection of materials for a future historian," it nevertheless contains, in addition to this, much that no British civil servant has so far unearthed, or is likely to in the future.

Let our friends smile incredulously, and our ill-wishers laugh at our pretensions "to penetrate the world-mysteries of Âryâvarta," as a certain critic recently expressed himself. Looking at it from the most pessimistic viewpoint, even in the event that our conclusions do not prove more trustworthy than those of Fergusson, Wilson, Wheeler, and the rest of the archaeologists and Sanskritists who have written about India, they will not be less susceptible to proof. We are daily reminded that we have rashly undertaken a task from which archaeologists and historians, aided by the influence and wealth of the Government, have shrunk in dismay, and that we have taken upon ourselves a work to which even the Royal Asiatic Society has found itself unequal.

So be it. Yet everyone remembers, and we more clearly than others, how a poor Hungarian, Csoma de Körös, not only without means, but a veritable beggar, set out on foot for Tibet, through unknown and dangerous countries, urged only by the love of learning and the eager wish to shed light on the historical origin of his nation. The result was that inexhaustible mines of literary treasures were suddenly discovered.

Philology, which until then had wandered in the Egyptian darkness of etymological labyrinths, and which expected the scientific world to accept its most fantastic theories, suddenly and without warning stumbled on the thread of Ariadne. Philology discovered that Sanskrit was, if not the forefather, at least—to use the expression of Max Müller—"the elder brother" of all the other ancient languages. There was found in Tibet an inexhaustible literature in a language whose written records were entirely unknown. Thanks to the extraordinary zeal of Alexander Csoma de Körös, that literature has been partly translated by him, and partly analyzed and explained. His translations prove to the entire scientific world that: 1) the originals of the *Zend-Avesta,* sacred scripture of the sun-worshippers, of the *Tripiṭaka,* that of the Buddhists, and of the *Aitareya-Brâhmaṇa,* were in the first place written in one and the same ancient Sanskrit language; 2) that all these three languages — Zend, Nepalese, and the modern Brâhmaṇical Sanskrit — are more or less dialects of the former; 3) that old Sanskrit is the origin of all the less ancient Indo-European languages, as well as of the modern European tongues and dialects; 4) that the three chief pagan religions — Zoroastrianism, Buddhism and Brâhmanism—are mere heresies of the monotheistic teachings of the *Vedas,* which does not prevent them from being genuine ancient religions and not modern substitutes.

The moral of all this is evident. That which could not have been achieved by whole generations of scholars, namely, penetration of the *lamaseries* of Tibet and access to the sacred literature of this wholly isolated people, a poor traveller, without means or protection, succeeded in doing; most likely because he looked upon the wild Mongolians and Tibetans as his *brothers,* and not as an *inferior* race. One cannot help feeling ashamed of humanity in general, and of science in particular, when one recognises that he who was the first to give to science such precious seeds, he who was the first sower of such an abundant harvest,

remained almost until the day of his death a poor and obscure toiler. On his way from Tibet, he walked to Calcutta
without a penny in his pocket. Then, at last, Csoma de
Körös became known, and his name was pronounced with
honor and praise, while he lay mortally ill in one of the
poorest quarters of Calcutta, a victim of his disinterested
love for science. Sick as he was, he started on foot, on his
way to Tibet, via Sikkim, and died at Darjeeling, where he
was buried.

It is of course evident that what we have undertaken
cannot be seriously outlined within the scope of a newspaper article. All we can hope to accomplish is to lay the
foundation stone of an edifice, whose later construction must
be entrusted to future generations. In order successfully to
refute the opinions established by two generations of Orientalists concerning the antiquities of India, not less than
half a century of tenacious labor would be required. And in
order to replace these opinions, one has to establish facts
founded not on the chronology and false evidence of wily
Brâhmaṇas, whose interest is to further the ignorance of
European Sanskritists (as experienced, to their sorrow, by
Lieutenant Wilford and Louis Jacolliot), but on irrefutable
evidence contained in the most ancient inscriptions, never yet
deciphered, the key to which Europeans have not yet found,
for it is hidden, as has already been stated, in other manuscripts *no less ancient,* and almost inaccessible. Even in the
event our hopes are realized and we obtain this key, a new
and difficult requirement will arise: to begin a systematic
refutation, page by page, of dozens of volumes of *hypotheses*
published by the Royal Asiatic Society. This would require
dozens of scholarly Sanskritists, constantly at work, and such
are, even in India, as rare as white elephants.*

Hence in describing the caves and other monuments of the
archaic epoch visited by us, I will limit myself to indicating

---

*Thanks to private contributions and the zeal of some educated
Hindu patriots, two *free* classes of Sanskrit and Pâli have already been
opened—one in Bombay by the Theosophical Society, the other in
Benares, under the leadership of the learned Râma-Miśra-Śâstrî. This
year, 1882, the former has already fourteen schools in Ceylon and India.

the most widespread ideas and the most generally accepted opinions among the archaeologists concerning such places. In any case, I reserve to myself the privilege of also pointing out their contradictory assertions and theories which prove, as surely as twice two make four, how little right they have as yet, regardless of all their authority, to demand for their theories anything more than ordinary attention. I hope to show by means of incontrovertible facts how far from any trustworthy conclusions with regard to, let us say, the cave-temples of Nâsik, our gentlemen, the archaeologists, are.

Greatly preoccupied by such thoughts, we, namely, one American, three Europeans, and three natives, occupied a whole coach of the great Indian Peninsular Railroad and started for Nâsik, one of the oldest towns of India, as already mentioned, and the most sacred of all in the eyes of the inhabitants of the Western Presidency. Nâsik borrowed its name from the Sanskrit word *nâsikâ,* meaning "nose." An epic legend assures us that Lakshmana, the eldest brother of the deified King Râma, here cut off the nose of the giantess "Śûrpanakhâ," sister of King Râvana, who stole Sîtâ, the "Helen of Troy" of the Hindus.

The train stopped six miles from the actual town. As we arrived late at night, we had to continue our journey at one a.m. in six two-wheeled gilded carts called *ekkas,* which are drawn by bullocks. In spite of the late hour, the horns of the animals were gilded and adorned with garlands of flowers, while brass bangles tinkled on their legs. Our way lay through uneven ravines full of ruts and thickly over-grown, where, according to the pleasant comment of our drivers, tigers and other four-footed misanthropes of the forests played hide-and-seek. We had no occasion to become acquainted with tigers that night, but, on the other hand, were regaled all the way with a concert by a whole com-munity of jackals. They followed us closely, piercing our ears with their wails, wild laughter and barking. These sweet animals are here so bold, and at the same time so cowardly that, though running around in packs strong enough to make a meal, not only of all of us, but of our gold-horned bullocks as well, none of them dared to come

any nearer than a few steps away. It was sufficient to lash
one of them with the long whip, with which we had provided ourselves for use against snakes, to see the whole horde
vanish away with incredible shrieks. Nevertheless, the drivers
did not overlook any of their superstitious precautions
against the tigers. They chanted "mantras" of exorcism in
unison, spread betel over the road as a token of their respect
to the râjâs of the forest, and, after every couplet, made the
bullocks kneel on their front legs and bow their heads low
in honor of the great gods, while our *ekka,* as light as a
nutshell, threatened each time to fall with its passenger
over the horns of the bullocks. This pleasant journey in the
darkness of the night lasted five hours, and we reached the
"Inn of Pilgrims" at about six in the morning.

The Nâsik's sacredness, as we learned, is not due to the
fact that here the trunk of the giantess was cut, but that
the town is situated on the banks of the Godâvarî, quite close
to the source of this river which, for some reason or other,
is called by the natives *Gaṅgâ* (Ganges). It is to this magic
name, no doubt, that the town owes is numerous magnificent temples, and the select class of Brâhmaṇas who have
taken residence along the banks of the river. Twice a year
pilgrims flock here to pray, and on these solemn occasions
the number of the visitors exceeds that of the inhabitants of
Nâsik (35,000). Very picturesque, but equally dirty, are the
houses of the rich Brâhmaṇas built on both sides of the
descending road that leads from the center of town to the
shores of the Godâvarî. A whole forest of narrow pyramidal
temples spreads out on both sides of the river. All these
pagodas are built on the ruins of older ones, which were
destroyed by the fanaticism of the Moslems. A legend tells
us that most of them rose from the ashes of the burned tail
of the monkey-god Hanuman, who was scampering through
the air from Lankâ, where Râvana, having rubbed the
brave hero's tail with some combustible stuff, set it on fire.
Hanuman, with a single leap through the air, reached
Nâsik, his fatherland. Here the noble adornment of the
monkey's back, charred almost entirely during the journey,
began to crumble into ashes; and behold, as the tail gradual-

ly was reduced to ashes, from every sacred atom fallen to the ground, there rose a temple . . . And indeed, when seen from the mountain, this collection of numerous pagodas, scattered in a most curious, anti-architectural disorder, looks as if it had been thrown down by handfuls from the sky. Not only the river banks and the surrounding countryside, but even the islands and rocks sticking out of the water are covered with temples . . . And every temple has its own legend, which every Brâhmaṇa, among this crowd of hereditary scoundrels, relates in his own manner, in the hope, of course, of receiving a suitable remuneration.

Here, as elsewhere in India, Brâhmaṇas are divided into two sects—worshippers of Śiva and worshippers of Vishṇu—and rivalry between the two has lasted for centuries. Though the neighborhood of the Godâvarî shines with a two-fold aureole of fame, owing to its being the birthplace of Hanuman and the scene of the early exploits of Râma,* the incarnation of Vishṇu, against Râvana, king of Ceylon, yet it possesses as many, if not more, temples dedicated to Śiva as to Vishṇu. The greater number of those consecrated to Śiva are constructed of black basalt. It is precisely this color, being the color of the singed tail of Râma's ally, which is the apple of discord. From the first day of their rule, the English inherited endless lawsuits between the fighting sectarians; cases were decided in one lawcourt only to be transferred on appeal to another, and always arising because of this ill-omened *tail* and its pretensions. This tail is a mysterious *deus ex machina* that directs all the thoughts of the Nâsik Brâhmaṇas *pro* and *con*. On the subject of this *tail,* more petitions on more reams of paper were written than in the quarrel about the goose between Ivan Ivanovich and Ivan Nikiforovich, and more ink and bile were spilt than there was mud in Mirgorod since the creation of the world. The pig that so happily decided the renowned quarrel in

---

*See *Journal of the Asiatic Society of Bengal,* Vol. XXIII, 1827, p. 353.

[This reference occurs in E. B. Eastwick's *A Handbook for Travellers in India,* Part II, p. 365, where the caves of Nâsik are described.—*Compiler.*]

Gogol's work would be a priceless blessing to Nâsik in this ticklish affair.* But unfortunately even a "pig," if it hailed from Russia, would be unthinkable in India, for the English would suspect it at once and arrest it as a *Russian spy* . . .

At Nâsik, they show you Râma's bathtub. The ashes of pious Hindus are brought hither from distant places to be thrown into the Godâvarî to be mingled forever with the sacred waters of the *Ganges*. In an ancient manuscript, mention is made of an order issued by the chief leader of Râma's army, who, by the way, is not referred to in the *Râmâyaṇa*. The order points to the river Godâvarî as the frontier between the kingdoms of Râma, king of Ayôdhyâ (Oude), and of Râvana, king of Lankâ. Legends and the poem of *Râmâyaṇa* state that this was the spot where Râma, while hunting, saw a beautiful antelope and, eagerly desirous of making a present of its skin to his beloved Sîtâ, crossed for the first time the frontiers of his own kingdom and entered the domain of an unknown neighbor. There is not the slightest doubt that Râma, Râvana, and possibly even Hanuman, promoted, for some reason or other, to the rank of a monkey, are historical personages who once had an actual existence.

About fifty years ago there were rumors that the Brâhmaṇas possessed many exceedingly valuable manuscripts. It was reported that one of these dealt in its entirety with the prehistoric epoch when the Âryans first invaded the country and began an endless warfare with the dark-skinned aborigines of Southern India. These rumors caused one of the "collectors," something like a district supervisor (as far as I can understand), to suggest that the Government force the Brâhmaṇas to search most carefully every corner of the pagodas and give up all such manuscripts; and furthermore, to break into their sanctuaries, and, disregarding all the protests of the superstitious fanatics, prove to them that the

---

*[This has reference to a story by the Russian novelist, Nikolay Vassilyevich Gogol (1809-52), entitled "How Ivan Ivanovich and Ivan Nikiforovich quarrelled with each other." Their differences were happily dispelled by the sudden appearance of a pig; they burst out laughing and became friends again.—*Compiler.*]

English are the *rulers* and not the *slaves*. Fortunately for the *rulers*, and perhaps unfortunately for the *slaves*, this foolish idea was never carried out. Fanaticism in religious matters is the only link which strongly binds together all these warring sects and castes. The English understand this well, and therefore never insult their *slaves* in things pertaining to religion. If not the Brâhmaṇas themselves, then at least their temples and altars are unquestionably *inviolable*.

The most interesting sights in Nâsik are its cave-temples, which are about five miles from town. Planning to visit them the very day after our arrival, I did not dream that the "tail" would again play a prominent part in our visit to Nâsik; and that in this case it would actually save me, if not from death, at least from very disagreeable and perhaps dangerous bruises. This is how it happened: as we had to climb a steep mountain road, we decided to ride on elephants. The best two in town, a male and a female, were brought to us, their owner assuring us that "The Prince of Wales himself had ridden them and was quite satisfied." For the whole pleasure — a round trip taking the entire day —we were to pay two rupees for each elephant; so we shook hands as sign of a bargain and started to make ready.

Our native friends, accustomed from infancy to balancing on elephants, immediately scrambled up on the back of one of them. They covered him like flies, casually settling down here and there, wherever they happened to alight; they held on by ropes, using their toes more than their fingers, and generally presented a picture of perfect contentment and comfort. We Europeans were given the female elephant, as being the tamer of the two; on her back were fastened two little benches with sloping seats on either side, without the slightest support for our backs. We looked with distrust upon this "perfected" seat, but had no choice. Our driver (*mahout*) placed himself between the ears of the huge elephant, whose actual size can hardly be judged by the wretched half-grown animals shown in itinerant European circuses. After the *mahout* had ordered the elephant to kneel, we somehow or other climbed on its back with the aid of a small ladder and a shameful feeling of

goose flesh. Our she-elephant answered to the poetical name
of *Chaṃchalâî-Peri* (the "active fairy"), and really was the
most obedient and the merriest representative of her tribe I
have ever seen. Clinging firmly to each other, we at last gave
the signal for departure, and the *mahout,* an iron javelin in
hand, goaded the right ear of the animal. First the elephant
raised itself on its fore legs, tilting us all backwards; then
it heavily rose on its haunches, and we rolled forward,
threatening to upset the *mahout.* But this was not the end of
our trials! The very first steps of *Peri* slithered us off in all
directions, like quivering fragments of jelly.

We stopped. Somehow or other we were picked up, partly
with the good-natured help of *Peri's* trunk, and the journey
was resumed. The very thought of five miles of this before
us filled us with horror, but we were ashamed to give up
the excursion and indignantly refused to be tied to our seats,
as was suggested by our laughing companions . . . However,
I had occasion to repent bitterly this display of vanity. This
unusual mode of locomotion was something incredibly fantastic and at the same time ridiculous. A horse carrying our
luggage trotted by the side of the elephant which was moving
with its measured gait and looked, from our unfamiliar elevation, no bigger than a donkey. Every step of *Peri* made
acrobats of us, forcing us to perform most unexpected
stunts. When she put her right foot forward, we dived
forward; when it was her left foot, we fell back like so many
sheaves of grain, all the while being tossed from one side to
the other. This experience, especially under a scorching
sun, soon became akin to a feverish delirium — something
between seasickness and a nightmare. To crown our pleasure, when we began to ascend a tortuous, stony little path
along the rim of a deep ravine, our *Peri* stumbled. This
sudden shock caused me to lose my balance altogether. I was
sitting on the hind part of the elephant's back, in the place
of *honor,* and began to roll down, unable to stop; no doubt,
in a moment I would have found myself at the bottom of
the ravine, with some unseemly damage to myself, had it
not been for the astounding instinct and understanding of
the clever animal. She put a halt to my fall from her

"slope," literally catching me in flight on her *tail*. Probably having felt that I was falling, she skillfully twisted her tail around my body, stopped short, and began to kneel down. But my natural weight proved too much for the thin tail of this kind animal. While *Peri* did not drop me, she hurriedly laid me down and moaned plaintively, probably thinking she had nearly lost her tail as a result of her generosity. This was apparently the opinion of the *mahout* who jumped off her head, hurried to my rescue, and then proceeded to examine the allegedly "damaged" tail of his animal. We now witnessed a scene clearly characteristic of the low cunning, slyness, greediness and, at the same time, cowardice of a lower class Hindu, an *outcaste*, as they are called here.

At first, the *mahout* coldbloodedly examined the tail and, to make sure, pulled it several times; he was about to return to his usual place, but upon hearing me unguardedly express my commiseration with regard to *Peri's* tail, he suddenly and most unexpectedly changed his tactics. He threw himself flat on the ground and rolled about uttering horrible groans. Sobbing loudly, he started to mumble and lament as if over a corpse, trying to convince everybody that "Maam-Saab"* had torn off his *Peri's* tail, that *Peri* was forever disgraced, and that her husband, the proud *Airâvata*, direct descendant of Indra's own favorite elephant, having witnessed her shame, would now renounce his spouse, who would have nothing left but to die ...

Thus yelled the *mahout*, paying no attention to the remonstrances of our companions. In vain we tried to persuade him that the "proud *Airâvata*" did not show the slightest disposition to be so cruel to his spouse, the kindly *Chaṃchalâî-Peri*, against whose flank, even at this critical moment, he was quietly rubbing his trunk, and that *Peri's* tail was undamaged and in place. All this was of no avail! At long last, our friend Nârâyaṇa, a man of unusual strength, lost his patience and had recourse to rather original

---

*I.e., Madame-Sâhib. The word Sâhib, pronounced Saab, is added here to every title and noun. They say, for instance, Captain-Saab, Colonel-Saab, Maam-Saab, etc.

means. With one hand he threw down a silver rupee, and with the other he seized the puny figure of the *mahout* by his *dhôti*,* and, lifting him, hurled him after the coin, head first. Without giving a thought to his bleeding nose, the *mahout* jumped at the rupee with the greediness of a wild beast springing upon its prey. He prostrated himself in the dust before us repeatedly, with endless "salaams," in token of gratitude; and without the slightest transition, expressed an equally mad joy, where but a moment ago was abject sorrow. To terminate the spectacle, and to show that the tail was really whole, thanks to the "prayers of the saab," he hung himself on it, like the bell-ringer on the rope of his bell, till he was torn away from it and made to regain his seat.

"Is it possible that a single miserable rupee can have been the cause of all this?" we asked each other in utter bewilderment.

"Your astonishment is natural enough," replied our Hindus. "It would be hard, especially for us, not to feel shame and disgust at the sight of such greediness and abasement. But do not forget that this wretched *mahout,* who most likely has a wife and children, nominally receives from his employer 12 rupees a year, and no board, while *in reality* he is more often paid by kicks than by money. Remember also the long centuries of oppression from his own Brûhmaṇas, from fanatical Moslems who regard a Hindu as no better than an unclean creature, and finally from our present, highly-educated, *humanitarian* rulers, the English, and maybe, instead of disgust, you will feel profound pity for this caricature of humanity."

But the "caricature" of humanity evidently felt perfectly happy and not in the least conscious of any humiliation. Sitting cross-legged on the roomy forehead of *Peri,* he was

---

Dhôti is a long piece of material used by Hindus to wrap their waist and upper part of the legs. With the poorer people, it is their only vestment, besides a similar rag on their heads.

telling her of his unexpected wealth, reminding her that she was a "divine" she-elephant, and ordering her to salute the saabs with her trunk. *Peri,* now in the best of spirits, after the gift of a whole stick of sugarcane from me, lifted her trunk backwards and playfully blew into our faces . . .

———————

—XI—

Leaving the world of modern "pigmies," of life's petty triffles, of degraded and humiliated India, we enter again the world of profound antiquity, the world of unknown India, great and mysterious . . .

The main caves of Nâsik are carved from a mountain called Pâṇḍu-Lena by the natives, which name indicates again the undying, persistent tradition spanning centuries of time which ascribes all such Cyclopean structures to the Pâṇḍavas, the five mythical(?) brothers of prehistoric times. In the unanimous opinion of archaeologists, these caves are more interesting and more important than are the caves of Elephanta and Kârlî put together. And yet — strange to say — with the exception of the learned and esteemed Dr. Wilson, who was prone at times to speak off the cuff — advancing popular suppositions as infallible axioms — not one of the archaeologists has been bold enough to decide to which epoch they belong, by whom they were erected, or even which of the three chief religions of antiquity their mysterious builders professed.

It is evident, however, that the caves of Nâsik were wrought by more than one generation and by men of more than one sect. The first thing that arrests the attention here is the crudeness of the original work, its huge dimensions and the worn character of the sculpture on the main walls, whereas the sculpture and carvings of the six colossi which support the chief cave on the second floor are magnificently preserved and exceedingly elegant. This circumstance would lead one to think that this cave was begun many centuries before it was finished. But when, even approximately, was that? A translation of a Sanskrit inscription on a portion of the work of a considerably later epoch (on the pedestal of one of the colossi) clearly points to 453 B.C. as the year of these additional structures. Such, at least, are the conjectures based on the astronomical data given on that inscription, and cited by Gibson, Bird, Stevenson, Reeves, and some other scholars educated in the Occident, and therefore free of the prejudices proper to native pundits. Moreover, the date of the conjuction of planets is obvious: it denotes either 453 B.C., or 1734 of our era, or again 2640 B.C., which latter is impossible, as the inscription speaks of Buddha and Buddhist monasteries. I quote some of the principal and more interesting sentences of this inscription, according to the translation first made by Dr. J. Stevenson and then corrected at the Government College of Sanskrit pundits at Benares:

To the Perfect Being. May this prove auspicious! By the son of King Kshaharâta, ruler of the Kshatriya tribe and protector of men, the Lord Dînîka, resplendent as the morn, a gift of a hundred thousand cows along with the river Banâs, and also a gift of gold, even by him the constructor of this holy place for the gods, and for the brâhmans to mortify the passions. There is not so desirable a place even at Prabhâsa, where hundreds of thousands of brâhmans go on pilgrimage to repeat sacred verses, nor at the pure city of Gayâ, where brâhmans go, nor at the steep hill at Daśapura, nor the serpents' field at Govardhana, nor at the city of Pratiśraya, where there is a Buddhistical monastery, nor even at the edifice built by Dîpanakara on the shore of the freshwater sea[?]. This is a place which confers incomparable benefits, wholly pleasing, well fitted for the spotted deer-skin [?] of the ascetic.* A safe boat has been provided by him, the maker also of a free ferry, which daily plies to the well-supported bank. By him also, the constructor of a house for travellers, and a public reservoir of water, a gilded lion [deer?] has been set up at the crowded gate of this Govardhana, another also at the ferry, and another at Râmatîrtha. For lean cattle within the bounds of the village there are various kinds of food, for such cattle more than a hundred kinds of grass, and a thousand mountain roots, given by this bounteous donor. In this very

---

*Indian ascetics cover themselves even today, à la Hercules, with the hide of wild beasts, usually tigers. [H.P.B.]

Govardhana, in the radiant mountains, the excavation was ordered to be made by the same charitable person. And these venerated by men, namely, the *Sun, Śukra,* and *Râhu** were in their exaltation in that year when the gift was bestowed. *Lakshmî, Indra* and *Yama* also consecrated it (in Vaiśâkha), and the couch was set up on the most fortunate day of the month, Bhadrapada. Thereafter, these, *Lakshmî, Indra* and *Yama†* departed with a shout of triumph for their excellent easy car, sustained by the force of incantatory verses, on the unbroken road.‡ When all their retinue had departed and was gone, there fell a shower of water before the army, which, being purified and having departed and having passed over with the thousand cows, approaches the village.§

The first caves are dug about two hundred and fifty feet from the base of a conical hillock. In the central one, some forty-five square feet in area, stand three statues of Buddha; in the lateral ones, a liṅga and two Jaina idols; while in the top cave there is the idol or rather the statue of *Dharma-Râjan* or *Yudhishṭhira,* the elder of the Pâṇḍavas, who has been deified and is worshipped in a temple of his own, erected in his honor between Peint and Nâsik. Beyond is a whole labyrinth of cells, where Buddhist hermits evidently lived. There is a huge statue of Buddha in a reclining posture and another of equally colossal proportions surrounded with pillars, the capitals of which are adorned with figures of various animals. Styles of differing epochs and sects are here mixed and intermingled like trees of various species in a forest.

It is a remarkable circumstance that almost all the cave-temples of India are dug from conical cliffs and mountains, as though the ancient builders looked for such natural pyramids purposely. I have already noted this peculiar and un-

---

*Râhu and *Ketu* are the fixed stars which form the head and the tail of the constellation of the Dragon; *Râhu* is also one of the nine planets. [H.P.B.]

†In other words the constellations of Virgo, Aquarius and Taurus, subservient and consecrated to these three among the higher deities. [H.P.B.]

‡The heavenly path. [H.P.B.]

§[Edward B. Eastwick, *A Handbook for Travellers in India,* 1859, Part II, p. 368.]

usual shape in describing our trip to Kârlî, and do not remember seeing it anywhere but in India. Is it a mere coincidence, or is it one of the rules of the religious architecture of those remote times? And who are the imitators — the builders of the Egyptian pyramids, or the unknown architects of the underground temples of India? In pyramids as well as in cave-temples, everything seems to be calculated with geometrical exactitude, and, just as in the case of pyramids, the entrances into the cave-temples are not at the foot but at a certain distance from the base of the hill.

It is well known that nature does not imitate art, but, to the contrary, the latter always tries to reproduce nature's own forms. And if, even in this similarity of the symbols of Egypt and India, nothing but mere coincidence exists, one will have to admit that coincidences are sometimes inexplicable. Subsequently we may advance more weighty evidence to the effect that Egypt has borrowed much from India. Let us not forget that the origin of the kingdom of the Pharaohs is entirely unknown to science, and the little that has been discovered, far from contradicting this theory, suggests India as the cradle and primeval fatherland of the Egyptians. In the days of remote antiquity, Kullûka-Bhatta wrote as follows in his *History of India*:

Under the reign of Viśvâmitra, first king of the Somavaṇśa dynasty, Manu-Vena, heir of the ancient kings, abandoned by the Brâhmaṇas, after a five-day battle, emigrated with all his companions, passing through Ârya and the countries of Barria, until he came to the shores of *Masra* . . . . . .*

And if we be answered that "Kullûka-Bhatta" is such an ancient historian that Sanskritists quarrel over him, unable to place him in any likely epoch, and therefore wavering between 2000 B.C. and the reign of Emperor Akbar (in the time of Ivan the Terrible), there are the words of a modern

---

*Ârya—Iran (Persia); *Barria*—an ancient name for Arabia; *Masr* or *Masra* is a purely Egyptian name; Moslems call Cairo by that name even today, disfiguring it into *Misro, Musr*, etc. [Cf. *Isis Unveiled*, Vol. I, p. 627.]

historian who has studied Egypt all his life (not in London or Berlin, like so many of his colleagues, but in Egypt itself), directly from the inscriptions of the oldest sarcophagi and papyri — we mean Heinrich Brugsch-Bey.*

Whatever relations of kindred may be found to exist in general between these great races of mankind, this may be regarded as certain, that the cradle of the Egyptian people must be sought in the interior of the Asiatic quarter of the world. In the earliest ages of humanity, far beyond all historical remembrance, the Egyptians, for reasons unknown to us, left the soil of their primeval home, took their way towards the setting sun, and finally crossed that bridge of nations, the Isthmus of Suez, to find a new fatherland on the favoured banks of the holy Nile.†

There is evidence that in the days of the eleventh dynasty the Egyptians traded with Arabia and on the shores of the Indian Ocean, and who knows from what immemorial antiquity! An inscription found on a Hammamat rock says that *Sankh-ka-ra,* the last king of the eleventh dynasty, sent a nobleman by the name of Han, to *Punt* or Pent(?). It states:

I was sent to conduct ships to the land of Punt to fetch for Pharaoh sweet-smelling spices which the princes of the red land collect out of fear and dread, such as he inspires in all nations.‡

Commenting on this inscription, Brugsch-Bey explains that:

Under the name of Punt, the ancient inhabitants of Kemi [Egypt]

---

*[Heinrich Karl Brugsch-Bey (1827-94) was a German Egyptologist who stayed in Egypt on two different trips and was Consul at Cairo in 1864-68. Professor at Göttingen, 1868-70. In later years, directed the School of Egyptology in Cairo and was Commissioner General of the Egyptian Government at Vienna and Philadelphia exhibitions, 1873 and 1876. Received, 1881, the title of Pasha. Chief work: *Geschichte Aegypten's unter den Pharaonen,* Leipzig, 1877, 1878; Engl. transl. by P. Smith, 2nd ed., London, 1881. Founded the *Zeitschrift für Aegyptische Sprache und Altertumskunde.—Compiler.*]

†[*A History of Egypt under the Pharaohs.* Translated from the German by Philip Smith. 2nd ed., London: J. Murray, 1881. 2 Vols. This passage may be found in Vol. I, p. 8.—*Compiler.*]

‡[*Ibid.,* p. 137.]

understood a distant land, washed by the great sea, full of valleys and hills, abounding in ebony and other choice woods, in frankincense, balsam, precious metals, and costly stones; rich also in beasts, for there were in it giraffes, hunting leopards, panthers, dog-headed apes, and long-tailed monkeys."*

Even the word for monkey in the ancient Egyptian language is *kaph* or *kaphi* (*koph* among the people of Israel), the purely Sanskrit word *kapi*.

Legendary accounts of a very ancient epoch in Egypt's history ascribed to this "Punt" (evidently India) a very sacred character, because Punt (or Pent)† was the primeval abode of the gods, who under the joint leadership of *A-Mon* [Manu-Vena of Kullûka-Bhatta?], *Hor* and *Hator,* left it to head *in the direction of the Valley of the Nile, and safely arrive din Kemi.*‡

No wonder that Hanuman should have such a family resemblance to the Egyptian *Cynocephalus,* and that the emblems of *Osiris* and *Śiva* should be the same. *Qui vivra verra! . . .*

Our return trip on *Peri* proved to be more pleasant. We had adapted ourselves to her gait and felt ourselves first-rate riders as we entered Nâsik. But for a whole week afterwards we could hardly walk because of pain in the waist.

---

*[*Ibid.,* p. 136.]

†*Pent*—from Pa-nuter, "sacred land," or the Egyptian "land of the gods."

‡From a monument of the XIth dynasty. See H. K. Brugsch-Bey.

—XII—

When asked which they would prefer if they had to choose
between blindness and deafness, nine people out of ten usually prefer deafness. And he whose good fortune it has been
to get but a glimpse of one of the fairy-like corners of India,
that land of lace-like marble palaces and enchanted gardens,
often reminding one of the most fantastic stage settings of
the Paris Opera — impossible, one would think, in nature —
would willingly add to deafness, lameness of both legs, rather
than miss such sights.

We are told that Sa'dî, the great poet, bitterly complained
of the indifference of his friends who were bored by his
endless and enthusiastic praise of his lady-love. "Had you
the chance and the happiness, as I have, to behold once
only *her* wonderful beauty," he said, "you would not fail
to understand my verses, which sing, alas, so poorly and so
feebly, the feeling of the soul-rapture which she produces
upon anyone who sees her even from a distance! . . ." I fully
sympathize with the enamoured poet, but cannot condemn
his friends who never saw his loved one, and that is why I
tremble in fear lest my enthusiastic rhapsodies on India bore
my readers as much as Sa'dî bored his friends. But what is
the poor narrator to do if he discovers in his "beloved" new
and undreamed-of charms? Her darkest aspects, repulsive
and immoral as they are, and sometimes even the most
terrifying characteristics—even these are full of wild poetry,

132

of originality, which is not met with in any other country. It is not unusual for a European unaccustomed to such, to shudder at the sight of some of the native scenes but, at the same time, these very sights attract and fascinate his attention, like some apparition of the night, so that he cannot tear his eyes away from them . . .

We had many of these experiences while our *école buissonière* lasted. We spent these days far from railways, that touch of civilization which suits India no better than a fashionable bonnet is appropriate to a half-naked Peruvian maiden, a "daughter of the Sun," in the time of Cortez.

Daily we wandered across rivers and jungles, passing villages and ruins of ancient fortresses, over local country roads between Nâsik and Jubbulpore, travelling by day in bullock carts, sometimes on elephants or on horseback, and at times being carried in *pâlkîs* (palanquins), and at nightfall frequently pitching our tent wherever we might be. These days offered us an opportunity to convince ourselves of the fact that man is able to surmount dangerous and almost fatal conditions of climate by mere force of habit, almost unconsciously. While we "white" people were on the verge of fainting, positively *roasted* under the unbearably scorching rays of the sun, in spite of thick cork *topis* on our heads and the protection of the canopy, and when even our native travelling companions wrapped an extra piece of muslin around their heads — the Bengalî *bâbû* travelled on horseback for endless miles bareheaded, with the vertical rays of the sun beating right down on him! He did not even have with him an ordinary *pagrî*, a piece of light material for a turban, let alone a hat. For hours he would ride with the crown of his head covered with nothing else but his thick crop of hair, and the sun seemed to have no effect whatsoever on his Bengal skull. These people never cover their heads, except on solemn occasions such as a *durbâr*, a wedding or a feast, when a turban is worn as a mere ornament, more or less as flowers are worn at a ball.

Bengalî *bâbûs* hold almost all the lesser civil posts, especially as clerks, and invade all the railway stations, the post and telegraph offices and the government's official places of

business. Wrapped in their white muslin vestment, thrown
over the shoulder like a Roman *toga,* their legs bare up to
the knees, their heads uncovered, they proudly loaf on the
platforms of railroad stations, or at the entrance of their
offices, casting contemptuous glances at the effeminate
adornment of the Marâthâs with rings on their fingers and
toes, and huge earrings in the upper part of their right ear.
Bengalîs, unlike the rest of the Hindus, do not paint sectarian signs on their foreheads; they allow themselves only
an expensive necklace, but even that is not common. And
yet, while the Marâthâs, with all their predilection for effeminate adornment, are justly considered one of the bravest
tribes of India (having displayed this more than once to the
English), and have proved themselves to be excellent and
most courageous warriors in many centuries of warfare,
Bengal, from time immemorial, *has never produced a single
soldier out of its sixty-five million inhabitants.* Not a single
Bengalî is to be found in the native regiments of the British
Army. This is a curious but nevertheless indisputable *fact,*
which we refused to believe at first, but which we had to
concede at last, when it was confirmed by many English
officers and by Bengalîs themselves. But with all this, they
are far from being cowards. Even though their *bâbûs* and
higher classes are effeminate, their *zamindars* (landowners)
and peasants are undoubtedly brave. A Bengalî goes out to
meet a tiger — the most ferocious tiger in all of India —
armed only with a club, and as composedly as he did with
rifles and daggers in days gone by.

Many out-of-the-way paths, many miraculously preserved
groves, which probably had never before been trodden by a
Western foot, were visited by us during these brief days.
And everywhere we were welcomed, thanks to the magical
influence of Gulâb-Lal-Singh who, while absent himself, had
sent his trusted servant to accompany us and guide us on our
way. Even though the wretched, naked peasants shrank from
us and shut their doors at our approach, the Brâhmaṇas
were as obliging as could be desired.

The surroundings of Khândesh, on the way to Thâlner
and Mhow, are in a delightful location. Nature, moreover,

WATER PALACE AT MÂNDU

GOLDEN TEMPLE AND LAKE AT AMRITSAR

has been richly adorned here by the art of man, and this art is especially conspicuous in Moslem cemeteries. At present, most of them are half-ruined and neglected, owing to the expulsion from these regions of Moslem princes and Khâns, and the majority of the Hindu population. Once rulers of most of India, Moslems are now oppressed and far more humiliated even than Hindus. Still they have left many indestructible monuments behind, among which are their cemeteries. This fidelity of the Moslems to their dead is one of the most touching traits of character of the sons of the Prophet. Their devotion to them after death, always more demonstrative than their love for the family while alive, seems to be concentrated on the last abode of those who have gone hence into a better world. In contrast to their notions of the paradise promised by Mohammed, which are coarse and material, the surroundings of their cemeteries are poetical, especially in India. In these shady, delightful gardens, amongst rows of white tombs crowned with turbans and covered from top to bottom with roses and jessamine, with cypresses all around, one may spend long hours most pleasantly. We usually stopped in them for rest, for dinner, or even overnight.

The cemetery near the town of Thâlner is particularly delightful. Among several historical mausoleums in a good state of preservation, the most magnificent is the monument of the family of the Killâdâr, who was hanged on the city tower in 1818 by order of General Thomas Hislop who, by the way, on the same day executed all the soldiers of the garrison who had surrendered, with the excuse that a conspiracy against him existed among them. Aside from this monument in honor of the unfortunate Killâdâr, there are four other mausoleums, one of which is celebrated throughout India. It is a white marble octagon, covered from top to bottom with carvings, the like of which could not be found even in the cemetery of *Père Lachaise*. A Persian inscription on its base reveals that it cost one hundred thousand rupees. By day bathed in the hot rays of the sun, its tall minaret-like outline stands out like a pyramid of ice against the cloudless azure of the sky; by night, in that peculiar phosphorescent moonlight proper to India, which has enthused all travelers and artists, it is still more dazzling and poetical. Its summit looks as if it were covered with light, freshly-fallen snow. Raising its slender profile above the dark green background of the shrubbery, it suggests some pure midnight apparition, soaring over this silent abode of destruction and death, lamenting the past that will never return . . .

In the vicinity of these cemeteries rise the Hindu *ghâts* . . . There is really something grand in this ritual of burning the dead — and the burning of the living in the not too distant past, but only in theory and not in practice. Witnessing this ceremony, and seeing how in the course of an hour or so after death nothing remains of the body but a few handfuls of ashes which an initiated Brâhmaṇa, performing the rites of death, scatters then and there to the four winds of heaven over the river, so that they will be forever mingled with the sacred waters, the spectator is struck with the deep philosophy underlying the fundamental idea of this rite. In scattering the handful of that which once lived and felt, loved and hated, rejoiced and wept, the Brâhmaṇa entrusts the ashes to the four elements: to *earth,* out of which it grew and developed little by little into a man, and which fed it for a long time; to *fire,* emblem of purity, that has just devoured the body, so that the spirit will be equally purified from all that is sinful, and may freely gravitate to the new sphere of post-mortem existence where every sin is a stumbling block on the way to "Moksha" or eternal bliss; to *air,* which was inhaled and thus sustained life; and to *water* which cleansed it physically and spiritually, quenched its thirst, and now receives its ashes into her *pure* bosom . . . (*Mantra XII*).

The adjective "pure" must be understood here merely in the figurative sense of the "mantra." Generally speaking, the rivers in India, beginning with the thrice sacred Ganges, are unimaginably dirty, especially near villages and towns. Some two hundred million people, in round numbers, cleanse themselves therein from tropical sweat and dirt several times a day; and, moreover, *castes* whose members are not worthy of being burned, such as śûdras, pariahs, mângs, etc., throw all their corpses into them. Furthermore, all castes, including Brâhmaṇas, throw children who die at less than three years of age into the rivers.

Let us wander along the shores of any river, but rather late in the evening, so as to spend the night there until daybreak. Only the rich, or those belonging to the highest castes are burned in the evening. Only for them are lit after sunset sandalwood fires beside the sacred waters; for them alone, mantras and incantations to the Gods are chanted. For ordinary mortals, for the poor *outcastes,* there is neither fire nor even an ordinary prayer. A *śûdra* is unworthy of listening even after death to the divine words from the sacred book of revelation, dictated at the beginning of the world by the four Ṛishis to Veda-Vyâsa, the great theologian of Âryâvarta. As he was not allowed during his lifetime nearer than seven steps from the temple, so even in the afterlife a śûdra will not be permitted to stand beside the "twice-born."

Brightly burn the fires, extending like a fiery serpent along the river. Dark silhouettes of strange, wildly fantastic figures silently move among them, either raising their thin arms toward the sky as if in prayer, or adding fuel to the fires and poking them with long iron pitchforks, until the dying flames flare up again, creeping and twisting, spattering in all directions melted human fat, and shooting upwards whole showers of golden sparks, which instantly vanish in the thick cloud of black smoke. This is on the right side of the river. Let us cross over to the left bank . . .

In the hours before dawn when the red fires, the black clouds of miasma, and the thin figures of the fakir-servants grow dim and slowly vanish after a last reflection in the dark mirror of the river; when the smell of burned flesh is blown away by the fresh wind which rises at the approach of dawn, and quiet settles over the *ghâts* until the next evening — at that instant a procession of a different kind appears on the opposite bank . . .

Sad, silent trains of Hindu men and women move in file, sometimes long, sometimes short, according to the mortality in town. They approach the river in separate groups, without weeping, and with no ritual of any kind. Swinging their burden by both head and feet, the carriers cold-bloodedly throw it into the yellowish-dirty water of the river. As it falls, the red rag is blown aside, and the dark green face of a young woman can be seen for an instant before vanishing in the muddy waves. Beyond is another group: an old man and two young women. One of them, a little girl of ten, small, thin, far from being fully developed, sobs bitterly. She is the mother of the dead child, whose body she will soon throw into the cold waters of the dirty river. Her weak voice monotonously resounds along the shore, and her trembling hands are not strong enough to throw the poor little figure, more like a tiny brown kitten than a human child. The old man tries to console her and, taking the dead body in his own hands, enters the water up to his waist, casting it into the middle of the river. After him both women get into the water just as they are, dressed or rather half-dressed, as usual, and, after plunging seven times in succession to purify themselves from the touch of a dead body, return to the shore and start for home, their clothes dripping wet. In the meanwhile, vultures, crows and other birds of prey, which had been circling all day over the river waiting for their booty, gather in black clouds over the bodies and retard their progress down the river. Occasionally some half-stripped skeleton is caught in the reeds along the shore or is wedged between two stones, sticking out from the shallow water, until finally one of the *mângs* — a wretched outcaste creature, living near the river, whose fate it is all lifelong, from the day of his birth to his last breath, to busy himself with this sort of unclean labor — comes armed with his long stick and, catching the skeleton by its ribs, picks it from under the stones or reeds and pushes it down the current on its way to the blue ocean . . .

But now let us leave the river bank, already blazing hot in spite of the early hour. Let us bid good-bye to the watery cemetery of the poor. Let us leave and go elsewhere . . . Disgusting and heart-rending are such sights in the eyes of Europeans. Unconsciously our swift-winged thought bears us to the far North, to the peaceful village cemeteries where, instead of carved marble tombs crowned with turbans, sandalwood fires, and a dirty river for a last resting place, there are but wooden crosses sheltered by old birch trees. How peacefully sleep our dear departed* under the luscious green grass! None of these ever saw, while floating downstream, giant palms, marble palaces, or pagodas covered with pure gold. But for all that, on their simple burial-mounds bloom violets and lilies of the valley, and in the springtime nightingales burst out in song in the old birch trees . . . As to ourselves, nightingales have not sung for us in many a year, either in the neighboring groves, or in our own souls. All of this is more remote here than anywhere else!

Let us stroll along this high wall of reddish sandstone. It will lead us to a fortress once renowned and drenched in blood, now, like so many others, harmless and half-ruined. Flocks of green parrots, startled by our approach, dart from every cavity in the wall, their wings shining in the sun like so many flying emeralds. We are on territory "accursed" by the English; we are in the land of Chândvaḍ where, during the Sepoy mutiny, the Bhîls rushed from their ambushes like an irresistible mountain torrent down into the valleys, not far from Sinnar, some twenty miles from Nâsik, cutting the throats of several dozen of their rulers, among them Captain Henry. *Tattva*,† an ancient Hindu work treating of geography in the time of King Aśoka (274-232 B.C.), informs us that the Marâthâ territory extends up to the wall of *Chândvaḍ* or *Chandor*, and that Khândesh is beyond the river. But

---

*[There is no way of translating literally into English the common Russian word *usopshiy* which is used for those who have died, and which means "he who is asleep," from the verb *usiplyat'* or *usipit'*, which means "to induce sleep" or "to have someone fall asleep." Another term, the one used here by H.P.B., is *pokoynik* which means "he who is at peace." It is of special interest to Theosophists to realize that the Slavonic and Russian languages connect the idea of death with both sleep and peace.—*Compiler.*]

†[It is not clear what particular work is meant here. *Tattva* can hardly be a complete and correct title, and something seems to have been dropped here, either by the proofreader or the printer.—*Compiler.*]

the English who do not recognize either the *Tattva* or any other authorities except themselves, ask us to believe that Khândesh begins at the Chandor hills. Therefore this "fortress," one of the most inaccessible "on account of its being fortified by nature herself from three sides," in the words of Colonel Wallace, had to be taken by the English in 1804 from the Marâthâ "rebels" who would not give it up; this was done with great trouble and many losses. And they would not have taken it, not for many years, had it not been for the Moslems, sworn enemies of the Marâthâs, who always defeated them. The Moslems finally disclosed to Col. Wallace the mystery of a certain passage under the gates of the fortress. The English forced the passage during the night, overcame the Marâthâs who were fast asleep, and have boasted of this ever after. Later, in a moment of careless generosity, they returned the fortress to the Holkar, on condition that he *pay the expenses* of the English soldiers quartered therein, even though they were not *in his service*. Later they regretted this act of kindness, and in 1818, seeing that the Holkar would not yield the fortress to them without a battle, they sent almost an entire army, under the command of Sir Thomas Hislop,* and thus reclaimed that which they had once granted.

-----

* [Sir Thomas Hislop, first baronet (1764-1843) ; general; with 39th at siege of Gibraltar, 1779-83; lieutenant-governor of Trinidad, 1803-11; commander-in-chief at Madras, 1813; led army of Dekkan in Marâtha war, 1817-18; won victory of Mahidpore, 1817; incurred blame for severity at Thâlner; left Madras, 1820.—*Compiler.*]

—XIII—

There is a whole city of cave-temples, known under the name of *Ankâi-Tankâi,* twelve miles southeast of Chândvaḍ. Here again, as elsewhere, the temples are about one hundred feet from the foot of the hill which is pyramidal. It would not be advisable to describe them in detail here because it is quite impossible to treat of this subject in a newspaper article. Therefore I shall merely note that in this case also all the statues, idols and carvings are ascribed to *Buddhist* ascetics of the first centuries after the death of Buddha. One would leave it at that were it not for the fact that the gentlemen-archaeologists are suddenly confronted here with a new and more serious difficulty than all the combined difficulties in regard to other points of contention. In these caves there are more idols designated *Buddhas* than anywhere else. They cover the main entrance, sit in thick rows along the balconies, occupy the inner walls of every cell, stand on guard like monster-giants at every entrance, and two of them sit in the main *tank* (reservoir), where waist-high spring water washes them century after century without any visible harm to their granite bodies. Among these *Buddhas,* some are decently clad with pyramidal, many-storied pagodas as their head gear; others are naked; some sit, others are represented standing; some are colossal in size; others are tiny; and some are of medium size.

All this, however, would not matter, even though we know

141

that the reform instituted by Gautama or Siddhârtha Buddha consisted precisely in waging a relentless war against the Brâhmaṇas and permanently uprooting idol worship. His religion remained pure for many centuries, *without the slightest admixture of idol worship,* until, in the hands of the lamas of Tibet, the Chinese, Burmese and Siamese, it was distorted and degraded by heresies. Later, driven out of India, persecuted by infuriated Brâhmaṇas, who by then had acquired the upper hand, it found a last refuge on the island of Ceylon. It flourishes there today like the legendary aloe which is said to blossom once in its lifetime, the main root dying, while its seeds, when their time comes to sprout, produce only weeds. But the main difficulty for the archaeologists does not consist in the idols ascribed to Buddhists, but in the physiognomies, the *type* of all these *Ankâi-Tankâi Buddhas.* All, from the tiniest to the largest, are Negroes, with flat noses, thick lips, facial angles of forty-five degrees, and curly hair! There is not the slightest likeness in these pure negroid faces to any of the Siamese or Tibetan Buddhas, which have Mongolian features with wide jaws and wide noses, and smooth, perfectly *straight* hair. This unexpected African type, not found anywhere else in India, upsets the antiquarians completely. No wonder the archaeologists avoid mentioning these remarkable caves; after the caves of Nâsik, those of *Ankâi-Tankâi* are a veritable Thermopylae for modern antiquarians.

We drove past Mâlegâon and Chikalvohol where we examined an exceedingly curious and very ancient temple of the Jainas, built without any cement whatever, of square stones which are so closely fitted one to the other that not even the blade of the thinnest knife can be inserted between them. The interior of this temple is richly decorated with gorgeous carvings. On our way back we did not stop at Thâlner, but went straight on to Dhâr. There we again had to hire elephants to visit the splendid ruins of *Mâṇḍu,* once a strongly fortified town, about twenty miles due northeast. This time we arrived speedily and safely. I mention this place as it is connected in my memory with one of the most remarkable sights ever seen by me, and which concerns that particular branch of the numerous Indian sects, which is usually called "devil worshippers."

Mându is situated on the crest of the Vindhya Mountains, about two thousand feet above sea level. According to Sir John Malcolm, this town was built in the fourth century A.D. (in 313), and for a long time was the capital of the Hindu râjâs of Dhâr. The historian Ferishta identifies Mându as being the residence of Dilâwar-Khân-Ghûrî, the first [Mohammedan] king of Mâlwâ, who flourished in 1387-1405. In 1526 the town was assaulted and captured by Bahâdur-Shâh, king of Gujarât; in 1570 it was retaken by Akbar, whose name and the date of his visit are inscribed on a marble slab over the main gate of the town.

A peculiar feeling, probably similar to the one experienced by some people on their first visit to Pompei, took possession of us upon entering this huge deserted city, called by the natives the "dead town." Everything indicates that Mându was once one of the largest towns of India. The town wall is *thirty-seven* miles in circumference, according to measurements taken in 1852. In this vast space, streets run for miles, and on both sides stand dilapidated palaces, and marble pillars lie scattered about. Remains of underground halls, in the cool semi-darkness of which wives of sultans spent the hottest hours of the day, peer from ruined granite walls. Further on are shattered steps, dry tanks, waterless reservoirs, endless empty yards, marble platforms and broken arches of majestic porticos. All this is overgrown with creepers and shrubs which hide the dens of wild beasts. Here and there a half-preserved wall of some marble or granite palace rises high over the general ruin, its empty windows thickly fringed with centuries-old parasitic plants, staring at us like sightless eyes, frowning at the troublesome intruders who have disturbed their rest. Still further, in the very center of the ruins, right out of the stricken heart of the sleeping town, out of the broad chest of the warrior-knight, where once so many passions, and so strong a life ran riot, a whole grove of cypresses springs forth . . .

In 1579 this town was called *Shâdiâbâd,* "the abode of

happiness." The Franciscan missionaries, Ridolfo Aquaviva,* Antario Monserrate, E. Henriquez, and other members of the mission sent that year from Gôa to seek various privileges from the Mogul government, described and mentioned it on innumerable occasions. At that time it was one of the greatest cities of the world; its magnificent streets and luxurious ways astonished the most pompous courts of contemporary India. It seems almost incredible that this city could now be a heap of rubbish, where a clear spot for our tent could hardly be found. At last we decided to pitch it in the only building which remained almost undamaged, the Jâmi'-Masjid, the "Cathedral Mosque," which rises on a granite platform about twenty-five steps higher than the square. The stairs leading to it, made of marble as is all else, are broad and almost untouched by time, but the roof has entirely disappeared, and so we would have been all night under the light of the starry dome of heaven had it not been for a set of circumstances which I will shortly relate. All around the main building, which stands on the rectangular square, runs a low gallery supported by several rows of huge pillars. Despite its being rather clumsy and lacking in proportion, it reminds one from a distance of the Acropolis of Athens.

From the steps where we settled ourselves, there was a view of the mausoleum of Hûshang-Shâh-Ghûrî, king of Mâlwâ, in whose reign the city attained the culmination of its brilliance and magnificence. It is a massive, majestic, white marble edifice, with a sheltered peristyle on pillars beautifully adorned with carvings; this peristyle once led straight to one of the palaces, but now runs beside a deep ravine, heaped with stones and overgrown with cactus. The

---

*[Father Ridolfo Aquaviva was a Jesuit missionary at Gôa. In 1579, Emperor Akbar expressed the desire to have two learned priests come to him and explain the Gospels. Aquaviva, together with Father Monserrate, were sent by the Portuguese government at Gôa and made their way to Akbar's Court at Fatehpûr-Sîkrî, where they arrived in February, 1580. They were received with great honor. Aquaviva was a great scholar who earned Akbar's esteem and lived long at his Court as an honorable member thereof.—*Compiler.*]

interior of the mausoleum consists of a large room the ceiling and walls of which are made of square slabs, covered high and low with precepts from the *Qur'ân* inscribed in gold lettering, and the middle of the room is occupied with the sarcophagus of the Sultan himself. Not far from this abode of death is the palace of Bâz-Bahâdur, all in pieces, covered with dust and overgrown trees.

Tired and ready to collapse from hunger and thirst after spending all day wandering through these ruins, we returned a little before sundown, carrying three dead snakes on our sticks like war trophies, and sat down to tea and supper at the entrance to our tent, already pitched inside the mosque. We found unexpected guests: the *patel* of the neighboring village — something between a tax collector and a justice of the peace — and two *zamindars* (landowners) had ridden over to present their respects to us and to invite us, as well as our Hindu friends whom they had known previously, to accompany them to their homes. On hearing that we intended to spend the night in the "dead town," they vehemently protested against it. They assured us that we had embarked upon a dangerous and unheard of venture; that two hours later the ruins would come to life, and from under every bush and every underground room of the ruined houses hyenas, cheetah and tigers were sure to emerge for their nightly brigandage, not to mention thousands of jackals and wild cats; and finally that our elephants would either run away or would be overpowered and eaten. We should get ready without delay and, leaving the ruins as fast as possible, go to their village which was about half an hour's ride. There everything was in readiness, and our *bâbû* was awaiting us.

Only on hearing this did we become aware that our bareheaded and cautious friend was conspicuous by his absence. Evidently he had gone into the valley some three hours earlier to visit his friends and had sent them to us.

The evening was so pleasant and we felt so comfortably settled, that the idea of upsetting all our plans for the morning was not attractive. Besides, it seemed plainly ridiculous that the ruins, in which we had wandered all day without

seeing anything more dangerous than the three snakes we
had killed, swarmed with wild beasts. So we continued to
thank them but refused to accept their invitation.

"But it is absolutely impossible for you to remain here,"
insisted the fat *patel*. "In case of an accident, I will be the
one responsible for you to the Government. Can you possibly
find it pleasant to spend a sleepless night fighting jackals
with your bare hands, if not something worse? . . . You do
not believe that you are surrounded by wild beasts, until
sundown invisible, it is true, but just as dangerous? Then
trust the instinct of the elephants, who are no less brave
than we are, but perchance more intelligent. Just look at
them now! . . ."

True enough, our grave, philosophical-looking elephants
behaved at this moment in a very unusual manner. Their
trunks lifted high in the shape of a question mark, they
snorted and stamped restively. A minute later, one of them
snapped the thick rope which tied him to a broken pillar,
as if it had been a rotten thread, his heavy body turning
suddenly to stand against the wind. He inhaled heavily with
his trunk and lifted his right leg as if ready to run . . . He
probably sensed a dangerous animal.

The Colonel stared at him through his spectacles and
gave a long drawn-out whistle.

"It really could be a serious affair," he remarked, "what
if tigers actually did assault us?"

"Yes, indeed," I thought to myself, "and Gulâb-Lal-
Singh is not with us now."

Both of our Hindu companions sat on the carpet cross-
legged and quietly chewed betel. On being asked their opinion, they said it did not concern them; they would fall in
with whatever we decided to do. But our other travelling
companions, the Englishmen, already scared, were hastily
preparing to depart. Five minutes later we were all astride
our elephants, and in about fifteen minutes, just when the
sun disappeared behind the mountain and twilight spread
rapidly all around, we passed through the gate of Akbar and
began to descend into the valley.

Hardly had we left the place, when a quarter of a mile

behind us, practically out of the very cypress grove we had just left, there resounded the shrieking howls of jackals, followed by such a loud, prolonged and air-shattering roar — the roar of disappointed expectation — that cold perspiration stood out on our brows. Our elephants sprang forward and almost knocked over the horses and their riders preceding us. For once, we, the riders, were out of danger, as we sat in a strong *howdah*, like a tightly locked tower.

"We seem to have cleared out just in time," remarked the Colonel, looking out the window at some twenty servants, brought by the *patel*, who were busily lighting torches.

In an hour we stopped at the gate of a rather large bungalow and were welcomed by the beaming countenance of our bareheaded companion, the Bengalî. After he had gathered us all in the courtyard and on the verandah, he explained that, knowing beforehand how our "American" pigheadedness would stand in the way of any warning, he had recourse to this cunning scheme, which happily, was successful.

"And now let us wash and have some supper," he said, and then added, turning to me, "you have wished for some time to be present at a real Hindu meal. Your wish is now about to be realized. Our host is a Brâhmaṇa, and you are the first Europeans to step over the threshold of his *family* home . . ."

—XIV—

What European ever dreamed of any country in the world where every step in the life of man, every happening, especially in the family life, the most insignificant deed is associated with some religious precept and *cannot* be performed except according to a certain procedure? In this country, not only all the most important incidents of life, all its outstanding events, such as conception, birth, the transition from one period of life to another, marriage, parenthood, old age and death, but even all the daily functions, physical and physiological, such as morning ablutions, dressing, eating and all that follows, from birth to the last breath, everything must be performed according to certain Brâhmanical routines, *on penalty of expulsion from the caste.*

The Brâhmanas may be likened to the musicians of an orchestra in which the different musical instruments are the numerous sects of the country. They are each of a different shape and produce varied sounds, yet all of them obey the same conductor. However widely these sects may differ one from the other in the interpretation of their sacred scriptures, and however hostile they may be to each other, striving to exalt their particular deity and to make it appear superior, every one of them, blindly obeying centuries-old customs, must follow, like musicians, the same directing wand — the *Laws of Manu.* Here is the pivotal point where they all meet and form a unanimous, single-minded community, a strong and unbreakably united body. And woe to

148

the one who either willfully or by chance produces a discordant note in that symphony! The elders (a hereditary position with the Hindus) and the high councils of each caste and sub-caste (of which there are a great many), whose members hold office for life, keep a tight rein on their community. Their decisions are without appeal, and this is why expulsion from the caste is one of the most terrible of punishments, entailing fearful consequences. The one so ostracized is worse off than a leper, the solidarity among the castes, especially in this regard, being something phenomenal, and comparable only to the solidarity among the sons of Loyola. If members of two different castes, even though united by the warmest feelings of mutual regard and friendship, strictly abiding by all the regulations, may not intermarry, dine, drink not so much as a glass of water or smoke a *hookah* together, it becomes clear how much more severe all these restrictions must be in the case of one ostracized. The miserable wretch must literally *die* in so far as everyone is concerned — the members of his own family as well as strangers. Even his own household, his father, mother, wife and children, are all bound to turn their faces from him, under the penalty of their being ostracized in their turn. There is no hope for his sons and daughters of getting married, however innocent they may be of the alleged sin of the father . . .

From the moment of ostracism, the Hindu simply ceases to exist for all those who knew and loved him. His mother, wife and children must not feed him, nor even let him drink from the family well. No member of his caste, let alone of any other, would dare to sell him food or prepare it for him. He must either literally starve or *pollute* himself still further by buying what he needs from *outcastes* or Europeans. When the Brâhmanical power was at its zenith, such acts as deceiving, robbery, or even killing the ostracized one was encouraged, as he was *beyond* the pale of the law. At present, of course, he is free from the latter danger, but even now, if he happens to die *before* he is forgiven and received back into the caste, his body may not be burned on the sacred pyre, and no purifying rites are given it.

"Mângs" will throw him into the bushes or into the water like a dead animal.

It is evident that against such a force — and it is the more frightful in its passive aspects because the law is power-less against it — neither Western education nor English in-fluence can be of any help. Only one thing is left: to repent, submitting to all kinds of humiliations, and often, in view of Brâhmanical greed, to face total ruin. I know personally several Brâhmanas who, having brilliantly passed the uni-versity examinations in England, have had to submit to the most repulsive conditions of "purification" on their return home, namely, shaving off half of their moustache and eye-brows, crawling naked on their bellies in the dust around pagodas, clinging for long hours to the tail of a *sacred* cow while reading prayers, and, finally, swallowing the excre-ments of this cow! * The voyage across the sea (*Kâla-pâni, i.e.,* "black water") is considered the worst of sins, and necessitates some of the most drastic purifications. A man who does that is considered to have polluted himself con-tinually from the first moment of his boarding the *bellati* (foreign) ship, to the moment of his return . . .

Only a few days ago a friend of ours, a doctor of juris-prudence, having finished his studies in England brilliantly, had to undergo this kind of "purgation," and it nearly cost him his reason. When we asked him why he submitted to this if, according to his confession, he had long ago ceased to believe in Brâhmanism and had become an ardent material-ist, he gave reasons which it would have been impossible to refute. "I have two daughters," he explained, "one five, the other six years old. If I do not find a husband for them, especially the elder one, in the course of this year, they will be considered overripe, and nobody would consider marrying them. Suppose I become ostracized; I thereby dishonor them both, make it impossible for them to find husbands, and render them unhappy for the rest of their lives. Also, my old mother is so superstitious that she would most certainly

---

*Called *pañcha-gavya,* literally "five cow-products" namely a mix-ture of milk, butter, curd, urine and excrement.

take her own life, because of the family dishonor; she has already more than once threatened to commit suicide . . ."

Some, perchance, may ask us why does he not, educated man as he is, sever all ties with Brâhmanism and caste? Why not join with other companions in the same circumstances? Why not form a whole colony with his family and relatives and side with civilization by becoming one with the Europeans?

This is a very natural question, but the answer to it is not difficult to find. It is somewhat like the celebrated reply of one of Napoleon's marshals; out of the thirty-two reasons why it was impossible to beseige a certain fortress, the first was absence of gunpowder, which made it entirely useless to enquire about the others. Similarly the first reason — among many others — why a Hindu cannot be *Europeanized* is quite sufficient and does not call for any mention of others. By cutting the Gordian knot, the Hindu would not only fail to improve his situation but would actually jump from one fire into a hotter one. Were he to have the mind of a genius, were he to rival a Tyndall in science, or be equal to a Disraeli or a Bismarck in politics, were he to belong to the most illustrious family, as soon as he gave up caste and kinsmen, he would at once be in the position of Mohammed's coffin, metaphorically speaking, and would hang between earth and sky.

"He left his own clan, and found himself unfit to join another," is a wise saying that seems to have special reference to these unhappy people. It would be vain to suppose that the rejection of both Moslems and Hindus * from civil service is merely the result of an unjust policy of fear which is loath to draw its professed enemies into the government of their country. Social ostracism and a feeling of enmity and contempt on the part of a "superior" for an "inferior" race (according to English notions) displayed quite frankly on

---

* Europeans very often make the mistake of confusing Hindu Moslems with *Hinduists* in India. The former are hurt when called Hindus and call themselves Hindu *Moguls*. They are Semites, while the Hindus are Âryans and differ from the former in everything.

the part of the English, plays a far more important role in this problem than is supposed even in England. The undeserved contempt which is shown for the natives (including Moslems) on every occasion, every year widens the gulf between both nations, which centuries will not suffice to close. Let me mention two examples of this.

We were visiting here with a very influential person, the editor of an English newspaper, and had an opportunity of making the acquaintance of a most remarkable young Moslem, Seyd M., belonging to the highest native aristocracy. The fact that he is welcome in a home frequented by the local English *beau monde* can be explained in two ways: first of all, Mr. Seyd M. is no ordinary man, but a gentleman in the full acceptance of the term; secondly, this curious circumstance can be explained by the fact that Seyd M., contrary to others, wears European clothes, was educated in England, and is not only a talented man, but one who has succeeded in making himself respected even by the English. An ardent patriot, he gave up his attorneyship, which promised for him both fame and considerable means, and entered civil service, accepting the position of judge in a small district in the hope of "improving, however little, the political and social situation of the natives," to quote his own words. A unique example among Indian Moslems, he makes no distinction between the Moguls and Hindus and defends with equal fervor the interests of both races. His love for Hindus is almost greater than his attachment to his own co-religionists. His mother was a Brâhmaṇa who became a Moslem . . .

"We natives are children of one and the same unhappy mother, India," he told us recently, speaking in his usual poetical Oriental manner. "Sons of one and the same sad destiny, we should bear it in mutual comradeship and not irritate the aching wounds by quarrels between adherents of two fanatical religions."

This was said in regard to a recent bloody conflict between Moguls and Hindus which took place in Benares during the religious festival of the former.

Seyd M. came to see us every day and usually began immediately to tell us about the "sores" of India, as he called them. We argued for hours, S. defending the English, M. trying to prove the opposite position, that of the natives, the injustice done them on the part of Anglo-Indian society, and the unbearable haughtiness of the British in India. On one occasion they started an argument more heated than usual on the subject of some new civil service regulation that had just been made public in Calcutta. M. asked why, for instance, of two employees, one English and the other native, of equal rank and occupying absolutely identical positions (namely, district judges), the Englishman receives 35%, and sometimes up to 60%, more in yearly pay than did the native? The former also receives additional funds for his summer vacation, so-called "camping-money" or "subsidy-money," while the native receives nothing beyond his wages. "And all this is India's money," he added, "and comes from the bloody sweat of the wretched milch cow of the English, a cow already so much milked that one wonders how her udder is still in place . . ."

S., a brilliant writer and orator, as familiar with the political trends of the Calcutta Government as he is of the contents of his own pocket, found himself thus placed against the wall, and not knowing what to reply, gave expression to a nonsensical paradox: "Let us not forget," he mumbled, "that *we* are *exiles* in this land, that you Hindus, according to your own confession, need us, and that *it would be unjust to make us serve your country without a good remuneration.* You, the natives, are obliged to pay us; after all our needs are greater than yours . . ."

M.'s countenance fell in amazement.

"Exiles?" he finally exclaimed, "You are exiles? But who asked you to come from across the ocean to save us? It is possible that . . ."

But he did not finish. Under the crossfire of our bewildered glances, following this comical outburst, S. started to laugh at himself. He evidently intended to sidetrack the delicate political argument. But M. would not allow it. Very obviously his heart was full, and so a few moments later he launched another attack.

"You see," he remarked, "we are old friends, and you look upon me as your equal, but this is not because my ancestors were for centuries high dignitaries of the Mogul empire, or because we are descendants in direct line from the daughter of Mohammed . . . . . But simply because in England I have become more or less of a *gentleman*, wear a black dresscoat, and, upon occasion, even straw-colored gloves. Otherwise, if in native dress, though it be more beautiful than your dark sacks, you would be ashamed to entertain me, especially to seat me at your table."

To the vehement protest of the host, he added:

"Do not argue, S., and especially do not speak for others, because I could prove you wrong right away, and among your people there are those in whose eyes even my black dresscoat does not redeem me. Yesterday, for instance, Lady K. did not accept my formal call. That was not so bad. But do you know what she asked Lord K.'s secretary to tell me? A most significant message, which has already circulated around town, and which outlines in a few words our political and social position. She ordered him to express her 'astonishment.' I should have known that Lord K., her high-born spouse and my superior, had left town three days ago, and that the 'wives' of dignitaries are not in the habit, either in England or India, of receiving anyone 'on business." In other words, she could not imagine that a native would 'dare' to make a call at an English home as if he were on a par with any other mortal, except on 'official business'."

"Lady K. showed thereby her natural stupidity," exclaimed Mrs. S. "No one else would have shown you such arrogance."

"Not at all," calmly replied the Moslem, "other ladies, and even their husbands, my own colleagues, have quite often shown me the same kind of entirely undeserved arrogance." And he mentioned several names. "And if *I*, in my position, exceptional for a native, am subjected to this, what can be expected by other natives who are less favored by fate and the Government?"

He sat leaning over his cup and talking quickly, evidently in complete self-possession; only the little spoon, with which he mechanically rapped the saucer, shook in his hand, and his black eyes were full of fire.

"I am ready to give my life for England which has educated me," he continued in the same tone of voice, "and to the Government to whom I swore allegiance and which I serve, and all for the sake of my beloved India. We as a people are unable now to rule our country without foreign help, that I know, even though we ruled it, for good or for ill, for centuries, and the land was richer and happier. But I realize that now, during the last century, we have degenerated, and English help is necessary. But if I swore allegiance to the Government, I did nothing of the kind in regard to society and private individuals . . . *and I hate them!* . . . Remember my words: If England ever has to fear a mutiny again, the exclusive cause will be English society, and it will occur as a result of the contemptuous haughtiness of the public officials who are sent here, and which drives the natives into a frenzy. They constantly prate to us about the tyranny and despotism of Russia. Do you know the answer to that from our Moslems, the descendants of the sultans, sardârs, heroes and greatest statesmen of bygone centuries? They say: "Yes, maybe the administrators of Russia are cruel, and its government hardly to be compared with the 'benign' government of Her Majesty, the Empress of India. But when we read and hear on all sides that such-and-such a general in Russia is a *Moslem,* and such-and-such a one is an Armenian, and in spite of this is the Commander-in-Chief of a whole army, while here the lowliest English soldier would rather desert than consent to acknowledge a *native* as commander, even though the latter were of princely blood, and comparing our sad fate with the fate and the hopes of any man of a different faith or tribe faithful to Russia, a question arises in our souls: 'Why are we the only ones to deserve such a humiliation, why do we find ourselves in a dark body? Realizing in silent despair the inescapable nature of our situation, why should we not envy at times the circumstances of our brother-Moslem in so-called *despotic* Russia! . . .' "

Here is our second example. The family of a well-known and learned doctor of medicine in Bombay, a native of Gôa, and bearing a Portuguese name, has been Catholic for three generations; the ancestors of both husband and wife

were, however, true and high-born Brâhmaṇas. Both of them
have been educated abroad and received excellent training.
The husband is a Knight of several honorary orders, a
member of several learned societies, and is highly regarded
in the Royal Asiatic Society. The wife is a young woman
twenty years old, highly educated and in possession of a
marvelous voice. *Neither of them is received in society.* At
their musical evenings on Tuesdays, with the exception of
a few journalists from the European *bohème,* you will not
find a single English merchant, let alone an Englishwoman.
"For goodness sake, who amongst us," explained some of
these liberal ladies and young girls, whose youth has been
spent in some second-rate store of Oxford Street, "would associate with such niggers?" . . .

The following remarkable fact will appear to our Russian
readers as strange and even monstrously incredible. The
chief barrier between this ex-Brâhmanic family and the
snobbish Anglo-Indian society is the *conversion to Christianity* of the former, even though a forced one, as were such
conversions in the last two centuries in Portuguese Gôa,
since they converted people by threat of the prison or the
Inquisition with its refined tortures. Not because they are
Catholics, but simply because *they used to be Hindus,* and
that in them flowed, as in the case of the despised half-
breeds of America, what the highly educated society calls
here in its expressive terminology—the blood of Ham;
because they are the descendants of a lower race (half-
castes) and on a par with Eurasians (a term formed from
European and Asian), who are equally despised by natives
and Christian Europeans. Were they merely idol worshipping Hindus, Pârsîs or sons of the Prophet—Moslems, they
would have a chance of being invited twice a year to one
of those tent-balls at Government House, when this mansion
is filled, like a keg of sardines, with thousands of natives
who are placed in rows along the walls like decorations and
promptly forgotten.

We have dwelt on this subject perhaps more than we
should have, in order to give a clear understanding of the
natives of India. Thus it is that the ill-fated Hindus prefer
temporary humiliation and all the physical and moral suf-

ferings of "purification," to the prospect of continued contempt until death.

A great many questions of this kind occupied our minds during the two hours which we spent before our dinner with the Brâhmaṇas. It appeared at first sight, a dangerous, almost impossible, breach of Manu's precepts — this dining with foreigners and people belonging to different castes, but this time, for once, it was easily explained. First, the stout *patel* was the *head* of his caste, and so was not afraid of excommunication; secondly, he had already taken all the precautions and the measures prescribed by law against being *polluted* by our presence; and thirdly, being a liberal at heart, and a friend of Gulâb-Lal-Singh, he had promised that he would show us all, in actual fact, how much sophistry and subtle cunning has been invented by adroit Brâhmaṇas in order skillfully to escape in cases of emergency, the iron hand of the law, while to all appearances adhering to its dead-letter meaning. Besides, our good-natured and stout host desired to obtain a diploma from our Society and become one of its members; he had heard that Col. O., the chief "tax collector" of his district, belonged to the American Society, and was anxious, therefore, to be of service to us.

Such were, at any rate, the explanations of our *bâbû* in reply to our expressed astonishment. It was up to us, therefore, to rejoice at the rare occasion and not to lose the opportunity. Whoever has been allowed not only to partake of a meal with Brâhmaṇas, but even to be present at one, becomes almost sacred in their eyes. Not only the host himself, but even all the members of his caste, look up on such a fortunate person as belonging at least *de jure* to the caste. How rare and almost impossible are such cases! . . .

[Pâtâni Prabhus and their history. — Visiting the patel's
house. — Various Brâhmaṇa ceremonies. — Ancient Hindu
knowledge unrecognized. — Dinanâth Âtmaram Dalvi, the
Mathematician. — Magnetic basis for certain ceremonies. —
Meal in a Brâhmaṇa family. — Bhûtas and Gandharvas. —
Dancing and singing.]

Hindus take food twice a day only (we are speaking here
of the well-to-do), at ten in the morning and at nine in the
evening; both meals are accompanied by complicated rites
and ceremonies. At other times of the day no one, not even
the children, eat anything, since eating without the mantras
prescribed by religion is considered a sin. Thousands of educated Hindus have long ceased to believe in these superstitious rites — remains of hoary antiquity — but are, nevertheless, forced to conform to them.

Shamrâo Rahunâthji, our host, belonged to the ancient
caste of Pâtâni Prabhus and was very proud of his origin.
Prabhus (*i.e.,* lords) are descendants of Kshatriyas (warriors), and their forefather was Aśvapati (700 B.C.), a
lineal descendant of Râma and Pṛithu, who, according to
local chronology, governed India in the Dvâpara and the
Tretâ Yugas.*

For them alone the Brâhmaṇas must perform purely
Vedic rites known under the name of the "Kshatriya rites."
They are now called *Pâtânis* (*i.e.,* the "fallen ones"), instead
of Pâthâris, and they owe this also to their forefather, King

---

*According to the chronology of the Hindus, this means in the Yuga
preceding the present *Kali-Yuga*, and in the one *before* it, as they divide
the *Mahâ-Yuga* or "Great Age" into four smaller periods (*Yugas*);
this in purely arithmetical terms would mean about two million years
ago!!

Aśvapati. Once, when distributing alms to holy anchorites, he inadvertently overlooked the great Bhṛigu. The offended prophet and seer cursed him, threatening him with a speedy end of his reign and the destruction of his entire posterity. Then the King, throwing himself at Bhṛigu's feet, implored his forgiveness. Bhṛigu finally consented to forgive him, but his curse had already taken root, and all he could do to remedy the situation was to promise not to let the King's descendants completely perish. As a result of this, the Pâthâris soon lost their throne and their power. Since then they have had to live "by the pen," in the employment of various governments, to exchange their name of Pâthâris for Pâtânis (fallen ones), and to lead a life of greater poverty than many of their former subjects. Fortunately, the forebears of our talkative Amphitryon became Brâhmaṇas, that is to say, "went through the golden cow."

The expression to "live by their pen" alludes, as we learned later, to the fact that from the beginning of British rule, almost all the scribes and small clerks in the Bombay Presidency are Pâtânis, just as similar posts are occupied in the North-West Provinces by Bengalî Bâbûs. In Bombay alone they number 5,000. They are darker in complexion than the Koṅkan Brâhmaṇas, but are handsomer and more intelligent. As to the mysterious expression, "went through the golden cow," it means the following: in exceptional cases and when willing to spend a large amount of money, not only the Kshatriyas, but even the despised Śûdras, may become, as it were, "sidewise" Brâhmaṇas. The true Brâhmaṇas, upon whom this metamorphosis exclusively depends, require them to purchase this right for several hundred, and sometimes several thousand, cows. Then an artificial cow is made out of pure gold and consecrated in various mystical ceremonies. The candidate is then made to crawl through her hollow body three times and, having submitted himself to this ordeal, immediately becomes a Brâhmaṇa. The present Mahârâja of Travancore, and even the well-known Mahârâja of Benares, recently deceased, were both Śûdras who had at one time acquired the coveted right in this manner.

We received all this information, as well as the historicolegendary chronicle of the Pâthâris from our most obliging host. Having asked us to prepare for supper, and promising to return for us in half an hour, the esteemed Shamrâo disappeared with the gentlemen of our party. Being left to ourselves, in the absence of the men, Miss B. and I decided to have a good look at what appeared to us to be an empty house. We took with us, however, the bareheaded Bâbû who could give us some explanations. Being a completely modern Bengalî, he despised the religious preparations for dinner and hence considered it useless to "prepare" for it. He went with us.

"Prabhus," if they are all brothers, always live together in the same bungalow, and every married brother has a separate room (if not a special dwelling in the yard) and a servant of his own. The habitation of our host was spacious, and was surrounded by smaller dwellings occupied by his brothers, while the main building was used for guests and contained a general dining room, a lying-in ward, a small chapel with idols, a room for those deceased, etc. As is the case with all the native bungalows, the entire ground floor was surrounded by a verandah (a covered gallery) pierced with arches without doors and leading to a large hall occupying the center of this floor. Around this hall, on all sides, were wooden pillars adorned with exquisite carvings; they upheld the ceiling of the upper floor and took the place of walls.

For some reason or other, it struck me that these pillars must once have adorned one of the palaces of the "dead town." Their carving was not in the least Hindu in style, and instead of gods, fabulous monsters and animals, the pillars were covered with arabesque murals of elegantly cut flowers and leaves. The pillars stood close to each other, but their *relief* work prevented them from forming an uninterrupted mass, so that there was too much ventilation; during the time we spent in the middle of the dining room, a strong cross current of wind blew at us from behind every pillar, and miniature hurricanes roared from all four quarters, arousing our old rheumatism and toothache, which had so far peacefully slumbered in India's climate. The façade of the house was thickly covered with iron horseshoes — the surest precaution against evil spirits and the *evil eye*. On the right of the façade an additional structure was added—a high room called "Ozri"; from it, as in all native houses, a staircase (carved as all else) led upstairs. At the foot, on a large couch without legs, hanging from the ceiling on iron chains, there lay an idol of full-grown size, which I first mistook for a sleeping Hindu and was about to retire discreetly. Upon recognizing our old friend Hanuman, I grew bold and started to examine him . . . Alas! Of the once complete god, only his head was left; the rest, which was supposed to represent the body, proved to be but a bag of old rags . . . On the left side of the verandah there was another row of rooms, each one for a special purpose. One of these was intended for giving birth; another for unfortunate widows; still another for those who had died; and finally a very large room, called "Vattan," was reserved for the members of the fair sex who, though not expected to hide behind a veil and spend their lives in harems, as Moslem women do, have nevertheless very little to do with men and keep entirely to themselves. Here women cook for the men, but do not dine with them; they are often held in respect by their husbands who sometimes show them a sort of shy courteousness; but nevertheless, they would not dare to speak to their husbands, not only before strangers, but even in the presence of sisters and mothers.

As for the Hindu widow, she is the most wretched creature on earth. As soon as a woman's husband dies, she must have her hair and her eyebrows shaved off for good. She must part with all her adornments: her earrings, her nose rings, her bracelets on arms and legs, and her rings on all twenty fingers and toes. She is literally *dead* to her family and to the rest of the world, and even a "mâng" will not marry her, as her slightest touch pollutes the man, and he must forthwith go and "purify" himself. The dirtiest work in the household is her duty, and she may not eat with the married women and the children. The "suttee," or the burning of widows, is forbidden, but the Brâhmaṇas have their own way, and the widows often long for the pyre.

At last, having examined the last room — a Hindu chapel, a sanctuary full of idols before which stood flowers, burning lamps and candles, where incense burned in a rich bronze vase, and the floor was thickly strewn with *tulsî* and other aromatic herbs—we decided to get ready for dinner. Having washed ourselves, we were requested to take off our shoes; such is the custom and there was nothing else to do but comply or refuse the Brâhmaṇa supper. A still greater surprise was in store for us, however. On entering the dining room, we stopped short: both of our European companions were dressed, or rather undressed, Hindu-fashion! For the sake of decency, they had kept on a kind of sleeveless knitted sweater, but they were barefooted, wore around their loins a snow-white *dhôti,* and looked like something between a white Hindu and a Constantinople *garçon de bain.* They were indescribably funny, and I know nothing more amusing than an European in this sort of attire. To the great discomfiture of the men, and I suppose, to the scandal of the grave ladies of the household, I burst out laughing. The forty-five year old Miss B. tried to blush, but instead followed my example. The worst had happened; let's see what followed . . .

Ceremonies and rites which have already been referred to, reach their culmination before every dinner and supper. A quarter of an hour before sitting down to a meal, every Hindu, young or old, has to perform *pûja* before the gods. He does not change his clothes, but takes off the few things which cover him during the day. He bathes by the well, *i.e.,* washes his hands, feet and face, loosens the long lock of hair at the top of his shaven head, and remains bareheaded;* to eat dressed or with covered head is considered a sin by the Hindus. Wrapping their hips in a white *silk dhôti* (silk possesses the property of repelling the evil spirits which inhabit the magnetic currents of the atmosphere, according to the *Book of Mantras,* Bk. V, verse 23) they go to make obeisance to the idols, and then sit down to the meal.

---

*Only *Bengalîs* do not shave their heads but wear their hair short; *Pañjâbîs* do not shave it either, but wear their hair as long as it will grow, and do not cut it off, but hide it during the day under their white turbans. *Râjputs* also keep their hair long, gathering it up on the back of the neck. But the *Marâthâs* and the *Dakhinîs* wear their hair like the Iroquois, leaving one long forelock, as used to be done by the Cossacks of Zaporozh.

I will now allow myself a slight digression, at least for the sake of the naturally occurring question, whether something deeper may not be hidden behind this apparent superstition concerning the spirits and the silk. Regardless of the obvious unwillingness on the part of scholars to relinquish their beloved notions that all the customs of the ancients and the pagans are based merely on *ignorance* and crude *superstition,* discoveries have been made for some time to the effect that some of these customs, which appeared so stupid at first sight, have originated in purely scientific principles. Why should we not suppose, for example, that through observation the ancients possessed full knowledge of the properties of electricity, and of its favorable effect upon the organs of digestion when in contact with the naked body?

Those who have studied the ancient philosophy of India, with a firm resolve to penetrate the hidden meaning of its aphorisms, have for the most part become convinced that the properties of electricity were known to a considerable extent, from the most ancient times, to such philosophers as, for instance, Patañjali. Charaka and Suśruta had propounded the system of Hippocrates several centuries before the time when the latter became known as the "father of medicine." The calculations in *Sûrya-Siddhânta* are indelibly imprinted on a stone which is held in the Badrînâth temple of Vishṇu, and show that the author knew and calculated the expansive forces of steam centuries ago. The ancient Hindus were the first to determine the velocity of light and the laws of reflection; and the table of Pythagoras and his celebrated theorem concerning the square of the hypotenuse are to be found in the ancient books of Jyotisha. Not so long ago, Occidental mathematicians named Hipparchus of Nicaea as the father of trigonometry, notwithstanding that all they knew about him was ascertained from the report of his pupil Ptolemy. Now an ancient manuscript has been found showing that the "equation of the center"* was known to the Hindus long before our era.

---

*[Difference between the place of a planet as supposed to move uniformly in a circle, and its place as moving in an ellipse.—*Compiler.*]

Even in our own day (in 1880)* there lives in India,
wasting his time as assistant judge in some out-of-the-way
place, a certain Dinanâth Âtmaram Dalvi (M.S.,LL.B. *i.e.,*
Master of Science and Baccalaureate of Jurisprudence), who
is possibly the greatest mathematical genius in the world.
According to Peile, director of national education in India,†
Dalvi proved (some three years ago) that the great Newton
was mistaken from beginning to end in his "Rule for
Imaginary Roots," and that the application of this New-
tonian rule does not bring about the intended result. The
same Dalvi blew the theorems of Professor James J. Sylvester, one of the greatest English mathematicians, into
smithereens.‡

---

* [This installment of H.P.B.'s story was originally published in the
Moscow Gazette on March 5, 1880, old style.]

† [Reference is to Sir James Braithwaite Peile (1833-1906), who
was the son of Rev. T. W. Peile. He was educated at Repton and the
Oriel College, Oxford; went to Bombay in 1856, on a Civil Service
assignment. Became Under Secretary to the Bombay Government, and
Director of Public Instruction, 1869-72. Later, Acting Municipal Commissioner of Bombay; Political Agent in Kathiawâr, 1873-78; Member
of Council, Bombay, 1883-86; Vice-Chancellor, Bombay University,
1884-86; Member of the Supreme Council, Oct., 1886 - Oct., 1887, and
of the Council of India, 1887-1902.—*Compiler.*]

‡In case (and this is bound to occur) someone among our Russian
mathematicians — followers of Sir Isaac Newton — "rises in anger"
against such an unwarranted (so far) desecration of the great mathematician, and doubts my assertion, I suggest that they get in touch
with the editorial office of the *Moscow Gazette* and ask it to notify
me of their doubts. I will immediately send to the above mentioned
editorial office several pamphlets of Âtmaram Dalvi, in which he proves
at length and irrefutably (according to the admission of the best professors) where the mistakes of Newton lie. The pamphlets will be sent
free of charge, for the sake of justice and my friendship for the author, whose genius is uselessly lost in the backwoods of India. The
pamphlets are published in English.

[James Joseph Sylvester (1814-1897) was a renowned mathematician. Matriculated at Cambridge in 1831. Being a Jew, he could not
take his degree, still less obtain a fellowship, due to entrenched prejudice.
Gained his first ordinary degree at Dublin. After the passing of the
Tests Act, he graduated B.A. at Cambridge in 1872, showing unusual

All this leads us to suppose that ancient Âryans, when instituting the strange custom of wearing silk "dhôtis" during meals, had something more serious in view than the repulsion of "demons." But it is interesting that even in our enlightened age there should be learned doctor-spiritualists who (like Dr. Eugene Crowell of New York) write entire treatises to prove that wearing tightly tied silk kerchiefs on their heads and chests is the only safeguard from evil demon-phantoms for so-called "mediums"; and while the esteemed Crowell has not, so far, demonstrated to the learned world that the phantom-spooks in general (the American ones especially) tremble before the product of the silkworm, nevertheless he explains clearly and logically the role of silk material in relation to electricity. And so . . .

The host came to fetch us, and we started for the dining room. In entering the "refectory," we immediately noticed the precautions taken by the Hindus against pollution. The stone floor of the hall was divided into two equal parts by a line traced in chalk, with strange Kabbalistic signs at either end. One part was destined for the hosts and those belonging to the same caste, the other for us. At the side was a third square for our travelling companions of another caste. Aside from this slight barrier, both halves were the same. Against the two opposite walls were narrow carpets with cushions and low stools to sit on. In front of each seat was an elongated figure on the bare floor, traced in chalk and divided, like a chessboard, into smaller quadrants, intended for various dishes and plates. These were of the thick,

---

pertinacity and courage. His entire life was spent chiefly in the study and teaching of mathematics. He was appointed professor of natural philosophy at University College, London, in 1837. Before 1870, he was recognized as one of the foremost mathematicians of the day, and was considered great as a maker of mathematicians no less than of mathematics. He is considered as the founder of invariant algebra in England. A prolific writer of mathematical papers, he was also a poet and a musician.

In the very first issue of *The Theosophist*, Vol. I, October, 1879, pp. 25-26, there is an article by D. A. Dalvi on "Âryan Trigonometry."
—*Compiler.*]

strong leaves of the East-Indian "teak" tree (*Butea fron-dosa*); larger dishes were several leaves pinned together with thorns, and saucers of one leaf with borders turned up. The entire supper was on display and was arranged in front of each seat. We counted forty-eight saucers made of small leaves, containing about a *mouthful* of forty-eight different dainties! The materials of which they were composed were to us *terra incognita,* but some of them tasted delicious.

The supper consisted strictly of vegetarian food; meat, fowl, eggs and fish were entirely absent from the menu. There were *chutneys,* fruit and vegetables preserved in honey and vinegar; *pañchâmṛit*—a mixture of pampello-berries, tamarinds, coconut milk, treacle and olive oil; *kushmer,* made of radishes, honey and flour; pickles and spices hot enough to burn your mouth, and so forth. All this was completed by a mountain of exquisitely cooked rice, and another mountain of *chapâtîs,* which are pancakes not unlike Georgian "churecks." The saucers stood in four rows of twelve each, and between the rows burned three aromatic sticks the size of a small church taper. Our part of the hall was brightly lit with red and green candles in *seven* huge strangely-shaped chandeliers, each of which represented a seven-headed cobra wound round the stump of a tree, and lifting its heads in all directions. Each of the seven mouths held a thin red or green wax candle, shaped like a corkscrew. Draughts blowing from behind every pillar fluttered the yellow flames in every direction, filling our high refectory with fantastic jumping shadows and causing our "lightly clad" gentlemen to sneeze profusely. Leaving the dark silhouettes of the Hindus in the shadows, this unsteady light made the two figures of the Europeans stand out like bright white spots, as if teasing them and laughing them to scorn . . .

One after the other, our hosts, and their relatives and friends of the same caste came in. They were all naked to the waist, and barefooted; their hair hung loose, and they wore the "triple" Brâhmanical thread over their shoulders and a white silk "dhôti." Every "saab" was followed by his own servant, who carried his cup, two silver, or even gold, jugs filled with water, and his towel. Having saluted the

CHAR-MINÂR AT HYDERÂBÂD

THE GHÁT AT HARDVÁR

host, they came to greet us in turn; with the palms of their hands pressed together, they touched their foreheads, their breasts, and finally the floor, bending low to the earth, and saying: "Râm, Râm" and "Namaste." * Then they sat down at their respective places, cross-legged and in silence. This reminded me that this ancient custom of greeting with the name of some ancestor pronounced twice has existed from immemorial antiquity.

When we were all seated — the Hindus, calm and stately, as if preparing for some rite, and we feeling somewhat awkward and not knowing what to do next, fearing innocently to commit some blunder and thus offend the hosts — there suddenly came from a dark corner the soft voices of a women's choir. About half a dozen *nâchnî*-girls (singers and dancers from the pagodas) began chanting in unison hymns and praises to the gods. To this accompaniment, famished and tired as we were, we began to partake of the rice; thanks to the instructions of the Bâbû, we did so with our right hands, because had we done so with the left, whole hosts of *râkshasas* (demons) would have been attracted to our feast, and by so doing we would have chased the natives away in terror. Of knives, forks and spoons, there was, of course, no trace whatsoever. Fearing to become unwittingly and inadvertently guilty of an indiscretion, I put my left hand in my pocket and firmly held my handkerchief as long as the dinner lasted.

Apart from the quiet singing which lasted but a few moments, the feast proved to be a silent one. It was Monday —a day of fasting—and the rule of silence during meals had to be observed even more strictly than usual. Ordinarily, a man who is compelled by some emergency or other to break the silence and to utter as much as one word, hastens to wet the middle finger of his left hand, which up to then had been behind his back, and with it to moisten both his eyelids. But a really pious man would not be content with only this purification; having spoken, he would leave at once, wash, and abstain from food the rest of the day.

---

*The first term is that of a hero made god; the second, literally translated from Sanskrit, means "I bow before you."

Thanks to this tomb-like silence, I had the opportunity
of noting everything that was going on with the greatest attention. Whenever I caught sight of the Colonel or Mr. W.,
who were stoking in rice by the handful, it cost me the
greatest of effort not to burst out laughing, for an irresistible
urge to do so took possession of me. They sat in imperturbable dignity and worked their elbows and hands awkwardly.
The long beard of the one was covered with grains of rice
as if with hoarfrost, while the other had the lower part of
his face messed up with liquid saffron, and green rivulets
of pickle juice streamed down their chests and to their
awkwardly drawn up knees. But I happily controlled myself
and directed all my attention to the quaint rigmarole of the
Hindus. I will try to describe the curious details of their way
of eating.

Each of them, sitting with his legs curled up under him,
held in his left hand the jug brought by the servant, and
poured some water, first into a cup, then into the palm of
his right hand. He then slowly and carefully sprinkled the
water round a leaf, holding all kinds of dainties, which
stood by itself (and was destined for the gods and the spirits,
as we learned later), chanting all the while a "mantra"
from the *Vedas*. Filling his right hand with rice, he repeated
a new series of couplets accompanied by intoning, then,
having placed five pinches of rice on the right side of his
own plate, he once more washed his hands (to avert the evil
eye), sprinkled more water around the plate, and, pouring
a few drops into his right palm, drank it slowly. After this
he swallowed six more pinches of rice, one after the other,
murmuring prayers all the while, and wetting the middle
finger of his left hand in the cup of water, moistened his
eyes. Finally, he hid his left hand behind his back, and began
to eat his supper with his right hand. All this took only a
few seconds, but was performed with great solemnity.

The Hindus ate with their bodies bent forward, throwing
the food up with their hands, and catching it in their mouths
with the skill of Japanese jugglers, with not a grain of rice
lost, and not a drop of the various liquids spilled. Out of
esteem for his host, and probably desirous of showing his
respect for India, our Colonel evidently tried to imitate all

their movements. He, too, attempted to bend his whole body forward, but, alas, his esteemed little belly proved to be a serious handicap. Losing his balance, he almost tumbled head first into all the dainties, but happily this time he got off with only his spectacles flying into a dish of sour milk and garlic. After this unsuccessful experiment, the brave American gave up all further attempts to become "Hinduized," and sat quietly.

Everyone concluded his supper, as customary, with rice mixed with sugar, powdered peas, olive oil, garlic and pomegranate. This last dainty is consumed hurriedly, nervously, with everyone glancing askance at his neighbor and almost in a race with him. They are all mortally afraid of being the last to finish, as this is considered an evil omen. At the end, they once more take some water in the palm of their hands, and, whispering a prayer over it, swallow it in one gulp. Woe to the one who may choke in so doing, for a *bhûta* (demon, spirit of the dead) has found lodgement in his throat, and he must run and be purified at the altar! The poor Hindus are very much troubled by the evil spirits of those who have died with ungratified desires and in the heat of earthly passion (the other troublesome deceased they do not recognize). Hindu spirits, if we are to believe public opinion, swarm around the living to try to satisfy their hunger by means of their mouths and to gratify their impure earthly desires with the help of living organs temporarily taken possession of by them. They are feared and cursed all over India; no means to get rid of them or to quiet the rampaging *bhûtas* are neglected.

The notions, ideas and conclusions of the Hindus on this point are diametrically opposite to the aspirations and hopes of Western Spiritualists. "A good and pure spirit," they say, "will not let his soul revisit the earth, if this soul is pure also. He is glad to die and unite the spirit (*âtman*) with Brahman, to live an eternal life in *Svarga* (heaven) and to commune with the lovely *Gandharvas* (singing angels or cherubim). He slumbers whole eternities listening to their heavenly song, whilst his soul (*jîva*) continues to purify itself from earthly dross in a body more perfect than the one the soul abandoned before." * But this is not what awaits the wicked soul. The soul that does not succeed in casting off earthly desires before death ensues, is weighed down by its sins, and, instead of reincarnating at once in some new form, according to the laws of metempsychosis, is doomed to wander on earth without a physical body. It becomes a *bhûta,* and its own sufferings will sometimes cause incredible suffering to its own kinsmen. That is why the Hindu dreads remaining *bodiless* after death more than anything else.

"It is better for one to enter the body of a tiger, a dog, or even a yellow-legged falcon, after death, than to become a *bhûta!*" an old Hindu recently told me. "Every animal, whatever it may be, possesses its lawful body and the right to make an honest use of it. Whereas the *bhûtas* are doomed *dacoits,* brigands and thieves, ever watching for an opportunity to benefit at someone else's expense. This is the most horrible, the most unimaginably frightful condition; it is *hell,* according to our views. What is this Western Spiritualism anyway? Is it possible that intelligent and educated English and Americans have gone completely mad?"

He simply could not believe that there actually were people foolish enough to love *bhûtas* and even *invite them to come to earth.*

After supper the men went to the well in the yard, and having washed, dressed themselves again. Usually at this hour of the night, they put on clean *malmalas* (tight, long shirts made of thin jaconet), turbans, and wooden sandals with knobs caught between the toes, which they always leave outside the door. Returning to the hall, they sit along the walls on carpets and cushions to chew betel, smoke hookahs and cheroots, listen to sacred reading, and watch the dances of the *nâchnîs.* This is the custom on ordinary

---

*According to their views, the spirit, *âtman,* a particle of the All, or Parabrahman, cannot be punished for sins in which it never participated. It is *manas,* animal intelligence and animal soul or "jîva," a half-material illusion or *mâyâ,* that sins and suffers, transmigrating from one body into another until purified. The spirit merely overshadows its earthly wanderings. When the *Ego* has been entirely purified, it permanently unites with its *âtman,* or spirit, and both gradually merge in Parabrahman and disappear.

days, but this evening (probably in our honor) they attired themselves richly. Many of them wore *dariyâi* of rich stripped satin, several gold bracelets, gold necklaces mounted with diamonds and emeralds, gold watches and chains, and white *djanvi*—Brâhmanical scarfs, as thin as a mist, embroided with gold, and worn over the shoulders. The fat fingers of our host and his right ear were ablaze with diamonds.

The women who waited on us, our hostesses who had disappeared after supper, came back half an hour later all dressed up, and were then formally introduced to us. They were five; the wife of our fat host, a woman of twenty-six or twenty-seven years of age; two other women somewhat younger, one of whom carried a baby, and who to our astonishment, proved to be the daughter of the hostess; then an old woman — the mother of the host; and finally a little girl of *seven,* the wife of his brother. Thus our hostess turned out to be a grandmother, and the little girl who was to enter into matrimony from two to three years later, may have become a mother long before she was twelve. They were all barefooted, with rings on their toes, and all, with the exception of the old woman, wore garlands of natural flowers round their necks and in their jet black hair. Their dress consisted of a short bodice (*cholî*), embroidered with gold, and worn next to the naked body, tightly covering their neck and breasts. This did not reach their *sârî* or skirt-like wrapper (if it is permissible to call it a skirt), whose upper part serves as a covering for the head and also as a mantle, at one and the same time, and boldly left exposed the dark waists of these beautiful women, which gleamed in the light as if cast in bronze. Their well-shaped arms were covered above the elbow with expensive bracelets, and so were their ankles. At the least movement, they all set up a silvery tinkling sound, and the little sister-in-law, not unlike a large doll on springs, could hardly move under her load of ornaments. The young "grandmother," our hostess, had a ring in her left nostril, which reached to below her chin and pulled heavily on her nose. Only when she took it off to enable her to drink tea, could we admire her remarkable beauty.

Then began some dances by the *nâchnîs,* two of whom were very beautiful. These dances consisted of more or less expressive movements of their eyes, ears, noses, heads, and of the whole upper part of their bodies generally. As to their legs, they either did not move at all or moved so fast as to appear lost in a cloud of mist . . .

That night I slept the sleep of the just.

———————

—XVI—

It is indeed pleasant, after many nights spent on the bare floor of a tent, to sleep in a bed, even though it be a hanging one, especially when this is accompanied by the realization that one is resting on the couch of a "god." This latter circumstance, however, was only discovered by me in the morning, when, upon descending the stairs I found the divine *général-en-chef* (Hanuman) had been deprived of his throne and discarded, rags and all, under the staircase . . . The Hindus of the nineteenth century are definitely a degenerate and blaspheming race!

It was later disclosed that, with the exception of an old sofa, this was the only bed in the house. Our two gentlemen had even a worse night; they slept in an old empty tower that was once the gopura of an ancient ruined pagoda situated behind the main building. They were so assigned with the praiseworthy intention of protecting them from the jackals, which steal by night into the rooms of the lower floor, where there are openings only, instead of doors and windows. The jackals, aside from their usual nightly concert, did not trouble them by their presence. But both Mr. W. and the Colonel had to fight all night with a *vampire*, which, in addition to being a large flying bat, was a "spirit," as they later learned to their sorrow. This is what happened.

The vampire flew noiselessly into the tower and, fluttering its cold, sticky wings, alighted on one or the other of the sleepers, evidently intending to feast on European blood. Ten

173

times or more they awoke and chased it away, but every time
unsuccessfully; as soon as they dozed off again, they would
feel its light, almost silent touch on shoulders, legs and chest.
At last Mr. W. caught it by a wing and skillfully twisted its
neck.

In the morning, boasting innocently of this exploit to the
host, they drew down on their heads the heavenly thunder.
The yard became crowded with people, and in front of the
entrance to the tower stood the inhabitants of the house,
with downcast heads. The old mother tore her hair in despair, and droned lamentations in every language of India.
What was the matter? Something terrible, which, when we
learned of it, threw us into deep consternation. By certain
signs, known only to the family Brâhmaṇa, it has been ascertained that our host's elder brother, the son of the frantic
old woman, had *transmigrated* after his death into the body
of this bloodthirsty vampire. For nine years the dead man
had existed in this new form, thus working out the requirement of metempsychosis. During the day, hanging by his
claws head down from a branch of the old pîpal-tree in
front of the tower (from time immemorial the abode of
spirits), he spent the hours between sunrise and sunset in
sleep. At night he visited the old tower and gave fierce chase
to the insects that swarmed there for their night's rest. Thus
the vampire lived, slowly redeeming old sins committed when
he had the shape of a "Pâtâni." And now? His lifeless body
lay at the entrance to the tower, with one wing already
devoured by rats . . . Choked by her tears the old woman
cast fierce glances, from under the covering over her shaven
head, on Mr. W., who, in his capacity of murderer, looked
utterly indifferent.

The affair grew involved and was becoming tragic. The
comic aspect was lost in the sincerity of the mother's genuine
sorrow. The crowd stood silent and curious, evidently not
daring to express its feelings before English "Saabs," but
looking at us askance, with no special good will. The family
priest and astrologer stood beside the old lady, *Sâstras* under
his arm and his wand in hand, ready to begin the ceremony
of purification of the tower. He had already made arrangements to cover with a piece of new linen the half-eaten and

ant-infested corpse of the revolting vampire, which was lying before him with its wings widely spread . . .

Mr. W. stood as before, whistling unconcernedly and with both hands in his pockets. Miss B. joined him and, ignoring the presence of our host who spoke English well, loudly proclaimed (precisely *à l'anglaise*) the ignorance and coarse superstitions of the "fallen race." W. did not reply, but smiled contemptuously. Our host then came up to the Colonel and with a low "salaam" very politely invited us to join him in a "few moments of talk."

"Well," I thought, "he'll ask us to clear out! . . ." It would seem, however, we had not at the time fathomed the metaphysical depth of a Hindu heart.

He began by delivering *ex tempore* a most florid preface. He reminded us that he, the host, was an educated man, a man with a *Western* upbringing. Owing to this, he was not positive that the body of the vampire was actually inhabited by his late brother. Darwin, and other great naturalists of the West, seem to believe in the transmigration of souls, but, as far as he understood, they did so in an *inverse* sense; that is to say, if a son had been born to him exactly at the moment of the unfortunate death of the vampire, this child, according to the latest scientific notions, would probably have in him much that was vampire-like, owing to the decaying atoms of the vampire being so near. "Is this not a correct interpretation of Darwin and his school?" he asked us.

We modestly replied that, having travelled almost incessantly during the previous year, we were not up-to-date on modern science, and had not heard about any such recent conclusion.

"But I have followed it," somewhat pompously rejoined the good-natured Shamrâo, "and thus I believe I have fully understood and duly appreciated its latest pronouncements. I have just finished reading the excellent *Anthropogenesis* of Haeckel and have pondered a great deal over his logical, scientific explanation concerning the origin of man from inferior animal forms through transformation. And what is this *transformation*, if not the *transmigration* of the ancient and modern Hindus — the *metempsychosis* of the Greeks?"

We could find nothing so say to dispute the identity and even ventured to say that, according to Haeckel, it *does* actually look like that.

"You see, then," he exclaimed joyfully. "It naturally follows that our ideas are neither as silly nor as superstitious as is maintained by some opponents of Manu. The Great Manu,* by the way, anticipated both Darwin and Haeckel. Judge for yourselves: The latter derives the genealogy or *genesis* of man from a group of 'plastides,' from the jelly-like *moneron;* this 'moneron,' through the *amoeba,* the *zinamoeba,* the *ascidean,* and finally the headless and heartless *amphioxus,* transmigrates in the eighth stage into a *lamprey,* and is eventually transformed into a vertebrate *amniota,* into a pro-mammalian, into a marsupial animal; and the *vampire* belongs to the species of vertebrates.—You, of course, being well read people, will not contradict that?"

We did not contradict it.

"Well, then, please follow me further . . ."

We followed, of course, with great attention, but were at a loss to understand where he was leading us.

"Darwin," he continued, "in outlining his teaching concerning the origin of species, follows almost word for word the 'palingenesis' of our Manu. Of this I am entirely convinced and am ready to prove it, book in hand. For instance our ancient lawgiver says, briefly: 'The Great Parabrahman commanded man to appear in the universe, after traversing all the grades of the animal kingdom, and springing primarily from the lowly worm in the deep sea mud. The worm became a snake, the snake a fish, the fish a mammal, and so on.' Is not this the basic idea at the root of Darwin's theory, when he maintains that the organic forms have been derived by means of a gradual transformation from simple species to more complex ones, from structureless protoplasm in the mud of the Silurian and Laurentian periods (the sea mud of Manu) to an anthropoid, and finally to man? . . ."

We agreed that it actually appeared so.

"But, in spite of all my sincere respect for Darwin and his

---

*["Manu" or the "Great Manu," throughout this chapter stands for *The Laws of Manu* or the *Mânava-dharma-śâstra.—Compiler.*]

follower Haeckel, I cannot agree with their final conclusions, especially with those of the latter," continued Shamrâo. "This impulsive and bilious German, copying so accurately the embryology of Manu and all the metamorphoses of our ancestors, loses sight of the evolution of the *human soul,* which, according to Manu, goes hand in hand with the evolution of *matter,* in all its transformations . . . The son of *Svayambhû* ('the uncreated one') speaks thus: 'Everything created acquires in the course of its transmigrations, in addition to the qualities of its preceding forms, new qualities, so that the nearer it approaches to the highest type on earth —man, the brighter becomes its divine spark,' and he adds: 'but once he has become a Brahmâ on earth (*i.e.,* has attained in the shape of *man* the highest form of the cycle of transmigrations), man enters the cycle of *conscious* transmigrations.' In other words, his future transformations will depend no longer on the blind law of gradual evolvement, but on his actions upon earth, for the least of which he will be either rewarded or punished. Therefore it depends on man's own will whether he will start higher on the road to *Moksha* (eternal bliss), passing from *loka* to *loka,** until he reaches *Brahma-loka,* or whether, owing to his sins, he will be thrown back by the law of retaliation. In that case he will be required to return to former animal forms, already once traversed unconsciously. And even if Darwin and Haeckel, as physicists, both lose sight of this, so to speak, the *second volume* of their incomplete theory, so cleverly 'filled out' in the teachings of Manu, still they do not deny it anywhere in their writings. Is that not so?"

---

*There are in the religion of the Hindus seven *chief* and a great many *less important* lokas. "Loka" means realm, locality. In general, lokas are worlds of purification, and some sects mean by them certain stars. Souls which are not too sinful and are freed from earthly transmigrations go to these worlds, gradually passing from one to the other, but always in the shape of man, although this shape grows and perfects itself in every new "loka." Such spirits, freed from earthly matter, become, according to the Hindus, *pitris* and *devas,* who are worshipped as the "spirits of the ancestors" (*pitris*) and to whom sacrifices are made. They correspond to the *planetary spirits* described by the mediaeval Kabbalists (*Vide* Heinrich Khunrath, *Amphitheatrum Sapientiae eternae,* etc., the writings of Paracelsus and others).

"It would appear they do not deny it."

"Why then," exclaimed he, in a suddenly aggressive tone, "why am I, I who have thoroughly studied the most modern and latest ideas of Western science, I who believe in its representatives, who, in their turn, confirm by scientific conclusions at least the *first half* (the evolution of the physical world) of Manu's teachings, why am I looked upon, I ask you, by our esteemed Miss B., as an ignorant and coarse Hindu, our *perfected* scientific theories as 'superstitions,' and we ourselves as the sons of a 'fallen inferior race'? . . ."

Poor Shamrâo stood there with tears in his eyes, as he thought of the *undeserved* accusation of the tactless Englishwoman. And we stood there, embarrassed and not knowing what to say.

"Mind you," he continued, "I do not dignify these popular beliefs by considering them 'infallible dogma,' I consider them mere theories, and seek to merge them and to make the ancient science harmonize with the new. I merely formulate 'hypotheses' like Darwin and Haeckel. Besides, I have heard that Miss B. is a Spiritualist; she believes in spirits, in *bhûtas*. And if a '*bhûta*,' according to her, were capable of entering a body of a medium, and to take possession of its organism for hours and even days, why then could not a *bhûta*, or even a less sinful soul, enter the body of a vampire? . . ."

In the face of such "over-simplified" logic, we knew not what reply to make, I confess, and so we preferred to avoid this delicate metaphysical question, and to apologize for the rudeness of miss B.: "She is an Englishwoman," we said, "and can hardly be changed; she did not wish to offend anyone, but simply gave expression to a thoughtless remark concerning superstitions," and so forth.

Little by little our host calmed down. He had just begun to explain to us, with even greater vehemence, how, on the basis of the law of "atavism," deeply thought over by him, which explains the hereditary transmission of qualities as it were by leaps, from the fifth ancestor in line to the tenth, he had arrived at the necessity of at least half-believing in the identity of his late brother and the late vampire . . . But suddenly Mr. W. very nearly ruined everything:

"The old woman has gone crazy! . . . ," he shouted across the yard to us. "She is cursing us, and insists that the murder of the vampire is only the forerunner of a whole series of misfortunes brought on her house by the son — you, Shamrâo. . . ," he went on rudely, addressing the follower of Haeckel. "She says you have polluted your Brâhmanical holiness by inviting us, *bellatis,* to take supper with you and spend the night in your house . . . Colonel, you had better send for the elephants, before we are thrown out or worse yet."

"For goodness sake!" exclaimed the confused Brâhmana, in his turn. "What can I do? She is an old woman; maybe with prejudices, but she is my mother . . . You are educated, learned people; tell me how to find a way out of this unfortunate situation. What would you do in my place?"

"What would I do, Sir?" exclaimed the irate Mr. W. "Were I in your place and believing as you do, I would not hesitate an instant; I would take a revolver and, in the first place, shoot all the vampires in the neighborhood, if only to rid my relatives of the disgusting bodies of these beasts; then, in the second place, I would use the butt of it to crack the skull of the rascal Brâhmana who invented all this nonsense. That is what I would do, Sir! . . ."

But this advice did not satisfy the poor descendant of Râma; no doubt he would have remained long undecided, talking to one or the other, torn between the sacred feeling of hospitality, the inborn fear of the Brâhmana-priest, and his own superstition, if our ingenious Bâbû had not come to the rescue. Learning that we were ourselves upset and had asked for the elephants in order to make our departure, the Bâbû persuaded us to stay, if only for an hour, saying that a hasty departure would be a terrible insult to our host, who was quite innocent in this entire affair. As to the foolish old woman, he promised to pacify her very soon; he had his plans all made.

With this end in view, he asked us to visit the ruins of an old fortress along the road and to await his arrival there. We obeyed, but moved on reluctantly and slowly, as we were exceedingly interested in his "plan." The men of our party were quite angry; Miss B. continued to be oratorical, and

Nârâyana, as imperturbably phlegmatic as usual, good-
naturedly teased her about the "spirits" in which she believed. Passing behind the house, we saw the Bâbû walking
along the wall with the family priest and vehemently discussing something with him. The shaven head of the priest
nodded in all directions, his long yellow garment flapped in
the wind, and his arms rose towards the sky, as if invoking
the gods to come down and witness his words . . .

"He won't get anywhere with that fanatic," remarked the
Colonel, as he lit his pipe.

We had hardly walked a hundred paces after this remark,
when we saw the Bâbû running after us and signaling us to
stop.

"Everything worked well," he shouted from a distance,
waving his arms and swallowing his words with laughter.
"You are to be thanked. You are the saviors and benefactors
of the late *bhûta* . . . You . . ."

And he sank to the ground holding his narrow, panting
breast with both hands and laughing until he made us all
laugh, before we knew what it was all about.

"Just think," he began, "it cost but ten rupees; I offered
five at first, but he was obstinate; however, he took the
ten."

And he rolled in laughter once more.

At long last, he explained his stratagem, which gives a fair
idea of the holiness of the Brâhmanas. He knew that generally the *metempsychoses* of the Shaivas (followers of Śiva)
depend upon the imagination of the family "gurus," who
receive for these precepts from 100 to 150 rupees a year
from each family. Such Brâhmanas are both astrologers and
manager-directors of all the religious rites established in the
family. The rites are associated with expenses which enrich
the pockets of the insatiable family Brâhmanas, and those
related to some happy event are better paid than those connected with unhappy ones.

Knowing all this, the Bâbû went straight to work; he
offered the Brâhmana five rupees if he would perform a
false *samâdhi,* that is to say, would feign an inspiration and
speak in the name of the dead son, declaring to the mother
that he, himself, had sought death for the body of the vam-

pire, that he wanted death in order to bring an end to this particular transmigration and to enter a *higher* one, that now he is better and he thanks the "saab" who freed him from his disgusting shape. Besides, the Bâbû had heard that the Brâhmaṇa desired to sell Shamrâo a calf which his she-buffalo was expecting almost any day, but the latter had refused to buy it. Now, what could be better? Let the reverend father-guru announce (under the influence of the same *samâdhi*) that the freed spirit intends to inhabit the body of the future baby-buffalo, and the old mother is sure to make Shamrâo buy the new incarnation of her eldest son. There will be rejoicings and new rites; the esteemed Brâhmaṇa will, on the occasion, get a nice little sum of rupees.

At first the guru had some misgivings, fearing to be found out, and called upon heaven and the gods to witness the fact that the vampire was actually inhabited by the son of the household. But later, when the Bâbû (well versed in all the Brâhmanical tricks) proved to him that that idea would not stand critical examination, as such a transmigration is not taught in the *Sâstras* — he gave in, merely requesting ten rupees and silence . . . Thus the deal was made and the old woman pacified.

When we returned to the tall gates of the house, Shamrâo met us with a radiant expression on his face . . . Afraid of being laughed at, or maybe at a loss to find in positive contemporary science in general, or Haeckel in particular, anything definite which could be referred to on the subject of this new transmigration, he did not explain why the affair had taken such a sudden turn for the better. He merely mentioned, akwardly enough, that his old mother, owing to some new and mysterious conjectures known to herself alone, had ceased to be apprehensive concerning her son's destiny, and then referred no more to this unpleasant little incident. He became even more friendly and happy, and entreated us for the pure love of science to go with him that evening to a religious *tamâshâ*.* A female *jâdûwâlâ* (sor-

---

*[*Tamâshâ* is a Hindustânî word derived from the Arabic, originally meaning "a walking about." It signifies a spectacle, a show, an entertainment; any occurrence that attracts and amuses spectators.— *Compiler*.]

ceress or conjuress), well known to the whole district, was then under the influence of *seven goddesses,* the seven sisters, all of whom in turn possessed her and prophesied through her mouth . . .

We gladly accepted and awaited impatiently the arrival of the evening.

———————

—XVII—

In order to erase the unpleasant impression of the morning's affair, Shamrâo invited us to sit at the entrance to his prayer-room and to witness him perform his morning rites and worship of the gods. With our love of knowledge, nothing could have been more welcome, and, having seated ourselves on the verandah, we watched him through the wide opening that took the place of a door . . .

It was nine in the morning, the natives' usual time for morning prayer. Shamrâo went to the well to get ready and "dress" himself, as he said, though an evil tongue would probably say "undress." In a few minutes, he came back with his head uncovered and wearing only a *dhôti,* as he had during dinner, and went straight to his idol room. The moment he entered, there was heard the loud sounding of a bell that hung under the ceiling of the prayer-room, and this tolling continued during the entire rite. The one striking the bell remained invisible, but the Bâbû explained to us that it was struck from the roof by a small boy.

Entering with his right foot, Shamrâo very slowly approached the altar and sat before it on a little stool with his legs crossed. Within the room, on the altar, which resembled modern semi-circular tiered shelves covered with red velvet, stood many idols. They were made of gold, silver, copper and marble, according to their importance and merit. *Mahâdeva* (Śiva) was of gold; Gaṇapati or "Gaṇêśa" (the son of Śiva, the god with an elephant's head) was of silver;

183

and Vishṇu was in the shape of *Śâlagrâma*, a round black stone from the river Gaṇḍakî in Nepal (in this form Vishṇu is called Lakshmî-Nârâyaṇa). Other gods, unknown to us, were there in the shape of large seashells, called *Chakras*. *Sûrya*, the god of the sun, and other gods and goddesses (*Kula-devas*, domestic gods), were placed in the second rank. The altar itself was sheltered by a cupola of sandalwood exquisitely carved. During the night, these gods and their offerings were covered by a huge glass bell, to protect them from rats. On the walls of the prayer-chamber hung many sacred images representing the chief episodes in the lives of the higher gods.

As we curiously observed every move, Shamrâo filled his left palm with ashes, all the while murmuring prayers, covered it for a moment with his right, then poured some water on the ashes and, mixing the two by rubbing his palms together, traced a line of the mixture by moving the thumb of his right hand from his nose upwards to the middle of his forehead, then from there to the right temple, then back to the left temple. Having completed the adornment of his face, he proceeded to rub the wet ashes on his throat, stomach, left arm, chest, right arm, shoulders, back, ears, eyes and head, in the order named; then, he went to the sacred bronze font filled with water that stood in a corner of the room, and plunged into it three times, *dhôti*, head, and all, after which he emerged looking like a fat Triton the sun had not yet dried out. Shaking his loose lock of hair, he twisted it in a manner which used to be called by Russian servant-girls of former days a *kudel'ka;* he then took water in his right palm and moistened his head with it. This operation concluded the first act.

The second act began with the prayers of *Saṃdhyâ* — religious meditations and *mantras* which pious people repeat three times a day, at sunrise, at noon and at sunset. He loudly pronounced the names of twenty-four gods, each name being accompanied by a stroke of the bell. This completed, he first shut his eyes and stuffed his ears with cotton, then placed two fingers of his right hand in his left nostril, and, having loudly drawn the air in through the right nostril, he stopped the latter with his thumb, tightly closing his lips, so as not to breathe. In this position every pious Hindu must mentally repeat a certain verse called the *Gâyatrî*. These are sacred words which no Hindu dares pronounce aloud; even in repeating them mentally, he must forcefully hold his breath, lest he might breathe some impurity. Bound by my word of honor not to repeat the entire verse, I can nevertheless quote a few incomplete sentences. The prayer begins thus:

"Om! . . . Earth! . . . Heaven! . . . May the adored light of . . . (this name must not be pronounced) illumine me. Let thy Sun, oh thou *only One,* illumine me, the unworthy . . . I shut my eyes, I plug my ears, I do not breathe . . . in order to see, to hear and to breathe thee alone . . . let our thoughts be illumined by (again the secret name) . . ."

It is curious to compare this Hindu prayer with that of Descartes, in his *Les Méditations*. It runs as follows, as readers may remember:

. . . . . I will now close my eyes, stop my ears, suspend all my senses . . . . . in order to contemplate for a while that perfect God, to consider at leisure his marvelous attributes, to admire and to adore the incomparable beauty of this immense light . . . .*

After this prayer, the Hindu quietly reads to himself other prayers while holding his sacred Brâhmanical thread between two fingers. Then, mixing some rice with sandalwood powder, he takes the jug of water standing on the altar and, washing off the old blobs, he daubs on new ones made of the dough he has just prepared. After this comes the ceremony of the "washing of the gods."

Taking the gods down one by one, according to their rank, he first dips them in the font of water and then bathes them in milk in another font by the altar. The milk is mixed with curds, butter, honey and sugar, so that instead of being given a washing, they are pretty much of a mess. But they are washed a third time in the first font and dried with a clean towel. When the gods are once more arranged in their

---

*[From the opening sentences and the last paragraph of his *IIIrd Meditation.—Compiler.*]

respective places, the Hindu traces on each of them the sectarian sign with a ring from his left hand. He uses white sandalwood for the *liṅga* and red for *Gaṇapati* and *Sûrya*. Then he sprinkles them with various aromatic oils and covers them with flowers that are fresh every day. The long ceremony is concluded by ringing a little bell as loudly as possible under their very noses, in order to "wake them up," as the Brâhmaṇas say, thinking perhaps, and not without reason, that the gods, being bored, may have gone to sleep. Noticing or imagining (which sometimes is one and the same thing) that the gods had awakened, he begins to offer them his sacrifices; he lights the scented candles and the lamps and wafts before them the incense burner, while snapping his fingers from time to time, as if warning them to "lookout." Having spread clouds of incense and fumes of burning camphor in all directions, he scatters more flowers over the gods* and, placing himself behind the little stool, offers the concluding prayers. He holds the palms of his hands over the flames of the tapers and lamps, rubs his face with them, and after walking three times round the altar, kneels three times and then retreats backward, facing the altar.

A little while before our host had finished his morning rite, the ladies of the house came into the prayer-room and, seating themselves on small stools they brought with them, began to pray and tell the beads of their rosaries. The latter play as important a part here as they do with the Buddhists. Each god has his own special beads, and the fakirs are covered with rosaries.†

We left the women to their prayers and followed Shamrâo to the cow stall. By means of this animal, worship is expressed to "nourishing-earth," or nature. After opening the door, he sat by the cow and proceeded to wash her feet, first with her own milk, then with water. He gave her some rice

---

*Each god and goddess has its own favorite flower.

†These rosaries are called *mâlâ*, and consist of 108 beads. They are made either of the black berries of a kind of wild-rose, known as *rudrâksha*, or of the light-colored tree called *tulsî*. Repeating their prayers while counting beads, very pious Hindus often hide their hands in a specially shaped bag called by them "cow's mouth" (*gomukha*).

and sugar in the palm of his hand, rubbed her head with sandalwood and other powders, and adorned her horns and four legs with garlands of flowers. Having then burned some incense under her nostrils and having brandished a burning lamp over her head, he walked three times round her and sat down to rest. There are Hindus who walk round the cow one hundred and eight times, rosary in hand. But our Shamrâo has a slight tendency to freethinking and has filled his head with Haeckel. Having rested himself, he filled a jug with water, dipped the cow's tail in it, and then drank it!...

In the same manner, he then performed the rite of worshipping the sacred plant *tulsî* * (the wife of Krishna) and the Sun, with only this difference: that, as he could not carry out the rite of washing this divinity, he stood on one leg, filled his mouth with water, and squirted it towards *Sûrya* three times, sprinkling us instead.

It is still a mystery to us why the plant *tulsî* is worshipped. All I know is, that although every year in September there is performed the ceremony of the wedding of this plant with the god Vishnu, yet *tulsî* bears the title of Krishna's bride, possibly because the latter is an incarnation of Vishnu. On this occasion, the Hindus (each of whom has a potted *tulsî* plant in his house) paint the pot in which the plant grows and adorn it with tinsel; the pot is then placed in the garden and a magic square is traced around it with chalk; a Brâhmana holds an idol of Vishnu in both hands and, standing before the plant, begins the marriage ceremony. The latter consists of a wedded couple holding a shawl between the flower and the god as if screening them from each other, while the Brâhmana mutters mantras, and women and young maidens (who are especially ardent worshippers of *tulsî*) throw rice and saffron over the god and the plant. When the wedding ceremony is concluded, the shawl is presented to the Brâhmana, the idol is placed in the shadow of his wife, the Hindus clap their hands, rend all ears with the noise of the tom-toms, set off fireworks, offer each other pieces of sugarcane, and rejoice in every conceivable way till the dawn of the next day ...

---

*Royal *basilicum*, or just basil.

By chance, last September, we witnessed this wedding in our own garden, where our *mâlî* (the gardener, a fanatical Hindu) would not have consented for any amount of money to permit foreigners to pollute by their presence his sacred *tête-à-tête* with the gods...

As evening closed in, we were again on elephants and ready to leave; but not for a long trip. It is only five miles to the lair of the old sorceress (the *Pythia* of Hindostan), and the road, though running through a thick jungle, is level and smooth. Besides, even the jungle and its ferocious inhabitants do not frighten us any longer. The timid elephants we had before had been sent home, and we were astride new ones sent by a neighboring Râjâ. These had more than once hunted tigers, and the roar of all the animals in the district would not frighten these old patriarchs of the forests. They stood in front of the verandah like two dark hillocks . . . So, we started! The ruddy flame of the torches dazzled us and increased the gloom of the forest which surrounded us on all sides, the bright light making it appear even more dark and mysterious...

There is something indescribably fascinating, almost solemn, in these night-journeys in India. Everything is quiet and silent; everything sleeps, both below us and above us. Only the heavy and regular thud of the massive tread of the elephants breaks the stillness of the night, like the sound of hammers upon the anvil in the underground smithy of Vulcan. From time to time uncanny voices and sounds are heard in the forest, as if someone were wailing among the scattered rocks. "It is the wind singing," we say, "a curious acoustical phenomenon." — "Bhûta! Bhûta!" whisper the awe-struck torch-bearers, brandishing their burning torches three times, swiftly spinning on one leg, and snapping their fingers to chase away the frenzied spirits. The plaintive wail is hushed, and once more we hear but the metallic whirr of the crickets, the mournful croak of a tree-frog, and the rapid beat of the grasshopper. At times all this suddenly stops, and then is resumed again, filling the forest with a melodious choir . . . Heavens! What teeming life, what stores of vital force are hidden under every leaf, under the smallest blade of grass in these tropical forests! Myriads of stars shine in the dark blue of the sky, and myriads of fireflies gleam with their phosphorescent sparks, like pale reflections of far-off stars, twinkling at us from the dark green bushes, as if showing us our way and lighting it for us ...

—XVIII—

Leaving the dark forest behind us, we found ourselves in a basin, fairly even in shape and surrounded on three sides with the same impenetrable forest, where even at noon the gloom is as deep as by night. We were now about two thousand feet above the foot of the Vindhya range, judging by the high walls of ruined Mându, which were straight above our heads.

Suddenly a rather chilly wind rose and nearly blew our torches out. Caught in the labyrinth of rocks and shrubbery, it suddenly wailed, angrily shook the green feathers of the blooming morinda, then, tearing itself free, rushed like a whirlwind around the basin and down the pass, howling and whistling, as if all the forest spirits wailed a funeral dirge for the mountain witches ...

"Here we are," declared Shamrâo, dismounting. "Here's the village, and we can't ride any farther."

"What do you mean? . . . and where is the village? . . . there seems to be nothing but forest here! . . ."

"You cannot see the village or the houses by night. The huts are all hidden among the bushes, and many of them, cut out of the rock, can hardly be distinguished from it even in daylight. Nobody here lights any fires after sundown ... they are afraid of spirits ...," he explained.

"And where is your witch? Shall we have to look at her in the darkness?"

Shamrâo cast a furtive glance around him, and his voice became noticeably tremulous as he replied:

190

"I implore you not to call her a *dâkinî* (witch). — She may hear you — We are not far from her now, though you'll have to walk about half a mile. Not even a horse could get through to her, let alone an elephant. There we shall find light . . ."

This was rather an unpleasant surprise — to walk half a mile at night in India, scrambling through thickets of cactus, in a dark forest full of wild animals! Miss B. positively refused to walk and declared she would not go, but would wait for us without dismounting her elephant, right in her *howdah*, where she could quietly sleep. And that's what she actually did.

Nârâyana, who from the outset was against this *partie de plaisir*, without explaining his reasons, told her she was very sensible in so doing.

"You won't miss a thing by refusing to visit the *dâkinî* . . . and I only wish everybody else would follow your example . . ."

"But what harm can possibly come from it?" remonstrated Shamrâo in a somewhat disappointed tone of voice, as he was the one to have first suggested this outing. "Quite apart from the fact that our guests will have an opportunity to see a most interesting spectacle—'the incarnation of gods,' a rare sight which not every European has a chance to witness — 'Kangâlin' is a holy woman . . . she is a prophetess, and her blessings, even if she is a pagan, can harm no one . . . I insisted on this excursion out of pure patriotism . . ."

"Saab," replied Nârâyana with a strange bitterness, "if your patriotism consists in boasting to your guests about the worst plagues of our downtrodden native land, almost stifled in filth, then why did you not use your power as a *patel* to gather together all the lepers of your district and to boast of *them* too?"

Fearing a quarrel between Hindus, the Colonel remarked that it was too late now to be sorry. Besides, without having much faith himself in the "incarnation of gods," he nevertheless knew that *demoniacs* are a fact even in the West. The court action that took place in Russia in connection with some peasants from Tihvinsk, who had burnt the witch

Agrafena alive, is one proof of the actual existence of a strange and mysterious disease called in the West "medium-ship" and in Russia "klikushestvo." From the scientific viewpoint, the Colonel wished to study psychic manifestations, whenever and under whatever shape they might take place . . .

Our procession in the dark of night would have been an amazing sight to our American and European friends. The road ran uphill along a narrow winding path. No more than two people could walk side by side, and there were thirty of us, including the torch-bearers. To judge by the fact that he immediately took command of our expedition, it is probable that reminiscences of night sallies against the Confederate Southerners had awakened in the Colonel's breast. It is true, of course, that his leadership was strictly limited. He had the rifles and revolvers loaded, dispatched three torch-bearers ahead of us to light our path—which they would have done anyway — and ordered us to advance! Now we had nothing to fear from the confederation of tigers and could proceed quietly. Winding like a fiery snake in the forest, our procession started slowly to crawl up the path.

It cannot be said that the company which appeared half an hour later at the den of the prophetess of Mându was especially noteworthy, either for their neatness or for the elegance of their costumes. My gown as well as the travelling shirts of both the Colonel and Mr. W. were nearly torn to pieces. The cacti extracted involuntary tribute from us all the way, and the Bâbû's disheveled hair swarmed with a colony of fireflies and long-legged grasshoppers, most likely irresistibly attracted there by the smell of coconut oil. The stout Shamrâo panted like a steam engine. Only Nârâyana, having had his say, reverted to his imperturbable indifference, resembling by day or night, but especially now, a bronze statue of Hercules armed with his mace.

At the last turn of the path, when we had to climb over huge boulders, we found ourselves skirting the level edge of a thick forest. When this last obstacle was overcome, our eyes, in spite of the torches, were suddenly dazzled with light, and our ears assaulted by most unusual sounds.

Another basin opened up before us, the entrance to which, out of the gorge we had just passed through, was hidden by the thick forest we had just skirted. We understood later how easy it would have been to wander round this enchanted forest for a week without even suspecting the existence of this glen, at the bottom of which we discovered the abode of the celebrated *kangâlin,* the sorceress and oracle of the entire district.

The "den," it so happened, was in the fairly well-preserved ruins of an ancient Hindu temple. Probably it had been built long before the "dead city," when the heathen were not allowed to have their own temples, and this half-ruined one stood under the wall of the town, but slightly out of line. The cupolas of the two smaller lateral pagodas had collapsed, and huge shrubs grew out of the altars of the temple. That evening, their branches were nearly hidden under a mass of brightly-colored rags, little pots and other talismans of popular superstition, the people seeing in them something divine . . . "Have they not grown in a sacred place? Does not their fiber carry sap impregnated with the incense of offerings and the exhalations of holy anchorites, who once lived and breathed here?" were the answers in question-form which the learned but superstitious Shamrâo gave to our queries.

The central temple, however, built of red granite, stood firmly, and, were it not for a closed door, we could have seen between its four thick pillars a deep tunnel dug under the mountain. No one knew what was behind the door. Shamrâo assured us that no man of the last three generations had ever stepped over the threshold of this thick door trimmed with iron, leading into the depths of the subterranean temple. *Kangâlin* lived there all alone and, according to the oldest people in the neighborhood, had *always* lived there. Some said she was three hundred years old; others alleged that a certain old man on his deathbed had revealed to his son that this old woman was none other than *his own uncle!* The latter had retired to a cave to work out his salvation and hew his road to *Moksha,* at the time when the "dead city" still numbered several hundred of its last inhabitants. The hermit saw no one, and no one knew then or knows now what he lived on. But once upon a time, very long ago, in the days when the *Bellati* had not yet taken possession of these mountains, the old hermit was suddenly transformed into an old hermitess, and from then on, continuing his pursuits, she speaks with his voice and often in his name, but, unlike her predecessor, receives worshippers.

Evidently we had come too early and the *Pythia* had not yet appeared. But the square in front of the temple was full of people, and a wild, though picturesque, scene it was indeed. An enormous bonfire blazed in the center of the yard and around it swarmed naked natives, like so many dark gnomes, adding to the fire branches of trees sacred to the "seven sister-goddesses." Slowly and rhythmically they all jumped from one leg to another, repeating in chorus one monotonous phrase, always the same, and with the identical tune, to the accompaniment of several native drums and tambourines. The hushed trill of the latter was repeated by the forest echo and mingled with the hysterical sobbing of two little girls who lay under a heap of leaves by the fire. They had been brought by their mothers in the hope that the "goddesses" would take pity upon them and would banish the two evil spirits possessing them. Both mothers, still young women, sat on their heels near their children and sorrowfully stared at the flames. No one among those present even so much as moved when we appeared; and during our entire stay with them, they acted as if they did not see us. Had we worn a cap of invisibility, they could not have behaved more strangely.

"They feel the approach of the gods . . . the whole atmosphere is full of their emanations," Shamrâo mysteriously explained, reverently observing those whom his beloved Haeckel might with justification have mistaken for the "missing link," the progeny of his *"Bathybius Haeckelii."*

"They are under the influence of *toddy* and opium," snapped the irreverent Bâbû.

True enough, those who did not take part in the "performance" moved as in a dream, while those who did reminded us of people possessed of St. Vitus's dance. One of them, a tall old man, with snow-white hair and thin as an skeleton, left the crowd as we approached, spread his arms like wings, and started twirling on one leg, loudly grinding his yellow teeth, long as those of a wolf. He was frightening and disgusting to look at. He soon collapsed and was calmly, almost mechanically, pushed towards the little girls by the feet (!) of the others. Yet more was in store for us. Our tale is not yet told...

Waiting for the appearance of the "prima donna" of this forest opera, we sat on the old trunk of a fallen oak, near the porch of the temple, ready to pelt our condescending host with questions. But we were hardly seated, when an anxious feeling of very real amazement and even horror made us shrink away...

I saw before me the skull of a monstrous animal, the like of which I could not place in my zoological reminiscences.

The head was much larger than that of an elephant skeleton... Yet it could only be an elephant, judging by the skillfully restored trunk, which wound down to my feet like a gigantic black worm. But an elephant has no horns, whereas this had four! The front pair rose from the flat forehead, curled foreward slightly and then spread out like the horns of a bull; and behind them there was another pair, massive in size, with a wide base like the root of a deer's horn; these gradually decreased toward the middle, where they branched out in both directions, and reached to such a height that they could have adorned the heads of a dozen ordinary reindeer. Pieces of yellow rhinocerous skin, transparent like amber,* were drawn over the empty eye sockets of the skull and small lamps burned behind them, which gave the head a still more horrible, a simply devilish appearance.

"What on earth is this?" was our unanimous exclamation. Even the Colonel had never seen anything like it, and did not recognize the beast.

"A *Sivatherium*," said Nârâyana. "Have you not seen the skeleton of these antediluvian animals in European museums? ... That is curious, their remains are quite numerous

---

*In Râjasthân shields are made of this skin. They cost a great deal and are worn only by the rich among the Râjputs.

in the Himâlayan mountains, though of course in fragments. They were named in honor of the god Śiva."

I confess, this was the first time I had occasion to see such a monster, which Senkovsky forgot to introduce us to in his antediluvian novel, in company with his mammoth who rescues the lovers.* Better late than never, however, and now we stood face to face with this interesting monster.

"If the tax collector ever learns of the existence of this skeleton in the den of your witch," remarked the Bâbû, "it won't adorn it much longer."

All around the skull, and on the floor of the portico, there were heaps of white flowers which, though not quite antediluvian, were totally unknown to us, who were ignorant of botany. They were as large as big roses and covered with the red powder of "lâl," the inevitable concomitant of every religious ceremony in this country. Beyond, coconuts were strewn about, and copper dishes filled with rice into which were stuck lighted candles of various colors. In the center of the porch was a queerly shaped coal-pot, surrounded with tall tapers in copper candlesticks. A small boy, dressed in a white garment, and white *pagrî* on his head, threw handfuls of incense and other powders into it.

"These people," said Shamrâo, "while they worship *Kaṅgâlin* as an incarnation of goddesses, do not belong either to her sect or to mine. They are devil-worshippers, and do not recognize the Hindu gods; they live in small communities scattered in the mountains and belong to one of the many Indian races known as *hill-tribes.* Unlike the Shânârs of Southern Travancore and Tinnevelly, they do not use the blood of the animals they sacrifice to the devils, nor do they build special temples to these *bhûtas,*† temples which they call *pey-kovil* or devil-houses. But for some reason or other, they imagine that the goddess Kâlî, the spouse of Śiva, from

---

*[Reference is to the Russian writer, philologist and Orientalist, Osip Ivanovich Senkovsky (1800-1858), who, in addition to being a prolific author, was professor of Arabic at the St. Petersburg University and founder of the well-known journal called the *Reading Library.—Compiler.*]

†These devils according to the Shânârs are not special spirits, but simply the spirits of evil people who have died.

time immemorial holds a grudge against them and sends subservient chosen evil spirits to torture them. Except for minor differences, they have the same beliefs as the Shânârs. They recognize no God and look *even* upon Śiva as an ordinary spirit. Their chief belief is in the souls of the dead. These souls, however righteous and kind they may have been in their lifetime, become evil devils immediately after death, being happy and contented only when they can torture both men and cattle. It is in this way that they are rewarded for their good actions upon earth. Adversely, if a man has been very wicked upon earth, he becomes willy-nilly a *good* devil and thus, because of his impotence suffers and becomes very unhappy. The results of this strange logic are not all bad, however. These primitive people and devil-worshippers are the kindest and most honest of all the hill-tribes in India, as they try in every way they can to become worthy of their great afterdeath reward — to become promoted into wicked devils."

Enjoying his own wit, Shamrâo laughingly told us this, holding his sides and trying to control his laughter in deference to the sacred place.

"A year ago I went to Tinnevelly on business," he continued. "Staying with a friend of mine, who was a Shânâr, I was allowed to witness one of their ceremonies in honor of the devils. No European has ever been allowed to attend such a rite — whatever the missionaries may boast — though there are converts among the Shânârs who have described it. My friend was a wealthy man and the devils most probably had it in for him particularly because of that . . . They tortured his family, poisoned his cattle, spoiled his crops, caused his coffee tree to rot, and persecuted his numerous relations, making them victims of sunstroke, madness and epilepsy, diseases over which they have special jurisdiction. These wicked demons settled in every corner of his spacious domain, in the woods, the rivers and even the stables. On account of this he covered his land with temple-pyramids made of clay; he anointed and whitewashed them, and adorned each one of them with a portrait of one of the devils — well, not exactly a portrait, but an outline of a human head; then he began to pray, humbly asking each one of the devils to draw with his own hand his likeness within the outlines, so that he might be recognized, promising henceforth to worship and honor each specific picture of the spirits as the rightful owner of the pyramid on which his portrait was drawn. And what do you think? Next morning all the outlines were found filled in. Each of them bore an incredibly good likeness to one or another of the neighborhood deceased. Almost all of them were recognized by my friend; among them, he found also a portrait of his father!"

"Well, did this please him?"

"Certainly he was pleased. At least he had learned how, at any time, to gratify the soul of every departed devil. He was not vexed at finding his father's portrait, as the old man had been irascible in earth-life, and once nearly broke both his son's legs, when, using all his might, he struck him with an iron crowbar . . . . Hence, he could not be a very dangerous devil. But one portrait, found on the most convenient and prettiest of the pyramids, greatly amazed my friend, and scared him stiff . . . . The whole district recognized an English officer, a certain Captain Pole,* who had passed away long before and had in his lifetime been a most kindly gentleman! . . . ."

"What? Do you mean to say that he even began to worship *him?*"

"That is right! Captain Pole was such a worthy, just and honest public servant, that, after his death, he would at once be promoted to the highest rank in the hierarchy of Shânâr devils. He remained the presiding devil of the entire village, and when I was there, the inhabitants of the whole district worshipped him. The *pey-kovil* dedicated to him stands next to the one of Bhadra-Kâlî (the Hecate of the Shânârs), whose place as a female devil in the "other world" was recently bestowed upon the wife of a certain German missionary, who had also been a most kindly lady in life and so became a very dangerous devil."

---

*A fact historically known all over India. Captain Pole is still one of their chief demons.

PORTALS OF THE CASTLE AT AMBER

SHEHER, IN JAIPUR

"But how are they worshipped? Tell me something about their rite."

"This rite consists mainly in dancing, singing and offerings. The Shânârs have no castes, and the sacred customs of the Hindus are not kept by them. They eat any kind of meat . . . The people assemble about a *pey-kovil* previously designated by the priest. There is a general beating of drums and the slaughtering of fowls, sheep and goats. When worshipping Mr. Pole, an oxen or cow is always killed as a sign of special respect for him, his nationality, and his earthly tastes . . . That evening the rites were performed by the chief priest. He came, holding a wand with little bells on it, his legs covered up to the knees with tinkling bracelets, his hair flowing, red and white flowers around his neck, and wearing a black mantle on which likenesses of some of the most frightful devils were embroidered. Accompanied by the sound of horns and drums, and the deep sound of a devil's bow*—the secret of whose production is known only to the Shânâr priests — he came forward, and, after waiting a moment, until Mr. Pole found it agreeable to possess his unworthy body, suddenly leaped in the air, approached the sacrificial cow and speared her on the spot . . . He then drank some hot blood and began to dance . . . And what a dance it was! You know, I am not at all superstitious . . . (I was glad that Miss B. was quietly sleeping on her elephant half-a-mile away!) but when I saw this priest as if possessed by all the demons of *naraka* [hell], whirling on the same spot with the amazing rapidity of a top, I almost became faint. Suddenly, accompanied by the mad howling of the crowd, he began to inflict deep wounds on his body with the bloody sacrificial knife. To witness him with foaming mouth and waving hair, bathing in the blood of the sacrificial animal, and mixing it with his own, was finally more than I could bear. I felt myself the prey of some hallucination; I imagined that I myself was spinning faster and faster . . ."

Shamrâo abruptly broke off his tale and remained motionless.

---

*A kind of *balalaika* with three thick strings, made, it is rumored, of human tendons, and played with a bamboo bow.

Before us stood *Kaṅgâlin*.

Her appearance was so unexpected that we all felt some-how confused. Carried away by Shamrâo description, we had not noticed how or whence she had come; had she risen from beneath the ground, we would not have been more unprepared, and her astonishing appearance would not have surprised us more. Nârâyaṇa stared at her with his large black eyes protruding, while the Bâbû clicked his tongue in confusion..

Imagine a skeleton seven feet high, covered with brown morocco leather, with a death's head of an eight-year-old child stuck on its bony shoulders! With eyes, so deeply set and at the same time so large, piercing through you so intensely with their devilish, burning flame, that you felt your brain benumbed under the influence of her glance, your thoughts becoming confused, and your blood freezing in your veins . . . I describe here my own personal impression, and that only partially. Both the Colonel and Mr. W. became pale, and W. even spat.

Of course this impression lasted but a moment, and when her deathly stare, and at the same time burning gaze, turned from us and towards the prostrate crowd before her, it vanished as swiftly as it had come. Still our entire attention was fixed on this remarkable creature . . .

Three hundred years old? How could one tell? Judging by her appearance, one might have conjectured her to be a thousand, with equal probability. We beheld a genuine living mummy or, rather, one endowed with motion. She was so utterly dried out that she seemed to have congealed since the days of creation. Neither time, nor the miseries of life, nor the elements themselves could any longer touch or affect this living statue of death. The all-destroying hand of time had marked her at the appointed hour, accomplished its work, and stopped short. It could not continue as its task was done. Thus appeared before our eyes the sorceress of the "Dead City."

And with all this, not a single grey strand! Her long, jet-black hair, shining with cocoa butter and giving forth a greenish sheen, fell in heavy thick tresses, straight as arrows, down her back and to her knees . . . Hair and nails, it is said, continue to grow on corpses, on vampires, in their graves, was the thought that crossed my mind, and I tried, to my shame, to examine the nails on the fingers and toes of this disgusting and frightful old woman . . . And what was she doing in the meantime? She still stood motionless, as if transformed into an ugly bronze idol, staring, her eyes burning like coals, into the crowd lying at her feet, slavishly prostrate in the dust. In one hand she held a small copper dish with a large piece of burning camphor, in the other a handful of rice. The pale yellow flame, flickering in the wind, almost touched her face, licked her chin and lit up her deathlike head, but she appeared not to notice the fire. Her neck, wrinkled as a mushroom, as thin as a stick, was surrounded by three rows of either copper or gold medallions, and her head, with a similar kind of snake. Her miserable likeness of a body, with ribs sticking out, was covered with a piece of saffron-yellow muslin.

The little girls raised their heads and suddenly set up a prolonged animal-like howl, their example being followed by the old man. The witch then tossed her head convulsively, and rising as if moved by some coiled spring, slowly began her invocation.

"*Angati enne-angati!* . . . ," * whispered Shamrâo who was perspiring profusely. "The goddess . . . one of the seven sisters, is about to take possession of her . . . look! . . ."

The advice was superfluous—we were looking with both eyes and at nothing else.

At first, the movements of the witch were slow, convulsive and somewhat jerky; then, gradually, they became more even; at last, as if catching the cadence of the beating drums, her long body leaning forward and writhing like an eel, she rushed with incredible speed round and round the blazing bonfire . . . A dry leaf caught in a whirlwind could not go any faster. Her bare bony feet trod noiselessly on the rocky ground. The black locks of her hair waved around her like so many snakes, writhing as if alive, and lashing the

---

*Literally, "it is entering man." The expression itself means that the spirit, demon, or some other invisible force is beginning to enter its chosen body.

sick people among the spectators, whose hands were stretched towards her. Anyone touched by one of the black curls of the Fury fell to the ground, shouting with happiness, thanking the goddess, and considering himself healed! . . . It was not the waving locks of the witch which lashed him, it was the *goddess* herself, one of the "seven," who touched the elected one ! . . .

Swifter and swifter fly her decrepit legs; the young, vigorous hands of the drummer can hardly keep up with her, and the old woman still rushes forward . . . Staring with her motionless, deathlike orbs at something invisible to others, but real to her, she glances but occasionally and for a fleeting moment into the faces of those present, transpiercing them with her gaze and at those upon whom she looks, she throws a few grains of rice. The small handful seems inexhaustible, as if the wrinkled palm contained the bottomless bag of Fortunatus himself. But lo, she suddenly stops as if thunderstruck!

After her mad dance around the bonfire, lasting twelve minutes by our watch, you would expect her to reel and fall! . . . No indeed. There is no sign of fatigue, not a drop of sweat on her deathlike face! She stops but for a minute, just long enough to allow the goddess to leap out of her. And then, in a jump worthy of a wildcat, she was over the bonfire and into the deep tank near the portico, up to her neck in water. Plunging once under the surface, where another of the sister-goddesses takes possession of her, she jumps out of the well and waits — the very personification of the Medusa's head . . . A little boy in white hands her another saucer of burning camphor, and she rushes headlong again.

For fourteen minutes, by the Colonel's watch, she races, jumps and leaps about, after which she plunges twice into the tank, to honor the *second* sister. Thus she increases the number of plunges with every "possession," until six disappearances under the water are counted.

We had not heard her voice yet. Her lips were tightly closed, and she did not open them. Exactly *one hour and a half* she had been racing and rushing about with all her might, without once pausing for breath. During all this period she stopped six times only, for a few seconds on each occasion. The "sisters" did not delay; they knew their business ... No wonder, since they are goddesses!

"She is a devil and not a woman!" exclaimed the Colonel in a low voice, seeing the head of the witch immersed in water for the sixth time.

"I'll be damned, if I know!" grumbled W., nervously pulling his beard. "All I know is that a grain of her cursed rice got into my throat and has stuck there ... I can't get rid of it ..."

"Hush, hush! Please! ..." whispered Shamrâo. "You'll spoil everything ..."

I glanced at Nârâyana and lost myself in conjecture ... His bronze features, usually so quiet and even severe, bore now the shadow of deep and real suffering. His lips were convulsively tightened. His half-opened eyes shone through their black eyelashes with the phosphorescent gleam of a wild beast, and his pupils, dilated as if by a dose of morphine and seemingly staring into the black forest before us, looked off into the far distance of unknown lands, perchance never yet seen by any man ... What is wrong with him, I thought? However, I had no time to ask him, as the witch, with water streaming from her, was again in full swing, madly chasing her own shadow. This time, however, her program was changed. She was not running, but leaping. Sometimes bending to the ground, like a black panther, she rushed toward some sick person and touched with her finger the forehead of the shaking worshipper, laughing inaudibly, and baring her teeth like a hyena. Then, again, as if shrinking from her own shadow, she whirled around it, beckoned to it, played with it, portraying some infernal caricature of Dinorah, dancing her "waltz with the shadow."* Suddenly she straightened herself and, in one leap, was again at the burning altar before the portico, where she prostrated herself, beating her forehead against the granite step. Another leap, and she was near the skeleton of the monstrous Śivatherium, prostrated before it, hitting the stone floor with the sound

---

*[In Giacomo Meyerbeer's comic opera entitled *Dinorah, oder die Wahlfahrt nach Ploërmel* (1859).—*Compiler*]

of an empty barrel striking the paved road. One last leap, and she stood upright on the head of the Śivatherium, in the middle of its four horns . . .

With a feeling of terror and disgust, which we no longer attempted to conceal, we instantly drew back — all of us except Nârâyaṇa.

He alone remained near the monstrous head; with folded arms, he looked straight into the face of the witch . . .

But what is this? Who suddenly spoke in that deep, base voice? It is her lips that moved; it is from the chest of this awful old woman that issued those quick, abrupt phrases, and the voice sounded hollow as if coming from beneath the ground . . .

"Hush, hush!" whispered Shamrâo again, his whole body trembling. "She is going to prophesy!"

"Maybe she — and maybe the 'uncle'," muttered W., showing his teeth and breaking into a smile which must have appeared devilish at this solemn moment to the plump fellow.

"Woe to you! — Woe to you! —" boomed the *voice*. "Woe to you, children of the impious 'Jaya' and 'Vijaya,'* of the mocking, unbelieving janitors of the great Śiva, you who are cursed by eighty thousand holy sages! Woe to you who believe not in the goddess Kâlî, you who deny us, her seven divine sisters! *Asuras* . . . meat-eating, yellow-legged vultures! Friends of the oppressors of our land! . . . Hounds who are not ashamed to eat from the same trough with the impure *bellatis!!* . . ."

"Your prophetess, it would seem, foretells the past," said Mr. W., philosophically putting his hands in his pockets. "She must be throwing a little stone in your garden, esteemed Shamrâo."

"Hm! . . . And into ours also," muttered the Colonel, somewhat embarrassed.

The unlucky Shamrâo, breaking out in cold sweat from horror, was running from one of us to the next, in the dark shadow of the wood where we had taken refuge, assuring

---

*The story about these two *Râkshasas*, or fallen spirits, will be told later. It is a most interesting one.

us that we were mistaken, that we did not understand the language well enough . . .

"It is not about you, believe me, not about you! . . . It is about me she speaks, because I am in the service . . . she is inexorable! . . ."

"Râkshasas! . . . Asuras!! . . . Daring to appear before us, goddesses . . . in *boots* . . . standing in shoes made of the skin of the sacred cow . . . may you be cursed . . ."

But her curse was destined to be stillborn. At that instant the enormous figure of Nârâyana fell shoulder first on the Sivatherium upsetting it, together with its trunk and the maddened *Pythia* sitting on top. A second later, and we thought we saw the witch flying through the air, with or without a broomstick — (Shamrâo ought to know more about this!) — in the direction of the portico, while a wide-shouldered Brâhmana, with shaven head, rolled head over heels into a hollow below . . .

Hardly another second had passed, before we came to the sad conclusion, judging from the loud clang of the underground door, and the ensuing general confusion, that the representative on earth of the "seven goddesses" had ignominiously fled, vanished forever from our inquisitive eyes into her subterranean kingdom . . . and that her hollow, unearthly and indeed subterranean voice, was in truth the voice of — someone's "uncle"! . . .

•　•　•　•　•　•　•　•　•　•　•　•　•

Oh, Nârâyana! . . . How carelessly, how disorderly, the worlds rotate around us! I began seriously to doubt their reality. From this moment I earnestly began to believe that all things in the universe are an illusion — a mere *Mâyâ*. I am becoming a Vedântin. I even doubt whether anything more objective may be found in the universe than the Hindu "witch" flying up the *chimney!* . . .

•　•　•　•　•　•　•　•　•　•　•　•　•

When Miss B. woke up, she asked what had taken place. The noise of many voices and the sound of the footsteps of the crowd of naked people, fleeing as they hurried towards the gorge, had awakened her. They all rushed away, it appears, without even looking back, as if afraid of being pursued, and seemed to be scared . . . .

After unburdening herself of her impressions, and having aired her false teeth in the light of the stars, with either a condescending smile or a yawn, she went back to sleep.

Next morning, at daybreak, we tenderly bade good-bye to the good-natured Shamrâo. He had had time to come to his senses after his defeat, and to recover from the shock of the previous night. The shamefully easy victory of Nârâyana weighed heavily on his mind. With the capitulation on the part of the "seven goddesses," who fled the field of battle at the first blow from an ordinary mortal, his faith in the "sisters" and in the holy hermit was badly shaken. Accordingly, he warmly shook our hands, albeit with some embarrassment. Accompanied by his and his family's best wishes, our elephants, with the heroes of this truthful narrative settled on their mighty backs, directed their heavy steps towards the high road and Jubbulpore.

———————

—XIX*—

As had been originally planned, the route of our pilgrimage of self-education lay in the North-West Provinces—this *status in statu* of Anglo-India, where the Viceroy is known but ignored, where his orders are received but are rarely carried out — provinces with a government that is despotic, suspicious and turbulent. But of this later.

In order to return to the Jubbulpore line, which we had left several miles from Nâsik, we had to go back to Akbarpur, then travel on country roads to the station of Sanevad, and take the train of the Holkar's line, which joins the great Indian Peninsular Railway. The great caves of Bâgh were but fifty miles away, to the east of Mâṇḍu, and a great attraction to us. We were undecided about taking the long way round and once more cross the Narbada. In the country beyond Khândesh, as in other places, our bâbû had "chums" which here actually means members of the same caste, and so we knew ahead of time that at Mâlwâ we would meet other omnipresent and serviceable Bengalî bâbûs, who are scattered all over the lands of Hindostan like the Jews in Russia. Also, our "regiment" was joined by a new recruit. The day before, we had received a letter from Swâmijî Dayânanda, brought to us by an itinerant and most

---

*[Misnumbered XVIII again in the *Russkiy Vestnik.—Compiler.*]

pious *sannyâsin*. It appeared that cholera was increasing daily at Hardwâr, and our collaborator whom we had not met personally, had postponed our meeting until the end of May, either at Dehra-Dûn, at the foot of the Himâlayas, or in Sahâranpur, some forty miles from the latter, where tourists are attracted by the cool charm of the surroundings.

In addition to the letter, the wanderer brought us, from the swâmi, a nosegay of the most curious flowers, which, I imagine, are totally unknown in Europe. They grow exclusively in a certain locality in the valleys of the Himâlayas, possess the wonderful ability to change their color after midday, and do not look withered when they dry. This charming plant (*Hibiscus mutabilis*) blooms between dawn and ten in the morning, while at night it appears to be nothing but a knot of pressed green leave. It is thickly covered with snow-white flowers similar to large white roses, which toward noon begin to redden, progressively becoming a deeper and deeper red, until towards four in the afternoon they become dark crimson like peonies. These flowers are sacred to the *Asuras*,* (a kind of *Peri* or angel in Hindu mythology) and to the God *Sûrya* (sun). The latter deity fell in love with an Asura at the creation of the Universe, and since then constantly whispers words of fiery love to the flower that shelters his beloved. But the Asura is a virgin and has dedicated herself from the beginning of time to the service of the goddess of chastity, the patroness of the monastic brotherhood. The love of Sûrya is in vain; Asura will not listen to him . . . Pierced with the flaming darts of the enamored god, the flower blushes and seemingly loses her pristine purity . . . The natives call this plant lajjâlu (the modest one).

We spent the night in the valley by a brook, having pitched our tents in the shadow of a figtree. The *sannyâsin*, en route to Bombay, had purposely gone out of his way in order to see us and to fulfill Svâmiji's request. He sat with us until long after midnight, telling us about his wanderings

---

*These *Asuras* should not be confused with those who are "demons," those whom the mythological history of India calls the first enemy to invade the land—probably the ancient Assyrians.

and the marvels of his native land, once so great, and of the heroic deeds of the old "Lion" of Pañjâb, Ranjît-Singh. Strange, mysterious characters are found among these pilgrims. Some of them are extremely learned, speak and read Sanskrit, apparently follow modern science and political events, and yet remain faithful to their ancient philosophical conceptions. Generally quite naked, except for a piece of yellow muslin around the loins (and that only by order of the police in the towns inhabited by Europeans), from the age of fifteen to the end of their days they walk from place to place, dying usually in advanced age, never giving a thought to the morrow, and living literally like the birds and the lillies of the field. They never take money, live on offerings, and are content with a handful of rice. All their worldly possessions consist of a small dry pumpkin to carry water, a rosary, a copper cup and a walking stick. *Sannyâsins* and Swâmis are for the most part Sikhs from the Pañjâb and are monotheists. They despise idol-worshippers and avoid them, though the latter very often use their titles.

Our new friend was a native of Amritsar, in the Pañjâb, and had been brought up in the "Golden Temple," on the banks of *Amṛita-Saras* (Lake of Immortality). The head *guru* or teacher of the Sikhs resides there. He never leaves the boundaries of his temple, where he spends his days in endless study of the *Âdi-Granth* — the sacred scripture of this strange, warlike sect. The Sikhs look upon him as the Tibetan lamas look upon their Talay-Lama. As the latter represents for the lamas the embodiment of the Buddha, so the Mahâ-guru of Amritsar is looked upon by the Sikhs as the embodiment of the founder of their sect, Bâbâ Nânak [1469-1538], although the latter, according to their ideas, never was a divinity, but merely a prophet inspired by the Spirit of the One God. Thus our *sannyâsin* was not one of the above-mentioned naked pilgrims, but a regular *Akâli*, one of the six hundred warrior-priests attached to the "Golden Temple" for the purpose of divine service and the protection of the Temple from the attacks of the greedy Moslems. His name was Râm-Ranjît-Dâs, and his outer appearance was in perfect accordance with his title of "God's warrior," as the brave *Akâlis* call themselves. His exterior

was very remarkable and typical: he resembled more a Hercules-like centurion of an ancient Roman legion than a meek
servant of the altar — even that of the Sikhs.*

Râm-Ranjît-Dâs approached us mounted on a magnificent horse and accompanied by another Sikh, who was
evidently either a servant or a novice, who in deference
stayed at some distance. The former was recognized by our
Hindu companions from a distance as an *Akâli,* owing to his
attire which was entirely different from the other natives.
He wore a bright blue sleeveless tunic, exactly like that seen
on the statues of Roman warriors; broad steel bracelets protected his huge muscular arms, and a shield was on his back.
A blue, conical turban covered his head, and round his
waist, instead of a belt, were several heavy steel circlets. The
enemies of the Sikhs assert that these sacred belts become,
upon occasion, more dangerous in the hands of an experienced "God's warrior" than any other weapon.

Is there anyone ignorant of the history of the Sikhs, the
most warlike and the bravest sect of the entire Pañjâb? The
word "Sikh" means "disciple." Founded in the fifteenth
century by the wealthy and noble Brâhmaṇa Nânak, the
new movement spread so rapidly amongst the Northern warriors, that in 1538 A.D., when the founder died, its followers
numbered one hundred thousand. At the present time, this
sect, closely knit by fiery religious mysticism and warlike
tendencies, is the prevailing creed of the Pañjâb. It is based
on the principle of theocratic rule, and its secret dogmas
are entirely unknown to Englishmen and almost so to
Europeans. Their teachings, ideas and rites are all kept and
carried out in greatest secrecy. All that is known is that the
Sikhs are strict monotheists, have no castes and recognize
none, eat everything that a European does and — a rare
exception among the Hindus — *bury* their dead. The second
volume of the *Âdi-Granth* teaches one: "to adore the One
God, to avoid superstitions, *to help the dead* [?], to lead a
strictly righteous life, and *to live by the sword.*" Govind-
Singh, the son of the Mahârâja, one of their great gurus,

---

*[H.P.B. refers at this point to her story *The Durbâr in Lahore,* in
Chapter II of which there is a description of the Sikhs.—*Compiler.*]

established the custom of never shaving their beards or moustaches or cutting their long hair, in order that they may be completely different from Moslems as well as Hindus.

After many desperate battles, the Sikhs, whose enemies were both Hindus and Moslems, emerged victorious. Their leader, the celebrated Ranjît-Singh, having secured supreme rule in Upper Pañjâb, concluded a treaty with Lord Auckland at the beginning of this century, in which his country was recognized as an independent state. But after the death of the "old lion," internecine troubles broke out among the Sikhs over this throne. Mahârâja Dalîp-Singh (his natural son by a public dancer) proved to be so weak that he allowed his Sikhs, who until then had been faithful allies of the English, to attempt to take Hindostan from them as they had once conquered border villages and fortresses in Afghânistân. The attempt ended disastrously both for the impetuous Sikhs and the weak Dalîp-Singh, who, in order to escape his soldiers and to earn the forgiveness of the English, became a Christian and was secretly sent to Scotland. His place was taken by Gulâb-Singh.* True to the promise and the political program of Ranjît-Singh, he refused to be a traitor, and as a reward received the charming valley of Kashmîr from the frightened English, and thereafter the Sikhs became subjects of the British like all Hindus.

This left the *Kûkis* — a branch from the broken old oak tree of Sikhism. The *Kûkîs* are a sect of the Sikhs, and the most dangerous element in the underground current of popular Hindu hatred. This sect was formed about thirty years ago by Bâlaka-Râma, and organized itself near Attock, in the Pañjâb, on the east bank of the Indus, where the latter, mingling with the waters of the Kâbul, becomes navigable. The aim of Bâlaka-Râma was twofold: to restore the religion of the Sikhs to its pristine purity and, at the same time, to organize a secret political body which would be ready for any emergency at a moment's notice. This brotherhood, consisting of more than 60,000 men, is united by some of the most terrible oaths and pledges: first, never to reveal their secrets, and second, never to refuse to act on an order

---

* [Not to be confused with H.P.B.'s travelling companion.—*Compiler.*]

from their leaders. In Attock itself, where there are not
more than two or three thousand people, including the inhabitants of the fortress, they are few. We were assured that
the *Kûkîs* are scattered throughout India. Their society is
so well organized that it is impossible to accuse them of any
unlawful act. Their leaders are also unknown.

In the course of the evening our *Akâli* presented us—not
from Svâmi Dayânanda, but from himself personally—with
a little crystal bottle filled with sacred water from the Lake
of Immortality. In case of pain, in the eyes or elsewhere,
he advised us to wet the ailing part with it, assuring us that
only a drop of it is enough to cure the most stubborn illness.
The water in the crystal jar was unusually clear and transparent. Either because the waters of the Amritsar *talav*
(reservoir) are constantly renewed by many springs, or
because of some other reason, the Lake of Immortality is
renowned all over India for its extraordinary clarity and
transparency, in spite of the fact that hundreds of people
daily bathe in it. When, later on, we visited this wonderful
lake, or rather a reservoir of 150 square yards, every little
stone and the smallest spot on it could be seen at a considerable depth, as if through the clearest glass. Amrita-Saras
is the most charming of all the sights of northern India.
The reflection of the "Golden Temple" in the crystal waters
of the lake is a fairy-like and rapturous scene. Only Aivazovsky could capture this picture on canvas.*

---

*[Reference is to the renowned Russian-Armenian painter, Ivan
Konstantinovich Aivazovsky, who was born at Theodosia, in the Crimea,
July 17/29, 1817, and died in 1900. He showed from early boyhood
unusual talent for drawing, and, through the influence of persons interested in him, entered the Academy of Art in 1833. He developed a
special aptitude for marine scapes, his first work being a study of "Air
over the Sea," which brought him a silver medal in 1835. From then
on he devoted himself exclusively to portraying the sea in its various
and ever-changing moods, a work in which his amazing memory of
what he had observed served him well. His journey through western
European countries in 1840, where he painted and exhibited, established
his reputation as an outstanding painter. His "Isle of Capri" (1843),
exhibited at the Paris Exposition, brought him a Fellowship in the
Academy of Art. In 1847, he became Professor of Art, and in 1857 was
decorated with the Legion of Honor. His exhibit in 1874 in Florence

We still had at our disposal seven weeks in which to travel from place to place, and could choose between the Bombay Presidency, the North-West Provinces and Râjasthân. Which to choose? Where to go? Faced with so many interesting places, like a well-known animal between its two stalls, we could not decide. We had heard so much of the palaces of Hyderâbâd and Golconda which transport the traveller into the fairy-like scenery of the *Arabian Nights,* that we began seriously to consider turning our elephants towards the Upper Sind going to Hiderâbâd, the territory of the Nizâm.

We wanted to see the "City of the Lion,"* which was built in 1589 by the magnificent Muhammad-Kulî-Kutb-Shâhî, who, surfeited with the world, grew weary even of Golconda and its fairy-castles and treasures. Hyderâbâd is famous for its edifices which are remnants of its past glory. According to Mir-Abu-Talib, the Keeper of the royal treasures, Muhammad-Kulî-Kutb-Shâhî spent the fabulous sum of £ 2,800,000 in the first years of his thirty-four-year reign on the embellishment of the town, though the actual work of construction did not cost him a single *pice* . . . Nowadays, with the exception of these reminders of greatness, Hyde-

---

aroused such enthusiasm that the Florentine Academy solicited his permission to paint his portrait for the Gallery of the Palace Pitti which houses the portraits of the most renowned painters since the Renaissance. His prodigious output resulted in several thousand canvases. Among his finest paintings mention should be made of: "Views of the Black Sea," "The Ninth Wave," "Chaos," "The Deluge," "Caucasus Range" and "Pushkin on the Shore of the Sea." Aivazovsky also became famous for his miniatures: he could paint with incredible speed and astounding perfection seascapes showing sailing boats, complete with their rigging and other minute details, and all on a canvas not much larger than an ordinary visiting card. He would leave this instead of his card whenever he called and found his neighbors away from home. A number of such miniature paintings were in the possession of various members of H.P.B.'s immediate family who lived at one time in the Crimea.—*Compiler.*]

Haidar means lion in Arabian, and *Âbâd*—an abode or settlement. Hyderâbâd was formerly known as *Bhâgnagar* (happy town), having taken its name from the favorite concubine of Muhammad-Kulî-Kutb-Shâhi, whose name was Bhâgmatî. The name of the town was changed on her death.

râbâd looks like a heap of rubbish and manure. On the other hand, eyewitnesses confirm that the "British Residency" is still renowned all over the country, and for good reason is called the Versailles of India. The history of this residency is very curious, and clearly portrays Anglo-Indian customs.

In 1788, no doubt imagining himself to be a caliph, *anch' io son' pittore* * — Residents are real caliphs — Colonel Kirkpatrick, an Irishman, at the time holding this lucrative position at the Nizâm's court, bethought himself to build a real Residency — of course at the expense of the ruler of Hyderâbâd. The edifice became one of the wonders of the world. It combines the enchanted gardens of Semiramis with the splendor of the French palaces of the period of the Regency. Twenty-two steps, each made of a single piece of rose granite, enormous in width, and adorned on both sides with huge sphinxes, lead to the portico, along the entire width of which gigantic Corinthian columns of pure marble rise to the upper floor of the main building. These columns are some eight inches higher than those of the famous "Hall of a Thousand Columns" in the Chidambaram Temple in the Madras Residency. The floors are of black and white marble. The Coat-of-Arms of the East India Company and of England are above every door; in some of these, pieces of real gold take the place of bronze lions. If the stairway leading to the portico is justly reckoned as "the finest and most gorgeous staircase in India," then the reception hall of the Residency may be the envy of any hall in the royal palaces of Europe. It occupies the full length of the façade of the palace, and on both of its sides stand, as in well-known cathedrals, two rows of marble columns. Just as in the Chidambaram Temple, where the "Hall of a Thousand Columns" is probably so called because it has 936, so the hall of this Residency is called the "Hall of a Hundred Columns," though it has only 32 in each row, making a total of 64 columns — quite a respectable number anyway. Apart from the columns with their carved marble and bronze workmanship, the hall has niches where statues of Hindu

---

* ["I too am a painter"—an expression attributed to Corregio on seeing a painting of Raphael.—*Compiler*.]

and Greek gods and goddesses have been placed — these, the production of the best Italian sculptors of the time. All the draperies are of purple velvet embroidered with gold. The furniture, of inlayed mahogany, is upholstered with the same material. Between the windows there are sixty mirrors, each of a single piece of glass the length of the whole wall, from ceiling to floor, set in the most expensive frames. The three chandeliers had been ordered from France for a fabulous sum of money, and the Hindus who built this palace worshipped them as gods. Such are the main features of this palace worthy of an Alladin, now used by the Residents, whose duty, according to the well-known excuse given by England when she took over the Indian provinces, is to stand as protectors of the downtrodden people and as mediators between them and the powerful râjans of India "who do not know how to rule." In the meantime, millions of people periodically die from *starvation,* while the lighting of the British Residency alone, on festive evenings, costs the Government, according to *official reports,* 1,000 pounds sterling a night . . .

Oh, Tartufe! Is not your name Great Britain? . . .

These, however, are mere trifles as compared to the past. In *A Handbook for Travellers in India,* by Edward B. Eastwick, we read as follows:

. . . . While the male visitors were received by the Resident, their wives were entertained by the Resident's lady, in a superb mansion attached to the Residency, called the Rang Mahall. This was built by Colonel Kirkpatrick, who formerly filled the office of English Minister at the Nizâm's Court. He married an Indian Princess, and built this palace for her abode. It was enclosed after the Asiatic manner by high walls, the centre containing a large marble basin filled with water, and fed by numerous fountains, lined with stately cypress trees. The pavilions, galleries, and terraces around were ornamented in the richest style of Oriental architecture, with a profusion of delicate trellis-work, painting, and gilding. As the entertainments were conducted in the Oriental fashion, Nâch [nautch] girls were commonly introduced, splendidly dressed; some of them have been known to wear £30,000 worth of jewels . . . .*

The glory of the East India Company, in the days when

---

* [Part I, pp. 83-84.]

its Residents were so "magnanimous" at the expense of the
princes, has now faded; now neither the Residents nor the
princes possess anything. Like the alchemists of old, the
English have melted all the gold of Hindostan in the hope
of finding the philosopher's stone of politics; they have even
ground into dust, burnt and reduced to cinders India itself,
this "most precious diamond in the British crown." They
will be lucky indeed if Afghânistân, instead of being "added"
for effect to their scorched diamond of India, does not grind
them into impalpable powder in its enchanted mortar . . .

Tales about the wonders of Hyderâbâd fanned our curiosity, and we felt an urge to see this wondrous land for ourselves. Both Nârâyaṇa and the Bâbû had been there several
times, and the former had relatives there. His stories and
descriptions had a special attraction for us, as he was acquainted with every corner of central India. His eloquent
narratives reflected with sadness all the great past of India,
great even as recently as the last century, when compared
with its present sorrowful condition. How low has this beauty
of the Orient fallen, she at whose feet yearned to sit all the
sages of Greece, and whose riches were envied by all the
rulers of the earth! . . . Trampled into dust, neglected,
everything in India is choked, withers away and disappears,
from the slightest national upsurge which is at once crushed
by jealous, suspicious England, down to the luxuriant virgin
forest . . . now felled by the hundreds of acres under the axe
of railway industrialists . . .

There was something unusually fascinating in these simple stories of the poor Hindu. Like the swan's last song, one
could hear in them the note of patriotism, crushed, restrained, to be true, but just as fiery as was the love for
their country of his glorious ancestors, a love which made
them sacrifice not only riches and their own lives, but even
those of their relatives, wives and children, to the glory of
the fatherland under the victorious banner of Śivâjî. In vain
do the English imagine that they have chosen a most prudent system of government, by means of strict measures and
Western education, on the one hand, and their disgusting
acquiescence in, and protection of, idol-worship. By means
of the former they successfully substitute positive atheism for

a false but nevertheless sincere religion; by means of the second they merely flatter the ignorant masses from whom they have nothing to fear. If there existed the slightest danger from these quarters, then the idol-worshippers, disarmed by them, would have long ago gained the upper hand over the hated *feringhees* and have drowned them in the sea — and this without any rifles or daggers, but with mere brass and stone idols sent here by the thousands every year from Birmingham. The danger, therefore, is from the educated patriots, whose most sacred feeling — love and devotion to the land — the English trample under foot on every suitable occasion. The more educated and trained the Hindu becomes, the more galling is the comparison of the present with the past.

Let us look at one of thousands of examples: the Hindus are especially proud of their ancient civilization, the glory of the land in the days when Europe was steeped in the darkness of the Stone Age. In the unanimous opinion of travellers and especially of antiquarians, the most interesting building in Hyderâbâd is the "Châr-Minâr," once upon a time a famous college in India, built [in 1591] by the Sultan Muhammad-Kulî-Khân on the ruins of a still more ancient college. It is built at the crossroads of the four main streets, on four arches, under which loaded camels and the turrets of the elephants pass freely. Over these arches rise several stories of the college building. Each story was once reserved for a separate branch of learning. Alas! Gone are the days when Indians studied philosophy and astronomy at the feet of their native sages. The many-storied edifice has been transformed by the English into a warehouse. The hall which served for the study of astronomy, and was filled with quaint, mediaeval instruments, is now used as a depot of opium; and the hall of philosophy contains huge boxes of liqueurs, rum, and the beverage of "widow Cliquot," prohibited by the *Qur'ân* and the Brâhmanas.

We had made final plans to start for Hyderâbâd, when some words from our cicerone and companions horrified us and disrupted all our plans. It would appear that during the so-called six "hot" months of the year, the thermometer stands in Hyderâbâd (Lower Sind) at 98° (Farenheit) in the shade, and the temperature of the water in the Indus reaches that of blood. As to Upper Sind, where the excessive dryness of the air and the aridity of the sandy soil make the climate of that land similar to the delightful temperature of an African desert, the thermometer reaches an unabashed 130° (Farenheit) in the shade. No wonder the missionaries experience only utter failure there; it is understandable that the most eloquent "description of hell" *à la* Dante, cannot produce anything but a "cooling" effect on the populace.

Realizing that no obstacle stood in the way of a visit to the caves of Bâgh, and that going to Sind was inconceivable at the moment, we regained our equanimity. Then, by general agreement, we decided to abandon the idea of any predetermined plan, and to travel as fancy led us. Accordingly, we dismissed our elephants the very next day, and a little before sunset arrived in *tongas* at the junction of the Wâgh and the Girna, two rivers famous in the annals of Hindu mythology, and as a rule conspicuous by their absence, especially in summer. Before us, like a monster crouching on the opposite side of the river, lay a mountain with four openings, as if blinking with its sunken black eyes in the dim mists of the twilight . . . These were the famous caves of Bâgh . . .

We could have crossed immediately with the help of a ferryboat, with a view to the more attractive plan of spending the night as we did at Kârlî, in the caves of ancient hermits, but our better judgment prevailed. Besides, our Hindus and even our *tongawallahs,* as well as the boatmen, refused point blank to accompany us; the former, because it was dangerous even in daytime to visit these caves without sending torch-bearers and armed *śikârîs* (hunters) ahead. This part of the domain of the Amjherâ râjan is overrun with wild beasts, especially tigers, which, not unlike the Bengalî Bâbûs, are met with everywhere in India. As to the boatmen, they protested on the ground that after sunset no Hindu would venture to approach within a mile of the caves. Only *belatti,* with their "silly geographical notions," would regard the Wâgh and Girna as merely ordinary little rivers; in reality they are the divine spouses, Śiva and Pârvatî. That was the first reason; and the second, the Bâgh tigers are no ordinary tigers, as the *saabs* think, but are the servants of the *sâdhus,* the holy wonder-workers, who have inhabited these caves for centuries; sometimes they are these very hermits themselves in the shape of tigers, and none of them, neither the gods, nor the *sâdhus,* neither the tigers nor their *were-shapes,** like to be disturbed at night . . .

There was nothing we could do about it. We cast one more sorrowful look in the direction of the caves, climbed again into our antediluvian carriages, and were off. The Bâbû and Nârâyana decided we would spend the night at the house of a certain "chum" of theirs, in the town of Bâgh, only some three miles from where we were.

Amazing and incomprehensible, like so many other things in India, is the geographical and topographical distribution of the numberless territorial possessions in this country. Political considerations seem to be always playing the French game of *casse-tête* here, forever changing the pattern, diminishing one part, adding another, taking away from the one, and giving it to another. What belonged but yesterday to this Râjan or Thâkur, is to be found today in the hands of some other. For instance, we were at the time in the *râj* or state of Amjherâ, in Mâlwâ, and were going to the little town of Bâgh, which also belongs to Mâlwâ and is included in the Amjherâ *râj.* Mâlwâ (as far as words are concerned) is an independent possession of the Holkar; yet the Amjherâ *râj* does not belong to Tukoji-Râo-Holkar, but to the son of the independent Râjâ of Amjherâ, who was, "by mistake," hanged by the English in 1857, at which time they "forgot" to return the râj to his heirs. The town and the caves of Bâgh belong, by a peculiar convergence of circumstances, to the Mahârâja Sindhia of Gwalior, who, by the way, does not personally own them, having made

---

*[The Russian word used here is *oboroten';* it defies any translation effort, but conveys the idea of "turning over," "turning into," and the like. The closest term in present day English is *were-animal,* from the Anglo-Saxon word *were* or *wer* meaning *man.* In connection with wolves the term of *werewolf* is of course the appropriate one, but it can hardly be used when tigers, leopards or jaguars are concerned, as is the case in the folklore of India, Assam, China and South America. —*Compiler.*]

a present of them, with their nine thousand rupees of revenue, to some poor relative. However, a certain Râjput
Thâkur took them from him and has not returned them.
Bâgh is situated on the road from Gujarât to Mâlwâ, right
in the so-called defile of Udaipur, and thus the latter is
owned by the Mahârânâ of Udaipur. Bâgh itself is built
on the top of a woody hillock and, being a disputed property,
does not belong to anyone in particular. But the small fortress, through the thick gates of which we presently drove,
and the bazaar inside, are the *private* possessions of a certain
"dhanî," the chieftain of the Bhilâlâ tribe, who was "a great
thief and robber," according to our Bâbû, and in addition
happened to be his "chum."

"But why do you take us to a man whom you consider to
be a thief and a robber?" we inquired timidly.

"He is a thief and a brigand only in a *political* sense.
Otherwise he is an excellent man and the truest of friends.
Without him, we would starve. The bazaar is his, you see,"
coolly replied the Bengalî.

The "chum" happened to be away, and we were received
by a relative of his who, we understood, was an assistant to
the *dhanî* (overseer). The garden was put at our disposal,
and hardly had our tents been pitched than people from all
sides began bringing us provisions. Each of them, on leaving
the tent, threw over his shoulder a pinch of betel and sugar,
an offering to the foreign spirits which were supposed to
accompany us wherever we went. Our Hindus begged us
not to *laugh* at any of this, saying it would be dangerous in
this out-of-the-way place.

It would have been useless to argue with these people.
We were in Central India, the very nest of all the superstitions of the land, and were surrounded by *Bhîls*. All along
the Vindhya range, from Yama on the west of the "dead
city," and throughout all Râjputâna, the country is thickly
populated with this tribe, the most courageous, robber-like
and superstitious of all the half-savage tribes of India. A few
words about them will be of some interest.

Orientalists think that the term *bhilla* comes from the
Sanskrit root *bil*, which means to fall away, to separate from.

Sir J. Malcolm thinks therefore that the *Bhîls* are sectarians who separated from the Brâhmanical creed and became outcastes. All this may be so, but their tribal traditions tell a different story. Of course, in this case as in others, history is tinged with mythology, and their genealogical tree can be traced only through a thick jungle of fancy. The absent *dhanî's* relative, who spent the evening with us, told us the following:

The *Bhîls* are the descendants of one of the sons of *Mahâdeva* (the god Śiva), by a lovely foreign woman with blue eyes and a white face, whom the god had met casually in a forest, on the other side of the *Kâlapâni* (black waters or ocean). Among the several sons born from this union, one, as handsome as he was vicious, killed the favorite oxen of Mahâdeva and was banished *beyond the sea,* to the Jodhpur desert. Exiled to its most remote southern corner, he married, and soon his descendants filled the country. They scattered along the entire Vindhya range, settled on the western frontier of Mâlwâ and Khândesh and later on the wooded and wild banks of the rivers Mahâ, Narbada and Taptî. They all inherited the beauty of their progenitor, his blue eyes and fair complexion and also his robber-like disposition and vices.

"We are thieves and robbers," naïvely explained the relative of the Bâbû's honest "chum," "because this was the decree of our forefather's father, the mighty Mahâdeva-Śiva. Sending him to the desert to repent, he (the god) told him: 'Go, cursed murderer of my innocent son, your brother, the bull Nardi.* Go and live the life of an exile and a brigand, a threat to your brothers . . .' How could we dare to disregard the orders of our great god? Our insignificant acts are

---

*It is strange that the bull *Apis,* the sacred animal of the Egyptians, is honored by the followers of Zoroaster, as well as by the Hindus. The bull *Nardi,* created by Śiva, is the emblem of life in nature, the son of the creating father, or his life-giving spirit. Ormazd creates the bull, and Ahriman kills it. Ammianus Marcellinus mentions in one of his works that a book exists in which the *exact age* of the bull Apis, the key to the mystery of creation and the computation of cycles, is given. The Brâhmanas also explain the allegory of the bull Nardi as pertaining to the continuation of *life* on our globe.

performed in accordance with the instructions of our *dhanîs*, and as these are the descendants of Nâdir-Singh, the first *Bhilâla* (the fruit of the union of the Râjput with a Bhîl woman), they are therefore looked upon by us as the direct intercessors between our people and Mahâdeva-Śiva . . ."

The authority of these "mediators" over the *Bhîls* is such that the most awful crimes are committed at a mere word from them. The tribe found it necessary to institute a council in every village, in order partially to restrain their power. This council is called *tadvi*, and sometimes succeeds in controlling the mad brigandage of the *dhanîs* or lords. However, their word of honor is sacred, and their hospitality knows no bounds.

The history and the annals of the Râjput princes of Jodhpur and Udaipur confirm the legend of the *Bhîl* emigration from their primitive desert, but nobody knows how they got there. Col. Tod is positive that the *Bhîls*, with the *Minas*, the *Maras* and the *Goands*, as well as the tribes which inhabit the Narbada forests, are the aborigines of India.* But why are the *Bhîls* so much lighter-complexioned and often blue or grey-eyed, side by side with the almost African types of the other hill-tribes? The fact that all these aborigines call themselves *Bhûmiputra* and *Vanaputra*, "sons of the earth" and "sons of the forest," while the Râjputs, their first conquerors, call themselves *Sûryavanśa*, and the Brâhmaṇas *Indu-putras*, descendants of the sun and moon respectively, proves very little. It seems to me that in the present case, their outward appearance, which confirms their traditions, is of much greater weight and meaning than philology. As very logically expressed by Dr. E. D. Clarke:†

---

* [*Annals*, etc., Vol. I, p. 526, ed. of 1894.]

† [Edward Daniel Clarke (1769-1822). English mineralogist and traveller, born at Willingdon, Sussex. Educated at Tonbridge and Jesus College, Cambridge. Travelled extensively in Europe, Egypt and the Middle East. Made important donations to Cambridge University, including a colossal statue of the Eleusinian Ceres. Appointed, 1808, to the professorship of mineralogy in Cambridge. Manuscripts collected by him during his travels were sold to the Bodleian library. He was one of the founders of the Cambridge Philosophical Society in 1819, and librarian to the university.—*Compiler*.]

By a proper attention paid to these vestiges of ancient superstition, we are sometimes enabled to refer a whole people to their original ancestors, with as much, if not with more certainty, than by observations made upon their language; because the superstition is engrafted upon the stock, but the language is liable to change . . .*

As of now, however, all we know about the history of these people is limited to the above-mentioned tradition and to the most ancient songs of their bards. These bards or *bhattas*, having settled in Râjasthân, visit the Bhîls every year, so as not to lose touch with the achievements of their countrymen. Their songs are history, as the *bhattas* have existed in the tribes from time immemorial, singing their exploits for future generations, this being their definite and hereditary duty. Let it be said, by the way, that there isn't a single tribe in India, however little of a war-like spirit it may have, but has its own native bards. The most ancient songs of the Bhîl *bhattas* point to a land "beyond the ocean," in other words, somewhere in Europe, as their origin. Some Orientalists, especially Col. Tod, seek to prove that the Râjputs, who conquered the *Bhîls,* are newcomers of Scythian origin, and that the *Bhîls* are the aborigines of India. In support of this, they present features common to both people, such as: 1) the worship of weapons — the sword, the lance, the shield and the horse; 2) the worship of, and the sacrifices to, the sun (which the Scythians, by the way, never worshipped, as their chief deity was the sword); 3) the passion for gambling (which is even greater among the Chinese and the Japanese); 4) the custom of drinking the blood of the enemies out of their skull (which is also practiced by some aborigines of America), etc.

This is not the place to enter into a learned ethnological discussion, yet one can hardly fail to notice how strange the reasoning of the scientists becomes when they have to defend some of their pet ideas. It is enough to remember how tangled and obscure the history of the ancient Scythians is, to realize how groundless it is to draw such deductions, merely on the foundation of the shaky historical data we

*Travels in Various Countries, etc., Part III, Vol. IX, Chap. ii, p. 41 [4th ed., 1816-24].

have, regarding the nations usually included under the generic term of *Scythians*. It is of course undeniable that there exists a great deal in common between the customs of the ancient Scandinavians, the worshippers of Odin (whose lands were actually occupied by Scythians more than 500 years B.C.), and those of the Râjputs. But this similitude gives at least as much, if not more, right to the Râjputs to point to *us* as "a colony of *Sûryavanśas* gone West," as for us to maintain that the Râjputs are "Scythians who emigrated to India." *

The Scythians of Herodotus and those of Ptolemy and Roman writers are two entirely different nationalities. The former gave the name of Scythia to the extension of land from the mouth of the Danube to the Sea of Azov (according to Niebuhr), and to the mouth of the Don (according to H. C. Rawlinson); whereas the Scythia of Ptolemy is a country exclusively Asiatic, including the whole of northern Asia between the Volga and Serikos (China). Furthermore, this Scythia was divided by the western Himâlayas, which the Roman historians called *Imaus*, into Scythia *intra Imaum* and Scythia *extra Imaum*. In view of such uncertainty, it may well be that the Râjputs are actually

---

*According to John Pinkerton, our contempt for Tatars would not be half as strong if we did not forget how closely related we are to them; that our forefathers came from Northern Asia, and that our customs, laws and mode of living were at first the same as theirs; in other words, that we are nothing but a colony of Tatars . . . . Cymrys, Kelts and Gauls, who conquered the northern part of Europe, are different names of the same tribe, whose origin is Tartary. Who were the Goths, the Huns, the Swedes, the Vandals, the Franks, if not separate swarms of the same beehive? The annals of Sweden point to Kashgar as the fatherland whence came the Swedes. The likeness between the languages of the Saxons and Kipchak-Tatars is striking; and the Keltic, which still exists in Brittany and in Wales, is the best proof that their inhabitants are descendants of the Tatar nation.

[John Pinkerton (1758-1826) was a Scottish antiquary and historian. He abandoned an early attempt in the profession of law and devoted himself to the study of poetry and ancient ballads, writing a number of works in that field. It is said that Gibbon formed a high estimate of his learning and historical abilities. Among his varied interests was geography on the subject of which he wrote the work entitled *Modern Geography digested on a New Plan* (2 vols., 1802).—*Compiler.*]

Asiatic Scythians and the Scythians — *European Râjputs.*

The present Râjput warriors, however, do not conform at all to the description Hippocrates gives us of the appearance of the Scythians: "The bodily structure of these men," the Father of Medicine tells us, "is thick, coarse and stocky; their joints are weak and flabby; their stomachs hang down; they have almost no hair, and they all resemble each other." Who, after having made the acquaintance of the warriors of Râjasthân, those well-proportioned men of gigantic stature, with their long hair and heavily bearded faces, would ever recognise them in the portrait of the Scythians drawn by Hippocrates? Besides, the Scythians, whoever they may be, *buried* their dead, which the Râjputs, judging by their most ancient annals, never did. The Scythians were a nomadic nation, and are described by Hesiod as "people living in covered carts and wagons and feeding on mare's milk." The Râjputs, on the other hand, have been sedentary people from time immemorial, inhabiting towns and having a history of their own at least several hundred years B.C. (before the time of Herodotus), and even if they celebrate the *Aśvamedha* (sacrificial offering of horses), they never touch "mare's milk" and despise the Mongolians. Herodotus tells us that the Scythians, who called themselves Scoloti, hated foreigners most of all, and chased them from their settlements, while the Râjputs are one of the most hospitable people in the world . . . Finally, history shows us clearly that the Scythians were at war with Darius (516 B.C.), and were then settled on their lands near the Danube. At the same epoch, the Râjputs were known to be in India and had their own kingdom. As to the *Aśvamedha* (sacrificial horse offering to the sun) upon which Tod bases his chief proof, reminding us that the Scythians also sacrificed horses — this rite is mentioned both in the *Rig-Veda* and the *Aitareya-Brâhmana.* According to Martin Haug, the latter was probably in existence some 2000-2400 years B.C.

I confess that this digression from the Bâbû's "chum" to the Scythians and the Râjputs of antediluvian times is a considerable one. To avoid putting the reader to sleep, I will now hasten to return to the caves.

While the local *śikârîs* under the leadership of the warlike

Akâli went to hunt for both real tigers and werewolves that may have been in the caves, our Bhîl got permission for us to be present at a wedding ceremony to be held in the town. A Brâhmaṇa was giving his daughter in marriage, and she was to be wedded that very day. These unfamiliar ceremonies were so interesting to me that the day went by like a flash. When we returned, it was too late to go to the caves, and so we postponed the trip until the next day. Meanwhile, I will describe the festivities we saw, the more remarkable because the rites of matchmaking, betrothal, marriage, etc., have not changed in India for the last two millenniums at least. They are performed according to the directions of Manu, and without the slightest variation upon the ancient theme. As far as its religious conceptions are concerned, India has crystallized, as it were, and whoever witnessed a wedding rite in 1879, saw it as it was celebrated in ancient Âryâvarta a thousand years before our present era.

—XX*—

A few days before we left Bombay we read two announce-
ments of marriages in one of the local newspapers: one was
the marriage of the heiress of a Brâhmaṇa, the other in a
family of fire-worshippers. The first announcement read:
"The family of Bimbay Mâvalankar, etc., are preparing
for a happy event. This respected member of our community, unlike the rest of the less fortunate Brâhmaṇas of his
caste, has found a husband for his granddaughter in a rich
Gujarât family of the same caste. The little Râma-bâi is
just *five* years old, her future husband is *seven*. The wedding
is to take place in two months and promises to be brilliant."
The second announcement referred to an accomplished
fact, and appeared in a Pârsî paper which strongly favors
reform and severely castigates its countrymen for their
"disgusting antiquated customs," especially early marriage. It justly ridiculed a certain Gujarât paper which ex-
travagantly described a wedding ceremony in Poona . . . The
happy bridegroom on this occasion, who had just passed his
fifth birthday, "pressed to his heart a *blushing* bride of two
and a half, entrusted to him by his mother-in-law"! . . .
The usual responses of the couple entering into matrimony

---

*[Misnumbered XIX in the *Russkiy Vestnik.*—*Compiler.*]

227

proved so indistinct that the priest of the Ghebers (the Mobed) had to address the customary questions to the parents: "Are you willing to have him for your lawful husband, oh daughter of Zarathusht (Zoroaster)?" and "Are you willing to be her husband, oh son of Ormazd?" . . . "The wedding preparations went off most successfully," sarcastically continued the paper, "the bridegroom was led from the room by the hand, in all the dashing appearance of his *toga virilis* and his tall turban, not unlike a sugar loaf, while the bride, who was carried in arms, greeted the guests, not with smiles, but with a dreadful howl, which made her forgetful of handkerchiefs and think only of her bottle, which she insistently demanded amidst frantic screaming, well-nigh choking under the weight of the family diamonds . . ." This was a Pârsî wedding, "which shows with the exactitude of a barometer the progress of our speedily developing nation," added the paper.

We laughed heartily on reading this, though we did not really believe that even in India there were such early marriages. We had heard of *couples only ten years old,* but it was the first time we had heard of a *two-year-old* bride. At Bâgh, we had an opportunity to become convinced of the measureless inventiveness of the Brâhmaṇas. No wonder they had established a law in ancient days which prohibits everyone, except the officiating Brâhmaṇas, from studying Sanskrit and especially from reading the *Vedas.* The *Śûdras* and even the high-caste *Vaiśya* were put to death in days of old for such an offence. The whole secret of this lies in the fact that the *Vedas* do not permit matrimony for women of from 15 to 20 years of age, and for men of age 25 or even 30. Having so arranged things that every religious ceremony should first of all fill the pockets of Brâhmaṇas, these parasites disfigured their ancient scriptures to suit themselves, and after gradually having burdened the Hindus with an endless series of rites, regulations, non-existent feasts, and the silliest of ceremonies, cunningly declared, in order not to be caught in a false interpretation of the sacred books, that it would be sacrilegious for anyone who did not belong to their camp, to read these books.

Among other "criminal inventions" (to use the expression

of Swâmi Dayânanda), here is one of the regulations from Brâhmanical books which is diametrically opposed to the *Vedas.* All over central India there is celebrated by the *Kadwâ Kunbîs* the so-called "wedding season" of the agricultural classes, to which belong all the *zamindars.* This season is celebrated only once in twelve years, but is nonetheless a field of abundant harvest for the Brâhmanas. All the mothers, both those of grown (*i.e.,* ten-year-old) children, and those of babes in arms, and even those of infants *not yet born,* are supposed to confer with the goddess *Mâtâ,* the patron saint of those newlywed — and this of course through her oracles, the Brâhmanas. *Mâtâ* is the patroness of all the four kinds of marriages among the Hindus: "the marriage of adults, of children, of infants, and of those *in utero.*" The latter is the strangest of all, because it is a gamble, and relies entirely on blind fate. Instead of the *future* fruits, it is *the mothers that are wed,* in other words those who are expectant.

Many a curious incident occurs as a result of these matrimonial parodies, but the Hindu national instinct is not disturbed by such unusual events. They remain calm and serene believers, showing on rare occasions only, and in most unusual circumstances, open antagonism for Brâhmanical institutions. Their faith apparently consists of a centuries-old fear in regard to the infallibility of the "elect of the gods," a feeling which unwittingly inspires both laughter and respect. As for the Brâhmana, as is well known, he will never allow provocation of blind and mocking fate to shake his dignity. If, for instance, *both wedded mothers* have boys, or if the newly-born are both girls, this is the will of Mâtâ; the goddess must have desired that, instead of a married couple, the two would be brothers or sisters, and their children, if they grow up, are acknowledged heirs to the properties of *both* mothers. In such a case, on order from the goddess, the Brâhmana breaks the marriage bonds, is paid for so doing, and the entire affair ends. But if the children are born of different sexes, then the bonds of marriage cannot be broken by anyone or anything, not even in cases of crippling, chronic disease or complete idiocy, in the case of either child.

In order not to have to revert to this subject, let me mention here some of the prevailing customs in India. With the exception of cases where the child is consecrated from the very first day of his life to one or another of the monastic fraternities, or is dedicated to one of the gods of the Trimûrti while still in the womb, no Hindu has the right to remain single. Religion prescribes matrimony for him so that he may have a son whose duty it will be to lead his deceased father into *svarga* (paradise), by means of certain obligatory exorcisms and prayers. Even the caste of *brahmachârins,* who take the vow of chastity, though they remain in the world and participate in worldly affairs, and thus are the only *lay*-celibates, are bound to adopt sons. The rest of the Hindus retain the state of matrimony until the age of *forty,* after which they have earned the right to leave the world, by consent of wife and family, and to seek salvation for their souls by retiring to the jungle and becoming ascetics. If a family has a crippled or otherwise defective child, this is no impediment to his getting married; all that is necessary is to find for himself a wife who is also crippled or defective. If his choice falls on a girl of his own caste, she must be a cripple, but in a different way. If, for instance, the bride-groom is blind, the bride must be either a hunchback or lame, she must not be blind too, or the other way round. But if the prospective husband is prejudiced and prefers a healthy and beautiful wife, he must make a *mésalliance;* in this case he cannot take a bride in his own caste, but is obliged to descend one step lower in the hierarchy of castes and to seek her outside his own circle; the latter will not acknowledge her and will not receive the unfortunate *par-venue.* All such exceptions depend, by the way, upon the family *guru*-Brâhmaṇa, inspired by the gods. So much for men.

But what a strange and incredibly unjust fate has befallen the women of India, in all that concerns their living conditions! The life of an *honest* woman, and especially of one who is pious and of firm faith, is one long series of fatal misfortunes. The more superior she is by birth and in social standing, the more wretched is her destiny. Only the *nâchnîs,* the dancing girls consecrated to the gods and serving in the

DELHI: MAUSOLEUM OF HUMÁYÛN

'ALÂ AL-DÎN'S GATE AT KUṬAB NEAR DELHI

temples (a hereditary position), can be said to be free and happy and live respected by others. They are *vestals* and the *daughters* of vestals, however strange the latter may sound. Hindu notions, especially on the question of morality, are quite original or, at any rate, "anti-Western," if one can express it that way. No one is more strict with regard to feminine honor and chastity than these people, but their Brâhmaṇas proved to be more cunning than even the Roman high priests and augurs. Rhea Silvia for instance, the mother of Romulus and Remus, was buried alive by the ancient Romans, in accordance with the custom of the vestals, for having committed her *faux pas,* even though Mars himself had taken an active part in it. Numa and Tiberius, as is well known, took every precaution to insure that the chastity of the priestesses would not become merely nominal. But the "vestals" on the banks of the Indus and Ganges are of a different mind on this subject from those on the banks of the Tiber. The intimacy of the *nâchnîs* with the gods (whom the Brâhmaṇas vicariously represent) cleanses them from every sin of the flesh and, at the same time, makes them above reproach and sinless. A *nâchnî cannot be* "a fallen woman," as other mortals may be, in spite of the crowd of "heavenly musicians" who swarm in every pagoda in the shape of baby-vestals and their little brothers. No Roman matron or even chaste Lucretia was ever held in such esteem for her good deeds, as is a *nâchnî* beauty covered with precious stones. This regard for the "favorites of the gods" is especially striking in the strictly native towns of central India, where the people have preserved intact their blind faith in the infallibility of the Brâhmaṇas.

But the fate of an *honest* woman of Hindostan is otherwise. Every *nâchnî* can read and receives the highest education, according to native standards. They all read and write Sanskrit and study the best literature of ancient India and her six chief philosophies, but specialize in music, singing and dancing.

Besides the "god-born" temple priestesses, there are also *public* nâchnîs, professional dancers, who, like the Egyptian "almeh," are available to others besides the gods, and these are also more or less educated. Hence, married women, afraid of resembling them, do not wish to learn what is taught to these despised creatures, who do not associate with the gods. If a Brâhmaṇa woman is rich, she spends most of her life in stupefying idleness; if she is poor, she fares still worse; her entire earthly existence is concentrated upon the routine and mechanical performance of rites. There is neither past nor future for her; only a tedious and monotonous present regulated by the clock and established centuries ago. And this only if everything is favorable, and she has good fortune and no family reverses. As to marriages based on love or free choice, no such question exists. The choice of her husband, limited as it is to her caste, is sometimes extremely difficult and, as a rule, very expensive, because in this country a wife is not sold, but her right to marry is bought. Accordingly, the birth of a girl is no joy, but a sorrow, especially if her family is not rich. She must be married not later than the age of seven or eight, as a girl of nine is considered an "old maid," is a discredit to her parents and is the miserable butt of all her more fortunate contemporaries.

If the English ever did any good in India, it is undoubtedly that they succeeded in suppressing, if not uprooting altogether, the terrible custom of *infanticide*. The killing of little girls was practiced almost universally throughout this country, but especially in central India, and this practice was prevalent among the tribes of Jâḍeja, once so powerful in Sind, and now reduced to petty brigandage. They were probably the first to introduce the practice. In ancient days this brutal custom — to dispose of daughters because of fear of having to arrange a marriage for them — was unknown to the Âryans. The ancient Brâhmanical literature shows that in the days of pure-blooded Âryans, woman enjoyed the same rights as man. Her voice was listened to in the state councils; she was free in the choice of her husband and was at liberty to stay single if she so chose. Many a woman's name plays a prominent part in the chronicles of the ancient Âryan land and has come down to posterity as that of eminent poets, astronomers, philosophers, and even sages and lawgivers. But with the invasion of the Persians in the VIIth century of our era, and later of the fanatical brigand-like

Moslems, all this changed. Woman became a slave, and the Brâhmaṇas took this opportunity of placing additional shackles on her. The position of the Hindu woman in the town is even worse than it is in the villages. Let us take a glance at some of the endlessly drawn out rites and rigmaroles.

The ceremonies preceding betrothal and marriage are exceedingly numerous and complicated. They are divided into three main groups: the rites *before* the wedding, *during* the wedding, and *after* the wedding has taken place. The first group alone consists of eleven required rites: asking in marriage; comparing the two horoscopes; sacrifice of a goat; fixing a propitious day by the stars; the invitation of the guests; building of the altar; purchase of the sacred pots for the household; sacrifices to the household gods; and, finally, mutual presents. All these must be accompanied by various religious ceremonies. As soon as the little girl becomes four years old, the father and mother send for the family *guru*-Brâhmaṇa, entrust him with her horoscope, which has been previously drawn up by the astrologer of their caste (a most important office), and send him to one who is known to have a son of appropriate age. The father of the little boy — advised beforehand — takes the girl's horoscope and, placing it before the family gods in the sanctuary, says: "I accept the *pânigrâha* . . . May Rudra (the Most High) help us!" * The matchmaker then asks: "When will the *lagna* (union) take place?" and bows out. A few days later, the father of the little boy gives the horoscopes of the bride and his son, the bridegroom, to his family priest, who takes them to the chief astrologer. If he finds them propitious — all is well; if not — the affair is dropped. The father of the bridegroom then sends the astrologer's decision to the parents of the girl, and the whole thing is forgotten. In a favorable case, however, the father and the Brâhmaṇa clinch the bargain on the spot. The Brâhmaṇa offers a coconut and a handful of sugar to the father, after which it becomes impossible to alter the promise, since the resulting Hindu *vendetta* would drag on for whole genera-

---

*Pânigrâha is a Sanskrit word meaning "hand in hand."

tions. After the sacrifice of a goat, the young couple is betrothed, and the astrologer fixes the day of the wedding.

All these ceremonies had been performed by the family
where we were supposed to attend a wedding at Bâgh. These
rites are especially sacred, and it is probable that we would
not have been allowed to be present at their performance.
We did see them later, however, in Benares, due to the
intercession of the Bâbû. The sacrifice of the poor goat is
most interesting, so I will describe it in detail.

A child of the male sex is sent to invite several "old"
married women (from 20 to 25 years of age) to attend the
worship of the household *lar* (the goddess-protectress of
the house) and spirits. Each family chooses a household
goddess of its own, which does not present any unusual difficulties since the gods and goddesses number 33 crores.
On the eve, a young goat is brought into the house, and
everyone lies down to sleep around it. Early next morning,
the reception hall on the lower floor is covered with cow-
dung, the favorite incense of Hindu goddesses. Exactly in
the center of the room, a square is traced in chalk in which
a high altar with the idol of the goddess is placed. Then the
goat is brought in and the patriarch of the family, holding
it by the horns, makes it salute the idol. Then the "old" and
young women, while singing marriage hymns, wash the
goat's feet, cover its head with red powder (the victim-to-
be butting all the while), swing a burning lamp under its
nose to drive from it the evil spirits, and finally step aside.
The patriarch then takes a bamboo fan, places some rice
onto it, and deceivingly puts it before the goat. Grasping
a sword, he then places himself on the right side of the goat,
and, as soon as the unsuspecting victim is occupied in grati-
fying its appetite with rice, the old man chops its head off
with a single deft stroke of the sword; holding it in
his right hand, he bathes the goddess in the warm blood
dripping from it . . . Everyone then sings in chorus, and the
betrothal is over.

The ceremonies with the astrologers, the exchange of
presents, and so forth, are too long to be described. Suffice
it to mention that therein the astrologer plays the double
role of a diviner and a notary. After a general invocation to

Ganêśa (the god with an elephant trunk), the marriage contracts are written on the reverse of the horoscopes; they are sealed and bear the name of the constellation propitious to the bridegroom and the bride. After this, a general blessing is pronounced. I will now pass to the wedding ceremony which we witnessed at Bâgh.

The bride looked to be about ten, and the bridegroom not more than fourteen years of age. The bride, seated on an elevated seat, wore a velvet skirt embroidered with gold, and covered with flowers and gold ornaments. Her small nose had a large golden ring threaded through it, with a brilliant stone which weighed her nostrils down. Her face was pitiful to see, and at times she cast furtive glances at us. The bridegroom, a stout, healthy looking boy, attired in a brocade coat, and wearing an Indra hat (*i.e.,* a turban made to resemble a many-storied pagoda), was on horseback, surrounded by a whole crowd of male relatives. The altar, already made, was erected on the steps of the house especially for the occasion. Its regulation height is three times the length of the bride's arm from the shoulder down to the middle finger, and it is made of bricks and whitewashed clay. Forty-six earthen pots, bleached and painted with red, yellow and green stripes (the colors of the Trimûrti) rose in two pyramids on both sides of the "god of marriages" seated on the altar, and a whole crowd of little married girls were busy pounding ginger in seven large mortars. When it was ready, the whole party of amazons rushed upon the bridegroom, dragged him off his horse and, completely stripping him, began rubbing him with ginger dipped in water. As soon as the sun had dried him, he was dressed again to the accompaniment of songs. While some of the girls were dressing him, others, armed with leaves of lotus twisted into tubes, sprinkled water over his head — an offering to the water gods.

We were told that all the previous night had been spent at the respective house of the bride and the bridegroom in performance of the culminating rites connected with the ceremonies begun several weeks before the wedding: invocation to *Ganêśa,* to the god of marriage, to the gods of the elements — of fire, water, air and earth; to the goddess of smallpox and other illnesses; to the spirits of ancestors and planetary spirits; to the evil spirits, the good spirits, and the family spirits . . . Suddenly music burst on our ears . . . Good heavens! What an infernal symphony! The earsplitting sound of tom-toms, Tibetan drums, Singhalese pipes, Chinese trumpets, kettle-drums and gongs on all sides deafened us, kindling in our souls hatred for humanity and its devilish inventions. *«De tous les bruits de monde celui de la musique est le plus désagréable»*, I recalled.

Fortunately, the agony did not last long, and we were rescued by the more pleasant choral singing of Brâhmaṇas and nâchnîs. The wedding was a sumptuous one, and so the "vestals" appeared in full array. A moment of silence, of restrained whispering, and one of them, a tall and beautiful girl with eyes big enough to fill half her face, began to run from one guest to another in perfect silence, rubbing their faces with her hand, and leaving traces of sandalwood and saffron powder. She glided towards us, too, noiselessly flitting over the dusty road with her bare feet, which were adorned with gold rings. Before we realized what was happening, she had daubed our noses — mine, the Colonel's and Miss B.'s — which made the latter sneeze loudly and wipe her face for the next ten minutes, while muttering and grumbling.

The Bâbû and Mûljî offered a more pleasant face to the little hand full of saffron and a smile of condescending generosity. As to Nârâyaṇa, at the very moment when, casting fiery glances at him, the vestal stood on tiptoe, ready to perform the *gulâl-pheṅknâ* * on him — he quickly drew away and with knitted brow half turned from her, getting his dose of saffron on his shoulder. The vestal frowned in her turn, but hiding her disappointment, merely gave him a scorching look and rushed towards Râm-Ranjît-Dâs. But here she met with even worse luck; his monotheism and his chastity offended, the "god's warrior" pushed the vestal so unceremoniously, that she was thrown against the vessels of

---

*[A Hindî term meaning "throwing gulâl" which is a particular colored powder which may be loosely called "saffron."—*Compiler.*]

the god of marriage, and nearly upset them. A dissatisfied murmur ran through the crowd, and we expected to be banished for the sins of the boisterous Sikh, when the drums suddenly rolled out again, and the procession moved on.

Leading everyone, the trumpeters and the drummers drove in a gilded cart, drawn by bullocks adorned from head to tail with flowers. They were followed by a group of pipers on foot, and after them came a third group on horseback hammering *gongs* with all their might. Following them came a procession of horses adorned with rich harnesses, feathers and flowers, two in a row, and bearing the relatives of the young couple. These were followed by a detachment of *Bhîls* totally without arms, since the English had just taken all battle armour from them, with the exception of bows and arrows. They looked as if they had a toothache, because of the way they had tied their white *pagrîs* up to their noses. After them walked ecclesiastical Brâhmaṇas, with aromatic tapers in their hands and surrounded by the flitting battalions of vestals, who performed their *glissades* and *pas* all along the way. These were followed by lay Brâhmaṇas, the "twice born." Then came the young bridegroom astride a handsome horse, on both sides of which walked two warriors armed with tails of *yak* (Tibetan ox) to chase the flies away. A naked Brâhmaṇa, perched on a donkey and holding over the head of the boy a huge Chinese umbrella made of red silk, brought up the rear of the bridegroom's group. Then came a cart drawn by bullocks, loaded with a thousand coconuts, and a hundred bamboo baskets strung on a red rope. The god who has marriage in his keeping rode in melancholic isolation on the back of an elephant led by its mahout on a chain adorned with flowers. Our humble party modestly advanced just behind the elephant's tail, and thus we closed the procession . . .

The rites performed along the way seemed endless. Extremely curious were the solemn "mantras" intoned before every tree and bush, every pagoda and tank, and finally before some sacred cows. When we returned to the house of the bride it was four in the afternoon, and we had arrived at six in the morning . . . Miss B. slept from fatigue and the

heat during most of the trip; the impetuous Sikh had gone
home long before and had taken with him Mr. W. and
Mûljî, whom the Colonel had nicknamed the "silent general," in memory of his surly President Grant. Our respected
leader was streaming with perspiration, and even the imperturbable Nârâyaṇa yawned and fanned himself. The Bâbû
alone looked as fresh as ever after a nine hours' walk, bareheaded, under the scorching sun of India; not a drop of
sweat showed on his dark-bronze face, which was as smooth
as satin! He bared his white teeth and played the jester,
declaiming verses from Stedman's *Diamond Wedding* . . .

The final marriage ceremony, after which the woman is
forever cut off from the external world, had just begun. We
kept our eyes and ears open and decided to observe everything more closely than ever. The bridegroom and the bride
were placed before the altar. With their hands tied by long
blades of *khus-khus* grass, the Brâhmaṇa led them three
times around the altar; their hands were then untied and
the priest mumbled a mantra. When he had finished, the
boy bridegroom lifted his diminutive bride and carried her
in his arms three times around the altar; then they both
walked three times around, the bridegroom preceding the
bride, she following him like an obedient wife. When this
was over, the young husband was placed on a high chair
by the entrance door, while the bride took a basin of water,
knelt at the feet of her future ruler, took off his shoes and,
having washed his feet, wiped them with her long hair —
a custom really most ancient, as we noticed. On the bridegroom's right sat his mother. The bride knelt before her also,
and, having performed a similar operation on her mother-
in-law's feet, she retired to the house. Then her mother came
out of the crowd and repeated the same ceremony on the
feet of her son-in-law and his mother, but without using her
hair as a towel. The wedding was over. The drums and tom-
toms sounded once more, and, half-deafened by them, we
started for home.

In the tent we found the *akâli* delivering a sermon to
Mr. W. and the "silent general," on the religion of "Nânak"
and all the soul-saving advantages of "Sikhism," as compared with the religion of the "devil-worshippers," as he

called the Brâhmaṇas. Our friend was right. Satan himself could not have devised, in his moments of genius, anything more unjust, more subtly cruel, than that which these "twice-born" infernal rascals had conjured up in regard to woman. *Complete, unconditional social death* is in store for her in case of widowhood, even if this occurs when she is but a five or three year old girl, and even in cases of betrothal, during which ceremony, as we have just seen, she is not even present, but is figuratively represented by the sacrifice of a goat. The male, on the other hand, has the right to have several wives, though it should be stated, in justice to the Hindus, that we have not yet heard of an instance of any of them having *more than one* wife, with the exception of the depraved princes and the Mahârâjas, trained in drunkenness and other charms of Western civilization by the Residents and their wardens, the English. In case of a widower, the man is required to enter into a second and even third marriage. No such law exists for the woman. For her, a second marriage is considered a great sin, an unheard of shame.

As I write these lines, agitators and opponents of the Brâhmaṇas have initiated a reform movement in Bombay, in regard to the remarriage of widows, and this is bound to shake the whole of orthodox India to its very foundation. It is now ten years since Mûljî-Ṭhâkur-Singh and other reformers raised this question (but only two or three individuals availed themselves of the opportunity. The struggle is one of life and death, a struggle that is silent and secret, but nevertheless fierce and obstinate. In the meantime, this is what every widow can expect; as soon as the corpse of her husband is burned, the widow must shave her head and remain shaved from then on. She is not allowed to wear any of her adornments; her bracelets, rings and necklaces are broken to pieces and burned together with her hair and her husband's remains. During the rest of her life, from head to foot, she must wear nothing but *white,* if she be less than twenty-five when widowed, and red, if older. The temples, religious ceremonies and society are closed to her forever. She has no right to speak to any of her relatives or to eat with them. She sleeps, eats and works separately, and her touch is considered impure for seven years. If a man, going

out to business in the morning, meets a widow first, he goes
home again and postpones his business for another day, as
meeting a widow is the worst omen. Caught in the false
interpretation of the *Vedas,* with the criminal intention of
burning widows in order to appropriate wealth, the Brâhmaṇas, unable any longer to carry out this cruel custom,
have revived the ancient precept which was but rarely put in
practice — and then merely in the case of *rich* widows refusing the last minute to be burned — and have applied it
to all widows indiscriminately. Powerless against British law,
they revenge themselves on the innocent and unhappy
women.

The story of how Professor Wilson caught the Brâhmaṇas
distorting the text of the *Vedas* and practicing deception
is most curious. For long centuries they cruelly burned the
wretched widows, appealing for justification to a certain
hymn of the *Ṛigveda,* and claiming to be rigidly fulfilling
the institutes of Manu, the interpreter of their revelation.
When the British government first declared its intention
to suppress the burning of widows, the whole country, from
Cape Comorin to the Himâlayas, rose in protest under the
influence of the Brâhmaṇas. "The English promised to uphold the policy of non-interference in our religious affairs,
and they must keep their word," was the general outcry.
Never was India so near revolution as in those days. The
English seeing that things were bad, did nothing. But Wilson,
the best Sanskritist of the day, did not consider the battle
lost. He searched the most ancient manuscripts, until he
became convinced that the alleged precept did not exist
anywhere in the *Vedas,* though in the *Laws of Manu,* the
infallible interpreter of the "revelation," it seemed to stand
out clearly, and had been translated accordingly by H. T.
Colebrooke and other Orientalists. The affair was becoming
embarrassing. An effort to prove that Manu's interpretation
was wrong would have been tantamount, in view of popular
fanaticism, to attempting to reduce water to powder. So Wilson set himself to study *Manu,* comparing the text of the
Vedas with the text of the lawgiver. And this was the result
of his labor: the *Ṛigveda* orders the Brâhmaṇa to place the
widow side by side with the corpse, *before* the pyre is lighted,

and then, after certain rites have been performed, *to lead her down from the funeral pyre* and loudly to sing to her the following verse from the *Rigveda* (X, 18, 8):

Rise up, woman, come to the world of living beings, thou sleepest nigh unto the lifeless. Come; thou hast been associated with maternity through the husband by whom thy hand was formerly taken.*

Then the women present at the burning rubbed their eyes with collyrium, and the Brâhmana addressed to them the following verse [*Rigveda*, X, 18, 7]:

May these women, who are not widows, who have good husbands, who are mothers, enter with unguents and clarified butter: without tears, without sorrow, let them first go up into the dwelling.†

It is precisely the last few words that were distorted by the Brâhmanas in the most cunning and subtle manner. The original of these words reads thus:

ârohantu janayo yonimagre.

which literally means: "first let the mothers enter into the womb of the altar" (*yonim agre—within* the altar). Changing one letter of the last word "agre," which they altered to "*agneh*" (fire), the Brâhmanas acquired the right for centuries on end to send the hapless Malabar widows into the *yonim agneh* — the "womb of fire." ‡

---

*[Horace H. Wilson's translation in the *Journal of the Royal Asiatic Society*, Vol. XVI (1854), pp. 201-14, in his essay entitled: "On the Supposed Vaidik Authority for the Burning of Hindu Widows, etc." — *Compiler*.]

† [Prof. Wilson's translation.]

‡ [We give below the transliteration in Roman characters of the original Devanâgarî of these two verses from the *Rigveda*:
 Imâ nâriravidhavâh supatnîrânjanena sarpishâ sam viśantu.
 Anaśravo'namîvâh suratnâ ârohantu janayo yonimagre (X, 18, 7).
 Udîrshva nâryabhi jîvalokam gatâsumetamupa śesha ehi
 Hastagrâbhasya didhishostavedam patyurjanitvamabhi sam babhûtha (X, 18, 8).

These are also given in the *Atharvaveda*, XII, 2, 31 and XVIII, 3, 57; there was a controversy between Colebrooke and Prof. Wilson about the translation of these verses, and Colebrooke was of the view that they gave authority for the practice of suttee (See *Asiatic Researches*,

Not only did the *Vedas* never permit the burning of
widows, but there is even a passage in the *Taittirîya-Âra-
nyaka* (VI, 10, 2) of the *Yajur-Veda* where the younger
brother of the deceased, or his disciple, or even a trusted
friend, in case no other relative exists, addresses the widow
in the following terms: "Arise, Oh woman! do not any
longer lie beside the lifeless corpse; return to the world of
the living, far from the deceased husband, and become the
wife of the one who holds you by the hand, and is willing
to become your husband." This verse shows that during the

Vol. IV, 1799,, p. 213). In doing so, he took the reading *jalayonimagne*
which is given by one of the commentators on law codes, Raghunandana, in his *Śuddhitattva*. This is a comparatively late work.

The reading which Prof. Wilson adopts and the translation he gives
of *ârohantu* . . . has the authority of the most famous of Vedic commentators, Sâyaṇa. None of the *Gṛihya-Sûtras* (ancient texts containing
procedures for ceremonies) nor *Dharma-Sûtras* (ancient law codes in
the form of aphorisms), except that of Vishṇu, gives any procedure for
suttee, which means that it did not exist then. But the later law codes
and then the commentators, including Raghunandana, began to pre-
scribe the use of these two verses for the performance of suttee.

There is a learned and interesting discussion on this complicated
subject in Dr. P. V. Kane's *History of Dharmaśâstra*, Vol. II, pp.
617-19 and 625-35 (Poona: Bhandarkar Oriental Research Institute,
1941). See also Dr. A. S. Altekar, *The Position of Women in Hindu
Civilization*, Benares, The Culture Publication House, Hindu University,
1938. Dr. Kane points out that Raghunandana could not have altered
the Vedic verse as thousands of people knew the *Vedas* by heart in
those days. Either the MS. of his *Śuddhitattva* is corrupt, or he made
an innocent mistake. He had no reason to change *agre* to *agne*, because
even the original reading had been taken as authority for *suttee* even
before Raghunandana's time by Aparârka and others. Dr. Kane points
out that the first verse has nothing to do with the widow but refers to
other women relations, friends, etc. As for the second verse, in ancient
times it was used to make the widow rise after she had been asked to sit
near the body of her husband, which might have had a symbolical
meaning or may have been a relic of pre-Vedic practice of suttee.
Later on the first verse was used in the suttee ceremonial which had
been created.

Cf. also John Wilson, *History of the Suppression of Infanticide in
Western India under the Government of Bombay*, 1855; Max Müller,
"Comparative Mythology," in *Chips from a German Workshop*, New
York, 1885, Vol. II, pp. 22 *et seq.*, and H. J. Bushby, *Widow-Burning,
A Narrative*, London, 1855.—*Compiler.*]

Vedic period a *second* marriage for widows did exist; and, furthermore, in several places in ancient manuscripts pointed out to us by Swâmi Dayânanda, we found orders to the widow "to gather and keep the ashes and bones of the husband for several months after his death, and to perform over them certain final rites..."

However, notwithstanding the complete exposure, and the scandal created by Professor Wilson's discovery, as well as the fact that the Brâhmanas had to bow to the double authority of the *Vedas* and *Manu,* the custom of centuries proved so strong that some *super*-pious Hindu women still burn themselves when they can. Only two years ago, on the death of Yung Bahâdur, chief minister of Nepal, his four widows insisted upon being burned. Nepal is not under British rule, and so the Anglo-Indian Government had no right to interfere.

—XXI*—

By four o'clock in the morning, we were crossing the rivers Wâgh and Girna, or rather, *comme couleur locale,* Śiva and Pârvatî. Probably, following the example of mortal couples, these "gods" must have been quarreling, as the crossing was certainly dreadfully rough, and our ferry, getting tangled in something at the bottom of the river, nearly upset us into the cold embrace of Mahâdeva and his snarling better half.

Like all the cave-temples of India, hollowed out by the ascetics, as I suspect, in order to test human patience, Bâgh caverns are at the top of an almost vertical rock. Since such inaccessibility does not prevent ordinary tigers, let alone werewolves, from reaching the caves and making their abode there, one would assume that this type of architecture was intended merely to tempt weak mortals into the sin of irritability. Seventy-two steps, cut out of the rock, covered with moss and thorny weeds, and with deep depressions, witnesses to the countless millions of pilgrim feet which in the course of two thousand years formed them—such is the main approach to the caves of Bâgh. Add to the delights of

---

*[Misnumbered XX in the *Russkiy Vestnik.* — Compiler.]

244

our ascent a number of mountain springs seeping through the stone steps, and no one will be surprised that we felt rather faint that morning under the weight of life and our archaeological difficulties. The Bâbû, who taking off his slippers, skipped over the thorns as lightly as if he had hoofs instead of human soles, laughed at the "feeble Europeans," and thus made us more irritated.

On reaching the top of the mountain, however, we stopped grumbling, realizing at first glance that we would receive ample reward for our fatigue. No sooner had we climbed a small terrace overhung by a projecting brown rock, than we beheld, through a rectangular opening about six feet wide, a whole series of dark caves. We were amazed at the somber majesty of this long deserted temple. Without wasting time on a closer observation of the ceiling over the terrace, which evidently served at one time as a verandah, or the portico with fragments of what used to be columns, like huge black teeth, protruding above us, and without stopping to examine the two rooms on either side of the old verandah, one with a brown idol of some flat-nosed goddess, the other with an image of Ganêśa, we ordered the torches to be lit, and entered the first hall . . . A tomb-like dampness met us. At our first word, everybody lowered their voices to a barely audible whisper. A hollow, prolonged and slowly dying echo made us all shudder with an uneasy feeling. "Devî! Devî!" exclaimed the torchbearers in humble and guttural voices and promptly threw themselves face down on the ground. In spite of the angry protest of Nârâyana and especially of the "god's warrior," they started then and there to perform a *pûja** in honor of the voice of the invisible goddess inhabiting the caves. The only light reaching the temple came from the entrance and made two-thirds of the hall appear by contrast as if plunged in still greater darkness. This hall, or central temple, is very large, eighty-two by eighty feet, and sixteen feet high. Twenty-eight massive pillars form a rectangle, six pillars in each face, and four corner pillars; four additional pillars prop up the center of the ceiling which, unlike Kârlî and Elephanta, is of heavily

---

*Ceremony of worship.

stratified rock, and would not otherwise be able to support at such great length the excessive weight of the mountain. The bases of the pillars consist of a plinth and two semi-circular toruses. The four middle pillars have rounded shafts with spiral ridges which gradually taper to the necks, changing from sixteen and eight-sided bands to square under the brackets, offering thus a very original and elegant appearance. Other columns, such as the two in front and back, are square to about a third of their height, then change from eight to twelve sides, and to circular with spiral ridges, then by bands of twenty-four and twelve sides to the square, ending under the architrave with elaborate ornamentation reminding one of the Corinthian style. Mr. W., a well-known architect by profession and an experienced artist, assured us that he had never seen anything more unique than these columns. He could not even imagine what instruments were used by the native builders to produce such results in solid rock. Just as is the case with all the other cave-temples in India, the history of which is lost in the darkness of the unknown, these are also ascribed by the Orientalist, Sir Wm. Erskine,* to the Buddhists, even though tradition points to the mythical Pândavas brothers as their builders.

Without mentioning the fact that Indian paleography contradicts by means of its newly discovered ancient inscriptions such an arbitrary conclusion, there exist many other reasons to doubt the correctness of the opinions expressed on this subject by the majority of English Orientalists. We shall mention but one of them now. Let us assume that the evidence adduced by the Brâhmaṇas is false, and that the Buddhists, as Stevenson and others would like to prove, professed their religion, built vihâras, and enjoyed

---

* [Sir William Erskine (1773-1852) was at first a lawyer's apprentice and went to India in 1803, where he practiced law. He was a member of Mountstuart Elphinstone's Committee for framing the Bombay Code of Regulations. He was especially interested in the Pârsîs and their culture. He returned to England in 1823. His literary works included a translation of Bâbar's autobiography from a Persian version (1826), and a *History of India under Bâbar and Humâyûn,* edited by his son in 1854.—*Compiler.*]

equal rights with other sects in India in the beginning of the sixth century of our era. On the other hand, however, the same Fellows of the Asiatic Society have decided long ago that the religion of Buddha, whose reform started precisely *against idol-worship,* had become distorted "not earlier than the fifth century." Prior to that time, as already shown, there was no Brâhmaṇa idol, nor could there be one, in purely Buddhist temples. How is it then, we may ask, that such a wealth of Brâhmanical idols exist in the cave-temples of Kârlî, Nâsik, Kânheri, etc., which came into being from the hands of the sculptor *simultaneously* with the walls of the building?

In the unanimous opinion of antiquarians, Kârlî was built between the third and the first centuries before the Christian era, certainly not any later than 95 B.C., and the caves of Nâsik in the first or second century of our era. Almost all of these idols are carved on the walls and form part and parcel of the cave-temples themselves. Would a Buddhist have dared in the first two centuries *before* and *after* our era to represent idols so contrary to the spirit of Buddha's teaching? The inscriptions found at Nâsik, as the antiquarians tell us, prove, for instance, that the famous monarch of Andhra, Gotamîputra, having conquered the king of Ceylon and driven out the Scyths, the Greeks and the Persians, founded at the same time a hospital for the sick and the handicapped, a school for archery, a college for the study of Buddhism, and another for the Brâhmaṇas, thus showing a very interesting example of love of humanity on the part of a tolerant and liberal ruler. This inscription proves also that: (1) the Buddhists lived in *friendly* relations (!?) with the Brâhmaṇas before being driven out of India and enjoyed the same rights with them, and (2) that gradually having accepted from the Brâhmaṇas their political views, they reverted to their former beliefs, merely adding Buddha to their idols, etc.

But this did not occur any earlier than the fifth century, you inform us!—Yes, not any earlier.—But the cave-temples, filled from top to bottom with Brâhmanical idols, were built, according to your own estimate, between the third century B.C. and the second century A.D.? — Certainly, we are unanimously agreed on that. How, then, do you *reconcile* the contradiction between the two *facts?*—We simply do not undertake that task, they tell us; we, authorities, determine and establish without appeal, and we leave it to others to explain away the seeming inconsistencies . . .

Cum grano salis, indeed! They give us the right to explain to them or to ourselves, but if the explanation deviates ever so slightly from their infallible conclusions, the one so explaining is at once branded as an ignoramus, and his criticism is paraded before the world as an insult to science. *Et c'est ainsi qu'on écrit l'histoire* (especially in India). It is likely that the same fate awaits the present modest remarks. Some of the Russian archaeologists will rise against the opinion advanced by us (*i.e.,* the opinion of native archaeologists), as it is diametrically opposed to that of Fergusson and the other great European oracles, concerning the cyclopean structures of archaic times.

In order to show once and for all the value of the opinions of that beacon-light among British architects, I will bring forward one more example. This great architect, but very mediocre archaeologist, proclaimed at the beginning of his scientific career, and does so now, that "all the cave-temples of Kânheri were built, *one and all,* between the fifth and the tenth centuries." That was his verdict. But unexpectedly Dr. James Bird, during his excavations in these caverns, found on a monument erected by Buddhists in one of their temples known as *tope,* a brass plate bearing an inscription. No complaint could be made against the fact that the inscription was a bit worn, since it stated in Sanskrit, as clearly as could be, that this *tope* was erected in homage to the *old* temple at the beginning of the year 245 (according to the Hindu astronomical era). According to Prinsep and Dr. Stevenson, this date coincides with the year 189 of the Christian era and thus irrevocably settles the problem, if not of the date of the structure itself, then at least of the year when the offering was made, therefore at a time when the cave was already looked upon as an *old temple,* as the inscription says. But to this Fergusson, without embarrassment, replies that *for him* old inscriptions *prove nothing at all* in problems of chronology, as they might be *lying,* and that he, Fergusson, "bases his views and conclusions concerning the antiquity of ruins *not upon inscriptions,* but upon architectural cannons and rules, discovered by himself."

At the present time, an argument rages between Fergusson and a doctor of law, the well-known Bâbû Râjendra Lâla Mitra of Calcutta, who is recognized in London as a most scholarly Indian archaeologist and antiquarian.* Râjendra Lâla points out that the "canons" fished by the esteemed English architect from the depths of his speculative knowledge cannot be applied to such ancient temples, often of an *unknown* architectural style, as are the "cave-temples" of India. Therefore, even my own voice, reflecting but little knowledge, has a right to proclaim that the proverb *vox et praeterea nihil* may be applied even to the voice of certain "authorities." And now, strengthened by this rather easy defeat of the opponents, I may say on my own authority that the theory which states that the Buddhists allegedly reverted to idol-worship, and that, therefore, the temples are Buddhist, contradicts the history of both the Buddhists and the Brâhmaṇas. The latter began to persecute and drive out of India the former precisely because they *opposed idol-worship.* As has already been shown above, those among them who fell away from the reform of the pure, though perhaps at first glance atheistic, teachings of Gautama Siddhârtha, remained in India; little by little they became mixed with the Jainas and later completely merged with them. And, of course, it is not these sectarians of the fifth century who built the temples some two or three hundred years B.C. It is not the Buddhists who became Brâhmaṇas, but rather

---

* [Râjâ Râjendralâla Mitra (1824-91). Hindu scholar and antiquarian educated at the Calcutta Medical College. Soon devoted entire attention to mastering Sanskrit, Greek, Latin, German and French. At twenty-two appointed assistant secretary and librarian of the Asiatic Society of Bengal, of which he became the President in 1885. Played prominent part in the second National Indian Congress. Through individual merit rose to the title of Râjâ in 1888, and became one of the most learned men in India at the time. Has written innumerable scholarly essays in the *Journal* of the Asiatic Society, and translated various Sanskrit texts for the *Bibliotheca Indica* Series. He was a Fellow of the Eastern Section of The Theosophical Society.—*Compiler.*]

the latter who followed the Buddha by the hundreds of
thousands. In such a case, why not rather suppose that if,
among hundreds of Brâhmanical gods, we find the figure
of Buddha * sometimes in the same temple, the latter instead
of being a Buddhist temple, is a Brâhmanical one, where the
builders—half-converts to Buddhism—added a statue of
Buddha—just another god—instead of imagining the contrary, which is quite illogical?

Moreover, though we examined more than once almost
all the chief so-called Buddhist "vihâras" of India, we never
met with one statue of the Buddha which could not have
been added at a later epoch, were it one year or a thousand
years after the construction of the temple. Not trusting our
own conclusions entirely, we took with us Mr. W., a well-
known and experienced architect, and we found everywhere,
in whatever temple it may have been, the Brâhmanical idols
forming a harmonious whole with the structure itself,
whereas the statues of Buddha were in almost every case as
if *added to it*, as for instance at *Chaitya-Gṛiha* in the temples
of Kânheri. Out of thirty or forty caves at Ellora, all filled
with idols, there is only one, the temple of the *Tri-Lokas,*
or "three worlds," which contains, instead of idols, statues
of Buddha and of Ânanda, his favorite disciple. There is a
direct inference in this case that this is a Buddhist vihâra.
It would be curious to learn the opinion of Professor Minayev concerning these caves, after his trip to India.

Directly opposite the entrance, a door leads to another
hall which is oblong, with two hexagonal columns and with
niches on the sides, containing statues, in a fair state of preservation, of goddesses ten feet and gods nine feet high.
Behind, a doorway leads into a room with an altar, which
is a regular hexagon, having sides three feet long, and protected by a cupola cut in the rock. No one ever has gained
admittance here, nor is admitted now, except those initiated
into the mysteries of the *adytum.* Cells of former priests

---

* All the figures of Gautama the Buddha are in sharp contrast with
the idols because of the invariable gesture: the right hand is raised
and has its palms outwards, representing the Buddha with two fingers
blessing the people.

surround it; there are about twenty of them. Having examined the altar, we were about to proceed further, when the Colonel, taking a torch from the hand of one of the servants, went with two others to look into the side-rooms. A few minutes later we heard his voice, loudly calling us from the second cell. He had found a secret passage and was shouting: "Let's go further! . . . We must find out where it leads to!"

"Maybe into the den of one of the werewolves! . . . Look out, Colonel, beware of tigers!" shouted the Bâbû.

But once started on the road to "discoveries," our President was not to be stopped. We responded to his call.

He had actually made a discovery, and upon entering the cell we beheld a most unexpected sight . . . Against the wall opposite to the entrance, two torchbearers stood motionless, as if transformed into stone caryatides, and from the wall itself, about five feet above the ground, protruded two legs clad in white trousers. There appeared to be no body attached to them for it had disappeared. Were it not for the fact that the legs were jerking we might have thought that the wicked "devî" inhabiting the cave had cut the Colonel into two halves and, having caused the upper part instantly to evaporate, had stuck the lower half to the wall as a token of her might.

"What have you gotten into, Mr. President?" was our unanimous outcry.

Instead of an answer, the legs became more agitated than ever and finally disappeared inside the wall; after this we heard his voice, as if it were coming through a long pipe:

"A room . . . a secret cell! . . . Come up, all of you! . . . There is a whole row of rooms . . . Here goes my torch! . . . Bring in some matches and another torch! . . ."

This was, however, easier said than done. The torchbearers refused point-blank to climb up there, and very nearly ran away in fright. Miss B. glanced with squeamishness at the wall covered with soot and then at her dress. Mr. W. sat down on a stone which had broken off a pillar and decided he would go no further, but would wait for us, while having a cigar in the company of the timid torch-bearers. There were several vertical steps cut in the wall at a later date than the cave itself, and on the floor there lay a large stone cut in an irregular shape which corresponded to the hole in the wall. The Bâbû explained in his picturesque language that this was the "stopper" of the secret passage. Examining it most carefully, we came to the conclusion that the mason-builders had intended to make it similar to, and even indistinguishable from, the unevenness of the rudely cut wall. We also found on it a sort of rod which was probably used to turn the stone around when there was occasion to open this entrance.

The first to climb into the hole, which measured about three feet in height and not over two feet in width was our muscular "God's warrior." As the hole came to about the middle of his chest when he stood on the broken piece of the column, our Pañjâbî Yeruslan Lazarevich* had no special difficulty in climbing up. He was followed by the Bâbû, who jumped with the agility of a monkey and, carrying a torch with him, lighted the whole room. Then, with the help of the *Akâli* pulling from above, and Nârâyaṇa pushing from below, I was safely made to negotiate the passage, though I got stuck in it for a while and badly scraped my hands against the wall. However trying archaeological explorations may be for a person of my weight, I felt confident that with two such Hercules-like fellows as Râm-Ranjît-Dâs and Nârâyaṇa, I could safely set out even for the summit of the Himâlayas. The last to climb up were Miss B., who nearly swallowed a heap of little stones and dust which fell into her invariably open mouth, and, after her, Mûljî. As to W., he remained hehind, preferring, this time, the cleanliness of his white trousers to the inspection of the sacred places of immemorial antiquity.

The secret cell proved to be a room of twelve feet square. Straight above the hole on the floor, on the opposite wall, and under the very ceiling, there was another similar open-

---

*[A hero of an old Russian tale from the seventeenth century known for his prowess and strength. It is most likely that the tale has an Iranian origin and the figure of Yeruslan has been adapted from Rustam, the legendary hero of the Persian epic *Shâh Nâmah* of Firdauzî.—*Compiler.*]

ing, though this time we did not find any "stopper." The cell was entirely empty except for black spiders as big as crabs. Our appearance, and especially the light which probably blinded them, produced a regular panic among them; they scrambled in hundreds over the walls, hung in mid-air, then fell on our heads. Miss B.'s impulse was to kill them, but this time the four Hindus strongly and unanimously protested against such an intention. The English lady was peeved and irked at this:

"I thought you were a reformer," she sneeringly remarked, addressing Mûljî, "but you are as superstitious as any idol-worshipper."

"Above all else I am a Hindu," replied the "silent general." "The Hindus consider it sinful before nature and before their own conscience to deprive of life any creatures instinctively running away from the strength of man, be it even a dangerous animal, let alone such a harmless one as is the spider."

"You are probably afraid of having to transmigrate into a black spider!" she retorted angrily.

"Hardly, but in case of necessity I would rather transmigrate into a black spider than into an Englishman," sharply replied Mûljî.

We laughed, all except the patriotic old maid. This time she was really angry and, under the pretense of being dizzy, she made her descent through the hole. We were getting tired of her, and so no one pressed her to stay.

As to us, we climbed through the second opening, this time under the leadership of Nârâyana. He had been here before and told us, in this connection, a very curious story. He assured us quite seriously that such rooms, one on top of the other, continue to the very summit of the mountain. Then they take a sudden turn and gradually descend to a huge underground dwelling—a regular cave-palace inhabited at times by râja-yogins. Wishing to leave the world for a time, and to spend a few days in isolation, the râja-yogins find these in this underground dwelling. Our president looked askance at Nârâyana through his spectacles, but remained silent. The Hindus did not contradict him.

The second cell was exactly like the first and had a similar opening in it. Through it we reached the third and sat
for a while to rest. Here I felt that breathing was becoming
difficult for me, but I decided that I was merely out of
breath and tired, so did not mention it to my companions,
and we started to climb into the fourth cell. The passage
into this one was about two-thirds filled with earth and
small stones, and we spent some twenty minutes clearing
it, before being able to crawl through it. As Nârâyaṇa had
told us, the cells were each one higher than the other, and
the floor of the one above was on the level of the ceiling of
the last. The fourth cell was in ruins, but two broken pillars
formed stepping-stones at the entrance of the fifth cell and
seemed to present but little difficulty. Here, however, the
Colonel stopped Nârâyaṇa, who had already started climbing, and declared that the time had come to hold a council,
or to "smoke the pipe of peace," as the red Indians say.

"If Nârâyaṇa is telling us the truth," he said, "our going
up and up in this fashion, from one opening to the next, may
continue until tomorrow morning."

"I told you the truth," said Nârâyaṇa almost solemnly.
"But since my previous visit here, I have heard that several
of the passages are now clogged, and this is the case with
the one in the next cell."

"Well, then there is no use trying to go any further. But
who has filled the passages? Or have they been crumbled
by the hand of time?"

"No . . . they have been filled on purpose. *They* . . ."

"Who are *they*? Or do you mean the werewolves?"

"Colonel!" said the Hindu with some effort — and one
could see by the gradually diminishing light of the torches
that his lips were trembling and that his face grew pale —
"Colonel . . . I am serious, I am not joking."

"I am not joking either. But who are *they*?"

"The *Brothers* . . . The *Râja-Yogins*. Some of them live
not far from here . . ."

The Colonel coughed, rearranged his spectacles, remained
silent for awhile, and finally remarked with a noticeable displeasure in his voice:

"Look here, my dear Nârâyana, I do not think that your intention is to mystify us . . . But do you really want to make us believe, or believe yourself, that anyone in this world, be it even an ascetic intent on finding salvation in the jungles, could live in a place that even the tigers do not frequent, and where even the bats are absent, on account of lack of air? Just look at our torches . . . Another couple of rooms like this — and we will suffocate!"

Sure enough, our torches were about to go out, and I found it more and more difficult to breathe. The men were breathing heavily, and the *Akâli* was loudly snorting.

"Nevertheless, I speak holy truth; *They* live further up — I have been there myself."

The Colonel grew thoughtful and stood near the opening, evidently undecided.

"Let's go back!" suddenly shouted the *Akâli,* "my nose is bleeding."

At this very moment, something happened to me that was quite unexpected and very strange. I felt all at once very dizzy and fell, rather than sank, half-conscious on the fragment of the pillar, right in front of the opening to the fifth cell. Another moment, and I felt an indescribably delicious, wonderful sense of rest, in spite of a dull pain beating in my temples. I vaguely realized that this was no mere threat of a faint, but that I had actually fainted, and that in a few moments I would die, if not taken out into the open air. And yet, even though I could not move a finger, nor utter a sound, there was no sense of agony and not a particle of fear in my soul — merely an apathetic, but unutterably pleasant feeling of rest, a complete quiescence of all the senses except hearing. For a moment I must have lost consciousness completely, and I remember how, just before, I had intently listened to the dead silence around me. Is this death? — was the thought that flashed vaguely through my mind. Then I felt as if mighty wings were fanning me from above. "Kind wings, kind, caressing, lovely wings," were the recurring words in my brain, beating like the regular movements of a pendulum, and for no reason I laughed inwardly at these words. Then I began to detach myself from the pillar and *knew* rather than *felt* that I was falling

down and down into some kind of abyss, amidst the hollow
rumblings of distant thunder. Suddenly a loud voice resounded near me, and I rather felt it than heard it with
my ear . . . There was something tangible in it, something
that instantly stopped my helpless descent, and kept me from
falling any further. This was a voice I had known for a
long time, a now familiar voice, but I had no strength at
the time to recognize to whom it belonged. Amidst the
thunder, this voice resounded rather angrily from a far
distance, as if from under the sky itself, and shouted in
Hindi:

"Tumâre yûṃ ânekâ kyâ kâm thâ?"—"What business
had you to come like this?" and all was silence again . . .

•　•　•　•　•　•　•　•　•　•　•　•

How they dragged me through five narrow holes will forever remain a mystery to me . . . I came to on the verandah
below, where the wind was blowing from all sides, and as
suddenly as I had collapsed in the foul air of the upper cell.
When I recovered completely, the first thing I saw was a
tall, powerful figure, clad from head to foot in white, with
a raven black Râjput beard, leaning over me. As soon as I
recognized the owner of the beard, I could not help expressing my feeling of sincere joy by exclaiming: "Where did
you come from?" It was our friend, Ṭhâkur Gulâb-Lal-Singh,
who, having promised to join us in the North-West Provinces, now appeared to us in Bâgh, as if falling from the sky
or growing out of the ground.

Indeed one could have expressed curiosity and have asked
how it was that he happened amongst us, and where he
came from, especially as I was not the only one surprised
at his presence. But my unfortunate fainting spell, and the
pitiable condition of the rest of the underground explorers,
were enough to discourage any immediate questioning. On
one side of me, Miss B. forcibly used my nose as a cork for
her bottle of *sal ammoniac;* on the other, the "God's warrior"
covered with blood as if actually having fought the Afghâns;
further on, Mûljî with a dreadful headache. Only the Colonel and Nârâyaṇa escaped with merely slight dizziness. As

for the Bâbû, no carbonic acid gas, it would seem, could put an end to him, no more than the fierce rays of the sun which were killing others on the spot; they both somehow or other glanced off his invulnerable Bengalî coat of skin. He was merely hungry . . . At long last, after a variety of confused exclamations, interjections and explanations, I was able to learn the following:

At the moment when Nârâyaṇa, being the first to notice that I had fainted, rushed to me and dragged me back towards the passage, the voice of the Ṭhâkur suddenly resounded from the upper cell and struck them with amazement. Even before they recovered from their surprise, Gulâb-Singh had jumped out of the upper passage, lantern in hand, and leaping down the next opening called to them to "hand him the bâi" (sister).* This "handing down" of such a heavy object as my ponderous body, and the whole of the proceedings as then pictured in my imagination, made me laugh heartily. Miss B., however, considered it her sacred duty to be hurt by this, even though nobody paid any attention to her. Passing their half-dead load from hand to hand, they hurried to join the Ṭhâkur, but the latter, according to their story, was able to act without their help, despite the difficulty presented by such a burden. By the time they succeeded in getting through one passage, Gulâb-Singh was already at the next; descending into one cell, they were just in time to see his waving white *sadra* disappearing in the passage leading to the next.

The Colonel, who is accurate to the point of pedantism and meticulous in all his observations, could not conceive how the Ṭhâkur could have managed to pass my almost lifeless body so dexterously from one end to the other of all these narrow openings! "He could not have thrown her down the passage before going in himself, or she would have broken her bones," he mused. "And it is still less possible to imagine that, descending first himself, he dragged her after him. Inconceivable! . . ." This idea harassed the Colonel for a long time, until it became something like the

---

* All our friends here, both Hindus and Buddhists, call us "brothers" and "sisters."

puzzle of which came first, the egg or the bird? As to the Ṭhâkur, he simply shrugged his shoulders when questioned closely, and replied that he did not remember. He said that he simply carried me out of the cells as fast as he could and did so the best way he could, that all the others were following him and therefore surely must have seen him, and that in moments when every second counts "people do not think, but act," and so forth.

All these considerations, however, and the difficulty of explaining the method of my removal, were questions that arose when there was time to think over what had occurred. As for the present moment, nobody could understand how Gulâb-Lal-Singh appeared at that particular moment and whence he came. When they all were down, they saw me lying on the carpet of the verandah. The Ṭhâkur was giving orders to two servants who had arrived on horseback from around the mountain, while Miss B., in an attitude of "graceful despair," her mouth wide open, stared with bulging eyes at Gulâb-Lal-Singh, whom she probably regarded quite seriously as being a "materialized spirit."

However, the explanation our friend gave us seemed at first quite simple and natural. He was at Hardvâr when Svâmi Dayânanda sent us a letter which postponed for a while our going to meet him. On arriving from Jubbulpore in Khandwâ by the Indore Railway, he had visited the Holkar on business, and, learning we were here, he decided to join us sooner than he had expected. Reaching Bâgh late the night before, he did not want to disturb us then, and learning that we would start for the caves in the morning, he went there quite early in order to meet us. And that was the whole mystery . . .

"The whole mystery?" exclaimed the Colonel. "Did you know beforehand that we would climb up into the cells, and so went there to wait for us?"

Nârâyaṇa was hardly breathing and was looking with almost insane eyes at the Ṭhâkur. But the latter did not even move a brow.

"No, I did not. But while waiting for you, I went to look at the cells which I had not seen for some time. I spent more time there than I expected and so missed meeting you . . ."

"The Ṭhâkur-Sâhib was most likely enjoying the fresh air of the cells," suggested the Bâbû mischievously, showing his white teeth in a grin.

Our president slapped himself on the forehead and jumped up.

"Exactly! And how could you have stood it for so long? How did you reach the fifth cell when the passage into the fourth was nearly closed and we had to dig it out?"

"There are other passages leading to them. I came by an inner passage long known to me," calmly replied Gulâb-Singh, smoking his *gargarî*. "Not everyone follows the same pathway," he added slowly and somewhat strangely, looking fixedly at Nârâyana, who almost cowered under his fiery glance. "However, let us go and have lunch in the next cave, where everything should be ready for us. Fresh air will do all of you good . . ."

Leaving the main cave, we found another similar one some twenty or thirty feet south of the verandah, which could be reached by a narrow ledge along the rock. Our Ṭhâkur did not let us enter this *vihâra*, fearing we might become dizzy after our unfortunate experience in the cells. We descended the stone steps leading to the river, which we had previously ascended, and, turning to the south, went around the mountain some 200 feet from the ladder, from there climbing to the "dining room," as the Bâbû named it. In my role of "interesting invalid," I was *carried* along a steep path in my folding chair, which I had brought from America and which never left me in my travels, and was safely deposited at the portico of the third cave.

This temple is of the same size as the first, but in spite of considerable signs of decay, is much less gloomy. Large portions of some exquisite water color paintings have been preserved on its ceiling. The walls, the tumbled down pillars, the ceiling, and even the interior rooms, which were more or less lighted by means of ventilators cut through the rock, were once covered with a varnished stucco, the secret of which is now known only to the Madrasîs, and which gives the walls the appearance of pure marble. As we entered we were met by the Ṭhâkur's four bodyguards, whom we remembered from our stay at Kârlî, and who bowed in the

dust to greet us. The carpets were spread and the lunch
was ready. Every trace of suffocation had left us, and we sat
down to our meal in the best of spirits. Our conversation
turned, of course, to the *melâ* at Hardvâr, which was frequently mentioned last year, even in the Russian papers, and
whence our suddenly appearing friend had just come. The
information brought us by Gulâb-Lal-Singh proved to be
most interesting, as he had left this gigantic religious fair
only five days before, and I wrote down immediately the
details of it as supplied by him.

In a few weeks we visited Hardvâr ourselves.

The recollection of this marvelous site (Hardvâr) evokes
in my mind the picture of the primitive earthly paradise.
I can write about it as an eyewitness.

Every twelfth year, which the Hindus call *Kumbha* (when
the planet Jupiter enters the sign of Aquarius), heralds an
especially auspicious day which the chief astrologers assigned
to the pagodas choose for the opening of the fair. Here
gather the theologians of all sects and pilgrims from all over
India, from princes and Mahârâjas to the last fakir. The
former come for the sake of religious discussions, each
representative and orator trying to prove the superiority
of his religion or philosophy while the latter come simply to
plunge into the waters of the Ganges at its very source; for
this performance an auspicious hour is also determined by
the stars. In speaking of the Ganges, an error should be
corrected. The name of the most sacred river of India has
been corrupted by European geographers. This circumstance
shows once more how little the character of Hindu religion
and traditions has been understood by our scholars, almost
up to the last decade. The conquerors of the land — un-
tutored Anglo-Indians — are not interested in anything of
the kind even now, considering the slightest attention to
"niggers" shocking and not respectable.

This river should be called either *Gangêsa* or *Gangâ,* as
the natives call it, but not *Ganges,* which is a masculine
form. "*Gangâ*" is sacred in the eyes of the Hindus, because
she is the greatest of all the nurturing goddesses of the country and a daughter of the old Himavat (Himâlaya), from
whose heart she springs forth for the salvation of the people.

That is why she is deified. And the town of Hardvâr, built at the source of the river, is looked upon by the natives as equally sacred.

Hardvâr is written *Hari-dvâra,* meaning the doorway of the sun-god or Krishna, and is also often called Gangâdvâra, the doorway of Gangâ; it is also known by the name of Kâpilâ, in memory of the ascetic Kapila, who lived here for a long time seeking salvation and left many miraculous traditions. The town is situated in a charming blooming valley at the foot of the southern slope of the Siwâlik range, between two mountain ranges which almost collide with each other. In this valley which is 1,024 feet above sea level, the northern nature of the Himâlayas vies with the tropical growth of the valley, and, in their effort to excel each other, they have created one of the most delightful corners of India. The town itself is a collection of ancient castle-like turrets of unbelievably fantastic architecture, of vihâras, of small wooden fortresses gaily painted like toys, of pagodas with loopholes, and little overhanging carved balconies; all of this is overgrown with such an abundance of aloes, roses, dahlias and showy cactus in bloom, that it is hard at first to tell a door from a window. The granite foundations of many houses are laid in the very bed of the river and during four months of the year are half under water. Behind this handful of scattered structures, higher up the mountain slope, cluster snow-white, stately temples. Some of them are low, with thick and wide side-walls, and gilded cupolas; others rise in majestic many-storied towers; still others have shapely pointed roofs, which look more like the spires of a bell-tower than like cupolas.

Strange and whimsical is the architecture of these temples, the like of which is not to be seen anywhere else. They look as if they had casually tumbled down from the snowy heights of the icy abodes of the mountain spirits — with which Himâlayan traditions are replete — and, standing there in the shelter of the mother-mountain, are timidly peeping over the head of the small town below, into the pure, cold waters of the Gangâ. Here the river is not polluted by the dirt and the sins of her million worshippers. Having held them for a while in her icy embrace, the pure maiden of the mountains carries her clear waves, transparent like crystal, through the burning plains of Hindostan, and it is only 348 miles lower down, near Cawnpore, that her waters begin to grow muddy and dark, until, on reaching Benares, they are transformed into a kind of peppery pea soup.

Once, while talking to a Brâhmaṇa of that town, who tried to convince us that the Hindus are the cleanest nation in the world, we asked him:

"Why is it, then, that in the plains, where people either do not wash at all or do so but little, the waters of the Gangâ are clear and transparent, while in Benares, especially towards evening, the river carries liquid mud rather than water?"

"Oh saabs, saabs," answered the old man mournfully, "It is not the dirt of the bodies of her devoted worshippers, as you think, it is not even the blackness of our sins, that the goddess (devî) washes off and carries away. It is," he whispered to us, lowering his voice and looking around him, "it is our suffering hidden for centuries, the burning pain of humiliation and persecution, and chiefly the feeling of despair and shameful helplessness against the usurpers of our native land, that muddy the sacred waters . . . These feelings, daily gushing from millions of Hindu hearts filled to the brim with them, have long ere this changed the waters and transformed them into black bile. They have poisoned them! . . . How could the goddess not pity us? . . . Of course she has become dark, but this is because of her sorrow for her children. Do you not understand? . . ."

Yes, indeed, we could well agree with the poor Brâhmaṇa; "our native land is overflowing with the great sorrow of its people," but this sorrow, no matter how much we may sympathize with it, seems to vanish at the source of the Gangâ. Quietly murmuring to the shore-reeds about the wonders she has seen on her way from the cherished Himâlayas to the estuary in the Bay of Bengal, the Gangâ rushes past Hardvâr, its aquamarine waves pure and un-defiled . . .

No wonder the Hindus see in the beauteous river the greatest and purest among their goddesses, especially at

LAHORE GATE AT THE PADISHÁH PALACE AT DELHI

OBSERVATORY OF MAHÁRÁJA JAI–SINGH II AT DELHI

Hari-dvâra, a place sacred to the god Krishna. Beside the "melâ" celebrated there once every twelve years, the pilgrims throng once a year, for a whole month, to the "Hari-kâpairâ" (stairs of Vishnu). Whoever succeeds in entering the water first, at the appointed day, hour and minute, will not only wash away all his sins, but also have all bodily ailments healed. This zeal to be the first costs many a life, owing to a badly constructed narrow stairway. In 1819, the East India Company, taking pity upon the pilgrims, ordered the removal of this ancient relic; and a new stairway, one hundred feet wide, made of sixty steps, was constructed.* The waters of the Gangâ, it appears, are endowed with their healing powers for one month only, and even then only at the first moment of a certain propitious hour, determined by astrologers, and which sometimes happens to be midnight.† You can imagine what takes place at the time appointed for the bathing, when more than two million people flock together! In 1819, some 430 people were crushed to death. But even after the erection of the new stairway by the East India Company, the Goddess Gangâ has carried on its virgin bosom many a disfigured corpse of her worshippers. No one pitied them; on the contrary, they were envied. A Hindu killed during such a purification is sure to go straight to *svarga* (paradise). In 1760, on the last day of the fair, the holy day of *Pûrvî,* two rival sects of mendicant hermits (*sannyâsins*) engaged, after a quarrel, in a "regular battle"; one sect was conquered, and 18,000 people were slaughtered.

---

* How dear to the heart of the Hindu must be the defunct "company," in spite of Warren Hastings and other exploiters, when compared with the present administration, can be seen from the following: the East India Company gave huge subsidies to the chief Brâhmanical temples, and, courting in various ways the Hindus, tried to win their good graces. The Imperial administration, on the other hand, has not only stopped all subsidies, but has devised this year, under the pretext of a lessening of the crowd at Hardvâr, to levy a fee on the pilgrims at the entrance of the town, as is the case at Elephanta. But considerable embarrassment followed. Not less than *two and a half million* people swept in, but only 290,000 pilgrims paid the fee. (See *The Pioneer* for February 19, 1880, "Official Report on the Hardvâr Mella".)

†According to Brâhmanical chronology, this month falls between March 12 and April 10th, and is called *Chaitra.*

"In 1796," proudly narrated our warlike *Akâli,* "the pilgrims from Pañjâb, all of them Sikhs, desiring to punish the insolence of the *gosâîns,* killed about five hundred of these heathens. My own grandfather took part in this."

As these figures are confirmed in official reports (see Edward Thornton's *Gazetteer of India*),* we had no reason to suspect our Sikh friend of exaggeration.

In 1879, however, no one was crushed to death or killed, but a dreadful epidemic of cholera broke out; fortunately, it did not spread further than halfway to Sahâranpur. We had reason to curse it, since it prevented us from going immediately to Hardvâr. However, there was nothing we could do about it, and so we had to bow to the inevitable. We had to be content with what we were told about old Himavat, until we could behold it ourselves.

After lunch we said good-bye to the "God's Warrior," who started on the road to Bombay. The worthy Sikh gave us all a firm handshake, and then, raising his right hand with palm forward and assuming a serious and solemn countenance, gave each one of us, in turn, his pastoral blessing, after the fashion of the followers of Nânak. When he approached the Thâkur, who was half-reclining on the ground and using his saddle as a cushion, his countenance suddenly changed. This change was so sharp and obvious that we were all struck by it. Up to that moment he quickly passed from one to the other, shaking hands with each and blessing them; but when his eyes fell on Gulâb-Lal-Singh who was casually observing the preparations for the departure, he stopped short and the solemn and somewhat proud expression of his face suddenly showed signs of embarrassment and humility. Instead of the usual *"namaste"* (I salute you), our *Akâli* most unexpectedly prostrated himself before the Thâkur. Reverently, as if addressing his own Amritsar guru, he clearly whispered: *"Ad'eya, sâdhu-sâhib, âsîr-vâd,"*† and remained on the ground.

---

* [Edward Thornton, *A Gazetteer of the Territories under the Government of the East India Company, and of the Native States on the Continent of India.* 4 vols., 1854, 1857, 1858; rev. ed., 1886.]

† "Salutations, holy Sâhib, please give your blessings!"

We were so astounded at this performance that we too felt somewhat embarrassed, but the face of the mysterious Râjput remained as dispassionate as ever, and its usual calm was unaffected. He slowly moved his eyes away from the river and directed them to the *Akâli* prostrated before him. He then simply touched his head lightly with the index finger, without saying a word, and, getting up himself, remarked that it was just about time for us to start . . .

All along the way, the Ṭhâkur followed our carriage on horseback, as it moved quite slowly through deep sand, and told us about the local traditions of Hardvâr and Râjasthân; about the epic legends that had grown up among the people from time immemorial, and the heroic deeds of *Hari-Kulas*,* the princes of the heroic race of *Hari* (the sun). This name of "Hari-Kula" gives cause for many Orientalists to suppose that some member of that family emigrated to Egypt in the dark prehistoric epoch of the first Pharaonic dynasties, and that the ancient Greeks, borrowing therefrom both the name and the traditions, built their legends about the sun-god *Hêrakleês*.† Ancient Egyptians deified the Sphinx under the name of "Hari-Mukh," or the *Sun upon the horizon*. In the mountain chain which fringes Kashmîr on the north, there is, as is well known, an enormous summit (13,000 feet above sea-level), shaped much like a head, which bears the name of *Harimukh*. This name is also found in the most ancient *Purânas*. Why should not the philologists do a bit of research into this curious coincidence of names and legends? The soil seems to be a very fertile one, to be sure . . . On the Himâlayan *Harimukh*, there is a sacred lake called "Gaṅgâ Bal" (place of Gaṅgâ), and popular superstition points to the huge head as the head of "Hari" — the god of the *setting sun*. Can this be a mere coincidence? I am bold enough to think there is just as much chance in this play upon names, as in the fact that Egypt,

---

*Literally, "Hari-Kula" means "from the family of the Sun." *Kula* means in Sanskrit "family name" or "nickname." Râjput princes, especially the Mahârâṇâs of Udaipur, are exceedingly proud of their astronomical origin.

† [Derived from the goddess *Hêra* and *kleos*, glory, fame. Hercules is the Latin equivalent of it.]

like India, held the *cow* and the *bull* sacred, and that the ancient Egyptians of the land of the Pharaohs had the same religious horror for the killing of cattle, namely, cows and bulls, as do modern Hindus.

In the evening, we found ourselves in some sort of clearing fringed with forest, and soon came to the shore of a large lake. Something took place here which at first sight would have appeared quite commonplace, but was in reality enigmatic. We had left our carriages. Near the shore, thickly overgrown with reeds (not the reed of our Russian conceptions, but rather one that corresponded to Gulliver's description of nature in Brobdingnag), stood a large, new ferryboat, tied to the reeds. There was no one near the boat, and the shore seemed to be entirely deserted. An hour and a half or two hours remained before sunset, and so, while our servants and the Ṭhâkur's bodyguards took our bundles out of the carriages and transported them to the boat, we sat on some ruins near the water and enjoyed the charming lake. Mr. Y. started to draw the landscape, which was really lovely.

"Don't hurry to sketch this view," said Gulâb-Singh. "In half an hour we shall be on the island, where there are much more beautiful views. We may spend the night and even the whole morning there."

"I am afraid it will be dark in an hour," said Mr. Y., opening his paint box, "and tomorrow we will have to start quite early."

"Oh, no! . . . we can stay here until three o'clock in the afternoon . . . It is only three hours to the railroad station, and the train leaves for Jubbulpore at eight in the evening. Besides," added the Ṭhâkur with his usual mysterious smile, "tonight on the island you will witness a curious and most interesting natural phenomenon. I am going to treat you to a concert."

We all pricked up our ears.

"What kind of an island are we going to?" asked the Colonel with curiosity. "Are we not going to spend the night here on the shore, where it is so cool, and where . . ."

"Where the forest swarms with playful leopards, and where the reeds hide snakes, you were going to say," smilingly interrupted the *Bâbû*. "Just look to your right, under the reed near Miss B.! Admire the happy family: father, mother, uncles, aunts, children," he began to count, "I even suspect a mother-in-law in this company . . ."

Miss B. looked in the direction of the reeds and, giving a shriek loud enough to be answered by all the echoes of the forest, made a headlong dash towards the *tonga* as if to an ark of salvation. No more than three steps from her there were some forty adult and baby snakes, their shining scales glittering in the rays of the setting sun. They were practising somersaults, coiling, uncoiling again, interlacing their tails, and presenting a picture of perfect and innocent happiness. The Thâkur who had just sat down on a stone beside Mr. Y., who was about to start drawing, left it and began watching the dangerous group of snakes, quietly smoking his constant gargarî (the Râjput pipe).

"Your screaming will merely attract from the forest the animals who are about to seek water here before nightfall," he remarked somewhat sarcastically to Miss B., who stuck her pale face distorted by fear out of the tonga. "We have naught to fear. If you do not bother an animal, he is sure to leave you alone, and will even run away from you, as much as you would from him . . ."

With these words, he lightly waved his pipe in the direction of the serpent family-party. As if thunderstruck, the whole living mass became for a moment motionless and then rapidly disappeared among the reeds with loud hissing and rustling.

"Now this is pure mesmerism!" exclaimed the Colonel, on whom not a gesture of the Thâkur was lost, and his eyes showed a special gleam from behind his eyeglasses. "How did you do it, Gulâb-Singh? How is this art to be learned?"

"How did I do it? I simply frightened them by the sudden movement of my pipe, as you saw. As to any 'art,' there is not the slightest 'mesmerism' in this, if you mean by that fashionable modern word what we barbarous Hindus call *Vaśkârana-vidyâ*, the science of charming people and animals by the force of will. Those snakes ran away simply because they were frightened by my motion directed against them . . ."

"But you do not deny, do you, that you have studied this ancient *art* and possess this gift?"

"Of course I don't. Every Hindu of my sect is duty bound to study the mysteries of physiology and psychology amongst other secrets left to us by our ancestors. But what of that? I am afraid, my dear Colonel," added the Ṭhâkur with a smile, "that you are rather inclined to view the simplest of my acts through the prism of mysticism. Nârâyaṇa must have been telling you all sorts of things about me. Is it not so?"

He looked at Nârâyaṇa who sat at his feet with a mixture of fondness and enigma in his expression. The Dekkan colossus, who rarely let his eyes wander from the Ṭhâkur, lowered them and remained silent.

"Oh yes," quietly, but very ironically, remarked Mr. Y., busy over his drawing apparatus. "Nârâyaṇa sees in you something more than his former deity Śiva; something just a little less than Parabrahman. Would you believe it? He seriously assured us at Nâsik that 'râja-yogins,' amongst them yourself (though I confess that I do not yet understand what a 'râja-yogin' really is), can, for instance, force one by their will alone to see, not what is actually before their eyes and what others see also, but that which is really non-existent, and is only in the imagination of the magnetizer or 'râja-yogin' . . . Ha, ha, ha! . . . If I remember right, he called it *mâyâ,* illusion."

"Well! You must have laughed at Nârâyaṇa, did you not?" the Ṭhâkur soberly inquired, fathoming with his eyes the dark green depths of the lake.

"Hm, yes . . . a little," evasively acknowledged Mr. Y. who by then, having sharpened his pencil and placed the drawing paper on his knees, attentively looked into the distance, choosing the most effective setting for his drawing. "I must confess I am a skeptic in these matters."

"And knowing Mr. Y. as I do," said the Colonel, "I can add that even were any of these phenomena to happen to himself personally, he, like Dr. Carpenter, would not believe it even then."

"Oh no! . . . Well, yes, that may be true. It may well be that I would not believe it, and I'll tell you why. If I saw before me something that did not exist, or rather existed only for me, however objective these things were for me personally, it seems to me that for the sake of mere logic I would be bound to suspect myself, before accepting a hallucination for something actual, and to assure myself that I am not insane, rather than permit myself to believe that that which I am the only one to see is not only actual, but the reflection of the thought directed by the will of another man, a man who thus for the time being governs my optical nerve and my brain . . . What nonsense! . . . Is there anyone who could make me believe that there exists in this world a magnetizer or râja-yogin who can force another, let us say *myself*, to see what he pleases, and not what I myself see and know that others see likewise?"

"Still, there are people who have complete faith in this, as they have become convinced that such a gift is possible," casually remarked the Thâkur.

"What if there are? . . . Besides those, there are twenty million Spiritualists who believe in the materialization of *spirits!* But do not include *me* among them."

"But you nevertheless believe in animal magnetism, don't you?"

"Of course I do . . . that is, to a certain point. If a person having smallpox or some other infectious disease can affect a person in good health, it would follow that a healthy person can transmit to a sick one the surplus of his health and cure him. But between purely physiological magnetism and the influencing of one individual by another, there is a great gulf, and I do not feel the need of crossing it on the ground of mere blind faith . . ."

"But is it so difficult to realize that that which one sees, or at least thinks one sees at the moment of hallucination, is merely the reflection of a picture created for this purpose in the mind of the one who is exercising his power over you? . . ."

"I am of the belief that in order to ascertain the facts of such a phenomenon it would be necessary first of all to acquire the gift of perceiving other people's thoughts, and thus become able to check on them without error. I do not possess such a gift . . ."

"There may also be other means of becoming convinced of the possibility of this phenomenon. For instance, if there appears before your eyes the picture of a landscape that actually does not exist, but is far distant and quite unfamiliar to you, although known to the magnetizer and, moreover, is the very one regarding which he had spoken to the skeptics ahead of time, saying that it would be precisely *that one*, and not any other, that you would see and describe. And then you actually describe it most accurately . . . is this not a proof?"

"It may be that such a transference of impressions is possible during trance, an epileptic seizure or somnambulism. I will not argue that point, though I am doubtful about it. But I am entirely convinced of one thing at least, and will vouch for it any time: in the case of a completely healthy man, under entirely normal conditions, magnetism cannot have the slightest effect. Mediums and clairvoyants are notoriously a sickly lot. I would like to see a magnetizer or 'râja-yogin' influence *me!*"

"Now, my dear fellow, don't boast like that!" interjected the Colonel, who until then had remained silent.

"There is no boastfulness in it. I simply vouch for myself because some of the best European magnetizers have tried their powers on me and failed every time. That's why I challenge all the living and dead magnetizers, and the Hindu râja-yogins into the bargain, to try on *me* the charms of their currents . . . That is just a fairy tale . . ."

Mr. Y. was getting quite excited, and the Ṭhâkur dropped the subject and talked of something else.

At this point, I will allow myself what seems to be a necessary digression.

Except for Miss B., no one of our party of tourists was either a Spiritist or a Spiritualist, least of all Mr. Y. We had long since lost faith in the pranks of departed spirits, though we admitted many of the mediumistic phenomena, but on totally different grounds than those of the Spiritists. Denying the intervention of "spirits," or even their presence, during the *tipping of tables* and other phenomena, we nevertheless believed — especially since coming to India — in the "Spirit" of living man, in its potencies and its innate, though until now *secret* (with very rare exceptions) and *latent* capacities; we believed that with a certain mode of living, this spirit — the divine spark — can become well-nigh extinguished in man, if not fanned out, and that contrarywise, man can develop in himself the strength of his spirit, performing henceforth phenomena far more amazing to the uninitiated observer than those accomplished by the entities * of the Spiritists which are later proved to be frauds. If gymnastics can not only increase the strength of our muscles tenfold, giving them an almost supernatural suppleness and elasticity (as we observe in the case of famous acrobats), then why should not the "spirit" do likewise as a result of certain training? We also believe, because we have become convinced of it, that this *secret,* unknown to, and denied by, our Occidental physiologists and even psychologists, is held in India, where it is hereditary and entrusted only to a very few.

Mr. Y. was a novice in our Society and denied the possibility even of such phenomena as those in the field of mesmerism. Trained in the Royal Institute of British Architects, from which he graduated with a gold medal, he left it as a skeptic mistrusting everything *en dehors des mathématiques pures.* No wonder he became upset when people bothered him with "fairy tales" . . .

I now return to my narrative.

The Bâbû and Mûljî had gone to hasten the servants loading the ferryboat. Everyone else had become very quiet, as if an "angel of peace" were passing. Miss B., overcome with heat and fright, had fallen asleep in the *tonga* and

---

*[H.P.B. uses here the untranslatable Russian word *kikimora* (pl. *kikimori*) which, according to popular belief, is a sort of "house sprite" which is especially good at weaving. It is significant to note that H.P.B., when writing to her relatives in Russian used the word *kikimora* whenever referring to the "entities" with which Spiritualistic mediums were dealing; she equates this term with a certain type of elementals.—*Compiler.*]

snored undisturbed. The Colonel, lying on his stomach close to the shore, amused himself by throwing stones into the water. Nârâyaṇa sat motionless on the sand, with his hands round his knees, plunged as usual in the mute contemplation of Gulâb-Lal-Singh. Mr. Y. sketched hurriedly and diligently, raising his head from time to time to glance at the opposite shore, knitting his brow in a peculiar fashion, entirely absorbed in his work . . . The Ṭhâkur went on smoking, and as for me, I sat on my folding chair, observing carefully everything around me, but soon found myself unable to keep my eyes away from Gulâb-Lal-Singh . . .

Who and what is this mysterious Hindu, after all, I wondered? Who is this man who combines in himself two entirely distinct personalities: the exterior, for ordinary eyes, for the world at large, and for the Englishmen; and the interior, spiritual, shown only to a few intimate friends? But even these intimate friends of his — do they know much beyond what is known to others? And what *do* they know? They see in him a Hindu who differs but little from the run of educated natives, except perhaps in outer appearance, and the fact that he has an even greater contempt than they for the social conventions and the demands of Western civilization . . . And that is just about all, unless one adds that he is well known in Central India as a fairly well-to-do man, a Ṭhâkur, a feudal chieftain of a *râj*, one of the hundreds of similar states in India. Besides, he is a faithful friend of ours, who has become a protector in our travels and a mediator between us and the suspicious, uncommunicative Hindus. Beyond this, we know absolutely nothing about him. It is true, however, that I personally know a little more than the others, but I promised silence, and silent I shall be. But the little I know is so strange, that it is more like a dream than reality . . .

Long ago, very long ago, more than twenty-seven years, I met him in the house of a stranger in England, where he had come in the company of a dethroned native prince, and our acquaintance was limited to two conversations which, although producing on me a strong impression by their unexpectedness, their strange character, and even their severity, have, nevertheless, like so many other things, sunk beneath the waters of Lethe . . .* About seven years ago, he wrote a letter to me, then in America, reminding me of our conversation and of the promise I had made. And now we meet again, this time in his own country — India! And what do you think! Had he changed in all these long years, had he aged? Not at all. I was young when I first saw him, and had time to become an old woman. As for him, he was a man of about thirty in those days, and seems to have remained that ever since, having arrested the progress of time . . . His striking beauty, especially his unusual height and stature, were so extraordinary in those days, that even the stodgy, conservative London press was moved to write about him. Journalists, still influenced by the poetry of Byron, now losing ground, praised in turn the "wild Râjput," even while being indignant at him for his point-blank refusal to be presented to the Queen, ignoring the great honor for which many a compatriot of his had come all the way from India . . . He was nicknamed then "Râjâ-Misanthrope," and social circles called him "Prince Jâlma-Samson," † inventing fables about him to the very day of his departure.

All this fanned in me a consuming curiosity, leaving me no peace, and causing me to forget all else.

And that is why I was now sitting in front of him, staring at him as did Nârâyana. I gazed intently at those remarkable features with mixed feelings akin to fear and inexplicable awe and reverence, as I recalled the mysterious death of the Kârlî tiger, my rescue a few hours before in Bâgh, and much else besides. He had only joined us in the morning of that

---

*[It is most likely that H.P.B. means by "a dethroned native prince" Dalîp-Singh, the deposed Mahârâja of Lahore (1837-1893), who sailed from India on April 19, 1854, accompanied by his guardian, Sir John Login, and arrived at Southampton on the SS Colombo, June 18, 1854. He was presented to the Queen on July 1st. The text of the present chapter was first published in the Moscow Chronicle on April 29 (o.s.), 1880. H.P.B.'s statement regarding "more than twenty-seven years" ago appears to be only approximately correct. It points to one of the early dates when she met Master M. in his physical body.— Compiler.]

†[The Sanskrit word jâlma means "full of contempt."—Compiler.]

day, and yet how many thoughts had been evoked in me by
his presence, how many enigmas he had brought with him!...
"What is all this about?" I almost asked out loud of myself.
Who is this being whom I met so many years ago, vibrant
with youth and life, and whom I am now meeting again
just as young and full of life, only still more austere, still
more incomprehensible? Could it be his brother, or even his
son, the thought suddenly flashed through my mind? No, it
is he himself; the same scar on the left temple; the same face.
But, just as a quarter of a century ago, not a wrinkle on those
beautiful, regular features, not a grey hair in his thick jet-
black mane; and, in moments of silence, the same expression
of calm on his dusky face, as if cast in bronze . . . What a
strange expression; what a quiet Sphinx-like face! . . .

"Not a very successful comparison, my old friend!" suddenly spoke the Ṭhâkur in a quiet, good-natured and somewhat derisive voice, as if answering my last thought, and
making me shudder all over. "It is inaccurate," he continued, "because it sins against history on two counts, First,
while the Sphinx is a winged lion, he is at the same time a
woman, and the Râjput Singhs,* while they are lions, never
had anything feminine in their nature. Besides, the Sphinx
is a daughter of Chimera, and sometimes of Echidna, and
so you could have chosen a more flattering, even though
less accurate, comparison!"

As if caught red-handed, I felt embarrassed, while he gave
way to his merriment, which did not relieve me at all.

"You know what?" continued Gulâb-Lal-Singh more seriously, as he rose. "Do not worry your head in vain. The day
this riddle is solved, the Râjput Sphinx will not cast himself
into the sea, and, believe me, the Russian Oedipus will gain
nothing from it either. You already know all that you can
ever learn. So leave the rest to fate! . . ."

"The ferryboat is ready! Come on! . . ." came the shouts
of Mûljî and the Bâbû from the shore.

"I have finished," said Mr. W. with a deep sigh, gathering his papers and paints.

---

*Singh means lion in the language of the Pañjâb.

"Let us see your work," insisted the Colonel and Miss B., who had just wakened.

We glanced at his fresh wet picture and froze in amazement. Instead of the lake, with its wooded shore receding in the bluish and velvety distance of the evening mists, we saw before us a charming seascape. Thick clusters of shapely palms scattered over the chalky yellow littoral protected a low native bungalow, not unlike a fortress, with stone balconies and a flat roof. At its entrance stood an elephant, and a native boat, tied to the shore, was bobbing on the crest of a foaming white billow.

"Where on earth did you get *this* view?" excitedly exclaimed the Colonel. "Not much use sitting in the sun, to draw pictures out of your imagination . . ."

"What do you mean out of my imagination?" said Mr. Y., fumbling with his papers. "Do you mean you do not recognize the lake?"

"What lake? You must have sketched while asleep?"

By this time, all our party had gathered around the Colonel, and the sketch was being passed from hand to hand. When it reached Nârâyana, the latter exclaimed aloud and stood still in utter amazement.

"This is 'Dayri-Bol,' the estate of the Thâkur-Sâhib. I recognize it. Last year, during the famine, I lived there for two months."

I was the first one to grasp what had taken place, but kept silent. Having packed his things, Mr. Y. approached us in his usual indolent and careless way, as if irked by the stupid onlookers who did not recognize the lake in the sea they were looking at.

"Now, that's enough of joking and inventing. It's time to start off. Give me back my sketch," he said.

But as soon as he got it and looked at it, he became frightfully pale. It was pitiful to look at his distraught expression. He turned and turned again the wretched piece of Bristol board in all directions, left, right, upside down, and could not control his astonishment. He then rushed like a madman to his drawing portfolio already packed away, and tearing off the string, turned the whole contents out, scattering in a few seconds hundreds of sketches and loose papers all over the place, as if looking for something. Failing to find what he wanted, he glanced again at his sketch, and suddenly covering his face with his hands, sank down on the sand, as if helpless and overwhelmed.

We all stood silently, exchanging occasional glances with each other, heedless of the Ṭhâkur who was already on the ferryboat and calling us to join him.

"Look here, Y.," kindly spoke the good-hearted Colonel, as if addressing a sick child. "Tell me, do you remember that *you* sketched this view? . . ."

The Englishman remained silent for quite some time; at last he answered in a hoarse voice, tremulous with emotion:

"Yes, I remember everything. Of course I sketched this view, and sketched it from nature. *I sketched that which I saw all the time before my eyes.* And that is precisely the most awful thing about it!" *

"And why is it so 'awful'? It is simply the temporary influence of one dominant will over another, less powerful. You simply acted under a 'biological influence,' to use the expression of Drs. Carpenter and Crookes."

"That is exactly what I fear. I recall everything now. I was sketching this view for more than an hour. I saw it from the very first minute on the other side of the lake, and seeing *it all the time* I did not find anything strange about it. I realized, or rather imagined, that I was drawing that which everyone else saw before them. I had lost every recollection of the shore as I saw it just prior to this, and as I see it again now. But how is this to be explained? Good God! Is it true that these cursed Hindus really possess the mystery of such a power? Colonel, I shall go mad if I am to believe all this! . . ."

"But as a result of this," said Nârâyaṇa with a triumphant twinkle in his sparkling eyes, "you will not deny any longer the great, ancient science of my country—*Yoga-Vidyâ!* . . ."

Mr. Y. did not answer him. Staggering as if drunk, he boarded the ferryboat, and evading the glance of the Ṭhâkur,

---

*Y. has kept this sketch, but never hints as to its origin.

sat down on the edge with his back turned towards us all and became absorbed in looking at the water.

«Ma chère», half-loudly whispered Miss B. to me in a mysteriously sounding voice. «Ma chère, mais Monsieur Y. devient vraiment un médium...»

In moments of excitement, she always addressed me in French.

"Please stop this nonsense. What do you mean by medium? You know I do not believe in spirits ..."

Receiving this rebuke from me, she turned to the Bâbû, who, for a wonder, had remained silent and, leaning against the railing, casually looked into the distance.

"Who but a departed spirit (*esprit désincarné*), who but the spirit of a former artist could have painted this fantastic view?" she exclaimed, opening her mouth wide.

"The devil!" abruptly replied the Bâbû. "Have not your compatriots decided long ago that we Hindus worship devils? One of our gods must have thrown a glamour over Mr. Y."

Had not the ferryboat, steered by the Thâkur's servants (there were no other boatmen in sight), arrived that very moment at the island, there would have been an argument between them. Fortunately we moored and the Bengalî jumped onto the shore.

«Il est positivement malhonnête, ce nègre là!» angrily muttered the old maid, loosing this Parthian arrow at him.

"Well, my dear," said I, stepping out with the others, "one such *nigger* is worth *ten* of your John Bulls ..."

—XXII*—

This island was a tiny one, and so overgrown with tall grass that, from a distance, it looked like a pyramidal basket of greenery floating in the midst of the blue lake. With the exception of some spreading groups of shady mango and fig trees, where a whole colony of monkeys were agitated at our appearance, the place was evidently uninhabited. In this virgin forest of thick grass, there was no trace of human footprint. Seeing the word "grass," the reader must not forget that I speak of *Indian* grass, and not that of European or Russian lawns, cut close; the grass *under* which we stood, like insects under a burdock, waved high its feathery multi-colored plumes, not only over our heads, but even above the white *pagṛî* of the Ṭhâkur and Nârâyaṇa, the former standing "six and a half feet in his stockings," to use the common English expression, and the latter hardly an inch less. Seen from the ferryboat, this grass looked like a gently waving sea of black, white, yellow, blue, but especially rose and green. In landing, we discovered that it consisted mainly of separate clumps of bamboo, mixed with the gigantic *sirkî* grass, which waved its fronds almost at the level of the mango and other trees.

It is hard to imagine anything prettier and more grace-

---

* [Misnumbered XXI in the *Russkiy Vestnik.—Compiler.*]

ful than the *sirkî* and the bamboos. Isolated tufts of bamboo, which in spite of its size is nevertheless really a grass, wave their green crests, like heads adorned with ostrich plumes at the least waft of wind. Every bamboo trunk, some five to eight inches in diameter at the root, grows up to 50 or 60 feet, with sections every two or three feet from which sprout forth a whole fringe of long, thin leaves. From time to time, when the wind came up, we heard a light, metallic rustle in the reeds, but, busy getting ready for our overnight stay, we did not pay any special attention to this.

While our *coolies* and servants were busy preparing supper for us, pitching the tents and clearing the road around them, we went to make the acquaintance of the monkeys. We never saw anything funnier. Without exaggeration, there must have been some two hundred of them. Preparing to go to bed, the monkeys behaved very decently. Every family chose a separate branch and defended it from the intrusion of other tenants on the same tree, but did so without conflict, limiting themselves to threatening grimaces. There were among them many mothers with babes in arms; some of them nursed the children tenderly and carefully, with all the earmarks of ordinary humans; others, after choosing a branch, jumped from one tree to another, with the child hanging on to the mother's tail; yet others, on all fours, with their heirs clinging to their stomachs, fussed about something, chattering and stopping every now and then to scold each other — a true picture of chatty old gossips on market day, repeated in the animal kingdom. The bachelors were absorbed in their evening amusement—athletic exercises performed hanging from the branches mostly by the ends of their tails. We particularly noticed one of them who seemed to divide the game between *sauts périlleux* and teasing a respectable looking grandfather, who sat gravely under the tree hugging two little monkeys. Swinging back and forth, the bachelor flung himself against him with full force, made faces at him, and bit his ear playfully, chattering all the time. We cautiously and quietly passed from one tree to another, afraid of frightening them away; but evidently the many years spent by them with the fakirs (who had left the island only a year ago) had accustomed them to people. They were sacred monkeys, as we learned, and did not show the slightest fear at our approach. They let us come quite close to them, and, having received our greeting, and some of them a piece of sugar cane, calmly looked us over from their branch-thrones, with affectedly folded hands and even with some degree of dignified contempt in their intelligent brown eyes.

Now the sun had set, and a hubbub arose in the trees. We were called to supper. The *Bâbû,* whose prevailing passion was (according to orthodox Hindus) a tendency to "blasphemy," had climbed a tree where, imitating every gesture and pose of his neighbors, he countered all the threatening grimaces of the monkeys with even more ugly ones of his own, to the pious horror of our *coolies.* After a while, he jumped off his branch and hastened us "homeward."

As the last golden ray vanished below the horizon, a transparent mist of pale lilac suddenly fell over the countryside. With every passing moment the tropical twilight dimmed, rapidly yet gradually losing its soft, velvet-like coloring, becoming darker and darker, as if an invisible painter spread one shade after another over the surrounding forests and water, quietly but steadily moving his gigantic brush across the wondrous background of our island . . . Feeble phosphorescent lights began to flare up around us; shining brightly against the dark trunks of the trees and of the stately bamboos, they vanished soon in the silvery, mother-of-pearl background of the opalescent evening sky . . . Another two or three minutes, and thousands of these fairy-like living sparks, heralds of the Queen of Night, were playing around us, flaring up and going out again, pouring like a rain of fire over the trees, swirling in the air, over the grass and the darkening lake . . . And now, behold the Night herself! Silently descending upon the earth, she assumed her sovereign powers. At her approach, all things calmed themselves and fell asleep. Under her cool breath, the activities of day ceased to be. Like a tender mother, she sang a lullaby to nature, lovingly wrapping it in her soft dark mantle, and, having lulled the world into slumber, she guarded its tired and sleeping forces until the break of dawn . . .

All nature slept, man alone was awake at this solemn evening hour, nor did we go to sleep. Sitting around the fire, we talked almost in a whisper, as if afraid of waking nature. Mr. Y. and Miss B. had retired sometime before, and nobody sought to prevent them. But we six—the colonel, four Hindus and myself—snugly sheltered under the fifteen-foot "grass," had no desire to miss this magnificent night by sleeping. Besides, we were waiting for the "concert" which the Ṭhâkur had promised us.

"Be patient," said he, "just before the moon rises, our musicians will appear."

The moon rose late, almost at ten o'clock. Just before her appearance, when the water of the lake began to grow lighter on the opposite shore, and the horizon grew perceptibly brighter, gradually assuming a silvery, milky tint, a sudden wind arose. The sleeping waves stirred again; they rustled at the feet of the bamboos, whose giant feathery heads swayed and murmured to each other as if passing on some instructions . . . Suddenly, in the general stillness, we heard again the same strange musical notes which we had noticed when first approaching the island on the ferryboat, as if all around us, and even above us, invisible wind instruments were being tuned, strings were being plucked, and flutes sounded. In about two minutes, just as another gust of wind forced its way through the bamboos, the whole island resounded with the strains of hundreds of Aeolian harps . . . And then suddenly, a wild, weird and unending symphony burst forth!

It resounded in the surrounding woods, filled the air with an indescribable melody which charmed even our spoiled European taste. Sad and solemn were its prolonged strains; now they sounded like the flowing measure of some funeral march, then, suddenly changing into a tremulous trill, they poured forth like the song of the nightingale, humming like the legendary self-playing zither,* only to die away in a

---

* [H.P.B. uses here the untranslatable Russian term "gusli-samogudi," a compound term which refers to a lagendary zither, dulcimer or psaltery, which in Russian folklore plays without anyone touching it. —Compiler.]

long sigh . . . At times they were like a long, drawn-out howl, heart-rending and woeful, as of a she-wolf deprived of her young; at times it rang out like Turkish bells, in a gay and rapid tarantella; then again was heard a sad song like that of a human voice, or the easy-flowing sound of the violoncello, ending in either a sob, or subdued laughter . . . And all of this was repeated in every direction by the mocking echo of the forest, as if hundreds of fabulous forest sprites awakened in their green bowers to answer the appeal of this wild musical revelry.

The Colonel and I glanced at each other, dumbfounded in our amazement. "How wonderful!" "What witchcraft!" we finally exclaimed, almost at the same time. The Hindus smiled and remained silent. The Ṭhâkur smoked his *gargarî* as peacefully as if he had suddenly become deaf. After a short interval, during which our minds unconsciously formulated a question in regard to this being perhaps another feat of magic, the invisible orchestra burst forth again and swelled with even greater abandon, momentarily almost deafening us. The sound poured out and rolled through the air like irresistible waves, arresting our attention. Never had we heard anything like this—to us an inconceivable wonder . . . Hark! Like a storm on the open sea, the wind whistling through the rigging, the roar of the maddened waves tumbling over each other! Or a blizzard on the silent steppes with a gale blowing . . .

> Like some animal it howls,
> Like an infant it cries!*

And now it is the solemn strains of an organ . . . Its powerful notes blend together, now spread throughout space, now cease, intermingle, and become entangled like the fantastic melody of a delirious dream, like some musical phantasy formed of the howling and whistling of the wind in the open.

But a few moments later, these sounds, so glamorous at

---

* [From a poem of Alexander S. Pushkin entitled *Winter Evening*, written in 1825.—*Compiler*.]

first, began to cut like knives through our brains. And it seemed to us as if the fingers of the invisible artists played no longer upon invisible strings, or blew into magic trumpets, but did so upon our nerves, straining our tendons and impeding our breath . . .

"For God's sake, stop this, Ṭhâkur! It's quite enough!" . . . shouted the Colonel, covering his ears with his hands. "Gulâb-Singh, order them to put a stop to this!"

At these words, the three Hindus burst out laughing, and even the sphinx-like features of the Ṭhâkur lit up with a merry smile . . .

"Upon my word," said he laughingly, "you seem to take me very seriously, if not for the great Parabrahman, then at least for some sort of genii, for a Marut, the lord of the winds and the elements. Is it in my power to stop the wind or instantaneously to uproot all this forest of bamboos? Ask me something easier! . . ."

"What do you mean by stopping the wind? And what of the bamboos? Do we not hear all this under some kind of psychological influence?"

"You will soon become unbalanced on your psychology and electro-biology, my dear Colonel. There is no psychology of any kind in this; simply a natural law of acoustics . . . Each of these bamboos surrounding us — and there are thousands of them on the island — contains in itself a natural musical instrument, upon which the wind, the universal artist, comes to try out his artistry after sunset, and especially so during the last quarter of the moon."

"Hm! The wind! . . ." murmured our somewhat abashed president. "But it's getting to be an awful noise . . . not particularly pleasant . . . Can anything be done about it?"

"I really don't know . . . But it's all right, in five minutes you'll be quite used to it, and you'll rest in the intervals when the wind momentarily falls . . ."

We were told that there are many such natural orchestras in India; they are well known to the Brâhmaṇas who call this wind in the reeds *vînâ-devas* (the lute of the Gods) and, making capital of popular superstition, say that the sounds are *divine* oracles. The fakirs of the idol-worshipping sects have added their own art to this peculiarity of the reeds,* and for this reason the island we were on is reckoned especially sacred.

"Tomorrow morning," said the Ṭhâkur, "I will show you with what consummate knowledge of all the laws of acoustics have the fakirs bored holes of varying size in these reeds. They enlarge the holes made by the beetles in any one section of the trunk, according to the size of the latter, shaping them into either a circle or an oval. This perfecting of a natural instrument can justly be looked upon as the finest example of the application of mechanics to acoustics. However, this is not to be wondered at. Our most ancient Sanskrit works on music minutely describe these laws and mention many musical instruments which are not only forgotten, but totally unknown at present . . . And now, if this too close proximity of the singing reeds disturbs your sensitive ears, I will take you to a meadow near the shore, some little distance from our orchestra. The wind dies down after midnight, and you will sleep undisturbed. In the meantime, let us go and see how the "sacred bonfires" are being lighted. As soon as the neighboring people hear the distant voices of the 'Gods' in the reeds, they gather on the shore, whole villages of them, light fires, and perform a 'pûja' (adoration of the island)."

"Is it really possible that the Brâhmaṇas manage to keep up such an obvious deception?" asked the astonished Colonel. "Even the most stupid must eventually learn who made the holes in the reeds and what the real cause of the sound is!"

"Possibly so in America, but not in India. Show even a half-educated native how it is done; tell him all about it and explain it . . . He will tell you that he knows as well as you do that the holes are made by beetles and enlarged by the fakirs. But what of that? The beetle was no ordinary beetle, but *one of the gods who incarnated in the insect for this special purpose* and the fakir is a holy hermit who acted in this case by the order of this god. That will be all you

---

*This variety of bamboo is constantly attacked by a certain small beetle, which rapidly bores large holes in the hollow trunk of the reed, and the wind is caught therein.

will get out of him. Fanaticism and superstition, which for centuries have permeated the masses, have become a necessary part of their physiological needs. Uproot these, and the people will have their eyes opened and will see the truth, but not before. As to the Brâhmaṇas, India would have been very fortunate if these scoundrels had not done anything worse than that through the centuries . . . Let the people adore the music and the spirit of harmony; there is nothing to fear in that."

The *Bâbû* then told us that in Dehra-Dûn this kind of bamboo has been planted on both sides of the central street which is more than a mile long. The buildings prevent the free action of the wind, and so the sounds are heard only when the wind blows from the east, which is very rare. A year ago, when Swâmi Dayânanda had arrived to camp there, and the crowd of followers gathered every evening around him, the bamboos decided to break into song, just as he finished his sermon in which he thundered against superstition. Tired out by this long lecturing, and not feeling too well, the Swâmi sat down on his carpet and remained motionless with eyes closed. The crowd imagined at once that the soul of the Swâmi, leaving the body, entered the reeds and was now conversing with the Gods through them. Many people, anxious to express thereby their devotion to the teacher, and probably to show him how fully they had grasped his teaching, hastened to perform "pûja" before the singing reeds.

"And what about the Swâmi? What did he say to that? . . ."

"He said nothing . . . You evidently do not really know him. Without saying a word, he jumped on his feet, and uprooting the first bamboo cane he happened to reach on his way, gave such a lively 'European *bakhshîsh*' * on the backs of the pûja-makers, that they instantly took to their heels. The Swâmi chased them for a whole mile, giving it hot and plenty to anyone in his way. He then spat and went

---

*Beating with a cane is called here by the people "European bakhshîsh" or "Bamboo bakhshîsh"; this latter expression is used all over Asia.

on his way. He is an awfully strong man, our Swâmi, and not inclined to useless talk," laughingly concluded the *Bâbû.*

"But in this way," remarked the Colonel, "instead of leading them on the road to the truth, he merely dispersed the crowd!"

"That simply shows that you know our people as little as your ally the Swâmi . . . He had hardly reached Patna, a place some 35 or 40 miles from Dehra-Dûn, than a delegation from the latter town, some 500 strong, arrived posthaste to entreat him on their knees to return. Among the petitioners were some whose backs were black and blue. They brought the Swâmi back with no end of pomp and circumstance, mounting him on an elephant, and spreading flowers along the road. Then the Swâmi formed a *samâja* (society), and there are now two hundred members in the "Ârya-Samâja" of Dehra-Dûn, who have forever renounced idol-worship and superstition."

"I was present," said Mûljî, "two years ago in Benares, when Dayânanda destroyed some one hundred idols and beat a Brâhmaṇa with the same stick. He dragged him out of the hollow idol of Śiva, where he was impersonating the god and begging money for a new suit of clothes for the idol."

"And the Swâmi did not have to pay for that?"

"The Brâhmaṇa hailed him into a court of law, but such a crowd of defenders and sympathizers turned up that the judge had to acquit the Swâmi, merely sentencing him to pay for the broken idols. Only one thing was not good: the Brâhmaṇa died that very night of cholera, and the opponents of the Swâmi loudly proclaimed that he died as a result of the *jâdû* (sorcery) practiced by Dayânanda Sarasvatî."

"And you, Nârâyaṇa, what do you know about the Swâmijî?" I asked. "Do you regard him as your 'guru'?"

"I have only one *guru* and only one God on earth, as in heaven," answered Nârâyaṇa somewhat unwillingly, "and I will never have another."

"And who is this *guru* and this God? . . . Is it a mystery? . . ."

"Thâkur Sâhib, of course! . . ." burst out the Bâbû. "For him both of these are blended in one . . ."

"You talk nonsense, Bâbû," coldly remarked Gulâb-Singh, "I do not consider myself worthy to be anyone's *guru,* let alone a God. Please do not blaspheme. Here we are! Let's sit on the shore," he added, pointing to the carpets that had been brought and evidently anxious to change the subject.

We had arrived at a small clearing near the lake some two or three hundred feet from the bamboo forest. The sounds of the magic orchestra now only reached us from time to time and then softly. We sat to the windward of the reeds; their sound was like a harmonious whisper, reminding one of the quiet tones of an Aeolian harp and having nothing harsh or unpleasant in it any longer. On the contrary, it only added to the poetical beauty of this colorful scene.

We sat on the carpets that had been spread out, and, seeing that I had been on my feet since four in the morning, I felt quite sleepy. The men continued to talk of the Swâmi and the "pûja," and I soon became so absorbed in thought that, as usually occurs, the conversation reached me only in fragments . . .

"Wake up! . . ." said the Colonel, giving me a little shake. "The Thâkur says you must not sleep in the moonlight . . ."

I was not asleep; I was simply thinking, though I felt groggy. I hardly replied, however, so drowsy can one become under such wondrous skies . . .

"Wake up, for heaven's sake!" continued the Colonel, "Just look at this moon . . . and the landscape all around us. Have you ever seen anything more wonderful than this panorama? Look . . ."

I looked and the familiar verse of Pushkin, "now the golden moon has risen . . ." came to my mind. Indeed this was a "golden moon." At this moment she poured forth a flood of golden light, showered it over the restless lake at our feet, and spread golden dust on every blade of grass, every pebble, everything around us, and into the far-off distance. Her silvery-yellow globe swiftly glided upwards into the dark blue sky, strewn with myriads of bright stars shining over our heads. However many moonlit nights we may

see in India, each time new and unexpected impressions
will be found . . . Such sights cannot be described; they
cannot be portrayed either on canvas or in mere words;
they can only be *felt*. What an inexpressible grandeur and
beauty!

In Europe, even in the south, the brightness of the full
moon usually dulls the stars around to a considerable
distance, so that even the largest among them are dimmed
by her brilliance. Here it is quite the contrary: she looks
like a large pearl surrounded with diamonds, rolling on the
blue velvet of the heavenly vault. It is possible to read a
letter written in small handwriting in her light and to perceive the various shadings of green in the surrounding vegetation — a thing unheard of in Europe. Cast a glance at the
trees during full moon, at the stately palms with their
fronds spreading outward like a fan! From the moment the
moon has risen, her rays begin to glide over every tree, like
a shimmering silvery scale, descending from its crest, lower
and lower, until the whole tree is bathed in a sea of light.
Without metaphor, the surface of the leaves appears all
night long to bathe in swirling, trembling waves of liquid
silver, whereas underneath they look darker and softer than
black velvet. But woe to the careless novice, woe to the
mortal who gazes at the moon with his head uncovered.
It is not only dangerous to sleep in moonlight, but even to
gaze too long at the chaste Indian Diana. Epilepsy, madness
and often death are the punishment wrought by her dangerous arrows on the modern Acteon who dares to contemplate
the cruel daughter of Latona in all her beauty. That is why
by day or night neither the Europeans nor the natives ever
go out without a *topi* or a *pagrî*. Even our Bâbû, who
spends whole days cooling himself bareheaded in the sun,
wore a kind of white cap during moonlit nights.

As the Thâkur had told us beforehand, the fires were
lighted one after another on the mainland, and the dark
silhouettes of the worshippers swayed to and fro. Their
primitive sacred songs and loud exclamations, *"Hari, Hari,
Mahâdeva,"* * reached us loudly and distinctly from the

Hari is one of the names of Śiva, and *Mahâdeva* means great god.

other shore. And the reeds, shaken by the wind, waving their slender stalks, answered with tender musical phrases . . . A vague uneasiness seemed to fill the soul, a strange intoxication could be sensed in these surroundings, and the idol-worship in these passionate deeply poetical souls, sunken in centuries-old ignorance, seemed less repulsive and more intelligible. A Hindu is a born mystic, and the glamorous nature of his land has made him a vehement pantheist.

Somewhere in the forest an *algojâ*, a kind of Indian reed-pipe with seven openings, was being played, and its sound startled a whole family of monkeys resting in the branches of a nearby tree. Two or three of them carefully slipped down and looked around as if waiting for something.

"Who is this Orpheus who is casting spells over the people?" we asked.

"Probably some fakir. The *algojâ* is generally used to invite the sacred monkeys to be fed. The community of fakirs, who once inhabited this island, has now moved to an old pagoda, not far from here in the forest. There they derive more profit from passers-by, and that's why they left the island . . ."

"Possibly because they were getting deaf," Miss B., who had just wakened and come towards us, ventured her innocent opinion.

"*À propos* of Orpheus," asked the Thâkur, "do you know that the lyre of this Greek hero and demi-god was far from being the first with the capacity to cast spells over people, animals and even rivers? *Kui*,* a certain Chinese 'musical artist' who lived a thousand years before the era ascribed by the scholars to Orpheus, expressed himself in these words: 'When I play my *King*, wild animals hasten to me, and range themselves into rows before me, spellbound by my melody . . .' "

---

*What a curious coincidence! *Cui* is the name of a famous musician from St. Petersburg; but neither animals nor people dance at his music.

[H.P.B. refers to César Antonovich Cui (1835-1918), Russian composer, son of a French officer who had been left behind in the retreat from Moscow in 1812. Beside his outstanding musical work, he was also a distinguished military engineer.—*Compiler.*]

"Where did you read that?"

"I could have read it in the words of your Western Orientalists, because this information can be found there. But I personally found it in an ancient Sanskrit manuscript (a translation from the Chinese) of the second century before your era. The original is in a very ancient work known as *The Preserver of the Five Chief Virtues,* a kind of chronicle or treatise on the development of music in China, written by the order of Emperor Huang-Ti many hundreds of years before your era."

"Have the Chinese ever understood anything about music?" said the Colonel laughingly. "In California and other places I heard some travelling artists of the Celestial Empire . . . Their musical cacophony could drive anyone mad . . ."

"That is exactly what many of your Western musicians say on the subject of our ancient Âryan music, as well as our modern Hindu music. But, in the first instance, the idea of melody is entirely arbitrary and, in the second, there is a good deal of difference between the knowledge of musical technique, and the application of this knowledge to the development of melodies which can be appreciated by both the educated and the uneducated ear. A musical piece may be excellent from the technical standpoint, and yet the melody itself may be entirely beyond the understanding of an ear that is unaccustomed to it, and even be unpleasant. Your most renowned operas, for instance, sound to us Hindus like a wild chaos, a cascade of unpleasant, harsh and entangled sounds, in which we do not see any meaning at all, and which simply give us a headache. I have more than once visited both the London and the Paris operas; I have heard Rossini and Meyerbeer; I wanted to become aware of my own impressions, hence listened with the greatest attention. I confess that I prefer our simple national melodies to the productions of your best European composers. The former are intelligible to me, while the latter are incomprehensible, and they affect me just as little as our national tunes touch you. But leaving the 'tunes' aside, I can assure you that not only our ancestors but even those of the Chinese were not inferior to you Europeans, if not in technical instrumentation, at least in musical 'technology,' and especially in their abstract conceptions of music."

"Maybe so with the Âryan sections of antiquity, but to concede the same in the case of the Turanians to which the Chinese belong, is a bit different," argued our Colonel.

"The music of nature has been everywhere the first step to the music of art. We prefer the former, and so we have held to it for centuries. Our musical system is the greatest art, if — pardon this seeming paradox — we are to avoid everything that is artificial. It disregards in its melodies any sounds that are not part of the living voice of nature. The Chinese do not hold to this. The Chinese system, for instance, comprises eight chief tones, which serve as a tuning fork for all derivative tones, which are accordingly classified under the name of their originators. These eight sounds are: *metal, stone, silk, bamboo, pumpkin, earthware, leather* and *wood.* So that they have metallic sounds, wooden sounds, silk sounds, and so forth. Thus they cannot possibly produce any melody; the result is complete chaos, as their music consists of an entangled series of separate notes. Their imperial anthem, for instance, is a series of long drawn-out sounds produced in unison. With us, however, everything is original and unique. We owe our music to living nature alone, and in no wise to inanimate objects. We are pantheists, in the highest sense of the word, and our music is, so to speak, *pantheistic.* But it is also highly scientific. Coming from the cradle of humanity, the Âryan races, who were the first to attain manhood, began to listen to the voices of nature, and found that both melody and harmony are comingled only in our great common mother. She has no false and no artificial notes, and man, the crown of her creation, desired to imitate her sounds. In their collectivity, all of these sounds (according to the assertion of your own physicists) blend into *one tone* which we can hear, if we know how to listen, in the ceaseless rustle of the foliage of great forests, in the murmur of the water, in the roar of the ocean and the storm, and even in the distant rumble of a great city. This tone is the middle 'F,' the fundamental tone of the whole of nature. In our melodies it serves as the starting

point, which is embodied in our keynote, and around which
are grouped all the other sounds. Having noticed that the
higher, middle and lower notes have their typical representative in the animal kingdom; that the goat, the peacock, the
ox, the parrot, the frog, the tiger, the elephant, and so forth,
have, each one of them, its special note, our ancestors have
given an attentive ear to this and found that everyone of
these notes corresponds to one of the *seven chief notes*. Thus
was the *octave* discovered and established. As to the subdivisions and measures, they also found their basis in the
complex sounds of the same animals."

"Concerning your ancient music," said the Colonel, "and
whether your ancestors discovered anything about it, I know
of course next to nothing, but I confess that, listening to the
songs of your modern Hindus, I would not suspect that they
knew anything about any kind of music."

"That is because you have not yet heard a real singer. Go
to Poona and visit the 'Gâyana-Samâja,' * and then we shall
resume this conversation. Until then, there is no use
arguing."

"The music of the ancient Âryans," suddenly interrupted
the Bâbû for the sake of his country's honor, "is an antediluvian plant which has almost entirely vanished from
India, but it is nevertheless well worth consideration and
study. This is definitely proved now by my compatriot Râjâ
Surendronâth Tagore,† who, according to the statements

---

*All over India musical societies are being organized for the restora-
tion of the ancient national music. One of these is the Gâyana-Samâja
in Poona.

†Râjâ Surendronâth Tagore is a doctor of music and has a number
of decorations, among them being those of the King of Portugal and
the Emperor of Austria, for his work entitled *On the Music of the
Âryans*.

[Râjâ Sir Saurindra Mohana Tagore (or Thâkura) (1840-1914)
was a younger brother of Mahârâja Sir Jotindra Mohana Tagore. He
was educated at the Hindu College and at sixteen began the study of
music, English and Bengalî. Founded in 1881, the Bengal Academy of
Music. He collected books and published a number of works on music
and musical instruments. He became a Doctor of Music at Oxford, 1896,
receiving later many titles of honor and being knighted.—*Compiler*.]

of the best musical critics in England, has firmly established the right of India to 'be counted as the mother of musical science.' Every school, whether Italian, German or ancient Âryan, arose in its own specific period, and has evolved in its own exclusive climate and in completely different circumstances. Everyone of these schools has its peculiarities and its charm for its followers, and our school is no exception. While you Europeans are used to the melodies of the West and are well acquainted with your own schools, our musical system, like many other things in India, is yet totally unknown to you. For this reason, I make bold to say, Colonel, that you have no right to judge it . . ."

"Don't get so excited, Bâbû," said the Ṭhâkur, "Everyone has the right, if not to judge, then to ask questions about a subject unfamiliar to him, otherwise he would never get the truth . . . If Hindu music belonged (as the Bâbû has pointed out) to an epoch as recent as that of European music, and if, besides, it embodied, as does the latter, all the virtues achieved by various musical systems in different epochs, then perchance experts would understand it and would better appreciate it. But our music belongs to prehistoric times. With the possible exception of the ancient Egyptians, who, to judge by the twenty-string harp found by James Bruce * in one of the Theban tombs, were also initiated in the mysteries of musical harmony, we Hindus seem to have been the only people acquainted with music at a time when all the other nations of the globe were still struggling with the

---

* [James Bruce (1730-1794) was a Scottish explorer in Africa. Educated at Harrow and Edinburgh University; examination of Oriental MSS. at the Escurial led him to the study of Arabic and determined his future career. Appointed as British consul at Algiers, with a commission to study ancient ruins. After some years of travel in the Middle East and in Abyssinia, he reached in 1770 the long-sought source of the Blue Nile, and also traced its course to its confluence with the White Nile. In 1774, while on a trip to London, he was met with incredulity concerning the story of his explorations, and soon retired to his home at Kinnaird. Published in 1790 his *Travels to Discover the Source of the Nile in the Years 1768-73*, in five octavo volumes, lavishly illustrated. The best edition of this work is the third of 1813. —*Compiler*.]

elements for the means of bare existence. We have hundreds
of Sanskrit manuscripts about music which have never
yet been translated even into present day vernaculars.
Despite all the conclusions of your Orientalists to the contrary, we believe implicitly in the great antiquity of the
treatises (from 4,000 to 8,000 years), and we will persist
in this belief because we have read them and studied them,
while the European scholars have not yet set eyes on them.
There are many such musical treatises, written at different
and very distant epochs, and they all agree in their evidence,
showing very clearly that in India *music was known and
systematized in times when the modern civilized nations in
the west of Europe still lived like savage tribes.* However,
all this does not give us the right to expect that you Europeans should like our music, as your ears are unaccustomed
to it and you are unable to understand its spirit . . . To a
certain extent we can explain its technique to you and give
you some idea of it as a science but nobody can create in you
that which the Âryans called *rakti,* the capacity of the
human soul to perceive and be moved by the combination
of the various sounds of nature — the *alpha* and *omega* of
our musical system — just as it is impossible to make us fall
into raptures over the melodies of Bellini."

"But why?" excitedly inquired the Colonel. "What is that
mysterious force in your music that can be understood only
by yourselves, Asiatics? Even if we differ from you in the
color of our skin, our organic mechanism is one and the
same. In other words, the physiological construction of
bones, blood, nerves, sinews and muscles which form a Hindu
has as many parts combined with each other, exactly after
the same plan and model, as the living mechanism known
under the name of American, Englishman or any other
European. They come into the world from the same workshop of nature and have the same beginning and the same
end. From the physiological standpoint we are duplicates
of each other . . ."

"Physiologically yes, and even psychologically, if education did not interfere, which, when all is said, influences
man's nature in one or another direction, affecting not only
his mental, but also his moral outlook; in some cases it

DELHI: DIVĀN-I-AĀM OR HALL OF PUBLIC AUDIENCE

DELHI: MOTÎ-MASJID—THE PEARL MOSQUE

entirely extinguishes his divine spark, while in others it fans it, transforming it into an inextinguishable beacon which serves as a lodestar for his mental capacity for life."

"Right; still this can hardly have so strong an effect upon the physiology of the ear."

"You are again mistaken. If, from the physical, or rather the physiological standpoint, the Hindu, viewed as a human machine, does not differ from a European, nevertheless as a result of an entirely unique education, mentally and psychically, especially the latter, the two differ diametrically from each other, being as it were, two different species in nature. Remember to what an extent complexion, bodily structure, capacity for reproduction, vital strength, and all the hereditary qualities of the purely physical functions alter with time as a result of climatic conditions, food and the everyday surroundings of man (the most recent scientific mask of your materialists, if I mistake not, intended conveniently to ignore the more abstract mysteries of being), and you will have answered your question. Apply the same law of gradual modification, instead of to the physical, to the purely psychic element in man, and you will observe the same results. Change the education of the soul, and you will change its capacity. In cases where formerly it found delight, experiencing something entirely inaccessible to another educated in a different manner, it finds now nought but boredom and confusion . . . For instance, you believe, and you do so on the basis of centuries-old evidence, that gymnastics, strengthening the muscles, not only develop the human body, but are capable of almost transforming it. We, Hindus, go one step further. We believe as a result of thousands of years of experimentation and objective demonstration, that there exist gymnastics for the soul, as well as for the body. This is our secret, the secret of the downtrodden Hindus enslaved by sheer animal force, and we do not allow anyone to penetrate this secret, except a handful of elect; but in due time, it may be demonstrated to you... What is it that gives to the sight of the sailor the quality of the eagle's sight, that endows the acrobat with the skill and the agility of a monkey, and the wrestler with muscles of iron? Practice and habit, you will say. Then why not suppose the same capacity in the soul of man as well as in his body? Is it simply on the ground that modern science denies the existence of the soul and does not acknowledge in it an entity distinct from the body? . . ."

"That will do, Ṭhâkur. You, for one, ought to know that I believe in the soul and its immortality . . ."

"We believe in the immortality of the *spirit* but not of the soul . . . However, this has nothing to do with our present subject. And so you must agree that every dormant capacity of the soul may be unfolded by practice to the highest degree of its strength and activity, and also that, as a result of disuse and lack of habit, every such capacity may become latent and even disappear altogether. Nature is so jealous of her gifts, that it is in our power systematically to develop or to destroy in our descendants — and this in the course of only a few generations — any physical or mental gifts, simply by practicing or by completely neglecting it . . ."

"Yes, but all this does not explain to me the secret charm of your national melodies."

"What's the use of going into details, when you can see that my explanation is a general clue to the solution of not only your problem, but of a host of others? Centuries have accustomed the Hindu ear's receptivity to one particular type of combination of audio-waves or atmospheric vibrations, while the ear of the European has been accustomed to another type; because of this, the soul of the former will experience delight when the soul of the latter will feel nothing, while the ear may feel pain. I could end my explanation at this point, as it seems simple enough and understandable, but I am anxious to awaken in you something more than the feeling of satisfied curiosity. What I have pointed out explains the mystery from its physiological angle only. It is as easily understandable as, for instance, the fact that we Hindus habitually eat with impunity quantities of spices which, even in small quantities, could give you inflammation of the intestines. Our auditory nerves, which at the beginning were identical with yours with regard to their capability, have altered as a result of centuries of training and have become as distinct from yours as our complexion and our stomachs. Add to this the fact that the eyes of our Kashmîr weavers, both men and women, are known to be able to distinguish three hundred hues more than the eyes of a European, as shown by your own most scholarly physicists and by the manufacturers of Lyons, and it will be realized how simple is the explanation of the problem. Force of habit, the law of atavism, anything you like . . . But you, coming from America to study the Hindus and their religion, will never understand the latter if you do not realize from the outset how closely and well-nigh indissolubly all our sciences are related, not to modern orthodox and ignorant Brâhmaṇism, of course, but to the philosophy of our primitive Vedic religion."

"But what, for instance, has music in common with the *Vedas?* . . ."

"A great deal — almost everything. As was the case with the ancient Egyptians and Chinese, so it is with us: all the sounds in nature, and consequently music itself, stood in direct relation to Astronomy and Mathematics, that is to say, to the planets, the signs of the zodiac, the solar and lunar currents and numbers; and especially to that, the existence of which your scientists have not yet fully ascertained: *âkâśa* or the ether of space. The doctrine of the 'music of the spheres' originated here, and not in Greece or Italy, whither it was brought by Pythagoras after he had completed his studies with the Gymnosophists of India. Most certainly this great philosopher, the only Western sage who revealed to the world the heliocentric system before Copernicus and Galileo, knew better than anyone, before or after him, how dependent is the least sound in nature on the *âkâśa* and its correlations. One of the four *Vedas,* namely the *Sâma-Veda,* consists entirely of hymns. It is a collection of *mantras* and incantations sung during the sacrifices to the 'gods,' that is to say, to the Powers of the Elements. Our ancient priests— even though their knowledge did not accord with the modern methods of chemistry and physics, knew a good deal that has not yet been uncovered by present day scientists. It is therefore understandable that these priests at times forced the 'gods' of the Elements or the blind forces of nature to answer

their prayers by various portents. Every sound in these mantras, the slightest variation in each, has its meaning and is
purposely where it should be; and, having a reason, it must
of course have its effect. As has been said by Professor Lesly,
'the science of sound is the most intangible, the most subtle,
and the most complex of all the series of physical sciences.'
If ever this teaching were recognized in all its perfection, it
was by our ancient Ṛishis, our philosophers and saints, who
left us the *Vedas* . . ."

"Now I begin to understand the origin of the mythological
fables of Greek antiquity," thoughtfully remarked the Colonel, "the tales about the pipes of Pan, his pipe of seven
reeds, the Fauns, the Satyrs, and even the lyre of Orpheus
himself . . . I know that the ancient Greeks knew little of
harmony and the rhythmical declamation of their dramas—
which probably never reached the heights of even the simplest of modern recitals, sustained as they were by only a
feeble lyre and the pipes of Pan — could hardly have suggested to them the idea of the all-enchanting lyre of
Orpheus. I feel strongly inclined to the opinion of many of
our well-known philologists and scholars. I suspect that
Orpheus, whose very name ὀρφνός, *i.e.*, dark-skinned, suggests
that even among the tawny-complexioned Greeks he must
have been even darker, was an immigrant from India. This
was the view of Lemprière and of several others . . ."

"Some day your suspicion may become a certainty. There
is not the slightest doubt that the purest and highest musical
forms of antiquity belong to India. All our legends ascribe
magical powers to music, which was a gift and a science sent
to earth by the gods. And while we ascribe all our arts in
general to divine revelation, music stands at the head of all
else. The invention of the *vînâ*, a kind of lute, belongs to
Nârada, the son of Brahmâ. You will probably laugh at me
if I tell you that our ancient *upgâtṛi* (singing priests), whose
duty it was to officiate during the *yajña* (sacrifice), knew
certain secrets of being so well that they were able to produce
by means of certain combinations, and, mark well, without
any trickery, phenomena which were regarded by the ignorant as manifestations of supernatural powers. The
phenomena produced by the *upgâtṛi* and the *Râja-yogins*

are perfectly natural to the initiated, however miraculous they may seem to the uninitiated."

"But do you really have no faith at all, none whatsoever, in our spirits?" insisted Miss B. who was quite afraid of the Ṭhâkur.

"With your permission, I have *none*."

"And . . . in mediums? . . ."

"Still less, my esteemed lady. However, as far as mediumism is concerned, for which we have had from time immemorial quite a different name, namely, *bhûta-dak,* literally, 'hostelry for devils,' * I do believe in it, as I do in all sorts of other psychic diseases. I sincerely pity the real mediums and try to help them when I can. As to the charlatans, I despise them and rarely lose an opportunity to unmask them . . ."

The scene in the witch's den near the "dead city" suddenly flashed into my mind; the Brâhmaṇa-oracle, caught and rolling down the hole, and the flight of the old woman herself. That which I did not understand then became clear to me now: Nârâyaṇa had acted under the orders of the Ṭhâkur . . .

"Our *Anga-tiene,*" continued the latter, "or those 'possessed' by this force unknown to the uninitiated—'force' in which spiritists recognize spirits; superstitious people, the devil; and sceptics deceit and trickery; while real men of science suspect it to be a natural force not yet discovered by them — are almost always weak women and children. You are trying to unfold and increase in them this dreadful psychic disease, while we are attempting to save them from that 'force' you know nothing about, and which it is useless to discuss now . . . We sons of India have been for ten centuries under the heel of various people, often inferior to ourselves . . . But the nations that have conquered us have

---

Dâk means a saloon or hostelry: and *bhûta* the evil soul of a dead man whose sins prevent it from rising to *moksha,* the heavenly abode, and which must wander upon the earth. There are no "devils" or fallen angels in Hindu philosophy.

conquered only our bodies, not ourselves.* They can never claim the upper hand over our souls! The Mayâvi-rûpa of a real Âryan is as free as Brahman, and even more so.† For us,

---

*The *Vedântins* or the followers of the philosophical system of Śaṁkarâchârya, rarely use the pronoun "I" when speaking of themselves, and say, for instance, "This body went," "This hand took" and so on, in everything concerning the physical or automatic actions of man. The personal pronouns "I," "he," are only used concerning mental processes, such as "I thought," "I wish to go," etc. To their eyes the body is but a shell, the outward sheath of the inner, invisible man, who is the real "I."

†*Mayâvi-rûpa* literally means illusion or Mayâvic body—the real *ego; Kâma-rûpa* is the body of desires or will, deliberately fashioned by our strong desire (endowed with creative power, according to the Hindus), our double which appears wherever it is sent by our desire. In life, man possesses just about as many such inner bodies as there are skins in an onion, each one more subtle and pure, and each one of them bears its special name and is independent of the body. After death, when the earthly vital principle disintegrates together with the body, all these interior bodies join into one aggregate, and, according to their deserts, either advance on the high road to *moksha*—such a soul is then termed *deva* (divine)—even though there are still a great many "stations" before the final liberation from the shackles of matter, or it becomes a *bhûta*, an evil soul, and suffers on earth, either wandering in the invisible world or transmigrating in various unclean animals. In the first instance, a *deva* will not have intercourse with the living. Its only link with the earth is its posthumous affection for those it loved in life, and over whom it exercises its protective influence even after death.

Love outlives every earthly feeling, and a *deva* can appear to its loved ones in their sleep, or as an illusion (*mâyâ*) for a brief moment, and in no other way, because the body of a *deva* undergoes a series of gradual changes from the moment it is freed from its earthly bonds. With every transition from one sphere to another, it loses somewhat of its objective nature, becoming more and more intangible. It is reborn, lives and dies in every new sphere or *loka*, which gradually becomes ever more subjective and pure, while it "dreams in the âkâśa," or ether, during its transition periods. Finally, being freed of the last earthly thought and sin, it becomes *nothing* from the substantial point of view. It is extinguished as a flame and, having become one with Parabrahman, it lives the life of the spirit, of which neither our material conceptions nor our language can give us any idea. But the "eternity" of Parabrahman, is not the eternity of the soul. The latter according to a *Vedântic* expression, is an eternity in *eternity*. However holy, the life of the soul has its beginning and its end, and con-in our religion and philosophy, our spirit is Brahman itself, higher than which there is only the unknowable, omnipresent and omnipotent spirit of Parabrahman. Neither the English nor even your 'spirits' can ever conquer our 'Mayâvi-rûpa.' It cannot be enslaved . . . And now let us retire for the night."

---

sequently no sins and no good actions can be either punished or rewarded in the "eternity of Parabrahman." This would be contrary to justice, "disproportionate," as the Vedânta expresses it. "Spirit alone lives in eternity and has neither beginning nor end, neither frontiers, nor limits, nor central point." The *deva* lives in Parabrahman as a drop of water lives in the ocean, till the next regeneration of the universe out of *pralaya*, a periodical chaos, a destruction or rather a disappearance of the worlds from the region of objectivity. With every new great cycle, the *Mahâ-Yuga*, it separates itself from the "eternal," attracted by existence in objective worlds, like a drop of water first drawn up by the sun, then starting downward again, passing from one sphere to the next, concreting itself, until it finally sinks into the dross of our planet.

Then, when a small cycle is over, it begins to ascend again on the opposite side of the circle. Thus it gravitates in the *eternity* of Parabrahman, passing from one conceptual eternity to another. Each of these "human" eternities, *i.e.*, *conceivable* to the mind, consists of 4,320,000,000 years of objective life and of as many years of subjective life in Parabrahman (when the individual character of the soul, according to the Vedânta, does not vanish, as is supposed by some European scholars), in other words altogether 8,640,000,000 years. This number of years in their estimation is long enough to redeem the most terrible of crimes and to reap the reward of any good actions performed in such a brief period as is the human life span. Only the souls of the *bhûtas*, when the last spark of repentance and of desire to atone for their sins has become extinguished, will eventually evaporate. Then their divine and undying spirit separates from the soul forever and returns to its primordial source; the soul is reduced to its primitive atoms, and the *Ego* is plunged into the darkness of eternal unconsciousness. Its identity is lost. Such is the philosophy of the Vedânta concerning the spiritual man. And that is why the Hindus do not believe in the return of souls to earth, except in the case of *bhûtas*.

— XXIII *—

[JUBBULPORE.—MARBLE ROCKS. — THE THUGS AND THEIR METHODS. — THE MADAN-MAHAL. — SUSPENSION OF BREATHING. — INCREDIBLE POSTURES OF THE FAKIRS. — DR. PAUL AND HIS TREATISE ON YOGA PHILOSOPHY. — METHODS OF HIBERNATION. — STAGES OF TRANCE ACCORDING TO DR. PAUL. — ALLÂHÂBÂD ON A SUMMER DAY. — THE UNDERGROUND RIVER. — ANCIENT MONUMENTS AND KING AŚOKA'S INSCRIPTIONS. — WHAT NIRVÂṆA IS. — CAUSALITY AND THE SPIRITUAL EGO.]

Leaving Mâlwâ and the "independent"(?) territory of the Holkar, we found ourselves again in strictly British territory, going by railway to Jubbulpore and Allâhâbâd. In the first town we stopped only a few hours, to look at the famous "Marble Rocks." Not wishing to lose an entire day, we left by boat, starting at 2 a.m., thus avoiding the heat and enjoying a splendid trip on the river two miles from town.

Jubbulpore, situated in the district of Saugor and Narbada, 222 miles from Allâhâbâd, was at one time owned by the Marâṭhâs, but is now British soil, as the English took it from them in 1817. As usual, they got it by cunning instead of force. They boast in their "History of India" that on December 19, 1817, General Hardyman, at the head of only 1,100 men, cut to pieces 5,000 Mârâṭhâs, the army of the Râjâ of Nâgpur, inflicting on them severe losses and taking possession of nine cannons and a large quantity of military stores, while themselves suffering *only two casualties* and *ten wounded*.† Tradition, however, tells

---

* [Misnumbered XXII in the *Russkiy Vestnik*. — *Compiler*.]
† See E. Thornton, *A Gazetteer of the Territories under the Government of the East India Company*, London, 1857, s.v. Jubbulpoor.

a different story. Under the pretense of negotiation, the Marâthâ leaders were invited by the English to a feast; the officers got them drunk with some concoction, while their soldiers performed the same operation in regard to the rank and file. In this manner, while they were half-dazed, the English were able to kill them and to take possession of the town.

This story, for the veracity of which I cannot vouch, as it appears altogether incredible and mean, was told us by a half-caste Portuguese (Eurasian), whose father, he said, had been an eyewitness of the event. It was related not as a censure of the English, but with some degree of pride, as a kind of hymn of praise to his European *compatriots*, who, as I have already mentioned more than once, despise half-castes more than they do Hindus, while the latter, in return, despise them and with compound interest.

The neighborhood of Jubbulpore is charming and of the greatest interest to the lovers of natural science. Both the geologists and the mineralogists find here a most fertile field for scientific research. The mountains, presenting an unusual variety of formations, provide granites of every variety, and the long chain of craggy rocks would keep a hundred Cuviers busy for life. The limestone caves of Jubbulpore are a true ossuary of antediluvian India; they are full of skeletons of monstrous animals, now completely extinct.

At a considerable distance from the other mountain ridges, and entirely by themselves, stand the "Marble Rocks," a freak of nature, of which there are many in India. On the flattish banks of the Narbada, overgrown with thick shrubbery, there suddenly rises, like a wart on the smooth cheek of Mother Nature, a long row of strangely-shaped snow-white cliffs. And what cliffs! . . . White and pure, as if moulded by human hand into some curious shape, they pile erratically one on the other and look rather like an enormous paperweight from the desk of a Titan. Halfway up the road, they appeared and disappeared for brief moments, with the sudden capricious turnings of the river, trembling in the pre-dawn mists like a distant, deceptive mirage on the horizon of the desert, until we lost sight of them altogether. But then, just before sunrise, they suddenly stood once more before our charmed eyes, floating above their reflected image in the river. Like an enchanted castle called forth by the wand of the magician, they suddenly sprang forth from the earth on the green banks of the Narbada, mirroring their virgin beauty in the calm surface of the lazy waters of the river, promising us both shade and coolness . . . And how precious is every moment of the cool hours before sunrise, can be appreciated only by those who have lived and travelled in this fiery land.

Alas! No matter how early our start, our enjoyment of the cool retreat beneath the rocks was of short duration. No sooner had we landed upon the magic shore, planning to have some prosaic tea in the midst of these poetical surroundings, than the sun leaped above the horizon and began shooting his fiery arrows at the boat and at our unfortunate heads. Pressing us from one place to another, it drove us at last even from under a high rock overhanging the water. The snow-white marble beauties became golden-red, pouring fiery sparks into the river, heating the sand on the shore, and blinding our eyes . . . No wonder legend points to them, and the people believe them to be, either the abode or the actual manifestation of Kâlî herself, the most cruel of all the goddesses of the Hindu pantheon. For many *yugas* this fierce spouse of Śiva has been engaged in a desperate conflict with her husband, who, in the shape of "Trikûṭeśvara" (three-headed *liṅga*) has claimed unlawful rights to rock and river, over which Kâlî herself presides.

And that is probably why something like underground cries can be heard every time the daring hand of an utterly irresponsible coolie, working in government quarries, breaks a stone from the white hip of the goddess. And the wretched stonecutter trembles and is torn between his fear of the inspector and the expectation of revenge on the part of the bloodthirsty deity. Kâlî is the patroness of not only the rocks but of the ex-*Thugs* as well—the stranglers, who quite recently struck lonely travellers with terror. Many a bloodless sacrifice have these *Thugs* offered on the marble altar of Kâlî. The country is full of blood-chilling tales about their accomplishments in honor of the goddess. These tales are too recent and fresh in popular memory to have become mere colorful legends, especially as they are confirmed by the official documents of the law courts and the inquest commissioners.

If England ever leaves this country (and she will not do so before her bone is thoroughly gnawed), the complete suppression of *Thugism* will stand foremost among the few services which she rendered to the land. Under this name, as everyone must still remember, was practiced in India during more than two hundred years the craftiest and the most terrible kind of homicide. Sometime after 1840, it was finally ascertained that its aim was simply robbery and brigandage. The distorted notion concerning the meaning of Kâli was simply a cunning pretext; in this case the goddess was nothing but a stage setting for the rascals. Otherwise, how is it possible to explain the presence of so many Moslems among her Hindu devotees? On the day when justice caught up with them, the majority of the "knights of the *rûmâl*"— the sacred handkerchief used in strangling the victims — proved to be Moslems. The most illustrious among their leaders were not Hindus, but sons of the Prophet, as for instance Aḥmad, and out of thirty-seven *Thugs* recently caught by the police, there were *twenty-two* Moslems. It is obvious of course that their religion, having nothing in common with the Hindu gods, played no role whatever in all of this; the motivating reason was merely robbery. It is true, however, that the final rite of initiation as a *Thug** was performed in the forests, before an idol of Bhavânî,† wearing a necklace of human skulls. Before this time, the *Thug* had to undergo a course of training which consisted of learning an especially difficult method of throwing the *rûmâl* around the neck of the marked and unsuspecting victim, and strangling him in such a way that death was instantaneous and without the slightest sound on the part of the victim. In this initiatory rite, the part ascribed to the goddess was made manifest by means of certain symbols, similar to those universally used among Freemasons, as for instance, an unsheathed dagger,

---

* The term *Thug* simply means thief or robber.
† Another name for the goddess Kâli, used by the Thugs.

a skull, and even the corpse of the slain Hiram Abif, the "widow's son," brought back to life by the Grand Master of the lodge. Kâlî was nothing but an imposing scenario used for another purpose altogether. *Thugism* was a freemasonry of its kind, with its own special signs of mutual recognition, passwords and jargon that no outsider could understand — and all this for criminal purposes. Freemasonry in our era, by the way, is quite a harmless pastime, except perhaps for the Mason's own pocketbook. Just as the Masonic "lodges" receive both Christians and Atheists, so the *Thugs* used to receive the thieves and robbers of every nation, and it is even reported that there were among them some English and Portuguese.

Poor, poetical Śiva, wretched Bhavânî! Popular ignorance has indeed invented a mean rôle in thus personifying these type-figures, so deeply philosophical and full of poetry and knowledge of nature! Śiva, in his primitive meaning, is at one and the same time the all-destroying and the all-regenerating power of nature. The Hindu trinity is an allegorical representation of the chief elements: fire, earth and water. All three, Brahmâ, Vishṇu and Śiva represent these elements by turn, in the various phases, but Śiva is much more the god of fire than Vishṇu; he burns and cleanses at the same time, creating out of the ashes, like the Phoenix, new forms, full of renewed life. Śiva-*Śaṃkara* is the destroyer and Śiva-*Râkshasa*, the regenerator. He is represented with a flame in his left palm, and with the sceptre of death and of resurrection (*śûlayudh*) in his right hand. His worshippers wear on their foreheads, between the brows, his symbol which consists of three horizontal parallel lines; it is traced with wet *ashes* (the remains of things burned in the fire), and these are termed *vibhûti* (purified substance). The color of Śiva's skin is rosy-yellow, gradually changing into flaming red. His neck, head and arms are wrapped round with snakes, emblems of eternity and constant regeneration. "As a serpent sloughs off its old, and reappears in a new skin, so man after death reappears in a new and purer body," say the *Purânas*. In her turn, Śiva's wife Kâlî is the allegorical representation of Śiva's earth, fructified by the flame of the sun . . . If her worshippers have allowed themselves to believe that she is fond of human sacrifices, it is only because the earth is fond of organic decomposition, which fertilizes her and helps her to call forth new and fresh forces from the discarded ashes of the old. The Śaivas, when burning their dead, place an idol of Śiva at the head of the corpse; but when, after gathering the ashes, they begin to scatter them on earth or water, they invoke Kâli, adorned with skulls, in order that the goddess may receive in her bosom ashes purified by the sacred fire and bring forth in them the germs of new life. But what truth is not distorted in the end by the coarse superstition of ignorance! Thus the perverted emblem fell into the hands of the *Thug* brigands. According to their understanding, the goddess requires human sacrifice, but at the same time hates bloodshed, so they decided to kill without soiling their hands.

We visited a very old man who was once a *Thug*. Having served his time on the Andaman Islands, he was later pardoned, owing to his sincere repentance and to some service he had rendered the Government. Returning to his native village, he peacefully settled down to end his days weaving ropes, a profession suggested to him, most likely, by some sweet reminiscences of his reckless youth. He first initiated us in the art of theoretic Thugism and then most kindly offered to show us his skill in practice, if we agreed to buy a sheep for him. He said he wanted to show us how easy it was to send a living thing into the hereafter in less than three seconds, the whole secrets of the art consisting in the rapid and skillful play of the finger joints of the right hand. As soon as the sign agreed upon, the fateful hooting of the owl (a bird sacred to Bhavânî-Kâli) was heard, a *Thug* stood behind each of the travellers who had fallen into the skillfully set trap, were they even as many as twenty. In a second the *rûmâl* was around the neck of the victim, the well-trained iron fingers of the *Thug* tightly holding the ends of the "sacred handkerchief"; another second and the joints of the fingers performed their artistic twist, pressing the cervix and the victim fell down helpless! Not a sound, not a shriek! . . . The *Thugs* worked as swiftly as lightning. The strangled man was immediately carried to a grave prepared beforehand in the forest, often under the bed of some brook or rivulet periodically in a state of drought. Every vestige of the victim vanished. Some thirty years ago, when no railways existed, and when there were no regular government systems, who would know or care about the disappearance of a Moslem or a Hindu embarked on a journey, except his own family or near relatives? Besides, the country is full of tigers, whose fate it is to be held responsible for the sins of others as well as their own. Whoever happened to disappear, the answer was invariably the same: "the tigers ate him."

This was a remarkably and efficiently organized system! Skillful accomplices, Brâhmaṇas, tramped all over India, visiting large cities especially, stopping at the bazaars, the social clubs of Asiatic nations, asking questions, and gathering information as to who was about to start on a journey and where they were going; they scared the would-be travellers with tales of *Thugs* and then advised them to join this or that travelling party, who, of course, were disguised *Thugs*. Having ensnared these wretched people, they advised the brigands and collected a commission in proportion to the total profit. For a long time these invisible and elusive bands, scattered all over the country and working in groups of from ten to sixty men, enjoyed freedom, but finally they were caught. The inquiry unveiled awful repulsive secrets; rich bankers, officiating Brâhmaṇas, râjâs of small domains, and even a few English government officials belonged to their bands. For its service in exposing this, the East India Company truly deserves popular gratitude in India.

We did not buy a sheep for the old brigand, but gave him some money. To show his gratitude, he offered to demonstrate for the Colonel all the preliminary sensations of the *rûmâl* on his own American neck, promising him, of course, to spare him the last, famous "twist." But our president generously declined . . .

On our way back we stopped at the "Madan-Mahal," another mysterious curiosity. It is a house built — no one knows by whom or for what purpose — on a huge rounded boulder. This stone (probably a relative of the *cromlechs* of the Celtic Druids) *wobbles in all directions* at the least touch, together with the house and whoever feels curious enough to venture inside it. Of course we were curious enough, and our noses remained safe thanks to the vigilance of Nârâyaṇa, the Bâbû and the Ṭhâkur who looked after us like tender nurses . . .

The natives of India are truly amazing people! I do not think there is anything in nature, however unsteady, that they cannot sit upon with the greatest of comfort, after finding their balance. A Hindu may jump up onto a post or an iron cross-rod somewhat thicker than a telegraph wire, grip it with all his ten toes, as long and tenacious as those of a monkey, squat down, and sit there for hours on end . . .

"Salaam, saab!" I once said to a venerable naked Hindu seated like a crow on a perch, near the sea. "Are you comfortable, uncle? Are you not afraid of falling?" "Why should I fall? . . ." seriously replied the "uncle," expectorating a red fountain of chewed betel. "I do not breathe, maam-saab! . . ."

"What do you mean you do not breathe? Can a man remain without breathing?" exclaimed I, somewhat surprised at such a piece of information.

"Oh, yes . . . I do not breathe now. But in some five minutes or so, I will take air into my lungs again; I will then hold to the post . . . And then I will again sit quietly without breathing . . ."

After this astounding physiological information we parted. We got no more out of the old man and left with the conviction that he could have earned a lot of money as an acrobat in any European theatre. This episode, however, threw all our "scientific" cogitations into a cocked hat.

We had recently heard that *yogins* and others who practice *gupta-vidyâ* (secret and sacred science) in India are known to have discovered the secret of not breathing for from 21 to 43 minutes at a time, while remaining alive! Some of them, as a result of years of constant daily practice, acquire the faculty of *hibernating*. They fall into a kind of sleep, as do certain animals, and remain in this condition without breathing and without the slightest sign of life, allowing themselves to be buried several weeks, and even months, and afterwards come back to life! . . . Eventually we witnessed this sort of thing ourselves, but at the time we received the old man's curious answer, we knew of the phenomenon merely from books, from the stories of travellers who were eyewitnesses to it, and from some of our acquaintances among the natives. On the testimony of Coathupe, an English surgeon, who for a long time disbelieved in the ability to suspend breathing, but who finally had to give in, "face to face with the fact," as he said, one such *yogin* known to him could remain without breathing from seven to twelve minutes. Physiology, however, definitely teaches that even in the case of healthy Arab and Sinhalese divers, suffocation occurs not later than one and a half, or at the most two minutes, after complete submersion of the body. Furthermore, while some of us believed in the existence of natural but hidden forces in man to be brought out only as a result of special "training," forces which science knows little about because of its extremely superficial acquaintance with Hindu *yogins* and conjurers, others, like Miss B., believed in Spiritism, and others yet, like W., believed in nothing at all. Still all of us, believers and unbelievers, protested this strange declaration. Was it possible for us to believe in such foolish things, we argued? Until then we were so naïve as to imagine that only sturgeons and such-like were clever enough to learn how to absorb as much air as possible, and to fill with it not only their stomachs but also their air-bladders, in order to become lighter than water and come up to the surface with that much more ease. What is possible to a sturgeon is impossible to man! . . . And even if it were possible for man to store air in unusual circumstances, such a gift must be rare and difficult to obtain. To use such an ability in order to perch bird-like on a post seemed to be unheard of foolishness! . . . We decided that the old man made an empty boast, probably with the object of laughing at the "white saabs." But we learned later that he had correctly described the necessary process for this sort of curious way of sitting.

In those days, however, we were inclined to resent explanations of this kind and interpreted them as mockery. But at Jubbulpore we witnessed a phenomenon which was even more curious. Strolling on the river bank, the so-called "fakir's avenue," the Ṭhâkur suggested we go into the courtyard of a pagoda. This is a sacred place and neither Europeans nor Moslems are allowed inside. But Gulâb-Lal-Singh said something to the chief Brâhmaṇa, and we entered. The yard was full of devotees and ascetics, among whom we specially noticed three ancient and perfectly naked fakirs. Dark, wrinkled, as thin as skeletons, their heads covered with a mass of white hair, they sat or rather stood in what appeared to us to be the most *impossible* postures. One of them *literally resting only on the palm of his right hand,* was poised perpendicularly with his head downwards and his legs upwards; his body was as motionless as if, instead of a live man, he were the dry branch of a tree. His head did not touch the ground, but was bent somewhat upwards in the most abnormal manner, and his eyes stared right into the sun. I cannot guarantee the truthfulness of some talkative inhabitants of the town who had joined our party, and who assured us that this ascetic spends every day of his life from noon to sunset in this posture. But I do know that we watched him exactly *one hour and twenty minutes,* and during the whole of this time the fakir did not move a muscle! . . .

The other stood on one leg on what is known as a "sacred stone of Śiva," about five inches in diameter; the other leg was curled up under his stomach, and the whole of his body was bent backwards into an arc; his eyes also were staring at the midday sun. The palms of his hands were pressed together as if in prayer . . . He appeared to be glued to his stone. It was impossible to imagine by what means a man could achieve this condition of equilibrium.

The third sat with his legs under him; but just exactly *how* he could sit was quite incomprehensible. His seat was a stone *liṅga,* not higher than an ordinary street post and not wider than the circumference of the stone of Śiva, in other words five or possibly seven inches in diameter. His arms were crossed behind his neck, and his nails had grown deep into the flesh of his shoulders.

"This one never changes his position," they told us, "he has been sitting in this position for the last seven years or so . . ."

"And how does he eat?" we asked in amazement.

His food, or rather drink, as it was milk, was brought to him once every 48 hours from the pagoda, and poured down his gullet with the aid of a bamboo tube. His disciples (every ascetic has his willing servants, candidates to holiness) take him off at midnight, wash him in the tank, and *place* him back upon his pedestal like an inanimate object, as he can no longer unbend his limbs.

"And how about the others?" we asked, pointing to two of them. "They look as if they would fall down. The least nudge would upset them, would it not?"

"Try!" suggested the Ṭhâkur. "As long as a man is in the state of *samâdhi* (religious trance), it is easier to break him to pieces like an idol made of clay than to move him from his place . . ."

To touch an ascetic in a state of trance is a sacrilege in the eyes of the Hindus, but evidently the Ṭhâkur was well aware of the exceptions to the general rule. He had another brief exchange of words with the sullen Brâhmaṇa who was accompanying us, and, after the consultation was over, told us that none of us would be allowed to touch the fakir, but that he personally had obtained permission, and so was going to show us something still more amazing. Saying this, he approached the fakir seated on his stone, and holding him carefully by his bony hips, lifted him and put him on the ground on one side. Not a joint moved in the body of the ascetic, as though instead of a living man it were a bronze or stone statue. Then he took up the little stone and showed it to us, asking us, however, not to touch it for fear of offending the crowd. The stone was round, flat, with rather an uneven surface. When laid on the ground, it could be set moving at the slightest touch . . .

"You see how unsteady is this pedestal chosen by the fakir. Under the weight of the ascetic, however, it is as immovable as if it were planted in the ground."

Lifting the fakir again, the Ṭhâkur placed him back where he belonged. In spite of the law of gravity which, to all appearances, should have acted upon his body and head bent backward in a long arc, the ascetic and the stone seemed to have become solidly joined to the ground, without the least change in position. How they are able to achieve this, they alone know. I merely state a fact and do not attempt to explain it.

At the gate of the pagoda we put on our shoes, which we had been told to take off before going in. We left this *holy-of-holies* of the centuries-old mysteries with our minds more puzzled than when we had entered it. In the "Fakir's Avenue" we found Nârâyana, Mûljî and the Bâbû, who had not been allowed to enter. All three of them had long before released themselves from the iron claws of caste, and openly ate and drank with us, and for this offence were "ostracized" and despised even more than the Europeans. Their presence in the pagoda would have polluted its holiness forever, whereas the pollution brought on by us would be only temporary; it would evaporate in the stench of cow-dung burnt after we had left — the usual Brâhmanical "incense of purification" — like a drop of dirty water in the rays of the sun.

India is a country of the unexpected; even from the standpoint of the ordinary European observer, everything here is topsy-turvy, from the shaking of the head which everywhere else is a sign of *negation,* but here an emphatic affirmation, to the host's custom of showing the door to the most pleasant guest, who, otherwise, would stay a week and might die of hunger rather than go without being invited to do so — everything here contradicts our Western ideas. To ask, for instance, how is the wife, even if you are well-acquainted, or how many children a man has, or whether he has any sisters, is highly offensive. Here, when you feel it is time for the guest to leave, you sprinkle him with rose-water, hang a garland of flowers round his neck, and pleasantly point to the door saying: "I now take leave of you . . . Come again!" The Hindus are a strange and original people, but their religion is still stranger and more incomprehensible . . . With the exception of certain disgusting rites of some of the sects and abuses on the part of the Brâhmanas, the religion of the Hindus must have a deeply and mysteriously attractive quality, if it can turn even an

Englishman from the path of truth. Here is something, for instance, that happened a few years ago.

There had appeared a very interesting and scholarly pamphlet, the contents of which were an affront to modern science. It was written in English and published in a small edition by a regimental physician and surgeon named N. C. Paul, G.B.M.C., in Benares. He was well known among his compatriots, the English, as a specialist in physiology and was at one time considered an authority in the world of medicine. The pamphlet treated of various instances of "hybernation" witnessed by the doctor among the ascetics, and the *samâdhi* and other phenomena produced by the *yogins*. Bearing the title *A Treatise on the Yoga Philosophy,* this pamphlet alarmed the representatives of European medicine in India, and a lively polemic between Anglo-Indian and native journalists ensued. Dr. Paul had spent thirty-five years in studying the incredible, but for him entirely indubitable, facts of "yogism." With perfect sincerity, and evident regret, he confesses the fact that he could never succeed in reaching the *râja-yogins,* but he established friendly ties with fakirs and *lay* yogins, *i.e.,* such as do not hide their rank and upon occasion will consent to permit a European to witness certain phenomena. Dr. Paul not only described some of the strangest among those he had witnessed, but even explained them. *Levitation,* for instance, something that stands in direct opposition to the accepted laws of gravity and which was vehemently denied by the astronomer Babinet, is explained by him quite scientifically. But it was chiefly his warm friendship with Captain Seymour which enabled him to penetrate some mysteries which, until then, were supposed to be impenetrable. Some twenty-five years ago, this captain produced in India, and more particularly in the Army, an unprecedented scandal. Captain Seymour, a wealthy and well-educated man, accepted the Brâhmanical creed and became a *yogin!* Of course he was proclaimed insane and, being caught, was sent back to England. Seymour escaped and returned to India in the dress of a *sannyâsin.* He was caught again, put on board a steamer, taken to London, and placed in a lunatic asylum. Three days later, in spite of bolts and watchmen, he disappeared from the institution. Later, his acquaintances saw him in Benares, and the Governor-General received a letter from him from the Himâlayas. He declared in this letter that he had never been insane, in spite of having been placed in a hospital. He advised the Governor-General not to meddle in his private affairs again and stated that he would never return to civilized society. "I am a *yogin*," he wrote, "and expect to attain what is the aim of my life—to become a *râja-yogin* before I die." The Governor did not understand, but dropped the matter. After this no European saw him except Dr. Paul, who, as it is reported, was in communication with him until his last days, and even went twice into the Himâlayas — ostensibly on *botanical* excursions. The chief inspector of the medical department, considering Dr. Paul's pamphlet as "a direct slap in the face of science in its physiological and pathological fields," ordered all published copies of it bought from private owners at a high price and publicly burned, as a sacrifice to science, no doubt. As a result of this, the pamphlet became a rarity. Of a few copies saved, one is to be found in the library of the Mahâraja of Benares and another was given to me by the Ṭhâkur.*

The train left for Allâhâbâd at eight o'clock in the evening, and we spent the night to six in the morning *en route*. Although we had a first class coach with room for ten, I felt sure that for various reasons I would not go to sleep that night. Accordingly, having secured candles for a portable lantern, I made ready to break the railway law during the night and to read Dr. Paul's pamphlet, as it interested me.

---

* [In the Catalog of the British Museum, the name of this physician appears as Navînachandra Pâla which may or may not be the Indian version chosen by him for his work among the natives. There is no readily available information concerning the original edition of his work, but the 2nd ed. of *A Treatise on the Yoga Philosophy* was published at Calcutta by the "Indian Echo" Press in 1883, as an 8vo booklet of 52 pages; a 3rd ed. was published by Tukarâm Tâtya, the indefatigable early worker at Bombay, in 1888.

Certain portions of the text of this booklet were published by H.P.B. in *The Theosophist*, Vol. I, September, 1880, and Vol. II, October and November, 1880, with comments by herself. This material may be found in Volume II of the *Collected Writings.* — *Compiler.*]

About an hour and a half before departure, we all went to dinner at one common table in the *Refreshment Rooms, i.e.,* the restaurant of the railway station. Our appearance caused an evident sensation. Our party which included four Hindus occupied the end of a table at which were seated some fifty first class passengers who all stared at us with undisguised astonishment and contempt. Europeans on equal footing with Hindus! . . . Hindus dining with Europeans! . . . The subdued whispers grew into loud exclamations, and one important-looking lady, unable to stand it, got up and walked away. Were it not for the impressive presence of some unquestionably familiar types, such as W. and Miss B., both English and the Colonel who was being mistaken by everyone for an English officer, a scandal would have been unavoidable. Two Englishmen came up to the Ṭhâkur and after shaking hands with him — another rare occurrence — took him aside as if to talk business, but actually to satisfy their curiosity; they happened to be acquainted with him. Not the slightest attention was paid to the other Hindus. Here we learned for the first time that we were under police surveillance. The Ṭhâkur, pointing out to us a captain of very rosy complexion, with a long blonde moustache and wearing a white summer uniform, quietly whispered to me: "Beware of him! . . ." He was an agent of the secret police from the political department and had followed us from Bombay. On learning this pleasant piece of news, the Colonel burst into a loud laugh, which doubly disturbed the natives from Albion who were engaged in eating. We learned afterward that all the servants in the hotel were *in duty bound* to spy. The custom in India is to have your servants accompany you even to a dinner; so a Hindu stood behind each of us, while behind the Ṭhakur were his four shield-bearers and two servants. The enemy was thus completely cut off by this army of naked-legged defenders, and the hotel spies had very little chance of overhearing our conversation. Besides, we had nothing to hide. But I confess that this state of affairs had a very bad effect on me. At last the uncomfortable dinner was over. Making myself at ease in the railway coach, I began reading the pamphlet . . .

Among other interesting things, Dr. Paul explains very

fully and learnedly the mystery of the periodical suspension of breathing on the part of *yogins,* and some other seemingly quite impossible phenomena which he witnessed himself many times. Here is his theory of "breathing" in brief.

The *yogins* have discovered the secret and have acquired the capacity of the chameleon to assume all the outward and visible appearances of plumpness and leanness. This animal, as is well known, appears at times very large when his lungs are filled with air; but when he releases the latter, he becomes quite insignificant in size. Many other reptiles acquire by the same process the ability to swim across wide rivers, as the need arises, and the surplus of air which remains in them after the blood has been fully oxygenated, makes them extremely lively, both on dry land and in water. The capacity of storing large quantities of air when necessary is the characteristic feature of all animals who are subject to *hibernation.* The ancient Hindu philosophers, observing this capacity, took advantage of it and perfected it. The method employed by the *yogins,* known as *Bhastrikâ Kumbhaka,* consists of the following:

The *yogin* who wishes to acquire this art isolates himself in an underground cave, where the atmosphere is more uniform and more moist than on the surface of the earth, and where, in consequence, the need for food is much less. Man's appetite is in proportion to the quantity of carbon dioxide he exhales in a given period of time. That is why *yogins* never use any salt and live on milk alone, which they take only once a day at night, spending their days in a semi-cataleptic condition. They move very slowly, in order to breathe as little as possible. Movement increases the amount of exhaled carbon dioxide, and so the philosophy of the *yogins* prescribes *avoidance of exertion.*

The quantity of exhaled carbon dioxide is also increased by loud and long talk and decreases when subdued so the *yogins* teach slow and quiet speech and often take the vow of silence. *Physical* labor increases the quantity of carbon dioxide also, while mental labor decreases it. Accordingly, the *yogin* spends his life in contemplation and deep meditation. The *yogins* practice two methods, *padmâsana* and *siddhâsana,* to enable them to breathe as little as possible. In the words of Śukadeva:*

> *Cross your legs; firmly straighten the neck and back; rest the palms of the hands on the knees; shut the mouth and begin to expire forcibly through both nostrils. Next inhale and exhale as rapidly as possible until you are fatigued. Then inhale through the right nostril, and filling the abdomen with the inspired air, suspend the breathing and fix the sight on the tip of the nose. Then exhale through the left nostril, and inhale through the left one. Suspend the breathing again and exhale through the right one. Then begin the process all over again, starting with the right nostril, etc.*

When the yogins are able to practice the above quiescent postures for the period of three hours [says Dr. Paul], they commence to practice *Prânâyâma,* a stage of self-trance, which is characterized by profuse perspiration, trembling of the system, and a sense of lightness of the animal economy. They next practice *Pratyâhâra,* a stage of self-trance in which they have functions of the senses suspended. They then practice *Dhâranâ,* a stage of self-trance in which sensibility and voluntary motion are suspended, and the body is made capable of retaining any given posture, the mind being said to be quiescent in this stage of self-trance.

The Yogins, after attaining the stage of *Dhâranâ* (cataleptic condition), aspire to what is termed *Dhyâna,* a stage of self-trance in which they pretend to be surrounded by flashes of eternal light or electricity, termed *Ananta-jyotis* (from two Sanskrit words signifying endless or all-pervading light), which they say is the universal soul. The Yogins in a state of Dhyâna are said to be clairvoyant. The Dhyâna of the Yogins is the *Turîya-avasthâ* of the Vedântists . . .

Samâdhi is the last stage of self-trance. In this state the Yogins, like the bat, the hedgehog, the marmot, the hamster, and the dormouse, acquire the power of supporting the abstraction of atmospheric air, and the privation of food and drink. Of *Samâdhi* or human hibernation there have been three cases within the last twenty-five years. The first case occurred in Calcutta, the second in Jaisalmer and the third in the Pañjâb. I was an eyewitness of the first case.

Some of the phenomena mentioned above were actually witnessed by Dr. Paul in their objective reality. There are others the reality of which he, having "seen so much that is hard to understand," neither believes nor denies. But he guarantees that a *yogin* can at will suspend and hold his breath for forty-three minutes and twelve seconds . . .

---

* A celebrated *yogin* and wonder-worker of the second century B.C.
[The work from which this passage is quoted may be Śukadeva's *Śukâshṭaka,* although this is not absolutely certain. — *Compiler.*]

Oh, Science! . . . Art thou also, like everything else, but *vanitas vanitatum?* Physiology, represented by Dr. Lefèvre and another doctor of medicine who quotes him, the learned Alfred Swaine Taylor, F.R.S. vice-president of the Royal Society of Physicians,* assures us that so far not a single diver, whoever he may have been, could sustain more than *two consecutive minutes* of complete submersion of the body. And the author adds that as long as man is not a fish, it is inconceivable that he would be able to remain under water even *another half-minute.†*

So then no argument will do us any good. Science has decided, and it is not for us, gullible profanes, to contradict it. But it is evident that nothing is known as yet in Europe about either the methods of the *yogins* or the means employed by the philosophers of India from immemorial times, gradually to "transmute," as it were, the whole organism of man. It follows that, at least in the case under discussion, all that our physiologists have the right to declare is limited approximately to the following: "The phenomena of life which we have studied, investigating them under conditions *known* to us, and which may be called normal or abnormal, we have studied well and fully guarantee the accuracy of our conclusions . . ." However, it would be well if they added: "But having no pretensions to assure the world that we are fully acquainted with all the forces of nature, known and unknown, existent or apt to be developed under conditions not yet known to us, we do not claim the right to impede in others their urge for bolder investigation in regions which we have not yet reached, owing to our great caution (and sometimes to our moral timidity), an urge for the discovery of higher, though rare, phenomena of human nature. Not presuming to maintain that the human organism

---

*[Alfred Swaine Taylor (1806-1880) was an English medical jurist who travelled and studied abroad. Prof. of medical jurisprudence at Guy's Hospital, lecturer on chemistry and innovator in photographic processes. Editor of *London Medical Gazette*, 1844-51, and author of several works, among them *The Principles and Practice of Medical Jurisprudence*, 1865 and 1873.—*Compiler.*]

†*Op. cit.*, Vol. II, p. 5.

is entirely incapable of developing transcendental powers, which manifest themselves only under rare conditions
unknown as yet to science, we do not wish to keep other
explorers within the limits of our scientific discoveries . . ."

By pronouncing this noble, and, at the same time, modest
speech, our physiologists (including our quarrelsome Dr.
Wm. B. Carpenter*) would at once gain the gratitude of
posterity. Their learned colleagues, no longer afraid to gain
the reputation (in spite of their past great services to
science) of gullible, irresponsible subjects in their dotage,
would undertake to investigate all such phenomena seriously
and impartially, instead of sureptitiously, as is being done
now by some of them, from fear of being discovered red-
handed. All the phenomena of Spiritualism would then pass
from the region of materialized "mothers-in-law" and
"grandmothers," as well as mere fortune telling, to the
region of pure psycho-physiological science, and the celebrated "spirits" would probably evaporate. The imperishable
Spirit which "belongeth not to this world" would then be
more accessible and more understandable to humanity. The
latter will comprehend the harmony of the whole when it
realizes how closely, how indissolubly, the visible world is
bound to the invisible. As expressed with deep understanding by one of the esteemed Russian scientists, Professor
Butlerov:† "all this is subject to knowledge, and the

---

* [Dr. William Benjamin Carpenter (1813-1885) was an English
naturalist and physician of considerable renown. A man of incessant
industry, he took part in many public movements, conducted deep-sea
explorations, and carried out laborious work mainly in zoology. He was
a voluminous writer of both books and scientific articles. His chief work
is entitled *The Principles of General and Comparative Physiology* published in 1839.—*Compiler.*]

† [Alexander Mihaylovich Butlerov. Renowned Russian chemist,
founder of the so-called "Butlerov School," b. Aug. 25/Sept. 6, 1828, at
Chistopol', Province of Kazan'; died Aug. 5/17, 1886, on his estate of
Butlerovka in the same Province. He was the son of a lieutenant-colonel
of modest means and was educated at home and in the Gymnasium of
Kazan', before entering the physio-mathematical department of the
Kazan' University. His unusual capacities resulted in a rapid progress
in his studies and a generous recognition on the part of his teachers.

increase of the sum-total of knowledge can only enrich and not suppress science. It has to be accomplished by means of strict observation, investigation, verification by means of experiment, and be guided by *positive scientific methods,* just as is the case in the establishment of all other natural phenomena. We do not appeal to blind faith, as has been done in the past, but to science; not to the denial of science, but to the broadening of its scope . . ."

Then indeed both Haeckel at the head of the evolutionists, and Alfred Russel Wallace at the head of the Spiritualists, would express complete satisfaction. What is there actually to prevent a man from having two principles in his essence; one purely divine, and the other purely animal? Really it does not behoove even you great scientists to "bind the sweet influences of the Pleiades," even if you choose "Arcturus and his sons" for guides on your way. Has it never occurred to you to apply to your own intellectual pride the questions which the "voice out of the whirlwind" once asked of long-suffering Job? Even though you have succeeded in catching

His University appointed him to its Staff to teach chemistry and physical geography. In 1854 he became Doctor of Chemistry at Moscow University and was retained there to teach Chemistry. During three separate trips abroad, Butlerov spent considerable time studying the progress of chemistry in Europe, and establishing personal relations with a number of outstanding scientists, such as Bunsen, Kekule and others. His scientific research laid the foundation of chemistry in Russia and coincided with the first marked development of organic chemistry in Europe.

It is of special interest to students of Theosophy to note his intense interest in Spiritualistic and allied phenomena. He became versed in the subject and approached it from the purely scientific viewpoint. On his initiative, there was organized in St. Petersburg in 1871 the first scientific committee for the investigation of mediumistic phenomena, which included Professors Ovsyannikov, Chebishev and Zion. He was also very active in the formation of another Committee for the same purpose, suggested by Prof. Mendeleyev and made up of members of the Physical Society at the University of St. Petersburg. He was a constant contributor to the Spiritualistic journal *Rebus* for which H.P.B. wrote. His articles on the general subject of mediumship and psychic manifestations were published at St. Petersburg in 1889, with reminiscences by his life-long friend and co-worker, Prof. N. P. Wagner— *Compiler.*]

leviathan in the watery deeps, by piercing his nose with a
hook, still, in the words of the *Book of Job* [xxxviii, 4, 17]:
"where wast thou when I laid the foundations of the earth?
. . . Have the gates of death been opened unto thee?" so as
to enable you to assert positively that *here,* and not *there,*
is the "abode of eternal light"? . . .*

"Allâhâbâd, . . . Allâhâbâd! . . ." the conductors cried.
It was six a.m. when our train, puffing and shaking, noisily
pulled into the magnificent station of the East Indian railway. This at once put an end to my reveries. All my travelling
companions woke and began to fuss about, excepting the
Thâkur, who had a habit of disappearing at the stations as
if swallowed by the earth. We were, however, accustomed
to his strange ways and did not even inquire about him. The
professor of Sanskrit, Pandit Sunder-Lal-Bhaṭṭachârya, was
waiting for us at the station and invited us all to his home.
A handsome and stately man, with muscular naked legs,
proudly draped in a red Kashmîr shawl, embroidered in
gold, and with a bright *pagrî* on his long, black hair—such
was our host. Here the types are quite different. The shaven
Marâthâ heads, crowned with their helmet-like turbans are
not to be seen any more. Long hair, black beards and
expensive shawls worn like Roman togas, with scarves on
the shapeless heads of the Benares Pandits, were now intermingled with the black coats *à la François I* worn by the
bareheaded Bâbûs and the white caps of the northern
Hindus. On the station platform the spying captain was
darting about, in his turn imagining us to be Russian spies
and probably thinking his dark glasses made him unrecognizable. However, we paid no attention to him, and left at
once in the carriages waiting for us.

In the very center of the native or "black" Allâhâbâd,†
in a real labyrinth of streets, lanes, alleys and gardens, stood
the house of Sunder-Lal-Bhaṭṭachârya to which we were
invited. It was about 8 a.m. The house was lost in the rich

---

*[The partial translation into English by Mrs. Vera V. Johnston,
published in 1892, does not go beyond this point.—*Compiler.*]

† All the cities were Englishmen live are divided into a *black* and
a *white* town. The Hindus are not allowed to live in the latter.

verdure of a thicket of teak trees; it seemed as though the sunbeams never reached the spacious and dark rooms of this house. In spite of this, we suddenly became aware of the intense heat. In the beginning of April, during the forenoon, the thermometer stood at 120° (Fahrenheit) in the shade. The scorching heat of the North-Western Provinces and of Râjasthân is entirely different from that of Bombay: in Central India perspiration runs off a man in streams, and in this moist, hot atmosphere one feels as if one were in a Russian bath, whereas at Allâhâbâd you never perspire, and this town seems destined to be the world's dryer, from the mummy-like ascetics, with whom the banks of the Ganges and the Jumnâ are strewn, to the planted feather-grass which is reduced to dust at the slightest touch. Here, for eight months of the year, there is a dry, fiery heat which seems to consume one internally, scorching the throat with every breath, and drying one out to the very marrow of one's bones like a burning desert wind; during such heat there is nothing to do but to sit motionless and avoid the slightest exertion. All the doors and windows on the verandah have shutters made of strongly fragrant *khus-khus* grass, abundantly sprinkled with water from the outside every five or ten minutes. The rooms are darkened until sundown, which makes it impossible for a European to do any work during the day.* Upon our arrival we seated ourselves on the carpets and rugs, and, half-reclining on the pillows made of

---

*The English are so permeated with the dead letter formality of their centuries-old national customs, that from the very beginning of their settlement in India until 1869, they never attempted to adapt themselves to climatic conditions, or to adjust at least the outward appearance of their courts of law; the judges and lawyers sat during the scorching heat in their enormous powdered wigs. Finally on an occasion in the summer of 1869, the presiding judge of Allâhâbâd, feeling he was about to faint, impulsively threw off his wig . . . . . Instantly all the other wigs followed suit. Not a single word was uttered during this performance. Realizing that a change in the old custom was unthinkable, they remained silent as if by mutual consent and have kept their silence to the present day. The law concerning the wigs has not been abrogated, but on entering the court everyone silently takes off his wig at the opening of the session, and this innovation has in its turn become a law.

palm leaves, were afraid to move. At times the breeze passing through the wet tissue of khus-khus wafted to our faces an aromatic coolness, while the *pankhâ*,* continuously waving over our heads, stirred the stuffy air and allowed us occasionally to breathe artificial air, instead of the scorching atmosphere.

We spent three days at Allâhâbâd. At three o'clock in the morning we went out to visit the town and its environs, returning at about 7 a.m. for breakfast; after that we all threw ourselves down on the rugs in the darkened hall under the *pankhâs*, and slept until four in the afternoon. Then, after some tea "with ice," we once again started on our expedition of studying antiquities and returned after 9 p.m. for our *dinner*. We never slept during the night but sat in the garden and *breathed* until dawn . . .

The town is situated on the southeastern boundary of the Doâb, the "Land of the Two Rivers," on a sandy promontory formed by the confluence of the Ganges and the Jumnâ. The latter has its source in a group of mountains called "Jumnâtri," in a spring bubbling among rocks covered with eternal snow, at a height of 10,849 feet above sea level. Here, at Allâhâbâd, both rivers are equally wide, but the Ganges is deeper and its waters are purer than those of the Jumnâ. They flow in a friendly way in the same river bed, side by side, but not blending their waters, so that the waves of the Jumnâ stretch like a blue ribbon along the yellow waters of the Ganges. The natives call this place *Trivenî* (the three rivers), as an underground river, the Sarasvatî, flows there also, a lost fugitive whose waters suddenly disappear in the

---

* *Pankhâs* are great fans. They are arranged in every room, especially in the bedrooms, and without them one could suffocate. They consist of lengths of cloth lined with cotton and stretched under the ceiling to the full width of the room, sometimes in several rows. They are set in motion by cords passing through the wall onto the verandah. Behind the wall, day and night sit *pankhâ-wallahs* (coolies), taking their two-hour turns in swinging the *pankhâs*. While this motion lasts, writing is impossible, as everything blows about the room; *pankhâs* are continuously raising a miniature storm, and in cast of heavy perspiration make it easy to catch cold.

desert of Sirhind. After irrigating the roots of the holy tree which grows in the underground caves (the "Catacombs of the Fort"), this river suddenly comes to light again from under a tower of the Allâhâbâd fortress and, as though ashamed of its conduct, swiftly flows away to one side; then, after forming a little island, it unites with its two sisters far below the town. A legend in one of the oldest *Purânas* * tells us the story of that river, assuring us that it is in reality the spouse of Brahmâ, Sarasvatî, "the Goddess of Knowledge and Secret Sciences," who had to blush from shame by reason of her own imprudence. One day, as she was slowly walking in the desert, a book in her hand, she was so deeply engrossed in reading she did not notice how a crowd of demons, noisily shouting, had surrounded her. Being ashamed of her negligence, she sank at once into the sands of the desert and, having disappeared from the surface of the earth, reappeared again only at *Prayâga* (the ancient name of Allâhâbâd), where she went on flowing side by side with her two worldly sisters.

The "White" town (where the Europeans live) is situated far away from the "Black" town of the natives. It has enormous, broad boulevards, crossing each other and lined with gorgeous trees which teem with jumping squirrels. Among spacious gardens, with yards protected on all sides by walls, are situated the bungalows of the English, which resemble out-of-town villas, rather than city buildings. The "White" town is not a town at all. With the exception of several wide squares, Allâhâbâd is like a gigantic park, 32 miles in circumference, in which, at a distance of a quarter of a mile from one another, are situated the villas mentioned above. Here a haughty colony of Britishers, longing for their foggy mother-country, tries to create around itself an artificial London. Here etiquette reigns like an implacable tyrant. The ladies, from early morning tightly laced in their corsets, spend their time in making ceremonious visits to one

---

Purâna means "olden" or "ancient." They are collections of the oldest religious legends of the land, which are highly revered by the natives.

another; twice a week there is held a high society formal
"*pûja*"—an official reception. Ceremonious dinners of close
friends are called "simple dinners"; but at these friendly
meals the men arrive in full dress and white neckties, and
the ladies in evening gowns and diamonds. And all this at a
temperature of 120°! . . . They dine at 8 p.m., and leave
for home at about 10 p.m., as here everyone gets up at five
in the morning. A most intellectual life in all respects! . . .
During our first stay at Allâhâbâd none of us dreamed it
necessary to leave our cards with the local goddess-patroness
of the province —Lady Cooper; for this reason our party
was looked upon with still greater suspicion. Who but
"Russian spies" would dare to show such contempt for the
representative in the North-Western Provinces of the Empress of India? . . .

On the first day we visited the fortress, having received
with great difficulty special permission from the commander.
Being probably afraid lest we should draw plans of the fortress, the English sent half a dozen spies to shadow us;
Moslem policemen followed us like shadows, and in the
distance could be seen our friend, the blond and rosy-cheeked
spy *en chef,* Captain Lang. He could have spared himself
the trouble; face to face with these ancient remnants of the
once sumptuous *Prayâga,* in turn the capital of Brâhman,
Buddhist and finally Moslem India, we were deep in contemplation of the past and quite forgetful of the present.

Prayâga-Allâhâbâd is one of the oldest places in India,
closely connected with its past and somewhat nebulous history. It was here that the Ṛishis of the Vedic period, the
great patriarchs and inspired poets of India, composed for
the first time their *Brâhmaṇa* commentaries. Inspired by a
zealous religious fervor — a feeling that is always dangerous
in its consequences for future generations, for, by carefully
keeping philosophical truths from possible desecration by the
ignorant masses, it estranges them from the latter, leaving
them to their own cogitations — the Ṛishis were the first
to sow in India the unfortunate seeds of idolatry. Concealing
under the poetical cover of allegories and emblems their
abstract ideas of the attributes of Deity, which they alone
perceived in their boundless world-contemplation, and endea-

DELHI: JÂMI‘-MASJID

KUṬB-MINĀR AT DELHI

voring to make these abstract attributes available to the masses, without profaning them, they very soon transformed each of these separate attributes into a special god or goddess. It is for that reason that the people "took unto themselves graven images." From that time on they saw truth in falsehood and falsehood in truth; the latter, however, remained entirely in the jealous hands of the ancient and learned clergy. We find a similar state of things in ancient Egypt, Greece, Chaldea — everywhere. No wonder that Sarasvatî, goddess of the secret sciences of nature, has to hide deep underground from the evil eyes of the demons of materialism; she manifests herself only to those who tirelessly and steadfastly pursue her and search out the pure sources of her living waters; in the world, however, and to the eyes of the superstitious masses, she appears riding on a proud peacock, whose tail, full of eyes, is spread in the sunshine, but whose real eyes are blind to daylight . . . It is only the former, those who are athirst for her teachings, that she caresses, quenching the burning thirst of her devoted followers, quieting their ceaseless longing for the unknown, which to all others is unattainable. But alas, the direct descendants of the Rishis of India and the Hierophants of ancient Egypt are few, while the name of the unworthy, allegedly "initiated," is legion.

The traditions of Râjasthân mention Prayâga as one of the oldest fortresses of the Râjputs. It was here that the Âryan Kshatriyas, following their military instinct, erected fortifications which later consolidated for them all their subsequent conquests in the upper valleys of the Jumnâ and the Ganges and enabled them for many centuries to hold in awe and trembling the whole of Lower Bengal. During the time of the Macedonian Empire, Prayâga was situated exactly on this spot, near the confluence of the two rivers. According to the ancient chronicle of the Jaisalmer princely family of Yadu, "the Prâchyas, descendants of *Pûru* from *Pûruyâga* (Prayâga), received Megasthenes, the ambassador of Seleucus, who was sent to conclude a treaty with Sandracottos, King of the Prâsii, in his *ancient* city." More than a thousand years later, in the seventh century, mention is made of a feast given by Sîlâditya to honor a Chinese traveller, the pious Buddhist Hiouen-Thsang.* In those days Buddhism, which had almost exiled the gods from India, was rapidly declining, and very soon after the above mentioned feast a mighty revival of contemporary Brâhmanism or rather Hinduism took place. But from the very earliest days of the Vedic period, and up to the time when this devoted Chinese traveller mourned the downfall of Buddhism, Prayâga never ceased to be, after Benares, the most sacred place in India; it was called the "field of happiness," where the widow's copper mite was esteemed just as highly as an offering of a *lakh* † of gold. The famous pillar of King Aśoka, erected 250 B.C., is standing even now in the middle of the fortress. There also, some 200 paces to one side, you can see the dark entrance to the underground caves, in one of which grows a thick tree, more like a stump, with several withered branches. Hindu Augurs say that these branches bear flowers once a year on the sacred day of Vishṇu.

On nearing the glacis of the fort our attention was directed to a heap of stones. On that spot once stood the mosque of Jâmi'-Masjid, erected in the time of Shâh-Jahân and renowned throughout India. The English, having forcibly and for no apparent reason taken it from the Moslems,

---

* [Hiouen Thsang (spelled also Hsüen Tsang, Hiwen T'Sang, Yüan Tsang, and Yuan-Chwang) was a renowned Chinese Buddhist traveller and scholar, born about 605 A.D. in the district of Keu-Shi near Honan-Fu. He adopted the monastic life, travelling over China, teaching and learning, and settling for a time at the capital Chang-gan where he became well known for his learning. In August 629 he started alone for India, plunging into the Gobi or Sha-mo desert. His journey was an epic in itself. He visited all the chief Buddhist shrines, staying for several years in some of them. He returned to his native land some fifteen years later. After several years of study and writing, Hiouen Thsang died in 664 in a convent at Chang-gan.

The best source of information concerning his life and extensive travels are: the *Ta-T'ang-Si-Yu-Ki,* or *Memoirs on Western Countries,* compiled under the traveller's own supervision by order of the great Emperor Tai-Tsung; and a *Biography of Hiouen Thsang* by two of his contemporaries, Hoeili and Yen-thsong. These works have been translated into French by Stanislas A. Julien in 1853 and 1857-58 respectively, under the general title of *Voyages des Pèlerins Bouddhistes.—Compiler.*]

†A *lakh* is equal to 100,000 rupees.

first turned it into barracks, later made it into a commisary for one of the regiments, and afterwards, when the regiment had left, for some mysterious strategical reason demolished it. "Shamefully and undeservedly did we deprive our Moslem subject of one of their revered shrines, without even giving them a rupee in compensation," writes Colonel Henry George Keene in his work *The Moghul Empire*,* Allâhâbâd was made the capital of the North-Western Provinces only after the mutiny of 1857. It became the residence of the authorities after they were cut to pieces at Âgra.

Beyond, to the north of the fortress, are the ruins of the *old* "white town." It was there that the mutiny of the 6th Bengalî Sepoy regiment of native infantry broke out the 5th of June, 1857. The officers assembled in the mess at the time, hearing the shouts and wild threats from outside, rushed out into the courtyard. They were instantly shot, some 23 of them, I believe. The mutineers ransacked the treasury, broke into the jail, set free the prisoners, burned down all the houses of the "white town," and murdered about a hundred Europeans. The remaining Europeans succeeded in finding refuge in the fortress, where four hundred Sikhs, always true to their word, protected them from their own people and thus saved the garrison, the women and children from certain death. Recognizing the Sikhs as the bravest people of India (with the exception of the Râjputs), the English — out of gratitude, no doubt — have attempted ever since in every possible way to disarm them, but do not do so outright. They cannot accept the idea that others can

---

* [Henry George Keene (1781-1864), English scholar, educated privately, partly by Menon, later one of Napoleon's generals. Went to India, 1798, as cadet in the Madras army, and, after some active duty with a Sepoy regiment, obtained an appointment in the Madras civil service. Entered college of Fort William, Calcutta, and in Jan., 1804 graduated with honors in Persian and Arabic and a gold medal in Mohammedan law. Returning to Europe, he graduated from Cambridge, 1815, and travelled on the continent. In 1824, he became professor of Arabic and Persian at the East India College at Haileybury, near Hartford. He resigned in 1834 and devoted the rest of his life to writing and study, mainly in the field of Persian history and culture. (*Nat. Cyclop. of Biography.*)—*Compiler.*]

be more honest than they and that there are such who can keep their word.

The fort of Allâhâbâd, as well as the fortified castle within it, were both built by the great Emperor Akbar about 1575 A.D. on the ruins of an ancient Buddhist town. Prayâga is the oldest capital of the lunar (or Somavanśa) dynasty of the Kshatriyas. None of the architectural beauties of Akbar's time — his high towers, the majestic cupola rising above the open-work galleries, the arcades and decorated walls, the little balconies which were seen and described by Heber, or any of the sights that so enchanted the bishop some 60 years ago — remain any longer. The hands of regular vandals — the Englishmen of the East India Company — tore down the balconies, pasted up, smoothed over and leveled the Mauritanian carvings of the exterior and interior walls, covering everything with stucco in the most hideous manner. One all-redeeming object remains in the fortress, the pillar of Aśoka, which has stood there for more than two thousand years.

Many columns exist, especially in Egypt, which are higher and more majestic than this one, but there is hardly another which could be of greater interest to an archaeologist or a philologist. Its inscriptions reveal to a patient cryptographer or philologist an entire panorama of the ancient world, as yet so little known to us. We can study in these inscriptions the innermost thoughts of the royal architects, follow the gradual change of ideas and conceptions, and witness more than twenty centuries of struggle between various peoples of differing religious views, who fought, brother against brother, from the dawn of history, and flooded the world with their blood, each of them in the name of that which he thought to be holy *truth* and which his brother considered to be sinful heresy.

The height of this pillar, excluding the base, is only 35 feet; it has a conical form, getting narrower towards the top; at the base, it is 3½ feet in diameter, whereas at the pointed top only a little more than two feet. The three different inscriptions belong to kings of three different epochs: Aśoka, Samudra-Gupta and Jahângîr, a Buddhist, a semi-

Brâhmaṇa and a Moslem, respectively. Aśoka erected the pillar in order to immortalize his edicts, issued to spread Buddhism. Samudra-Gupta, in the second century of our era, used the opportunity to engrave on it the inventory of his vast possessions in India, which stretched from Nepal to Dekkan and from Gujarât to Assam. Finally the pillar, which in the meantime had fallen and been forgotten, was replaced on its former base and cleared of the dust of centuries by the Mogul Emperor, Jahângîr, who engraved on it the date of his ascension to the throne (1605). In addition to these inscriptions, there are numerous others containing the names of potentates, pilgrims, Brâhmaṇas converted to Buddhism, and the many travellers from the first century of our era to the last.

King Aśoka's inscriptions on the pillar are strikingly different from the others; first, because they are often found on many other monuments, and secondly, for the reason that they invariably commence with the stereotyped phrase: "Devânampiye Piyadasi lâja hevaṃ âhâ" (the Beloved of the gods, King Piyadasi). History tells us that King Piyadasi inherited his throne in Ceylon from his father 236 years after the birth of Gautama (Buddha). A fervent Buddhist, he persuaded the Hindu King Aśoka (called also Dharmâśoka) to send his second son Mahinda and his daughter Saṃghamittâ, accompanied by monks and nuns, as pilgrims to spread Buddhism all over India. According to the *Mahâvanśa,** the religious zeal of the old king and his sons for the new teaching was so strong that even Queen *Anulâ,*

---

*George Turnour translated from the Pâli this oldest of all the manuscripts of Ceylon. See his *The Mahâwanso,* Ceylon, 1837.

[George Turnour (1799-1843) was an English Orientalist, born in Ceylon and educated in England; entered Ceylon Civil Service, 1818, and soon became a renowned Pâli scholar, devoting his attention to the native records of the Island. He was the first to publish authentic facts as to the origin and progress of the Buddhist religion in Ceylon. The first Pâli text to be translated was his work, *The Mahâwanso,* in Roman characters and with translation (Ceylon, Cotta Church Mission Press, 1837). Turnour rose to the Supreme Council of Ceylon, and died at Naples.—*Compiler.*]

at his suggestion, went as a pilgrim to preach the religion of truth, accompanied by *bhikshus* (mendicant monks) who were her own subjects, and later herself became a *bhikshunî* (nun).* Aśoka who probably regarded King Piyadasi as an apostle of Buddha, refers to him constantly in his inscriptions. "Thus says King Devânampiya Piyadasi . . ." was used as a sacramental introductory phrase to every new paragraph.

I quote here a few excerpts from some of the more interesting inscriptions on this pillar:

> Thus spake King Devânampiya Piyadasi:—In the twenty-seventh year of my anointment.† I have caused this religious edict to be published in writing. I acknowledge and confess the faults that have been cherished in my heart. From the love of virtue, by the side of which all other things are as sins—from the strict scrutiny of sin,—and from a fervent desire to be told of sin; — by the fear of sin and by very enormity of sin:—by these may my eyes be strengthened and confirmed (in rectitude).
>
> The sight of religion and the love of religion of their own accord increase and will ever increase; and my people whether of the laity (*grihasta*), or of the priesthood (*ascetics*)—all mortal beings, are knit together thereby and prescribe to themselves the same path: and above

---

* [The original Russian text of this entire paragraph is rather confused and contains obvious errors which are somewhat difficult to disentangle. We have tried to clarify the meaning by making as few corrections as possible.

Aśoka was king of Magadha in India and Devânampiya-Tissa was the brother of a sub-king of Ceylon called Mahânâga. The latter was married to Anulâ, the daughter of the king of Ceylon whose name was Mutasiva. According to G. P. Malalasekera's *A Dictionary of Pâli Proper Names*, Devânampiya-Tissa and his sister-in-law were converted to Buddhism by Mahinda, the son of Aśoka. After Anulâ and her five hundred women had heard Mahinda preach, they wanted to become Buddhist nuns. Samghamittâ, Aśoka's daughter and Mahinda's sister, was asked to come to Ceylon from India and ordain them. She brought with her a branch of the Bodhi-tree.—*Compiler.*]

† Compare for verification with the *Journal of the Asiatic Society of Bengal*, Vol. VI, No. 67, July, 1873.

[H.P.B. quotes here from pp. 581-84, where may be found an account by James Prinsep, Secretary of the Asiatic Society, entitled: "Interpretation of the most ancient of the Inscriptions on the pillar called the lât of Feroz Shâh, near Delhi, and of the Allâhâbâd, Radhia and Mattiah pillars, or lât, inscriptions which agree therewith."— *Compiler.*]

all, having obtained the mastery over their passions, they become supremely wise. For this is indeed true wisdom: it is upheld and bound by (it consists in) religion—by religion which cherishes, religion which teaches pious acts, religion that bestows (the only true) pleasure.

Thus spake King Devânampiya Piyadasi:—In religion is the chief excellence:—but religion consists in good works:—in the non-omission of many acts: mercy and charity, purity and chastity—(these are) to me the anointment of consecration.* Towards the poor and the afflicted, towards bipeds and quadrupeds, towards the fowls of the air and things that move in the waters, manifold have been the benevolent acts performed by me. Out of consideration for things inanimate even many other excellent things have been done by me. To this purpose is the present edict promulgated; may all pay attention to it (or take cognizance thereof), and let it endure for ages to come: and he who acts in conformity thereto, the same shall attain eternal happiness (or shall be united with Sugato).

---

*Sumaṅgala, Buddhist High Priest of Ceylon, explained this phrase in one of his letters to me, by saying that Piyadasi was the first one to ask to be anointed again at his consecration to Buddhism, in the name of these seven chief virtues. [H.P.B.]

[Unnanse H. Sumaṅgala was a renowned Ceylonese Buddhist priest and scholar. He was born on January 20, 1827, in the village of Hikkaduwa, Ceylon, the fourth son of Don Johannes de Silva Abeyewera-Gunawardana; was a precocious child, and his parents saw at a very early age what the trend of his life was likely to be. When five years old, he was already dedicated to the monastery, and at the age of twelve was admitted to the Order as a *samanera* or novice; it is recorded that in his studies he already then surpassed those who were far older than he. He placed himself under the tuition of a Sanskrit pundit, a Brâhmaṇa from India, and made very rapid progress. When 21, he went to Kandy, the ancient capital of the Island, and received the full ordination of a monk at the hands of the Chief High Priest. He astonished his examiners by the depth of his scholarship, the wide range of his reading, and the ease with which he handled both Sanskrit and Pâli. He then returned to his native village where he was appointed as tutor to the monks, spending there twelve years of his life. Transferred later to a higher appointment at Galle, where he spent the next six years as priest in charge of the temple, continuing also as tutor to the monks. Having special aptitude for languages, he learned Elu, the classical language of Ceylon, English and French.

After six years at Galle, he was elected High Priest of the Srîpada —the temple of the Holy Footprint on the mountain of Adam's Peak. At a later date, he became also High Priest of the District of Galle, and Examiner-in-Chief of the candidates for ordination in Ceylon. In 1873, he moved to Kotahena in Colombo, and shortly afterwards to Maliga-

There follows an enumeration of the nine sins. They are known under the name of *âzinave,* and, according to the teachings of Gautama the Buddha, one must avoid them: "anger, cruelty, theft, pride, envy, despondency, drunkenness, adultery, murder." * On the western side of the pillars are engra ed the rules concerning the relation of ascetics to punishments in the name of the Buddha, and the amnesty of criminals during three special days. Which days these are, is not stated. On the southern side we find the enumeration of the birds and animals which it is sinful to kill; then follows the most interesting inscription, which throws a

---

kanda, where he founded the Vidyodaya College for monks, of which he remained Principal during the rest of his life.

Sumaṅgala was a voluminous writer, but his works are mostly unknown in the West. He was a friend of F. Max Müller, Prof. Rhys Davids, Prof. C. R. Lanman of Harvard, Sir Edwin Arnold and Sir Monier-Williams. His first contact with Theosophy took place in 1880, when the Founders first visited Ceylon. From then on a strong friendship existed with them, and he speeded Col. Olcott on his mission to Japan in 1889 (See the Colonel's *Old Diary Leaves* for complete account).

When quite old, Sumaṅgala fell down a short staircase, rising one morning in the dark, as he always did, and fractured his hip bone. The shock was too much for the aged body, and he passed away nine days after, April 30, 1911. The ceremony of cremation at Colombo was the greatest they ever had, and all combined to render him their respects. He was succeeded as Principal of the College by his pupil Ñanissera.

For all practical purposes, Sumaṅgala was the Head of the Southern Church of Buddhism, as a whole. He was also one of the Honorary Vice-Presidents of the Theosophical Society, and both Founders held him in the greatest esteem.—*Compiler.*]

* [The closing portion of this inscription is as follows:

"Thus spake King Devânampiya Piyadasi:—Whatever appeareth to be virtuous and good, that is so held to be good and virtuous by me, and not the less if it have evil tendency, is it accounted for evil by me or is named among the *âzinave* (the nine offences?). Eyes are given (to man) to distinguish between the two qualities (between right and wrong): according to the capacity of the eyes so may they behold. The following are accounted among the nine minor transgressions:—mischief, hard-heartedness, anger, pride, envy. These evil deeds of nine kinds shall on no account be mentioned. They should be regarded as opposite (or prohibited). Let this (ordinance) be impressed on my heart, let it be cherished with all my soul."

—*Compiler.*]

bright light on the whole life of this royal apostle of Buddhism. It says:

Thus spake King Devânampiya Piyadasi: — In the twelfth year of my anointment, a religious edict (was) published for the pleasure and profit of the world; having destroyed that (document) and regarding my former religion as sin, I now for the benefit of the world proclaim the fact. And this (among my nobles, among my near relations, and among my dependents, whatsoever pleasure I may thus abandon), I therefore cause to be destroyed; and I proclaim the same in all the congregations; while I pray with every variety of prayer for those who differ from me in creed, that they following after my proper example may with me attain unto eternal salvation; wherefore the present edict of religion is promulgated in the twenty-seventh year of my anointment.

Thus spake King Devânampiya Piyadasi:—Kings of the olden time have gone to heaven under these very desires. How then among mankind may religion (or growth in grace) be increased? Yea through the conversion of the humbly-born shall religion increase.

Thus spake King Devânampiya Piyadasi:—The present moment and the past have departed under the same ardent hopes. How by the conversion of the royal-born may religion be increased? Through the conversion of the lowly-born if religion thus increaseth, by how much (more) through the conviction of the high-born, and their conversion, shall religion increase? Among whomsoever the name of God resteth (?) verily this is religion (or verily virtue shall there increase) . . . .*

In this case the "name of God" is a synonym of "Nirvâna," the meaning of which (notwithstanding the views of

---

*The occurrence of the word *God* in a Buddhist inscription became a constant source of dispute among Sanskrit scholars. "Buddhists are atheists; they believe neither in God, nor in the immortality of the human soul," many say. "This expression of Piyadasi is *a reminiscence of his former religion*—an erroneous utterance." I permit myself to express my firm assurance that such a view is absolutely false. A Buddhist, if he is educated at all and acquainted with the *Sûtras*, the pure philosophy of the Buddha, believes both in a deity—though an impersonal one, it is true—and in a life after death. My conviction is based not on personal deductions, but on five years of constant correspondence with the learned Buddhists of Ceylon and Burma, who are members of The Theosophical Society. It is not the fault of Buddhism if to this day our scientists cannot understand its subtle and abstruse metaphysics.

[This Inscription may be found on the eastern side of the pillar, and the translation occurs on pp. 596-99 of Prinsep's account—*Compiler.*]

Eugène Burnouf, Barthélemy Saint-Hilaire * and Co., or
even those of Professor Max Müller) has constantly eluded
Sanskrit scholars and interpreters of Buddhism. It is not
correctly understood to the present day, because it is defined
and argued about on its *dead letter* meaning solely.

The most learned Buddhist priests of Ceylon, Burma and
Siam protest against these various interpretations. It is true
that the Buddhists do not believe in God as an individual,
as a personality independent from the universe, but their
summum bonum, or *Nirvâna,* is identical with the *Moksha*
of the Brâhmaṇas. It is the final union of an infinitesimal
particle, which in its separateness is limited, with the boundless and limitless *whole;* it is eternal and conscious life for
the soul in the quintessence of the divine spirit. The soul
is a temporarily separated spark, attracted by, and merging
again into, the shoreless, flaming ocean of the *Universal
Soul* — the primeval source of *All.* But such a final absorp-
tion of the individual soul, purified from all that is earthly
and sinful, in the "Soul of the Universe" (Anima Mundi)
does not mean the disappearance or "complete annihilation"
of the human soul. In expounding to us this theory, the young
Singhalese Dhammapadajoti, a very learned monk, crushed
a little glass bulb filled with mercury, and dropping it onto
a saucer began to swing it from side to side. The globules of
mercury separated from each other, but at the slightest contact with other droplets blended together again. "Here you
have Nirvâna and the souls," said he.

"Why then is it deemed so difficult to attain Nirvâna?"
asked one of our party. "With the existing mutual attrac-

---

* [Eugène Burnouf (1801-1852), French Orientalist who deciphered
the Zend manuscripts brought to France by Anquetil Duperron, laying
the foundations for a knowledge of that language. He also published
the Sanskrit text and a French translation of the *Bhâgavata-Purâna* and
an important work on Buddhism entitled *Introduction à l'histoire du
Bouddhisme indien.*

Jules Barthélemy Saint-Hilaire (1805-1895) was a French philosopher, scholar and statesman who took active part in the political life
of his country, in addition to his scholastic research and writings. He
published two works on the subject of Buddhism: *Le Bouddha et sa
religion;* and *Du Bouddhisme.—Compiler.*]

tion every soul, on account of its identical nature with the *Universal Soul,* once freed from its earthly fetters, should be able to enter into Nirvâna."

"Certainly; but this mutual attraction exists only on condition of absolute purity of the separate particles. See what will happen now!"

Having sprinkled some ashes and dust on another saucer, he dropped the globules of mercury into this dirt and added a drop of oil. The globules, formerly so lively, were now resting quietly on the bottom of the saucer, thickly covered with dirt. Vain were the attempts to roll them closer to the larger drop of pure mercury; they would not blend with it . . .

"Such are the consequences of earthly pollution," explained Dhammapadajoti. "As long as the soul is not cleansed of the last earthly particle, it cannot enter Nirvâna, nor live the eternal life within the divine essence."

"You believe then in life beyond the tomb?"

Dhammapadajoti laughed, with what seemed to be a slight contempt.

"We believe in it, of course, but we try to avoid its lasting too long, as this would mean a heavy, though perhaps deserved sorrow, in punishment for our sins. To live means to feel and to suffer; not to live, but to rest in Nirvâna, is synonymous with eternal beatitude."

"But this would mean that you are seeking to *annihilate* the soul?"

"In no way; we only seek to annihilate the sufferings which are inseparable from individual life; we try to attain unconditioned felicity in the union with the Supreme Universal Soul. It is only the Whole that is infinite and perfect; in separateness every particle becomes finite and full of imperfections and defects."

I leave all further explanations to the metaphysicians. My aim is merely to prove that our greatest authorities on the philosophy of Buddhism are dealing with it in the dark. Here is another proof: in the first volume of his lectures, *Chips from a German Workshop,* in the chapter on "The

meaning of Nirvâna," * Professor Max Müller, in an indignant answer to some opponent, is trying to show on the
basis of the fact that the word *Nirvâna* means something disappearing or extinguishing itself like the flame of a candle,
that this meaning alone clearly explains the Buddhist religion. According to him, the Buddhists believe in the annihilation of the individual soul and strive after one thing
only, namely, some day to cease to exist. In this article of
Max Müller's, Buddha appears either as an "atheist" or an
"egotist" (in the metaphysical meaning of the words). He
preaches beatitude, "a relapse into that being which is
nothing but itself" [p. 288]. But to the great surprise and
even grief of his followers, who had already become used
to the *mot d'ordre* of the eminent scientist that all the Buddhists are "atheists and nihilists," the esteemed philologist
suddenly makes an unexpected *volte face*. In 1869, in a
public lecture at Kiel, at one of the meetings of the "Association of German Philologists," Max Müller announced before
a large assembly his "opinion of long standing" that *atheism
has nothing whatever to do with the teaching of the Buddha,*
and that it is definitely a great mistake to think that *Nirvâna*
really means the annihilation of the individual soul.†

Taking this into account, would anyone disagree with us,
that the "great scientists" very often abuse their authority?
Professor Max Müller, we must remember, was just as much
of an authority in matters of philology and ancient religions
in 1857 as in 1869. To assert dogmatically that the ancients
believed so-and-so, one must first fathom the depth of their
thought and understand not only their language, but their
unique metaphysical ideas as well; this can be done only by
comparing *all* the ancient philosophies, as each taken separately is entirely incomprehensible . . . "But this," we may
be told, "is what our philologists are now doing, with Professor Max Müller at their head." Yes, but unfortunately so
far their successful comparison has been concerned only
with the dead letter; the living spirit has constantly eluded

---

* [Vol. I, pp, 279 *et seq.* Lecture of April, 1857.]
†See *Trübner's American and Oriental Literary Record,* October 16,
1869, pp. 562-63.

them in the stuffy and foggy atmosphere of materialism . . .
Only the careful study of the *Sûtras,* the preaching of
Gautama the Buddha (the first volume of the *Tripiṭaka* or
"The Three Baskets"), and of the third volume of the same
work, "The System of Metaphysics" of Kaśyapa, the friend
and disciple of the Buddha (a work that throws new light on
the teachings of the Buddha and thus completes them), could
illumine the darkness called Buddhism or the "Philosophy
of Buddha." In the *Sûtras* the reality of the objective world
is called the illusion of the senses; the actuality of form and
of every substance is shown to be dangerous illusions; even
the seeming reality of the individual or the *ego* is rejected.
But precisely *that,* the existence of which is denied by all
contemporary materialists, that which they try to erase from
the face of the earth by calling it mere raving, unfounded
speculation, the *Sûtras* declare to be the "only reality in the
world of illusions," and the "metaphysics of Kaśyapa" explain to us why this is so. This reality is the *spiritual ego*
of man, an ego entirely separate and distinct from matter,
even the most sublimated. *Causality* alone is reality, because
it has neither beginning nor end, neither past nor future,
existing forever in the present, and all its actions are but
temporary and secondary phenomena, "flashes of lightning
in an ocean of electricity." Everything passes away, everything changes in its objective form and, being subject to
division in time and to mensuration, is all illusion; *causality,*
however, is limitless and infinite and cannot be measured;
thus *it is the only reality.*

Nirvâna is *nought* because it is *all.* Parabrahman has
neither consciousness nor will, as it is *absolute* "universal
consciousness" and *unconditioned* will. The infinite, begin-
ningless and causeless Monad of Pythagoras is the *primal
cause* of all; after the creation of the triad, the *monad* which
"dwells in darkness and silence," re-enters once more into
its invisible and intangible abode. And yet, according to
Proclus, it is this Monad that is the "eternal God" and the
whole Universe gravitates around it. Hebrew Kabalists also
conceive their *Ain-Soph* as unconscious and devoid of will,
as it is the *causeless cause,* and the literal translation of the
word *Ain* implies the negation of the following word —

nought. "The spirit has no outward form and thus it cannot be said to exist," teaches the Buddhist work *Prajñâ-Pâramitâ* (Perfection of Wisdom).

"What is Nirvâna?" asks King Milinda of the *arhat* saint Nâgasena. "Why do the fruits of the *four* paths of virtue lead to Nirvâna? What is the cause of its existence?"

"The path to Nirvâna may be pointed out, but its cause is not known to anyone," answers the sage.

"Why?"

"Because Nirvâna is causality itself. That which constitutes Nirvâna — beyond all formulation — is a mystery which apart from its own nature cannot be attained by the human mind. The eye cannot see it, the ear cannot hear it, the nose cannot smell it, the tongue cannot taste it, nor the body feel it."

"Therefore, oh Nâgasena, Nirvâna does not exist?"

"Great King, Nirvâna *does not exist,* but it *is.*"

It is high time, however, to return to our world of "illusions" and to proceed with our examination of the column of Aśoka.

—XXIV—

[THE AKSHAYA VAṬA. — THE KHUSRU-BÂGH. — THE IDOL OF HANUMAN. — BÂBÂ SANNYÂSIN. — HERB MEDICINE.]

Around such monuments as the pillar of Aśoka there are always old specimens of the *pîpal* (*ficus religiosa*), the direct offspring of the Bodhi-tree (the "tree of knowledge"), which, according to tradition, was beloved by the founder of Buddhism. Such a tree grew also near the pillar, but it is no longer there; it was cut down by the English, as usual without any apparent reason. In the cave, however, one can still see the *Akshaya Vaṭa* ("undying banyan"). Hiouen-Thsang saw this tree in the beginning of the VIIth century; but in those days it no longer belonged to the Buddhists, and the catacombs, after centuries of silence, once more resounded with the exclamations of the Śaivas and became again the scene of bloody rites in honor of the god-destroyer. In the days of the Buddhist pilgrims, this banyan, an enormous tree with widespread green branches, stood at the entrance to the main underground cave. Now, however, all that remains is an old blackened stump with a few dry branches, in the fourth underground hall. The Brâhmaṇas tried to persuade us that the tree was transplanted by the god Śiva himself: having broken off the upper portion of the trunk, he divided it into two, planting one at Gayâ, and the other as Jagannâtha.

We went down into the cave by way of a slippery stony stairway, covered with moss. Gravely shaking his shaven head, the naked Brâhmaṇa led the way, lighting it with a smelly oil torch; on both sides of the steps dirty and disgust-

341

ing fakirs sat motionless in various positions, their long hair, uncombed for years, twisted into a knot. Genuine ascetics never sit in populated places, but dwell either in the solitude of the forest or in the courts of the temples, where no unsympathetic eye can reach them, as for instance at Jubbulpore. In the center of the first hall, which was low and surrounded by pillars, stood an enormous linga, ornamented with wreaths of gorgeous roses; at the sides were niches with idols and their picturesque painted representations. The stone idols were covered with moisture; big drops of water, oozing through from the underground river Sarasvatî, dripped from the blackened walls. It was impossible to distinguish the inscriptions, on account of the dimness of the torchlight. As the majority of them had already been translated, we were not especially concerned. There is a strong suspicion that in the seventh century these caves were level with the surface of the earth, and only later, as a result of the dampness and the accumulation of centuries of debris, began to settle and are at present underground. The immortal tree *Akshaya Vata* is mentioned by Hiouen Thsang and the historians Rashîd-al-dîn and Abu'l-Raihân [or al-Bîrûnî], all of whom call it the oldest tree in India.

We passed through about twenty chambers but, except for the tree, saw nothing of interest. Behind the tree can be seen a large opening to a tunnel, which according to the Brâhmana, leads to Benares. "All the saints," he said, "went through this passage on their way to pray in the holy city. As they went, they talked with Sarasvatî . . ."

We preferred the bridge over the Jumnâ to this dark passage and crossed it to the other side of the river. This bridge is one of the greatest triumphs of Anglo-Indian engineering art. It has two levels and spans the widest stretch of the confluent rivers, being 3,331 feet in length. The vehicles and people on foot use the lower level, while the railroad crosses over on the upper. We happened to cross simultaneously with the train and were nearly deafened by the noise.

Not far away from the railway station there is an ancient portal with a high arch, which leads into a well-kept garden.

The outer walls are thickly covered with clinging vines and gorgeous roses. In *Khusru-Bâgh* (garden of Khusru) are the tombs and monuments of the prince of the same name, of his mother Shâh-Begum, and of many other historical personages. Khusru was the grandson of the great King Akbar and the son of a Râjput woman, the daughter of the Mahârâja of Amber, known all over India for her beauty and her witchcraft; the latter probably because she bewitched Salîm, the son of Akbar, a Moslem, and, after driving away all his other wives, remained his one and only wife for the rest of his life. Be that as it may, after sunset neither Hindu nor Moslem will go within a mile of *Khusru-Bâgh,* for they say that all the descendants of Akbar, headed by the Emperor (though he himself is buried at Âgra), assemble here each night to hold their post-mortem *durbâr.*

The history of this kingly family, beginning with the Emperor Akbar himself, is most curious. A descendant of Pârsîs, whom the Moslem conquerors never succeeded in wholly converting to their religion, Akbar was not even nominally a Moslem. Judging by his biography, he hated the religion of the Prophet; having become the Emperor of India, he persistently endeavored to weaken the influence of Islam and to introduce at least some of the elements of fire-worship. This is proved by the names he chose for his grandchildren. Khusru or Hosroi ("pretty face") is an ancient name of the Persian Achaemenid Kings, the same as "Cyaxares" of the Greek classics and the Biblical Ahasuerus. This name, so beloved by the followers of Zoroaster, became hereditary among the descendants of Akbar. Salîm, who was later Emperor of India under the title of Jahângîr, was the commander of the fort of Allâhâbâd during the later years of Akbar's life. Passionately devoted to his wife, the princess of Amber, as well as to his son by her, Khusru, he was entirely under the influence of her adopted brother, the famous Râjput Râjâ Mân-Singh. The latter wished to elevate to the throne his nephew Khusru and to set Salîm aside. An awful slaughter followed, in which Salîm, with the help of his other son Khurram (born from a concubine) took possession of the throne ... Then his wife, Shâh-Begum, mother of Khusru, after placing a curse upon him and all

his posterity, committed suicide by taking poison. Khurram,
who reigned in Dekkan, subsequently murdered his brother
Khusru in 1622. This is the story of the curse: having broken
a string of pearl over the head of the Emperor, Shâh-Begum
exclaimed: "Let each pearl become a year of suffering,
tears and death! . . . May the last of thy descendants perish
in as many years as there are pearls now falling upon thy
accursed head! . . ." There were 252 pearls. It happened in
1605; precisely 252 years later, in 1857, the last two princes
of the family perished at Delhi, shot by the English, and,
as the story has it, smeared by the executioners with pork
grease. The last Emperor of Delhi, Abu'l-Zafar, a poet
renowned all over India and called the Hindu Hâfiz, had to
leave his country the same year, going into exile at the Cape
of Good Hope, where he died an unnatural death, of course.*
No wonder popular superstition has peopled the tombs of
Shâh-Begum and her sons with awesome phantoms.

The tomb of Khusru, whom his father and brother made
a martyr after disposing of him, is a sumptuous marble building with a cupola reminding one of the Tâj Mahal of Âgra.
The tomb itself is underground, and the cenotaph, a tall and
beautiful monument, is covered with inscriptions. Beyond,
there stands a square two-story building of peculiar architecture; it is the mausoleum of Shâh-Begum, the witch.
Facing it stands the building and monument of "Tamboli-
Begum" or *Istambuli*-Begum, a Christian princess brought
from Constantinople and strangled by her rival. All this is
thickly covered with roses and cypresses, and the shady
paths of the garden are considered to be the coolest spot
in Allâhâbâd.

The next morning we went to visit the "abode of Hanuman" on the bank of the Ganges and some other curiosities
of Allâhâbâd. The "Abode" proved to be an open square
room paved with stones of granite and built some twenty

---

* [Reference is here to Abu'l-Muzaffar Sirâj al-Dîn Muḥammad
(1775-1862) who reigned at Delhi under the name of Bahâdur Shâh,
and who used the name of Zafar for his poetical work.—*Compiler.*]

feet underground. Above it rises a cupola resting on four pillars, some ten feet above the ground and without walls, so that the crowd could easily admire the sleeping monkey-god below from all sides. A few broad and gloomy steps lead down, but only the Brâhmaṇas who guard the peace of the idol can make use of them. The most curious thing, more so even than the idol itself, is a long and wordy inscription in three languages, English, Hindî and Urdu (the tongue of the Moslems), placed there by the municipality. This inscription strictly forbids the Christians, and especially the Moslems, "any profanation of this Hindu sacred object, as for instance throwing stones in the sanctuary, approaching it in boots, laughing loudly, making indecent remarks, which might hurt the feelings of the worshippers of the *god* or show *squeamishness*" (I translate this sentence literally). Notwithstanding this prohibition and even the threat of fine and imprisonment, after giving the Brâhmaṇa a rupee, we quietly approached the columns without taking off our shoes. Then we looked down: an idol of enormous dimensions — some 20 feet — and of bright red color, with a crown on his monkey head, was lying asleep on his back with his raised knees far apart, his tail curled in a ring, and his cheek on the palm of his left hand, while his right hand held a sceptre. A holy lantern was hanging over his nose, and he was covered with flowers. Asking of what material the idol was made and receiving from the Brâhmaṇa the reply that he "was made of nothing," but is "the living body of a god," we were not satisfied with such an enigmatical answer. But what could we do? From the day Hanuman fell asleep in his hole no one but the initiated Brâhmaṇas were allowed to enter. To throw a stone at the sleeping god, and then judge by the sound it produced, would be a crime, foreseen by the municipality, which might lead to a fine of 100 rupees. It was then, however, that our president, like a real inventive Yankee, rose to the occasion: having taken out of his pocket a handful of copper and silver coins and lowering his hand through the railing, he dropped, as though accidentally, but really as an experiment, one *anna* on the very stomach of the god, keeping his eyes the whole time on the Brâhmaṇa, who was attentively watching him

and who at once slyly asked, if the 'saab" would not like
it brought back: "No," answered the President, "whatever
happens to drop should remain as an offering to Hanuman."
Thus encouraged, the Colonel threw another coin, this time
taking his aim. Having scored a hit on the very nose of the
god, but without the expected sound, he began to throw
more coins, harder and in quicker succession, until finally,
after throwing more than a dozen, one coin clinked as
though it struck some metal surface. When he stopped,
satisfied with his discovery, the Brâhmaṇa asked him to
throw some more coins into the mouth of Hanuman, meekly
stating that such a game is very pleasing to the *deva* . . .

From Hanuman we went to greet "Bâbâ Sannyâsin." To
avoid any misunderstanding, I hasten to say that this "Bâbâ"
has nothing in common with the Russian word for "peasant
woman," but on the contrary is an old Hindu and, judging
by his age, a most respectable one. People assert he is 250
years old, but he himself says he was born so long ago that
he has forgotten the actual date of his birth. Whatever may
be the facts, the "Bâbâ" is an historical personage and esteemed even by the English who for once, to the astonishment of the Indian people, showed gratitude toward him
for his services. True enough, their thanks have been
limited to the fact that they did not shoot the "Bâbâ" out
of a cannon, or hang him, or even put him in prison; but
even that counts for a great deal in India. They presented
him with a stone, a yard and a half square, on which he has
now been sitting for exactly 53 years hardly ever rising; and
the same municipality provides him with a little board bearing an inscription. The fact is that this old "Bâbâ" is closely
bound, for the English, to the memory of the mutiny. He
saved the life of many Europeans during those awful days,
hiding them in the hole under the stone which he never
leaves, and in which he keeps his medicines and talismans.
Twice he was nearly killed himself but even so he did not
betray those he was hiding.

The "Bâbâ" is a Sikh from the Pañjâb, a follower of
Nânak. Not far from the fort, on the blazing banks of the
Ganges, sits this venerable man, totally blind and absolutely

white. Gravely draped in a piece of white muslin, with his long silver-white hair, he appears on a calm day to be more like a marble statue, than a living being. Here is the text of the generous inscription, placed by the city government some six feet from the old man:

"Bâbâ Sannyâsin, a descendant of Pañjâb. A man tried and known for his strict honesty, incapable of any imposture. He has rendered many services to the Government. He has sat on this stone since the fifth of July, 1827. He became blind in 1839 from sitting constantly in the sun and from the reflection of the light on the water. The passers-by are not allowed to disturb him. People who want to talk with him must take off their shoes or boots. By order of the Allâhâbâd municipality, October, 1858."

Having taken off our shoes, we approached the old man and greeted him with the words: "May Râja Nânak dwell with the blessing of the gods in *Svarga* (paradise)." The Ṭhâkur, whom, to our great astonishment, the blind man recognized at the distance of some ten feet and loudly greeted with a blessing, at once entered into conversation with him. We learned that the blind Sikh eats and rises only once a day at midnight; with the help of his disciples he first immerses himself in the sacred water of the Ganges; then, having bathed, he eats a handful of rice with milk and, covering himself with a new piece of muslin, he takes his seat again until the next midnight. Under the blazing sun, in the midst of thunderstorms, in the pouring rain of the monsoon, the old man sits day and night bareheaded, with not even a piece of muslin between the sky and the crown of his head. His disciples assured us that he never sleeps; at least no one of them ever saw him lie down and if he does sleep (a fact which is denied by his disciples), he does it in a sitting posture and with open eyes, and with nothing to lean upon. The pieces of muslin which he never wears more than 24 hours are sometimes sold for a high price to the neighboring people, who firmly believe in their healing power, after the Sikh had used them for just one day. The proceeds are given to an institution for waifs, which is supported exclusively by the Sikh, and to which children, numbering at times as many as 300, are admitted irrespective of their faith. The same institution receives all the other offerings of money and kind which are made very generously to the Sikh, whose own needs consist only of rice, milk and some five yards of white muslin. Often he interrupts his long contemplation by addressing one of his disciples and occasionally sending him miles away into a forest for some object, as for instance a root of some plant, a flower or a stone, giving him at the same time detailed instructions. Once the collector's wife had a bad carbuncle on her leg; being on the verge of death, the English doctors wanted to amputate her leg, to avoid gangrene and ultimately death; she sent her husband to ask the advice of the old man. The husband was an atheist and a skeptic and did not believe in the Sikh any more than he did in his own clergyman. He went, however, to see the old man, like Nicodemus, during the night. Hardly had he begun to explain the case, when the old man interrupted him, sending him home: "Your Maam-saab is worse, you must hurry to her," said the blind man, "and give her this grass to smell, all night long; early next morning you will receive from me (the Sikh) an ointment, which will heal your wife's leg."

The puzzled collector took the grass, a dried bunch that had been dipped in the water of the Ganges, and on his return found the whole household in consternation: his wife was dying, if not already dead. Forgetting his skepticism, the collector put the bunch of grass close to her nose; his wife at once regained consciousness and, towards morning, fell peacefully asleep. Meanwhile the old man called in his eldest disciple (who was the one to tell us this story), ordered him to ford one of the tributaries of the Jumnâ, to enter the forest to the right, follow the third path, count off twenty-three mango trees, and under the twenty-fourth, on the south side, *to look for something* by the root of the tree. There, some two inches underground, in an old deserted ant hill, he would find the claw of a tiger, which he should bring back. The disciple left, followed all the directions, and brought the claw back to his teacher. The Sikh ordered this claw to be first charred in a fire and then pounded into a thin powder; he then added various herbs and made an ointment of it; then he sent it to the collector with special instructions. A week later "maam-saab" came herself to thank the blind man.*

Everyone with whom we talked about the Sikh spoke of him with the greatest respect, and the Hindus and even the Moslems did so with reverent fear.

---

*This story was confirmed to us by the collector's wife's sister. The wound, which seemed incurable by any of the remedies known to science, healed entirely in three days.

—XXV—

The people of India never do anything by half; they are
either out and out fanatics or absolute atheists. Their love
as well as their hatred knows no bounds and when a Hindu
calls you, without being forced to do so, a "brother" or a
"friend," this is no mere phrase. All our companions were
"reformers" (as they call them here) and had long ago cut
all ties with the Brâhmaṇas and with all sects, but they were
mystics, believing in the higher spiritual development of the
human being and thoroughly convinced that such a development can place man nearly on a level with deity, if he really
deserves it. At the same time, while harboring both uncouth
fanatics and educated, highly exalted mystics (as for instance
Nârâyaṇa), the crowd of "freethinkers" (as they call themselves) is increased yearly by recruits of the school of Charles
Bradlaugh and Lewes* from among the young students. During the last decade, under the "beneficent" influence of educa-

---

*[Charles Bradlaugh (1833-1891), English freethinker and politician.
From 1860 he conducted the *National Reformer*, and in 1874 became
associated in this work with Mrs. Annie Besant. His political career was
full of combativeness, but he gained popularity because of his un-
questioned sincerity and his gift for popular oratory. Mrs. Besant's close
alliance with him terminated about 1885, when she drifted, first into
socialism and later (1888) into Theosophy as a pupil of H. P. Blavatsky.
George Henry Lewes (1817-1878), British philosopher and literary
critic whose chief work was *The Problems of Life and Mind* wherein
he claimed a place for introspection in psychological research. He also
wrote a number of popular works on science.—*Compiler*.]

tion (more strictly English than Western), something phenomenal has been taking place; the whole generation educated in city schools and colleges is graduating as irrevocable atheists. Exceptions are extremely rare.

The English policy is never to meddle under any pretext with the purely religious questions of a conquered country. One is apt to suspect that such a rule is rather the result of cowardice than of liberalism on the part of the government; but in one respect it is very reasonable, as it serves as a sort of "balm" for the aching political sores of the country. The Anglo-Indian press, with *The Pioneer* at its head, tries constantly in various ways to remind its readers that "the British Government is *absolutely incapable* of introducing an element of religious bigotry into the domain of its clearly outlined policy."

Following this golden rule, and possibly also in order not to hurt "the Christian feelings" of their higher officials, all the offices of presidents, directors or principals of native colleges are filled with carefully selected and confirmed materialists. As such offices, owing to their serious and responsible nature, are always important and of pecuniary advantage as well, it may be easily understood that they are reserved exclusively for the English; to a native, no matter how much more learned he might be than his English superior, such a position is inaccessible.

On the other hand, the missionaries of different sects, whose name is legion, are denied the right of entry to the colleges. In consequence of the above-mentioned policy, they live among the very slums of society, among the *pariahs* and the *mângs,* who are excluded from all Brâhmaṇa sects. Living in constant struggle and dissention among themselves, they literally *buy* converts, to harm one another; pariahs and mângs, all of whom are either devil-worshippers or have no religion whatever, may be converted for money, and often for a loaf of bread, into almost anything one chooses. It can be definitely stated that there is not a single Hindu convert to Christianity, who is not a thief, a scoundrel, a drunkard, and upon occasion a murderer. The missions in India are the greatest profanation of Christianity. No European family would hire a convert as a servant in their house, irrespective of advantages. The missionaries have their own schools, but the latter, as well as the results, are humbug. The Hindus who are keen on free education send their children to the *padri* up to the age of 5 or 7 and occasionally 8; soon after, these same half-educated children are generally married: once married the young couple naturally cannot easily be persuaded to return to school. All further hopes of voluntary conversion are thus shot to pieces.

Among the Catholics, the situation is even more hopeless on this score. The rich and self-supporting Jesuit College of St. Xavier in Bombay, instead of enlightening the people or dispelling the darkness of ignorance and educating the younger generations of pagans, merely confuses them completely. The students of this famous college are graduated from it with an utter scorn for the religion and the customs of their ancestors — the usual system and a well-known trick of the sons of Loyola; at the same time their hatred for the Roman Catholic faith is even keener, perhaps, than that for the Christian religion in general. Not having any chance in British India to convert the natives by force, as they love to do, the Jesuit fathers appear in this country under such a cynical and disgraceful cover, perverting in such a coarse manner the understanding of truth and honesty, rather shaky already, among the native boys, that under their supposedly *Christian* tutelage, the net results are worse than those achieved under the freethinking system of such learned atheists as the principals of the Bombay and Lahore colleges. Last year one of them constantly preached to his pupils, who long before had fallen victim to the teachings of Huxley and Tyndall, the famous statement of Professor W. K. Clifford * to the effect that if it is right to call any

---

* [William Kindon Clifford (1845-79). English mathematician and philosopher, educated at King's college, London, and at Trinity college, Cambridge. Professor of mathematics at University college, London, 1871, and Fellow of the Royal Society, 1874. Died rather early of consumption. As a philosopher, his name is associated with two expressions of his coining, "mind-stuff" and the "tribal self." He was a man of extraordinary acuteness and originality. Most of his works were published after his death, such as *Lectures and Essays* (1879). His wife became a well-known novelist.—*Compiler.*]

doctrine immoral, then, it would be correct to point out as most immoral the doctrine which says that Providence or destiny outside of ourselves can overrule us,* in other words, the teaching which recognizes a power higher than man himself. More farsighted critics tried to explain this phrase as having a political aim. "The English have conceived a very subtle scheme," said a young man to me, slyly smiling, "they evidently want to impress upon us the idea that they alone represent Providence and the all-powerful, all-destructive as well as recreating hand which governs the destinies of our people. We have nothing to expect, it seems, either from our own gods, or from the God of the *padris*."

From the psychological point of view, therefore, India presents an unusually interesting picture. With the exception of a small handful of "reformers," the country is divided into two hostile camps: the *fanatics* and the *ultra-skeptics*. The former, full of superstitions, see divinity in everything: in a tiger, in a cow and her tail, in a tree, in a crow, and in any pest; the others, equally full of what I take the liberty of calling *scientific superstitions,* deny everything but matter. That which was looked upon by their forefathers as the immortal soul, "young India" considers to be merely the interaction of carbon, oxygen, hydrogen and nitrogen; something that exists merely as a result of the combination of these elements, and which disappears with the disappearance of the causes, viz., gases. Man is the progeny of the *cosmic gas,* of a "fiery cloud," they repeat with Tyndall; from this gas originate not only the material forms, "not alone the exquisite and wonderful mechanism of the human body," but even human mind, emotion, intellect, will, and all their dependent phenomena, viz., our philosophy, our poetry, our science and art. Plato, Shakespeare, Newton, Raphael — all that they gave to the world, was once included in the gas in a concealed and potential state.†

---

* *Fortnightly Review,* Vol. XVI, New Series, December 1874, page 730. [This idea is summarized from Clifford's article on "Body and Mind,"—*Compiler.*]

† "Scientific Use of the Imagination," by Prof. Tyndall. [This essay may be found in his *Fragments of Science,* Vol. II, pp. 101 *et seq.*, 1892 edition.—*Compiler.*]

"Wonderful are thy works, Oh Tyndall!" exclaim the young Hindus in chorus, bowing before this luminary of science.

Notwithstanding all this, however, both parties, the orthodox as well as the atheist, are inwardly hostile to their rulers. The ardent fanatics, driven by the Brâhmaṇas to a high pitch of exaltation, very naturally will never be reconciled in the depth of their hearts with a government that grants them in their own country only negative privileges over the missionaries of a faith that is hateful to them. As to the camp of the *materialists,* it is yearly strengthened by a number of Hindu graduates who have brilliantly finished their studies and are cast into the ocean of life by universities and colleges, literally without a rudder or compass and without any hope in this life, as they are prevented by the prevailing political situation from taking part in the government of their own land. They have no faith in a future life, ashamed to believe in it as did their "silly forefathers," they being the followers of our European "Apostles of the Intellect." There remains nothing for them in this life. Thus in the latter part of the 19th century we find them rephrasing in various ways the well-known saying of the Epicurean school: "Let us eat, drink and be merry, for tomorrow we shall all be reduced to carbonic acid, water and ammonia!"

Taking the liberty for this digression, I am not departing from my narrative. I merely wish to give my Russian readers a picture of what the English have made of India and prepare them for a clearer understanding of the discussions we had on many occasions with the learned pandits.* Having heard of our arrival, these pandits and other native philosophers came to us in great numbers — some of them from Benares, especially to meet us. They spoke perfect English; like our friend Shamrâo, they had read Moleschott and Büchner, knew by heart and understood Herbert Spencer, Lewes and John Stuart Mill; they raved about Huxley and Tyndall and worshipped Darwin as presented by his apostle Haeckel.

Pandit is a scholastic degree in India which corresponds to a doctor of philosophy.

They had not succeeded, however, as our naïve Shamrâo had, in selecting from this scientific bedlam the ideas most akin to the ancient philosophies of their own country, rejecting the rest and arriving at their own understanding. They had not preserved even a spark of that invincible and inextinguishable faith, which no Büchner can ever snuff out; faith in a Supreme Power and a life after death. No matter how distorted this faith may be at times, how ludicrous a poor, uneducated, and at the same time over-educated, Shamrâo might seem, in calling his salad of Manu and Haeckel "the new religious philosophy," as we listened to the learned ravings of the Allâhâbâd and Benares pandits, we often mentally drew a comparison between them, and certainly not in favor of the latter.

Returning from our visit to Bâbâ-Sannyâsin, we found awaiting us at Professor Bhattachârya's a crowd of pandits. They stayed in the garden with us late into the night. We had come from America to study the philosophy of their ancient and contemporary religions, and they had come to stare with undisguised amazement at "Westerners," who were silly and senseless enough to prefer Kapila and Patañjali to Huxley and Tyndall, and the philosophy of Manu and Buddhism to the positivism of Auguste Comte. Having renounced all religious faith, they, however, did not dare to renounce their caste and the rules of the latter. Ashamed of bearing even secretly an image of some deity in the depths of their hearts, they shamelessly wore the red and white sexual symbols of Śiva and Vishnu painted on their foreheads. They ridiculed all things divine and at the same time feared men and public opinion. Isn't this often the case with us Europeans also?

Naturally we began to talk about their ancient philosophy, about Rishis, Yogins and ascetics. The pandits were quite frank with us and, with a pride deserving a better cause, exposed the moral wounds inflicted on them, and constantly aggravated by the skillful hands of their English "principals." How could these ravings of old metaphysicians and theologians interest us, they asked? Who but bigots, fakirs or half-witted ascetics could see any meaning, for instance, in

the Triune Divinity? Bâbâ-Sannyâsin was an old fool, and
the fakirs, diving into the Ganges to be purified of their
sins and remaining under water until they were in danger
of drowning, while repeating their mantras thrice, should be
sent by the Government to the workhouse . . .

Our arguments and opposition irritated some of them
extremely. Finally an old stately Hindu, draped in a white
shawl embroidered with gold, with golden rings on his toes,
an enormous symbol of Vishnu on his forehead, and with
a golden *pince-nez*(!), turned to me with a direct question:
"Is it possible that you, having lived so long in America,
the country of Thomas Paine, still believe in some deity?

"I must confess I do, and am not at all repentant of my
ignorant weakness," was my answer.

"And you believe in the existence of the human 'soul'?"
he asked again, this time with a half-controlled smile.

"Yes, I do; and though it may seem extraordinary to you,
I believe also in an *immortal* Spirit . . ."

Then the young master, nervously playing with the rings
on his toes, put to me a new and rather curious question:

"So you take Huxley for a quack or a fool?"

Now it was my turn to stare in utter astonishment.

"And why so?" I inquired of the *pince-nez.*

"Because either he, an acknowledged authority, knows
what he is talking about, or he must be a charlatan, discussing things he does not understand."

"Huxley, as a naturalist, physiologist and scientist," I said,
"I not only recognize, but acknowledge his learning, considering him one of the greatest authorities of our day, as far as
purely natural sciences are concerned; but as a philosopher,
I have no high regard for him."

"It is hard to deny logical deductions based on *facts* . . .
Did you read his article in the *Fortnighly Review* on the
automatism of man?"

"I believe I did, and I even remember some of his wonderful sophisms . . . But what of that?"

"This, that the professor *unquestionably* proved in it that
a human being is nothing but a conscious and self-conscious

automaton;* and to this statement he added in his *Lay Sermons* that man is the most cunning of all nature's clocks, but nothing else." †

I admit I grew a little tired of this discussion. I glanced at Gulâb-Lal-Singh. He sat with knitted brows, taking no part in the conversation. Knowing his contempt for modern materialism, I wanted to make him join the discussion. As though understanding my thoughts, he came to my aid.

"Permit me to answer you for our guest, pandit Sâhib. I read the article you mentioned but a short time ago and possibly I remember better the learned sophistry of Huxley; I am ready to consider the more striking ones. It is quite true that Huxley calls man an 'automaton' and 'a piece of nature's clockwork.' Here it is not a matter of words, but whether Huxley has proved his assertion. I will show you that not only has he failed to prove it, but that he contradicts himself in a most childish way."

The man with the *pince-nez* simply jumped at this heretical assertion against science. "How was it possible? Where has the great Huxley contradicted himself? Do tell us! . . ."

"If you will allow me, I will explain it to you; nor will it be very difficult. You forget that, having undermined the dignity of man by applying to him the epithet of 'automaton,' possibly out of consideration for the general public that is not yet ready for his great ideas, or the little weakness of his *non-scientific* brethren — those whom Herbert Spencer describes as being left behind in the modern rapid movement of conquest in natural philosophy, and therefore out of touch with physical sciences — Huxley condescendingly adds something very strange. Calling man an 'automaton' he magnanimously admits at the same time that this machine is 'to some extent provided with free will, as in many cases

---

Fortnightly Review, Vol. XVI, New Series, November, 1874, p. 577. [See his essay entitled: "On the Hypothesis that Animals are Automata, and its History," pp. 551-80.—*Compiler*.]

†*Lay Sermons*, p. 164. [Huxley said in his essay on "The Scientific Aspects of Positivism": "Does human nature possess any free, volitional, or truly anthropomorphic element, or is it only the cunningest of all Nature's clocks?"—*Compiler*.]

man is able to do as he likes.' * Isn't that so, if you remember?"

"I think it is," said the *pince-nez,* somewhat confused.

"Then if that is so, we must take this assertion to be a
concession to an old superstition, offered by the professor
to the public to sweeten the bitter pill because otherwise
it would appear that Huxley, the greatest modern scientific
authority, is simply contradicting himself . . . However, even
you must admit that man has free will."

"Certainly. But where do you see the great contradiction
here?"

"Well, isn't it clear to you, that by adding the last phrase,
Huxley, like a Japanese suicide, kills himself and his theory,
and that the skillfully invented word 'automaton' is transformed thereby into an absurdity? . . . First, according to
his idea, man is literally, no less than a rabbit or frog,
a simple 'automaton,' deprived of all free will; then it is
granted that in certain cases he can act according to his
choice and finally, that his *'volition* counts for something
in conditioning the course of events.' † As a result, man
remains, after this learned explanation, just what he always
was, namely, *a thinking being endowed with free will.* This
'automaton' possessing free will is certainly an interesting
and unexpected discovery in the field of natural science,
as has been pointed out by Dr. Elam.‡ Neither a skeptic nor
a believer would imagine that free will is anything other than
the faculty of acting according to one's own choice! . . . Thus
the 'automaton' falls to pieces and we see that it would do
Huxley no harm to learn a little logic from our Kaṇâda or
other philosophers whom you scorn."

"Well, suppose you are right in this," stammered the disconcerted scholar. "Let us take another example: Tyndall,
for instance, who repeats practically the same idea: 'matter
and only matter contains all the promise and potency of
terrestrial life'; this is what he declared at the Belfast meeting before a selected and informed public, in 1874. This

---

Fortnightly Review, ibid., p. 577.
†T. H. Huxley, *Protoplasm: The Physical Basis of Life,* p. 16.
‡[Dr. Chas. E. Elam (1824-89), specializing in epilepsy.—*Compiler.*]

MOTÎ-MASJID AT ÂGRA

JÁMI'-MASJID AT ÁGRA

happy expression: 'In matter I discern the promise and potency of every form and quality of life,' brought him the enmity of all old-fashioned dreamers, but has circled the world and has become a vital watchword of physical science!"

"And you might add that it was futile for the religious world to be so startled about it. In another lecture, Tyndall, like Huxley, contradicts his happy expression. Why not look into his 'Scientific Materialism,' his answer to a criticism by Dr. James Martineau* of this expression that shocked the whole world! There he clearly confesses that our inner consciousness belongs to quite *another* class of phenomena whose relation to physical science is unthinkable (!?);† having now divided the phenomena of life into *two* classes, instead of *one,* the esteemed materialist begins to talk about the gulf which lies between them, which is unbridgeable and 'which will forever remain intellectually *impassable.*' Alas, where is it now? And what became of the alleged omnipotence of matter?"

The pandits exchanged looks. They were seemingly stunned. To hear such patriarchs of science, as Huxley and Tyndall, accused of not knowing themselves what they intended to teach others, and to be unable to defend these apostles of positive science, was sad and insulting. Our party felt triumphant . . .

---

*[James Martineau, (1805-1900). English philosopher and divine whose influence as a preacher was mainly exercised at Liverpool. Became professor of moral philosophy in Manchester college, 1840; continued in the same capacity later in London. His most stimulating works are his sermons, publ. as *Endeavours after the Christian Life* (1843 & 1847), and *Hours of Thought* (1876 & 1879). As a divine, he hated both sacrosanct priesthood and enforced uniformity. He trusted rather statesmen than ecclesiastics and his ideals were very high both about religion and about the state.—*Compiler.*]

†[This lecture or essay was entitled "Materialism and its Opponents," and appeared in the *Fortnightly Review,* Vol. XVIII, New Series, November 1, 1875, pp. 579-99. It was supposed to be the text of the Introduction to his forthcoming *Fragments of Science,* where it appears, however, as an essay under the title of "Scientific Materialism." The actual words of Tyndall are: "The passage from the physics of the brain to the corresponding facts of consciousness is unthinkable" (p. 589).—*Compiler.*]

"And now," continued the Thâkur, "to prove the weakness of their theories, allow me to quote in my turn the words of a naturalist, equally learned and as well known as these two. Do you remember what Du Bois-Reymond says about the phenomenon of consciousness? 'It will remain absolutely and forever inconceivable that a number of carbon, hydrogen, nitrogen and oxygen atoms should be otherwise than indifferent as to their own position and motion, past, present or future.' These same words are also quoted by Tyndall.* And the latter adds to them his own argument: 'You cannot satisfy the human understanding in its demand for logical continuity between molecular processes and the phenomena of consciousness. This is a rock on which materialism must inevitably split whenever it pretends to be a complete philosophy of the human mind.' † Notwithstanding this full confession in one article, the same author in another article, entitled 'Scientific Materialism,' writes without hesitation about the 'relations of physics to consciousness,' referring to them as to something 'immutable' and positive."

"All the other authorities of science uphold the same idea," rather timidly rejoined the pandits, "even Virchow does so."

"Far from all," interrupted the Colonel, "only some of them, and they are not numerous."

"Just so. It is quite sufficient to have merely a superficial acquaintance with physiology and pathology," added Gulâb-Lal-Singh, "to realize that not only 'immutable,' but even exceptional relations between pure physics and physiology are very difficult to find, let alone in the case of psychical phenomena. As to Virchow, in demolishing Haeckel's *Anthropogenie*, he, at the same time, even though indirectly, also demolished those who supported his work at its appearance."

Fortnightly Review, Vol. XVIII, New Series, November 1875, p. 585. [It is stated there that Du Bois-Reymond's words are from his Address to the Congress of German Naturforschers, Leipzig, 1872.— *Compiler.*]

† [p. 585 also.]

"It is a great pity," the pandit in the *pince-nez* murmured, "for in this case Virchow is at variance with one of the greatest thinkers of his own country, namely Büchner. The latter writes in his *Kraft und Stoff* (p. xxvii of the Preface) : 'The naturalists merely prove that there are no other forces in nature besides the physical, chemical, and mechanical...'."

"I do not doubt that Büchner wrote that, and that your memory is excellent," said the Thâkur somewhat ironically. "He said even more than that! Thus, for instance, as if repeating the words of Manu, he says: 'All natural and mental forces are inherent in it [nature]; in matter alone can they manifest; matter is the origin of all that exists ... Nature, the all-engendering and all-devouring, is its own beginning and end, birth and death. She produces man by her own power, and takes him again.' * But Manu, while saying the same thing,† by merely asserting that all that is *seen* originates from an *unseen,* but *conscious* force, stands from the point of view of logic as well as philosophy a hundred times higher than all the Büchners past and present. That some naturalists and so-called philosophers assure us

---

* [These quotations are taken from the English translation of Büchner's work, published under the title of *Force and Matter*, ed. by J. F. Collingwood, London: Trübner & Co., 1864. They occur on page xxvii of the "Preface to Third Edition," and pages 34 and 88 of the text, respectively.—*Compiler.*]

† "Out of its own (Brahman's) essence condenses the universal ether —the materialisation of his will, the seen and the unseen, the tangible and the intangible matter, and decomposes at his breath into fire, air, earth and water. Out of the earthly vapor (the breathing of Brahman) originate all beings and things, organic and inorganic, out of the seed thrown into the earth and impregnated by the divine breath and originated in the infinite and boundless matter—the universal seed." Having given the Universe time to develop according to the laws of transmutation (evolution), the Highest Ruler, impregnating after each pralaya (period of universal destruction, or to be more exact, disappearance of the world from objective into subjective) the radiant egg of nature, after having gone through its transformations once more merges itself with the Universal Soul—Parabrahman (*Manu*, Book I).
Brahman is the universal embodiment of Parabrahman, and a god in the form of Nature. The unseen and formless spirit impregnates only the radiant womb (egg) from which issues the bisexual Brahmâ, or the creative force of Parabrahman, at the beginning of every new cycle.

that outside this triple material force there are no other forces in nature, is a fact known to everybody. But that they will ever *prove* their hypotheses by direct scientific confirmation, that I absolutely deny . . ."

"Should we really then, in this 19th century of ours, prefer Manu to Büchner and Huxley?"

"If Manu teaches us fundamentally the same principles as the contemporary Western scientists, why not? You cannot deny that Manu *anticipates* in his teachings nearly everything that is being preached nowadays by the evolutionists —'apostles of the intellect,' who present their theories as something entirely new. And if Manu succeeds where these apostles of matter fail, and therefore prefer to deny; if Manu logically proves the necessity of a relation between spirit and matter and, using the words of Patañjali,* supports this relationship by experiments demonstrated on man's twofold nature, this highest sanctuary of spirit and matter, then I positively assert that Manu stands incomparably higher than our contemporary science, at least in everything that concerns both purely spiritual nature and human physiology."

"You are advising us, I think, to return to idol-worship," ironically said one of our opponents.

"In no way. Our ancient philosophers never taught us to worship idols. It would be useless anyway, as you yourselves worship Vishṇu and Śiva as well as other gods, whose symbols you have not yet wiped from your faces . . . If you have decided to do away with all the customs of ancient times, why not part also with those symbols of paganism?"

"This . . . this is a caste custom . . . and has nothing to do with idol-worship," stammered the abashed pandit.

"How is that? Have you forgotten or possibly never knew, that according to the teachings of the Brâhmaṇas the castes were established by the gods themselves; that the gods were the first to conform to caste rules, and that the heads of idols are daily decorated with the symbols of their respective sects?" implacably continued the Ṭhâkur.

---

*Patañjali was the founder of the *Yoga* system of the psychological development of man by means of a gradual change of the physical nature.

"But even our best philosophers probably wore these symbols," replied the pandits. "If we believe in Darwin and Haeckel, it is perhaps only because these scientists amplified and fully developed the materialistic conceptions of Kapila and Manu. The Sânkhya of Kapila, for instance, is no less an atheistic philosophy than Haeckel's *Anthropogenie*."

"You have probably forgotten the teachings of Kapila ... Whereas Haeckel sees force and the power of creation in matter alone, Kapila deems it impossible to ascribe anything to *prakriti*,* without the co-operation of *purusha*.† He compares them thus: *prakriti* is a man with healthy legs, but without head or eyes, and *purusha*, a being with eyes and brain, but without legs or motion. That the world might evolve and finally produce man, *purusha* (spirit) had to get on the shoulders of the headless *prakriti* (matter) ; only then was the latter endowed with the consciousness of life and reason, while *purusha* received the faculty to move by means of *prakriti's* legs and thus to manifest its existence. If *purusha* is impotent in its manifestations and is, as it were, merely a non-existent abstraction, without the help of the objective form of *prakriti*, the latter is even more so; without the aid of the spirit and its vivifying influence, *prakriti* is no better than a lifeless heap of manure."

"We also heard that you are interested in ancient Zoroastrianism," another pandit inquired of me. "What is your opinion of *Sûrya*, the sun, as a deity?"

"According to my opinion, it is better to believe in *Sûrya*, than in nothing at all. The sun that warms and feeds us, giving life to all earthly nature, is much better than Büchner or the Fellows of the Royal Society, before whom you perform your 'pûja,' as though they were deities."

"But once we believe in Sûrya, why not return at once to the worship of all the 330 millions of our ancient gods, Kâlî, Krishna, or even Hanuman?"

"I am not advising you to believe in either the one or the

Prakriti is plastic matter, nature in its chaotic and undifferentiated state.

†*Purusha* is the intangible spirit that does not manifest itself in nature otherwise than through *prakriti* or matter, which it vivifies.

other," I had to say, to defend myself. "I am speaking relatively and repeat that it seems to me better to believe *even* in Hanuman, than, for instance in the *Bathybius Haeckelii,* or in the mythical tailless anthropoid whom Haeckel is offering us as our ancestor . . ."

"He proves what he asserts . . . Haeckel begins the evolution of being from primordial atoms and logically develops the gradual transformation of the original protoplasm . . ."

"Let him develop it as much as he likes. In my opinion the *mucus* and all the protoplasms of Messrs. Lorenz Oken * and Haeckel are no cleverer ideas than the primitive ooze and the monsters which, according to Berosus, in his ancient fable about the creation of the world, populated it . . ."

The pandits finally left, carrying with them the firm conviction that we were ignorant reactionaries.

"Well, well, what a sweet 'Young India' you've got," said the Colonel. "They gave me a headache with their nonsense . . ."

"You can thank the English for it," replied the Ṭhâkur. "It would be unfair to call us to account for other people's sins."

---

* [Lorenz Oken (1779-1851) was a German naturalist whose real name was Ockenfuss. He became professor of medical sciences at Jena and later in life professor of natural history at the University of Zurich. He was a prolific writer on various subjects connected with his profession.—*Compiler.*]

—XXVI—

Once more we are in the dark and stuffy railway coaches. In five minutes the train, with a deafening noise, will dash across the long bridge over the Jumnâ, and six hours later we will be in Cawnpore, where the bloodiest page in Anglo-Indian history was enacted. Our barelegged friends, the pandits, in their gold-embroidered shawls, saw us off; a few Bengalî Bâbûs joined them, bareheaded and wearing their snow-white muslin togas. At some little distance we could see the figure of the "chief spy"; we saw him settle down in the next coach, accompanied by a large basket filled with bottles of whisky and soda and a box full of ice. The Thâkur left the day before with Nârâyana to prepare a place for us "which never yet had been trodden by the foot of an Englishman — and never will be" (so he said). Meanwhile we have to content ourselves with this promise and not even ask him any questions, especially in the presence of Mr. Y. and Miss B., who, though theosophists and our friends, are nevertheless English. One can positively state that in India no person belonging to this race will ever be made a saint . . .

The coaches have dark green windows, otherwise the passengers might be blinded. When they are pulled down, they are replaced by movable frames made of khus-khus

365

grass. A special hydraulic apparatus, fixed on both sides of the window frame, pours water on the frames with each turn of the wheels, which causes them to turn round in the window as fans, intended to let the fresh breeze generated by the train in motion enter the coach. But alas, having travelled no more than a couple of miles, I nearly burned my fingers touching the shutters; the water was really hot from the sun. Last year in June (this was told us by the Frenchman, Moncoutier, the manager of the Keller Restaurant, a few minutes before the train left the Allâhâbâd station), the family of a colonel arrived on the noon train. When the passengers began to leave the train, two young boys, crying and howling, jumped from the colonel's coach. Lying inside the coach were found the colonel, dead drunk, and his wife, a sickly woman some 22 years old, dead. The doctors decided that death had come from apoplexy caused by the heat. Moncoutier, himself, had lost both of his sons (12 and 14 years old) who had run out in the sun for a few minutes. The poor Frenchman told us this story with tears in his eyes, while fussing behind his counter, and sold us some cigarettes at triple price, constantly urging us to partake of a glass of absinthe or vermouth. «Ah, le gredin de pays!» he repeated, half sobbing, «Un vrai enfer, quoi!... Et puis, pas un de ces cochons d'Anglais qui sache un mot de français. Oh, que je voudrais donc voir un jour les Russes ici!...»

We laughed, but thought it better not to take part in his dangerous wishes. Turning, we noticed behind us our blond spy, being served by the waiter some "refreshing" drink from a bottle of rum. This time poor Moncoutier must have been mistaken as to Englishmen not understanding French. Returning to Bombay some two months later, we did not find the Frenchman behind his counter; his master, Keller, had sent him to some other distant station, as a punishment for his "chatter."

The day before we left, the Thâkur brought us a bunch of fresh leaves and asked us to try them. Their taste reminded one of sorrel and produced a cooling sensation like mint. He made us solemnly promise to keep a small piece of these leaves in our mouth during the whole trip to Cawnpore and throughout the day's heat. "As long as you chew them like betel the heat will have no harmful effect on you," he said, "and at times you may feel too cool." True enough, from that day on we no longer felt the heat. But we did not succeed in persuading Mr. Y. to keep this grass in his mouth, and as for Miss B., she kept spitting it out, and both of them nearly fell ill from the heat. I sincerely regret that I have no right either to describe this grass or to send some of it to Russia for examination. The Hindus are a strange people, and even the Thâkur, the best and noblest of all Hindus we ever met, and our most devoted friend, was not free from some peculiarities. He appeared to conceal the knowledge of his country, especially such facts as would be looked upon by science as fabulous. In answer to our question as to why he did not want to enrich Western science with a new discovery, so useful in this hot country, he merely smiled enigmatically and remarked that this grass grows only in India and is difficult to find even there, and that it was impossible to save everyone anyway. "Western science is rich enough without our crumbs," he added, "and you, who have taken *everything* from us, should leave us at least these crumbs."

Cawnpore for some time was a place without a history, and before the English chose it in 1777 as an advance post for one of their Indian garrisons, it was utterly unknown. The railway station is situated outside the town; we were just planning to take two guilded *gârîs* drawn by oxen, when the Thâkur's servant announced that his *mahâ saab* (master) had sent a European coach to meet us. It was a gaudy crimson-lined four seater, at the back of which were two *syces* in their red, gold-embroidered coats and turbans, looking like two big drops of blood; four similar-looking men, long-legged and fleet-footed, wearing liveries, were the runners, who ran in front of the carriage. Add to these, four Râjputs on horseback, the bodyguard of Gulâb-Lal-Singh, and you will understand why, on entering the carriage, the Colonel remarked; "If, in some magic way, we could find ourselves in New York, people would probably take us for charlatans selling toothpaste and magic powders." But we were in India, and there people almost prostrated themselves at this magnificent sight.

The first object which attracted our attention was a large,

empty, dark red brick church, without windows or doors, with a high, pointed steeple. This building served for some three weeks as an inadequate fortress for a garrison which had taken refuge in it at the outbreak of the mutiny on June 6, 1857 and was eventually murdered to the last man.

What was the true cause of this bloody mutiny? Europe reads English accounts and imagines that it reads history. It never occurs to anyone to ask whether among the many accounts of the mutiny there is a single truthful and dispassionate one. No one asked the Hindus what truth there was in the accounts of their conquerors, which of the two belligerent sides was guilty of the greatest crimes, and which committed the most bestial cruelties, the educated and humane Europeans or the wild natives driven to desperation. We gathered many *facts* concerning this, and not from just one, but from many persons who had no way of being in collusion with each other before answering us. Their answers were on all major points strikingly similar; for that reason we believed them, rather than all the "histories" of the 1857 mutiny taken together. Cartridges greased with pork tallow was the reason for the mutiny among the *Moslems,* and cowhide "straps," which exasperated the Hindus, were but the last drop, which made the vessel of gall overflow.

Sometime before the mutiny, there lived at Biṭhûr, a large place situated on the right bank of the Ganges some 12 miles from Cawnpore, a Hindu of an ancient and proud family, called Dhondu Pant, better known under the name of Nâna-Sâhib. He was the adopted heir of the last peshwa (the royal head of the Marâṭhâ Confederacy) Bâjî Râo, after whose death he inherited all his estates, treasures and possessions. Some Englishmen, more conscientious than the rest, confess that this young man, the cousin of the Mahârâja of Sind, had good reasons for hating the Government. In his official report, Lt.-Colonel G. M. Sherer wrote, for instance, the following important words: "This man had a claim to which we Britishers with the unsympathetic demeanor common to all successful people, paid no attention whatever." Having been adopted in 1832 as a mere child, Nâna-Sâhib was brought up fully convinced that he would inherit the title and rights of the peshwa, an honor which, owing to the

English, was in reality more nominal than actual, but flattering to the one who had a right to it. Five years before the mutiny, the old Bâjî Râo died. Right after his death, the government of Lord Dalhousie, seemingly without any reason, announced that the title of peshwa was abolished and that Prince Dhondu would inherit only the private property and estates of his father. Accordingly, the pension of the old Râjâ was stopped, the army was ordered not to salute the heir, and even some old and obsolete artillery guns, which formerly had been magnanimously left to the dethroned prince and which gave him much pleasure in his old age, were now taken away from Nâna-Sâhib. During more than four years the young prince spent his money in vain endeavors to force the directors of the Company to cancel their unjust decision. Instead of firmly but kindly telling him that his efforts were in vain, the directors simply put him off and threatened to deprive him even of his private heritage. Nâna-Sâhib had two sisters, one 12 and the other 13 years of age; the eldest was a beauty, and both of them were married. Having gone, one day, on a pilgrimage with their nurses and servants, the two women were assaulted by drunken officers, who rushed into the front courtyard of the cave-temple just at the moment when they, undressed, had entered the holy *tank,* and violated them. The unanimous account is that the two girls were killed by the hand of Nâna-Sâhib himself and *at their own insistent request.* After killing them, he drank a drop of blood from each one of them and swore to avenge them on the wives and daughters of the English, or to die himself. Nâna-Sâhib had a devoted and trusted friend, a Hindu, who formerly had been converted by force to Islam, but who, having fled from Hyderâbâd, had found refuge and protection with Nâna-Sâhib and returned to his former religion. The English knew him under the name of 'Azîm-ullâh-Khân. 'Azîm was the right-hand man and the secretary of Nâna-Sâhib. In the beginning of 1853, 'Azîm was sent to England to try and secure the help of Parliament. Nowadays the English make him out to be a sort of waiter and purveyor for the harem of Nâna-Sâhib, though the latter, after his father's death, was consecrated as a *brahmachârin,* a lay monk without even a single wife, let alone a harem. The English complain of 'Azîm in their "histories," calling him "a tiger in human form"; they accuse him of having been a spy at Sebastopol, who had seen the English weakness and tried to exaggerate it in the eyes of his compatriots, who thus dared to mutiny; finally, 'Azîm-ullâh-Khân is accused of having taken part in "the plot organized in Turkey against Great Britain and of having secretly been to Russia." However, during the stay of 'Azîm-ullâh in England, his picturesque costumes, jewelry, shawls and diamonds enchanted not only the local ladies, who went mad over him, but the high officials as well. He was received in the best society of London and Brighton, and all the papers praised his elegant manners and his education . . . How then is it possible to call him now a "vile lackey"? Some of the distinguished ladies were even preparing to fulfill their promise to come and visit his master, Prince Nâna, on his estates near Biṭhûr, when the mutiny broke out earlier than expected, thus ruining Nâna-Sâhib's plans.

It can be positively asserted that Nâna-Sâhib, as well as all the chief conspirators, was inspired much more by feelings of vengeance and hatred toward the English, than by a hope for a political upheaval. Of course, had the plans of Nâna-Sâhib succeeded, the Mogul and Marâṭhâ dynasties would have once more been restored in India. But the insatiable feeling of vengeance, the passionate desire to dishonor England by violating her most eminent women and daughters, violating them (according to the expression of the one who gave us these details) so that "the act should become historic and would be glorified in tradition as the just vengeance of a Marâṭhâ prince, all the way to the next *pralaya*" —that was the main and chief incentive. 'Azîm-ullâh-Khân played his role so skillfully that no less than fourteen distinguished ladies of the London court (as said above), enchanted by the Asiatic diplomat, were ready to visit the den of the beast that was lying in wait for them, and their arrival at Biṭhûr was to have been the signal for the general uprising. Blind fate — *Kismet* — saved them of course, but did not save their Anglo-Indian sisters.

Nâna-Sâhib followed the motto of the vanquished goddess

of Virgil. He actually "raised hell," as some of his biographers graphically describe it, calling in the help of all the demons of Eastern vengeance . . .

Having mortified him in every way, having deprived him first of his sisters, then of his title, his pension and his honors, the English, with a confidence worthy of innocence and a clear conscience, considered, because of some skillfully planned banquets staged by Nâna-Sâhib, that the heir of the peshwa was their greatest friend. Expecting daily that the Sepoys of his regiment would revolt, following the example of their comrades, General Wheeler,* as late as May 26, called on Nâna-Sâhib at Bithûr to "help him quiet the Sepoys and prevent a mutiny." Nâna appeared at once and brought with him two hundred of his five hundred bodyguards and the three or four guns he still had. He was appointed to guard the treasury and settled in his own house at Navâbganj. He was thus acquainted with all the transactions between the civil and military authorities and made arrangements together with the English for a "refuge" for the women and children . . .

On June 6th, when the Sepoys revolted, instead of murdering their officers as happened in other places, they only sacked the treasury, and then marched towards Delhi to join the main corps of the mutineers. The English, having fortified the church, locked themselves in it and in the supply barracks and magnanimously turned over to Nâna-Sâhib, who swore "eternal friendship," the arsenal, the powder magazine, the artillery and all that was left of the treasury, empowering their "true ally" to defend them from his own people. Only then did Nâna throw off his mask. He ordered the Sepoys to return, and on the very next day, June 7th, opened fire on his "friends," but then suddenly stopped: a devilish thought struck the Marâthâ. Sudden death without

---

* [Major-General Wheeler was an army officer in the East India Company's service, in charge of the garrison at Cawnpore at the outbreak of the Sepoy Mutiny, when he was already 75 years old. He held out against the Sepoys at Cawnpore for three weeks in June, 1857. Surrendered on assurance of safe conduct to Allâhâbâd, but was killed by Sepoys along with others of the British garrison when embarking in boats.—*Compiler.*]

suffering would not be a punishment. He began to play with his prisoners like a cat with a mouse; knowing how many provisions were stored in the barracks, he decided to starve the English ... Two weeks later, out of 250 men of the garrison who had entered the fortifications, there remained only 150, and out of 380 women and children there remained less than half. Corpses putrified without being buried before the eyes of those who outlived them. It was an appalling and frightful agony.

Finally, Nâna decided to finish them off. He sent word on the 26th of June that if the English would trust him, he would save those still alive. The garrison, preferring a quick death to the tortures of starvation, accepted the offer. Then the dethroned prince ordered some barges to be made ready, telling his prisoners he would land them at Allâhâbâd. On the morning of the 27th, a party of Englishmen was allocated thirty barges. As soon as they took their places, the boatmen set fire to the straw awnings over the boats, and the Sepoys began to shoot at the prisoners. Out of thirty boats, only two succeeded in extinguishing the fire and reaching the middle of the river, which at that spot is about a mile wide. One of them sank, owing to bullet holes, the other was miraculously saved, but of the twenty-eight passengers only four were alive the next morning, having found shelter in the rushes. Those who did not drown were dragged out of the water and led back to the shore. Nâna himself did not take any part in all these proceedings. It is said that he announced the same morning he would give up the prisoners to fate and his people: happy would be those who could escape; those who had to perish, even he himself could not save; to this he added that any "white" who managed to escape would be wise never to fall into his hands again, as in such a case he would be executed. All the men who escaped from drowning were shot dead; the women and children were locked up in another building, called "Savada-Kotti," not far away from the station, where they were left to live for some ten days. Nâna might have possibly pardoned them, had not the following taken place: on the tenth of July, while passing by Biṭhûr with a strong party of refugees of both sexes from Fatehgarh, Colonel Smith was seen on the river by the sentinels. The boat was captured, and about fifty persons, women and children included, were made prisoners. In the morning they were driven on foot to Cawnpore, in scorching heat, to be presented to Nâna-Sâhib. Instead of keeping quiet and accepting their fate of life or death, the English, according to hearsay, began abusing Nâna-Sâhib, calling him, among other things, an "illegitimate son," an offence which the proud Brâhmaṇas punish by death. The men were led out into the market place and shot dead, while the women and children were added to the other prisoners. All of this terrible period is enveloped in mysterious darkness. Not one of the prisoners remained alive to tell the story of what really happened, but it must have been something appalling and beyond description . . .

Probably if he could have avoided it, Nâna-Sâhib would not have executed the women and children, whom he kept alive as long as he was in power. But on the 15th of July, he lost the battle at Aundh and had to flee. It is said that in a moment of mad frenzy, during the last night of his power and his presence at Cawnpore, he avenged his sisters: he admitted a crowd of Sepoys (Moslems and Hindus), drunk with *bhâṅg* and opium, to the house where the European women were imprisoned, just a few hours before the execution. It is also related that four men, Judge Thornhill, Colonel Smith and two others, were purposely left alive to witness this national disgrace. At dawn, the men were dragged out into the street and murdered, then came the turn of the 250 women and children. Their bodies were thrown into a deep "well" famous forever after.

It would be useless to continue this story, as all of Europe knows the rest. I will merely add some details which have not before been given. When Cawnpore was once more taken by the English and quiet was restored (it happened the evening of the same day), Nâna-Sâhib was no longer there; he had disappeared leaving no trace. It is well known that for some time the English exhibited a prisoner in an iron cage, whom, in the absence of the genuine, they tried to palm off as Prince Dhondu; finally they were forced to set him free, as the whole of India laughed at it. Meanwhile, people say that Nâna-Sâhib is still alive, and some have not yet lost hope of seeing him once more in India. As to the prisoners, the collector, Lt.-Colonel G. M. Sherer, tells us the following:

> In driving up to the house of murder we found blood more than 10 inches deep. We looked into the well and the whole awful scene was clear to us: there was no one to save. It was a sight at the mere thought of which even in our day, in far distant England, people shudder and their hearts bleed. The well was deep but narrow; looking into it we saw it filled to the top with corpses, absolutely naked. There was 253 of them.

This is the story of an English witness. But he does not relate how the next morning the people of Cawnpore were gathered together and *every tenth man* shot dead; he is silent about the fact that, having caught several hundred men (probably mostly innocent), they made them *lick the caked blood on the floors of the room;* silent also about the fact that this blood was *licked* by some five hundred men, prevented from getting up from the floor for 48 hours, that two-thirds of them died from vomiting and the other third were clubbed to death by the English; and finally, that not merely a few dozens of mutineers were loaded into guns and fired off (which is confirmed from English sources), but that *several thousand men died that way,* is left unsaid.

Lord Canning* ordered all the "white" corpses to be left untouched in the well which was filled with lime and earth. The square was turned into a garden, and the famous memorial monument of 1857 was erected over the well.

We visited the garden immediately after leaving the station. It is shady, full of cypresses, weeping willows and other beautiful plants and flowers; but neither the architecture of the chapel, nor the walls of the garden, nor even the monu-

---

* [Charles John Canning, Earl Canning (1812-1862). Educated at Eton and at Christ Church, Oxford. Under-Secretary for foreign affairs, 1841-46; postmaster general, 1853-55. Assumed the governor-general-ship of India, 1856, and was confronted with a number of administrative difficulties and wars, including the Mutiny, in all of which he showed himself as very able. Created Earl, 1859. Engaged in reorganizing the financial, legal, and administrative systems of India, 1859-62. —*Compiler.*]

ment over the well are appropriate to the great tragic event or worthy of the sums of money spent in the fulfillment of Canning's idea. The statue represents a coarse figure of an angel with his hands held open, palms down, as though he felt cold and was warming them at an open fireplace. The statue is the work of Baron Carlo Marochetti * and represents, according to his idea, "the Angel of Compassion." But why this pose should represent *Compassion* and not something else, is hard to say. The statue is placed within a granite enclosure with an iron railing around it; in front, marble steps lead to a wicket gate in the railing; this is even more ridiculous, as it would seem that in a structure having no roof a gate had no place, the more so as it seems to be hanging between heaven and earth. A person wishing to approach the monument has to descend other similar steps inside the railing; and only then could a "passer-by," now in a square hole with the monument in its middle, stand in front of the pedestal and really look at it, though he certainly would not be moved. Right in front of him he would find written in white raised letters on a pink background around the whole pedestal the legend of the mutiny. This legend is curious indeed. It seems to be a collection of all the choicest *unprintable* swearing and damning of the pagans. Prince Dhondu Pant (Nâna-Sâhib), robbed and exiled from his hereditary estates, is delivered therein to "eternal fire," as being a "seditious and vile slave who dared to rebel against the lawful government of *God's chosen people*" — the English "God's chosen people"! All sympathy, all deep grief for the undeserved suffering of the unfortunate martyred women and children — all such feelings must disappear in reading the disgraceful imprecations of this haughty and pompous inscription. One forgets the presence of the remains that rest beneath; there is left before the eyes but this proud inscription, which smacks of Phari-

---

* [Baron Carlo Marochetti (1805-67). Italian sculptor, born at Turin. Studied chiefly at Rome, 1822-30; lived in France, 1832-48. His "Fallen Angel" was exhibited in 1831. In 1848, he removed to London, where he executed statues of Queen Victoria, Lord Clyde and Richard Cœur-de-Lion. He died in London.—*Compiler.*]

seeism on the part of haughty and cruel fathers, brothers and sons! In all the garden, among dozens of memorial inscriptions, positively not a single one from the New Testament can be found. The spirit of the ancient Israelitic intolerance and vindictiveness, the rule of "an eye for an eye, and a tooth for a tooth," reigns despotically in this garden of death and Puritanism. Be that as it may, in mourning the innocent dead one cannot help but recognize in that terrible tragedy the working of a just "law of retaliation." "What you sow that you shall reap," I seemed to hear in the rustling of every weeping willow over the grave, and the distant murmur of the creek. Great and terrible are the sins of Nâna-Sâhib, but who would dare to assert that his acts were not called forth by the bloody tears and the groans of the 200 million people in a country which was trampled under the foot of her conqueror, a people despised, starved to death by the hundreds of thousands during the last long century? And would our Christian readers believe that some unknown hand had written the following words on many a tomb, words so befitting the sacredness of the place. "The pride of a race is justified, whose voice proclaimed to every Asiatic: *Hic niger est: hunc tu, Romane, caveto.*" *

The Colonel, a most humane man among the liberals, who once shed his own blood for the liberty of real *negroes* (the "tribe of Ham," as they were called then by the American preachers), was really beside himself. Finally we stumbled over the monument of some sergeant with the following inscription. "Oh God! You made me inherit impious pagans; destroy them, obliterate them from the face of the earth, and may the *damned* Philistines perish; and You, Oh God! shed lustre over Your *own* people!" All these inscriptions with their false humility seemed to me so disgustingly Jesuit-

---

* [Expression of Horace meaning: "That man is black (in the sense of knave, not good): Roman, beware of him!"

According to the *Handbook for Travellers in India*, etc., ed. by Sir A. C. Lothian (London: John Murray, 1955), the marble memorial by Marochetti has been removed from its original site over the well in the Memorial Gardens to the churchyard; and the Gardens have been renamed the Municipal Garden and have become a public park.— *Compiler.*]

ical, so full of secret hypocrisy, that I hastened to depart and called our English companions to leave the garden. I positively felt that the very next moment I would no longer control myself and would state in the presence of the guard what I thought of the English, living or dead, and in addition would fall upon the "blond spy," who followed us as our shadow. We were already prepared for exasperation from the very first moment we approached the monument; having admitted us Europeans we were told that our friends, the Bâbû and Mûljî, would have to remain in the garden, *outside the gates,* which were then closed in their faces. In answer to our protests, the old watchman silently pointed to an inscription nailed to the gate. In large letters it stated the prohibition to "Hindus, pagans and Moslems to approach the garden enclosure."

Miss B. shed bitter tears and blew her nose over every monument. With great difficulty, we dragged her away from a monument consisting of two marble lovers over a double grave, whose "spirit," according to her idea, was "soaring that very moment" above her *topi* and her veil, wet from tears. She felt very grieved and even hurt when I told her that, as far as I was concerned, there was nothing soaring around her, except the "spirit of conceit and British haughtiness and Phariseeism."

«Ma chère», sobbed she, «vous n'avez vraiment pas de cœur...»

"Maybe so," said I, "but then I have what you apparently are lacking: j'ai du nez . . ."

We then returned to our Hindus.

—XXVII—

About four miles from Cawnpore, on the rocky right bank
of the Ganges, in the midst of a dark and virgin forest, some
wonderful old ruins stand. They are the remains of a number
of ancient cities, built on top of each other. Of the topmost
one there now remain only some colossal blocks of former
walls, embrasures and temples, and the ruins of once magnificent palaces, one or two rooms of which, or rather the walls
thereof, have been preserved here and there. Over these
walls, the poor natives built roofs of foliage and settled in
them, gradually transforming the ancient town of Jâjmau
into a village. The ruins cover many square miles, but the
natives gather only in some parts of them, leaving the rest
to the undisputed possession of the monkeys. History (English history) is silent about these cities, ignoring the Indian
legend that Jâjmau stands on the site of her sister and rival,
Asgarta, the City of the Sun.* The latter, according to the

---

*[The term *Asgarta* used by H.P.B. occurs also in *Isis Unveiled*, II,
31, where it is spelled *Asgartha* and is part of a quote from Louis
Jacolliot. Its original usage, allegedly in the *Purânas*, has not been sub-
stantiated, and demands further research. However, the most interesting
aspect of it is that it bears such a remarkably close resemblance to the
Norse mythological term *Asgard* or *Asgarth*, properly *Âsgarthr* (from
âss, a divine being, and *garthr*, an enclosure), which occurs in both the

378

ancient *Purânas*, was built by the Sons of the Sun, two centuries after the conquest of the island Lankâ by King Râma, in other words 5000 years B.C., according to the reckoning of the Brâhmanas. The past history of Jâjmau, which was sacked many times by invaders coming from beyond the Himâlayas, is absolutely unknown to European historians. This mysterious city, which "remembers not its parentage," is mentioned but once in the autobiography of Bâbur (Zahîr-ud-dîn-Muhammad), the Mogul emperor who lived in the beginning of the sixteenth century.* He says that during one of his numerous campaigns against the Afghâns, the latter sought shelter and tried to fortify themselves in the ancient town of Jâjmau. But Humâyûn, his son, defeated them. These ruins are among the numerous places in India utterly unknown to the English, both as to their past and, one must add, their present.

The road to Jâjmau is awful. We rode on elephants and it is thanks only to the steady step of these clever animals that we frequently avoided hurtling down deep ravines, or being caught by our hair on the branches, like modern Absaloms. Slowly and carefully the elephants stepped along the edge of the precipice; they stopped at every low hanging branch and tore it off with their trunks, before going further. The branches, in fact, did not hinder the elephants, but they

---

Older and the Younger *Edda*. The *Aesir* (pl. of *âss*) were the chief gods of the Teutonic pantheon and included such figures as Odin, Thor, Balder and others. *Asgard* was the abode or citadel of the gods, situated at the zenith and which could be reached only by the bridge *Bifrost*, the rainbow. It is also represented as rising from the center of *Midgard*. In *Asgard* is the *Ithavoll*, where the gods hold assembly at the base of the tree Yggdrasill. There are in *Asgard twelve* mansions or realms of the gods, a legend which contains an echo of an esoteric truth concerning the inner structure of the universe. Whether this legend has its counterpart, or indeed origin, in any of the known *Purânas*, is something left to be ascertained by some competent scholar.—*Compiler.*]

*The Emperor Bâbur, a famous literary man of India, was the nephew of the Samarkand Sultan and a direct descendant of Tamerlane; he conquered Kâbul in 1504; in 1519, he conquered the Pañjâb, and in 1526, Delhi. He was the first to organize communication and mail service betwen Âgra and Kâbul, and while in India, wrote his autobiography or memoirs, renowned for their wealth of historical data.

were taught to do that and cleverly followed the directions
of their riders. We rode for some three miles through woods
and over rocks before reaching the first ruin, most of the
time along such narrow paths that not even a small native
shell-like *ekka* driven by oxen could have negotiated them;
from one gully into another, from one ravine into the next,
we finally came to some inhabited buildings; then we struck
a wider road and looked around. We were amazed at the
sight! There was not a single human being to be seen, but
on every ruin, on every piece of wall or ancient fallen column,
there sat dozens and dozens of monkeys. Without exaggerating, they must have numbered several thousands. The
inhabitants complain that they steal most of their supplies;
that no matter how carefully they may hide their millet or
corn, or any vegetables, it will surely be stolen during the
night by these forest "Dacoits." And yet no native would
dare to throw even a stone at a monkey; here monkeys are
sacred, as is the case everywhere, "deva-saabs," "master-
gods" literally. The inhabitants die of hunger but the monkeys thrive.

On the fringe of the forest flows the Ganges; on its right
bank you can see even now the remains of huge ancient
marble steps, the width of which would seem to indicate they
were intended for giants. The whole sandy bank for several
miles, and the forest itself, are covered with numberless
fragments of columns, of carved broken pedestals, idols and
bas-reliefs, sunk deep into the earth. The outlines of the
carving, the style of the architectural remains, the very size
of the ruins produces an impression of something grandiose
and unexpected, even on those who have seen Palmyra and
the Egyptian Memphis. It is hard to understand why these
ruins have never been described, especially as they are at the
very walls of Cawnpore. In the comprehensive work *Concerning the Territories Acquired by the East India Company,*
they are mentioned in only a few words: "Jâjmau, formerly
a town, is now a village with a dilapidated bazaar. The local
legends say it was built on the ruins of two other cities. The
distance from Calcutta is 620 miles; lat. 26° 26′, long.
89° 28′." That is all. And yet under Jâjmau lies buried one
of the oldest cities of ancient India . . . It is sufficient to

cite the following example to prove its antiquity. Some years ago, after a severe hurricane, several large and old banyans were felled, and some others torn up by their roots. At the extremities of the latter were found pieces of carved marble around which the roots had grown. People dug deeper and discovered, some four yards underground, the tops of ruins of enormous buildings. The question, however, is not so much as to these building themselves, but rather how many centuries it must have taken, first, to deposit a sufficient amount of alluvial soil on the banks of the Ganges to come up to the level of these buildings (some of which are 300 feet high), and furthermore to cover them with four yards of earth; and second, how much time must have elapsed between this event and the time when the banyans, now some 1,200 years old, began to send their roots into this alluvial deposit? To judge by the concentric rings of the trunks,* it has been shown that these banyans were not less than twelve centuries old, and the forest has other trees that are even older. One group of these *Ficus indica,* especially, amazed us by their size, perhaps only a trifle smaller than that of the famous banyan on the banks of the Narbada, near Broach, which is called by the people "Kabîr-Bad." The latter is an historic tree. It was 700 years old at the time when Alexander of Macedonia and his whole army rested under its shade. At present, it consists of 356 stout trunks and about 3,000 smaller ones, and some two hundred years ago another army, 7,000 men strong, rested beneath it.

We camped in and wandered about the forest for three days. The Thâkur was familiar with all its nooks and paths and kept his word. He showed us the way into places where no Englishman had ever been; one such place was a dark underground tunnel some 140 feet beneath the earth. We went there before dawn, when everyone else was still sleeping.

---

*As has been ascertained, trees grow in width by adding a new layer annually, each new layer forming a new ring around the tree, so that by counting these rings it is possible to tell its age fairly correctly. Adamson found near Gorée a *baobab* which was five or six thousand years old. Humboldt mentions it as the oldest tree on earth. Some of these *baobab-*trees are 90 to 100 feet in circumference.

Except for us, the Ṭhâkur had only Nârâyaṇa to escort him
and his faithful servant, the old and gray-haired Râjput,
who accompanied us all the way from Bombay. Mr. Y. and
Miss B. stayed at Jâjmau with the Bâbû and Mûljî and
did not even know when we left or where we went. This
underground journey was to me, as well as to the Colonel,
the most interesting event of our whole trip, probably because of its mysteriousness . . .

We had to cut through the thicket for more than an hour,
frightening monkeys that were waking, and threw at us all
sorts of indescribable objects. Like a flock of forest demon-
gnomes, they snapped their teeth at us and peeped with their
sharp glittering eyes from behind every bush. Finally we
entered a narrow gorge entirely overgrown with shrubbery,
but had no time to notice whether it was a natural or an
artificial one. The Ṭhâkur led the way, then came I, followed by Nârâyaṇa, while the Colonel and the Râjput
servant brought up the rear. Going in single file, we were
silent, as the road became very difficult, and it was no time
for talking. Finally we began to descend steep, winding steps,
at the bottom of which we entered a little glade. On our
right, against a lonely rock, stood a small hut, which we
entered. It was not light in the forest, as the day had only
begun to dawn; but here in this hut, sheltered by thick
banyans and backed by the rock which served as a sort of
wall for it, complete darkness reigned. The Râjput struck
fire and lighted a covered lantern which he gave to the
Ṭhâkur. Then, taking the lantern in one hand and my hand
in the other, he passed with me, as it seemed to me in this
Egyptian darkness, right through the wall. Either because
of the novelty of the situation, or as a consequence of
constant nervous strain, I must confess that on entering that
underground region — unknown to the rest of the world —
I felt very much alarmed; however, a feeling of curiosity
and shame prevailed and I silently followed him. The lantern
feebly lighted our way, throwing but a solitary sharp beam
in front of our feet; all around us impenetrable darkness
reigned. I was irresistibly drawn by the hand of a powerful
figure of a giant, all dressed in white, and whose face appeared to me now darker than night itself . . . He walked

swiftly and with no hesitation. Everyone kept silent, and even our footsteps seemed to produce no sound on the even and soft ground of the passage, as though we were walking on a thick carpet. Notwithstanding the solemnity of our procession or the Radcliff surroundings, the Colonel, even now, could not keep from joking. "It's a wonderful dark cabinet for calling forth spirits . . . What a pity we have no medium with us," we heard him suddenly say. In spite of the jocular tone, the mere sound of his voice in this silence made me, and him, shudder. His voice sounded hollow and strained, and at the same time seemed drawn out and coming as if from somewhere above; it rushed far, far ahead, awakening along its path the sleeping echo . . .

All at once the Ṭhâkur stopped, strongly grasping my hand.

"What is it? Are you actually and seriously *afraid?*" he asked suddenly, contemptuously stressing the last word, "Your hand trembles as though you had fever!"

I felt the blood rush to my face at this *deserved* rebuke; but I acted as any other person would have in my place: "reared up inwardly" and tried to excuse myself.

"I am not afraid . . . there would be no reason to be . . .," I muttered, feeling in the darkness the eyes of Gulâb-Singh fixed on me. "I simply feel tired . . ."

"Women," calmly whispered the Ṭhâkur to himself, with some condescension and bitterness, and slowed his steps.

Having no sufficiently weighty proof to the contrary, and unable to object to this new offence, which was as much personal as directed against my whole sex, I swallowed it meekly and was silent. We walked in this manner about a quarter of an hour or even more, on even and soft ground, somewhat sloping, and through a passage that seemed to me to be rather high-vaulted; my old friend continually held me by the hand, the Colonel was already beginning to puff loudly, and I was inwardly grumbling at my lack of strength and the rebuke I had received. The Ṭhâkur stopped, lifted the lantern high, and opened its shutters. We saw in front of us a smooth wall of rock. Not a single fissure was to be seen.

"Look here," said Gulâb-Lal-Singh to the Colonel," and see this proof of the mechanical wonders our ancestors performed who, according to European opinion, were unacquainted with science. I'll bet you anything that the best mechanics of the West would not succeed in finding the secret of this door! I want to prove to you now that this is no rock, but a door . . ."

Our inquisitive president, who once had received a medal for the best thesis in mechanics at the Rensselaer Polytechnic Institute of Troy (New York), began carefully to examine the wall. His efforts were a complete failure. Neither his knocking nor his fumbling led to any conclusive result. Meanwhile, taking advantage of the light of the opened lantern, I examined our surroundings. It was a sort of semi-circular room with rocky walls and a ceiling at an enormous height; the floor looked as if it were strewn with black powder.

"If you can believe my word," finally remarked the Thâkur, who was patiently watching the Colonel's investigations, "I can tell you that this passage was excavated and built many thousands of years ago. As you may see," he added, while leaning his shoulder against the corner of the rock, "the Sons of the Sun were well-acquainted with the principle of the lever and the rules of the center of gravity long before Archimedes. Otherwise how could they have invented this? . . ."

Pressing with his shoulder and turning some unnoticed joint-pin, he produced noiselessly and slowly an opening of some two feet in width and of his own height, not unlike the modern American doors which slide up to their locks inside a wall. But in this case, the door had no handle nor was an opening visible inside the wall . . .

We all stepped through, and the Thâkur, applying pressure again and moving *something* imperceptibly, closed the wall. Notwithstanding the insistent questioning and curiosity of the Colonel, he declined to tell us the secret. "It ought to be sufficient that I prove to you that these secret underground passages have existed for many thousands of years in India," he said, "and untold thousands of people have found a refuge here at different times, with the help of those who knew of their existence. Not many of those individuals are left today," he added with what seemed to me a tone of sorrow in his voice. "They did not succeed in saving against her will one of the bravest and noblest women of India, the last of the great heroines of our 'mother'! * In a few minutes we will sit down for a rest, and then I will tell you an episode of the last mutiny. In Europe it is almost, if not entirely, unknown . . ."

We now walked along a broad and high-vaulted corridor. The latter probably had some sort of connection with the outer world, as the air, though somewhat damp, was fresh in spite of the fact that we were 140 feet underground. Our path continued downhill; and not until the end of the third corridor, beginning with the cave, which I will now describe, did it begin to go uphill again. It was evident that parts of these passages existed at the time when Asgarta, among other cities, was a flourishing town on the surface of the earth. On both sides of the corridor we saw many openings in the shape of oblong squares, which led into other side passages; but the Thâkur did not take us there, remarking that they led to dwellings which apparently *sometimes* were occupied. That this underground tunnel had been visited only recently was evidenced by the fact that I found an old crumpled envelope with some hieroglyphic signs on it, but of quite a modern pattern and even with glue on the flap. The whole passage, with its corridors, as far as we could judge, was some five or six miles long. Having walked for some three miles counting from the secret door, in other words about halfway between the two passages, we came to an enormous natural cave, with a little lake in its center and benches hewn out of rock all around it. In the water, right in the middle of the little lake, stood a granite column with a pyramidal top and a thick and rusty chain twisted round it. While in the passage, we had noticed at times that the darkness grew less intense and a sort of dim light came from the top; in the cave, however, which was probably

---

*Speaking about their country, the Hindus always call India their "mother."

the lowest point of the underground tunnels, it was as dark as in the pyramid of Gizeh. But here the Ṭhâkur had prepared a surprise for us. He gave the old Râjput some order in a dialect unknown to us, and the latter, as if endowed with the eyes of a cat, went into the darkness, fumbled for something in a corner, and proceeded to light several torches, one after the other, placing them into iron rings fastened in the wall. Very soon the whole cave was blazing with light. Then, tired and quite hungry, we sat down on the rim of the lake and took up our basket of provisions.

I will now try briefly to tell the history of this cave and the episode referred to by the Ṭhâkur, concerning the mutiny of 1857. The latter belongs to history, though the English tried to distort the accounts of it, as they have distorted and even *concealed* many other facts of this, to them, disgraceful epoch. Having learned these facts first from Gulâb-Lal-Singh, we later heard some very interesting details concerning them from several old Hindus, some of whom had been eyewitnesses to the events; and on one occasion we heard about them from an Englishman, an old Anglo-Indian officer.

The *Purâṇas* recount the following sad story about the end of the ancient city of Asgarta. Sudâsa-Ṛishi was the sacred head of the "Brahmâtma," * and his brother Agastya was the Mahâ-Kshatriya (the great warrior-king) of Asgarta. In their absence, the Kingdom was ruled by the Mahârânî (the great queen) who was formerly a *kumâraka* (Virgin of the Sun) in the temple of *Sûrya-Nârî* (Sun-Nature). Her beauty captivated the king; at the very moment when she was about to offer herself on the altar of fire (religious cremation), he took advantage of the ancient custom giving to kings the right of saving Hindu vestals from death and claimed her as his wife. There had been previously another suitor, the king of Himavat, but she refused him, preferring death in the fiery embrace of her husband-god, the sacred fire. The insulted trans-Himâlayan king swore vengeance. Many years later, when King Agas-

---

* "Soul of Brahmâ," the highest religious dignity.

tya was at war in Lanka (Ceylon), his vanquished rival, profiting by his and his army's absence, invaded Asgarta. The queen defended her city with the courage of despair; finally, however, the city was taken by storm. Then, having assembled all the "Virgins of Sûrya" from the temples, the wives and daughters of her subjects and her own children, in all 69,000 women, including the *kumârakas,* the queen locked herself in the enormous underground temple of *Sûrya-Nârî;* ordering sacred pyres to be built along the passages she burned herself and all the other women and all the treasures of the city, leaving to the conquerors but the empty walls.

When the king returned and found, instead of his palace, wife and children, nothing but ashes, he at once set out to pursue the victorious army. Having overtaken it, he defeated it, took the king and 11,000 men of his army prisoners, and returned to the ruins of Asgarta. Here he forced the prisoners to build on the site of the old city a new and more beautiful one, and then, when the work was finished, he ordered them to erect in the middle of the city, in front of the temple of Nârî, a funeral-pyre sufficiently large to take care of 11,000 men. It was there that the king of Himavat and all his warriors were burned alive amidst the curses and insults of the people of Asgarta, to avenge the death of the Queen.

According to tradition and the ancient chronicles, the underground tunnels we had just passed through, as well as that portion of them which was still ahead, on the other side of the cave, are the ones in which the queen had burned herself. The soft soil under our feet which I mistook for fine black sand consisted of the ashes of 69,000 women and *kumârakas,* or Virgins!

Such is the legend. And now for some factual events! Twenty-two years have elapsed since the following took place, and all the details of the tragic epic are still fresh in the memory of the people, both at Poona and at Gwalior.

On the road from Âgra to Saugor lies the territory of Jhânsi. It is situated now in the English Province of Bundel-khand, but in 1854 it belonged to the independent Marâthâ peshwa. The Râj of Jhânsi consists of two sections divided

by a narrow strip of land which belongs to the territory
of the native Râjâ or Ṭhâkur of Tehrî. To the north of
Western Jhânsi are the boundaries of Gwalior and Datiâ,
to the east, those of Tehrî, to the south and west, those of
Gwalior again. In 1832, according to the statistics of the
East India Company, the Râj contained 956 villages and
286,000 inhabitants, scattered over 2,922 square miles. It
yielded a revenue of about 18 lakhs of rupees.* Formerly a
part of the property of the Râjâ of Orchhâ, who belonged to
the family of the princes of Bundelâ, it was ceded at the time
of Śivâjî to the peshwas, and was ruled by their Subahdârs
(governors). In 1804, the English concluded a defensive
alliance with one of these vassals of the peshwas; and in
1817, when the allies and friends, in accordance with their
usual method, deprived the peshwa of all his rights, he
ceded (!!!) to them among other things the possession of
Bundelkhand; then the Company drew up another treaty
with the Subahdâr of Jhânsi, according to which he was
declared an independent Râjâ, "having the right to leave
his inheritance to his children, and should he have none, to
his nearest heirs," on condition that he pay the Company
74,000 rupees a year. In 1832, Prince Râm-Râmchandra-
Râo was formally acknowledged as the Râjâ. In 1835, however, he died without any direct male heir, leaving his throne
to his granddaughter, the week-old child of his daughter,
with the understanding that the husband chosen for her
should inherit the throne. The Company, however, notwithstanding the clauses of the treaty, the will of the people,
or the Indian laws of successorship, which do not allow lepers
to reign, chose the uncle of the deceased Râjâ, Raghunâth-
Râo. This leprous, half-demented and sickly Râjâ died three
years later. This was the opportunity for which the Company
had waited. Under the pretext that the natives did not
know how to manage the affairs of their own house, and
pretending all the time that they sought a decent heir for
Jhânsi, the English took possession of the Râj in 1843 and
granted a pension to Lakshmî-Bâi, Râm-Râmchandra-Râo's
married granddaughter (and direct heir), and to her husband

---

*2,800,000 rupees.

Gaṅgâdhara-Râo. The latter died in 1854, three years before the mutiny, leaving a widow and a son, the latter holding all the hereditary rights to the throne of his mother and great-grandfather. The English, however, declared him *illegitimate* and even deprived Lakshmî-Bâi of her pension. She was 16 years old at the time. It was she whom the Thâkur had in mind, when he spoke of the greatest heroine of modern India.

Mahârânî Lakshmî-Bâi was the cousin of Sindhia, the Mahârâja of Gwalior, and of Nâna-Sâhib. At the very beginning of the mutiny, when the latter threw off his mask, she publicly took his side, and assembling an army of 22,000 men at Jhânsi she prepared herself to support him to the end. It is said that Nâna-Sâhib succeeded not only in winning over the army of Gwalior, but Sindhia himself. In the ensuing litigation, however, the Mahârâja succeeded in proving he was legitimate and the fact that the accusation originated with his enemies. Having received word that the army of Sindhia was ready for action, and in agreement with Nâna-Sâhib, the Mahârânî marched at the head of her army to Gwalior, the capital of Sindhia, where she expected to find the entrance to the fortress open, and the army and people ready to proclaim their independence. According to previous arrangements, this Hindu Joan of Arc was to take possession of Gwalior in the name of Nâna-Sâhib and, when the whole affair was over, to return to Sindhia his property. But matters turned out differently. The *Divân* (prime minister) on whom all their hopes were based, expecting him to prepare everything and inform the army and the people, turned traitor to their cause. Mahârâja Sindhia was absent at the time, being with the English. Instead of opening the gates to Lakshmî-Bâi and her army, the *Divân* locked himself up and warned the British, in the meantime threatening his own soldiers with the vengeance of the Mahârâja and his allies in the Company. The soldiers wavered and upon hearing the prearranged signals during the night, did not know what to do. Meanwhile the "Queen of Jhânsi," * finding the gates were not open and suspecting

---

*She is thus called by the people.

treason, stormed and broke into the city from the other side. People say that some other secret passage had been opened for her.

Then began a reign of terror in the city, which lasted a whole week until the English arrived post haste. Lakshmî-Bâi executed most of Sindhia's army, killing every man who as much as hesitated in joining her cause. The *Divân* was able to flee.* When the English army came to the rescue of Gwalior, a *brahmachârin*, dressed as a *sannyâsin* (ascetic), offered the Queen shelter, telling her that otherwise she would certainly perish. He implored her to follow him with her son to the vicinity of Cawnpore, where she would find in the caves of Jâjmau both friends and complete safety. But Lakshmî-Bâi proudly refused the offer, telling him she did not fear death and even preferred it to life, owing to her country's disgrace. There took place outside the city gates and the fortress, which our heroine had not had time to occupy, a battle that was to remain memorable for years. The Mahârânî personally led her troops into battle astride a maddened horse. At first the soldiers were panic-stricken, and the young recruits, unaccustomed to regular service, started running away. Spurred by the resoluteness of despair, she, with a handful of followers, defended the position for three hours against an enemy three times as strong. Finally, noticing that her forces were beginning to dwindle, she ordered her followers to build a pyre on the spot and make all necessary preparations to light it at a given signal. "Brothers," she exclaimed, according to an eyewitness, "I swear by the shades of all my ancestor-warriors who died in honest combat, to die before the hand of a *bellati* shall touch a single thread of my *sârî*. Swear also that in case I do fall, you will burn my body and will not permit the enemy to touch even my ashes!" They so swore, and Lakshmî-Bâi galloped on horseback into the thick of the battle. They say that the same mysterious ascetic once more offered to save her at this solemn hour, but she again refused. Popular rumor, always exaggerating, tells of her killing with her own hands several hundred Englishmen! That she killed a number of them is

---

* He is still alive and receives from the English an enormous pension.

AGRA: THE TAJ MAHAL

DISTANT VIEW OF THE *TÁJ MAHAL*

as true as the fact that the English have carefully hidden the records of this disgraceful event. Finally her horse, in sudden terror, bolted so that the Mahârânî lost the reins. In a few bounds, the maddened horse carried her back to the wall of the city, where, hit by an enemy bullet, it fell, throwing its rider. The Mahârânî, however, was not killed. She did not lose consciousness, but probably broke her legs. They leaned her against the wall and she continued to give orders. Having noticed that some Englishmen who had seen her fall were hastening to capture her, and that her retinue had been cut off from the way to the pyre, she made a sudden decision and gave her last order. While some of her followers held back the enemy, the others placed her on a heap of hay, covered her with straw and dried branches, and set them on fire. Then they threw themselves against the English and were cut to pieces, thereby giving the fire time to complete its task and reduce the Mahârânî to ashes . . .

"These noble ashes, worthy of uniting with those of the Queen of Asgarta, rest here, and surely no human hand will ever disturb them," concluded our guide.

We went out of the caves by another passage which led uphill. The road sloped gently, and our feet trod, as before, on ground which was as soft as a carpet. Finally, after turning sharply to the right, we came to a solid wall similar to the first, with this difference: instead of sliding into the side wall, this closing stone went down, to open the entrance, leaving a low wall some foot and a half high, which we had to step over. Behind this wall, in a small cave, there is a deep well. Here, all around us, over 16 square miles, are buried the ruins of the sleeping city of Asgarta.

To reach the surface we had to climb three consecutive series of endless steps. Once again a sort of door — a stone between two rocks, turning on an unseen pivot — and we entered another cave; the light, though dim, blinded us after eight hours of darkness. Emerging into the fresh air we felt as a person would on coming out of a chilly cellar and stepping into an oven. The heat was unbearable. Everything in the forest was asleep, and, except for the ceaseless noise of the crickets, absolute stillness reigned. Even the monkeys

slumbered amidst the foliage. It was noon, and, threatened
with sunstroke, we had to wait in the shade for the midday
heat to abate. Some ten paces from us stood an old dilapidated temple of which nothing was left but the *gopura,* the
gate-tower with a room or two inside. It was there that we
sought shelter from the unbearable heat, and our entrance
disturbed hundreds of multi-colored parrots, whose bright
wings glittered in the sun like a moving rainbow . . . We
were home in time for evening tea.

To recount our underground trip in greater detail cannot
be done for many reasons, the main one being the fact that
this locality is absolutely unknown; in addition, much of
what we saw and heard there is so strange that I probably
could not find words with which to describe it accurately.
Other underground tunnels also exist, for instance at Amber,
near Jaipur, that have never yet been visited by any other
Europeans but ourselves; then there is also the underground
passage leading far out under the sea at Elephanta, where
having descended for some two miles, we, and our Pârsî
guides nearly suffocated. These passages, however, are known
to the English, though they have never visited them. As to
the underground of Jâjmau, to my great astonishment and
in spite of my frequent questioning, I found them to be unknown to the English. No wonder, then, that the Ṭhâkur,
who made us promise never to give a hint as to the road
leading to them, was so sure of the fact that they would
remain undiscovered by the English. The Hindus are in
general a very secretive and mysterious people;* but among
them, the Ṭhâkur was more mysterious than any of them.
Not long ago, intending to describe this trip, I asked him:

"Would you mind if I told my Russian readers about the
underground tunnels of Jâjmau?"

---

*They are so secretive that notwithstanding all the endeavors of the
police in general and the detectives in particular, the English have not
been able to understand the following fact: how could the news during
the mutiny of 1857, *without telegraph or railways,* spread as quickly as
it did from one end of India to the other? No sooner did anything happen at Calcutta than it was known a few hours later some 2,000 miles
to the north and discussed in the market places, whereas the English

"Certainly not," he said, "if you will trust your memory."

"I do trust my memory. But you said that the English do not even suspect their existence? What if they should read my article and make note of these facts? They avidly read all Russian papers and translate at once into English everything that in any way concerns India or even Asia in general."

"Well, what of that? Let them take note of these facts."

"But what if they should go looking for these caves and find them?"

Gulâb-Singh blinked strangely and looked at me either inquiringly or a bit contemptuously.

"What is there so strange in my words? I think the supposition is very plausible."

"*Very*," underscored the Thâkur, "but only from the European point of view, and not from our own. Permit me to take the liberty to say that I probably know a little better than you do, not only the English, but human nature in general. And having studied it, I can tell you ahead of time, there are nine chances out of ten that in reading your story the Englishmen will think it a tale of your invention. They are too proud and boastful a people to concede that there exist places in their dominions of which they have not heard, and where they have no guards stationed."

---

learned about it a whole week later. Sir John Wm. Kaye in his work, *The History of the Sepoy War in India, 1857-1858* [Vol. I, p. 491], mentions this as a "fact unaccountable to the Government." "At the time when our staff was murdered at Allâhâbâd," writes Major Morel, "I was at Madras. The following morning, on June 8, I received a visit from a Brâhmana known to me, who told me the whole story. Not believing him, I ran to the Governor. Nothing was known there. Officially we learned the news only six days later!" (*A Few Days in 1857 in India*).

[Sir John William Kaye (1814-1876), English military historian who served for some time as secretary of the political and secret department of the India Office. He was a voluminous writer and a constant contributor to periodical literature. His best known work was *The History of the Sepoy War in India, 1857-58*, in three volumes. The work was continued by Col. G. B. Malleson, and was completed in six volumes in 1890.—*Compiler*.]

"But what of the *tenth* chance; what then?"

"Then they will go looking for the caves and will find nothing."

"How can you be so sure of that? . . . The underground passage does exist . . . It has not disappeared from the face of the earth, has it? . . ."

"Just because it actually *does* exist, they will not find it. Now, in case you had invented it, the English would surely find it, even if they had to excavate it themselves . . . They would do so to frighten the natives, and so prove their prowess at home. 'You see what fine chaps we are! Nothing escapes our all-seeing eye!' They did invent forged political correspondence and caught alleged political criminals by bribing escaped thieves; and all this merely to justify reports invented by them and which they had sent to themselves."

"Now one last supposition! They, *i.e.,* the Government and its spies, know that you were with us at Cawnpore and Jâjmau . . . I shall describe this as it took place . . . If they should bother you and insist on your showing them the caves, or, pardon me, if they should try *to make you* tell them the secret . . . what will you do then?"

The Thâkur laughed that silent laugh which always made me shiver.

"Do not worry. It can never happen. But in case they get the idea of 'bothering' me, I can warn you in advance that it will be *you* and not *I*, who will be in a false position. You can be sure I will not utter a single word under such circumstances and will leave my defense to the collector of my district and to those inhabitants who know me personally. The collector, Mr. V., will report, that *from March 15th and up to June 3rd, 1879, I did not leave my 'Râj,' and that he called on me twice a week during that time*, and the inhabitants, mostly English, will confirm it." *

---

* [Writing in the *Bombay Gazette*, March 5, 1881 (Cf. *Collected Writings*, Vol. III, "A Berlin Mare's Nest"), H.P.B. definitely states that she *was* at Cawnpore in the summer of 1879, "and with a Hindoo gentleman, among others, named Thackersey (since deceased to our regret). The party visiting Jâjmau, included besides the latter, two English friends, an Assistant Magistrate, a Collector of the N.W.P. and his brother, an Anglo-Indian Engineer: the Political Department de-

Having said this, he got up, mounted his horse, took his leave, and rode away, tossing this parting remark in a rather jeering tone:

"How do you know, perhaps I have a *twin* brother whose existence is as little known to the outer world as the caves themselves? . . . Put that down also; otherwise even your own countrymen will take us and our Theosophical Society for an enlarged edition of Munchausen."

They surely will.

This had already happened once to the Thâkur. People once saw him in Poona, where he went about openly for a whole month. But when the authorities wanted to involve him in some political offence, the collector, the municipality and *two missionaries* bore witness that Gulâb-Lal-Singh had not left his estate for the last six months. I merely state the fact, as usual without attempting to explain it. This happened less than a year ago.

---

tectives, or police (I could never make out which) following us in those days of blessed Conservative trust like hawks poised for a swoop which was never made . . ."

While H.P.B. says that "the letter about the Cawnpore caves, with an invitation to the Russian public by the 'Thâkur' to view them and himself, was but a study after Baron Munchausen," she nevertheless affirms "her belief, or rather knowledge, of such 'mysterious passages'."—*Compiler.*]

—XXVIII—

At last we are at Delhi, the great city of the Moguls. While other cities and places of India held us under the enchantment of a fairy dream with visions of all that was beauteous in architecture, Delhi will always remain in our memory as the embodiment of a seemingly invincible yet vanquished giant, the sleeping Samson, deprived of his locks by the hand of the treacherous Delilah. Nowhere throughout despoiled India will you find so many proofs of the greatness of the Moslem Empire, nowhere else will you feel impelled to bow in reverence to the memory of the great masters who created the "Nâdir-Shâh Mosque," the tower of Kuṭab, the Delhi palace, and above all the Tâj Mahal of Âgra.

Delhi rose before us from behind a hill, a few moments before sunset, and suddenly wakened in me the memory of the gold-and-pearl capital of Mohammed's paradise, as described by the Prophet. During one of his divine excursions into this heavenly region, newly discovered by him, the poet-Prophet had occasion to see, and later to describe for

396

us, an angel, the lower part of whose body was of fire, while the upper part was of transparent ice; the two warring elements were thus peacefully united without the least harm to each other. I thought of this angel at the first sight of the ancient capital of Shâh-Jahân. Could Mohammed have prophetically seen modern Delhi at sunset, you might imagine his angel of "fire and ice" was but an Eastern and very realistic metaphorical description of this city. Flooded by the golden and purple light of the setting sun, the lower part of the palaces, mosques and minarets of Delhi, all built of red sandstone, appeared like an enormous flaming bonfire, from the bosom of which rose high into the transparent and darkening azure of the evening sky the upper parts of these buildings, massive, gleaming white marble cupolas, minarets, towers, and what not . . . And over the whole scene, as though it were the head of the angel, towered, on a rocky mount, Jâmi'-Masjid, the chief mosque of the city, placed so very high that its foundations are thirty feet above the highest roof of Delhi. With its numberless towers, crenelated walls and minarets surrounding a striped apex of black and white marble, consisting of three cupolas, this mosque is certainly the most unique, if not the most beautiful, in India.* The sight was gorgeous and drew from us all a unanimous exclamation of amazement.

The ancient town, on the ruins of which Shâh-Jahân built Delhi in the seventeenth century, was called in Indian history Indraprastha, and later Indrapat. Its founder was King Yudhishthira who died, according to the ancient Brâhmanical chronicles, in the year 3101 B.C. Prior to the Christian era, the history of the city is enveloped in impenetrable darkness in the midst of which, here and there, a few points of light stand out in the shape of events the historical authenticity of which can be verified by comparison with facts known from the history of other people. The chronicles of Indrapat, from beginning to end, certainly

---

*Jâmi'-Masjid was founded by Shâh-Jahân in the fourth year of his reign (in 1633) and completed in the tenth. Its estimated cost was about 100,000 pounds sterling for material alone; the actual labor of construction cost nothing.

do exist, but they are in the hands of the Brâhmaṇas, who conceal them, as they do many other facts, under the pretext that, as long as *kali-yuga* (the Black Age) lasts, the Âryans should not disclose their history to their "white" enemies. And as there remain 427,012 years before the end of this period, which means the beginning of the next one, that of *satya-yuga,* the learned Orientalists will have time to grow old; consequently, it will not be our generation to which the mysteries of ancient Indian history will be disclosed. The European scholars take revenge upon the Brâhmaṇas by rejecting their data and denying the historical validity of even the few facts which the native historians consent to disclose to them . . . . What is generally known, in spite of them, can be told in a few words. But even that is un-usually interesting because of the many events that read almost like a fairy tale.

Passing over an interval of many centuries, we find Indrapat established as the capital of King Anangpâl Tomar, in the 11th century A.D. Then follows a long period of uncertain history. The Brâhmaṇas do not allow the profane behind the scenes, but tell both friends and foes about the wonderful riches and the civilization of this capital of North-Western India, and translate whole pages of their chronicles.

About the year 980 of our era, the Râjâ of Indrapat is mentioned as a member and ally of the native confederacy which was first vanquished by the Râjâ of Pâñjab, Sabuk-tigîn, and later defeated by Mahmûd of Ghaznî in 1008. Finally, at the time of the invasion of India by Shihâb al-dîn Muḥammad of Ghûrî in 1191, we find Indrapat one of the four great powers of India, called in 1193, Shihâb al-dîn, the Empire of Delhi. The Moslem historian Ferishta tells us that the Sultan of Ghûrî took this Empire from Prithivî-Râjâ, a Râjput prince who lost the battle, notwithstanding his 200,000 mounted men and 3,000 elephants. However, these allegedly "historical" data are confused and obscured to such an extent that in the chronicles of Ajmer we find the opposite assertion, namely, that it was not Prithivî-Râjâ who was vanquished, but Shihâb al-dîn Muḥammad whose head was cut off, the latter being stuffed and kept for many centuries in the armory of the Râjput kings. On the other hand, these same chronicles tell us that a few years later, as a result of a quarrel between the confederates, Kutb-al Dîn Aibak, a Ghûrî general, actually conquered the defenders of Indrapat and founded therein an independent Moslem dynasty [1206 A.D.], known to Oriental historians as that of "the Slaves of the Sultans of Ghûr." From then on this unfortunate empire was thrown from hand to hand like a ball. In 1290, the Khaljî, a "tribe of adventurers" from Afghânistân (according to the same chronicle), murdered the sovereign of Delhi, Kaikubâd, and gave the country to their own chief, Jalâl al-dîn Fîrûz Shâh, and thus established the Khaljî dynasty, which reigned until 1321 and ended with the murder of Sultan Kutb-al-Dîn Mubârak. The Empire then passed into the hands of Ghiyâth al-Dîn Tughluk, the founder of the Tughluk dynasty. Then Tamerlane invaded India and reached Delhi in 1398, marking his achievement by the massacre of 100,000 Hindu prisoners. "High towers were erected of their heads, and their carcases were left a prey to the birds and beasts," says the historian. Like a devastating thunderstorm sweeping over the length and breadth of India, Tamerlane soon relinquished Delhi, leaving the whole country to oblivion. During the next 50 years a deathlike silence reigned over this city, where no single living soul was left. In 1450, Buhlûl, the chief of the Pathâns (the Afghân tribe of Lodî), once more took possession of the abandoned town and country. His grandson, Ibrâhîm, was vanquished and killed in the battle of Pânîpat by the famous Sultan Bâbur in 1526. It was at that time that the last dynasty of Bâbur established itself on the throne, under the title of *padishâhs,* and the city was renamed Shâhjahânâbâd, in honor of its latest founder. But even that dynasty knew no peace. The son of Bâbur, Sultan Humâyûn, was vanquished in 1540 and exiled from India by Sher-Khân-Sûr of Pathân; it was only through the help of Persia that he regained his throne in 1554. Emperor Akbar, alone, knew how to raise his Indian kingdom to the highest pinnacle of power and might; having at his disposal an army of 4,400,000 men, he was able to secure the great Empire of Delhi for his posterity,* an empire which brought the dynasty a yearly revenue of £37,724,615, until the year 1707. After that time and until the year 1803, in other words for more than a century, this unfortunate country was the scene of perpetual wars. Her Great Moguls lived through every kind of disaster. Paṭhâns and Sikhs, Nawâbs, Marâṭhas and Râjputs, in turn, invaded the country, put out the eyes of the kings, burned them alive, alternately conquered and lost the city of Delhi. Finally, the kindhearted East India Company took pity on these poor sovereigns and decided to save the dynasty, *albeit against its will*. With praiseworthy self-denial, unique in history, General Lake marched up to the walls of Delhi in 1803. There he took advantage of either the over-confidence or perhaps the negligence of the French adventurer, Louis Bourguien,† who commanded the Marâthâ army, and with great impartiality drowned in the Jumnâ river the Frenchmen, Marâṭhâs and Paṭhâns besieging the town, as well as the Moguls defending it, to whose rescue he had allegedly come. He then took possession of the town, and the English have kept it ever since. From then on the poor descendants of Bâbur fared from bad to worse. The great *dies irae* came to them and lasted until 1862, when, as a result of the mutiny, the last of the nominal "Great Moguls," Bahâdur Shâh II, left his place of exile and imprisonment on earth—for the lofty Paradise spheres of his Prophet. This at least is our hope for this miserable, demoted Mogul. He suffered enough to have merited at least this one privilege out of the many he had been promised.

Nothing can compare with the beauty of not only the

---

*See M. Elphinstone's *History of India*, where he quotes the words of Abu'l Fazl.

† [Louis Bourguien was a Frenchman who went to India with Admiral Suffrein. Enlisted in Calcutta in the service of the East India Company. Engaged for some years in various political and militaristic struggles and adventures. For a while held command of Sindia's troops, until defeated by Lake at the battle of Delhi, September 11, 1803. Surrendered to Lake and was sent to Calcutta. Returned to France with considerable wealth, and was heard of no more.—*Compiler*.]

secluded places and historical monuments of the half-ruined city of Delhi, but of the general surroundings and the city ramparts. The latter, still formidable to the sight, and shaded by thick acacias and date palms, eloquently remind the tourist of their former grandeur and of the glorious knightly times when the sentinels of the invincible Sultans Akbar and Aurangzîb stood guard thereon. In our days, there remain under the mournful shade of the dark *salvadoras* only the scattered minarets of the tombs and the lonely monuments of the heroes gone to their eternal rest ... We shall long remember the sad and mysterious dale of Kuṭab. Along this valley, in an unbroken file seven miles wide and more than thirty miles long, are scattered on the banks of the Jumnâ the ruins of not only one, but of *several* ancient and modern towns. It is an entire epic poem in marble, a poem of the glorious past of numberless generations of heroes . . . . . From the Garden of Shâlamâr under the city wall and almost halfway out to Âgra, the whole valley is strewn with cyclopic structures and crumbling buildings of a more recent era: once formidable fortresses of the Râjput Kings; palaces, marble walls of which seem to have been wrought by the hands of fairy beings; tile towers, granite fortifications and other buildings strangely shaped. One can see sumptuous mausoleums, large as temples, with their gigantic gates and arches, as though the five millions of the army of Xerxes rendered military honors to all buried there; ruined obelisks—the relics of massive Paṭhân architecture; rooms of kingly palaces now transformed into huts and free lodgings for the pariahs, with brick walls all covered with precious enamel and wonderful mosaics; ancient golden cupolas, from the cracks of which whole forests of cacti have grown; fragments of walls which look like beautiful Venetian lace work, and ruins of ancient pagan temples consecrated to unknown gods, with altars showing paintings the colors of which are as bright and fresh as though they had been painted yesterday! . . . . . At every step there are ruins; wherever one looks, one sees some tumbled-down wall, an overturned statue or a broken column . . . . . And over this marvellous and strange world of well-nigh living ruins, there reigns day and night a

deadly silence. What a strange scene of devastation! When
we found ourselves in it, we thought we had wandered
into the fairy kingdom of the "Sleeping Beauty."

Not so long ago, less than a quarter of a century, this
valley, from the town itself to the tower of Kuṭb-Mînâr, nine
miles from the nearest city gate, was the home of luxury,
delight and power. It was strewn then with the villas of
rich courtiers and dignitaries of the Great Mogul. At
present, however, it has been transformed into the abode
of utter decay and is appropriately called by the people
the Valley of Death. Pedestrians as well as horsemen shun
it; tourists alone dare to tread this accursed ground. Its
once gorgeous mansions are demolished, their mosaic walls
are cracked and groan as they suffocate in the embrace of
wild cactus. Because of its thorny branches, the walls have
not entirely collapsed, but remain standing like martyrs
sentenced to death . . . . . Every emperor of the mighty
dynasties of the Paṭhâns, Râjputs and Moguls erected here
some monument to himself. One can go in any chosen
direction, for 25 miles around, and find no end to this most
unusual and strange world of ruins.

For five days we roamed among them. Leaving the house
at dawn, we lunched and dined amidst these relics of past
ages, not returning until evening. A sad and melancholic
feeling takes possession of one upon entering this deserted
valley, the last resting place of so many generations! Everything is quiet, deathlike and silent around you . . . . . Not
the slightest sound reaches you even from the distant city-
walls, where rise solemnly, among minarets and monuments,
heavy English fortifications from every bastion of which
stare nine cannons, like watchful eyes of the enemy. Occasionally something moves under your very feet; it is a
porcupine disturbed by the unfamiliar sound of human
steps; raising his needles in all directions, and sniffing like
a frightened cat, it rolls away like a ball. At times a flock
of peacocks flies over, glittering in the sun like a shower of
multicolored sparks; or a shy doe looks at you from behind a dark green aloe; or some lizard darts in the grass, its
rainbow-tinted back glistening in the sun. Not a sound is to
be heard. From time to time you may perceive a slight

rustle in the midst of the heavy silence, followed by the fall of a little stone; this is the hand of implacable Time, ceaselessly busy at its destructive work in the "Valley of Death," loosening brick after brick, stone after stone, from the mosaic walls of former palaces, like so many marble tears falling on the blood-red foundations. Century after century they fall, until palaces and walls have been reduced to dust....

Yes, the proud city of Delhi did fall, but it fell as only giants do—as Samson did, a victim of treason and of his own over-confidence. He fell asleep in the embrace of Delilah, whom he had cherished and bejewelled for so many years, and in whose faithfulness he was foolish enough to believe. The East India Company, true to her "historical vocation," acted, therefore, as a veritable Delilah. Not only did she connive in his voluptuousness, but dragged him down the road to insane depravity. In the last years of its *independence,* sheltered under the wings of Delilah, Delhi had surpassed ancient Rome in debauchery and effeminacy . . . Taking advantage of its temporary weakness, Delilah sheared the helpless giant's hair, put out his eyes and turned him over to the Philistines. And yet, how they appeared to love each other! A warm friendship had bound them together, England-Delilah and the handsome Indo-Mogul! One can judge of the coquetry of the former by the following account. Colonel Skinner, a hero of the East India Company days, lived in India for 45 consecutive years. Having settled down in Delhi, he forgot all differences between the various religions, became a devoted Moslem and married several wives. Having refused to allocate from government funds a small sum towards the building of a Christian Church, he erected soon after, apparently at *his own expense,* a very costly mosque and, somewhat later, a temple for the Hindus. The building of a church at Delhi, he wrote in his report, "would justly arouse resentment on the part of the Great Mogul and his people." We were also shown at Delhi some two dozen pagan temples and mosques which contained precious bronze bells, silver idols, costly chandeliers and lamps of artistic design, and even altars with the names of their donors engraved on them. All these objects were "offerings of gratitude," freewill gifts *from the English to the idols and to Mohammed,* as a result of a *vow* "on deliverance from serious illness" and other calamities . . . . . The names of the donors are all European.

But in our day this is all changed. There is no longer room for hypocrisy; instead of lavishing feats worthy of Lucullus and use of mere flattery, Albion-Delilah has placed her heavy foot over Delhi, as well as its neighbors, and the Moslem city has been suffocated. The Great Mogul has disappeared; so have his effeminate courtiers. *Les apparences sont sauvées,* and nothing else is required. The Moguls no more knew how to govern than did the Nawâbs of Oudh in former days, and *in our day the unfortunate Teibo,* King of Burma.* The philanthropy of the English has not permitted them in the past, nor will it permit them in the future, calmly to witness a martyred people under a despotic rule. They are the God-sent saviors of all the Asiatic peoples, the friends of suffering humanity.

On the way to the valley of Kuṭab [Kuṭb], I wrote in pencil, on an old monument by the ancient fortress of Fîrûz Shâh, the famous verse of Dante, the inscription over the Gates of Hell, which aptly applies to the lonely valley and the road leading to it:

> Per me si va nella città dolente,
> Per me si va nell'eterno dolore,
> Per me si va tra la perduta gente . . . . . †

---

*More than once we had the opportunity of talking with Buddhist monks just returned from Burma, about the libelous reports of "crimes" and "atrocities" ascribed to the king of Burma by the English journals. They all assured us that they knew nothing of these. These Buddhist were peaceful English subjects from Ceylon; they were well-pleased with the government of their country and devoted to the English, a fact that is easily understood when you think of the despotic, bloodthirsty and fanatical Dutch and Portuguese. But these Buddhists never read the newspapers and so could not understand the deceitful policy of their rulers, the motto of which should have been the French saying; *"Quand on veut tuer son chien on dit qu'il est enragé."*

† [*La Divina Commedia,* Canto III, 1, Inferno.]

Hardly had we time to take a few steps, when, turning around, I caught a glimpse of the blond mustache and the rosy face of the highly honorable spy, Captain L. He stood in front of the monument with the penciled inscription and scratched the back of his head. Then, taking out pencil and paper, he carefully copied the inscription, so that Dante will be read once more by Lord Lytton and perhaps even by Beaconsfield himself . . . . .

Some traveller once said about the Moslem tombs of the noblemen of India: "If you wish to get a true idea of them, you should imagine London's St. Pauls' Cathedral, as though made of marble and standing in the midst of a large garden with the ornate gates of old York as an entrance; or imagine a number of cupolas placed on tall and graceful pillars and arches, inlaid with tiles painted in colors of the most brilliant metallic sheen — green, azure, golden and bronze-violet, pristinely beautiful and just as perfect as they were on the day when they left the sculptor's hand." Such structures are literally strewn all around Delhi. The work on some of these tombs is so delicate and fine that at sunset the marble walls seem as transparent as an alabaster lampshade . . . . .

Having admired the *Lât* of Fîrûz Shâh (an enormous column of red standstone, which, in spite of the fact that, in falling, two thirds of its length sank into the ground, is 37 feet in length and six and a half feet in circumference at its pointed end), we went to see the Mausoleum of Sultan Humâyûn, so often represented on the famous brooches of Delhi. It stands on a marble platform 200 feet square, supported on all sides by arcades, with four flights of granite steps leading up to them. Each arch shelters a number of tombs, and high above them stands the Imperial Mausoleum, a magnificent building of red stone, trimmed with white marble. The style of architecture is purely Saracene. Inside the Mausoleum is a round chamber in the middle of which stands a marble sarcophagus. From the flat roof of the monument you have a splendid view for many miles around. We brought with us a telescope and could clearly distinguish, without loss of precious time, the monument to Nizâm al-dîn, a saint who spent his long life on manure and now after his death rests on precious marble and porphyry.* We also saw the mausoleum of Princess Jahânârâ, the daughter of the unfortunate Shâh-Jahân (the poetical legend concerning her and her monument is told later), and the last luxurious mansion of Safdar-Jang, the great *vizir* of the Empire in the eighteenth century and the ancestor of the last unlucky king of Oudh. Whole cities of mausoleums and sarcophagi of precious marble—that is all that remains of what was once the most wealthy of Moslem empires! "Those white monuments you see in the distance," an unusually candid English judge said to me recently, "positively produce in me a feeling of unaccountable fear and make me nervous, when I sit in the evening alone on my balcony . . . . . They seem like an army of the dead in their white shrouds, who have come to demand an account of the fate of their descendants . . . . ."

In "Chândnî-Chauk" stands the beautiful Imperial palace, described by Bishop Heber as one of the noblest kingly residences ever seen by him, "far more impressive than the Kremlin, though in some details yielding to Windsor Castle." A naïve nationalistic boast! According to our opinion, which includes the opinion of English artists and the architect W., this palace is far superior to any European palace, ancient or modern, as much in its originality and beauty, as in its solidity. One of the arches of the great tower in the central court is succeeded by a long vaulted aisle like the nave of a Gothic cathedral, arousing the admiration of experts. One arch follows after another, making this passage like a tunnel than an annex . . . . . In the center there is an open octagonal granite court, every inch of which is of minute inlaid work, similar to mosaic and representing flowers and fruit made of colored marble and other stones. The "Diwân-i-Khâs" (Hall of the Imperial Council) is a white marble pavilion surmounted by four cupolas of the same material, with arches and columns beautifully carved, and all covered with golden arabesques,

---

* [Nizâm al-Dîn Awliyâ', whose real name was Muḥammad b. Aḥmad b. 'Alî al-Bukhârî al-Badâ'ûni. He lived in the period of 1238-1325. —*Compiler.*]

flowers of mother-of-pearl, carnelian and malachite, and with inscriptions from the *Qur'ân* in Persian letters of the most exquisite design. The rich foliage made of pure silver which once adorned the ceiling has been torn down by the conquerors, and the lovely pavilion is now the abode of bats and owls. Of the same style is the octagonal pavilion in the midst of the sumptuous but now neglected garden, as well as the "Motî-Masjid" — the twin sister of another Motî-Masjid (the *Pearl Mosque*) in Âgra — the Court Chapel of the Emperors; and in the "Hall of Public Audiences," there stands the throne of the Great Moguls, with a mosaic representation of a spread peacock's tail. Only recently has this throne been cleaned of pigeon's droppings which had thickly covered it.

Having driven past a pretty mosque with a whole cluster of minarets, mirroring themselves all day long in the waters of the river, we stopped near the great mosque of "Jâmi'-Masjid." Its enormous square foundation or plinth is of red sandstone and the walls look like those of a fortress. On each corner of the terrace stands a tower, the marble cupola of which rests on slender red columns. From three sides incredibly wide marble steps lead up to the three main gates. It is a long climb; when you have reached the top, the roofs of the city lie below. As for the fourth or central gate opening to the east, it is so sacred that no one is allowed to approach it. The three gates lead into a court 450 feet square with open arcades, surrounded on three sides with rows of red columns; in the middle of these is a large reservoir of marble which can be filled from several springs in the valley, by means of a special device. Facing in the direction of Mecca stands the mosque known as "The Beauty of the East." Its entire façade is covered with thick white marble plates, and all along the cornice are inscriptions from the *Qur'ân*, inlaid in black marble letters ornate with gold, four feet high. The three enormous cupolas are striped with the same black marble, while the minarets are red and white. Each one of the towers is a wonder of beauty.

It was Friday and also some holiday; in the courtyard which could accommodate some 12,000 people, there were crowds of the faithful. Our Hindus did not follow us, but remained downstairs with some acquaintances, or one of the numerous relatives of the Bâbû. We remained in the mosque but a few minutes as Mr. W. and the Colonel, to their great indignation, were made to take off their shoes and both felt they were catching cold walking over the chilly marble floors. The floor of the mosque looks like a chessboard of black and white . . . . .

A few hundred steps from the city wall stands the observatory, as enormous as everything else. It was erected [1742 A.D.], as were a number of other observatories, according to the plans of the famous Râjâ of Amber, Jay-Singh II, a learned astronomer and astrologer in the beginning of the eighteenth century, the same who, according to the will of the Emperor Muhammad-Shâh, revised the local calendar. In addition to an enormous sundial, we found in this courtyard, which was as large as a city square, some "azimuth circles," so Gulâb-Singh told us, and also some curiously shaped gnomones used for measuring altitude and many other awesome astronomical instruments. The entire courtyard is full of curved walls, of triangular stones with steps leading into empty space, with quaint geometrical figures made of granite "for local astrologers," as we learned later; and all of it is covered with incomprehensible signs, fearful symbols and figures, with which the Ṭhâkur alone was familiar, while we, miserable profanes, stood confused and returned home with headaches.

"Kutb-Mînâr," a column situated nine miles from town, is considered the highest in the world, even now, though it has settled deep into the ground and part of its top was sheered off by lightning. The column is 238 feet high and, according to local tradition, was used by court magicians for their friendly intercourse with "planetary" spirits. As a matter of fact, to judge by its height, one can easily suppose that these inhabitants of the elements often stumbled over it and tore their wings on its sharp points. Possibly they sent lightning just to destroy it? . . . . .The column tapers regularly from the base to the top where, prior to the destruction of the cupola, there was sufficient room for 12 magicians, each one having 12 books of "exorcisms" with him. The walls are covered with Kufic inscriptions and gigantic letters cut several feet into the stone. Red from top to bottom and reaching to the clouds, the "Kutb-Mînâr" seems from afar like a monstrous exclamation mark of blood, placed over the "Valley of Death."

Around the column are a number of pillars, arches and smaller columns. Each one of these fragments has its own and frequently a non-Moslem style, rather than that of the Hindus, which alone is sufficient evidence of their antiquity and to the time that must have elapsed between the various styles. A little to one side, by itself, stands a remarkable building of four stories, shaped like a pyramid at the top, surmounted with a cupola, and with terraces seeming to spread like a flat mushroom. This is the "College of Akbar," renowned for its exquisite carvings and built by him for the assemblies of "wise men," especially invited from all parts of the world for "religious discussions."* This building opens onto its lower terrace, and its walls are covered with paintings, mosaics, bas-reliefs of inlaid work of every description, and niches with endless rows of geometrical designs and inscriptions in raised work on a golden background; it is a magnificent introduction to the gigantic column itself.

Five days had rolled by like a single day, and we were to leave that evening for Âgra, the ancient capital of Akbar. Parting perhaps forever from the Valley of Kuṭab [Kuṭb], we went to take a rest for the last time in the shade of the enormous column. No one knows when, by whom, or for what purpose it was built. The black marble floors of the four balconies around it are covered with the same curious signs as those on its inner spiral staircase. The four rooms of the column, one on each floor, have low openings leading to the balcony, and there are always visitors who are anxious to climb the staircase. We refused, however, to ascend to the clouds: I for personal reasons which had

---

*It is a known fact that the Emperor Akbar never was an orthodox Moslem, but searched for truth throughout his long life in different religions, constantly wavering between Christianity, Islam and the religions of the Pârsîs and the Brâhmaṇas. He was one of the great astrologers of his time.

better remain unmentioned, and the others on account of
laziness or simply satiety. We really, all of us, began to feel
the symptoms of an illness which might be called "ruin
indigestion." We began to have nightmares in the form of
towers, palaces and temples; fleet-footed minarets chased
us, and the black marble sarcophagi danced a dance of
death around us . . . . . . The Thâkur, however, accompanied by Nârâyana-Krishnarâo, went up, leaving us under the guardianship of the latter's brother-in-law, Bâbû
Nârâyana-Dâs-Sen, who began immediately to frighten
Miss B. by telling her stories of ghosts and spirits which frequent the column of Kutb-Mînâr.

It is probable that even our Marâthâ Hercules saw
something very frightening in the mysterious column, because when they both came down half an hour later, the
Thâkur seemed more serious and stern than ever before;
while the swarthy cheeks of Nârâyana were of the color of
earth, and his lips trembled nervously.

"Look," whispered the irrepressible Bengalî to Miss B.
"I am dead sure Thâkur-Saab called forth one of his ancestors for Nârâyana . . . . . . Look at his frightened face!"

Something deeply painful and even ominous shone in the
black eyes of the Brâhmana . . . . . . But he at once lowered
his eyes and, making a visible effort to control himself,
kept silent . . . . .

I wanted to interfere and stop the untimely teasing on
the part of the Bâbû, but the Thâkur gave me a warning.
Without changing the conversation he deftly turned the
trend of our ideas from this delicate subject into an entirely
different direction . . . . .

"You are right, Bâbû," said he thoughtfully, without paying the least attention to the obvious irony of the Bengalî,
"in the whole of India there isn't a place better suited for
calling forth the memory of the great deeds of former days
achieved by *my* Râjput ancestors, than is this tower. Here,"
he continued pointing toward Delhi, "the generals and
princes of Râjasthân, at the end of the seventeenth century, were finally dethroned and deprived of their rightful
kingdom, the inheritance of their fathers . . . . . . It was

here that the fanatical and cruel Moguls, taking possession of the throne by sheer cunning, deliberately turned the last bloody page of the history of India as a great and independent land! . . . . . . Yes!" he exclaimed suddenly, with eyes glowing like burning coals and seemingly overcome by a heretofore repressed and therefore even more intense impulse of anger. "Yes! . . . . . . It was only the depravity and effeminacy of this accursed race, which opened wide the doors to the European conquerors! . . . . . . It was the Moguls alone that ruined our India! If this generation of harems had not settled in our fatherland, we would not have had a single Englishman here now! . . . ."

Mr. W. knitted his brows and, turning towards the wall, seemed busily occupied in examining the Kufi inscriptions. Miss B., however, her fur rubbed the wrong way, and with patriotic zeal deserving of a better cause, rushed to do battle.

"Oh!" ironically exclaimed the old spinster, making use of all the tones of her discordant national tongue, "Oh, oh, do you really mean to say that *we* would not have been able to master even you, the Râjputs? . . . . We, the English, were *never* vanquished by *anyone;* and we never yielded a territory we had once occupied! . . . . ."

I really began to fear for this silly woman. I never yet had occasion to see in human eyes such an ominous and sombre light, as burned now in the dilated pupils of the proud Thâkur. But he was silent and only looked at her. Thus must have stared the Sphinx at his future victim before the solution of his enigma . . . . .

Fortunately the Colonel rose to the occasion and saved us all with a fortuitous diversion.

"You English were never vanquished, were you?" he asked, laughing good-naturedly. "Except by us Americans you ought to add . . . . . Remember the dressing down we gave you between 1775 and 1783, when we chased you from our shores for good . . . . . . And then again in 1812, when to each American who lost his life there were *eight* Englishmen killed! . . . . . You shouldn't, my dear Miss B., forget historical facts even for the sake of patriotism."

The Colonel was not mistaken in his magnanimous plan.

These few words were quite sufficient to call forth a whole storm of indignation directed against him and accompanied, as usual, by a deluge of hysterical tears. The Englishwoman was daily becoming more unbearable to us . . . . .

In his capacity as president of the Theosophical Society, the Colonel had several times intended to tell her in earnest that she should return to Bombay where, in the familiar and sympathetic sphere of tradesmen grown rich and haughty English ex-shoemakers, she would feel calmer and happier. But I always protested. No matter how unbearable her company was to us, still, being English, both Miss B. and Mr. W. were doubtless of some use to us, due to the silly suspicions and persecutions on the part of the police. This spying, awkward and stupid as it was, attempting but unable to keep itself secret, annoyed us more and more each day. The presence of two English people, both such fervent patriots, not only could be useful in the future but exposed the Anglo-Indian administration in its silliest light . . . . .

True to his usual custom, the Ṭhâkur came to see us off at the railway station, took leave of us, and promised to meet us, *possibly* at Âgra, but at all events at Bhurtpore. And so we parted.

During the trip Nârâyaṇa was quite unlike himself and seemed to experience the weight of some awful pressure or sorrow. The Bâbû, on the contrary, was as excited as the devil before the liturgy.* Mûljî was silent as usual; Mr. W. was pouting on behalf of Miss B. who was gnashing her teeth most of the way; the Colonel snored in a corner of the carriage; as for me, I was deep in thought, deep enough to be literally "not here" . . . . . . What had happened between the Ṭhâkur and Nârâyaṇa? . . . . . What was their secret? . . . . . Who knows! . . . . .

Similar to the day when we arrived at Delhi, the sun was again just about to set, sinking in the molten gold of the clouds, and far away towards the horizon could be seen the magnificent "Kuṭb-Minâr," already half-shrouded in the purple of the evening shadows, its upper portion burn-

---

*A Russian proverb.

ing like a fiery pillar in the gold and orange brilliance of the sunset.

Emperor Akbar, India's King Solomon, was, by virtue of his wisdom, the greatest and most beloved Mogul ruler of India, the only one whose memory is as dear to Moslems as to Hindus. The latter love him possibly even more than the former, as he was always partial to their cause. Akbar the Magnificent, the Blessed, Akbar the Beloved of the gods and "the Beauty of the Throne of the World"—these are the epithets linked to his name. Among the natives the town of Âgra is known even today as *Akbarâbâd*. As to the number of his wives, he surpassed even Solomon. What matter the 800 legal wives and the 300 concubines of the latter, when compared with the 5,000 wives of Akbar? The native chronicles assert that it was to these ladies alone he owed his power and greatness. Having once decided to get possession of the whole of India, the Great Padishâh married in turn the daughters of every one of his new allies in order to strengthen his alliances. As soon as he learned that such and such a Râjâ or neighboring prince had a daughter, he offered at once to marry her. How was it possible to refuse such a suitor as the Emperor Akbar? In this way, having created a whole army of ally-fathers-in-law, he guaranteed himself peace and insured his country from invasion. The wives were contented and happy, and no one seemed to envy any other. Each one of them had her own room in the palace and her own special privileges. Now all that remains of this family palace are ruins.

Akbar is said to have belonged to the fourth generation of Mohammed's descendants; for that reason the orthodox people forgave him much, though he sinned greatly against his religion. His greatest offenses were his doubt and his constant search for *truth* "as though the whole of divine truth were not centered in our Blessed Prophet," to use the words of one of his historiographers. He had a passion for the study of philosophy and profound reverence for ancient manuscripts, setting aside large sums of money for the oldest scriptures concerning the "six great religions of the East:" Christianity, Islam, Judaism, Pârsîism, Buddhism and Brâhmanism. He had reverence for all six, but did not be-

long to any one of them.* It is said that after his death
there were found a great number of manuscripts written in
his own hand, and what is even more astonishing, that they
exist even today. He was born in 1542 and died in 1605,
having reigned almost half a century. I cannot refrain from
telling a strange story I have heard, though it may be but
a legend or a mere fable. But as it is closely connected with
Russian history and exactly tallies with the dates of its most
important historical events, and mentions a well-known
Russian princely family, I will tell it just as I heard it myself, without embellishments.

Like all people in India, Akbar blindly believed in astrology and magic. During his youth as a prince he had
once befriended some pale-faced young man who had somehow or other come to his palace. Later the youth disappeared, and no one but the prince knew who he was and
where he had gone. But after the accession of Akbar to the
throne, the youth reappeared and acquired a great influence
over the emperor. No one knew his real name or whence
the mysterious foreigner came, and at a court always full
of foreigners and "wise men from the East, West, South
and North," no one at first paid any special attention to
him; soon, however, envy grew, and people began to un-
dermine the emperor's favor for him. People began to say
that the youth was a despicable slave, a prisoner from the
Far North, who had been given to Akbar by a Paṭhân
chieftain of Afghânistân. Finally, the intrigues grew so bitter that his life was endangered. The emperor became

---

*Akbar, though his Moslem subjects looked upon him as a saint and
miracle-worker, was far from favoring Islam; often, when in need of
money, he coolly took it from mosques and sacked their treasuries for
the benefit of his cavalry. Nor were the Christian missionaries more
fortunate than the Moslem *mullahs*. He not only adored the sun and
prayed to it four times a day, but set himself up as an object of worship. "He studied magic and surrounded himself with men dedicated to
Satan—men who worked various evil miracles in the name and with
the help of the evil forces." (From the Accounts of the Gôa missionaries
in *Murray's Discoveries*.)
[Reference is here to the work by Hugh Murray, *Historical Account
of Discoveries and Travels in Asia*, etc., Edinb., 1820. 3 Vols. The subject is treated of on pp. 95, 100-103, 176.—*Compiler*.]

alarmed, and one fine morning the youth disappeared again, as mysteriously as he had formerly appeared. To impress his subjects and to warn them, Akbar pretended he did not know whither his favorite had vanished; he ordered the enemies of the youth to appear before him, and the same morning several heads fell. Twelve years later a man, still looking young, whom the old courtiers recognized as the lost youth, once more appeared at court. A manly, dignified and thoughtful individual, he was introduced to the courtiers by the emperor himself as a learned astrologer and *guru* (teacher); now the court bowed more or less sincerely and with some awe before the foreigner, as the fame of the young astrologer had preceded his apparance at Âgra and people had already spoken of him in reverent whispers with subdued fear. "The pandit Vasishtha Âjânu-bâhu* studied the secret sciences of *jâdû* and *yoga-vidyâ* (black and white magic) with the *jinn* themselves in the fastnesses of the Himâlayas, near Badrînâth, and the Great Emperor himself chose him as his *guru*. Allah is great! This foreigner is the possessor of the ring of Sulaiman (Solomon), the ruler of all the *jinn* (spirits). The Orthodox should avoid offending the pandit!"

The chronicles assert that pandit Vasishtha Âjânubâhu remained with Akbar until the latter's death, and then, being himself of a very advanced age, disappeared—no one knows where. Before leaving, he is said to have called his disciples together and uttered the following remarkable words: "Vasishtha Âjânubâhu is leaving and soon will retire from this decrepit body; but he will not die and will reappear in the body of another Âjânubâhu, greater and more famous, who will put an end to the Mogul rule . . . . .†

Âjânubâhu is a name consisting of two Sanskrit words: *âjânu*—"reaching down to the knees" and *bâhu*—"arm."

†Sivâjî, the hero and conqueror of the Moguls, and the founder of the Marâthâ dynasty, who was born in the second quarter of the 17th century and ascended the throne of the Peshwas in 1664, received the name of "Âjânubâhu," on account of having very long arms. Tradition asserts that Sivâjî was the incarnation of a powerful "magician from the Far North." He was born 17 years after the death of Akbar, most likely in 1622.

Âjânubâhu II will avenge Âjânubâhu I, *whose country was humiliated and sacked* by the hateful sons of the pseudo-prophet." Having uttered these words, blasphemous to the ears of his disciples, the old magician disappeared—"and may his name be damned," adds devoutly the Moslem author.*

The reader should keep in mind the above underlined sentence and the chronology of the events. Perhaps our recent discovery does not mean anything, but the coincidence and the names are very significant. In any case it is of more than ordinary interest to *Russian* readers. There are as many legends about pandit Vasishṭha as there are trees in the virgin forest; from among them I have chosen but one which directly concerns our subject. That this pandit was a Russian, taken prisoner as a boy by the Tatars during the victory of Ivan the Terrible over the Golden Horde in 1552, near Kazan, seems to me now beyond doubt. As to the question who actually was this legendary "pandit," and what he had in common with certain Russian princely families, I leave it to the reader himself to decide. Our tale is not ended; the most curious part of this wonderful story has not yet been told and certainly the mere name of *Âjânubâhu* does not mean much. It is a name generally given here to all those proficient in "secret science." Popular tradition asserts that a person predestined to be "the ruler of the mysterious forces of nature" is born with very long arms . . . . . We return now to our story.

During the storming of Delhi in 1857-1858, when the English at last burst into the city, the following historical event took place. The town was captured, but the old king had disappeared and could not be found anywhere. Finally, as is usually the case in such difficult situations, a Judas-like traitor turned up among the Moguls. For a bag of gold and promises of pardon and pension, the father-in-law of the heir apparent, Mirza Elahi-Buksh, with the help of a man called Rujjub-Ali, a *munshî* (teacher), betrayed the Great Mogul and delivered him, and four other princes

---

Legends of the Mogul Empire. A collection of traditions translated from the Urdu and Marâṭhâ tongues.

of the Delhi dynasty of Shâhzâda, into the hands of the adventurer, Hodson. The king was found hidden where no one would have discovered him; had he not been betrayed, he would have had time to escape into the Himâlayas. It was ascertained that he had succeeded in sending to the princes a certain box of treasures and documents, so Captain Hodson—the mention of whose name alone makes the English army blush with shame, something which does not happen often — started in pursuit of the princes. They were found hidden in the neighborhood of Delhi, in one of the secret hiding places among the tombs of the "Valley of Death." It was difficult to capture them alive, as they and all their companions were prepared to blow themselves up, yet Hodson wanted to get safe possession, if not of the princes themselves, at least of the treasures which were in their keeping. He therefore resorted to cunning. Having promised to pardon them *in the name of the Government* and to guarantee their lives and complete amnesty, he persuaded them to surrender and told them he would take them to the city. It is quite sufficient to read the *Sepoy War*, by Sir John Wm. Kaye,* a witness to these events, to learn the details of what then happened. Despite all his promises, the scoundrel Hodson ordered the palanquin of the princes to stop, and had them get out and stand in front of him, being on horseback in the middle of the road. Suspecting treason, the princes got out alone, leaving a servant with the treasure-box and a small ancient silver trunk in the palanquin. Then, while pretending he wanted to talk to them, his soldiers, at a given sign, slaughtered them and all their followers like sheep. Hodson then rushed to the palanquin, but there was neither treasure box, nor trunk, nor man to be found. During the turmoil and while the murder was going on, the Sepoy disappeared and no one ever heard of him again. What happened to the treasures—I have no way of knowing. But as to the trunk with the documents, some traces of it were found. According to reports, one of the parchment rolls is now in the possession of a chieftain in the North-Western Provinces. The manuscripts are partly

---

*Vol. III, pp. 642 *et seq.*

in Persian, and partly in Hindî, each one of them
bearing the personal seal of the Emperor. They contain
records, notes and documents, which in their fullness form
a sort of notebook of the Emperor Jalâl al-dîn Akbar. About
their existence and the contents of one of them I learned
in the following curious way. One of the members of our
Theosophical Society, a close relative of the individual who
is the possessor of the mysterious roll, wished to learn from
me if among our Russian princely families there were any
by the name of "Vasishṭha Âjânubâhu."

"No, I never heard of such a name," said I. "We have the
name Vassiliy but not Vasishṭha; as to 'Âjânubâhu' I never
heard it before. But what does the name mean? *Âjânubâhu,*
translated from Sanskrit, means 'long-armed,' I believe
(*âjânu* —reaching down to the knees, and *bâhu* — arms).
Wasn't that the name of Śivâjî, the great Marâṭha ruler
and the founder of their kingdom? Do you mean him? . . ."

"No, not quite. Have you in Russia the name of *Longimanus?*"

"No, not that either; but we have the name of Dolgorukov, which is the literal translation of the Latin *Longimanus* and the Sanskrit *Âjânubâhu.*"

"Now at last we have reached the point," remarked my
friend, "where everything is clear to me . . ."

"As far as I am concerned, it seems as obscure as ever! . . ."

It was then that I learned from him the story of the pandit
Vasishṭha and Akbar and the episode about Delhi just
narrated by me. For quite some time he had been interested
in the memoirs of Akbar. Knowing several languages well,
he had studied the notes of the emperor, and being acquainted with the legend about the astrologer Vasishṭha at
Âgra, he at once noticed that one of the notes concerned this
mysterious person. He had to refuse my repeated requests
to see the manuscripts, as the latter were hidden in a secret
place known only to one man, his eldest brother. He promised, however, to translate for me one of the entries of
Akbar which he had copied for his own use. He kept his
promise. This is the text written according to the Moslem
chronology in the 938th year of the Hegira.

I transcribe it from the English translation of my friend.*

Note 1. "In the beginning of the full moon of the month of Marana, of the year 935 (1557), there was brought from Ghaznî by the Pathân Âzaf-Khân, from "Ulamam" (?) a young *Moskovite.* He was captured and enslaved in the Kipchak Khanate (the Golden Horde) near the *village* of Kazan (?), during those days when Shaitan in the form of the Moskovite Czar was said to have defeated the Khâns . . . The name of the young Moskovite, translated into our *Hindî* tongue (*i.e.,* Sanskrit) is Kosr Vasishtha Âjânubâhu,† also *Longimanus* in the tongue of the Portuguese *padris* (missionaries). He is the son of the old Kosr (prince) murdered in the Kipchak Khanate . . . Vasishtha spoke thus: 'I know my own Moskovite tongue; also the tongues of Iran and Pathân. I was taught astrology and *wisdom* in the province of Gilan (on the Caspian Sea). From there I was once more taken to Iran, where I served King Tahmâsp. The Padishâh grew angry on account of a bad dream he had and gave me as a present to Âzaf-Khân. I want to study the wisdom of the Sûfîs and the Samans [probably the Buddhists] and I want to get the *shast* [a chain, but in this connection a talisman] with the Great Name on it . . .' Let him study." And a little further: "Sent to Kashmîr."

Note 2. "Came back for consultation, received Allâh-u-Akbar.‡ Vasishtha discovered the great name *He*§ and he initiates the Sûfîs of the blessed Râbia.‖

---

*[Having no access either to Akbar's original text or to the English translation of H.P.B.'s friend, we had to translate these excerpts of Akbar's Notes from H.P.B.'s own Russian rendering.— *Compiler.*]

†This would mean in Russian translation Prince (Kosr) Vasishtha (or Vassiliy) Long Arms or Dolgorukov!!?

‡The symbolic motto of Akbar, carved on a talisman and which was granted by Akbar only to renowned magicians and astrologers to wear on their turban, as a sign of merit.

§*He* or *Nei*, which translated means Ît, or the Deity.

‖*Râbia*, a woman, was the founder of the mystical sect of the *Sûfîs* and lived in the first century of the Hegira. The Persian poet Hâfiz belonged to this brotherhood.

In the year 968, there is a note seemingly in the handwriting of the Emperor himself: "Great is Vasishtha Âjânubâhu! . . . He holds in his hands the moon and the sun.
He threw off the *taklîd* (collar) of deceiving religions and
discovered the real wisdom of the Sûfîs as expressed in
the following stanza:

> The lamp and its light *are one,*
> Only fools see in the idol and its Brâhmaṇa
> Two objects distinct from each other . . .*

•   •   •   •   •   •   •   •   •   •   •   •

Thus end these notes. Who this Vasishtha Âjânubâhu was
will probably remain forever an unsolved enigma. If he was
one of the Princes Dolgorukov made prisoner by the Tatars
at the time of Ivan the Terrible, this fact ought to be mentioned at least in the chronicles of that family, if not in
general history. That he was a Russian was proved to me
by the fact that in a line "written in an unknown language,"
and exactly *drawn* by my friend from the parchment, I saw
and recognized the signature "Knyaz Vassiliy"; this was
written in old Slavonic letters and in an unskilled hand, just
as our ancestors wrote three centuries ago; the signature
is not easy to read, but the work *Knyaz* and the name
Vassiliy can be easily recognized by any Russian.

"Wonderful are thy mysteries, oh gray-haired and silent
antiquity!" And the more we study it in India, the stronger
grows my unshakable conviction that we Russians, as well
as prehistoric Russia, Bulgaria and all the Slavonic nations
in general, are much more closely related to Âryâvarta than
is known to history or even suspected by modern Orientalists.

I have had more than one occasion definitely to assert
in these pages that I have not the slightest intention of
competing with the learned ethnologists and philologists;
but, notwithstanding their authoritative conclusions, I can-

---

*This is the pantheistic idea of the Sûfîs and the Vedântists about
the oneness of the whole world. The Universe is *One;* forms and shapes
of both the objective and the subjective worlds are only waves of one
and the same ocean. The Deity is in the Universe and the Universe is
in the Deity. Outside of that there is nothing, not even chaos.

not help contradicting them at every step, noticing how often and to what degree their deductions, seemingly so logical and brilliant when away from India, appear weak and improbable to one who studies this country on the spot and takes into consideration not only local traditions, but the way they dovetail with those in places far removed one from the other. I recognize that my actions in such cases contradict strictly scientific principles and the methods evolved by modern philology; I realize that by pointing out the phonetic similarities of different tongues apart from all other considerations, I sin against the basic rules of etymology established by strict philologists and accepted without protest in Europe by the followers of their schools. Professor Max Müller has a perfect right to look at me with a contemptuous smile and even to call my opinion a "wild one" and my theories *unwissenschaftlich;* still, in spite of his severe disapproval (which by the way I have happily outlived), every time I am present at the discussions of the pandits in their Sanskrit tongue, or hear from our esteemed friend and ally Swâmi Dayânanda * his frequent appeal to his disciples: "dehi me agnim," *give me fire,* in the simplicity of my uneducated spirit I cannot help exclaiming: This

---

*Alas, the "esteemed friend and ally" has since turned into a dangerous enemy! Fanaticism and bigotry got the upper hand. Contrary to the original program, the Svâmi *requested* that "The Brotherhood of Humanity"— The Theosophical Society, should accept as members "Âryas" exclusively, *i.e.*, persons having renounced their former religion, and who had unconditionally accepted the faith of Hindu Vedists. Once a Vedântist himself, he now opposes the Vedânta—the best and purest of all Indian philosophies—and substitutes for it the *Vedas* in their dead letter form, which he interprets according to his own wishes and tastes. This new Luther of the East developed little by little into a Calvin, and now rapidly follows the path chosen by the followers of Loyola. Becoming convinced that neither Colonel O. nor I would ever consent to be publicly converted into "Ârya-Samâjists," nor acknowledge him as the *infallible* Pope, he grew so angry that he began publicly to call us "*nâstikas*" (atheists) and then anathematized us. The Thâkur, defending us, declared him possessed with the "mania of power." In this way the Swâmi lost about 45 individuals, English and American, who formerly acknowledged him as their *teacher*, and our Society acquired about 100 members of the "Ârya-Samâja," who came from his camp into ours.

sounds quite Russian!* . . . To quote a Russian saying: "If
you live simply, you will live a century," in which I would
replace the word "live" by the word "think." At such times
I cannot help thinking that more apt than all the learned
philologists of the world, from the point of view of ordinary
common sense, are the words of one of my Russian lady
relatives, a clever, educated and very observing woman,
though not learned in Sanskrit, who recently wrote in one
of her letters to me: "You, my dear, can defend the
Brâhmanical *Trimûrti* and can rave about its secret meaning as much as you like; but there can hardly be any doubt
that your *Trimûrti* in Russian translation means simply
three snouts (*tri mordi*)." She was quite right; the word
"mûrti" means in Sanskrit both face and idol; and "Trimûrti," literally translated, means *three images,* the three-
fold representation of Brahmâ, Vishṇu and Śiva. For that
reason I can neither agree with the great Max Müller nor
believe him, when he says that "in the German language
the percentage of purely Sanskrit words is much greater
than in the Slavonic or Russian." The more so as in childhood they made us conjugate the German verb *geben,* and
we couldn't help feeling that the imperative form "gib mir
Feuer," in spite of philology, resembles "dehi me agnim"
as little as the esteemed professor in evening dress would
resemble the Tibetan Talay-Lama without any. The Georgian tongue, we are assured by present day encyclopaedias,
on the authority of philologists, is full of pure Sanskrit
grammatical forms, while the Russian is full of Scandinavian, Tatar, Finnish and other non-Slavonic roots. But
the question is: could not the Russian language have acquired these "non-Slavonic roots" in the later historical
periods of its development, and *only for the reason* that
these "*non*-Slavonic roots" of the Scandinavian, Tatar,
Finnish and other languages are merely dialects or, according to the expression of Max Müller, primitive derivatives
of Sanskrit (I must ask our *Turano-Semitophils* to excuse
me in advance for this unscientific hypothesis) — Sanskrit,

---

*[The Russian words for this are *day mne ogon'*, or *ognya*—Compiler.]

MAUSOLEUM OF AKBAR AT SIKANDRA

PALACE OF DURJAN SAL AT BHURTPORE

if not in its completed and perfected form, then at least as the primitive tongue of two-thirds of humanity. This question was never even touched upon by the philologists, let alone resolved. One must not forget the highly important fact that Russia has no monuments or inscriptions whatsoever which would indicate the different stages of development of the Russian language.

All this is *my* private opinion, however, and should not concern the reader. Therefore I will leave this question for the time being and resume my narrative about India, as she appears in our day.

Âgra, like many other cities, was built on the tombs of its numerous predecessors. The present state of the city, aside from the magnificent historical buildings and monuments, which chiefly belong to the Moguls, is lamentable. Dirt, stench and, to judge by the outward appearances of the dwellings, an awful state of poverty reign everywhere in the Moslem part of town. The Hindus here have become like Moslems and have entirely lost their original traits. Âgra is the entrance to Râjasthân, a sort of anteroom in which the owners do not actually live but pass through occasionally. The English, as in all other cities, have isolated themselves from the natives by a Chinese wall of barracks and haughtiness and live entirely separate. They have their own quarters —where no "nigger" would dare to settle—far from the Jumnâ and the Tâj Mahal; the latter is not far from *Motî-Masjid* known among the people by the poetical name of the "Pearl Mosque." Both the *Masjid* and the *Tâj* can be literally and without any Oriental exaggeration compared to pearls lying in a heap of manure.

What a beautiful pearl the latter is! Having exhausted all my eloquence in describing Delhi, I have now to describe this eighth wonder of the world, the Tâj Mahal, and feel myself entirely unequal to the task. Were it possible to evoke from the mysterious realm where the likenesses that once had their fleeting existences upon earth endure — a realm disclosed by the Alchemists and the Kabalists — the most poetical dreams of Michelangelo, then perhaps an adequate vision of it could be created by one who had never seen it. He would then picture to himself a grandiose mausoleum, as large as a Gothic cathedral and finished like a precious royal crown; he would see its four pearl-white domes at the corners of a quadrangle, in the midst of which rises fifty feet higher the shining central dome, crowned with two gilt globes and a gilt crescent,* glowing in the soft azure of the sky. Far removed from any other building and surrounded with beautiful gardens, the Tâj Mahal stands alone in its indescribable beauty, on the banks of the blue Jumnâ, mirroring its pure and proud image . . . The building is so perfect in its architectural dimensions, so enchanting and complete in the finish of its slightest detail, and at the same time so grand in its simplicity, that one feels oneself at a loss to decide what to admire most — its plan, its workmanship, or the materials of which it is made! . . .

These materials are masses of expensive white marble, sometimes intermixed with black and yellow marble, mother-of-pearl, jasper, agate, emerald, aquamarine, pearls and hundreds of other stones. White marble prevails, however. In the entire building, from the top of the cupola down to the last inch of the foundations, *there cannot be found a single nail,* or a single atom of glass or wood. Even the waterpipes are of marble, and the walls are so perfectly polished that they mirror on their shining surfaces the most fleeting shades of sky and foliage, reminding one rather of mother-of-pearl than of marble. We could hardly believe that the Tâj was the work of human beings, and were quite ready to credit the local legend, which assures the faithful that the inconsolable caliph was raised by a dervish Saint to the abode of Mohammed in Paradise, where Allah himself ordered Archangel Gabriel to outline the plan of one of his dwelling places.† It was according to this plan

---

*This dome is 70 feet in diameter and rises 260 feet from the foundation of the lower terrace.

† [This, of course is merely the product of imagination on the part of devotees. A man like Shâh-Jahân who, to assure his succession to Jahângîr's throne, strangled to death one brother, allowed his father-in-law to blind another, and had his henchmen dispose of a third, who took a grisly pleasure in watching the torture of criminals, can hardly be suspected of any "heavenly" visions or spiritual inspirations. Of the manner in which the design of the Tâj was obtained and just

that the Tâj Mahal was built over the body of Mumtâz-i-Mahall, the beloved of the caliph, known as *Arjmand-Bânû,* "The Crown of the Seraglio."*

Approaching from the side of the Jumnâ, the first thing

---

exactly who was responsible for the outline of the noble building, there are no direct records. What evidence there is, is contradictory. On the one hand, there is the contemporary statement of Father Sebastian Manrique of the Society of Jesus, who visited Âgra in 1640, during the period of construction, who definitely affirms that models were prepared and submitted to the Emperor by a Venetian jeweller named Geronimo Verroneo, who was residing in the Mogul capital at the time and who died at Lahore in that year and is buried in the old Roman Catholic cemetery at Âgra (cf. *Travels of Fray Sebastian Manrique 1629-1643,* tr. by C. E. Luard and H. Hosten. London: Hakluyt Society, 1927, 2 Vols.; Vol. II, note pp. 174-77.). The ultimate authority for this statement is Father Josef da Castro, another Jesuit, who was Verroneo's executor, and who died at Âgra in 1646. On the other hand, indigenous documents have been preserved containing a detailed account of those employed on the building, all of whom were Asiatics, with no indication of any European intervention. The testimony of the Tâj Mahal itself shows it to be in all respects the natural evolution of existing styles, true to tradition and unaffected by Occidental influence. —*Compiler.*]

*The history of India is so tangled and uncertain, that some historians assure us that Mumtâz was the granddaughter of Akbar, while others say that she was only the wife of his grandson Shâh-Jahân, the father of the famous Aurangzîb. The latter version is unquestionably the right one.

[*Mumtâz-i-Mahall* literally means "the distinguished one of the palace" which was a title of the consort of Shâh-Jahân. *Tâj Mahal* is a corruption of this Persian term.

Mumtâz-i-Mahall, born in 1593, was the daughter of Âzaf-Khân, the brother of Nûr-Jahân (1577-1645), and the famous empress-wife of Shâh-Jahân (r. 1627-1658). Her grandfather was Mirzâ Ghiyâth Beg, either a Persian from Teheran or a native of Western Tartary. He came to seek his fortune in India and rose to power under the title of I'timâd-al-Dawla, "Lord High Treasurer." When he died, his son Âzaf-Khân succeeded him. Mumtâz married Prince Khurram, known later as Shâh-Jahân, in 1612, at the age of nineteen. She was his second wife and bore him fourteen children; she died in childbed at Berhampur in 1631, at the birth of her eighth son. This was in the second year of Shâh-Jahân's accession. Her body was brought to Âgra and first laid in the garden. According to Tavernier, it took twenty-two years (1630-52) to build the Tâj, and some 22,000 workers were engaged in its construction.—*Compiler.*]

that strikes the eye is a massive quadrangle made of blinding
white marble, 964 feet in length from east to west and 329
feet in width from south to north — a platform or pedestal
truly worthy of such a monument. The base of it is of red
sandstone, but is hardly noticeable, being hidden by the
green shrubbery of the shore. On each side are separate
mosques, also built of sandstone, with *appliqué* designs of
black and white marble, and with three white domes each.
These mosques, however, do not seem to belong to the
monument itself and look more like two sentries forever
standing on guard. On the first platform and terrace, some
400 feet square and 60 feet high, also made of white marble,
rises the mausoleum. At the four angles, sparkling in the
sunshine like ice towers, are tall and wonderfully graceful
minarets, each 137 feet high, made of the same material and
with similar cupolas. The imperial mausoleum with the
cenotaphs stands on the northern side of the quadrangular
terrace. Magnificent gates with arches lead up to the main
building; the red walls of these are covered with mnemonic
inscriptions taken from the *Qur'ân,* in *appliqué* work of
marble: farther on is the garden, divided into separate
squares, with fountains in marble basins surrounded with
beds of the rarest flowers, and with old cypresses, whose dark
shade harmonizes perfectly with the over-all view of the
white building. Right in front of the entrance, a long and
shady avenue ends in a wide marble staircase of two flights,
leading to the upper platform, the floor of which consists
of enormous white marble slabs enclosed in a border of
black marble.

As you reach the upper platform, some forty steps ahead,
you behold the mausoleum itself, and the sight is enough
to stun anyone . . . You feel as though it were a dream, a
sudden vision belonging to another, better and purer world;
you try to come to your senses again, to convince yourself
you are not dreaming, that what you see is a reality, and
not a phantasy of your imagination, a vision from the
Thousand and One Nights! I have seen the Cathedral of
St. Peter in Rome and those of Cologne and Strasbourg; I
have admired to my heart's content the productions of the
best-known Italian artists; but never did I see a single

monument, a single statue, painting, or temple, which made a stronger impression on me than did this building, conceived by Moslems whom I do not particularly like, and erected by unknown hands. It is said that for 22 years 20,000 workmen worked constantly on this mausoleum, and that, without counting the labor and material which did not cost anything, the building cost 3 million pounds sterling. The correspondent of the *Illustrated London News,* the well-known journalist Simpson, who is also an artist, architect and archaeologist, upon returning to England last year from Kâbul, told me he would not undertake to build such a monument for all the treasures of Golconda. "There are no such artists any longer in our cold and all-denying world," said a modern artist. "To polish this marble alone would require a Phidias and a Benvenuto Cellini, with a Michelangelo to help them! . . ." This opinion is not in the least exaggerated.

You are facing the marble façade of a temple, grandiose in its graceful simplicity. Its walls are entirely white and smooth. Only under the arch and above the wide portico can you see ingenious decorations made of the same material, like transparent embroidery turned into stone, representing flowers, fruit and arabesques; over the cornice of the dome and along the side walls you see also a thin border of inscriptions from the *Qur'ân* in enormous gold letters. The portico leads directly into the large inner hall of the mausoleum, surrounded by corridors and side-aisles. Everywhere the same blinding white walls and panels of mosaic, the same garlands of beautiful flowers made of precious stones in *pietra dura.* Some of them look so perfectly natural, the artist has copied nature so marvelously well, that your hand involuntarily reaches to assure yourself they are not actually real. Branches of white jasmine made of mother-of-pearl are winding around a red pomegranate flower of carnelian, or the delicate tendrils of vines and honeysuckle, while some delicate oleanders peep out from under the rich green foliage. And all of this is superimposed over white marble, not like the microscopic Florentine mosaic, but in the style of the *Oriental* mosaic of India, which uses pieces of such a size and form that they do not spoil the wholeness of the precious stones. Every leaf, every petal, is a separate emerald, amethyst, pearl or topaz; at times you can count as many as a hundred of them for one single bunch of flowers, and there are hundreds of such bunches all over the panels and perforated marble screens. A mysterious half-darkness reigns in this abode of death, so we could not at once realize the amount of treasure buried here with the imperial couple. But the torches lit up the hall and suddenly millions of sparks flashed from the precious stones, making us exclaim in amazement.

The ceiling under the dome, lighted by the daylight from the Gothic windows of pierced marble tracery, is thickly covered with similar flowers and fruit made of multi-colored stones; but instead of a smooth surface, the mosaic is super-imposed on marble, so that from a distance it actually re-sembles a flowery bower of living plants rather than cold stone. Having once seen the Tâj, the tourist will read with-out a smile the eloquent story told by a devout native his-torian who concludes his description with the following naïve assertion: "There is no doubt whatever that the plans of this Pearl of the East, of which we, Moslems of India, are justly proud, were from the very beginning destined by the great Prophet to inspire the faithful with the right idea of the blessed abodes in Paradise."

Right under the center of the dome stand two cenotaphs, enclosed in a pierced marble tracery, six feet high, similar to others in the mausoleum, and covered from top to bottom with precious designs of flowers and a border reminiscent of lillies. The carvings are so minute and graceful that in spite of being several inches thick, the screen of marble tracery looks exactly like lace. The cenotaphs, four in num-ber, though only two of them contain the bodies of the royal couple (the beautiful Mumtâz-i-Maḥall and her faithful husband, here and hereafter, the caliph Shâh-Jahân), are each made of a single piece of white marble.* The two

---

*Two cenotaphs with bodies in them stand in the lower burial crypt situated on the lower floor under the two platforms; above them, in the hall of the mausoleum, on the upper floor, are the two empty cenotaphs.

cenotaphs of the upper hall are splendid examples of simplicity and are in striking contrast to the marble screens covered with precious stones. From the portico we went down some broad steps into the burial crypt where the other two cenotaphs stand side by side. The tomb of the empress is covered with numberless arabesques, mosaics, precious stones and verses from the *Qur'ân*. The tomb of the caliph is a little higher, but simpler. Like the upper cenotaphs, these two are enclosed in wonderful lattice-work, but without any mosaics. The ceiling has a vault like that of the upper floor, but is not decorated; the hall itself is octangular. Day and night this dark hall is lit by silver and golden lamps; on Fridays the faithful bring numerous offerings to their "caliph"; these, of course, find their way into the pockets of the *mullah,* as all the repair work and safeguarding of the mausoleum are taken care of by the government.

Having visited the mausoleum, we climbed the northern minaret by a winding staircase and remained there resting for about two hours. It was difficult to part from this marvelous scene. From the minaret one can see the surroundings of Âgra spread over many miles. Scattered along both banks of the twisting silver ribbon of the Jumnâ are the great monuments of the Tîmûr dynasty—fortresses, palaces, mosques, towers . . . The city viewed from that height loses its dirty appearance and seems submerged in the green foliage of shrubbery and trees. It would be an anticlimax to describe anything else at Âgra after having seen the Tâj. Motî-Masjid, the "Pearl Mosque," whose beauty is generally highly praised, may well be remarkable from the standpoint of architecture; but it can hold the attention of only those who have not yet seen the mausoleum. Columns, cupolas and white marble, especially large blocks of it standing on platforms built of red sandstone — such is the description in brief of the palaces and the other mosques of Âgra.

Living quite close to the *Tâj Mahal,* we visited it daily and used its shady, cool gardens as our drawing room. Sitting there we listened to local legends and breathed more freely

than in the stuffy *dâk-bungalow*,* erected by the government
in one of the ancient mausoleums and mosques, near the
gates of the Tâj. In the same mosque, over the burial hall,
the English have arranged "*a dancing hall for picnics,*" an
act "of very doubtful tact and delicacy," according to the
expression of R. Gordon Cumming.

"Imagine the feelings of us Europeans and Christians,"
adds the author, "if some New Zealanders, after having
conquered us, would start dancing their war dance in *our*
mausoleums, or rather in our much less romantic cemetery
chapels!"

Without making any comments of my own, I purposely
quote one of their own countrymen, in order to show the
English that it is not only the Russians, whom they generally suspect as spies, who notice and point out to the world
their repulsive egotism and lack of consideration for the
feelings of their conquered peoples. It is not the Russians
but they, themselves, who arouse the just hatred of the
Asiatic people by means of such dangerous behavior.

It is said that after the death of his beloved Mumtâz,
the idol of his heart, the poor caliph was overcome by a
profound melancholy. Presently there appeared a dervish-
saint who suggested to him the building of such a monument in memory of his beloved as would astonish the
whole world and promised him in this the protection of the
Prophet. The dervish kept his word. According to the
original plan, the caliph had planned to erect a similar
mausoleum for himself, on the opposite bank of the Jumnâ,
and to connect the two monuments by a white marble
bridge. But long before the Tâj was completed, the emperor
fell ill and was on the verge of death. Then his four sons,
the children of Mumtâz, without waiting for his death,
started a war among themselves for the possession of the
throne. Aurangzîb was the victor in this reverent filial
tournament and locked up his three brothers, as well as his
own son, in the fortress of Gwalior — a sort of Indian

---

*An inn where free lodging is afforded. Charges for board are very
low for travellers who do not have their cook and servants with them.

Bastille, where the close relatives of the Mogul caliphs were often imprisoned. As to his father, the poor widower Shâh-Jahân, he imprisoned him in the old fortress of Âgra, where the dethroned emperor spent seven years and where he finally died, his only consolation being that he could see the mausoleum of his beloved wife from his window, grieving, however, that the work had been stopped. He should have looked upon his imprisonment, however, as a very natural event, inherent in the very nature of things. Not a single emperor, excepting Akbar, had yet ascended the Mogul throne without bloodshed and the imprisonment of all the pretenders who at one time or another had stood in the way. Shâh-Jahân himself ascended the throne over the dead body of his brother whom he had killed with his own hand, in spite of his sincere regret. Such is *Kismet*. His father, Jahângîr, the son of Akbar, impaled more than 800 relatives of the Tîmûr dynasty, before he could peacefully settle down on the family throne.

After the death of his prisoner-father, Aurangzîb, as a true Moslem and devoted son, rendered all possible honors to the parent who could no longer be dangerous to him. He buried him next to "the Crown of the Seraglio" and completed the mausoleum with the money of some grandees murdered for the occasion. He even surpassed his father in extravagance, by erecting in front of the existing gate leading into the garden, another made of *pure silver,* with whole chapters from the *Qur'ân* carved on it, and decorated like the goblet of Benvenuto Cellini. Describing these gates, the chronicles of the Portuguese missionaries of Gôa say they were built by the devil himself and finished in one night; but in this the pious *padris* are probably mistaken . . . It was also by the order of the same emperor that a wicket, which has now disappeared, was made out *of one single piece of agate* of such beauty and value that, according to the words of the same veracious historians, "it was the production of Hell." But if that is really so, the fate of these two treasures only confirms the saying that "the devil makes no presents, but only lends." A mere quarter of a century later the triumphant Marâthâs carried away the gates and coined rupees out of them; as to the wicket, they made a

screen of it for Śiva in the temple of the Mahârâja of
Gwalior. No one knows today what has become of the
wicket. It is conjectured that it was again removed, this
time by the Mahârâja of Bhurtpore, who has it buried
somewhere in the enchanted gardens of Dîgh. But he died
suddenly, and the secret of the hiding place of the wicket
died with him.

Even today in Âgra you can hear dark rumors among
the people and traditions about the "secret" power (even
more so than the manifest one) of Akbar. The emperor
was not only a great statesman and general, but had also
been initiated into the dark science of necromancy and
magic. At his death, he predicted that the greatness of his
dynasty would come to an end in the fourth generation
succeeding him, in the reign of his great-grandson, and he
promised to appear before the then reigning emperor. He
kept his word. This is the way it happened . . .

The great caliph appeared to Aurangzîb the "Splendid"
in the famous fortress of Âgra, which he had erected, and
which was known as the fort of Akbar. This happened about
1680. "The Splendid" one was sitting one fine morning on
his throne in the "audience hall," where once upon a time
sat his ancestor, judging cases of right and wrong with no
regard to any canon of laws. History does not tell us in
what state of mind he was, nor what state his courtiers were
in. Probably, not unlike another orthodox Khân, the caliph
was sitting "with his eyes cast down and smoking his pipe."
For the last decade the Moguls had been constantly and
badly beaten by the Marâthâs, and the poor faithful were
very much depressed, the more so because the Marâthâs
were under the command of the invincible Śîvajî, the Dekkan Ilya Muromets. Âjânubâhu II, according to the
prophecy of pandit Vasishṭha, was threatening to grab with
his "long arms" all the conquered kingdoms of India * and

---

*Aurangzîb, calling himself haughtily "Conqueror of the World,"
had a golden globe carried in front of him as a symbol . . . . But to
prove humbly to the world that he had so far only conquered three-
quarters of it, he used to tear off a corner of every sheet of paper he
used in his correspondence.

thus avenge the *land* of Âjânubâhu I. Suddenly Aurangzîb (literally the "Beauty of the Throne") began to tremble like an aspen leaf and jumping up silently, with eyes full of terror, pointed out something in a corner of the room to his courtiers. The courtiers could see nothing, but they all heard a loud voice, sounding like that of an old man, utter the words: "Sorrow . . . misfortune to the great house of Tîmûr! The end of its greatness has come! . . ." The Emperor fainted. He swore later that he saw the shade of his ancestor Akbar, who repeated the awful prophecy which, according to tradition, he had already uttered on his death-bed . . .

From that time on, all went awry in the kingdom and it eventually fell to pieces. Aurangzîb died in 1707, and with the "Beauty of the Throne" disappeared also the grandeur of the dynasty.

At first we did not believe this story, but after visiting the "audience hall" and seeing the corner in which Akbar appeared to his great-grandson, we had to surrender before the evidence of the facts.

In the city of Âgra, in the fortress of Akbar, there was an armory, the contents of which the Sepoys availed themselves of during the mutiny of 1857 to use it in murdering the English. The armory has now been transferred to the "audience hall" and the latter made into a fortress within a fortress, the weapons being held behind 77 locks. In my humble opinion, the English should behave themselves and not dance in the mausoleum of the caliphs; that would be the best precautionary measure.

The fortress stretches for a mile along the river bank and has walls 85 feet high and of unusual thickness, calculated to frighten anyone who would besiege it . . . but only those who might come without the help of up-to-date artillery. With the help of the latter, this stronghold, which was further fortified in the last twenty years, would no more be able to hold out than it did in 1803, when Lord Lake, with a limited number of ancient guns, on the very first day of the siege, forced the capitulation of its 6,000 Marâthâs. Among the treasures of the "armory," which we were not allowed to enter this time, are the two halves of the

exquisitely carved gates, 12 feet high, inlaid with expensive
mosaics, and adorned with coats-of-arms made of pure
silver. A strange metamorphosis that no one can explain,
happened to these gates which have their own history. They
were made of sandalwood and filled the air with a delightful fragrance. They were said to have once been the ornament of the great Brâhmanical pagoda of Somnâth, but in
997 were carried away by the Afghân Sultan Mahmûd of
Ghaznî, who in the same year invaded and sacked the whole
of Gujarât, in order to punish the pagans and make himself
rich with booty. These sandalwood gates were considered a
chef-d'œuvre of native carving; they were venerated and
treasured by the people of India to such a degree that
Mahmûd ordered them, at great expense, to be taken to
Ghaznî, where they were honored by being placed at the
entrance of the Sultan's own mausoleum. The presence of
so sacred an object in the eyes of the Hindus at a Moslem
burying place was an eyesore to the Brâhmaṇas, and was
meant to remind the people of the supreme power of the
Mogul rule. The Brâhmaṇas tried many times to take them
by force and even attempted to steal them, but all in vain.
They had already cost many lives, but still remained. Thus
800 years elapsed, until Lord Ellenborough,* who conquered
Ghaznî, beheld the famous bone of contention. Having heard
their history, he conceived the idea of proving to the Moguls
that they were no longer the masters of India, and that the
English had taken their place. In accordance with this
intention, he ordered the gates to be taken to Âgra. This
was accomplished at great cost and with considerable difficulties, and the whole undertaking was cursed by the
English soldiers. The Hindus, however, were triumphant.
"The gates of the Somnâth temple are now of even greater
historical value," says the *Guide to the Curiosities of Âgra.*

---

*[Edward Law, Earl of Ellenborough (1790-1871), governor-gen-
eral of India (1841-44) succeeding Lord Auckland. His second wife
was the notorious Jane Elizabeth Ellenborough (ca. 1807-81) from
whom he was divorced by act of Parliament. She eventually married
Sheikh Midjwal el Mezrab and resided for many years in the desert near
Damascus. —*Compiler.*]

"They are a monument to the victory of Lord Ellenborough and his proclamation at the end of the Kâbul War; at the same time, they are a rare object of art, added by us [*i.e.,* the English] to so many other treasures."

Among numerous other visitors, all agog with amazement, there once came to admire the gates a Mr. Simpson, an accurate and sagacious Scotsman whose name we had occasion to mention before. Having critically examined them, he suddenly declared the gates to be substitutes, to the great horror of the English! According to all ancient descriptions, the gates taken by Sultan Mahmûd had nearly all the 33 million Indian gods represented on them. On these, however, the carving was of a purely Mohammedan style. Great excitement followed; everyone rushed about, not knowing what to do. Finally there came an order from Calcutta to examine the gates through a microscope. Alas! The examination proved in the most undeniable manner that these gates, brought at such a cost, and visited by hundreds of tourists from distant lands, were not even of sandalwood but of ordinary pine! . . . Had this discovery been made some years later, I could wager that the English press would have accused Russia of having stolen the real gates! . . . In our day the poor gates stand in a dark corner, covered with dust, and quite forgotten.

The "Great Temple" of Somnâth, the Indian Osiris, the god that judges the souls of the dead and decides their future form of existence according to the law of metempsychosis, is one of the largest and richest in India. It is situated in Gujarât on the coast of the Indian Ocean. In the days of Mahmûd this temple had 2000 priests, 500 dancers (*nâchnîs*), 300 sacred pipers and 300 barbers. Having heard of its wealth, the Sultan decided to look at it and to share the booty with the god. On entering the temple, he saw an immense hall with a vault supported by 56 silver columns, and with golden idols of gods all along the walls. Ordering his soldiers to load the latter into his baggage train, Mahmûd came up to the larger idol of Somnâth, and, without uttering a word, broke off its nose. The Brâhmaṇas then threw themselves down upon their knees in front of him and begged him to spare their god, offering so great a

sum of money if he desisted that his vizier advised him to
accept the offer. But the Sultan was a strict Moslem and
refused the offer, which act was rewarded by the Prophet.
When Somnâth was broken to pieces, there was found inside
it an immense treasure consisting of pearls and diamonds,
amounting to ten times the value of what had been offered
by the Brâhmaṇas. Thus virtue was once more triumphant
on earth.

The palace itself in which Shâh-Jahân was imprisoned
is now in ruins. Upon leaving it, we crossed a court and
entered the *zenânâ* (harem), in the middle of which Tavernier saw in his day a bathing pool, 40 feet long and 25 feet
wide, made of gray marble. The walls of the numberless
rooms are covered with thousands of convex mirrors in
Persian style; everything here is again of white marble — the
pillars, what not . . . Separate charming pavilions hang
like stars of lace over their red pedestals, surrounded by
openwork balconies covered with green vines. All these
wonders of architecture, where once people lived, suffered
and loved—all these are now empty, deserted and as if
slumbering in an endless sleep . . . The green parrots alone
disturb the solemn silence of this uninhabited part of the
fortress, awakening the lazy echoes, and blue-winged birds
sometimes build their nests among the niches of the panels,
each separate piece of which is a marvel of carving. On
a moonlit night these scenes are full of enchantment. Just
as though the Frost King had flown through the kingdom
of the "Sleeping Beauty" and covered the buildings with
hoar-frost ornaments . . . This fairy workmanship seems
more like miniature carving in ivory than any marble cutting known to us in Europe.

In the same fortress, only a stone's throw from the Tâj
Mahal, stands "Motî-Masjid," the mosque erected by Shâh-
Jahân during his seven years' imprisonment. The mausoleum, which we had visited first, prejudiced us against everything else, the "Pearl Mosque" included. The latter, however, is truly a most precious pearl among the mosques.
Perfect in its architectural form, surrounded by a highly
poetical atmosphere, white like newly-fallen snow, without
the admixture of any other colors, the mosque attracts the

attention of the visitor and deserves his sympathy because of the sad legend which goes with it. People say that the idea of building this beautiful mosque belongs to Jahânârâ, the favorite daughter of the imprisoned Sultan. Seeing the sufferings of her father and his inconsolable grief, the princess, who insisted on being imprisoned with her father, persuaded him to spend his time in erecting the mosque, which she thought would dissipate his melancholy. It is said that in consenting to this plan the dethroned Sultan exclaimed in deep heartfelt sorrow: "Let it be as you wish it, my daughter; and let the future holy mosque be named 'The Pearl' . . . As the real pearl owes its inception, its development and its beauty within the shell to the sufferings of the oyster, so Motî-Masjid will owe its existence to the hopeless grief experienced by the unlucky father of the cruel Aurangzîb!" Thus did his dream-mosque, the progeny of so many bitter hours of seclusion, all at once come into existence, as though a tear of the "angel of fate," the angel whose duty is to record in the book of repentence all earthly sufferings and sorrows, fell and froze at the feet of the Tâj Mahal.

Later on we saw at Delhi the last abode, the tomb, of the Sultan's faithful daughter—Jahânârâ; outwardly it is a proud sarcophagus of white marble with sculptural ornaments and mosaics like all other monuments; but inside the mausoleum there is a little cool, green garden, with simple flowerbeds daily watered with utmost care by an old bent Mogul, a half-wit who lost his mind as a result of the horrors he experienced at Delhi. A living ruin among dead ruins, this old man is the very imbodiment of unfailing love and devotion to the fallen house of the Padishâhs — the last and only descendant of a long line of faithful servants of the Sultans, who escaped the fate of all the others because he was decrepit and insignificant. He was about a hundred years old. Shaking and quivering on his old bony legs, he led the way into the mausoleum, pointing out to us on one of the walls an epitaph written by Princess Jahânârâ herself, just before her untimely death, and carved on her tomb according to her wish. She requested that only flowers and grass should mark the place where her body would lie.

"Let only flowers created by the hands of Allah mingle with the remains of the mortal pilgrim—Jahânârâ . . . They are the best possible ornament of the last abode of the soul, freed from all earthly fetters," says the inscription. We gave a few coins to the bony old man; the devoted servant hid them in the tall grass and, patting the marble sarcophagus with his trembling hand, began to murmur, addressing himself to the dead princess: "I will buy you, Begum-Hanum, some fresh flowers; I will plant new roses in place of the withered ones . . ." I remembered this scene in the Tâj Mahal, when the *mullah* of the place, growing fatter and richer by the hour, was annoying us by constantly begging for "one more rupee, just one more" for his caliph. Here the poor old man, whose ebbing life-force was centered upon the tomb of the princess, deceased some 200 years, and merely because she was an ancestor of his beloved, murdered masters, appeared before my imagination as one of the last examples in our time of the sincere love and devotion of our "lesser brothers."

In the harem section of the spacious fortress, one can see at every step sealed rooms, secret hiding places, and underground passages, built centuries ago and now unexpectedly discovered by the English. What awful and bloody scenes took place in this fortress! How many victims, how much suffering, and how many forever buried mysteries! . . . English soldiers who live here are said to be in a state of constant dread because of their superstitions, which no punishment, however severe, can prevent. As an Irish sergeant told Mr. W., "Who would like to spend night after night among *pagans* of the other world, killed unbaptised and related to 'Old Harry' (the devil)? Blessed St. Patrick himself would be no help here!" After traversing a whole series of corridors, we were shown a place where English engineers pierced a wall and found a secret room over the river; in it were three smiling skeletons of a young man and two women, one old and the other young. The latter was richly dressed and covered with jewels. They had been immured here and left to die of starvation. As if to increase their last tortures to a *nec plus ultra* of refined cruelty, there was a hole in the middle of the room, opening onto a deep well with gurgling water, but protected by a thick iron grating . . . In one of the underground passages was found a well-nigh bottomless abyss, across the opening of which lay a thick beam. Over this beam were hanging like bunches of dry grass about a dozen female skeletons! . . . How many young lives were lost by falling off the beam into the awful dark abyss, no one but the Angel of Death knows for certain. Azrâil, however, does not disclose his secrets, especially to us unbelievers as, according to the request of Mohammed, he no longer appears in a visible form* . . . Thus the harem life appears to be most attractive, and we can only envy the happy Zuleika.

In another part of Âgra, workmen digging out a basin found not long ago the remains of a large palace, and finally uncovered the entrance to one of the underground rooms, known as *thikânâ* (cool dwelling), where landlords spent the hottest part of the day. They became interested in a wall which proved to be a double wall; in between was a narrow corridor, where five skeletons stood in a row, chained to the wall, and dressed in gorgeous raiment. Three of them, it would appear, belonged to the high aristocracy: a young man and two women, one on each side of him, with long black braids. Their dresses and veils were embroidered with gold; on their hands and ankles were golden bracelets and around their necks precious chains, strings of pearls and other talismans. The latter obviously proved their magic power to safeguard from danger! . . . All these treasures were sold by the government for £2,000. Two other skeletons were those of old women, probably servants.

About nine miles from the city, in a clearing of the garden, in a village called Sikandra, the great Emperor Akbar is buried. His mausoleum is a miniature second edition of the fortress itself. It occupies forty acres of land and stands in a garden or rather a walled park, several square miles in size. The mausoleum stands on the topmost of four

---

*Before the time of the Prophet, teaches the *Qur'ân*, he appeared in bodily form to claim his victims, and it is only owing to the request of Mohammed who wanted to free humanity from such a dreadful sight, that this angel arrives nowadays unseen and unheard.

gradually diminishing terraces, having the usual minarets with cupolas at each corner. The cupolas are covered with tiles of mosaic, green and blue with gold. It is inconceivable that neither the colors nor the carvings should not have deteriorated at all in three centuries, especially in a climate where heat and humidity ruin in a year's time some of the most durable work of European artists.

Upon the sarcophagus are carved in Persian letters of gold the ninety-nine virtues of Allah. On three sides of the lower terrace of the mausoleum are colonnades with numerous arches, covered with inscriptions from the *Qur'ân* and the more recent curses upon the unbelievers; all this is laid in black marble. Between every two columns there is a window of the usual Indian architectural style — a sort of stone lacework. As the sister of R. Gordon Cumming, the Scottish Nimrod of modern England, very justly said, this stone lacework finally begins to impress one as being something commonplace. "But if we could transport one of these windows," she goes on to say, "into some Christian cathedral, what a crowd would be pressing to see it, and what exclamations of delight and amazement would be heard from the experts! Here in India, however, such work is only the accomplishment of *despised niggers* and our haughty Britisher will hardly even look at it!"

This is the opinion of a patriotic English woman.

Next morning we left Âgra quite early; so early that the dawn had not yet cast its rosy light over the snow-white Tâj Mahal . . . We had to drive twenty-four miles before luncheon, which was to be prepared for us in Fatehpûr Sîkrî, the most famous ruins of the North-West Provinces, where our friend and protector, the Thâkur, was expecting us. Gulâb-Lal-Singh did not turn up at Âgra, a place which he for some reason or other hated, though he had half-promised to come. We were quite accustomed, however, to his strange ways, to his sudden appearances and disappearances, and never questioned him.

In the morning we left British territory and entered the classical country of Râjasthân, a land though not entirely free and independent, yet one with which the English have to reckon. In Bhurtpore, for instance, the native state bordering on Âgra, there is neither a political resident, nor even a single Englishman, whether in the town itself or in the neighborhood. The Anglo-Indian Government and Bhurtpore have only a political interrelationship. Râjasthân was the Thâkur's native country of which he is so proud; its history has been traced by English Orientalists 600 years before Xerxes, and by Tod as far back as 3,000 B.C. It is the land of historical and mythical heroes, of reckless bravery and chivalrous feelings toward women, who are so little esteemed and often despised and down-trodden in the rest of India . . . Here Gulâb-Singh was at home and was preparing a warm welcome for us. We now seemed to breathe more freely . . . Hardly had the rattling and dilapidated coaches of the Jaipur train pulled up at the Fatehpûr station, than all of us except the two Englishmen exclaimed with joyful relief. In no time, the servants of the Thâkur, who had appeared as though risen from below ground, transported our baggage to carriages sent to meet us by the *Divân* (Minister) of the Mahârâja of Bhurtpore. "His Highness is at Hardvâr on a pilgrimage, but the *Divân* is at your disposal and ordered us to prostrate ourselves before our American brethren-Sâhibs," said a tall young Râjput, with long hair and white turban. "The carriages are at your service."

Then came the Thâkur-Sâhib on horseback, escorted by a bodyguard of half a dozen broad-shouldered, bearded men, with long, waving hair, whom we had never seen before . . . The dark silhouette of the man on horseback was thrown into sharp relief against the cloudless dark blue sky, and his enormous figure reminded me of the equestrian monument of Peter the Great. All of us were pleased . . . Miss B. alone, with her usual tact, turning round and addressing either the envoy of the *Divân* or perhaps the tails of the horses, exclaimed in a sad tone of voice: "Great Heavens! what sombre and wild surroundings! People say the Râjputs are awful bandits . . . Wouldn't it be dangerous for us to go alone into this country? . . ."

I felt an irresistible urge to strangle the tactless fool, but restrained myself and, feeling shame in the presence of the Râjputs, looked at the Ṭhâkur who had just reached us.

Gulâb-Lal-Singh was quietly stroking his mustache. But in his seemingly casual glance at the Englishwoman I caught the same lightning-swift expression of controlled anger, nay, I would even say, hatred, as at Delhi some days before. This anger or hatred was at once mirrored in the pale face of Nârâyaṇa-Kṛishṇarâo.

"Calm yourself!" said the even and somewhat sarcastic voice of our friend. "You forget that Râjputâna has the honor of being under the protectorate of Great Britain . . . The perspicacity and fatherly vigilance of the latter have no bounds, just as its warm care for us miserable . . . bandits . . . Look around, your government does not lose sight of any of us for one moment, so anxious is it that we should not fall into evil hands! . . ."

He pointed towards the railway station. There on the platform, fussing over his baggage and the box with whiskey and soda, we saw the blond spy in his white uniform.

———

—XXIX*—

The days and weeks passed quickly, and even more quickly did we change our places of residence; but even though we lost no time, we saw barely a twentieth part of the famous historical places for which India is renowned. Meanwhile, the heat grew more intense every day. Early in the beginning of May, as a rule, it reaches its climax throughout most of Hindostan. Râjasthân during this deadly month is really as hot as hell even for India, and Allâhâbâd itself may seem cool in comparison. Now, when around St. Petersburg and Moscow the fields are just beginning to don their green raiment, and the lilac bushes are still quite bare, on the scorched fields of Râjputâna everything is sad and roasted to a crisp, and the earth's surface is like toasted bread left too long in the oven and crumbling to pieces. Its enormous plains, scorched and sad-looking in their brownish-yellow color, where they are not too densely inhabited, remind one of the Russian steppes: the same dry feather grass, the same frequent mirages on the red-hot horizon.

Like an old woman shriveled to the marrow of her bones, slumbers the tired and withering nature of India, enduring to the end its "hot season," under the scorching rays of the merciless sun. Spring, summer, autumn, winter are for

---

*[Misnumbered XXIII in the *Russkiy Vestnik.* —*Compiler.*]

443

the native mere words without meaning. The Hindu knows only three seasons of the year, and speaks of them as the "hot season," the "cold season" and the "rainy season." In about three or four weeks, in the bright sapphire sky, cloudless for nine months of the year, the first rain clouds will appear. Thunder will roll, and cyclones and devastating hurricanes will rage on the coasts of Bengal. Human beings will perish, buildings will be torn down; but in exchange, the hurricane from the south will bring on its powerful wings the longed-for *monsoon*, laden with the fragrances of Ceylon and Southern India. And after two or three days of torrential downpour, the whole of India from the Himâlayas to Cape Comorin will blossom forth again. The flooded valleys of Râjasthân will look like a sea from the depth of which rise but the rocks of the Ṭhâkurs with their half-ruined fortresses and castles. These rocks, now scattered like hideous warts over the face of *Sûryavanśa* — "The Race of the Sun" — will be washed clean and be covered with blossoms, and all of nature will rejoice . . . The cuckoo, the bard of love in Hindostan, the bird consecrated to Kâma, the god of love, will burst into song. Mists will rise from the earth — the most fragrant of all the aromas of nature, according to the Hindu, and weddings, banquets and feasts will take place everywhere.

Now, however, before the arrival of the rain, the "beloved of the earth" according to the Greek poet, Râjputâna could offer us no more than she herself possessed. Everything was scorched, and there was really nothing further left to burn. Miss B. was right, the first sight of the surrounding country was not favorable. All was death and silence; on the bare fields, the familiar figure of the farmer, a poor black skeleton, digging like a mole nearly all the year round, was no longer seen . . . He had nothing to do until the first rain came. During such heat even the all-enduring camel lies down wherever he can; his cud loses its taste and he either sleeps soundly day after day, or simply dies. Everything in nature seems dead and congealed, and its activity is revealed only in death or putrefaction . . . During such days, birds fall to the ground, dying by the dozen. The general silence is interrupted only by the long and sad shrill of the falcon which seems to hover in the hot currents of air; sometimes on a small hillock some vultures, surrounding carrion, stand motionless with their heads down, not even touching their favorite food, content merely to dream about it. Death in every form soars over the head of the European. It blinks at him from the shimmering heat-waves, presaging sunstroke; it stalks him in a railway carriage, threatening death by "heat apoplexy," as it is called by doctors in India, and which is caused by the scorching air currents produced by the motion of the train, or by the oppressive temperature at home. It awaits its victims in every dark and comparatively cool corner, where poisonous centipedes, scorpions and even snakes are attracted by the dampness of the water-cooled shutters and doors.

Death in India misses no single chance; it is the best ally of the native as it often rids him of the tyrant. It watches the Anglo-Indian from every corner; any means to that end are good. The ever-perspiring Englishman finds it everywhere; in the artificially cooled *pankhâ*, the Indian *perpetuum mobile*, under the motions of which he eats, sleeps, drinks, swears, fights and performs his official duties, as well as in every iced drink. Pneumonia or cholera often end his career in a couple of hours.

All this we knew as we had been warned of the Râjputâna heat. But all had gone well so far, and this impunity made us rash. At Delhi the Thâkur told us: "Do not be afraid; *I vouch* for you two, and if both Englishmen will listen to my advice, I will vouch for them also." We were thus quite reassured.

The Thâkur, little by little was gaining an ever greater influence over our will and thoughts (I speak about the Colonel and myself). Having swayed our minds and our souls and excited our curiosity to the utmost, he made us feel that at the slightest motion of his hand we would be ready to follow him anywhere, through fire or water, without the least hesitation; yet, having finally entirely subdued our volition, he evidently did not want to make use of his power . . . Always calm and friendly to everyone, with us he seemed to be at times even more so, but still as secretive as with anyone else in regard to his mysterious and undeniable

knowledge of the "secret science." That he knew of our
intense wish to learn from him and to receive an explanation
of his extraordinary psychological powers, of which we had
absolute proof, is just as unquestionable as the fact that he
knows at this very moment, if he so wishes, though in Tibet,
every word of what I am writing. But knowing this, he
was silent. At times it seemed to me as though he were
studying us, wanting to assure himself as to what extent
he could trust us, and I was afraid to speak about him even
with the Colonel. Though belonging to our "Society," he
remained but an ordinary member, refusing the title of
"honorary member of the General Council," which had been
repeatedly offered him. One of the General Councillors of
the Theosophical Society in London, a Lord and an Earl,
a man known as one of the most learned Fellows of the
Royal Society, having heard of the Ṭhâkur, wrote last year
to another member of the Council of our Society, the editor
of the chief government newspaper: "For heaven's sake,
ask the Ṭhâkur to tell me whether there is any hope for me
to attain the goal I have been vainly striving for these last
15 years . . . Spiritism has treacherously betrayed me. Its
phenomena are facts; their explanation—*rubbish.* How can
I renew my former contact with the person I used to speak
to so freely across three thousand miles, each of us sitting in
his own room? . . . It has all ceased now; he does not hear
me and even *does not feel me* . . . Why? . . ." When I
transmitted the letter of the editor to the Ṭhâkur, Gulâb-
Singh asked me to write down the following, which he
dictated to me: "My Lord! You are an Englishman and
your daily life runs according to the English pattern. Ambition and Parliament began the work of ruin, the meat you
eat and the wine you drink finished it . . . For the assimilation of the human soul with the Universal Soul or Parabrahman, there is but one narrow and thorny path, and this
you will not tread. The material man killed in you the
spiritual. You alone can resurrect the latter; no one else
is able to do so for you . . ."

Skeptics and materialists, those who take the phenomena
of spiritism for the *work of the devil,* and those others,
who are quite sure that after death nothing remains of us

but "weeds," according to the expression of Bazaroff,* will of course not believe any of this and will either laugh at us, with our Thâkurs and Lords, or even shun us. To all of this we have been long accustomed. Earnest people on the contrary, scientists, men experienced in *mediumistic* phenomena, like Professors Butlerov, Wagner, Zöllner, Wallace and others, who were conquered by facts and who acknowledged them as such, these men of learning, who have become cognizant of the existence of a force capable of tying knots on an endless cord, will believe in the *reality* of the strange and inexplicable phenomena seen by us in India. On one point only will we disagree with them: they believe that the unknown force that causes transformation of matter at spiritistic *séances* belongs to *spirits,* while we do not believe that the dead have an active power in interfering in such cases, and ascribe this power to the spirit of *living man.* Which one of us is right or wrong, time alone will show. Men must first become convinced of the objectivity of such controversial phenomena, and only then attempt to explain them. Spiritism has been most seriously harmed by the theories of people who believe in it.

What is said above is no digression, but a necessary explanation of what is to follow. My *Letters from the Caves and Jungles of Hindostan* are no mere geographical and ethnographical descriptions of India, with some fictitious heroes and heroines woven into them, but a diary of the chief members of the Theosophical Society with whose ideas both spiritualism and materialism in Europe — but especially the untidy Orientalists—have already begun to reckon.

Embarrassed by the conduct of Miss B., and ready to take our seats in the carriage of the Mahârâja of Bhurtpore, we were startled by contact with it. It was an enormous half-opened prehistoric *landau* quite comfortable and seating six or even eight easily. But while waiting for our arrival, the seat had been turned into an Inquisition chair, where formerly victims were slowly roasted . . . One could have baked an omelette on the steps and other iron parts

---

*[One of the characters in I.S. Turgenyev's (1818-83) novel, *Fathers and Sons.—Compiler.*]

of the vehicle, and at the touch of one of its sides I very nearly lost the skin of the palm of my hand. I drew it away in horror and did not dare to sit down; even the brave Colonel hesitated. Such a vehicle can only be used by Beelzebub, the Prince of Hell!

"You cannot use this carriage before evening," remarked the Ṭhâkur, knitting his brows. "You will have to spend the day somewhere nearby. Go to the station restaurant, while I fetch a covered vehicle . . ."

A council meeting followed. To the fairy gardens of Dîgh, with its 600 fountains (the historically renowned heritage of the Bhurtpore Mahârâjas), it was 18 miles; to the capital of the state—5 miles. The train was late and it was already 10 A.M. To drive in the midday heat, when we were already dizzy from it, would have been sheer folly. Even the Hindus, everybody, in fact, but the Ṭhâkur, grew pale, their faces turning an earthly color, and were fanning themselves with their scarves. The Bâbû alone seemed to be quite blissful. Bareheaded and fidgety on the front seat of the carriage where he had already climbed, he plunged through the waves of the red-hot air as a swimmer would dive through the cool waves of a river, assuring us that it was not so hot after all, and that in Bengal such a day would have been considered by many people to be a cool one.

While the Ṭhâkur gave his orders, and two of his body-guard galloped away to get a carriage, Miss B., near collapse from the heat and picking quarrels right and left, deemed it her duty to become offended at the words of the Bâbû:

«C'est du persifflage, cela!» she kept repeating. "He is cool when we are all dying from heat!"

"What does it matter to you? Can you prevent a man feeling other than you feel yourself?" I said persuasively, foreseeing a new quarrel between them.

"He is doing it on purpose! He is making fun of us," said the old maid, grumbling. "He, like all other Hindus, hates us Englishmen. He is happy when we suffer."

"You are not right in thinking that," ironically remarked the Bâbû from his seat. "I do not hate our *good* rulers at all. But when they are hot, I am always cold and *vice versa* . . . Sit down beside me and I will fan you with your fan . . . You know how I . . . esteem you! . . ."

"Thank you," she exclaimed. "Sit in the sun, which is powerless only against such as you . . . regular amphibious creatures," she suddenly added in her rage.

"Salamanders, you mean?" retorted the Bâbû jokingly; "don't make any mistakes, *chând kâ tukṟâ** Saab! . . ."

"I care not for your corrections, even if I am mistaken!" she said angrily, getting quite pale. "It is not your race that should give lessons to the English!"

"I would seriously advise you to be more careful in such heat," interrupted the Ṭhâkur, getting off his horse and emphasizing his last words. "The least excitement can be fatal in our climate, which even English rule has not been able to subdue."

And once more the same piercing lightning appeared in the half-opened eyes of the Râjput and his nostrils slightly quivered at the feeling of disdain which sounded in her words, "your race." But the infuriated Englishwoman could no longer be held in check. She began complaining that it had been fraud alone that made her come into a land where there was not a single Englishman to defend her, where the natives made fun of her and insulted the greatness of the whole English race including the queen, in her person. She finally began to talk such nonsense, that we looked at her in amazement, as if she were a lunatic. Mr. W. seized her by the arm and tried to take her to the restaurant. He was very much embarrassed, but, as an Englishman, he probably thought it beneath his dignity to try and make her reasonable, and thus indirectly seem to be on the native's side in a quarrel with a daughter of the "higher race."

This, however, was to be the last quarrel and its consequences proved to be quite unexpected. The unfortunate Bâbû, the involuntary cause of the tempest, intending to make peace with Miss B. "for the sake of the Society," as he latter said, made matters worse instead of better.

Miss B. led by Mr. W. was on her way to the station; I,

---

*This means when translated: "madame piece of the moon"; it is a reverential and flattering expression in Hindî.

standing under an enormous parasol that had been opened
over the Colonel and myself, was waiting to get back the
opera glass and satchel we had left in the carriage, when
Nârâyaṇa-Kṛishṇarâo-Mûljî and the Bâbû, as though by
mutual consent, came up to the Colonel and begged his
permission to return to Âgra by the same train, in order
to go home. Our esteemed president waived both arms in
absolute refusal. He was not going to part with them for
anything . . . This quarrel was a lot of nonsense and would
be forgotten the next hour . . .

"Not for anything! I would rather go back myself with
you," he said, loudly.

At the first words of this conversation, the Englishwoman
had pricked up her ears. Having gotten the trend of it,
she tore herself away from Mr. W., and, running up to us,
blurted something to the effect that "those gentlemen
Hindus (accentuating ironically the word *gentlemen*) were
anticipating her own request."

"We can no longer maintain the harmony needed for
travelling together," she said. "Let the president now choose
between the members: Europeans or *Asiatics*."

I was quite enraged at this new offense and was about
to answer her as she deserved, when I felt the gaze of the
Ṭhâkur fastened upon me. The President was coughing and
adjusting his glasses — a sign that he was preparing an
official resolution. As long as he had anything to say I
had no right to interfere . . .

"There can be no choice here," he began slowly, but
angrily, shaking the hot ashes of his pipe onto the cushions
of His Highness's carriage. "All the members of the Society
placed in New York under my care, *without distinction of
race or religion,* are equally honored by myself and are
dear to the general Society. I therefore refuse to choose, but
I sustain my right to settle quarrels between members.
I heard every word of your rather loud talk and must confess
that I do not find it to be a quarrel at all! . . . Our esteemed
Miss B. lost her temper and said some rude things (he ac-
centuated the word *rude*) to the Bâbû. The latter remained
silent and acted like a gentleman. I hope Miss B. will
understand that it was *he* who was insulted and not *she,* and

in his person the rest of the native members; I hope she will add her own apologies to mine, in asking them to forget this silly incident and request our dear and esteemed friends not to leave us . . ."

Miss B. was shaking with anger.

Standing a few feet from me, resting his elbow on his saddle, the Thâkur had his eyes fixed on her—an ominous phosphorescent glow within them. Nârâyaṇa, his head bent down, was silent, but on his lip, which he bit, there was a large drop of blood . . .

"What? Do you mean it is for *me* to ask *his* pardon?" burst out the old maid, "For me, when he . . ."

"Not to ask pardon, but to give him your hand in sign of peace between you," interrupted Mr. W.

He was quite pale and spoke with obvious effort. His innate honor was struggling with his national haughtiness which latter unfortunately prevailed. Catching the infuriated look of his compatriot, he then added:

"Excuse my interrupting, but I permit myself to interpret the President's wish *only* in the sense I have just pointed out. Because . . . you must agree . . . that in spite of the fact that American ideas of decency are diametrically opposed to ours (*i.e.,* English), I could not possibly suppose even for an instant such an absurdity, that it could occur even to the President to ask a lady, *an English lady,* to beg pardon of a . . . of a . . . man!" he finally concluded with some difficulty, evidently substituting the last word for some other he fortunately succeeded in swallowing.

"There is your Universal Brotherhood," I thought to myself.

"Why not?" answered the Colonel quite calmly. "You may suppose it, as it was precisely such an *absurdity* that I had in mind."

"But I am not thinking of requesting any excuses, nor even hope for them," the Bâbû interrupted good-naturedly. "I don't understand even yet what I did to offend the esteemed Miss B., for whom I have always had regard as for my own mother . . ."

Lightning striking at the feet of the forty-five-year old spinster would not have had as much effect as this innocent word "mother," so good-heartedly uttered by a twenty-year-old boy. Knowing her weakest point, I really became frightened, thinking she would pounce upon the Bâbû like a wild cat. The Ṭhâkur, throwing aside the bridle of his horse, came up a step or two, looking at the angry English woman with a glance even more steady than before.

She grew purple in the face. The veins of her neck were swollen like cords, and she screamed, foaming at the mouth:

"What? *Mother!* . . . Mother . . . You call me . . . You must know, sir," she suddenly added, haughtily straightening herself, "that you have to esteem me not as your mother, but as a member of the *great* nation, which keeps down your de . . . despised ra . . ."

The Ṭhâkur suddenly and rapidly stretched out his hand toward her . . . and uttering incoherent sounds she all at once collapsed like a sheaf cut down, convulsively shaking, and found herself in the arms of Mr. W., to whom Gulâb-Singh had adroitly tossed her falling body.

"Just what I expected and warned her of," quietly and calmly said the Ṭhâkur, bending over her jerking body. "It is sunstroke. Take her into the ladies' room!"

In all of Bhurtpore, and probably in the whole kingdom of the Jâṭs, with a population of about 100,000, there are no European physicians, but only native "ḥakîms" (doctors). To go anywhere that day was unthinkable; and so, having dismissed our carriage until the next morning, we carried the poor Englishwoman into the tiny room of the telegraph operator, in the equally tiny railway station, and tried to bring her round by our own means. But the station had no ice, the first remedy for sunstroke. Remembering the box of whiskey and ice belonging to the blond spy who followed us, we sent Mr. W. to tell his compatriot about our misfortune and ask him to yield to the dying Englishwoman a small portion of his stores until they could bring us ice from Âgra. The spy politely listened to the request and — refused! A piece of ice would not be of much help and he himself might fall ill from the heat . . . Then the Bâbû, whom Miss B. had insulted, had recourse to the last remedy and saved both her and us. With Nârâyaṇa, he ran into the fields and brought back a whole armful of grass called *kusimah.* This grass, acting like nettles, covers the body with an eruption at the slightest touch and forms large blisters. Without explaining this, he asked me to put on my gloves and rub the legs of Miss B. with the *kusimah.* His own hands and face were already swollen with blisters, but he paid not the slightest attention to it. I must confess that I carried out his order with fierce zeal. I somehow hoped . . . *felt* rather, that the Thâkur would not allow such a tragic end as the death of an Englishwoman on our trip. To inflict upon her an unpleasant but healthy itching, however, which would last for some days, was a comforting thought to me. After five minutes of rubbing, the legs of the Englishwoman were covered with blisters, but as a result she opened her eyes and had the satisfaction of seeing (I hoped so at least) "the son of the despised race" nursing her. The Bâbû, however, did not confine himself to this; while Mr. W., her compatriot, snored in the neighboring room under the pretext of being tired and not feeling well, the little Bengalî did not leave her for an instant. He was the one who constantly changed the packs of ice over her head, the ice which we received towards evening by telegraphing for it to Âgra, and left her only next morning after an English doctor had arrived by the first train.

Having heard of the strange remedy of the Bâbû, the doctor muttered something to himself and then declared that even the *kusimah* can be useful as a remedy to draw the blood from the head. Ordering his patient to be taken back to Âgra and later, as she grew better, back to Bombay, he took from us 50 rupees and went to his luncheon, while waiting for the next train; *en passant* he asked Mr. W. to see to it that the "niggers" should not bother him. Mr. W., feeling my eyes fixed upon him, blushed but promised the doctor to accede to his request, and made no further remark. He had to leave with Miss B., as we could not send her alone in such a state and could not leave ourselves without having visited Svâmi Dayânanda.

But let us now return to the events that took place some hours previously. The evening before, after the catastrophe, when the patient had fallen asleep, four of us, the Thâkur, the Colonel, Nârayâna and myself, were sitting together

near the tents which had been pitched for us behind the
little garden at the station. The tents belonged to the
Thâkur; they had somehow suddenly appeared, as though
by magic, and were very odd. Under other circumstances,
their construction would have attracted the attention of
our president, always eager for novelties, as they contained
several rooms, a little corridor around them, a bedroom,
a drawing-room and even a small bathroom, all furnished
with Eastern furniture. But at this moment he was much
too excited. He was preoccupied by one single thought—his
duties and responsibilities as president of the Society and
the realization that there had been a quarrel in our party,
and that one of its members, no matter how guilty, was in
danger of death. The uncertainty of the future and the
sincere grief about the actual impossibility of creating peace
between the two elements of the Society under his direction
and care, as antagonistic to each other as are the haughty
English and the natives, acting upon each other like water
and fire, producing steam at the least contact, gave him no
rest. He was pacing up and down, the poor Colonel, under
the cover of the central tent, in a state of great anxiety;
the Thâkur, calm and undisturbed as ever, sat on the carpet
smoking at the entrance of the tent. Finally, in despair, the
Colonel began a monologue.

"No doubt, Miss B. is an awful, an awful woman—an
egotist and as excitable as . . . as . . . a Mexican mare! . . . ,"
he cut short, not finding a better simile. "All that is true.
Besides she is English, haughty and starched like her own
petticoats, ready to burst at any moment like the frog in
the fable, from personal pride and national conceit! . . .
In other words, she is plain silly! . . . However, she is a
Fellow of our Society! . . . Isn't that so?" he ended by
addressing me.

"As long as she remains a Fellow of our Society there
won't be much sense in it," I answered, "as she does not
keep the statutes herself and confuses others."

"She is nevertheless a useful Fellow of the Society," retorted the Colonel, "useful precisely because she is English
and a patriot. She and Mr. W. are our defense . . . a sort
of living protest against, for instance, that idiot over there

ELLORA CAVES: KAILÁSA TEMPLE

DIVÁN-I-KHÁS AT DÍGH

in his white uniform, who is now drinking his twentieth *peg**
on the verandah and mistakes us for spies, like himself . . .
If she dies, what shall we do?"

"Don't worry, Colonel, she will not die," casually remarked
the Ṭhâkur.

"She won't! . . . Do you vouch for it, my dear Ṭhâkur?"
exclaimed the American joyfully.

"To vouch for the life or death of a sick person would
be too daring on my part, not being a doctor," replied the
Râjput, laughing. "But judging by many years of experience,
if she lived through the first half-hour and no symptoms of
some other illness appear to complicate the sunstroke, the
main danger can be considered passed."

"And you . . . pardon me, my dear, my highly esteemed
friend, you won't *assail her with other similar symptoms?*"
asked the Colonel, mysteriously looking around and bending
low over the Ṭhâkur.

I was sitting on the other side, leaning against a post,
silently listening. The words of the President made me
shudder; they seemed to be an echo of my own unexpressed
thoughts and deeply buried feelings, a faithful echo at that.
Nârâyaṇa, with an extinguished *bîrî*† in his mouth, stood
next to Gulâb-Singh. I saw a shadow cross his face, and he
swiftly looked at the Colonel. In this glance I clearly read
anger and a silent reproach for the insolent question.

In the deep, dark and abysmally enigmatic eyes of the
Ṭhâkur, I did not now catch that burning, sudden flash
of light which, like lightning behind the clouds, lit them
up when Miss B. made a silly and offensive remark about
the natives; I did not see in them this time that spark,
which I must confess always frightened me, arousing in me
a feeling of supernatural fear, a feeling of which I was
ashamed, but which I could not overcome. Now his look
was quite calm and indifferent; he merely smiled somewhat
ironically . . .

"In other words, your question is a direct accusation that

---

*Whiskey and soda with ice.

†*Bîrî* is a small native cigar made of the green leaves of the mango
tree.

it was I who made her ill in the first place?" he asked the
Colonel, looking straight into his eyes.

The Colonel blushed, but did not attempt a useless denial.
He frankly looked with his somewhat blind but honest eyes
at the Ṭhâkur and haltingly confessed:

"Yes, it is thus that I understood this unfortunate event
. . . But you must not call it an accusation."

"Hm! It can't be said, however, that such a suspicion is
especially flattering," the Râjput added smilingly, after a
short silence, looking into the distance. "Avenging yourself
upon a woman for her silly language by threatening her with
death is even less a habit of the *robber* tribes of Râjasthân,
than of the civilized Europeans. But I cannot condemn you
for such a thought, for knowing that you had arrived at an
exaggerated idea of my . . . psychological powers, I had
nevertheless left you to draw your own conclusions and
deductions . . . You are right in your own way."

The American lifted his clear blue eyes and, thoughfully
stroking his beard, meekly remarked:

"We came to India across a distance of 10,000 miles to
study psychology and all that relates to the *spiritual* being
of man . . . and . . . in compliance with your call. We chose
you as our *guru* (teacher), and now that we have discovered
in you alone the embodiment of the 'secret science,' will
you turn away from us?"

There was a very sad note in the voice of our president.
The Ṭhâkur quickly looked up at him and, after a pause,
answered quite calmly and even kindly: "It is true that
I have been initiated in that which is known to us as
gupta-vidyâ—secret science . . ."

"These sciences are then known to you? You have finally
decided to acknowledge this to us, your ignorant but wholly
devoted disciples?"

"I never tried to make a secret of it and could not have
done so even if I wanted to. I am a *brahmachârin.** But this
term and the one of 'secret sciences' often mean a great

---

*A kind of lay monk, consecrated from birth to celibacy and to the
study of the *siddhis* — the science of theurgy or white magic and
wonder-working.

deal, and their meaning is very elastic. Many thousands of years have elapsed since the glorious days of the Rishis; India has fallen and degenerated," he added sadly. "Now you will find *brahmachârins* in every large city who substitute for a legal wife not permitted to them by caste rule a secret harem — the *zenânâ* — and who are usurers; you will often meet charlatans preparing and selling love potions in the name of the 'secret sciences'! Would you try to chase after these also and honor them for their name only? . . ."

I could not help looking at the Colonel, and we both felt embarrassed. Before we left Bombay, after great precautions and persistent requests, a certain great *sâdhu* (saint) and alchemist, as he was represented to us by Mûljî and others, was brought to us. The "saintly" anchorite emitted a most offensive odor and made all sorts of strange noises with his mouth and nose, but all of this was ascribed by the Colonel to his renunciation of all earthly interests, as well as to his saintliness. Having received from us, including the "silent general," several hundred rupees with the promise of transforming them into an "elixir of life" and a protective powder against all ills, and having publicly accepted signs of servile devotion on the part of the Colonel (this time with the rightful indignation of the Englishwoman), the saintly old man left us for his unknown retreat; *en nous disant: «je reviendrai! . . .»* as runs the line in the *Favorite*.* We are still waiting . . .

"What are the 'secret sciences'?" continued the Thâkur, turning our attention from this unpleasant memory. "To me and to all those who have dedicated their lives to them, these secret sciences contain the key to all nature's places of concealment and to the worlds both seen and unseen. This key, however, is much more difficult to discover than you may think. *Gupta-vidyâ* is a two-edged weapon and you cannot approach it without at the very outset sacrificing all earthly things, nay, even reason itself, as she overwhelms and destroys anyone who does not succeed in subduing her. Ancient fables are not built on imagination alone. In our

* [*La Favorita*, an Italian Opera (1840) by Donizetti. —*Compiler.*]

antediluvian Âryâvarta you will also find the Sphinx, similar to the Egyptian one, and for every single Oedipus there are thousands of victims. This science is especially dangerous to you, Europeans and whites. That is why I hesitate to accede to your determined but foolish desire even to try a period of probation."

"Thâkur, for the sake of all that is dear to you," exclaimed our president in an imploring voice, "I beg you in the name of our entire Society, in the name of science and the whole of humanity! . . . You know that I am not a coward. I do not set a high value on life, and if even towards its end I do not catch a glimpse of the truth, well then . . . the sooner this end comes . . . the better! . . . If you but once show me the path that leads to truth, I swear never to betray it . . ."

The Thâkur's reply was slow in coming.

"All right," said he suddenly, to the great joy of the Colonel, "now that you probably will be free tomorrow from your two English people, I will invite you to my own estate at D. You have two weeks left before your trip to Svâmi Dayânanda. At home I will subject you, Colonel, to a small preliminary test. If you are successful, you will be my *chela* for seven years. If not — well, then everything will remain as of old. Do you consent?"

"With pleasure, with pleasure," exclaimed our Colonel joyously. "And you will see, Thâkur, that I will not fail in any test."

At the end of this talk, the Thâkur asked me to go to ascertain the condition of Miss B. The other three, namely, Gulâb-Singh, the Colonel and Nârâyana locked themselves in the tent. When I returned an hour and a half later, two bodyguards were marching up and down in front of the closed entrance, and three others were lying motionless across the entrance. In going to my own tent in the darkness, I nearly bumped into the blond spy, recognizing him rather by his strong breath of liquor than by his dress or figure. He evidently was trying to listen to what was going on, and quickly disappeared into the darkness on my arrival.

An hour later somebody knocked at my door. I had not yet retired, having intended to go once more to our unfortunate Miss B. Hearing the knock, I was about to utter the usual "come in," when suddenly, as though out of the ground, there appeared before me two stately and hairy Râjputs who stood at the entrance like statues, leaning on their rifles and looking at me inquiringly. I must confess that this sudden appearance embarrassed and puzzled me. They could not understand me and I could not understand them, and our talk might have thus lasted until morning were it not for the angry voice of our esteemed Colonel heard on the other side of the tent.

"What the devil?" he was shouting, "Do they take me for a leopard, that they do not let me come near the tent! . . . Come out for a moment," he shouted with the clear intention of being heard by me. "Look at what they are doing! . . . What does this mean, are you under arrest or what!"

Like lightning the thought flashed through my head that the English spy, the one I had just seen almost on my doorstep, was mixed up in this business. It was a silly but not an improbable idea, which was, however, instantly dispelled when I started towards the one and only door in reply to the Colonel's call. My hairy Râjputs not only let me pass without opposition, but at my approach prostrated themselves like crabs upon the sand, in sign of submission and devotion, so that I practically had to walk over their heads. As I emerged, I saw a sight which reminded me of certain American ballet scenes, representing a dance of the redskin Indians on the war path. Three other Râjputs, just as heavily armed and just as hairy as the others, with their three crossed swords held in their right hands, and holding in their left hands shields made of rhinoceros hide, were barring the way to the Colonel. Their energetic tactics were accomplished in utter silence and with an expression of complete devotion on their faces. If the Colonel made a step to the left, they would also jump to the left and meet him with their shields; were he to go to the right, they would do the same and again meet him with the impassable wall of their shields. The moment they saw me, they at once put down their arms and stood like statues.

Happy to see me, the Colonel told me that he had some

very important news, and would explain later the strange
conduct of the Râjputs; he was about to enter my tent, when
Nârâyana called him.

"Colonel-Saab," he called out gently, "wait a moment!
Thâkur-Saab has sent me to you."

"What is it? What has happened?" asked the Colonel
inquiringly.

"Mahâ-Saab (the great lord, *Monseigneur*) ordered me
to tell you that you had better not go in to *Bâi-Saab*. We
are in Râjasthân and here ideas about etiquette are different from those in Europe, and even from our own . . . in
Central India. Do not enter; if you do, you will shock them
more than I can tell you . . ."

"But why, who can be shocked? Besides who are these
strange men anyway?"

"These men are sent here by the *Divân* of the Mahârâja
of Bhurtpore; they are bodyguards, a sort of guard of honor
for Madame-Saab," answered Nârâyana. "The whole country will feel shocked. No one can enter a *zenânâ** after
sunset."

"*Zenânâ?* But where did you find a *zenânâ?*"

"The quarters of *Maam-Saab!*"

The Colonel whistled long and loud.

"Hey-dey! Do women of her age still live in *zenânâs?*. . . ,"
he exclaimed, his eyes popping, and bursting into irreverent
laughter. I myself laughed at his frank remark.

"It is not a question of age, Saab," seriously remarked
Nârâyana, "but of esteem for the female sex. The older the
woman, the more she is esteemed by the Râjputs."

"Well, if I should not enter, I won't," good-naturedly
remarked the Colonel. "I nearly suspected them of planning
to rob me and just could not understand why they were
dancing before me! . . . Well, let's walk towards the station
and I will tell you my news on the way. We can also enquire
about Miss B. while there."

"Do you know," he added in a joyful whisper, as soon
as Nâyârana left, "the Thâkur will let me have my first
trial?"

---

*Zenânâ is a "harem," or women's quarters.

"Yes, I know. I was present when he promised it, if you succeed in your first test."

"No, but I mean something else altogether. He has allowed me to try the *Kumbhaka* and *Pûraka* whenever I want to do so."

"Heavens," I exclaimed in horror. "Will you be hanging down and without breathing for hours? You will certainly have a stroke! . . . Have you lost your mind?"

"Why a stroke? All depends on one's will power and that I have never lacked," answered the Colonel, a little hurt.

"Well, do as you like . . . Only be sure he is not making fun of you . . . He simply wants to show you how utterly unfit a European is for the goal of Hindu asceticism . . ."

For the first time since we met, the esteemed American almost picked a quarrel with me over that remark. "You seem to envy me," he kept repeating, in spite of my assurance that I really did not see what there was to envy in hanging head down like a bat; that anyone could hang himself in this fashion if he wished; and, finally, that he was courting trouble and everyone would laugh at him. Nothing worked, my reasons did not convince him. He had come here to study the "secret sciences" and would certainly do so.

"What have you decided now?" I said somewhat angrily. "Do you want to become a fakir painted with cow manure, or a *râja-yogin?* You have either forgotten or simply do not know that the former know as much of *gupta-vidyâ* as yourself, while the real *râja-yogins,* like the Ṭhâkur, do not hang head down and feet up, and do not turn their brains upside down."

The last argument seemingly struck home.

"How is that? Didn't the Ṭhâkur practice the 86 postures prescribed by the 'Yoga' of Patañjali?"*

---

*This philosophical system of asceticism in India is the most difficult to grasp. As in the Chaldean Kabbalah, on the pattern of which Shimon ben-Yohai outlined in the first century A.D. the Hebrew Kabbalah, and in some alchemical treatises, every word in it bears another meaning in accordance with a certain key. It is generally understood that the key is in the exclusive possession of the *râja-yogins,* and the Brâhmaṇas do not have the slightest idea as to the real meaning of these teachings.

"That would be quite like him, wouldn't it? He who speaks with such contempt about the folly of the *hatha-yogins*, those who follow only the dead letter of Patañjali's teachings and stand for days on their heads, let their toenails grow into the ground, or hang on an iron hook passed through their thigh and the skin of their back, with the hook fastened to a *chakra*,"* I replied, losing my patience.

"Why then does he allow another to do so?"

"He allows it just to get rid of you, as your insistence annoys him; and he probably wants to teach you a lesson . . . Don't get angry, Colonel. Where did you ever see a fakir or even a simple *bairâgin-gosâin* (mendicant monk) with a paunch like yours?"

He was again offended and even grieved.

"I can lose weight; I simply want to prove to him *my will power,* and also to show that Hindus are not the only ones worthy of being initiated into the secret sciences."

"It is not by means of such feats that you will prove that! I know him better than you do. Don't delude yourself with vain hopes! Thank fate for the fact that though both of us belong to the hated and despised 'white race,' he sees better than anyone else the warm devotion we have for him, and, maybe even more on account of our sincere sympathies for his people and respect for his country, makes such an unheard of exception for us. Do not request from him that which he cannot and dares not give, but be satisfied with the crumbs he throws to us along the way."

"But why, tell me why?" insisted the Colonel. "Hasn't he disciples?"

"He has them, but not such as we, children of a rotten civilization, heirs to all the vices of the West. Look at Nârâyana; the poor boy is a mystic and a fanatic by nature; he lives and breathes only for the Thâkur and is ready at

---

*The *chakra* is a thick pole, having four horizontal movable cross planks fastened to it. Around such a pole you can see at times a dozen fakirs hanging on hooks fastened through their flesh, often bleeding. The government has prohibited the public showing of *chakras* at religious meetings, but they still exist in the sacrificial courts of the temples, where the English are not allowed to enter. The fakirs swing around the *chakra* like chunks of raw meat, until they fall off.

the least hint from him to sacrifice 10,000 lives if he had them. But even he will never be admitted as a *chela* in spite of being a native Hindu."

"But how do you know! Did he say so? . . ."

"No, he did not, but I know it for the simple reason that I understand Patañjali better than you do and am not in India for the first time. The unfortunate Nârâyaṇa *cannot become a râja-yogin because he is married.*"

"But he is married so far only nominally; his wife is only 11 years old. It is merely an engagement."

"Has the Ṭhâkur the right to ruin the life of a young and totally innocent being? Is he that kind of man? You forget that if Nârâyaṇa deserts her now, she will be disgraced for the rest of her life. Not alone she, but all her relatives up to the seventh generation will lose their caste . . . She will have her head shaved as a widow and the least contact with her will be *impure.* Her misfortune will at once be accounted for as a sin committed by her in one of her previous lives, and she will not even be cremated after death, but thrown to the jackals."

"Unfortunate young man!" exclaimed the Colonel with sincere sympathy, forgetting for the moment his own grief and not realizing to what extent I had diminished by this example his own chances of success.

"Well, possibly luck will smile upon him . . . she may perhaps die?" he naïvely added.

"Poor little Avani-Bâi!* Aren't you ashamed to wish for her death?"

"I don't wish it at all . . . but anything may happen . . . after all, my only wish is for his good . . ."

He hardly had time to finish the last words, when something quite unusual happened. We were standing in the backyard of the station and were talking nearly in a whisper; the Ṭhâkur's tent was at least 200 feet away. All at once, as though coming out of the thick foliage of a mango tree over our heads, we heard the clear and sonorous voice of

---

Avani means *"stream," "river"; Bâi* means *"sister"* and is added to every woman's name by both Pârsîs and Hindus.

Gulâb-Singh answering the egotistic remark of the president, who stood petrified . . .

"He who would build his own happiness on the misery of another, can never become a *râja-yogin!* . . . ," said the *voice* clearly.

Heard at first right over our heads, the last words of the sentence, as if gradually withdrawing, sounded somewhere in the distance and finally blended with the doleful howl and laugh of the jackals in the far-off fields.

The Colonel ran back as fast as his short stubby legs could carry him towards the tent of the Thâkur, where he found him at supper with Nârâyana and two other Hindus. The Thâkur was about to finish his evening ration of milk, the only food he ever took (as far as we were able to observe in all the weeks of our travel together). To the question of the Colonel as to whether he had just now left the tent, a negative answer was given by all those present. The Thâkur had not left his rug from the time the president had been trying in vain to enter "Bâi-Saab's" tent . . .

"I looked at him as though I were momentarily crazy," the Colonel told me later, "while he sat there, calm and indifferent, as usual, staring at me with his wonderful eyes, as though he were analysing and examining my soul down to its very bottom! . . . And do you know what he said in reply to my exclamation that I *thought* I heard his voice in the station courtyard? 'Quite possible, my dear Colonel. The unseen corridors of eternity and of the boundless space of *Âkâśa* * are full of all the voices of nature — of the past and of the present. It is quite possible that you ran into a congealed wave of my voice and, setting it in motion, evoked an echo in one of these corridors . . . Remember, nothing is ever tracelessly lost in nature; therefore, never mention, *nor even utter in thought* anything you would not care to see later inscribed on the tablets of eternity . . .' The devil take me, if I can understand this living riddle which we all call the Thâkur! Who and what is he? . . ."

---

* *Âkâśa* is the ether of our scientists, and sometimes even more, which cannot be described in our language and for which there is no adequate term as yet in Western metaphysics.

Next day, we placed Miss B., weak but already quarrelsome, in a railway carriage and sent her back to Âgra, accompanied by Mr. W. and the doctor. To the farewell greetings of the Bâbû, who had looked after her and nursed her until morning, she answered with a benevolent but haughty and rather cold bow. She did not shake hands with any of the Hindus; Mr. W., however, shamed by our presence, hurriedly and as if hiding it, shook hands with all of them, except the Thâkur who was not present at this farewell. The doctor lifted his hat slightly, and with an unlighted cigar in his mouth turned to the "silent general" with an implied *order* to get him a light. But he was stunned by the Colonel who, looking boldly at the doctor and at the "spy" who had just made his appearance on the platform, took Mûljî's arm and loudly shouted: "Hey! Who's there? Send a *waiter* here!" Miss B. fell into my arms in tears, and in spite of my rather cold reception, wiped her nose on my blouse for two whole minutes.

Finally the last bell freed us from this unsympathetic element, and we felt as though a mountain had fallen off our shoulders. We were left alone with our Hindus and the Anglo-Indian spy. The latter, however, mysteriously disappeared somewhere the very same day and, as we learned later from the Thâkur, was replaced by Moslem spies until our return to British territory.

In the evening of the same day we left for the capital of the Mahârâja, where we spent the night in the palace of the independent Indian prince. That story, however, and the narrative about our further adventures are yet to come.

End of Part I.

PART II*

— I —

The small dominion of Bhurtpore, at one time a kingdom with its kings and queens, is known only for its Semiramis gardens and its city of Dîgh. Its râjâ is extremely proud of his independence in the presence of his less fortunate brothers, the râjâs of the other states in Râjputâna, forgetting that he owes this independence in reality to the completely

---

*The publication of the Second Part of these letters was begun in 1883. Due to circumstances beyond the control of the author and the editorial office, printing was discontinued after the second press-signature. Having received the sequel of these letters, we resume their publication, not as a continued supplement but as separate articles which eventually in their entirety will constitute the Second Part of the work entitled *From the Caves and Jungles of Hindostan*. The first letter cut short in the middle of the text is reprinted in its entirety for the sake of the continuity of the whole.—EDITOR, *Russkiy Vestnik*.

467

isolated geographical position of his territory. There is neither a Resident, nor any other British official at Bhurtpore, for the simple reason that, gripped in the clutches of Âgra, Jeypore and Alwar, this small state is like a prisoner surrounded by closed ranks of soldiers and has, therefore, been freed of the superfluous sentinel, who would have had to perch himself on the shoulders or head of the captive. In spite of this circumstance, the population, or rather the upper classes (Kshatriyas, the warrior caste) which outnumber the lower, despise, with a pride worthy of the Spanish hidalgo, the Marâthâs and even the Râjputs whom they have now ceased to fear. Utterly ruined by the English, they are content with little and live in their "Kingdom of Peacocks" (so named because in the Bhârata valley alone as many as 6,000 sacred peacocks have been counted) happily and without concern. An active and, at one time, a warlike people, they have since 1826, when Lord Lake* destroyed their capital after taking it by storm, sunk into a kind of comatose condition and literally spend their entire lives in religious festivals and offerings to the gods. Bhurtpore is a nest of bards whose sacred hymns glorify, from morning until night, the heroic deeds of gods and mortals. For this reason, out of seven hundred thousand inhabitants occupying a space about 77 miles long and 50 wide, four hundred thousand *brahmanize,* doing exactly nothing, while three hundred thousand spend their lives dragging water from the lakes of Dîgh to distribute it on their shoulders to irrigate 1,978 square miles. Except for these lakes, which occupy in all but a few miles, there is not a drop of water to be had in the entire dominion.

The Râjâ and ninety-nine percent of the inhabitants are Jâts. This tribe, which at one time composed the overwhelming majority of the population of Râjasthân, are "the aborigines of the scorched plains" stretching along the Indus

---

*[Gerard Lake, first Viscount Lake of Delhi and Leswarree (1744-1808); lieutenant and captain, 1762; major-general, 1790; member of Council of India, 1800; developed military resources of the East India Company, and assisted Wellesley in breaking up the Marâthâ confederacy, 1803.—*Compiler.*]

and its tributaries. Tod asserts, and proves in his own way," * that the Jâṭs are of the same stock and tribe as the Getae, Massagetae and the Jutes of Jutland and, therefore, also the Anglo-Saxon conquerors of England. He even finds "an exceedingly strong family resemblance" in the lower part of the jawbone (*sic*) and, in all probability, the ears, between the white-headed Jutlander, his ruddy cousin John Bull, and the black-as-the-ace-of-spades Jâṭ. There is nothing ingenious in this. Under the despotic decrees of Messrs. Philologists, Ethnologists and Anthropologists, our poor Mother Nature has naught left but to remain silent.

One thing is certain: the Jâṭs are one of the most ancient people of India and, although "aborigines" to the Râjputs who came after them, are not the actual aborigines, but are themselves newcomers in respect to the real aborigines; namely, tribes which are now scattered all over India, hiding in inaccessible mountain gorges, forests and jungles. Their traditions indicate, as does history itself, or more correctly those pages torn to shreds which go under the name of history among us, that the Jâṭs are a tribe whose advance colonies came to India prior to the time of Cyrus from beyond the Himâlayas, probably from beyond the Oxus (the present Amu-Darya). In the fourth century, history finds the Jâṭ Empire in the Pañjâb, but does not state the period of its founding nor does it give any information about the first appearance of the Jâṭs. Tod also wishes to prove their identity with the *Asii* of the Oxus, the tribe which overthrew the Greek Empire in Bactriana.† These very *Asii*, he says, are the ancestral tribe, a branch of which invaded northern Europe and settled, among other places,

---

*See *Journal Asiatique*, Paris, Vol. X, May, 1827, 281-91.
[Ref. is here to Col. Tod's article entitled "De l'origine asiatique de quelques-unes des anciennes tribus de l'Europe, etc."—*Compiler.*]

†The *Asii* (Gr. *Asioi*) are mentioned by Strabo in his *Geography* (Book XI, viii, 2), as the people who took away Bactria from the Greeks. Malte-Brun (originally Malthe-Conrad Brunn) speaks of them as *A-si* or *Ases* of Bukhara; he calls them also *Asiani*. Cf. his *Précis de la géographie universelle*, 4th & rev. ed. by J. J. N. Huot. Paris, 1836-37; Vol. I, Book 17, pp. 460, 468, 469. Mention of them is rarely made by later writers.—*Compiler.*]

in Jutland. Of all the tribes existing today in India, and to which historians wish to attach the Scythians as ancestors, the Jâts are the most likely to fit the hypothesis. The outward appearance of the Scythians, as we find it described by Herodotus, is sharply imprinted upon them. Squat, thickset, hirsute, with strongly developed muscles—this description fits the Jâts as much as it fails to fit the tall, well-shaped Râjputs and Bhîls. It is enough to glance at the purely Greek profiles of the Râjputs to be convinced of the impossibility of deriving Scythians from them. It is just as absurd as unloading the Sikhs of the Pañjâb, the colossi with aquiline noses and a purely European type of face, into the general "Scythian pit" just because, prior to their conversion to monotheism, they used horses as sacrificial victims. According to the general opinion of Orientalists, the Sikhs and Râjputs are among the handsomest types of the human species.

Under the "beneficent rule of England" (a stereotyped expression), a large part of Râjasthân has now mixed within itself pure Râjputs and Jâts, and their *thâkurs* and *zamindârs* enjoy equal rights or, what is perhaps more true, equally do not enjoy any rights outside those of the average landowner and proprietor of his own estate. Public opinion, however, which rarely errs, has dug an impassable chasm between the Thâkurs of Râjput and those of Jât blood. The Jât Thâkur is a feudal baron who plunders by night. The Râjput Thâkur is a knight, *un chevalier sans peur et sans reproche,* in the full sense of the word. In order to appease the former and thus provide itself with faithful allies, the government while forbiding plunder by day, *de jure,* has permitted it *de facto,* having allowed the plunderers, like the Bedouin *sheiks* in Palestine and Syria, to collect indemnity from the incoming caravans and travellers, in order to guarantee the latter full safety from the Bhîls. But the Râjput Thâkurs did not accept a single one of the favors offered them. Ruling and governing almost autocratically a handful of their own subjects, they practically never ride beyond the boundaries of their villages and, frequently, not even beyond those of their castles. Proud and untamable, unable at present to wage war with one another, they have apparently resigned themselves to their fate, and associate only with the Râjâs to whom, like vassals, they are obliged to pay taxes in people and money. With the English they have almost no direct dealing, but in case of need conduct their affairs through the ministers of their suzerain, the Mahârâja.

As elsewhere, the "superior race" of conquerors here played the role of Cains in relation to the innocent Abels. They have shuffled India as though it were a deck of cards so that now a man is a stranger to his kin. What a pity to see this little corner of Bhârata, now known as Bhurtpore, which formerly had flourished under the Râjput, and even the Moslem kings, discarded like a charred piece of mouldy biscuit, in the dust of ancient palaces and temples. As late as the beginning of the present century, there was still a magnificent water supply from the inexhaustible lakes of Dîgh piped through the entire country, and Bhurtpore was considered to be one of the important granaries of India. The country flourished and was green the year round. But, in 1825, the insatiable troops of the East India Company appeared under the leadership of Lords Lake and Combermere.

The city is built in the lowlands, and the waters from *Motî Jhil* (Pearl Lake), the enormous lake now filled-in and non-existent, and which was on a higher level, could at any time upon discretion be let into the fortification ditches, flooding them, and thus making the town impregnable. Since 1805, the English have attempted to take Bhurtpore by storm four times, and each time they have been thrown back with huge losses. For twenty years, every military stratagem, at which the benevolent British are so clever, had been used in order to take possession of the Peacock Kingdom, with its salt lakes and commerce yielding 170,000 pounds sterling annual revenue, but it was only in 1826 that they finally succeeded. According to the accounts of the *Divân,* and particularly of the aged tutor to the Râjâ, the responsibility for the destruction of the city lies on the conscience of its patron, the god Krishna. During the first siege, native soldiers who served in the British ranks swore that they saw Krishna over the city, in the air, "clothed in the yellow robe of an ascetic and armed with his own special accoutrements — a bow, a mace, a conch and a sacred pipe"; as a result of this they ran away. But in 1826, the deity was negligent . . . The superstition of the Jâṭs may be compared only to the superstition of the Dravidians of Southern India. It is a kind of enchanted and bewitched world. To spend several days among the Jâṭs is like reading fairy tales day and night . . . At every step there is a shrine with its particular legend where there are prominently displayed knights and gods with goddesses, always in the roles of good and evil magicians, as in the stories of Perrault, where virtue inevitably triumphs and vice is always punished . . .

"Do you see those demolished fortress walls over there, on the bulwark where that huge tree with golden flowers is growing?" the *Divân's* envoy asked us.

We were approaching the capital of Bhurtpore; in front of us rose mountains of rubbish, debris of the once famous fortifications, and beyond them, in a dirty and oppressive basin, the city spread itself, a collection of half-demolished miserable huts. On the flat terraces of the houses stood ugly idols among which the peacocks strolled pompously, their hundred-eyed tails sparkling in the rays of the setting sun.

"I see it . . . What is there so wonderful about that tree?" asked the Colonel, squinting.

"At present, nothing," answered the official, sighing. "But those golden yellow flowers, those innumerable clusters of fragrant little cups, they are the tears of Krishṇa . . . Seeing that the English had cut off the road to the pond for our engineers, and were crossing the city ditch, the *deva* (god) threw his mace in despair under the feet of the first detachment, and immediately a tree grew up in that place. Then like fine rain, holy tears dropped down onto the tree, and a flower grew from every drop."

"Instead of crying, it would have been better had the god not been negligent, and had then and there twisted the neck of the whole detachment," scoffed the Bâbû through his teeth.

The youthful Râjput riding on horseback near the carriage merely lifted his eyes at the Bâbû. There was a silent reproach in his pitch-black eyes.

"You are a Bengalî and . . . probably a *nâstika?*" * he asked, cutting the Bâbû short.

"Yes and no," replied the Bâbû, a bit embarrassed by the direct question and still more by the fixed stare directed at him by Nârâyana. "I am from Bengal, but belong, or rather *belonged,* to the Chârvâka sect, the Lokâyatikas.† But now," he hastened to add, "I am a Theosophist and am ready to believe what our president commands."

We laughed, endeavoring to turn the frank avowal into a joke. To all appearances, it made a bad impression on his religious comrades. They most likely had not until then known that our thoughtless Bâbû belonged to this sect, which is so despised by other Hindus. Fortunately for him, the Thâkur was absent. After mounting us and sending us off in the custody of his horsemen, he himself, as usual, had vanished.

Bhurtpore is built upon ruins, the last remains of which do not contain even the ashes of the ancient capital founded by the hero Bharata. The present capital is just a century old. As if ashamed of its present miserable appearance, the Mahârâja's castle is hidden amid the ruins of ancient bastions and towers, tightly choked by creepers. It is surrounded on all sides by towers and surviving domes on the flat terraces of the old fortress with its numerous embrasures and, according to the comment of Fergusson, presents "an awful medley of architectural styles," from the Saracen to the Jât.

Nâstika—an atheist.

†The Chârvâka teaching is based on a *Sûtra* (writing) of Brihaspati, and the short *Catechism* of Chârvâka, the Epicurus of India, known as *The Aphorisms of Brihaspati*. The followers of these deny all the *pramânas*—the sources of true knowledge—acknowledging only *pratyaksha* (knowledge by means of the senses alone) and four *Tattwas* (eternal principles), that is, four Elements from the totality of which reason emerges or, rather, animal instinct, which becomes reason only in man. They teach that the soul does not differ from the body, that it develops and dies with it. *Chârvâka-darśana* is the most extremely materialistic school of India.

After going through several ancient arched gateways and half-demolished walls, on the stumps of which sentinels either were fast asleep or smoking *chelum,* we arrived at the castle. The Mahârâja was not there, as he had gone with his retinue upon a pilgrimage to Hardvâr.* For the first time since our arrival in India, we were entering the inhabited palace of a Râjâ and, of course, were expecting to see something magically beautiful. Our disappointment was complete! . . .

It was a huge structure, like all palaces of Râjâs, and quite depressing. Blackened by smoke, with mouldy walls, it had an endless row of galleries, verandahs, towers and turrets, stairways and corridors. Within were nondescript rooms without end, and from the first to the last, from the durbâr "throne" hall to the smallest closet under the eaves, resembled the storeroom of a dealer in antique furniture. There were uncarpeted stone floors everywhere, extremely uneven and most likely unswept since the Râjâ's departure, as every step raised a cloud of dust that made us sneeze and cough. The rooms were cluttered with odds and ends in various states of disrepair; there were rows of armchairs and couches of every variety and era, which once had been gilded but were now bare, and which were upholstered in expensive but faded brocades. On the walls, cheap German cuckoo clocks hung (we counted eight of them in one room!), mechanical pictures of moving boats with music, side by side with enormous and expensive mirrors from the ceiling to the floor. In the library, which was of precious crystal and magnificently carved rosewood, there were some six or seven sixpenny-volumes of a broken set of James' novels. Placed all around, as if on sale, stood lady's full length swinging mirrors, the surface of which, as a result of years of dampness, resembled geographical maps, and distorted our reflections as if making faces at us along the way. This is what we found within the palace of an independent Râjâ!

---

*In India all Râjâs, greater or lesser, make pilgrimages to holy places at least once a year. They ordinarily complete at least part of the journey on foot, dressed in the poor garb of a pilgrim-ascetic, barefooted, and with the symbols of their sect painted on their foreheads.

Having noted, very likely, the absence of any rapture on our candid faces, the bearded Jât who had met us at the porch to show us the *imperial* chambers, intent upon making us change our opinion about the splendor of the palace, escorted us to some *secret* corner room which was visited, as he informed us very confidentially, by all the English *badâ-Sâhibs* (big lords) and praised by them very highly. This room, which he asked the old male servant to unlock with some special secret key, with musical accompaniment, was hung all around with pictures in the French style and of the most illicit subject matter. The Colonel barely restrained himself from giving the Jât a verbal thrashing, and Nârâyana, hardly glancing up, dashed headlong out of the room and relieved his chaste heart by means of a whole stream of words, which we did not understand, but which evidently made a profound impression on the bearded confidant. He became terribly embarrassed and hastened to lock the "secret" room, uttering something in the nature of an apology. We understood but one thing: all the *badâ-Sâhibs*, the *feringhees*, and even the *Maam-Sâhibs*, their ladies, visited this *European* "museum" and invariably laughed merrily. After this shock, however, the bearded fellow hastened to withdraw, leaving us to the care of the old male nurse, or tutor, of the Râjâ.

Everywhere there was the same dirt, dust, lack of taste, desolation and dilapidation. The Mahârâja himself does not occupy his "imperial" chambers; they are intended to captivate the foreign white barbarians. For some time past, he has settled himself with half a dozen wives in the *zenânâ*. Unfortunately, in India neither the Râjâs nor the princes set an example of virtue to their subjects. Excepting the former, the natives from the highest Brâhmana to the lowest *coolie* are strict monogamists, whereas their Mahârâja-sovereigns, to the very last one, adhere to polygamy. These potentates were born and live, so to speak, beyond caste, for the majority of them never had any caste. The grandfather of the *Holkar* of Indore was born a simple shepherd; the *Gwalior* of the Sindhia family is the great-grandson of a footman. In 1714, his great-grandfather Rânâji, the first Sindhia, served as the trusted servant of the peshwa, who took him from a plain peasant family, and in 1782 the natural son of Râṇâji, Sindhia, became Mahârâja of Gwalior. The *Gaekwars* of Baroda, as their very name implies, were cowherds a hundred years ago; the present young Gaekwar—chosen by the government upon the banishment of the unfortunate Malhâr-Rao,* who was charged (and completely unjustly) with attempting to poison Colonel Robert Phayre, the political Resident † —is the son of a simple coolie, a distant relative of Malhâr-Rao, etc. If we are to believe them, the Moslem Râjâs alone, descend, every one of them, from Fâṭimah, the daughter of the Prophet, and their feminine strain, from Mohammed's mare (*sic*), though the method of evolution from the latter has not yet been entirely explained. On the other hand, the Mahârâṇâ of Udaipur, the sovereign of Mewâr in Râjasthân, without exaggeration and with no intention of jest, descends almost from Adam. In any case, the genealogy of this imperial house has been proclaimed by the British government as absolutely correct and legal; and this genealogy indicated Ikshvâku, the son of Manu, the great mythical lawgiver of Âyrâvarta, as the primogenitor of these Mahârâṇâs. Ikshvâku was born over 2225 years B.C. One can bet that in all of Europe not a single family would be found older than this one. *Sûryavaṇśas,* the descendants of the Sun, have the inalienable right, supported by the genealogical tree acknowledged by the English, to disdain the most ancient English families. In due time we shall discuss in more detail these haughty remains of a vanished greatness, which has gone never to return!

"An old curiosity and bric-a-brac shop," muttered the still

---

* [He died in exile at Madras in 1893.—*Compiler.*]

† [Sir Robert Phayre was born January 22, 1820; educated at Shrewsbury; entered the East India Company's service, 1839, in Bombay; took part in the first Afghân war and the Sind campaign, 1843; also in the Persian war, 1857; was Quarter Master General of the Bombay Army in the Mutiny, 1857-68; commanded the Sind frontier force, 1867-72. Resident at Baroda, 1873. His life was attempted by poison in 1874. Commanded a division of the Bombay Army, 1881-86, retiring in 1886. General, 1889. Died Jan. 28, 1897. —*Compiler.*]

angry Colonel, as he glanced around. "But where is Ṭhâkur-Sâhib?" he inquired unexpectedly. "Are we not going to see him any more today? . . . Nârâyaṇa . . . Mûljî! . . . Do you know where the Ṭhâkur is?"

"*Mahâ-Sâhib* (the great lord) never enters the palace of the rulers of Bhurtpore," Nârâyaṇa whispered into our ear. "He went on ahead to Dîgh and awaits us there for *chota-hâziri* (breakfast) tomorrow."

"Hm!" grunted the president, while examining a Chinese porcelain mandarin with a broken nose. "That means the evening is lost. Do you know, my dear Nârâyaṇa, why Ṭhâkur-Sâhib avoids the dwelling of the local Râjâ?"

The Marâṭhâ noticeably became perplexed.

"I do not have the right, Colonel, to meddle in . . . and discuss . . . the private affairs, particularly the actions, of the *Mahâ-Sâhib*," he finally answered, falteringly.

But the Colonel's curiosity was not of the kind which could be stopped by a reprimand. He turned to the Râjâ's old tutor, who was creeping along behind us surrounded by janitors with bunches of keys, and repeated the question to the old man. The old Jâṭ, upon hearing it, suddenly became even more troubled than Nârâyaṇa.

At first he was completely lost. Then he started bowing servilely and assuring the Colonel that he, an American *Sâhib*, was the "protector of the poor" and "the benefactor of widows and orphans." After this he cleverly avoided the direct question as if suddenly realizing that the sun had already set, and it would get dark immediately. It ended with his escorting us to our quarters, instead of answering the question. The Colonel was left high and dry.

We were put up in a huge separate wing connected to the main building by a covered terrace, directly from the roof of our quarters. Our rooms, though less encumbered with furniture, were nonetheless in an inconceivable state of disorder. Here too, as inside the palace, was a jumble of the most varied decorations. Potbellied armchairs with uncomfortable backs, which in all probability had been brought from England by the defunct Company, seemed to withdraw and stand aside, like thoroughbred Englishmen "of the

superior race," from cleverly carved chairs of dark wood,
the work of "the inferior race." Blades of grass were growing out of the deep dirt-and-dust-filled crevices of the
broken-down billiard table. Console tables with cracked
marble slabs on gilded crystal legs supported expensive
antique mirrors which had grown askew with time. The
walls were covered with life-sized oil portaits of Râjâs,
next to which hung cheap wood-engravings of English
manufacture depicting hunting scenes with lords and ladies
mounted on crimson horses, accompanied by pale-pink and
green dogs running after them. On a partition between the
corners of the dining room, beneath another wood engraving
of French character, representing a skating tournament of
ladies with noses hidden in muffs, oversized calves, and shod
in light blue boots, were about two dozen pictures of the
so-called work of Delhi, carelessly leaning against the wall.
On heavy parchment with gold inscriptions in Urdu —
evidently the legends concerning the subject matter — and
with verses from the *Qur'ân,* they portrayed various historical *durbârs* of Mogul and Indian Râjâs and sovereigns.
On one of them, about a yard square in size, there were
some 80 human figures represented. With the exception of
a small figure in a light blue uniform, epaulettes, and sport-
ing a red moustache, all of them stood obediently with arms
folded against the chest and bodies bent in the direction
of some Râjâ seated upon a throne. The eyes were dazzled
by one single look at this group painted in most glaring
colors and, like all Eastern productions, without any shadows
and without priming. The room was lit by a single large
suspended copper lamp; the flame of the wick, which was
immersed in the most primitive manner right into the coconut oil, was fanned in all directions by a draft coming
through the apertures and openwork doors and illumined
the objects very dimly. Neither the Colonel nor I paid attention to this picture, half-pulled out from behind the
other pictures of *durbârs* and hunting scenes that were
standing upside down.

It was obvious that efforts were made to receive and entertain us in European fashion. The dinner table was found
to be in the possession of a whole colony of red ants, and

as it proved to be impossible to get rid of them without accidentally killing some, a crime according to the laws of Manu, and which the Jât tutor hesitated perpetrating, another table was brought in for us. The marble table of magnificent mosaic work atop three partly broken gilded legs immediately collapsed under the weight of a whole pile of plates, to the horror of the servant-tutor, who saw in this fall an obvious omen of someone's sudden death. To the unconcealed disgust of our Hindus, we were brought a basketful of French wines and liqueurs, and to the indescribable astonishment of the old Jât tutor, the merry-making beverages were immediately banished with shame by the Colonel. The teacher could not understand how the *feringhee-Sâhibs* could refuse the wine and vodka. His amazement knew no bounds when, to complete the eccentricity which obviously appeared as wild folly to him, we asked him to let us eat dinner in the native fashion, seated on pillows and with plane tree leaves in place of dishes and plates . . .

It was only eight o'clock in the evening when, after having finished our meal on the floor in the questionably pleasant company of two huge centipedes, which hid themselves from our pursuit in the bedroom prepared for me, we began to drag, with all possible caution, several of the shaky armchairs onto the verandah, where we finally sat down intending to breathe in the evening air after a sultry day. Our group was soon joined by two visitors, the *Divân's* assistant or secretary, who had escorted us from the station in the morning, and a most corpulent Bengalî Bâbû who was the school inspector for the Mahârâja, the only people in Bhurtpore who spoke English. The Colonel overwhelmed them with questions. Within an hour, we knew no less than they did of the inside gossip of the Mahârâja and the Peacock Kingdom.

Among other bits of historical information, we learned that the present Râjâ, who is claimed by the English to be the real, lawful heir to the throne, is, in the eyes of his subjects, an usurper, though not he but the government is blamed for this crime. In 1825, upon the death of Baldeo-Singh, the *râj,* according to the law, was supposed to go to his brother, Durjan-Sâl; first, because the sons of Râjâs cannot be their heirs and ascend the throne only for lack of brothers and nephews (sons of sisters but not of brothers) and, second, because the deceased Râjâ had only one son and that one was illegitimate. Durjan-Sâl had a large party and the *Laws of Manu* backing him, but the East India Company had soldiers with cannons and the rights of the cleverest if not the strongest. Furthermore, then as now, John Bull insisted on his right to be the universal defender of the weak and the innocent and, under the pretext of being the protector, to devour the weak and the innocent together with their kingdom. Uninvited guardians appeared here also. Their policy consists in allowing power only to those Râjâs who have been educated solely by them, according to the wise pattern of Metternich in relation to Napoleon II, the unfortunate imperial prince. Like the Duke of Reichstadt, all these Indian Râjâs perish *à la* Marquis de Sade, thanks to their English tutors, who from the very first day lead them inconspicuously down the path of early ruin via debauchery and drunkenness.*

Thus, notwithstanding the fact that Durjan-Sâl had already been enthroned by the choice of the people, there appeared in 1826, without any obvious reason, an army of 20,000 men and 112 cannons to save the illegitimate prince, who was a minor. The army was repulsed with great losses, it is said, "by the god Kṛishṇa himself and the sacred pea-

---

*The young Râjâ of Cooch-Behâr, whom I meet every summer at Simla, Darjeeling, and in the Mysore Hills, has now become a pureblooded Englishman. He drinks champagne by the barrelful; presents valuable bracelets, necklaces, and brooches to all the *belles de la saison*—the *Maam-Sâhib* and *Missy-Bibi*—who greatly honor him by waltzing with him; and is ruining himself through sports and revelry. He does all this not only with the consent but with the approval of his tutor, Colonel X., who never leaves him, and the Râjâ is not yet twenty years old! Even youthful maidens are not ashamed of accepting expensive gifts from him! It is obvious what kind of an administrator the Râjâ of Cooch-Behâr will be. Should he crack his head or become devilishly drunk, then the benevolent ruling fathers will, first, take the entire management of the kingdom into their hands under the pretext that they are the lawful guardians and, afterwards, secretly *annex* it. Everything is in order, and all proprieties have been observed.

cocks of Sarasvatî," twenty thousand of which descended upon the army, perched upon the soldiers' heads, and started recklessly to peck out their eyes. That time the English failed to take the city by storm. But they returned in a month and (I translate the words of the Bhurtpore Chronicles) "taking advantage of the fact that Krishna was at the time performing *tapas*," * or more likely, due to the swiftness of their action, the army blocked the Râjâ's engineers from the safe road to the pond, as already stated above, and then slaughtered some 9,000 innocent inhabitants, according to the testimony of the narrators. After this, the English caught Râjâ Durjan-Sâl, who was fleeing with his wives and two sons, and banished the unfortunate prince to Benares, magnanimously allotting him 50 pounds sterling (500 rupees) a month for maintenance. The Râjâ died in 1851, leaving two sons and a countless number of grandsons. The miserable pension was divided among the sons and the Mahârânî-mother. The descendants of Baldeo-Singh have one by one died, which has been very advantageous for the government.

I shall now allow myself a slight digression and run ahead of the story for a moment, for the sake of clarity.

In 1880, at the time of our sojourn in Benares, we became acquainted with the Râjâ's sole surviving grandson. All the rest had died of starvation. The visiting-card that was sent us read:

"*Râo Krishna Deva Sûrya Singh. Grandson of the Mahârâja of Bhurtpore.*"

Râo Krishna proved to be a highly educated and handsome young man. Furthermore, we immediately recalled at the time that he was the hero of a mysterious, though highly improbable, story which had been told us at Bhurtpore by our two visitors, and which I now relate.

His father, son of the banished Râjâ, while dying from starvation (the pension had conveniently ceased, because of the insurrection of 1857), had studied photography and supported himself by taking pictures of pilgrims on the holy

---

*Religious meditation enjoined for all gods and men; self-immersion in Brahman, who resides in the heart of every mortal.

banks of the Ganges, and scenes of various temples. He did
not have the means to pay for the education of his only son
and the government refused to help. Religious to the point
of fanaticism, he departed one fine evening—the day of a
lunar eclipse, a most important holiday for Hindus—for
the temple of his patron, Krishna. Despite the neglect
shown by the *Avatâra* of Vishnu to the capital of his father's
former kingdom, he had not ceased to make sacrificial
offerings to Krishna whenever he could. That evening,
the pockets and the stomach of the ill-fated son of the
Mahârâja were both empty. Squatting on his heels before
the idol and fingering his rosary, he fell asleep from grief.
Some learned materialists and physiologists have expressed
the opinion that visions appear to mortals only upon a tightly stuffed stomach, but this time there was an exception in
favor of the starving one. The youthful god appeared to
him in a dream and, pointing to the dense tree in the garden
of the miserable hut occupied by the Râjâ, said to him:
"Dig under that tree at the time of every full moon and, as
long as you remain faithful to me, you will find 1,000 silver
rupees every month on the south side of it." Awakening and
realizing that it was full moon that very night, the prince-
photographer entered his home, armed himself with a spade,
and started digging. Krishna had kept his word and a
thousand rupees were found. Then, in a burst of gratitude,
the prince vowed to make a yearly pilgrimage with his son
to a well-known shrine near Hardvâr, in honor of the
favorite god of gopîs (shepherdesses). The following month
at the full moon, the same thing occurred — a thousand
rupees were found under the tree. His only son, Râo
Krishna (the latter name had been added to the first by
the father, in gratitude to the divine patron), was only eight
or nine years of age. Every month the god Krishna placed a
bag of rupees under the tree, and every year the father and
his son made a pilgrimage to the distant temple, barefooted,
staff in hand, and in the full raiment of Indian ascetics —
namely, the light and primitive attire of Adam.

And now I ask the reader to get ready for the incredible
story alluded to above. In spite of their improbable character, such stories are very common among the two hundred

and fifty million native population of India, and there is nothing incredible about them to the natives.

When Râo Krishna had reached his fourteenth birthday, his father, as usual, took him on the annual pilgrimage. That year a violent cholera raged among the pilgrims, killing its victims in less than an hour. They died in swarms like flies along the road. In the glade of a Deodâr forest, the youthful Râo also fell ill. The father, terrified and desperate, observed that the boy was dying. Other pilgrims and *sannyâsins* walking with them noticed this also and immediately dispersed, in order not to become defiled by contact with the corpse if they rendered aid. There remained but a group of worshippers who watched from a distance. It was they who spread the news all over India of what took place right before their eyes.

The lad died and the father's cries of despair and helpless grief filled the whole forest. He implored his comrade-pilgrims at least to help him erect the funeral pyre for the cremation of the corpse. Finally, two of them decided to suffer defilement and approached. The boy lay blue and completely dead. All the rites prescribed by Manu were performed over him. Several hours went by, the pyre was ready, and all that remained to be done was to lay the dead body on it. Suddenly, the pilgrims saw a new and, to them, utterly strange individual who had appeared from no one knew where. He was an aged ascetic over a hundred years old. The sacred triple cord over his shoulder indicated that he was a Brâhmaṇa, and the painted black and white mark on his forehead, showed that he belonged to the Vedânta sect called *Advaita*.* Quietly and barely shuffling his feet, he approached the corpse which lay at one side, and, bending over the face of the deceased, he stared at him a long time without touching the body. The father and other pilgrims, seeing the triple cord, dared not draw near but watched the silent scene from a distance. Furthermore, the

---

*The *Advaita* (non-dualist) sect is opposed to the *Dvaita* (dualist). They do not acknowledge gods, but Parabrahman alone, the universal divine essence, which on account of its omnipresence is indistinguishable from the essence of the spirit of man.

old father was so grief-stricken that he probably would have paid no attention to the man, had not something very strange happened. The ascetic, who up to then had stood motionless, began to sway little by little and to bend lower and lower towards the deceased. Two or three seconds more, and the pilgrims saw the decrepit body quiver and the legs give way . . . Falling suddenly to the ground with a thud, the aged man, like a cut sheaf, lay stretched beside the dead youth and . . . at that very moment, the latter raised his arms, sat up, looked about him wildly, and to the horror of the pilgrims, silently beckoned them to him with his hand . . .

After the first minute of confusion and terror had passed, the father rushed forward with a cry of joy to his resurrected son, and the other pilgrims approached also. Upon examining the body of the ascetic, they found it to be stiff and dead. But strangest of all was the fact that he appeared to have died several hours previously. His body showed all the symptoms of cholera — the black spots, the swelling and contorted limbs. The body of the youth, however, which had seemingly begun to decompose but a short while before, was free of all these symptoms — which had vanished without leaving a trace. His body was clean and appeared perfectly healthy. It was as though the old man and the youth had exchanged organisms . . .

The moral and explanation of this are as follows: everything in the world is *mâyâ*, illusion, and we should not believe even in death. The Hindus are deeply convinced of the secret power of *mantras* and *mantrikas* (prayers of exorcism and exorcists) and also of the ability possessed by the adepts of the secret sciences to occupy, in case of need, and without ceremony, the bodies of other people during the sound sleep, the illness or even the death of the latter. Thus, they explain the incident with Râo Krishna to the effect that the aged ascetic was tired of dwelling in his own decrepit and frail body. Besides, he was probably touched by the despair of the bereaved father. Because of this twofold reason, and assuring himself that the boy was dead, the revered ascetic recited a *mantra*, oozed out of his own skin and entered into the body of the deceased which, by so doing, he revived. Thus "everyone won, both sides were satisfied, and no one was the loser."

"What do you mean, no one was the loser?" we argued with the narrators. "The boy kept a live body or, rather, the decrepit old man obtained for himself a new one, but Râo Krishṇa certainly lost his spiritual personality, the individuality of his immortal soul!"

"A very faulty reasoning," the Vedântists answered us then as they did later. "The belief in the individuality of our spirit and in its own personal identity is, of all the delusions, the strongest and the most dangerous one. According to us, it is a terrible *heresy*. The immortal spirit in man is not separated from the Universal Spirit."

"Then, according to you, Parabrahman dwells in me also?" I asked them.

"It is not It in you but, so to speak, you in It that has eternal being, and your spirit (*âtman*) is in no way different from the spirit of another human being . . . But the soul, the seat of your own personal intelligence, is, of course, yours."

"Thanks for that much . . . Doesn't it add up to the same thing?"

"Of course it isn't the same! You see, the soul (*manas*, or the vital soul) cannot be immortal like the spirit. Spirit is a part of the divine, uncreated Parabrahman, without beginning or end, but mind, having a beginning, must also have an end. *Manas* is born, develops and dies; hence it cannot be immortal. For example: take with your hands some drops of water from the ocean, press them together in the palm of your hand, and let the person next to you do likewise. These hands are completely distinct one from the other; one is white, the other is dark brown; neither the one nor the other is immortal, for sooner or later they will both revert to dust, while the water in both palms, being from the one limitless, infinite ocean, the personification in our case of Parabrahman, must return in one or another aspect to its primary source, to the one *Paramâtman* (the highest universal soul) . . . Do you understand?"

"I understand exactly nothing, but that doesn't mean

much. You keep on believing for your health's sake, but I shall wait a while."

Thus our Hindu-theosophists taught us, in support of the narrated story. This, however, is the teaching of Vedântists who are the followers of Śaṃkarâchârya, the greatest adept and yogin of southern India. The Dvaitas, Viśishṭadvaitas and Brahmos reject the above and believe in a divine personality, *Íśvara,* distinct from the human soul.

In those days of our early travels, we were not yet familiar with this doctrine nor with the event or even with its hero, who is the first to deny its veracity, though he remembers his so-called death. We, therefore, reacted with much doubt to the story and thus greatly offended our friends.

"This obviously is freethinking," they reproached us in chorus. "Such *facts* are known all over India, and there have been many, many such *historically* known cases. The great Śaṃkarâchârya himself, the expounder of the Vedânta, several times in his life inhabited the bodies of Râjâs in order to correct their wrongs and help the people. Recall his argument with the goddess Sarasvatî."

To assure us of the truthfulness of the narrated event, they told us the following from the biography of the great *achârya* (teacher).

In the *Śaṃkaradigvijaya* by Mâdhava (VIII, 34), there is a story about how he outwitted Sarasvatî, the goddess of secret sciences and wisdom. Once in the form of an ordinary mortal, the goddess entered into a scholarly dispute with Śaṃkarâchârya. She wished to prove to him that there were in the world facts about which even he did not know. Having received satisfactory answers to questions on a variety of subjects of learning, Sarasvatî suddenly nonplussed him by demanding a definition of the *science of love,* about which Śaṃkarâchârya, as an ascetic and yogin from the age of eight, could, of course. know nothing. Then, so as not to disgrace himself before the witnesses, Śaṃkarâchârya asked for a postponement of one month. The goddess, convinced that no *sannyâsin* dedicated to celibacy and chastity was in a position to answer her questions, agreed to the postponement and celebrated her victory in advance.

LUCKNOW: THE GREAT IMÁMBÁRAH

TEMPLE AT BHUVANEŚVAR

But the great commentator on the *Upanishads** called to his aid *Jñâna-Kânda*. This *Kânda* is the secret science or the correct understanding of the *Vedas,* something accessible only to a very few select ones (*râjâ-yogins*), while *Karma-Kânda* is that teaching of the *Vedas* which is available to the ignorant majority, who are incapable of receiving truth other than through exterior ritualism and the crude worship of form and the dead letter. Thus with the aid of *Jñâna-Kânda,* Samkarâchârya won the day. He departed immediately with his disciples for the Eastern part of Amrita-pura, where Râjâ Amâraka had just died and, after mingling with the crowd of grieving courtiers, decided upon the most practical course of action in the situation. One had only to glance at the beautiful body of the deceased and to see the despair of his ninety-nine wives, to be convinced that the Râjâ had been a master in the *science of love.* After having entrusted his disciples with the care of his own body, temporarily to be abandoned, Samkarâchârya (or rather his soul) slipped out of his "sheaths"† and entered into the lifeless *sheaths* of the Râjâ. The illusion of resurrection was complete. In one month Samkara-râjâ had learned the "science of love" to perfection, and not only had he learned it, but he wrote an excellent treatise on it in two parts. In the first part, he describes love in most brilliant colors and eulogizes the attraction of this illusion in *ślokas* (verses) as ardent as they are erudite; in the second, all the arguments, all the brilliant sophistry of the first are demolished and shattered to dust by the author. He annihilates the arguments of his first dissertation and points to the bitter fruit born of the

---

* The *Upanishads,* the third subdivision of the *Vedas,* are also called *Rahasya,* or mystical teaching. It is necessary to have the key to the secret meaning in order to understand perfectly these metaphysical conceptions of the mind of man. As correctly remarked by Professor Monier-Williams, the *Upanishads* are the only religious school worthy of the profound thinkers of India. They are the sacred books of all the educated natives. The Commentaries on the *Upanishads* by Samkarâchârya are the foundation stone of the *Vedânta* (*i.e.,* "the crowning or end of all earthly knowledge").

† *Kośa* (sheath) is a term used by the Vedântists when they speak of the body of flesh.

attractive flower of the insidious "tree of love." Under the
wise government of Râjâ-Śaṃkara in the "sheaths" of Râjâ
Amâraka, the people were happy; the cunning Brâhmaṇas
however, familiar with *Jñâna-Kânḍa,* suspecting the truth,
and wishing to take advantage in every way, and as long as
possible, of the government of such a wise man, resorted to
craftiness. In order to obstruct the return to his own body
of the one who possessed the body of the deceased and apparently resurrected king, they issued a secret edict ordering
the immediate *cremation of every dead body found in their
land.* In this manner, acting without the knowledge of the
king, they figured that the body of the adept whom they
did not know, the *râjâ-yogin* who so timely inhabited the
corpse of their former handsome but stupid Râjâ, would
perish also. The "sheaths" of Śaṃkarâchârya, though under
the faithful protection of his disciples, were found, and the
body was thrown on the funeral pyre which had been prepared. However, thanks to *Yoga-Vidyâ,* Śaṃkarâchârya felt
at once that something was wrong with his rightful "sheaths,"
and immediately perceived that they intended to force him
to remain in the body of the Râjâ. So without delay, he
slipped out of the *kośa* which did not belong to him and,
now leaving the Râjâ's empty hull to its inevitable fate,
returned to his own body, which he found already surrounded by flames. It was only because of its surrounding
coat-of-mail, so to say, made of incombustible, though invisible, material, that it was not consumed. Upon returning to Benares, he astounded even the goddess of the secret
wisdom, Sarasvatî, with his profound knowledge concerning the "science of love." She acknowledged herself defeated
and declared Śaṃkarâchârya a great *Ṛishi* (sage and saint).

It is understandable that if the most sacred of the Hindu
Śâstras and *Purânas* (ancient traditions), and even the
Upanishads, which are considered by the Brâhmaṇas to be
divine revelation, are full of such stories about the soul
slipping out of one body into another, it would be unjust
to accuse the Hindus, even the most educated among them,
of superstition. For the belief in such miracles is natural
and sacred, and I cited this episode from the life of Śaṃkarâchârya, acknowledged by the Orientalists as one of

the most remarkable philosophers of India, as an example justifying the native belief in what *we* look upon as stupid superstition. Here the religious feelings of both Hundus and Râjputs are offended at every step. Their sacred *pîpal*, the refuge for pure spirits, falls daily under the axe of the English planter; the peacock, the bird consecrated to Krishna, is shot under the very nose of the natives, with equally cool indifference as if it were a crow. The English do not, and do not wish, to understand that every blow of the axe and every bullet leaves a mark in the heart of the devout Hindu, widening more with every hour that abyss of hatred in the soul of the defenceless native, which the English themselves have dug with their own hands. To what extent the English are aware of this, is easily discernible in their own statements:

He is unphilosophical and unwise who treats such prejudices with contumely: prejudices beyond the reach of reason. He is uncharitable who does not respect them; impolitic, who does not use every means to prevent such offence by ignorance or levity. It is an abuse of our strength, and an ungenerous advantage over their weakness. Let us recollect who are the guardians of these fanes of Bal, his *pipal*, and his sacred bird (the peacock); the children of Sûrya and Chandra [the sun and moon], and the descendants of the sages of yore, they who fill the ranks of our army and are attentive, though silent, observers of all of our actions: the most attached, the most faithful and the most obedient of mankind! Let us maintain them in duty, obedience and attachment, by respecting their prejudices and conciliating their pride . . . . Let the question be put to the unprejudiced whether their welfare has advanced in proportion to the dominion they have conquered for us,* or if it has not been in the inverse ratio of this

---

*However strange such an admission may sound, it remains and will remain a fact: "the conquerors of India" are not the English, but the Hindus. Recently, the Bengalîs, at the point of raging despair as a result of the daily unbearable insults both in print and deed, published a pamphlet addressed to the newspaper *Englishman* (Calcutta), in which they refute, point by point, the *imaginary* conquest of India by the English and call it "boasting," proving this with official reports and the correspondence of the Anglo-Indian Government with the *Foreign Office*. The pamphlet was issued under the title of *Our Conquerors, Who Are They?* Refuting the loud assertion that "we belong to the higher race of conquerors and will not allow the Government to subordinate us to the jurisdiction of people who belong to

prosperity . . . . . For the good of ruler and servant, let these be rectified. With the utmost solemnity I aver, I have but the welfare of all at heart in these observations. I loved the service, I loved the native soldier. I have proved what he will do, where devoted, when, in 1817, thirty-two firelocks of my guard attacked, defeated, and dispersed, a camp of fifteen hundred men, slaying thrice their numbers . . . . .

What says the Thermopylae of India, Corygaum? Five hundred firelocks against twenty thousand men! Do the annals of Napoleon record a more brilliant exploit? . . . . .*

Well, they have received and are receiving each day the thanks of 60,000 Anglo-Indians, led by all the English newspapers of India, particularly the *Englishman*. In 1857, disrespect and daily insults provoked the mutiny of the Sepoys. At the present moment, in 1883, a revolt of the Bengalî Bâbûs has broken out, and asserts itself with greater force daily! However, the consequences of the first meeting of Anglo-Indian planters and shopkeepers in the Calcutta City Hall, after the so-called *Ilbert Bill* became known to them, were not limited to general skirmishes and innocent quarrels

---

the *lowest*," the author of the pamphlet says: "To this boastful *vae victis* which has been buzzing in our ears from the first day of resistance to the Ilbert Bill, we reply once and for all the following: 'you did not conquer India, nor did your European soldiers, but our Sepoys, the Hindus did, and we challenge you, summon you as a whole nation, to refute this if you can!' " Furthermore, the author enumerates all the places conquered by the Hindus for England, from Plassey to the latest revolt when England was rescued by the Sikhs. He reminds the Anglo-Indians of the words of many a general, words which are in print and now belong to history. Thus Lord Macaulay compares the loyalty of the Sepoys to Lord Clive with the loyalty of the 10th Legion to Julius Caesar, and of the Old Guard to Napoleon; the author repeats also the comparison made by the same historian between Hindu Sepoys and the soldiers of Moritz of Saxony, and the words of Cornwallis reproving the English soldiers and praising the Hindus: "*A brigade of our Sepoys could easily make anyone Emperor of Hindostan,*" etc. (See J. W. Kaye's *Lives of Indian Officers*, "Life of Cornwallis," p. 75.)

The Black Act which restricts the freedom of the press has been repealed and the English *nolens volens* have swallowed the bitter truth.

*Col. James Tod, *Annals and Antiquities of Râjasthân*, Vol. I, pp. 74-75.

only. The legal and meritorious wish of Lord Ripon, nick-named "Babû Ripon," finally to render simple justice to the natives by granting their educated judges in the service of the Crown equal rights with the English judges, called forth an unheard-of storm, unexpected by all, from the *non-civilians,* namely, the above-mentioned planters and speculators who were not in the ranks of the civil or military services. The civil servants and the military followed the latter, some secretly, some even openly. Such insults and ridicule were hurled on the innocent Bâbûs that one had to be a *Hindu,* and to have the patience of the meekest mule, to swallow them daily and hourly, with hardly any reply, while holding a defensive attitude in the meantime. But the hurricane is growing in strength. At first it spread from Calcutta into all the cities and hamlets of Bengal, so that at present there is no town or village which does not echo the cries of the outraged Bâbûs. The matter has already reached Parliament. There has appeared in the newspaper *Englishman,* under the pseudonym "Chai-Chi-Chfu," something in the nature of an advertisement: "Wanted by several Eurasian families a large party of water-carriers, scavengers, coachmen, *sweepers of butcher shops,* etc.; only Bengalî Bâbûs will be hired. The advertisers prefer retired collectors, judges and lawyers of the Crown," and so on in this vein. At this the fury of the outraged Bâbûs and, in fact, of the entire nation reached its limits, and similar affronts began to appear in reply. In Parliament, Mr. O'Connell, one of the leaders of the Irish Party, called the attention of the House to this "undeserved insult." The Assistant Secretary, Mr. Cross, replied that he had read the "dishonorable lampoon," that instructions had already been sent to the Anglo-Indian Government, and that the *Englishman* would in all probability be brought to trial for inciting racial antagonism among people already mutually hostile. Meanwhile, having cooked his porridge, poor "Bâbû" Ripon does not know what to do with it. The suggestion without action simply inflamed our Bâbûs still more. The daily, weekly and monthly publications have been filled with this matter for over three months. The unfortunate Râjâ Siva-Prasâda, who dared to say a few words against the *Bill* in the Viceregal Council, was burned

and is still being burned, in effigy of course, in all the cities
of India. Everywhere there are *monster-meetings,* protests,
addresses and fiery speeches. Groans and rumblings of all
kinds fill India. The native press, for the first time since
the day of its inception, has risen as one man, and in the
Anglo-Indian camp the Amazonian *Maam-Sâhibs* and
Missy-Bîbî have gone to the aid of their husbands and
brothers. In answer to a petition *against* the *Ilbert Bill*
embodied in the "ladies address to the Queen," with six
thousand signatures obtained through the solicitation of
the fair (but highly ill-tempered) sex, the native women
reply in an "address" to Her Majesty *in favor* of the *Bill,*
with 300,000 signatures on it. They protest at the same time
against the systematic series of insults to Her Majesty's
subjects.

All this, however, concerns the question of the *Bill* above.
At the time of the climax of this affair, something far worse
suddenly happened, about which, of course, all our readers
have already learned from the newspapers. This matter
appears even more serious, and only Providence knows how
it will end. Because of a penny candle, Moscow burned;
because of an old stone idol, a *Śâlagrâma,* the hearts of all
Hindus, unbelievers as well as believers, burn with an un-
quenchable hatred for the English, This insult, however, is
not of a political, but of a purely religious, character about
which even such unbelieving *nâstikas* as our Bâbû have
become aroused. "The point lies not in the idol," they say,
"but in the affront to an entire nation." Norris, a judge of
the Superior Court, while in the process of adjudicating
some dispute concerning the possession of the above-mentioned idol, ordered it brought to his judicial chambers with
the consent of both parties, as he now explains. But in the
eyes of the entire nation such an action was unheard-of
and intolerable. Native newspapers divided their attention
between the *Bill* and the idol. All the Pandits, Brâhmaṇas
and Śâstrîns* rose. Menacingly, an army made up of yogins,

---

*Learned Brâhmaṇas who know *by memory* all the *Śâstras, Purâṇas*
and *Vedas.*

sannyâsins and the entire brotherhood of monks and mendicants also rose. The government became seriously alarmed. But if, according to the saying, an Englishman invariably gets off scot-free, then the Anglo-Indian "most likely has the very devil for a nursemaid." Things quieted down for about two days after a promise not to repeat a similar offence, when suddenly and unexpectedly the thunder struck for a third time. The editor of the journal *Bengalî*, it was said, had offended the Supreme Court, by printing a censure of Judge Norris' action pointing out that, according to law, he had no right to summon the revered idol and thus defile the holy relic. Norris was offended on behalf of "the majesty and inviolability of the Court," as the Anglo-Indian newspapers assured us, and "wanted to take revenge on the whole of India in the person of an educated and influential native," according to native progressivists, who then and there brought to light the judge's action, pointing out how he threw up his hat at the meeting against the *Bill* and berated the natives. The editor, Bâbû Surendro Nâth Bannerji, was condemned to prison for two months. What happened after this is hardly possible to relate. Within 24 hours the Bâbû literally became the hero of all India. He "is a martyr for our Mother India; he is suffering for all the people *and for the cowardice of all the others*," etc. Condolences are being received from every town in India and large sums collected for "the martyr." Literally *millions* of signatures are being gathered for a petition to be presented to Parliament, and several lawyers and speakers have already been sent to London . . .

How will it all end? Great is that politician, or shall I say that prophet, who could lift the curtain that hides the future of this case. Everything depends on the heart of India— Calcutta. Shameful and sad as it may be to brand an entire nation of sixty million with one stroke of the pen, truth compels me to say frankly that, aside from several exceptions, the Bengalî Bâbûs are not men at all, but some sort of rich pastry made with coconut butter. The leaven has risen and is working for the time being; but it will fall again and ferment for another whole century . . .

But, goodness gracious! Where have I wandered? In what

far horizons have I lost myself. It is difficult, when writing of the past, not to linger in the present, particularly when the matter concerns a people full of excellent qualities, with a heart as gentle as a baby's and the head of a sage, but as spoiled also as a baby, not by indulgence but by the cruel thrashing of an unbidden and unloved stepmother . . . I shall now return to the superstitions of this strange and completely exceptional people.

It is hardly possible to relate even some of the stories told by the school teacher and the Jât about the ability of the Hindu spiritual *Ego* to receive and return mutual visits and to make itself at home in the bodies of others. It would require a special book with a supplement of selected tales from *Baron Munchausen*. However, having been nourished for four years on similar narratives, with indications of the *facts* in each, that is, *of other persons inhabited by the souls of the living (sic)*, it is perhaps not *I* but my European *sheath* that writes these irreverent remarks. At times my head spins, things get muddled in my brain, and I even confuse, and do not seem to recognize, my own personality. In the presence of such extraordinary tales, I was not prepared to declare mentally to myself that I was actually *myself*, and not (as in one of Mark Twain's stories) my own twin brother who drowned beside me in the bathtub . . . Thus from eight o'clock in the evening to way past midnight we sat on the verandah, listening to one story after another, each more extraordinary than the one that preceded it.

Finally, our guests asked permission to leave. Only then did we realize that we ourselves were to blame for their long visit: *we had forgotten to ask them to leave!* In India, if the host does not take care of sending his guests off in time (the European, with the phrase, "I hope you'll drop in soon again," and the native, with an offer of betel to chew, after sprinkling the guests with rose water), the visitors out of politeness are prepared to stay the whole night. This is a most unpleasant duty, and at first it embarrassed us dreadfully. Now we are used to it and even find the custom very convenient, all the more so since such a delicate problem here does not even call for any of Demian's fish soup.* On the contrary, the guests themselves bring presents in the form of fruit, sweet spices and flowers and would run away without looking back if offered anything. The rigid rules of the inexorable caste system do not allow them to touch even a glass of water. When a European has been offered water in the home of a Hindu, the glass or other dish used is immediately smashed to smithereens as if it were forever defiled. The courteous European always breaks it himself.

The guests were already preparing to leave, when the Colonel, who is fervent and stubborn in dispute like a regular Yankee, smilingly remarked to the Jâṭ and to the school teacher:

"Thank you for the visit and for the information furnished. However, forgive me, but I somehow cannot believe that the soul of a living person could take possession of the body of another whenever it wanted to."

"We do not assert that *every* soul can do it, but only the *mayâvi-rûpa* (the body of illusion, *périsprit*) of an initiated yogin."

"I firmly believe in their strength and secret power," interrupted the Colonel, more serious now. "I believe because I personally became convinced of all this upon my arrival in India. But that the soul, even of the mightiest of adepts, be he as wise as Solomon, could at choice occupy another body — I cannot believe! You make of them regular werewolves! . . . In like manner, if you please, every *yogin* might be capable of turning into a crocodile, a cat, or a frog, as in the stories of our Redskins . . . That's the devil of a thing!"

"Do not argue, Colonel," said Nârâyaṇa, who so far had been silent. "Do not argue, you cannot know to what extent *their* power reaches, and to . . ."

"But everything has its limits!" interrupted our president with a slight note of vexation in his voice. "Well, for

---

* [Referring to the fable by the Russian writer Krilov, in which the oversolicitous and overhospitable host, Demian, stuffs his guest with fish soup to the point that the latter, grabbing his belt and hat, hastens home never to set foot again in Demian's house.—*Compiler.*]

instance, take our Ṭhâkur . . . I believe in his science, deep
knowledge and psychic power, as I believe in my own
existence . . . Do I have to believe therefore that, taking
advantage of the body of a dead rat, he is capable of crawling into it also? Ugh! what ugliness!"

He even spat which, for some reason, made me recall Mr.
W. and his argument with the Ṭhâkur on the shores of
the lake.

"Only *jâdûgars,* sorcerers, and Tibetan *dugpas* and
shamans turn into rats and tigers," exclaimed Nârâyaṇa,
almost angrily, flashing his eyes. "The great Saab would
never condescend to this, but if he should want to do so,
then, of course . . ."

The ponderous sound of powerful wings two steps away
from us suddenly interrupted Nârâyaṇa before he had finished. He shuddered and cast a staring glance into the
corner of the verandah. A magnificent peacock, which
had probably been awakened by the loud voices of the
disputants, flew down from the roof and landed heavily
on the ground before Nârâyaṇa, proudly spreading out its
luxurious tail into a fan . . .

The Colonel roared with laughter.

"Now then, maybe you think, my poor Nârâyaṇji, that
our Ṭhâkur is in that peacock? Perhaps you are ready to
convince both yourself and us that Gulâb-Lal-Singh purposely transformed himself into a peacock in order to stop your
indiscret disclosure of his power! Ha, ha, ha! . . ."

Our president shook with laughter, but Nârâyaṇa did
not even smile. We noticed to our surprise that even the
Bâbû remained serious. The others affected an air of indifference and ease which evidently they did not feel. Only
the stout teacher snorted and smirked, having tried for
several minutes to put in a word. Finally, he succeeded in
taking advantage of a momentary silence and coughed
meaningfully.

"The Colonel-Saab does not believe our stories about the
transmigration of souls from one living body into another,
and yet right in front of him, if we are to believe all India,
there stands, so to speak, a living example," he said loudly.

"Ask whom you wish, and everyone will reply that in the *young* Ṭhâkur, Gulâb-Lal-Singh, resides the soul of the old ruling Ṭhâkur, his grandfather, and that he . . ."

The Colonel and I pricked up our ears and listened, trying not to let slip a single word. I even stopped breathing . . .

"Do finish!" impatiently exclaimed our president to the suddenly silent teacher who appeared as if considering something.

". . . that the Ṭhâkur, while still living . . ."

But apparently we were not destined to hear the end of this interesting bit of information. Suddenly on the roof above our heads the shrill cries of peahens resounded, and something fell at the feet of the teacher, once more squatting, striking the stone floor with a hollow sound. In the semi-darkness, and before we could examine the shape of this new phenomenon, the obese pedagogue jumped on his chair with the elasticity of a rubber ball, breaking it to pieces, and almost shattering himself with it. Landing somehow on his feet, he leaped to one side and in a scared falsetto shouted at the top of his voice:

"A cobra, a cobra, beware of the cobra!"

Our small Bâbû, who believed as little in the *Laws of Manu,* which forbade the killing of any living creature whatsoever, including tigers and bed bugs, as he did in werewolves, rushed at once with the speed of a monkey to the aid of his countryman. Snatching from his hands a thin bamboo walking stick he grabbed the snake, probably more frightened than we were, by its tail, and with the other hand, armed with the walking stick, broke its spine; then, stepping on its head with his heavy boot, he finished it by beating it. We found a peacock's egg in the mouth of the unpleasant creature, which explained to us both the visit of the peacock-werewolf and the appearance of the cobra. Its mouth stuffed with an egg which it could not swallow, and probably feeling itself powerless against the attacking peahens, the cobra fell off the roof in fright.

We laughed a bit over the superstition of Nârâyaṇa and Mûljî and, bidding the guests farewell, entered our dining room. Taking advantage of our absence and probably expecting to earn some *bakhshîsh* the following morning, which even imperial servants expect, the *court* domestics had tried to set the rooms in order. Their main effort at tidying consisted of covering the billiard table with an old chintz blanket full of holes and distributing the pictures of Delhi along the tables and windows. One of the pictures particularly caught the eye. It had been placed on a table which stood under a mirror hanging on the wall opposite the entrance. Our esteemed president walked up to it mechanically and, raising his glasses to his forehead, began examining the numerous figures of the depicted *durbâr* by the light of the large lamp which stood on the table. While waiting for him to finish the inspection, I sat by the window, extremely tired and yawning.

There was stillness all around. Bhurtpore was asleep, our companions had left, and the peacocks on the roof were also asleep, having quieted down after the excitement. Only we were not asleep, and Nârâyana, who was still sitting on the verandah steps, his head bowed. He never retired before we did and was obediently at our services at all hours of the day and night. Whether he did this as a result of the Thâkur's wishes, or of his own good will, we never did find out. But from the very day of our departure from Bombay, just as soon as the heavy snoring of our good-natured leader was heard coming from the Colonel's room or tent, Nârâyana would lie down across the path leading to the door of my temporary bedchamber and would not move from there until morning. A fortunate people are the Hindus in this respect! They are comfortable everywhere, from the summits of the Himâlayas to the red-hot earth of the plains of Hindostan. The wealthiest Râjâ would not agree to sleep in a bed for anything; a bit of carpet — and a bed is made. The climate means nothing to them. A muslin *dhôti** and a shirt, bare legs and feet, and an equally bare chest — this is their attire in all seasons and in all climates.

Dhôti is a piece of muslin eight to ten feet long which takes the place of breeches for men, and of a skirt for women.

The Hindus — Bengalîs and Madrasîs — who arrived with me at Darjeeling last October, dressed the same as they did on the scorching shores of the Hûgli in Calcutta, without adding a shred to their costume in Sikkim, where I grew numb from cold and dampness and shivered under blankets and fur-lined coats. For them 8,000 feet above sea level, or merely a few inches above it,* made no difference, and they bathed twice a day in the half-frozen icy mountain streams, with the same pleasure as they did in the heated water of their holy *tanks* on the plains of Bengal. Never did any of them get sick, even with a cold. In reply to my request for an explanation of this secret invulnerability, they laughed, assuring me that it was very simple: "You, white saabs, wash your bodies with soap and rub them with all sorts of poisonous essences, whereas from the first day of our birth our mothers rub us with coconut oil after bathing, and we continue this procedure every morning during the course of our entire life. Every pore of our body is permeated and filled with a substance which does not admit either dampness or cold inside the organism . . ." I leave it to the physiologists and allopaths to judge of the correctness or error of this view. The latter will probably say that this is a harmful custom, that oil blocks natural perspiration, etc. Maybe so, but our delicate *grandes dames* could envy the skin (if not the color) of the lowliest coolie or the plainest peasant woman of India. Their skin is softer and finer than any satin or velvet and besides, as is obvious, is not subject to cold, as is our own.

Suddenly, from somewhere, several roosters began to crow.

"Go to sleep, Nârâyana," said I, turning to the Marâthâ who was sitting on the steps. "Listen, the Jât roosters have already begun to sing. Colonel, you go, too! You prevent Nârâyana from retiring," I added getting up. "Good night, saabs! . . ."

There was no answer whatever to my polite farewell and

---

*The highest place in Calcutta—Clive Street—is only 27 feet above sea level at low tide.

I turned, surprised, toward the Colonel. He was standing in the same place, holding a picture in his hands, with his back half turned to me, and was so absorbed in the contemplation of the *durbâr* that, in bending over the lamp, he hardly noticed that his baldness was the only safeguard against the inevitable burning of his hair.

"What's the matter with you, Colonel?" I asked again. "Have you fallen asleep over the lamp? Heavens! Why don't you answer! What is the matter with you?"

I rushed to him, really frightened. The thought of "sheaths," "werewolves," and various other wonders of India flashed through my mind.

Glancing at his face, I became still more frightened. Red as a boiled crab, with white spots on his face from which fell large drops of perspiration, he stood there, resembling a statue of terror. In his wide-open eyes, fright, amazement, and a kind of helpless confusion were clearly evident. I noticed that he was holding the picture right side down and that his terrified gaze was directed to the reverse side of it.

"What do you see on the back of this parchment that's so terrible?" I continued, shaking him by the arm with all my strength. "At least, say something!"

My esteemed president uttered something in the nature of a weak bellow and pointed with the finger of his left hand to the gold inscription in Urdu. Being unfamiliar with the hooks of that dialect, I understood exactly nothing.

"What's written there? Tell me!"

Instead of a direct answer, he whispered in a weak voice, "Nârâyana, Nârâyana, come here!"

In a second, our faithful travelling companion stood beside us and gazed at him with the same astonishment as I did.

"I do not know these letters very well . . . I may possibly be mistaken . . . Read it, Nârâyana, my son, read it," he whispered quietly in a low tone.

"Durbâr of Shâh-'Âlam. The transference by His Majesty the Padishâh Diwânî, of Bengal, and also of the provinces of Behâr and Orissa, to the East India Company. The meeting of the Râjput Ambassadors . . . Peace-making . . . by the will of the Blessed Prophet Mohammed . . . after the bitter defeat at Patna in 1173, painted by Aḥmad Din in 1177."

"What's so terrible about that? What concern of ours is their misfortune?" I asked.

"What concern of ours?" the Colonel almost yelled. "Ours? Ours? You shall see right away what concern! According to the Hegira, this was in 1177, was it not?"

"It seems so," answered Nârâyana, looking at him with astonishment.

"Well, 1177 of the Hegira . . . what year would that be according to our European chronology?"

Nârâyana thought for a moment and then replied:

"The year 1765, it seems, that's about 114 years ago . . ."

"The year 1765! One hundred and fourteen years!" shouted the Colonel, red in the face and strongly emphasizing each syllable. "Yes? Well, then just look, both of you . . . recognize and call by name! After that only one thing remains for me—to order myself placed in the lunatic asylum! . . ."

Quickly snatching the painting from Nârâyana's hands, the Colonel turned it picture upward and, pointing to the figure standing beside the Padishâh, whispered in a hoarse voice:

"Look, here, here *he* is . . . without a doubt it is *he*. Is there another one like him in the whole world? It is *he!*" repeated the Colonel, pointing with his finger.

We looked, and I admit that the surprise took my breath away and chilled my blood . . . The picture swayed markedly in Nârâyana's hands.

Before our eyes, among seventy or eighty figures of Moslems and Brâhmaṇas of the Court near the throne of the Padishâh stood, unquestionably, the figure of Ṭhâkur Gulâb Singh! . . . Actually, as the Colonel had expressed it, was there another one in the whole world that looked like him? It was *he!* It was a portrait of his double, if not of himself. Without mentioning the fact that the great height of the figure raised it a whole head above the rest of the figures, it was the sole portrayal in the picture that was completely free of the servile poses of the other courtiers. The English officer barely stood out from under the elbows of the magnificent, bewhiskered *sardârs*, and the hatred

of the artist pushed him back completely into the background. Only the figure of the one in whom all of us immediately recognized Gulâb Singh, towering high above
the crowd, was prominent by its proud bearing. Even his
pose was his own peculiarly characteristic one; he stood
with arms crossed on his chest, quietly looking into space
over the heads of the courtiers. The costume alone was
different. A Râjput turban with a small feather plume,
elbow-length steel gloves, a kind of coat-of-mail, several
daggers at the waist, and a shield of transparent rhinoceros
hide at his feet . . . But the long wavy hair, the beard, the
face, the stature left no doubt that it was he, our mysterious
and unfathomable protector . . .

"But this is impossible, inconceivable!" said the Colonel,
still very perplexed, breaking the silence. "How can any-
body figure it out? The man doesn't look forty, and yet his
portrait appears on a painting made over a hundred years
ago!"

"It is probably a portrait of his grandfather," muttered
Nârâyana, as if apologizing for the Ṭhâkur.

"Grandfather?" scornfully shot back our President. "And
why not your grandfather or mine? . . . Are there actually
such family resemblances! . . . No . . . no . . . It isn't
his grandfather, nor his great-grandfather, but he himself.
I begin to wander in my mind," said the Colonel pulling
himself together. "Really, if the picture is not a counterfeit,
then it is . . . *impossible!* . . . Tell me," he said suddenly
to me in a comically imploring voice, "tell me . . . it *is*
impossible . . . Isn't it?"

"I do not know, Colonel . . . For several days now I have
been losing the ability even to think. It seems that . . . but
don't ask me. Better ask him directly . . . if you dare . . . ,"
I added mentally, feeling, I don't know why, angry with
the poor Colonel.

"No, no! It is impossible," he continued to reason as if
to himself. "Impossible! Therefore, let's stop the conversation."

"Maybe, it really is his grandfather," I commented. "Do
you recall the school inspector starting to tell us something
about him. But he said . . ."

I was simply shocked by the look that Nârâyaṇa threw me. Just as I uttered my first words he glanced at me with such a scorching and painful reproach that I felt my words stop in my throat.

But even the simple hint had already taken effect.

"Great heavens! I had almost forgotten!" exclaimed the Colonel, striking his forehead. "But the problem becomes more difficult then . . . Just think," he continued, as if talking to himself, "if the Ṭhâkur and his grandfather . . ."

"That's enough!" I announced definitely. "If you really respect him, don't forget what he has frequently advised us to do: not to listen to various rumors, nor to try to find out anything whatsoever about him. I at least have sufficient respect for him not to go against his wishes. Until tomorrow, gentlemen!"

I entered my room and lowered the door curtain. In a few minutes everything quieted down in the adjoining room, and within a quarter of an hour the familiar snoring with the accompaniment of a whistle began to be heard.

•   •   •   •   •   •   •   •   •   •   •   •

What was that? An apparition, a reality, or simply a fantasy, a dream? . . . The stuffiness was terrific and I could not fall asleep. The *pankhâ*,* rhythmically rocked by two coolies on the verandah, was wafting hot instead of cool air. It was like the hot air of an oven blowing into my face... I was not asleep, that's a fact. There was my *ayah* (maid), coiled up into a ball like a black cat, sleeping on the carpet at the foot of my bed . . . There was my sun *topi*, which had fallen on the floor, rolling back and forth with the swaying of the *pankhâ*. No, I was not asleep . . . But what was that? Why did it seem to me as if I were seeing through the thick curtain of the door and able to distinguish

---

* In every bedroom in India a board with a wide, thick flounce extends above the bed and across the entire room. Opposite the bed there is an opening in the wall through which is drawn the rope that moves the *pankhâ*. Coolies swing it all night long. Otherwise, any European would suffocate.

in the dark all objects, furniture, Nârâyaṇa who was sleeping, or at least lying across the doorway, and even the picture of the *durbâr* which the Colonel had left on the table . . . In the adjoining dining room, it became lighter and lighter as if the moon, emerging from behind dark clouds, were shining into it. Who was that? . . . Could it be the Ṭhâkur? But he was in Dîgh!... There he was, quietly and noiselessly approaching the sleeping Nârâyaṇa and touching his shoulder. Nârâyaṇa jumped up and I saw him bow before the *Mahâ-Sâhib,* touching the latter's feet with his folded palms. The Ṭhâkur extended his hand toward the picture, and it instantly disappeared before my eyes . . . after gleaming with what seemed like a million electric sparks. Everything became confused and blurred and then I opened my eyes in the morning at the call of my *ayah,* who quietly and with endless *salaams* wakened me saying that the carriage was ready and the *Colonel-Sâhib* was already awaiting me.

"What a strange but surprisingly clear dream!" I thought to myself as I sat down in the gilded carriage sent for us by the *Divân.*

— II —

The smooth and level road from Bhurtpore to Dîgh flew past like a dusty ribbon amid endless steppes and small water holes. Our gilded carriage, dating from the time of the King of Yore and followed by a long line of small *juts* drawn by briskly trotting pygmy-steers, sped along to the accompaniment of the whoops and cries of the coachmen and runners. The procession brought to mind the travels of "Puss-in-Boots" through the property of Marquis Karabas. As in Perrault's* story, the peaceful settlers we met along the road, on seeing our triumphant procession surrounded by a guard of honor (the half-dozen brigand-like Jâṭs on sorry nags with spears, pennants and shields), bowed low to the ground, timorously making way for us and rendering us all possible honor. We rode in this fashion for about two hours through desert areas, without the least sign of vegetation, surrounded on all sides by swamps, ditches, and small salt lakes. Finally we arrived at the gigantic gates of Dîgh, which has been correctly named "The Oasis of Bhurtpore."

What an unexpected change of scenery! As if by the waving of a magic wand, in the midst of scorched fields and swamps covered with centuries-old green scum, there

---

*[Charles Perrault (1628-1703), French author whose fame is mainly due to his popular tales and fables.—*Compiler.*]

rose before us an enchanted castle-fortress with towers, turrets, and hanging Semiramis gardens.

We entered the half-ruined small town—if two dozen stone turrets may so be designated—and started the ascent to the fortress. The little town found refuge under the protection of a majestic monument of the greatest antiquity, so great that the minds of contemporary chroniclers, losing themselves in the obscurity of an unfathomable prehistoric past, feel powerless to determine its beginning.

The ancient names for Dîgh — "Dîrgha" and "Dîrgha-pura"—are frequently mentioned in the *Skanda-Purâna* and in Chapter IV of the *Bhâgavata-Mâhâtmya*. Dîgh, the old, prehistoric Dîgh that lies in dust under the present one, is more ancient than Lucknow, the former "Lakshmanavatî" of hoary antiquity, the capital city of King Lakshmana, brother of Râma, built *sixty centuries* ago, as explained to us by Nârâyana, our walking encyclopedia.

Contemporary Dîgh "was founded by the Jâts, foreign *Scythians* from the far North," say the Anglo-Indian historians. Dîgh, according to popular belief, was built by the sorcerers who had come with the Jâts, and who erected the former powerful fortress with its enchanted castle and delightful gardens — *in one night*. Like everything that is built in such haste, Dîgh, in spite of its impassable water-filled ditches, and its inaccessibility during nine months of the year, both to its own people and to the outsiders, proved to be, however, but a *mâyâ*, an illusion, to the red-haired conquerors. During the flooding of the rivers and the hundreds of small lakes in the Bhurtpore steppes, a whole ocean is formed around the small town, and at such times it is really inaccessible to the enemy. But though the English, as the proverb says, had to sit awhile by the sea, they waited long enough for favorable weather. In December, 1804, General Frazer besieged Dîgh and took it by storm; then, after completely demolishing it, generously returned "the oasis" to the Jât Râjâ. At present there is not a stone left of the fortress walls. In a corner towards the southeast the *Shakh-Burj* of the modern Dîgh sticks out. This is a huge cliff, the spacious square of which is now surrounded by a green hedge instead of bulwarks, though retaining a bastion in each of its four corners. Within the square, however, which rises high into the air, there remain three walls from the fortifications, twenty-one feet in thickness, bespeaking even now their glorious past. In the western corner of "the fortress," is the palace of the Râjâ with its sumptuous gardens, sacred peacocks and fountains. This palace and garden constitute the main attraction for tourists.

Contemporary travellers have unanimously decided that, with the exception of the "Tâj Mahal" at Âgra, the "Dîgh" palace is the most magnificent building in India: the same huge marble halls with walls inlaid with a mosaic of expensive stones; the same style of architecture in the towers; the same amazingly delicate workmanship in the lacy openwork of the white marble balustrades, terraces and stairway railings.

An amazing subject is the Englishman both at home and in his "Colonies"! With all his haughty conceit and his demands that he, John Bull, be considered the foremost representative of the human family, he has not yet fully realized the truth of the proverb contained in his own popular saying: "It is a foul bird that defiles its own nest." He is justly proud of India, calls her "the most precious pearl of the Crown of Great Britain," gloats over her like a miser over his treasure, yet he hates the Hindus, the lawful children of her soil, despising and at the same time fearing them more than a cruel stepmother! Poor, unfortunate Brâhmaṇas, wretched Śûdras, and you, Pariahs, and other outcastes, considered lower than any earthly vermin, who would not pity you from the bottom of his heart? The malicious spite of the Indo-Britishers extends not only to the present generation of Hindus of all castes and tribes but, in its insatiable contempt for the subjugated descendants, vents this base and petty feeling, exalted in self justification by them to the level of race feeling, upon their distant forefathers as well.

It is ridiculous and distasteful to read the comments and conclusions on archaeological lines by the various civil employees in their *allegedly scientific* articles about India. The authors actually strive to belittle the natives even of

the *Mahâbhârata* period, showing them to be a race completely incapable of fine arts. There is no such creative
faculty, they tell us, among the present (oppressed and
starving) Brâhmaṇas; therefore it could not have existed
before, runs the logic of these "fiction-writers," who forget
so conveniently that we see the same thing among contemporary Greeks and even degenerate Romans. Consequently, among the hundreds of stately temples that are still
being found every year in the impassable jungles of Central
India, there is not a single historical ruin that an Anglo-
Indian would consider as the work of pure native art. In
places where, obviously, *non*-Moguls had built (as, for
instance, the temples scattered over Râjputâna and Mewâr),
the clever, though baseless, hypothesis about the Greek and
Italians is immediately trotted out. In the *Purâṇas* mention
is made of the "Yavana" captives who were put to work
by the conquerors. "It is they who are the builders of these
temples." In saying this, it is overlooked that the name
"Yavana" was given by the Brâhmaṇas not only to the
Greeks and Ionians, but also to other foreigners, among
them the Scythians. There is no great harm in that; but
it is the Greeks, don't you see, who, stranded in India from
Macedonian times, most assuredly built the Temple of
Kârlî and even the oldest *vihâras* of Elephanta and Ellora.
Not the slightest data exists to warrant such a conclusion.
It is contradicted by the *Purâṇas* and other chronicles, as
well as by all the traditions of India, *even the Laws of Manu
themselves.* Immutable and inviolable, they forbid the hand
of a *mlechchha* (unclean foreigner, a *non-Brâhmaṇa*), just
as much as the hand of an impure *pariah,* to touch the
smallest stone among those prepared for the sacred structure. Otherwise, "in case of such desecration," we read in
Manu, "the Temple, though almost finished, must be
destroyed, as regards that portion of it which was touched
by such a hand; its material must be purified, and only then
may the building be continued." (*Mânava-dharma-śâstra*
and *Vâstu-śâstra*).

But all these arguments have no value whatsoever in the
presence of the partiality and obstinacy of the Indophobes.
The *Purâṇas* are lying; the *Laws of Manu* were written

and subjected to *forgeries* by the Brâhmaṇas after the conquest of India by the Moguls, and so forth. In short, the Hindus, "neither ancient nor contemporary, could ever create anything like these wonders of architecture." Could indolent parasites ever erect such transparent, ethereal and phantom-like walls, yet as strong as rock? Could they possibly conceive the plan of these chambers and palaces, of these open-work balustrades, that appear in the blue sky of Hindostan, like Venetian lace on the light blue satin dress of a beautiful woman? Now really, could they?

We will admit, of course, that not only the "eighth wonder of the world," the Tâj Mahal, but also all the palaces, monuments and pagodas, as well as all the mosques, of Lucknow, Delhi and the North-East Provinces were built by the Moguls and the fugitive Greeks; and that the hand of Brâhmaṇas never touched these buildings, unique in their style and beauty, the like of which is not to be found either in Greece or in the midst of the ruins of ancient Rome. But who were the builders of, and whose hand carved, the granite walls of the Temples of Ellora and Jaisalmer, the Jaina Pagoda of *Aṛhai din kâ Jhomprâ,** and others less remarkable — these stone sculptures, the perfection of whose design and finish send the English (those, of course, who are competent to judge them) into indescribable rapture and amazement? Such work can only be seen on silver and gold in the production of Benvenuto Cellini; but even in Italy nothing like it will be found on granite or marble. Whose hands labored these granite blocks, adorned from top to bottom with carving? If not those of the Hindus, then, we must suppose, those of the *"magician-yogins."* In the presence of such blind hatred, the English, driven into a corner by facts, would sooner believe, I am afraid, tales about "magicians" than give due justice to the Brâhmaṇas.

What is said above should be applied only to those monuments which are embellished with the gods and goddesses of the Hindu pantheon — subjects which are loath-

---

*"Refuge of two-and-a-half-days"—a name given to the Temple on account of the legend that its *yogi-magician* builders, after erecting it in 60 hours, lived in it but two-and-a-half days and then disappeared.

some to Moslems, who consider, as do the Hebrews, the representation of any human figure as the greatest "abomination" and sin. But the English* would find it not less difficult to deny the participation of the Hindus in the building of even temples and monuments in the "Saracen" style. The working hands that labored over them belonged, nonetheless, to the *native* artists and not to the alien Moguls; and, if the Greeks ever built anything in India, they surely built according to Hindu plans and not those of the Moguls, and this for the following reason:

The Moguls, as everybody knows, were always (at least in India) great artists in matters of destruction and bloodshed; they did not engage in fine arts, though some of their caliphs supported the latter and were authorities on them. The Spanish Moors and Saracens who built the Alhambra are not a case in point, however, if for no other reason than because the Moguls who conquered India were neither Moors nor Saracens like the enlightened knight Saladin. To a very large extent they were not Arabs at all but simply the forefathers of most of the present hero-robbers of Kâbulistân and the Hindu-Kush, which means barbarous tribes of Central Asia who had then been recently converted to Islam, as well as Afghâns and ancient Turkmen. In the Moguls of India, the pure Turanian and Mongol type predominates to the present day, and in order to be convinced of this, our opponents are invited to look at the Moslem population from Bombay to the Northern Provinces. Their sparsely bearded (if not completely beardless) faces, with high cheekbones like those of the Kalmucks, show the complete absence in them of the Semitic element.†

From Muhammad-ibn-Kâsim, who had conquered Sind for Caliph Omar II in 711 A.D. (in the 90th year of the

---

*As, for instance, the architect-archaeologist Fergusson and his admirer Simpson, an artist and now a correspondent for the *Illustrated London News* in Central Asia.

†For five years we have constantly inquired of our Moslem acquaintances their origin. Wherever we met the Âryan or palefaced type with regular features, we discovered their forefathers to be *Hindus who had been forcibly converted to Islamism by the Moguls.*

Hegira) to the end of the reign of al-Mansûr (775),* in other words, for more than half a century, there were no Moslems in India; they had conquered Sind and had left. The caliphs who followed were too busy with Western Christians and Caspian Huns to think of India. In those days, the *real* Saracens battled with and defeated Roderick, the last Goth of Andalusia, and struggled with, and were defeated by, Charles Martel at Tours in France. But in India at that time they had not even made an appearance. As mentioned above, it was the Afghâns† and the peoples of Central Asia in general (whose descendants still plunder there) who made up the caliphs' armies, and who later conquered India. They finally did so in 975 A.D., *i.e.*, 150 years after Hârûn al-Rashîd, a contemporary of Charlemagne, made a gift of Sind, Hindostan and Khûrâsân to his second son, al-Ma'mûn.‡ Then Hindostan was actually settled by *Moslems*, but not at all by enlightened Saracens. With the exception of the kings, direct descendants of

---

*[Al-Mansûr, meaning in Arabic "victorious," is a surname which has been assumed by many rulers. In this case reference is to Abû Ja'far'Abd Allâh b. Muhammad, second caliph of the Abbasid House, b. 712 A.D., who reigned 754-775 A.D. and founded Baghdad in 764. —*Compiler.*]

†If we are to believe the historian Ferishta, the Afghâns may well prove to be, if not the ancient, then the present "Arabs" of Egypt, *i.e.*, the *Copts.* He says that when the Afghâns first fell into the hands of the Moslems, they were living around Kûh-i-Sulaimân. That was in the year 62 of the Hegira. Ferishta writes: "The Afghâns were Copts under the rule of the Pharaohs, and many of them had embraced the Law of Moses. The majority of them recanted and, returning again to their gods, left Egypt and wandered until they reached Hindostan[?], finally settling on the outskirts of Kûh-i-Sulaimân. Kâsim (Muhammad-ibn-Kâsim, Omar's commander-in-chief and the conqueror of Sind) visited them and converted them to the true faith. In 143 of the Hegira, the Afghâns had already conquered the provinces of Kerman, Peshâwar and many other neighboring countries."

Could it not be because of the conversion to the Law of Moses that the Afghâns are suspected of being one of the ten lost tribes of Israel? Concerning the Afghâns, we will have something to say further on.

‡[An Arabic surname meaning "in whom men trust." Reference is to 'Abu'l-Abbâs 'Abd Allâh b. Hârûn (786-833 A.D.), seventh of the Abbasid Caliphs.—*Compiler.*]

Mohammed through the caliphs of Baghdad, the rest of the Mogul population, the people and the army, were the dregs of Islam from Central Asia.

Knowing all this, must we believe the Orientalists who are trying to convince us that, instead of the Hindus, it was the Moguls and the fugitive Greeks who labored over these artistic wonders? That instead of the descendants of the glorious Rishis and of whole generations of mathematicians, geometricians and poets, having built these edifices which are matchless in their originality, it was the brigand tribes of Central Asia, who to this day have not the slightest idea of art? Where the Arabian element has settled and has predominated through the centuries, the Moslems have never built, and are not building now, the like of such tombs, palaces and mausoleums, as we now find in India alone. There is nothing resembling the Tâj Mahal, the tombs of Akbar and the Caliph Humâyûn, the mosques and palaces of Delhi, Lucknow and Dîgh, either in Persia or in contemporary Egypt, either in Syria or Baghdad, nor even in semi-Europeanized Turkey. Let anyone look at the monuments and palaces of Southern India; at the fretwork and sculptural ornamentation of the temples of Madhurai, Śrîraṅga, and others in the Madras Presidency; at the pyramidal block of the great Tanjore pagoda, the oldest in the land. Two hundred feet in height, covered with statues of gods, goddesses and *Avatâras* twice the size of a human being, with its gigantic ox of black granite in front of the façade and its sculptural ornamentations on columns and ceilings, this pagoda is considered "one of the finest productions of the art of Brâhmaṇa India" (Bishop Heber). Did the Moslems build that too? Let those who deny to the Hindus any talent take a trip through the length and breadth of Râjputâna, Mewâr, Sind and Mâlwâ, as we did. Let them look at this huge expanse literally sown like a field of peas with the ruins of Hindu temples, fortresses and palaces — and then decide who built them. Here in Râjputâna and Mewâr, the Moguls did not tarry long, for the simple reason that they were thoroughly thrashed, contrary to their fate in other portions of India. Here they built nothing, though they laid waste many things. Yet it is precisely here that the tourist will find, on the half-demolished temple walls, such sculpture and molded work, such a variety of art objects, that even Homer's description of Achilles' shield may well lose by comparison.

Who among Europeans ever heard of the Temple of Barolli near Chitor, so famous in the Chronicles of Râjasthân? It was discovered in the midst of a dense forest and described by Colonel Tod and Captain Waugh. I take the liberty of relating a few excerpts from the description of these officers. They will show better than anything else the difference between the opinion of educated, unprejudiced Englishmen in the days of the East India Company and the opinions of contemporary "petty shopkeepers" in India. The latter, sent from London to *destroy* and *appease,* judge everything native merely by the reaction of their own shallow, envious, puny minds, thus injuring truth as well as science.

. . . . . the temple of Barolli suddenly burst upon my view from amidst the foliage that shrouded it . . . . We instantly dismounted, and by a flight of steps attained the court of the temple. To describe its stupendous and diversified architecture is impossible; it is the office of the pencil alone, but the labour would be almost endless. Art seems here to have exhausted itself, and we were, perhaps now for the first time, fully impressed with the beauty of Hindu sculpture. The columns, the ceilings, the external roofing, where each stone presents a miniature temple, one rising over another, until crowned by the urn-like *kullus* [kalaśas], distracted our attention. The carving on the capital of each column would require pages of explanation, and the whole, in spite of its high antiquity, is in wonderful preservation. This is attributable mainly to two causes: every stone is chiselled out of the close-grained quartz rock, perhaps the most durable (as it is the most difficult to work) of any; and in order that the Islamite should have some excuse for evading their iconoclastic law, they covered their entire temple with the finest marble cement, so adhesive, that it is only where the prevalent winds have beaten upon it that it is altogether worn off, leaving the sculptural edges of the stone as smooth and sharp as if carved only yesterday.*

. . . . The doorway, which is destroyed, must have been very curious, and the remains that choke up the interior are highly interesting. One of these specimens was entire, and unrivalled in taste and beauty.

---

*This cement was removed after Śîvajî, the Marâthâ put an end to the dynasty and house of Tîmûr, two century ago. [H.P.B.]

The principal figures are of Śiva and his consort, Pârvatî, with their attendants. He stands upon the lotus, having the serpent twined as a garland. In his right hand he holds the *dumroo* [ḍamarû], or little drum, with which, as the god of war, he inspires the warrior; in his left is the *cupra* [kapâla] formed of a human skull, out of which he drinks the blood of the slain. The other two arms have been broken off: a circumstance which proves that even the Islamite, to whom the act may be ascribed, respected this work of art. The "mountain-born" is on the left of her spouse, standing on the *coorm* [kûrma], or tortoise, with braided locks, and earrings made of the conch-shell. Every limb is in the easy flowing style peculiar to ancient Hindu art, and wanting in modern specimens. Both are covered with beaded ornaments, and have no drapery. The firm, masculine attitude of "*Bâbâ Adam,*" as I have heard a Râjpoot call Mahâdeo, contrasts well with the delicate feminine outline of his consort. The serpent and lotus intertwine gracefully over their heads . . . . . Captain Waugh is engaged on one of the figures, which he agrees with me in pronouncing unrivalled as a specimen of art. There are parts of them, especially the heads, which would not disgrace Canova. They are in high relief, being almost detached from the slab . . . .

On the right is the shrine of *Trimûrti*, the triune divinity. Brahmâ's face, in the centre, has been totally obliterated, as has that of Vishṇu, the Preserver; but the Destroyer is uninjured.* The tiara, which covers the head of this triple divinity, is also entire, and of perfect workmanship. The skill of the sculptor "can no further go." . . . . . The whole is colossal, the figures being six feet and a half high . . . . . The roof of the *munduf* (*pronaos*) [maṇṭapa] . . . cannot be described: its various parts must be examined with miscroscopic nicety in order to enter into detail. In the whole of the ornaments there is an exact harmony which I have seen nowhere else. Even the miniature elephants are in the finest proportions, and exquisitely carved†

Twelve pages describing the *dii minorum gentium* and other wonders of Barolli follow and Tod concludes:

. . . it would require the labour of several artists for six months to do anything like justice to the wonders of Bûndi.‡

No indication has been left to posterity as to when this temple, little known even in India, was built or by whom.

---

*This *Trimûrti* is represented with three faces (*mûrti*) though but one head.

†Col. James Tod, *Annals and Antiquities of Râjasthân*, Vol. II, "Personal Narrative," pp. 670-74 [ed. of 1894]. Tod lived as a political agent in Râjputâna, never leaving it for twenty-two years.

‡*Op. cit.*, p. 677.

A certain Râjâ Hûn is the legendary hero of this locality. Even Tod, however, who has written two thick volumes to prove that the Râjputs are Scythians, that Mahâdeo-Śiva is Adam, and that Manu is Noah, has not succeeded in incorporating the Huns into the mythology of the Hindus. The Company's political agent to Râjputâna did accomplish one thing: he found in the temple at Barolli an inscription on the bas-relief of Mahâdeo, and translated it with the date on it—the 13th of *Kârttika* (the month dedicated to India's Mars) of the era of Śâlivâhana, 981 or 925 A.D. In this inscription mention is made of the offering to Mahâdeo (the patron of the Yogins) by "his slave" (the name has been erased by the hand of time) of the necessary sum for the repair of *his ancient temple*.

If in the year 925, almost a thousand years ago, and some fifty years *before* the Moslem invasion of India, the temple at Barolli was already considered "ancient," then it was obviously not built by the Moguls, and still less by the Greeks. Neither in the architecture nor in the sculpture of this entire mass can be found any characteristic reminiscent of the Hellenes. There is not even a suggestion of the Doric, and still less of the Ionic, style. Everything about it is unique, everything is in pure Hindu style.

Apologising for this lengthy digression, but without promising never again to fall into my habitual error, I would like to explain the reason for it. First, as I was to visit this temple only at a later date, I would have had to describe it just the same, and my narrative, after so many other descriptions of temples, would have probably appeared monotonous; and second, I wanted to be supported in this case by the evidence of the Anglo-Indian archaeologist and dignitary, well known as an accurate writer, to the effect that I am not partial to India but merely render her justice. Tod lived for many years in India, and the delight breaking through every line of his description of the wonders of ancient Indian art is much more significant than mine.

Moreover, the very question as to who built all of this in India, the Moguls or the Hindus, served, in the first hours of our arrival at Dîgh, as the cause of a very unpleasant acquaintanceship which ended in an equally unpleasant quarrel.

We had barely ascended the terrace and entered the hall when we found, to the great displeasure of our entire party, two unknown Englishmen. Coming from Jaipur on their way somewhere else, they had stopped at Dîgh to lunch at the expense of the Mahârâja, and to partake of the gratuitous liqueurs and champagne. With the latter they had obviously already become acquainted, as they had apparently shed the customary haughty reserve of the sons of Albion. Forgetting their "etiquette," they nodded to us as we entered, and even started a conversation with O., all the while looking askance, however, at our native companions and winking at the Colonel. It is possible that this was simply a good-natured joke on their part, but their grimaces seemed very insolent and particularly insulting to the Hindus. I immediately left with Nârâyana to inspect the "chambers," while O. remained with the Englishmen in the Durbâr Hall, where the latter had seated themselves before we did at the table prepared solely for us. There was no other table, either large or small, in the entire palace, the dusty and spacious halls of which looked like a marble wilderness. We just had to wait. The Englishmen, however, left in an hour or two, but even in that short time they had succeeded in offending our friends and in having an encounter with me personally.

When I came back in an hour, having grown tired of walking through countless corridors and up and down stairs, they were still at the table arguing with O., who was defending the ancient arts of India and, in general, taking the natives' side. Our Hindus were sitting on mats in another room, gloomily listening to the conversation. Nârâyana, noticeably sullen and bored from early morning, went directly to his comrades without passing through the hall, and I myself sat down at the very end of the table for my coffee, having decided not to take any part in the conversation. Not possessing the good-natured patience of our respected President, I felt I would become indignant if I had to argue with them, and therefore remained obstinately silent. My caution was not crowned with success; the Colonel spoiled my plan.

Having forgotten the name of a famous geometrician of ancient India, he raised his voice and called for help from Nârâyana and the Bâbû, and ended in bringing both of them from the adjoining room. While he was explaining to them whom he wished to recall, one of the Indo-Britons, after casually looking me over, turned to me directly.

"*Your servants,* of course?" he asked disdainfully nodding his head towards Nârâyana and Bâbû.

I erupted from indignation and annoyance at this obviously *deliberate* impertinence.

"Servants! . . . You are mistaken. Both gentlemen are our dear friends and brothers," I said, strongly emphasizing the word "gentlemen."

Insolence and effrontery are quick to develop in Indo-Britons. My reply brought forth loud laughter from both of them. "Friends . . . that, maybe, is possible, as there can be no argument about taste," the Englishman drawled out bitingly, while slowly finishing his glass of iced champagne. "But, how can they be 'brothers'? You are surely a native of Europe?"

"I take it I am, but fortunately for me I am not an *Englishwoman.* Consequently, I am proud of the privilege of calling these two native gentlemen, not only friends, but also *brothers*," I replied very sharply, looking straight into the eyes of the tall and insolent fellow.

It was his turn to become enraged.

I do not know what he was about to say in reply, for his friend gave him no time to collect his thoughts. Grabbing him by the arm, he dragged him almost forcibly to the other end of the room, where he immediately began to impart something to him in a whisper. I guessed that he was explaining to him about our Society and telling him who I was. And so it proved to be.

At the first words of our outspoken exchange, the dark faces of the natives turned rather green, and their eyes flashed with the unkind, phosphoric sparks, so familiar to me. They stood like two immovable statues . . . Only the Colonel became disturbed, hastily rising from the table.

The Englishmen picked up their hats and bags and, nodding to O., started to leave. The older of them obviously wished to avoid an unpleasant quarrel and, muttering something about not arguing with women, started for the exit. But my opponent, excited by the champagne and my rebuff, did not subside. Halting in the center of the hall and tottering a bit from intoxication, he made a half-turn in my direction and, haughtily turning his head towards me, said angrily over his shoulder: "I have just found out that you are *that very Russian lady* about whom our newspapers had so much to say as a warning to the *government* . . . Now your *brotherly* relations with, and your feelings for, the *black rabble* have become clear to me. Allow me to inform you that, in spite of the gratitude you have just expressed to Providence for *not* being born an Englishwoman, it is safer, I can assure you, to belong to *our* nation than to *yours,* at least *here, in India,*" he added significantly.

"That is very probable. But, just the same, I am happy and proud that I am *not* an Englishwoman," said I, rising and restraining myself as much as I could.

"In vain, for *our government does not like to allow Russians,* even ladies, *to fraternize much with Asiatics who have been conquered by us.*"

"What is this, a joke or a threat?" interrupted the Colonel, his face changing.

"Of course it's a threat," I commented laughingly. "Have you forgotten that we have already received actual evidence of this, and that the Anglo-Indian government, either from stupidity or from cowardice, has sent its military spies, *officers,* to follow us like shadows from the very moment we left Bombay? . . ."

"Be careful . . . and be more discreet in the choice of your words!" the Englishman uttered through his teeth even more haughtily, being by now completely infuriated. "Do not depend on the patience of our government, whose action and politics you allow yourself to censure . . . you had better learn, if you have not already, *that there is no room for Russians in our British dominions* . . . Do not forget this on another occasion."

TEMPLE OF MAHÂDEVA AT KHAJURÂHO

MADHURAI: SOUTH TOWER OF THE TEMPLE OF MÍNÂKSHÍ

"It is you who forget yourself, sir!" furiously exclaimed the Colonel, who had lost all patience. "You are insulting a woman and threatening her! . . . Moreover, she is a citizen of free America and *not a Russian* at all, that is, not *the kind* of Russian you take her to be," he corrected himself, having met my indignant glance.

"Excuse me, Colonel. Leave me the right, I beg you, to defend myself . . . First of all, *I am Russian*. I was born a Russian and I shall die a Russian. I am a Russian in my *soul*, if not on my passport . . . You should be ashamed! Do you really want these gentlemen to leave with the impression that I am ready to renounce the country of my birth, and even my nationality, in the face of their foolish exhibition and impertinence?"

"That might have been more prudent, if you please," cuttingly commented the other Englishman.

"More prudent possibly, but in no way more honest. In any case," I added, turning to the first one, "I am extremely sorry if your remark that there is no room for Russians in the British dominions is a *fact* and not just idle insolence on your part. In *our* Russian dominions, for example in Georgia and in the Caucasus, there is room for every foreigner, even for *scores of English paupers* who come to us without boots and leave with millions in their pockets . . ."

Quarreling does not seem to be sobering, but rather an aid to champagne. My opponent now sat completely drunk and his friend replied for him.

"Every country has its own political views on things. Your remark proves nothing against the policy of the Anglo-Indian government."

"To you, possibly not. But on the other hand, to *us* foreigners, and most likely to your native subjects, it proves clearly one point: that while your Messrs. Englishmen are afraid of Russians in your own colonies, the Russians are not afraid of you. It is a mere trifle, not worth talking about."

Seeing the distorted face of the defender of British privileges at hearing these words, I called the Hindus and, turning my back to the others, went into the garden. Nârâyana's eyes were bloodshot; the Bâbû, whose face was dripping with perspiration from controlled fury, dashed out and started jumping and snorting with his clothes on, under the high splashing fountain, shouting from under the water spray, across the whole garden: "Oh, to freshen and cleanse myself at least a little of the atmosphere defiled by the *baḍâ-Saabs!*"

I was inexpressibly grieved, not for myself, of course, but for these innocent and offended Hindus, condemned by some fatal power to eternal and in no way merited abuse. That I was being taken for a spy became obvious now, a fact which under other circumstances would have made me laugh. Even now I felt only contempt for the "victor" who was so cowardly as obviously to be in fear of the influence of a single woman on the minds of the "conquered" millions. At another time, I dare say, it would have even flattered my ego and, generally, would have been very funny, had it not been so sad, and in addition to that even dangerous. I feared that, instead of rendering the Hindu members of our Society a service, I might become the pretext for their persecution and for various excuses on the part of their "rulers," owing to the sole fact that I was *Russian.* Russia and everything Russian are a constant nightmare for Anglo-India. The closer to the Himâlayas, the more violently does the Russian "house-demon" choke every Britisher at night. Fear, it is said, has large eyes, and it can make black out of that which is white.

At the very inception of our Society in India, I began hearing rumors of the displeasure of various dignitaries in whose offices many of the Bombay native Fellows of the Theosophical Society served. "The mighty ones of this world," the *baḍâ-Saabs,* advised their timid subordinates "not to be too friendly with the newly arrived *adventurers* from America."

In a word, the situation was very unpleasant.

I sat down on the bench near the fountain, where the Bâbû was now shaking himself in the sun like a drenched cur. Nârâyaṇa remained dead silent. Glancing at him, I was stunned: The dark circles under his large eyes had darkened more deeply, his teeth were bared like those of a wild beast, and he shivered as if in fever . . .

"What is the matter with you, Nârâyaṇa," I asked, frightened.

For a whole minute, he did not answer; his strong white teeth merely gnashed a bit harder... Suddenly he squatted on the sand of the footpath and at once somehow fell face downwards into the flower-bed of brilliant bright-red *arales,* the flower dedicated to the goddess Kâlî ...

Whether the favorite flower of the bloodthirsty goddess of revenge aroused our gentle, patient Nârâyaṇa, or something else instilled an awful thought into him, he raised his head and, fixing his bloodshot eyes on me, asked in a changed hissing voice:

"Well, do you want me to kill him?"

I jumped as if stung.

"What do you mean? Come to your senses! Is this drunken braggart worth honest people risking their necks because of his insolence? You're either joking or raving, my dear!"

"It isn't he, not he . . . In his face I see but his nation, hateful to us. Killing him, I would avenge years of suffering, humiliation . . . deadly insults . . . I would avenge my many friends and, in addition, the insult rendered *you!* . . ." he exclaimed in a voice husky with despair.

"Stop it! Can you really imagine that I feel seriously insulted? Why I am simply laughing at his foolish behavior! . . ."

But he did not hear me. Lowering his head on the crushed plants, as if turning to an invisible interlocutor under the ground, he continued speaking in the same changed husky voice. It was as if he were pouring into the bosom of Mother Earth a suddenly cresting wave of suffering, full of impotent bitterness that had been boiling in him all this time . . . I had never seen him in such a disturbed state. He seemed inexpressibly pitiful to me, but at the same time positively frightening.

"What has happened to him," I thought. "Could this really be the result of that most stupid episode?"

"They have offended you . . . because of *us* . . . because of us alone," he continued half-whispering. "And that is not all! You will soon be followed . . . Pursued . . . Leave us, turn away from us . . . Tell them you were joking, were laughing at us, and they will forgive you; they will start entertaining you and offering you their friendship and society . . . But you will not do that, otherwise the *Mahâ-Saab* would not treat you as he does . . . Therefore much grief awaits you in the future—grief and slander! Yes, it is dangerous to be friends with the poor Hindus! There is no happiness for the sons of *Kali-Yuga,* and he who offers us his hand is a madman, for sooner or later he will have to pay bitterly for his transgression! . . ."

I listened with amazement and almost terror to this unexpected, incoherent speech, but could find nothing to say to console him, and so I remained silent. Involuntarily, I started to look around for the Bâbû. He lay on the bench, some thirty steps from us and, drying himself in the sun, must have been dozing.

"Do not be angry with me, *Upâsikâ,** and forgive me for disturbing you," Nârâyana spoke again, but now in a more even and quiet voice.

"Angry with you, my poor Nârâyana? What for? You were only joking, were you not?" I interrupted him, not knowing what to say.

He raised himself a little, and again sat on the footpath in his customary pose. Hugging both knees with his powerful arms and resting his chin on them, he now sat rocking himself back and forth, staring at the crushed *arales.* He obviously was struggling to control himself and finally succeeded. His voice was no longer hoarse nor did it tremble, but when he spoke again, there was heard so much genuine suffering in that voice that I involuntarily shuddered.

"No, I was not joking," he said slowly and firmly. "One word, and I would have killed him. Does it not all come to the same thing? My life, one way or the other, has been lost . . ."

"But why? What has happened? It can't be that you would be so disturbed because of that one fool. Tell me, it is not because of him, is it?"

---

*Upâsikâ—literally, a "female student of philosophy" under the guidance of a *Guru,* or "teacher," usually from the brotherhood of monks. *Chela*—a pupil and student of the secret sciences and a mystic.

"No, not because of him *alone*," he whispered barely audibly. "Just the same it would be easier for me, could I, before dying, kill *at least one individual of this race, so intolerable to us!!*"

"Kill! How easily you say that! It's a horrible crime! What would the Ṭhâkur say? . . ."

"He would say nothing! What do I matter to him!" he uttered still more quietly.

"But you are . . . his *chela?*"

He shuddered and was completely crushed as if someone had pierced his heart with a knife. He bent over still lower on his knees, and there suddenly broke loose from his chest such a cry of despair that I was completely at a loss . . . I felt myself becoming pale and in no condition to endure this scene any longer.

"No, I am not his *chela.* He refused me . . . He has dismissed me! . . ." sobbed the pitiful giant like a five-year-old child.

So that's what it is, I suddenly realized to myself. That means the Englishman was nothing but the last drop in an overflowing cup! And suddenly I recalled a vision, a dream, that I had seen, or thought I had seen, the night before at Bhurtpore, in which Nârâyaṇa was hugging Ṭhâkur's knees. But that was only a dream! Or had all this actually happened, and had I really witnessed the scene?

"When did he refuse you?"

Hasty steps were suddenly heard. Nârâyaṇa jumped up and, bowing quickly, said to me in a whisper: "I beg of you, keep my secret inviolate! Not a word of this to *anyone* . . . I shall still be of use to you, but do not tell Mr. O . . . I am leaving!"

But he did not make it.

"Why have you buried yourself here as if summoning submarine *bhûtas?*" the Colonel's voice unexpectedly resounded near us. "Where is Nârâyaṇa, and where is the Bâbû?" he continued as he approached us in company with the "silent general." "Ah! there they are! Do not hide yourselves. Both braggarts have left, and proved to be very decent fellows . . . We parted as friends. I assured them of

your forgiveness also, I explained to them much of what they
did not know; for instance, the principles and aims of our
Society . . . They became interested and even admitted they
had been mistaken."

"What people and what a place to proselytize in!" I
sadly remarked, interrupting this torrent of words. "Possibly
you wish to add to our Society these two 'patriots and
thinkers'? Don't blush and be embarrassed, my dear President; you'd better agree with me that they would be a
splendid pendant for Mr. G. and Miss B."

Mr. G. was, and still is, a rather important official in
the Northern Province of Hindostan. Pretending to be an
enthusiastic follower of the great philosophy of the Hindus,
he secured fellowship in our Society at the time we were
still in New York. Reaching India, we discovered that there
was no more ferocious Indophobe in the whole country than
Mr. G.; that he hated the natives, and had dishonored two
Brâhmaṇa families (*with impunity,* as is always the case
in such instances); and, above all, that a series of derisive
and slanderous letters against Theosophy and ourselves,
which had been published in 1879 and 1880 in *The Civil
and Military Gazette* of Lahore, were the work of this
"patriot and thinker," as the Colonel referred to him in
New York, delighted with this "most wonderful and honorable Anglo-Indian co-Fellow."

"There you are again, recalling old events," muttered the
Colonel in confusion. "What of it! Who is there that never
makes mistakes? Surely I don't claim to be an infallible
Pope! Not all Anglo-Indians are villains and traitors."

"Certainly not all, but I wager there couldn't be found
more than two dozen Anglo-Indians that respect Hindus
. . . As I see it now, it is necessary to be very, very careful
here . . . Why are you laughing, Mûljî?" I asked the
"silent" one, who had a broad smile on his face.

"At your generosity, Maam-Saab. *Two dozen* Englishmen
in India who respect us, niggers? Isn't that too many?"

"Indeed!" snapped the Bâbû who had awakened and was
completely dry. "Had we even 'two dozen' such, I can
assure you that everyone of the 250 million Hindus, 'regardless of caste or religion'," he said, quoting from theosophical

statutes, "would pray, and perform *pûja* every morning and evening to the Calcutta *badâ-Saabs* and others!"

"I have only known one during my whole life, and they wanted to commit him to an asylum, but, fortunately for him, he died," blurted out Mûljî.

"Who was he?" inquired the Colonel inquisitively.

"Mr.Peters, the former Collector at Madhurai, in the Madras Presidency. He died more than twenty years ago, when I was still a boy."

"What was Mr. Peters' guilt?"

"He started as a materialist, like our Bâbû here, but ended as a *pûjist* (worshipper of idols)."

"As 'our Bâbû' does not intend to do yet," coolly replied the Bengalî to this personal reference. He was occupying himself with pasting sticky flower petals on the nose of Kâlî, whose idol rose above the *arale* shrubs.

"He became a *pûjist*? What do you mean by that? Tell us his story more explicitly," insisted the Colonel, who had pricked up his ears.

"All right, Mr. President, except that I do not know how to narrate."

However, he related it to us just the same, and the "story" proved to be a most curious one. I shall tell it in my next letter, just as I then jotted it down from the words of the narrator. The story is known to everyone in Madras.

— III —

[THE STORY OF MR. PETERS. — THE AUTOBIOGRAPHY OF THE GODDESS MÎNÂKSHÎ. — BHÛTAS AND PISÂCHAS. — BRÂHMAṆAS AND THEIR REVENUES. — UNDERGROUND RIVERS. — MÎNÂKSHÎ SAVES MR. PETERS' LIFE. — PROFOUND THOUGHTS HIDDEN BEHIND EXOTERIC MYTHOLOGY. — THE HINDU TRIMÛRTI. — GODS AND THEIR INNER MEANING. — THE VEDÂNTA ON THE THREE KINDS OF EXISTENCES. — AGNOSTICS AND PANTHEISTS.]

I will now detail what Mûljî related to us "about the Anglo-Indian who loved the Hindus."

Mr. Peters was the Collector for the holy city of Madhurai, the Mecca of Southern India. An ardent archaeologist and admirer of ancient manuscripts, he needed the assistance of the Brâhmaṇas in the search and translation of them; consequently, though it is possible that at first he did not love them, nevertheless, he associated with the Hindus and did not oppress them as did his own colleagues. A thorough materialist at heart, he laughed at their superstitions and prejudices; his attitude, however, was exactly the same towards the Christian religion and so the Brâhmaṇas did not pay much attention to it. "Nâstika" (atheist), they used to say, and dismissed him with a wave of the hand. But soon all of this changed and Mr. Peters surprised both the people of India and his own compatriots.

Here is how it happened.

One day an unknown yogin came to ask for a personal interview. Having obtained permission to appear before the bright eyes of Mr. Collector, he handed him an ancient manuscript and explained that he had received it from the goddess Mînâkshî herself (one of the comeliest forms of

Kâlî) who, he said, had ordered him to give it to Mr. Peters. The manuscript was written on an *olla** and its appearance was so archaic that it inspired involuntary respect on the part of the antiquary. The Collector, who was proud of his knowledge in the field of ancient letters, was delighted and immediately wished properly to reward the hermit. To his great surprise, the *yogin,* with great dignity, refused any payment. Then he astonished him even more. Like almost all Anglo-Indian officials, Mr. Peters belonged to the Masonic Lodge. Unexpectedly, the hermit gave him the most secret sign and, having uttered the well-known formula of the Scottish Rite, "I have not so received *it,* nor shall I so impart *it*" (*i.e.,* the manuscript was not given for money), quickly disappeared.

Peters became thoughtful. Sending a *Sepoy* in pursuit of the guest who had vanished, he engaged himself at once, with the aid of a Brâhmaṇa pundit, in the deciphering of the manuscript and in its translation. The *yogin,* of course, was not found because, in the opinion of Mûljî, who in this instance was but echoing the belief of the whole city of Madhurai, he was a temporary embodiment of the goddess Mînâkshî herself. From diligent study of the *olla,* the Collector found much that was interesting about many things.

According to the assertions of the pundit, the manuscript was the *autobiography of the goddess Mînâkshî in her own handwriting,* in which she spoke about her manifestations, powers, qualities, and her character in general. According to her own statement, the goddess possessed powers (*śakti*)† of the most pleasing variety, and few were the wonders she could not promise her favorites. Too blind a faith in her personal power was not even expected; it was sufficient *to love the devatî* (goddess) sincerely and ardently, as a mother is loved, and she would extend her patronage to the worshipper, take care of, love and help him.

"Oh you, *fish-eyed one!*" whistled the incorrigible ma-

Olla—palm leaf which has been dried and prepared for writing.
†*Śakti* means literally "force," the feminine principle in male gods. Its common meaning, however, is *power* or *might.*

terialist, Peters, when he heard the above from the lips of the pundit.

This epithet, however, was not insolence on his part. Literally translated, "fish-eyed" is the name of the goddess, from *mîna*—"fish," and *akshî*—"eye."

"But what or who is the goddess Mînâkshî?" the European laity will ask us.

Mînâkshî is the selfsame Kâlî, namely, the creative power or *śakti* of Śiva, his feminine principle and aspect—impregnated with his spirit, and one of the numerous manifestations of his spouse Kâlî.

Every deity of the vast pantheon of India, female or male, is in its primary aspect, namely, at its first separation from the purely abstract principle, the "One and Impersonal," which they call *Parabrahman,* always neuter. But in its earthly manifestation, it appears twofold, like the first-begotten Adam and Eve; the feminine half, separating from the masculine, becomes a goddess, while the other half remains a god. The universal divinity, Parabrahman, is ɪᴛ, but its twofold energy, which afterwards begets a countless number of gods and goddesses, is *he* and *she*, namely, bisexual. From the principal gods, Brahmâ, Vishnu and Śiva, and their *śaktis,* other gods are begotten in their turn. These latter, however, are not direct descendants as one might think, of the divine spouses, descendants which in the pantheon of the Brâhmaṇas may have a completely separate and distinct place from others: they are the same first-begotten gods and goddesses, who masquerade and present innumerable "aspects" or countenances of themselves.

Therefore even the sanguinary goddess Kâlî, the mightiest of all *śaktis,* appearing under one of her own aspects, such as Mînâkshî for example, changes her personal attributes completely and becomes unrecognizable. It would be untimely and boring to explain here the process of such a transformation. It will be sufficient to say that Kâlî, when transformed into the Mînâkshî of Madhurai, becomes the most peace-loving of goddesses, possessing all the best qualities: meekness, long-suffering, magnanimity, etc.

Mînâkshî is the patroness of the city of Madhurai, which is built according to the plan of the temple of Śrîraṅga—a square divided into a great number of inner squares, or enclosures, in the center of which appears the famous Temple of Mînâkshî. The goddess, in spite of her inner qualities and, possibly, as proof that she has neither vanity nor pride, is in her outer image far from beautiful— her eyes resembling fish, whence the appelation of "fish-eyed." According to her worshippers, she naturally possesses extraordinary power. The unfortunate ones who are possessed by *piśâchas*, "demons," are brought to her in throngs for healing. There are a great many such possessed people in India, because the pious Brâhmaṇas include in the category of "possessed" even such as are called in Europe "mediums." In India, the right of citizenship is permitted to phenomenal manifestations only in the presence of the *yogins, sâdhus,* and other wonder-workers initiated into the "secret sciences." Everything which occurs *with the will of the person,* and which we call demoniacal, is attributed by the Brâhmaṇas to the unseemly behavior of the *piśâchas.*

But what is a *piśâcha?*

Piśâchas are the "spirits," *esprits frappeurs,* of the Spiritualists, but not in the complete structure of their unveiled personalities. Only that part of a human soul becomes a *bhûta* (earthly spirit) or a *piśâcha* which, upon separation from the immortal spirit after death, usually remains in an *invisible* form (being frequently *sensed* by the living) in the atmosphere of the place where it moved and had existence during the life of the body. After the death of a human being, everything that is *divine* in him departs into a higher, purer and better world. *Only the dregs of the soul* which are held back by this atmosphere remain behind, *i.e.,* the soul's *earthly passions,* which find a temporary abode in the semi-material "double" of the deceased that has been expelled from its habitat by the decomposition and complete destruction of the physical envelope; and it is this fact which delays the final dissipation of the "double," causing it to suffer. An after-death state such as this causes much distress for the family of the deceased and is regarded as a great misfortune by the Brâhmaṇas, hence the Hindus take all possible precautions to avert such an unwelcome event. It happens most frequently, they think, as the result of *a sinful thirst for life,* or of a particular passion of the deceased for somebody or something from *whom* or from *which* he did not, and even after death does not, wish to part. Therefore, the Hindus try to remain indifferent to everything and to avoid all attachments, fearing, more than anything else in the world, to die with an *unsatisfied* desire and, consequently, becoming a *piśâcha*. Natives of all castes and sects detest "spirits" and, believing them to be *piśâchas,* or demons, they attempt to exorcise such as quickly as possible.

How strange this tribute to Mînâkshî: Daily in the courtyard of her *pagoda,* throngs of possessed Hindus may be seen. Some of them crow like cocks and bark like dogs, as they do in our own Russia; but mere mediums are even more plentiful, those who are simply seers of ghosts, and *soothsayers* in whose presence various phenomena and a variety of devilry take place. Just as soon as the one possessed by a *piśâcha* is brought before the fish-eyes of the goddess, the demon begins to shout (through the mouth of the one possessed, of course) that he will immediately vacate the lodging occupied by him, if only the goddess will give him time . . . The sick person is led away and as a token of his having kept his word, the *piśâcha,* true to his word, throws a tuft of hair, which is always plucked by him from the head of his victim, in front of Mînâkshî, in farewell. According to reports, such bunches of hair, seemingly coming from nowhere, fly around in the temple from morning until night, before the very eyes of the amazed people. Excellent mattresses could be made with them if the Brâhmaṇas did not burn them with great ceremony.*

Flocking to the temple by the thousands and hundreds of thousands, the pilgrims provide the temple with enormous revenues, and its officiating Brâhmaṇa-oracles are considered to be the richest in India. Excluding the Temple of Mînâkshî, there are only five such lucrative *pagodas* in the

---

*If we are to believe the stories, it is very dangerous to touch this hair. Mûljî, when he was a chaste youth, stole such a tuft of hair from the Temple of Mînâkshî, and the *piśâcha* immediately took possession of the boy. "Thanks to *devatî,* I finally got rid of the devil," related the general.

entire Madras Presidency, namely, the renowned temples of Tirupati, Alîgarh, Vaidêśvaran, Kôvil and Svamimalai. The first two are consecrated to the god Vishṇu, and the last three to Śiva. On ordinary weekdays, from 3,000 to 10,000 rupees are collected in the *pagodas daily;* during holidays, the daily revenue surpasses all belief, frequently reaching from 25,000 to 50,000, and even up to 75,000, rupees *a day!* These figures are not exaggerated, but are a well-known fact to the Anglo-Indian Government. Not in vain have the Madras authorities gnashed their mean little teeth for a long time at the colossal *pagoda fund* of Southern India.

Malicious tongues assure us that only due to a compromise did this celebrated "fund" escape for a time the bitter fate which threatened to land it under the complete management of the administrators of Madras. In the nick of time, it occurred to the wealthiest of all the demon-curing *pagodas,* Tirupati, to present 40 lakhs of rupees (4 million rubles) to the above-mentioned administrators, after apportioning the amount, according to rank, among the members of the legislative council, an action which spared the other *pagodas* for several years.

It is embarrassing even to relate such a rumor. What? Englishmen accepting a bribe! Who in Europe does not know, chiefly from the London papers, that only in barbarous, semi-Asiatic Russia are there still such monstrous anomalies of our century as *bribe-taking officials* (see *The Pioneer* and *Bombay Gazette).* Is it possible to believe that the Anglo-Indians—those sober, temperate warriors and officials, the former destined to be known from now to the end of time as the "Spartans of the Afghân Thermopilae"— could have dared to take *a bribe!* And could Englishmen *pur sang,* the Englishmen of London, worthy sons of a nation whose representatives in Parliament severely punish "greediness for extortion" in their neighbors and the smallest departure from truth and honesty in other nations, have ever permitted it in their own Anglo-Indians! Unthinkable, simply absurd. We must not believe it because such a sensible nation would not express so much ardent indignation in the press and Parliament over "Russian extortionists," if it were guilty of the same sin . . . As a result of this reflection, we have decided to consider the Brâhmaṇas' accusations as an abominable slander coming from ungrateful heathens, and to return to the story about Mr. Peters.

Alas, this "story" cannot be attributed to slander, as was the "bribe of the forty lakhs of rupees offered by the Temple of Tirupati" to the instigators of the celebrated Ilbert Bill. The heathen grave of the esteemed Collector, with its pagan symbols, is seen to this day at the gates of Madhurai, and at the sight of it the cultured officials, successors to the deceased, blush.

They blush because Mr. Peters belonged to the same cultured class of officials (only not in relation to bribes), and because he not only did not look askance at the *pagoda* funds, but even added to them from his own pocket. All this was the result of the fact that, after having read the manuscript about Mînâkshî, for some reason or other his soul was moved by such great virtue, and he decided to get better acquainted with the goddess. In spite of considerable study of Hindu philosophy in the past, he did not share their views on "obsession," and did not include the feminine healer thereof in the province of philosophy; on the contrary, he amused himself with, and made fun of, such nature beliefs. But from the day he received the manuscript, he began visiting the Temple, and made an effort to collect all the existing legends about the goddess.

Among such legends gathered by the scholarly Collector, one proved to be unusually interesting and, though the British geologist-ethnographers give but scant attention to it, Mr. Peters classified it as a historical event. Moreover, it was set forth by the goddess herself in her "autobiography." By Peters' own wish, the manuscript was buried in the tomb where his ashes repose.

The Vaigai River, on the southern shore of which the city of Madhurai is situated, belongs to the so-called *antar-vâhinî nadî*, namely, rivers which flow *underground* from their source to their outlet in the sea, in short, subterranean streams. Even during the monsoon season, when the countryside is flooded with torrential rains and the river overflows its banks, the river bed dries up in three of four days, and only its rocky bottom remains. However, by digging any time of the year just two or three feet underground, excellent water may be obtained, enough not only for the indispensable needs of the city, but also for the irrigation of the fields of the entire district.

Such hermit-rivers are very few in India and, consequently, they are considered very sacred. As is generally known— or is it, perhaps, known only to a few—every temple and hill, every mountain and wood in India, in short, every locality and every building which is considered sacred for some reason or other, has its own *Purâna* (history or chronicle).* Written on ancient palm leaves, it is always carefully preserved by the officiating Brâhmana of one or the other of the *pagodas*. Sometimes the Sanskrit original is translated into the vernacular, and both texts are preserved with equal reverence. On the anniversary of holy days in honor of such "river-goddesses" and "hill-gods" (to them a river is always a *goddess*, and a hill, a *god*), the manuscripts are brought out, and these local *Purânas* are read at night to the people by the Brâhmana, accompanied by considerable ritual and the necessary commentaries pertaining to them. In many temples, on the Hindu New Year's Eve,† the almanac for the following year is also read to the people by the *Brâhmana-astrologer*.

These almanacs indicate accurately the position of the planets and stars; they distinguish the *fortunate* from the *unfortunate* hours of each of the 365 days of the forthcoming year and predict the date, and even *the hour of the day*, when there will be rains, winds, hurricanes, eclipses of the planets or the sun, and various other manifestations of nature.‡ All this is read in front of the

---

Purâna means literally, "ancient," but is also a synonym for *history*.

†In March or April, depending on the sect.

‡Our astronomers predict the hour and minute of eclipses no less successfully, we take it, than the Brâhmana-astrologers. But it is strange that the latter seldom make mistakes in often foretelling for a whole year ahead the dates and even the hours of unexpected hurricanes and rains, which (particularly the latter) very rarely occur out of the rainy season. Here is what the Mahârâja of Travancore writes about these Brâhmana-astrologers in his article, "The Borderland between Matter and Spirit:"

"Astrology, so much scouted by moderns, has still its hold upon

patron-god or patron-goddess of the temple. The crowd listens reverently to the prophecies of the idol who speaks through the lips of his Brâhmaṇa about famine, wars, and other national calamities; afterwards, the astrologer and the Brâhmaṇa bless the crowd and, upon dividing the rice, fruit, and other edible offerings brought for the idols, among the poorest, permit them to go home.

Collector Peters found in the "autobiography" of Mînâkshî a *Purâṇa* about the *antarvâhinî nadî*. With the aid of his pundit, he translated it from the Sanskrit into *Telugu*, and it is read to this day in the temple of the kindhearted goddess. The following is a brief summary of its contents:

This *Sthûla-Purâṇa* explains the cause of the subterranean course of the river Vaigai and, in addition, gives proof of the deep trust of the goddess Mînâkshî in Mr. Peters, to whom she chose to confide the episode of her early youth and love for her spouse Śiva.

Kulaśekhara,* the valiant King of Madhurai in the adolescent days of the chief gods, and his spouse (whose name has not survived in history), found themselves rewarded for long years of continual *tapas*† and pious works by the birth

---

mankind, and belief in it may often be seen in the most unexpected quarters. A European friend told us the other day that some years ago he was going to a lumber depot in the heart of the forests and situated on an islet formed by two branches of a large river. It was perfectly dry weather and the streams were quite dry. Happening to meet an astrologer on the way, he was warned that three days hence there would be heavy rain and a terrible flood in the river. There wasn't a cloud in the sky; pooh-poohing the prediction, he went on to the lumber depot. The result was, rain came in torrents on the predicted day, the river flooded over, cutting off all communication, and washing away much valuable timber, and compelled him to live most miserably in an improvised log-hut on the most elevated part of the islet for several days. *He*, for one, professes belief in *astrology*, however much astrologers may be impostors in many cases. We have known instances in which the date of childbirth and the sex of the child have been foretold with perfect correctness." (*The Theosophist*, Vol. VI, No. 2, Nov. 1884, p. 41, 2nd column.)

*The literal translation of this name is: "the head of the family jewels."

†*Tapas*—ritual prayers in various postures.

of a charming daughter. She was the fruit of hundreds of their past *janmans* (reincarnations) in the outer shape of other personalities, for this daughter was the celebrated, fish-eyed Mînâkshî. The goddess did not become a goddess at once, but as the result of piety in many of her former existences, during the course of which she supplicated Śiva and Kâlî — the first, to honor her by selecting her as one of his spouses, and the other, to make the supplicant one of her own *aspects*. Finally, Sundarêśvara* fulfilled her ardent prayer and announced to Mînâkshî that he would marry her.

The king, Kulaśekhara, began magnificent preparations for the wedding feast. Overflowing with pride at the thought that he was being honored with such a divine son-in-law, he beseeched Śiva to bring a large retinue with him from the most eminent lords of Kailâsa.† *Bhûmi-devî* (the earth goddess), he said, though her fecundity and innate patience were proverbial, would not have time to generate enough *devas* for the wedding, in the addition to the mass of sinners (not to mention the animal and other kingdoms) which she has daily to bring into the world; therefore if Śiva does not take pity, the wedding feast would be lacking in splendor and there would be no one to eat the food prepared.

The bridegroom promised to satisfy the ambition of his father-in-law, but when he descended from Kailâsa to "sweet earth," ‡ instead of the expected resplendent retinue, he brought with him only one misshapen dwarf, *Kuṇḍôdara.*§ The chosen father-in-law took this as mockery and became very vexed. But what can the anger of a mortal mean in the eyes of a god? Śiva, upon reading the thoughts of Kulaśekhara, smiled and merely said: "King, feed my little courtier!" The Râjâ, very grieved by the fact that there

---

Sundarêśvara—"the Magnificent Lord," a name of Śiva, one of the *ekâdaśa Rudras*, or "eleven Rudras," Rudra meaning literally *destroyer*, conqueror of sin.

†*Kailâsa* is that part of heaven which is the favorite abode of Śiva and his domicile.

‡*Madhurai* means "sweet earth."

§*Kuṇḍôdara* means "large abdomen."

would be no one to eat his feast, ordered his *pradhâna mantrin* (prime minister) to see that the dwarf was well-fed. But when the latter began to eat, he devoured not only the *delicacies* which had been prepared at the palace, but all the supplies as well, even the entire year's reserve of the town of Madhurai; thereupon, swallowing all the stored water in the wells and fountains. Still crying for more water, the dwarf was then led to the shore of the River Vaigai. Its water proved to be insufficient for quenching Kundô-dara's thirst. In one gulp he drained the river to its bed. whereupon the river-goddess had to save herself by flight into the bosom of the earth.

That was the lesson Śiva taught his father-in-law, who had given no thought to the poor whom he could have fed with the food prepared for the wedding, but had preferred to have the dignitaries of the court eat it. Ever since then, the dwarf, under the guise of his *barrel-bellied* stone idol, has been sitting on the bank of the dry river, awaiting its annual appearance during the rainy season. Kind Mîn-âkshî, pitying the fate of the Madhuraians, prevailed upon the goddess Vaigai to return from the bosom of the earth and to flow towards the sea one yard underground, and permitted the dwarf to drink all the water of the river just once a year. Since then she has been the patroness of the city.

Shortly after making frequent visits to the temple, Peters, who had become immersed in the study of the glorious deeds of the mighty *devî* and astounded by her virtues, began to find something engaging in the expression of the fish-eyes of Mînâkshî. It seemed as if her hideous mouth would spread into a benign smile upon the approach of the Collector. He became used to her ugliness. A bachelor and with simple tastes like all scholars, Peters, who at first had begun to study the religion of the Hindus for the sake of science and, possibly, from boredom as well, began to be drawn, little by little, into their complicated, head-splitting philosophy, and soon became an actual *Śâstrin*.* He ceased

---

*A theologian knowing by heart all the *Śâstras*, or theological treatises.

making fun of the pious Brâhmaṇas and began to fraternize, and to surround himself, with them.

Among the latter there was a *mantrika,* a Brâhmaṇa of the Temple of Mînâkshî, whose duty consisted of uttering mantras and other magic prayers before the goddess. Soon he became the *alter ego* of the Collector. Finally, one fine day he brought the Collector an idol of Mînâkshî, and the bronze image was placed in the host's bedroom. Knowing him to be an archaeologist, the few Anglo-Indians who lived in Madhurai paid no particular attention to this.

One night, Mr. Peters, who always slept very soundly, saw his goddesss in a dream. The fish-eyed apparition tried hurriedly to wake him, bidding him to "get up and get dressed." But even such a summons as this could have no effect on the sound sleep of the Collector. Then *in his dream* it appeared as if the goddess herself began dressing him in haste; the holy hands of Mînâkshî were not squeamish even about pulling his boots over his feet, boots which were made from *sacred* cowhide. (This is the reason that in the eyes of the Brâhmaṇas boots are the most defiled article of European apparel.) Having dressed her admirer, she touched his forehead, saying, "Save yourself through the window. Jump, or you will perish! . . ." She then vanished, and Mr. Peters woke up.

The Collector's house was on fire. The flames were already licking the walls of his bedchamber with their greedy tongues, and the only door leading out of the room was ablaze. Without deliberating, he jumped out of the window and thus saved his life. The house was built on the bank of the river, but at the time of the fire, as usual, the Vaigai was absolutely dry. Suddenly, to the amazement of the crowd gathered there, the water began to ooze through the river bed and to rise rapidly to the very verandah of the burning house before their very eyes. Thanks to this unexpected help, the fire was soon put out and many objects of Mr. Peter's priceless collection were saved. Only papers and documents of great value to the Government had been consumed.

This fact is stated in the Collector's own handwriting, over his own signature, and is confirmed by the testimony of his assistant, his clerks, and many of those present at the scene of the fire; furthermore, it is entered in the officially sealed book in the city archives, where the curious document may be found to this day.

Strangest of all was the fact that Mr. Peters, according to the testimony of his valet and his own recollections, went to bed on the eve of the conflagration undressed and unshod, but upon jumping out of the window, found himself dressed and with his boots on. In addition to all this, he did not jump from the first floor empty handed *but with the heavy bronze idol of Mînâkshî under his arm.* This inexplicable fact, which he related himself hundreds of times, caused everyone to smile and shake their heads. "The esteemed Peters," they said, "was simply drunk that evening and probably fell asleep as he was, even to his boots." But the Brâhmaṇas and the native population were triumphant, firmly convinced that *he had been dressed and saved by the Mahâ-devatî,* the "great goddess" herself.

It is evident that Mr. Peters was also fully of this opinion, judging by the unforeseen results of this event: He suddenly became extremely devout, if it is at all possible to use this word in connection with the object of his piety, and in the words of Mûljî, from a complete materialist was actually "transformed into a *pûjist.*" Peters began honoring the goddess Mînâkshî no less than any Brâhmaṇa. He gave up his service and, upon retirement, clothed himself in the attire of the *bairâgins,* to daily perform the religious rites prescribed by the *Sâstras,* and finally gained among the populace the reputation of being a "white saint." He grew fond of the Hindus and became such an ardent defender of them that his memory still lives in the hearts of the grateful natives, and his name is uttered with the greatest respect by all pilgrims who come to worship.

As a result of this unusual "occurrence," the Government proclaimed him insane and appointed a commission of psychiatrists to dispatch him to England for a cure. But even here the "goddess" did not betray her admirer. The doctors and experts evidently fell under the influence of Mînâkshî's *dhâraṇâ* (magnetic influence), for instead of a testimonial to his mental derangement, they gave him a clean bill of health, stating that the ex-Collector's reason was found to be completely sound. After his return to Madras, they again confirmed their testimony. Peters had influential friends in England and independent means, so he was left in peace. When he died many years later, it was his wish that his ashes be buried in a place from which one could see the temple of his goddess. And so it was done. He was buried, after cremation, on a hillock from which the golden *stupa* (cupola) of the eastern tower of the temple is seen as clearly as if it lay in the palm of one's hand. The granite mausoleum still towers to this day, and pilgrims come to visit the grave of the "white saint." *Peter's Tomb* is one of the curiosities of Madhurai, and the tourist who wishes to have a view of the city and the temple sets out for this well-known hillock. The latter is located on land belonging to the Temple of Mînâkshî, otherwise the tomb and the monument would have been taken down, and the ground leveled, long ago.

Anglo-Indians, however, "who were *not* fond" of the Hindus would have found it beyond their strength had they been obliged to proclaim insane all those among them who, though they did not love the natives, nevertheless did believe in the power of their gods and goddesses, however strange this may appear. All these eccentric people, upon inquiry, appear to have left the ranks of the materialists; they are all *ex*-atheists and positivists! For example, here is what the Mahârâja of Travancore, the most educated of all Indian princes, wrote about another Collector whose name he did not wish to reveal:

"A certain Collector of a certain district in the Madras Presidency had a family of several daughters but not a single son. Having had, in the course of his official life, to associate with native gentlemen of all shades of faith, he was advised by several natives to take sea-baths at Râmeśvaram to get a son! Of course, he derided the proposal, but thinking that a sea-bath could do no harm he did bathe at Dhanushkoṭi.* *And he had a son shortly after!"†*

---

*The Temple of Râmeśvaram at Dhanushkoṭi is a place of pilgrimage visited by the natives under vow, *in order to have sons.*
†*The Theosophist*, Vol. VI, No. 2, Nov., 1884, p. 41, 2nd col.

Some Anglo-Indians turned to Mohammedanism; others, who were not accepted into Hinduism by the Brâhmaṇas, became, from grief, either *Vallabhachâryas** or devil-worshippers.

Madhurai is not far from Madras. When we visited there some two years later, and soon after settled at Adyar on the shores of the river, one of the old Brâhmaṇas who had known Peters personally told us a great deal about him.

"The goddess revealed herself to him," he said, among other things, "in her *actual primordial essence; otherwise* he would have never worshipped her as he did."

In answer to our comment that even though they, the Vedântins, speak a great deal about the *Oneness* of Para-brahman, their worship of idols disproves and contradicts this Oneness in their teachings, he replied:

"*Devatî* (goddess) is an idol only in the eyes of the ignorant *śûdra* (lower caste); for the initiated *śâstrîns,* Mîn-âkshî, like other divinities, is simply *one of the bricks of the common edifice,* the name of which is *Sat,* Be-ness."

This explanation and the expression "brick," seemed at the time very unsatisfactory to us and, to me, exceedingly ludicrous. Later, however, I better understood its significance.

Prior to my serious study of the *Vedas* and, in general, of the symbolism of Brâhmanical beliefs, I frequently asked myself the question: By virtue of *what* could such intelligent people and genuine thinkers, as the authors of these highly remarkable and original systems appear to be — to those who have studied the *six* main philosophical schools of India — have fallen into *polytheism* and its outer expression through worship of idols, or have allowed it in the masses, no matter how ignorant the latter might be? For a long time I could not account for this strange predilection. I could not explain to myself, even superficially, why, for example, Keshub Chunder-Sen, the well-known, highly

---

*The *Vallabhachârya* sect is the most immoral. It recognizes as its sole head the pontiff, who enjoys absolute connubial rights over the wives and daughters *of all* Vallabhachâryas without exception.

educated Bengal reformer, a man who at one time had charmed Queen Victoria * by his conversation and his views, and all London high society by his unusual, fascinating eloquence — why even this mystic, the head and *leader* of the Brahmo-Samâja, could not throughout his life reject his goddess *Durgâ*. At times it seemed simply disgusting to listen to him and to read in the press how, in his mystical semi-delirium, he jumbled Mohammed, Buddha, Chaitanya and Durgâ! But now I understand, and sincerely regret my vociferous censure of this reformer who is now deceased. He was an ardent monotheist, but he was born a Hindu and remained one to the end. The following explanation of this riddle may possibly prove to be of some benefit:

In the strange mythology of the Brâhmaṇas — which at first glance is even more legendary than Greek mythology — and, generally, in their still stranger conception of the world, a profound philosophy is nevertheless concealed. The outer form of idolatry is but a curtain which hides the truth, like the veil of Isis. This truth, however, is not given to all. For some the curtain hides, not the countenance of Isis, but merely empty space receding into what for them is impenetrable darkness; for others, however, light pours forth therefrom. For those not endowed by nature with that innate, inner sense possessed by some, which the Hindus so rightly call "the third eye" or "the eye of Śiva," it is better by far to be content with the fantastic patterns upon the curtain; such cannot fathom the depth of the impenetrable darkness, nor fill empty space. But he who is possessed of the "third eye" or, speaking more clearly, who is capable of transferring his vision from the grossly objective to the pure innermost, sees light within the darkness, and in the seeming emptiness discerns the *Universe*... Inner self-awareness will show him infallibly that the presence of God *is* felt here, but cannot be communicated, and that the expression of this in concrete form finds its excuse in the ardent desire to convey this feeling to the masses. Thus, though still censuring in

---

*Keshub Chunder-Sen always called the Queen his "mother." The members of the Brahmo-Samâja sect are considered to be, and are called, the Indian "Unitarians," being semi-Christians.

his soul the form of worship, he will no longer laugh openly at idols and at the belief in them of those who, unable to penetrate beyond the curtain, are satisfied with the exterior form only because it is difficult for them, if not completely impossible, to arrive at any kind of suitable conception of the "Unknown God."

In order to show graphically that all the 330 million gods of India together point to *One* Unknown God, I shall try to speak more plainly. For this it will be sufficient to tell one of the allegorical stories of the ancient Brâhmaṇas from the *Purâṇas,* a story which, apparently, has not yet reached our Orientalists. It is quickly told.

Towards the end of the last *pralaya* (*i.e.,* the intervening period between two creations of our world), the Great Râjâ who abides in the eternity of endless space, wishing to give to the coming people some means of knowing him, built a palace upon Mount Meru out of his *inherent qualities* and established residence therein. But when people once again inhabited the world, this palace, one end of which rested upon the right and the other upon the left "boundlessness," proved to be so vast that the little folk did not even suspect its existence; for them the palace was the celestial firmament, beyond which, according to them, there was nothing. The Great Râjâ, perceiving the difficulty and taking pity on the little folk, decided to reveal himself to them, *not in his entirety, but in parts.* He demolished the palace created out of his qualities and started throwing one brick after another on the earth. Each brick turned into an idol: a red brick, into a god, and a gray, into a goddess; and each of the *devatâs* and *devatîs* who had embodied themselves in an idol *became endowed with one of the innumerable qualities of the Mahârâja.* At first the entire pantheon consisted of only the superior qualities. But people, taking advantage of impunity, became more depraved and more evil . . . Then the Great Râjâ sent *karman* (the law of retribution) to earth. Karman, which does not spare even the gods, changed many of the qualities into instruments of punishment; and it is thus that destroyer-gods and avenger-gods appeared among the all-forgiving, benevolent divinities.

This story, related to us by a Brâhmaṇa from Madhurai,

explains why he called the goddess Mînâkshî "a brick" and, in addition to this, indicates the unity at the bottom of all this polytheism. Between the *dii majores* of holy Mount Meru — the Olympus of India — and the *dii minores,* the difference in individual essence is not great. The first are the direct rays, and the second are the fragmented, refracted rays of the same luminary. What in reality are Brahmâ, Vishnu and Śiva? They are the threefold ray issuing directly from "the luminary of the universe," *Svayambhû,* the *power* or *spirit* that vivifies and fecundates matter, the latter personified in Sarasvatî, Lakshmî and Kâlî, the three representations of *prakriti* (matter), the three goddesses of the three gods. These three pairs, synthesized in *Svayambhû,* the *"Unmanifested* Deity," are the symbols that personify its unseen presence in all the manifestations of nature. In short, Brahmâ and Sarasvatî, Vishnu and Lakshmî, Śiva and Kâlî represent in their totality *spirit* and *matter* in their threefold quality — *creation, preservation* and *destruction.*

Vishnu is one, but he has 1,008 names, each one of which is the name *of one of the qualities of the One.* The personal qualities of Vishnu are embodied in their turn in the secondary gods of the Hindu pantheon. Thus, becoming a separate personality from Vishnu (while Vishnu himself is only the personification of one of the *seven* chief qualities or attributes of Svayambhû), each personification is called an aspect or "appearance" of Vishnu, Brahmâ or Śiva — in short, of one or the other of the *chief* gods and goddesses. All of them have many names which are repeated parrot-fashion by the officiating Brâhmana of one or another sect, but each name had a deep significance in the days of antiquity. Svayambhû is the first emanation or ray of Parabrahman, the Divinity *without attributes;* it is the first breath of its spirit; and it is *Trimûrti,* the synthesis of the three spiritual powers in union with the three material powers. It is from the qualities of these three pairs that are born the lesser gods, *dii minores,* who in their turn represent the qualities of the greater gods.

Thus the seven primary colors of the prism into which the *colorless* ray is decomposed, give rise, upon further blending, to secondary composite colors and are diversified *ad infi-*

nitum. The Brâmaṇas say that the god *Sûrya* (the sun) has seven sons, whose offspring comprise a good third of the pantheon of *devas;* and the god of air, *Vâyu,* is the father of the seven primordial syllables and the seven musical tones in which are generated, and from which issue, all possible combinations of sounds in the harmony of nature.

In ancient India, religion was closely connected with the contemplation of nature. Universal truths and the very essence of *Truth* were personified in Deity. Every manifest truth, no matter what it consists of, has a direct relationship to divinity or *self-existent* truth. In the pantheon of the Hindu religion only the outer method of expression is really crude and, as a rule, has a repellent and caricatured form.

The natural inference to be drawn from all this is that the pantheism of India, which has outwardly deified all the crude forces of nature, as if personifying only the outer forms, is tied in with the realm of physical knowledge, of chemistry, and particularly of astronomy, and presents in itself something in the nature of poetical materialism — a continuation of Chaldean Sabaeanism. However, if we cast aside its outer form, which has led the ignorant masses to the most repugnant worship of idols, and penetrate to the primordial source of the myths of pantheism, we shall find therein neither gods nor even outer worship of various objects from the kingdoms of nature in their ordinary forms, but rather a worship of the *omnipresent* Spirit, equally immanent in the smallest blade of grass as in the power that begot and stimulated it to growth.

Such is the simple and natural explanation of the 33 *crores** (330 million) gods in India. These gods were begotten and endowed with being as a result of the blind endeavor to personify that which cannot be personified, thus giving rise to "idols." In the course of time, the cornerstone of the philosophic and religious world-conception of their wise men found itself in the hands of the ambitious, coldly calculating Brâhmaṇas, who broke the stone into chips and ground it into dust for the convenient assimilation by the masses. But for the thinker, as well as for every *unprejudiced*

---

*A *crore* is equal to 100 *lakhs* or 10 million.

Orientalist, these misshapen chips, as well as their finely crushed gravel, are, nonetheless, from the very same stone — attributes of the manifested energy of Parabrahman, the One that forever Is, without beginning or end.

The Brâhmaṇa-Vedântists postulate three kinds of existence: *pâramârthika* — the *real*, the true; *vyâvahârika* — the *conditioned* and practical; and *prâtibhâsika* — the *illusory*. Parabrahman is the only representation of the first and, therefore, is called *Sat*, "that which really is" or the *One-Existent;* to the second class belong the gods personified in diverse forms, the *personal* souls* of mortals, and everything that is manifested and phenomenal in the world of subjective feeling. This class, having received existence in the imagination of the ignorant masses, has a foundation no firmer than that which we see in dreams; but in view of the actuality of the practical relationship of the people to these gods, their existence is allowed *conditionally*. The third class of existence includes such objects as mirages — mother-of-pearl mistaken for silver, a coiled serpent mistaken for a rope — and even man, in one of its subdivisions. People *think*, imagine that they see the one or the other; consequently, for him who sees it and imagines it to be so, it *actually does exist*. But since this actuality is only temporary and the very nature of the objects is ephemeral, and thus conditioned, therefore in the last analysis it follows that all this actuality is merely an *illusion*.

All of these conceptions not only do not interfere with the belief in the personality and oneness of deity, but also serve as an impassable barrier to atheism. There are no atheists in India in the sense in which we Europeans use this term. *Nâstika* is an atheist in the sense of *non-believer in gods and idols*. This is known to everyone in India, and we have become completely convinced of it. The atheists, and even the *agnostics* of the West are a long way from the *Nâstikas* of the East. The former crudely deny everything except matter; the latter, namely, the Hindu materialists, the *Nâstikas*, do not at all deny the possibility of the exist-

---

*According to the teachings of the Brâhmaṇas, the *personal* soul or *earth* consciousness is distinguished from our immortal "spirit."

ence of that which they do not understand. The true philosopher will understand the *spirit* and not the letter of
their denial. He will be easily convinced of the fact that
if they, in referring to the abstraction called Parabrahman,
teach that this principle is "without volition and without
activity, devoid of sensation and of consciousness," they do so
precisely because, according to their understanding, *the
One,* under that name, is *unconditioned* volition, activity
without beginning and *without end, self-existent* self-consciousness, self-apprehension and self-awareness.

It follows that the pantheists of India, in retaining their
idols, sin merely by an overdose of religious, though badly
applied, feeling. In addition, after the total destructiveness
and absolute non-creativeness of *animal* materialism in
Europe, such pantheism appears as morally and spiritually
refreshing, a blossoming oasis in the midst of a barren, sandy
desert. Better to believe *at least in one of the qualities of
divinity,* personifying and worshipping it under that particular guise which represents to each one, according to the
power of his understanding, the most convenient semblance
and symbol of the *All,* than to deny the *All* under the pretext
that it cannot be proved by scientific methods, and to
believe in nothing, as do our learned materialists and
fashionable agnostics.

From the above point of view, and though we may be
surprised and even sincerely amused at the originality of his
choice of an object for worship, we will understand why
Mr. Peters was changed, so suddenly and unexpectedly,
from an ardent materialist of the school of Mill and Clifford
to a pantheist and even a *pûjist.**

And now we shall return to Dîgh.

---

*From the word *pûja,* meaning the worship of gods by established
rules; not prayer, but ritual.

— IV —

[THE PLEASANT GARDENS OF DÎGH. — THE VEDÂNTA TEACHINGS
CONCERNING THE NATURE OF MAN AND THE UNIVERSE. — THE PRIN-
CIPLES OF MAN'S CONSTITUTION. — A DISCUSSION WITH THE ṬHÂKUR
ON MAN AND HIS POST-MORTEM STATES. — THE SÛTRÂTMAN. — SLEEP
AND DEATH. — ÂNANDA SVÂMI AND THE COLONEL'S DELIGHT. — WHAT
IS A RUDRÂKSHA? — THE ŚÂLAGRÂMA.]

Mûljî's narrative, related in great detail by him, but considerably condensed by me, came to a close at the dinner hour, about five o'clock in the afternoon; of this we were not aware.

An unbearable sultriness lay about us. The day we spent in Dîgh had been so hot that one could suspect *Sûrya* of wishing to burn alive all the Jâts that worshipped him, and with them us sinners, who had cursed his overly-ardent caresses so frequently . . .

The scorching rays poured like molten gold over the cupolas and the marble walls of the kiosks and lay like blinding spots on the drowsy waters of the ponds, shooting forth death-dealing darts on the living and the dead. They even drove the flocks of parrots and peacocks, with which the gardens of India teem as our Russian kitchen gardens do with sparrows, to hide in the very thickest of the shrubs. An impenetrable silence lay around us . . . Everything slept, everything languished and burned . . .

Even prior to the beginning of the narrative about Mr. Peters, however, we took refuge in the tall central marble summerhouse that was almost hidden in the densest part of the garden and there, without venturing to leave the blessed shelter we had found, delighted in its comparative coolness.

547

Surrounded on all sides by the water of a small reservoir in the midst of which it towered, the spacious summerhouse, shaded by creeping aquatic plants, offered us shelter in which we felt neither the great heat nor exhaustion. For several yards around us there was shade and coolness. An inferno blazed beyond the boundary of the miniature mirror-like pond; the ground cracked and split from the fiery kisses of the frightful spring sun, whose rays licked the still luxuriant, though seared, vegetation of the garden with their flaming tongues. The roses crumpled and fell; even the lotus and water lily curled the edges of their hardy thick petals into little tubes, as if fastidiously avoiding the burning touch. Only the orchids, "the flowers of passion," * raised their variegated, insect-like little cups to drink in this fiery stream as other flowers drink in the cool dew . . .

What a delightful, unique garden! Laid out on a bare cliff, in a space about two hundred and eighty yards deep and one hundred and seventeen wide, it includes within itself more than two hundred large and small fountains.

The superintendent, a sugary old man who resembled a eunuch, assured us that "not all the fountains were active," that many were choked and damaged, but that on the day of the reception in Dîgh, for the Prince of Wales, if I am not mistaken, there had been six hundred of them. However, we were completely satisfied with even two hundred of them. For several rupees, the gardeners made it possible for us to be in the midst of delightful coolness the entire day, and to stroll, on a moonlit night, along an avenue bordered by two continuous rows of tall gushing fountains, instead of trees. Nothing could be equal to the effect of these two walls of spraying water scintillating in the moonlight like diamonds and iridescent with all the tints of mother-of-pearl. A wonderful little corner, but one that has been forgotten by everybody, and which is visited by no one except Anglo-Indian officials passing through accidentally,

---

*Passion flower, so named because this species of orchid opens fully only in the heat of midday, and not at all, as many have asserted, because its petals, supposedly, bear a resemblance to the cross, nails, and crown of thorns.

who are always willing to accept the entertainment of the native princes and, in gratitude, to slander them at the crossroads.

The Mahârâja of Bhurtpore himself does not as much as peep into Dîgh. The potentate of the Jâts, a nursling of the Government, prefers the fizzle of champagne to the murmuring of the fountains in his own charming palace, and there is no sweeter melody for him than the sound of a bottle of cognac being uncorked . . .

Thus, the shady old garden grows rampant in its wild beauty, deserted by people but, on the other hand, left at the complete disposal of a whole army of magnificent, though also wild, peahens. Hundreds of these favorite birds of Juno (who is called *Sarasvatî* in India) fill the paths, strolling about pompously, with their long tails sweeping the dust accumulated through the years. They stud the trees from top to bottom and, thanks to their presence, the old garden from afar frequently takes on the appearance of an enchanted wood in a fairy tale. The shaggy trees, flooded by the dazzling sunlight, seem to breathe while moving and swaying, and from behind their dense foliage, thousands of sparkling curious eyes peep out, reflecting hues of sapphire and gold . . . These are the eyes scattered on the tails of the peacocks moving in the branches.

Stepping out onto the terrace overlooking the garden, I could not for some time account for this strange phantasmagoria, and descended the steps in order to examine the wonderful spectacle more closely. My curiosity was immediately punished by "assault and battery." The ponderous flight of a peacock that had slipped off a tree, frightened by my sudden appearance, interrupted my reflections about the wonders of India, having knocked the topi from my head and me off my feet. I solaced myself by an exploration of the garden, but the Bâbû took revenge for my fall by plucking half a dozen feathers from the tail of another peacock, one which was guiltless, "in remembrance of Dîgh"! . . .

The garden is crisscrossed in all directions by narrow paths, which are cleaned and freed of accumulated refuse only before the arrival of "notable guests," as the gardener explained to us, from which we drew the conclusion, with our discerning perspicacity, that we did not belong to this fortunate category. In every corner, as well as in the heart of the garden, the motionless waters slumber peacefully in their marble basins under blankets of thick slime. The fountain reservoirs, ponds, and miniature lakes have become a mass of green scum, and only the waters of the ponds nearest the palace are kept clean, adding much to the general beauty of this little corner. Irrespective of the obvious neglect, the octagonal basin in the center of the garden with the cool kiosk that sheltered us from the heat, was particularly beautiful. Surrounded by smaller basins with tall gushing sprays from baskets of luxuriant tropical flowers, we were blissfully happy the whole day, sitting in the kiosk as if in a submarine kingdom. Four avenues of fountains led to the pond, cutting it crosswise, and four small bridges of marble fretwork led to the kiosk.

Exhausted by conversation, we now sat in silence, each one brooding over his own thoughts and pursuits. I was reading, thinking more of the Ṭhâkur than of the contents of the book, while the Colonel slept. Sitting on a bench against the wall, his head thrown back on the dense creeping greenery and his long grey beard protruding, our esteemed chief, Colonel O., snored quietly. Nârâyaṇa and Mûljî squatted on the floor, while the Bâbû, perched caryatid-fashion on the pedestal of a broken idol, now missing, slept also.

Thus we sat, drowsy, silent, and motionless, for quite some time. Finally, towards half-past-five, the slumbering garden gradually began to waken; the heat abated, the peacocks emerged from their corners, and flocks of golden-green parrots called to each other from the tree tops . . . A few more minutes — and the sun would disappear beyond the boundary of the briny lakes, and nature, exhausted for the day, would rest until the following morning and cool off until the next fiery ordeal.

I abandoned my book to observe how everything around us began to breathe and move. The garden was changing from a fiery furnace — like Daniel's — into the grove of a classical idyll: it lacked only the playful, dancing nymphs

MADHURAI: HALL OF A THOUSAND PILLARS

AN OLD FORT AT MATHURĀ (MUTTRA)

and the gay pipes of Pan. The transparent liquid of the pond now reflected only the light blue sky and the vain peacocks, perching for the night on the carved balustrades of the little bridge. In preparation for their coming slumber, they moved their tails like Spanish ladies do their fans, opening and closing them over and over again, and admiring their reflections in the water. Finally, the sun, flashing its last golden sparks, vanished, and a gentle breeze enveloped us. It was so pleasant, so cool in the summerhouse, that we definitely refused to dine in the stuffy hall of the palace and decided to ask for *khânâ* (dinner) in the arbor, sending the Bâbû as an envoy upon this mission.

Under the pretense of fearing vengeance from the peacock whose feathers he had plucked, and which, according to his own assertion, he recognized among those perched on the balustrades, the restless Bengalî selected the most direct way, by impetuously diving straight into the pond from the pedestal instead of taking the path over the little bridge. The sudden splash of water wakened and frightened the sleeping Colonel, who immediately and anxiously inquired whether the Bâbû was in any danger of drowning.

"Better to drown than to risk the vengeance of a '*were-fowl*'," shouted the scoffing skeptic, snorting and choking with water.

"What 'werefowl'?" inquisitively asked our President, who had been set at ease by the fact that the water barely reached the Bâbû's chest.

"The cursed peacock! You see, it's the very same "werefowl" that tumbled down onto the verandah at Bhurtpore yesterday evening!" shouted the Bengalî, as he walked with difficulty across the slimy bottom of the pond. "I myself saw him wink at Mûljî about me."

"He is always throwing stones into my garden," commented "the general," frowning. "Has this *nâstika* ever really believed in anything? He is always laughing at everything and everybody."

"Well, now you, too, can laugh at him. Just look at that figure!" I replied, bursting into laughter.

Really, the Bâbû presented the most curious sight. He had crawled out of the mire with great effort and, having clambered onto the high parapet of the pond, left large puddles of greenish mud on the white marble behind him. Covered with slimy weeds and mud, he had lost all human semblance.

"You look like a drowned man, my poor Bâbû," I laughed at him. "How is it possible to feel such attraction to water? This is the second time for you today. Beware you do not become a water *piśâcha* after death and, also, do not drown sometime . . ."

"What I was, that I am, and that I will be," was the reply I received from him, a quotation from the aphorisms of his all-denying sect. "Dust I am and dust I shall be, and drowning, they say, is a most pleasant and easy death, *Maam-Saab* . . ."

"Everyone sees what you *are*. What you *will be,* that I do not know. But that you surely were a Newfoundland pup in your former existence, that is certain," replied Mûljî, avenging himself.

But the Bâbû did not hear the remark made under his breath at his expense. Somewhat embarrassed by his appearance, he took to his heels and dashed straight towards the house.

Had I possessed the gift of foresight, as Nârâyaṇa somehow imagined that I did, I would have sooner swallowed my tongue than to have uttered my last comment. Poor, gay, unconcerned boy! . . . Did he foresee then that such an early and agonizing death awaited him in the turbid yellow waves of the Ganges? To this very day I cannot recall without emotion the poor Bâbû and the happy weeks of travel we had spent together, though five years have elapsed since, and almost two years from the day of the fateful event. How frequently, too frequently indeed, since that time, have I dreamt in my restless sleep of that emaciated, small, and semi-childish figure all covered with dark green slime from the pond of Dîgh! I fancy in my dreams that his once sparkling eyes, which used to be full of good-natured merriment, but are now glassy and lifeless, stare at me, and I clearly hear again the familiar chuckling voice in reply to my unconscious prophetic warning, "Do not drown sometime," answering with an equally prophetic note: *"What*

I was, that I am ... Dust I am, and dust I shall be ..."—
and I awaken trembling with horror at the recollection!...*
In thinking over the past, I often ask myself the question:
"Is it true, that all that remains of him is ... *dust?*" And
at once I recall an argument between Nârâyaṇa and the
Bâbû, and the Thâkur's replies to our questions. This argument started between them a few days after the one—so
memorable to me—spent at Dîgh.

I shall relate the remarkable conversation *in extenso,*
hoping that it will be interesting to the serious reader, not
so much because it settled the questions that had bothered
me for a long time, but because it explains the peculiar point
of view of the Vedântins on life after death, its mysteries, and
the soul of man in general.

With a view to a fuller explanation, I venture to make
a few preliminary remarks, thus making the conversation
that follows more intelligible to the reader. Otherwise, it
would be extremely difficult for those unfamiliar with the
philosophy of the Vedântins (of the *secret* school), and
particularly with the complex theory of the soul and its
significance in eternity, to follow the many different terms
for the "spiritual man." The latter are as innumerable, as
are the names of their gods — these being masks — because
every *aspect* of the soul (or, more accurately, of the unified
spiritual *aggregate,* which is called by the Vedântins the
real man or the "spiritual individuality," whereas his
perishable body of *earthly* personality is considered as an
illusion), each one of its qualitative modifications has its
own particular descriptive name. For example, they divide

---

*The young lad drowned in 1883 in an awful and, at the same time,
stupid manner. Between Dehra-Dûn and Hardvâr, the Ganges is not
yet a river, but a shallow and exceedingly rapid stream. It can be
crossed at one place by means of a small bridge, and those who have
a horse lead it by the reins close to the bridge and through water which
does not reach even to the knees of the animal. But the Bâbû, in spite
of a warning, conceived a desire to cross the river on horseback. The
horse stumbled and fell; the Bâbû became entangled in the stirrups
and could not free himself. The stream, according to accounts, rolled
both of them more than a mile to the edge of the waterfall, where the
rider and horse both perished. His death, it goes without saying, was
attributed to "the anger of the gods"!

the "earthly personality" into three main groups: spirit, soul
and body, and then subdivide these groups into seven compound powers or principles. The first two, spirit and the
"divine soul" (the vehicle of the spirit), are impersonal and
devoid of qualities *per se*, and the remaining five are called
kośas, i.e., "sheaths" or "envelopes" of the various spiritual
and earthly qualities of man, therefore personal and qualitative. Thus *manomaya-kośa,* in literal translation, would mean
"sheath of illusory cognition," *i.e.,* seat or receptacle of the
purely earthly and, therefore, *illusory* conceptions of man.
This *kośa* is the envelope *of the conceptions of his earthly
mind,* in conjunction with the activity of our five sense
organs, which, obscuring the pure divine mind with their
gross earthly conceptions, transform every truth into a
mirage.

This theory is particularly difficult for those who, while
admitting the creation of a separate soul for each man,
reject at the same time the theory of his numerous reincarnations and thus repudiate *emanation,* the most essential point of the pantheistic teaching of India. In reading,
for example, about the *septenary* constitution of man, it
might be supposed that there reside in us seven personalities,
each one distinct from the other ("seven demons," according to the expression of a Russian Theosophist), which appear in their numerical sequence like the thin skin of an
onion, becoming more ethereal and subjective in proportion
to their distance from the outer and coarse envelope, namely,
the body. The philosophy of Vedânta preaches, however,
nothing of the kind. All these *kośas* are devised for the
purpose of elucidating its doctrine of the complete unity
of Parabrahman, the basis and *substance* of the entire *manifested* universe. If this doctrine of the begetting of the
qualitative universe from spirit devoid of all qualities were
not explained by means of emanations, the doctrine would
remain completely incomprehensible to the pantheists themselves.

Spirit is one and indivisible, while the souls of mankind
represent a countless number of separate units. These souls
are emanations, "spirits from spirit." But as the impersonal
Unconditioned Be-ness, devoid of all qualities, cannot mani-

fest personally, the reverse side of Parabrahman, *Mûla-prakṛiti*,* its co-eternal power or energy, the *root* of all that exists, is postulated. Inseparable from Parabrahman, *Mûla-prakṛiti* constitutes with it the *invisible universe*. That which becomes separated is not *Mûlaprakṛiti*, but only the light or the radiance from "the light of the universe," and it is this that is the emanation which becomes the *visible* universe. But here again a difficulty arises: where is there room for the *visible* universe? How can anything be put in a place that is already occupied, even in boundless space, if this space is in fact the Omnipresent *Sat* itself? Finally, how can qualitative substance be abstracted from spirit that is devoid of all qualities, namely, from that which appears to our conception as *nothing?*

The Vedântins solve this difficulty thus: the *visible* universe is nothing but a *delusion* of our senses, a temporary illusion of the equally temporary and deceptive concepts of *earthly* man, who himself is an illusion and merely a *kośa* or sheath of the spiritual man and, therefore, of the only *real* individuality. The visible universe as well as objective man do not exist in reality, for everything that is visible and cognizable by means of the testimony of our five senses is *self-deceptive*, because *Sat* alone is all that exists and is.

Yet before changing from the *real* "nothing" even into an *illusory* "something," such a transformation must take place gradually. "The radiance from the light" is neverthe-less Parabrahman without qualities and, consequently, in-capable of action. Thus the *shadow* — also "illusory," of course, for a shadow does not exist without an object, and Parabrahman is bodiless—begins to transform itself, through the gradual differentiation of its unconscious activity (*nota bene:* unconscious only in our conditioned understanding of self-consciousness) from that which is without quality and impersonal into that which is qualitative and personal, namely, into visible worlds at first, and later into man as well. But man, and the worlds, would not have been created

---

*Mûlaprakṛiti means literally the "root of matter," *i.e.*, the pri-mordial essence of substance. But since Parabrahman is the ALL, this root is that very Parabrahman also.

at a stroke even in that coarse envelope in which we *imagine* we see him. He was formed and constituted in the following order:

GROUP I.

1. *Brahman* or *Âtman,* a ray of Parabrahman, or Spirit.

2. *Buddhi*—its *vâhana* or receptacle, the carrier of the spirit; the highest or divine soul.

(This dual unit is the *root* of man, though to our understanding this unit, *impersonal* and *without quality* in itself, appears as a pure *abstraction.* Its individuality begins to be outlined, only after many incarnations; just as *Buddhi,* in order to acquire even spiritual qualities, must harvest them, after the death of the earthly personality, from the first principle of Group II—*Manas.*)

GROUP II.

3. *Manas*—the seat of the mind. In conjunction with *Kâma-rûpa* (see below), this is the actual earthly personality, the *Ego* of man or of the body which that personality inhabits; it is called *human* or *earthly* soul when considered as separate from *Buddhi* or the "divine soul." However, in union with *Buddhi,* it is called *Sûtrâtman* (thread-soul), as it alone, of all the three groups, follows the first group in all its earthly incarnations, merely changing its own personal qualities.

4. *Kâma-rûpa*—"the seat of desires." This principle survives man, and together with the

5. *Mayâvi-rûpa,* "the phantom body" or the *double* of the personality, disappears in time. After the death of man, these 4th and 5th principles become *piśâchas,* or those "materialized spirits" in which the Spiritualists see the souls of their deceased, and the Brâhmanas—*demons.*

GROUP III.

6. *Jîva,* or life: "the vital principle."

7. *Sthûla-śarîra,* or the physical body of man, the mask of the soul.

This last group is the most transitory of all "the illusions" and disappears without leaving any trace after its disintegration.

Thus we see that the three groups with their seven divisions are all summarized in the "divine soul." The impersonal unit without quality has to acquire individuality and spiritual qualities from each new *manas, i.e.,* from the rational *Ego,* and not in one, but in an innumerable series of its incarnations. Before this unit is ready to become a *godlike* personality, worthy to unite even temporarily with *Sat** and to cease being an "illusion," it must pass through all the stages of human suffering; experience personally all that is experienced by helpless humanity; make a personal effort toward cleansing itself of earthly dross, while extracting from the personalities inhabited by it only the highest spiritual qualities, *if such are to be had;* and to be tested like gold by fire. Each new incarnation is a new step towards purification and perfection. All this is intended so that after many ages even past humanity shall truly live as much in God, as God shall live in future humanity, "in the seventh," according to the Vedântins *of the secret school,* who call present humanity the *fifth.*

The following conversation with the Thâkur will now be more intelligible to the reader.

"Master," asked Nârâyana of the Thâkur in the midst of a heated argument with the poor Bâbû, "what is he saying, and are we to believe it? . . . That exactly nothing remains of a man after his death? That his body, as he claims, simply falls apart into its component elements; and that which we call soul and he, 'temporary self-consciousness,' evaporates, vanishing like vapor from boiling water which has been allowed to cool?"

"What is there so strange in that?" the Thâkur answered.

---

*Sat is a word almost untranslatable into European languages. Here *Sat* signifies *the One-Existent reality,* outside of which everything is only illusion, or self-deception, *Sat* is the eternal, boundless *essence* of everything, in eternal and limitless space, where there is no room for anything except *Sat.* In short, *Sat* is the One Be-ness or unconditioned spirit without qualities—*unmanifested* divinity.

"You see, the Bâbû is a *Chârvâka** and, therefore, says only that which any other *Chârvâka* will tell you."

"But, *Chârvâkas* are liars! There are others who believe that the man is not his physical envelope, but consists of his mind, the seat of his self-consciousness. But can self-consciousness ever forsake the soul after death?"

"In *his case* it can," answered the Ṭhâkur calmly, "because *he sincerely and firmly believes in that which he now professes.*"

Nârâyaṇa threw an amazed and perplexed glance at the Ṭhâkur, but the Bâbû, who was rather afraid of the latter, threw us a triumphant smile.

"How is that? Does not the Vedânta teach that 'the spirit of the Spirit' is deathless and that the soul of man does not die in Parabrahman. Are there any exceptions?"

"In the fundamental laws of the spiritual world there can be no exceptions, but there are rules for those who see, and rules for those who do not."

"I understand that. But in such a case, as I told him, the 'complete and final disappearance of his self-consciousness' is no more than the aberration of the blind man who, unable to see the sun, denies that it exists during life . . . but will see it with his spiritual eyes beyond the grave."

"He will see nothing at all. Having denied it during his lifetime he will not see it beyond the grave."

Noticing that Nârâyaṇa was dreadfully perturbed, and also that both the Colonel and I stared at him in expectation of a more explicit answer, the Ṭhâkur continued, obviously unwillingly.

"You speak of 'spirit from Spirit'—of Âtman, and confuse the spirit with the soul of the mortal, the *Manas.* Undoubtedly Spirit is deathless for it is without beginning and, therefore, without end. But the discussion is now not about spirit, but about the selfconscious human soul. You confuse it with the former, while the Bâbû denies both the one and the other, the spirit as well as the soul. Both of you misunderstand each other."

---

*Chârvâkas are a sect of Bengal materialists.

"I understand him, but . . ."

"Don't you understand me? I shall try to express myself more clearly. The whole gist of your question is to learn whether complete loss of self-consciousness and self-perception after death is possible, even in the case of a deep-rooted materialist? Is that so?"

"Yes, because he completely denies everything that constitutes unquestionable truth for us . . . that in which we all sacredly believe."

"Very well. To this, believing just as sacredly as you do in our teaching which regards the *post-mortem* period, or the interval between two lives as *temporary* state, I reply positively by saying: Whether this intermission between two acts of the illusion of life lasts one year or a million, that *post-mortem* state may, without any breach of the law, prove to be completely like the state in which the human being finds himself in a dead faint. The Bâbû, therefore, *is right* in his own case."

"But why? . . . How is that, since the laws of immortality, as you tell us, admit of no exceptions?" . . . asked the Colonel.

"Certainly they do not — *for all that really exists*. He who has studied *Mundakôpanishad* and the *Vedântasâra* should not even ask that . . ."

"But *Mundakôpanishad* actually teaches," timidly commented Nârâyana, "that between *Buddhi** and *Manas*,† as between *Îsvara* and *Prajñâ*,‡ there is, in fact, no more difference than *between a forest and its trees, or between a lake and its waters.*"

"Perfectly true, because one or even a hundred trees withered because of lack of life-giving sap, or uprooted, cannot prevent the forest from still being a forest."

"Yes . . . but Buddhi in this simile represents the forest,

---

*The "divine soul" of man.

†*Manas*, as the seat of the terrestrial mind, gives rise to a perception of the Universe that is based on the evidence of that mind, and does not arouse spiritual vision.

‡*Îsvara* is the collective consciousness of the *manifested* deity, *Brahmâ*; and *Prajñâ* is its individual wisdom.

and *Manas-Taijasa** the trees. If the former is immortal,
how can *Manas-Taijasa*, being the same as *Buddhi*, entirely
lose its consciousness until its new incarnation? . . . That
is what perplexes me . . ."

"Needlessly so. If you would endeavor not to confuse
an abstract representation of the whole with its casual modifications. Remember that if it can be said of *Buddhi* that
"it is unconditionally immortal," the same cannot be said
of the *Manas,* or of *Taijasa.* Neither of these [neither *Manas*
nor *Taijasa*] can exist apart from the divine soul [*Buddhi*],
because the first is a qualificative attribute of the terrestrial
personality, and the second is identical with the first, but
with the light of *Buddhi* reflected on it. *Buddhi,* in its turn,
would remain only an *impersonal* spirit without this element,
which it borrows from the human soul, which conditions
and makes of it something *seemingly separate from the
Universal Soul* for the entire duration of the cycle of human
incarnations. Had you said, therefore, that *Buddhi-Manas*
can neither die nor lose consciousness either in eternity or
during its transitory periods, you would have been right,
according to our teaching. But to apply this axiom to its
attributes is the same as if you insisted that, since Colonel
O.'s soul is immortal, therefore the bloom of his cheeks must
also be immortal. It follows that in your comprehension you
have obviously confused the essence with its manifestation.
You have forgotten that, in association with *Manas* or the
'human' soul alone, the radiance of *Taijasa* itself becomes
a mere question of time, for both immortality and consciousness after death become, for the *terrestrial* personality
of man, simply conditioned attributes depending on the
conditions and beliefs created by the personality itself
during the life of its body. *Karman* (the law of retribution)
acts incessantly, *and we reap in our after-life only the fruit
of that which we have ourselves sown in this.*"

"But if my *Ego* can, after the dissolution of my body,

Taijasa means "the radiant," as a result of its union with Buddhi;
Manas-Taijasa means radiant mind, the human reason illuminated by
the light of the spirit, while *Buddhi-Manas* is "revelation of the divine
plus human intellect and self-consciousness."

find itself in a state of complete unconsciousness, what punishment for the sins of my life can there be in this *for me?*" asked the Colonel, thoughtfully stroking his beard.

"Our philosophy teaches that punishment overtakes the *Ego* only in a future incarnation and that after death it receives only the reward for the *unmerited* sufferings endured in terrestrial life. As you see, the whole punishment *consists of the absence of any reward and the utter loss of the consciousness of one's bliss and rest. Karman* is the child of the terrestrial *Ego,* the fruit of the actions of its personality, visible to all, and even of the thoughts and motives of the spiritual 'I.' But it is also the tender mother who heals the wounds inflicted by her in the previous existence, before she begins to torture the *Ego* anew by inflicting upon him new ones. If it may be said that there is no grief or misfortune in the life of a mortal which is not the fruit and direct result of some transgression in his former existence, on the other hand, not having preserved the least recollection of it in his present life, and feeling that he does not merit such punishment and, consequently, suffers *unjustly,* this alone is sufficient to entitle the human soul to the fullest consolation, rest and peace in its *post-mortem* existence. To our spiritual selves, death always comes as a deliverer and friend; like the placid sleep of an infant, or a sleep of blissful fancies and dreams."

"But as far as I can remember, the periodic incarnations of the *sûtrâtman** are likened in the *Upanishad* to the terrestrial life alternating between sleep and waking. Is that so?" I asked, wishing to resume Nârâyaṇa's first question.

"Yes, that comparison is a very correct one."

"I do not doubt it. But my understanding of it is hazy.

---

*In the Vedânta, *Buddhi,* when united with the spiritual qualities, perception and understanding of those personalities in which it has been embodied, is called *sûtrâtman,* which literally means "thread-soul," because the entire long series of human lives is strung on this thread like pearls on a string. In union with *sûtrâtman* and hanging from it like a pearl on a thread, so to speak, *Manas* must become *Taijasa* (radiant), in order to attain eternity and to become aware of itself therein. Frequently, however, as a result of sin and association with the purely earthly mind, this very radiance disappears.

After sleep, another day commences for man, but man, both in soul and in body, is still the same as he was the day before, whereas at every new incarnation, a complete change takes place not only of the external envelope, sex, and personality but apparently of all his spiritual qualities as well . . . How can this comparison be true in the light of the fact that people, upon rising from sleep, remember well not only what they did yesterday but also what they did many days, months, and even years before; whereas in their present life they do not preserve the slightest recollection of any of their past lives? A person who has awakened can, I grant you, forget what he saw in his dreams, but he knows just the same that he has slept and that he existed during sleep. About our past life, however, we do not know even that much. How is that?"

"There may be those, perhaps, who do know," somewhat enigmatically replied the Ṭhâkur, without answering the direct question.

"I suspect so . . . but it is *not we* sinners. Therefore, how are we who have not attained *samma-sambuddha** to understand the simile?"

"By studying it and more correctly understanding the characteristics and the three kinds of sleep."

"Well, that is rather difficult. Even our greatest physiologists have become entangled in this question and, failing themselves to explain sleep, have only added to our confusion," laughingly said the Colonel.

"Because, instead of their own task, they undertook the duty of the psychologists, of which there are none in Europe, at least not among the scientists. The Western psychiatrists are those same physiologists, only under another name, and they function on the basis of principles still more materialistic. Just read Maudsley, and you will see that they treat illnesses of the psyche without believing in the existence of the soul."

---

*The knowledge of one's past incarnations. It is said that only yogins and adepts of the secret science attain this complete insight into their *entire* past, by means of great ascetic achievement.

"But we have strayed from the subject of our inquiries, which, it would seem, you do not wish to explain to us, Thâkur-Sâhib. You appear to confirm and approve the Bâbû's theory, and he, strongly entrenched on the ground that we know nothing of either our past earthly life or our after-death state, seeks to prove that there is not and cannot be any kind of consciousness beyond the grave."

"Again I say that the Bâbû is a *Chârvâka* who repeats that which he was taught. I confirm and approve, not the system itself of the materialists, but only the correctness of the opinions of the Bâbû himself on that which concerns his personal state beyond the grave."

"According to that, it would appear that people like the Bâbû must be an exception to the general rule."

"By no means. Sleep is a general and immutable law for man, as well as for every living terrestrial creature, but there are different types of sleep and a greater variety of dreams and visions."

"He, however, not only denies consciousness in the life after death and in its dreams, using the language of the *Vedântasâra,* but also rejects immortality generally, as well as the survival of his own spirit."

"In the first instance, he acts completely according to the canons of contemporary European science, which is founded on the testimony of our five senses. In this, he offends those only who do not share his opinion. In the second instance, he is equally correct: without preliminary inner perception of, and faith in, the immortality of his soul, the latter will not become *Buddhi-Taijasî,** but will simply

---

*It means that, without complete assimilation with the *divine* soul, the *earthly* soul or *Manas* will not live a conscious life in eternity. It becomes *Buddhi-Taijasi* (or *Buddhi-Manas*) when its aspirations during life draw it from the earthly towards the spiritual world. Then, nourished by the essence and permeated with the light of its own divine soul, *Manas* disappears into *Buddhi,* becomes *it,* preserving only the spiritual awareness of its terrestrial personality. Otherwise, as merely *Manas,* i.e., human opinion founded on the testimony of the physical senses only, our earthly or personal soul falls, as it were, into a sound sleep without dreams and without consciousness, until the next incarnation.

remain *Manas,* and for *Manas* alone there is no immortality possible. *In order to live a conscious life in the world to come, one has to believe first of all in that life during terrestrial existence.* Our entire philosophy about the *post-mortem* consciousness and the immortality of the soul is built on these two aphorisms of the secret science. *Sûtrâtman* always receives according to its deserts. Following the dissolution of the body, there commences for it a period of fully awakened consciousness, a state of chaotic dreams, or an utterly dreamless sleep. If your physiologists find the cause of dreams and visions in an unconscious preparation for them during the waking hours, why cannot the same be admitted for the *post-mortem* dreams? I repeat that which *Vedântasâra* teaches: *death is sleep.* After death, before the spiritual eyes of the soul begins a performance according to a program learned and very often unconsciously composed by ourselves: the practical carrying out of either our *correct* beliefs or the illusions that we ourselves have created. These are the *post-mortem* fruits of the tree of life. It is evident, of course, that belief or unbelief in the fact of conscious immortality is unable to influence the unconditioned reality of the fact itself, once it is recognized; but the belief or unbelief in it on the part of each separate personality cannot fail to give color to that fact in its application to each of them in particular. I trust you understand now!"

"I begin to understand. Materialists, disbelieving in everything that is not verifiable by their five senses and so-called *scientific* reasoning, and rejecting every spiritual manifestation, point to earthly life as the sole conscious existence; therefore, according to their belief, or rather unbelief, will it be unto them. They will lose their personal 'Ego' and will plunge into dreamless sleep until a new awakening. Is it so?"

"Almost so. You can add that the Vedântins, recognizing two kinds of conscious existence, terrestrial and spiritual, speak of the latter only as an *irrefutable* reality; terrestrial life, as a result of its changefulness and transitory nature, is merely an illusion of the deceptive senses. Our life in the spiritual spheres must be admitted as reality by the fact alone that our changeless, infinite, and immortal 'Ego,' the *sûtrâtman,* dwells in these spheres; whereas with every new incarnation, it dons a temporary and transitory personality completely distinct from the preceding one, in which everything except its spiritual prototype is doomed to utter destruction, leaving no trace behind."

"Excuse me, Thâkur, but can my personality, my conscious terrestrial 'Ego,' perish, not only temporarily as in the case of the materialists, *but even without leaving any trace behind?*"

"According to our teaching, it *must* so perish, and in its entirety, all except that principle in it which, having united itself with *Buddhi,* has become purely spiritual, forming with it henceforth and forever an indestructible whole. But in the case of an out-and-out materialist it may happen that, since absolutely nothing from his personal 'I' had been reflected in *Buddhi* either consciously or unconsciously, the latter would have no occasion to carry away a single particle of this terrestrial personality into eternity. Your spiritual 'I' is immortal; but from your present personality, it will carry away with it *that only which merits immortality,* namely, the aroma alone of the flower that has been mown by death."

"Well, what of the flower, the terrestrial 'I'?"

"The flower itself, as all past and future flowers that have blossomed and will have to blossom on the mother bough, the *sûtrâtman,* all children of one root or *Buddhi,* will return to dust. As you doubtless know, your real 'I' is not the *body** now sitting before me, nor is it your *Manas-Sûtrâtman,* but the *Sûtrâtman-Buddhi.*"

"But this does not explain to me why you term the life after death immortal, infinite and real, and the terrestrial life a *phantom,* for, according to your teaching, it appears that *post-mortem* life has also its boundaries, and though of longer duration than terrestrial life, must also end."

"Undoubtedly. The spiritual *Ego* of man moves in eternity like a pendulum between the hours of birth and death. But

---

*The Vedântins feel such complete scorn for the physical envelope that in speaking of purely automatic acts of the body, they do not use the pronoun *I,* but say: "This body walked," "These hands made," etc. Only when they speak of mental actions, do they say, "*I* thought," "*I* wished," etc.

if these hours, marking the periods of life terrestrial and life spiritual, are limited in their duration, and if the very number of such stages in eternity between sleep and awakening, illusion and reality, has its beginning and its end, on the other hand the *spiritual* pilgrim is eternal. Therefore the hours of his *post-mortem* life when, disembodied, he stands face to face with *truth,* and not the mirages of his transitory earthly existences during the period of that pilgrimage which we call the 'cycle of re-births,' are the *only reality* in our conception. Such intervals, their limitation notwithstanding, do not prevent the *Sûtrâtman,* while ever perfecting itself, from following undeviatingly, though gradually and slowly, the path to its last transformation when, having reached its goal, it becomes a 'divine' being. These intervals not only help towards the attainment of the goal, but without such limited intervals, *Sûtrâtman-Buddhi* would never reach that goal. *Sûtrâtman* is the actor and its many and varied incarnations are the parts it plays. I presume you would not call these 'parts,' and still less their costumes, the individuality of the actor himself. Like the actor, the soul is obliged to play during the cycle of necessity and to the very threshold of *paranirvâna,** many parts which

---

*There is a vast difference between *nirvâna* and *paranirvâna.* Nirvâna is that spiritual life which every *personal* soul of the *sûtrâtman;* such as soul A. or soul B. (except, as has been shown, the souls of the materialists), lives after every disembodiment, and which is decreed by the law of compensation (*karman*) as a result of its personal earthly sufferings. *Paranirvâna* is that blissful state which awaits the *sûtrâtman* in its completeness, *i.e.,* together with all the personal souls strung on this *thread.* "Soul" is an incorrect expression, and I use it for lack of a more appropriate term in our language; instead of "personal souls," it would have been better to say "the *aroma* only of the personal souls," to use the Thâkur's expression. Upon "the dissolution of the world" (*pralaya*), all these "aromas," having blended into one, form the one "divine man," who *dwells in Parabrahman* eternally; while each soul of the personality taken singly, lives only temporarily in the ray of divinity, the *Âtman-Buddhi.* The difference between *nirvâna* and *paranirvâna* is analogous to that between the state of the soul *before* and *after* the Day of Final Judgment.

[At the beginning of this footnote, the term *nirvâna* seems to be used for the idea of the *devachan;* there is a confusion of terms here, the cause of which is difficult to determine. —*Compiler.*]

frequently may be unpleasant to it. As the bee gathers its honey from every flower, leaving the rest as food for earthly worms, so does our spiritual individuality, the *sûtrâtman,* gather only the nectar of the spiritual qualities and self-consciousness of every terrestrial personality into which *karman* compels it to incarnate, finally blending all these qualities into one whole, and emerging then as a perfect being, a *Dhyâni-Chohan.** So much the worse for those terrestrial personalities from which it could collect nothing. Such personalities, of course, do not consciously outlive their terrestrial existence."†

"Accordingly, for the terrestrial personality, immortality is still conditional? Is immortality itself then *not* unconditional?"

"Not in the least. But immortality cannot touch the *non-existent.* For everything that exists as *Sat* or emanates from *Sat,* immortality and eternity are absolute. *Mûlaprakriti* is the opposite pole of Parabrahman, yet both are one. The essence of *all* this, *i.e.,* spirit, force and matter, is without end and without beginning, but the form, the exterior, acquired by this triple unity during its incarnations is, of course, simply the illusion of our personal conceptions. Therefore, we call the life beyond the grave a *reality,* and the terrestrial life, including the terrestrial personality, an *illusion.*"

"But why, in such a case, call sleep the reality, and waking the *illusion?*"

***Dhyâni-Chohan, esprit planétaire,* "issuing from Parabrahman, and merging again with it," after the cycle of life.

†The philosophy of the *secret* Vedânta does not believe in hell and does not concede punishment in a spiritual world for earthly transgressions. Man, it says, is born helpless, a plaything of outer circumstances which are not dependent on him, even though he is endowed with free will. He suffers innocently so much in this world, that infinite mercy gives him complete rest in the world of *shades;* and only subsequently, in the following earthly life and in a new incarnation, will he bear the due punishment for the transgressions in his previous *role.* The selection of every subsequent life and the punishment are determined and carried out by *karman,* "the law of retribution." This is proved by the fact that people, apparently innocent, suffer constantly on our earth.

"The comparison is made to facilitate the grasping of the subject; from the point of view of terrestrial conceptions it is a very correct one."

"Then again, if life beyond the grave is founded on justice, on merited recompense for all terrestrial sorrows, and if the *sûtrâtman* makes use of the smallest spark of spirituality in each of its incarnations, then how can it be admitted that the spiritual individuality in our Bâbû — he has left and we can speak of him without restraint — the individuality in this so ideally honest, noble and infinitely good lad, in spite of all his belief, should not pass into immortality but perish like the 'refuse of a flower?'" I commented.

"Who, but himself, consigned him to such a fate? I have known the Bâbû from childhood and am completely convinced that the *sûtrâtman* will reap from him a plentiful harvest. Although his belief and materialism are far from being a mere pretence, nevertheless, *he cannot* die forever and in the entirety of his personality."

"But, Thâkur, you have just now confirmed the correctness of his views about his personal condition after death, and these views are that his *entire consciousness* will disappear after death . . ."

"I confirmed his views and comfirm them anew. One can sleep and miss several stations while travelling on a railway journey and, nevertheless, without having the slightest awareness *of them,* awaken at a subsequent station and reach the destination of the journey in a conscious state. Do you find fault with the simile between sleep and death? Just recall that three kinds of sleep are known even to man: the deep and dreamless sleep; the chaotic sleep, with confused dreams; and finally, the sleep where dreams are so real and lucid that they become, for the time, completely real to the sleeper. Why, then, can you not admit that the same takes place also with the soul when freed of the body? Upon separation from the body, there begins for the soul, depending on its merits and mainly *its faith,* a life either completely conscious or semi-conscious, or it falls into that deep, dreamless sleep which is without awareness and is comparable to the state of *non-existence.* This is the enactment of the 'program' I spoke about, created and prepared beforehand by the materialists themselves. But materialists vary. An evil man, or even just a downright egotist, who adds to his complete unbelief an indifference for the whole world, must certainly drop his personality forever at the threshold of death. There is nothing that binds it to its *sûtrâtman*, and with its last breath every connection between the two is broken. But such as the Bâbû will sleep through and miss only one 'station.' The time will come when he, too, will perceive himself again in eternity and repent that he lost even one day* from the life eternal."

"But would it not be more correct to say that death is birth into a new life or, still better, a return once more to eternity?"

"Actually, it is so, and I have no objection to the rephrasing. But with our conditioned concepts about material life, the words 'living' and 'being' are quite inapplicable to the purely subjective state of *post-mortem* existence and, if they were used in our philosophy without a firm knowledge of all its elucidations, the Vedântins would very soon come to the strange ideas now prevalent among American Spiritualists, who preach about 'spirits' entering into marriage both among themselves and with mortals . . . Among Vedântins, just as among true and not merely nominal Christians, the life beyond is that realm where there are neither tears nor sighs, and where no one can intrude and where no one marries . . . It is just because the life of the

---

*In answer to the remark frequently made to the Vedântins, that hundreds and thousands of such earthly lives spent by the *Sûtrâtman* or *Ego* of man, amount nevertheless, to complete disappearance of every personality instead of immortality, they usually reply: "For comparison with eternity, take the life of man on earth, a life made up of so many days, weeks, months and years. If the personality has preserved a good memory in old age, it can vividly recall all the outstanding days and years in the life just past. But even if it has forgotten some of them, does it not really still remain the same personality? And so it is with the divine *Ego* at the end of the cycle of incarnations. Each separate life will be for it similar to each separate day in the life of man."

disembodied soul, while possessing all the vividness of reality as in certain dreams, is devoid of every grossly objective form of terrestrial life, useful only for corporeal senses, that our philosophers have compared it to dreaming during sleep. And now, it seems, I have explained everything . . ."

We separated, but this conversation penetrated deep into my soul, and I never forgot it. That day I almost quarreled with the Bâbû over his *Chârvâkian* pranks; despite all his good qualities, there was some chord lacking in this Bengalî, and I decided to leave him to his own fate. However, after his early death, I frequently, oh! so frequently, regretted my indifference.

We had barely finished dinner in the summerhouse, when it was announced that a certain young man in yogi attire, sent by "Thâkur-Sâhib," asked permission to see us. At the mention of the Thâkur's name, the Colonel, who had already inquired several times about his *guru* (teacher), but received no satisfactory answer from Nârâyana, hastily jumped up from the table.

"Let him in, let him come in!" exclaimed the Colonel in delight. "I am sure it is his *chela,* whom he promised to send upon his arrival home, particularly for the purpose of my special instructions in *prânâyâma* . . ." *

"What! Do you intend taking your first lesson immediately after dinner?" I inquired.

"Of course, if only the *chela* is agreeable to it . . . Why lose precious time?"

"You could easily have a stroke on a full stomach... You are simply going out of your mind with your passion for *yogism.* Remember what I told you . . . when I warned you at the station near Bhurtpore . . ."

"I remember, I remember," our president replied, evidently offended. "I thoroughly understand and have long been aware of the fact that, for some reason or other, you do not want me to study the mysteries of ancient India . . ."

---

*The original method of instructing the candidates in yoga. The process consists of gradually accustoming oneself to suspended breathing, by means of certain mantras.

"And what sort of mysteries are these? Simply juggler's tricks, and for you they are completely superfluous and even dangerous . . ."

"I trust that the Thâkur is not harboring any harmful designs against my life or even against my health," he replied sharply.

I waved my hand.

"Colonel," said Mûljî to him quietly, "Maam-Saab is right. *Prânâyâma* is to be studied from earliest youth and . . ."

But he had no time to finish. The Colonel's scowling face lighted up with a smile of happiness. Before us stood Thâkur's messenger, who, barefoot, had slipped across the bridge noiselessly in the dark.

He appeared before us suddenly, as if grown from the marble floor of the kiosk. He stood at the entrance, immovable, with eyes lowered and arms crossed on his breast, the flickering candlelight swaying in the breeze playing over him. Long fantastic shadows slid over his face and white attire, giving his small, slender figure, almost transparent in its leanness, something strange and unearthly in its contour.

"*Sarvabhishṭa, Muṇḍaka!*" (may all your wishes be fulfilled) — his soft, calm voice, gentle as a maiden's, was heard to say in the Tamil vernacular.

Each of us answered his greeting according to his knowlege and ability. Mûljî and Nârâyaṇa muttered something in Sanskrit (very likely some formal greeting), covering their ears with their palms and bowing low: the Bâbû bared his teeth and placed his palms together; I myself mumbled the customary English greeting through my teeth.

The Colonel, on the other hand, distinguished himself, surprising those present and sending me into fits of laughter. He bent low and, having covered his ears with his palms according to the example of the two Hindus, suddenly flattened himself in front of the youth standing humbly before him, and almost thrust his nose onto the lad's bare feet.

We all rushed to him, thinking that he had slipped and

fallen while bowing so very low. But he nimbly jumped to his feet and welcomed the envoy once again. Saying "salaam," and touching his forehead with his right hand, he invited him with his left hand to the bench at the table, with all possible signs of servile respect, just as if he were receiving a prince of the blood.

"What are you doing, Colonel?" I asked him quietly in French. "He may think you are laughing at him."

"For heaven's sake, don't say a word! I recognize him . . . although the Thâkur merely hinted to me about him. He is not a simple *chela*, not a disciple, but an adept of the 'Brotherhood of the Grove.' * Did you not hear him greet us in the Tamil vernacular?" whispered the Colonel in reply, also in French.

"Well, what does that prove? He . . ."

"Pardon me, *madame et monsieur,* for interrupting you. But I speak French, being a native of Pondicherry," said the newcomer, to our sudden amazement, in the same soft voice using the language of Victor Hugo, and without the least note of mockery, which would have been so understandable in his case.

I could not contain myself any longer and burst into laughter that resounded through the whole garden; the Colonel, however, became angry for some reason, although concealing rather skillfully his unpleasant discomfiture.

"Ah . . . you are from Pondicherry? I am very, very glad, indeed! That means it will be easier for us to understand each other . . . I had fears at first that we might not . . ."

"I also speak English," answered the same voice.

"Excellent!" exclaimed the Colonel, suddenly and obviously losing some of his veneration before such vast worldly education, detrimental, as he supposed, to the mystical sciences. "Wonderful! Sit down here at the table and let's get acquainted. You came to us from Thâkur-Sâhib?"

"Yes, it is he who sent me to you."

"Are you his *chela*? . . . Oh, yes, forgive me, by the way,

---

*The *Brotherhood of the Grove* is a well-known, though secret, society of mystics in the Madras Presidency.

for taking you for one of the Brotherhood of the Grove. I supposed . . ."

And without saying what he supposed, the Colonel burst into a gay, though constrained, laughter.

"You do not have to apologize because you surmised correctly. I actually do belong to that Brotherhood."

I felt very sorry for the Colonel, so completely was he embarrassed at this new defeat. Without taking his eyes off the face of the youth, the poor president stared at him from behind his glasses with a most perplexed look, as if he were seeing a phantom standing before him. I, too, gazed at him with the greatest curiosity, and behind me, the Hindus — Mûljî and the Bâbû — did likewise. Nârâyaṇa alone remained sitting, sadly hanging his head and gazing, it seemed, only *into himself,* without noticing anything or anyone.

"You . . . you are one of those amazing adepts . . . You are a *sâdhu?* . . . I just knew it . . . I had a presentiment of it! . . ."

"*O my prophetic soul!*" quietly remarked the Bâbû, quoting Hamlet.

"So far, I am only a candidate, a humble *śishya,** Colonel-Sâhib, who is at your service and to whom Ṭhâkur-Sâhib entrusted your preliminary training, if you permit."

The stranger spoke quietly, seriously, and with great dignity. There was not the slightest smile on his youthful, almost childlike face, which had not the least trace of beard except for a barely noticeable down on the upper lip. To judge from appearances, he seemed no more than sixteen years of age. Only by examining more attentively his remarkable face, undoubtedly of the Dravidian type, could one notice signs of manhood on it. He sat at the table with the bright light of the lamp falling upon him, making it possible for me to scrutinize his features more closely. He was shorter and, in general, of even a slighter build than

---

*A *disciple* of a higher degree, a student of the "secret sciences," who has surmounted all the trials except the last which would make of him a *sâdhu.*

our small Bâbû. His hands, small as those of a ten-year-old girl, lay on the table, and the color of their satin skin reminded me of beautiful bronze hands on a paperweight. He had an oval face, striking in its leanness and tenderness, with a small straight nose, a small mouth with thin lips, and unnaturally large eyes and heavy eyebrows, as black as if he had daubed them with tar. All this was framed by a leonine mane of curly ringlets that fell loosely over his ears, forehead and shoulders. His dress, like our Bâbû's on a hot day, consisted of several yards of thin white muslin, under which could be seen the angular contours of his emaciated frame. Two deep furrows between the brows, similar folds at the corners of the mouth and eyes, eloquently contradicted the first impression of youth. We learned later that he was well over thirty years of age.

He sat motionless, as if reverently waiting to be questioned, and calmly gazed with an inscrutable look at the Colonel. If it had not been for the slight movement of his necklace made of *rudrâksha* seeds,* one might have taken him for a stone statue, so deathly still was his face.

Rudrâksha is the seed, or rather the kernel, of the fruit of a tree growing in the Himâlayas and the Nîlgiris, mostly in Nepal. A necklace or a string of beads made of such kernels is the most precious and most difficult thing to obtain in India. The natives consider a *rudrâksha* sacred and only yogins have the right of wearing it around their necks or even of touching the seed, because of its wonderful magic qualities. *Rudrâksha* is a compound word meaning "the eye of Rudra" (Rudra is one of the names of Śiva) and only the *three-eyed* adepts of the secret sciences, those who by long years of asceticism have acquired the "third eye" of Śiva (*i.e.*, clairvoyance and the gift of prophecy, the symbol of which is *rudrâksha*) are acquainted with all these qualities. Whole volumes in Sanskrit and Tamil are devoted to the description of this talisman and to instructions on how to distinguish good seeds from bad ones, etc. The magical qualities of the *rudrâksha* depend on the age of the tree, the soil, the surrounding forest and even the *personal qualities* of those who gather them. "To a wicked man the *rudrâksha* will bring evil instead of good." Only a few trees of the species bear fruit, and from these more than 90% are of no use for such purposes—their fruit either falls before ripening, or becomes overripe; the most useful seeds are those which, being ground on the trial-stone, leave a gold dust: the princes and Râjâs of India pay exorbitant sums for them, from 1,000 to 5,000 rupees for each seed, while the best, which have

A rather embarrassing silence followed. The Colonel, who had already suffered three rebukes in a row, was fingering his spectacles, putting them on and taking them off, rubbing them, but not saying a single word, forgetting not only to express his joy at the news, but even to thank the newcomer for undertaking the responsibility of his "preliminary education."

"What will this preliminary education consist of?" I thought to myself. "Everybody will laugh at him!"

"I have a letter for you from Thâkur-râjâ and a small present," said the messenger, breaking the silence.

Thrusting his hand under the muslin garment, he pulled out of its folds a sealed envelope and a small box and put them in front of the Colonel. At the sight of them, our president at last came to and regained his normal state of mind.

"Ah! I am very, very thankful to you . . . . my *guru*! . . ." answered the Colonel, smiling joyously. "You will permit me?" he asked, pointing to the letter.

The *guru* bowed slightly and made a gesture of assent, which would have done honor to any marquis in a Paris salon, so dignified and graceful was it.

The letter was unsealed and first read silently: its contents were then communicated to us. It was short, but contained many interesting items of news for us all.

"I am sending you, dear Colonel," wrote the Thâkur, "the instructor in the sciences which interest you, as I promised. Subramaṇya-Muruga-Ânanda-Svâmi (you may call him for short Ânanda-Svâmi) is young, but he has already reached the last step but one towards the inner temple of the *gupta-vidyâ*. He is a member of the Brotherhood of the Grove, therefore well-acquainted with all the methods of

---

one *mukha* (cut) or *indentation* on the kernel cannot be secured for even 10,000 rupees. Such *rudrâkshas* are found only on a few trees in Nepal, and then only one or two on a tree, in several years. The unripe seeds (red, brown, grey and yellow) have no value at all; it is only the *black* ones that are precious. The Mahârâja of Nepal paid 10 lakhs (one million rupees) for half a dozen such genuine seeds. They are of the size of a small nut and have an uneven surface like the stone of a peach.

the different systems, as they are practised by the various sects. Not being a Hindu you cannot follow, of course, any of the special methods of the sects, but you will have a choice among the teachings of the best schools and thus will be able to learn much . . . I sincerely regret that even in the case of your full success through the *trials,* you nevertheless will not be able to belong to our *âśrama;** you are married, the father of a family, and a worldly man — three insurmountable obstacles on the road to râja-yoga."

At this phrase, the Colonel slightly stumbled, and for a second his voice became unsteady. Like an echo, a hardly discernible but mournful sigh, more like a groan, could be heard in the far corner . . . Looking swiftly around I saw a tall figure on the bridge, disappearing into the darkness.

Poor Nârâyaṇa, I thought to myself, and asked the Colonel to continue his reading. No one paid any attention to this sigh evoked by sorrow; no one, except, it seemed to me, the newcomer. His heavy eyelids lifted and he cast a quick glance from under the thick fringe of his eyelashes towards the bridge. The enigmatic expression of those blue eyes, dark as night, impressed me so much, that thinking of its meaning, I did not hear the end of the Ṭhâkur's letter and had to ask the Colonel to give it to me to read.

". . . However," I read further, "if you should emerge victorious from the trials, this will not prevent me from looking upon you as my *chela* in some respects. But do not expect to become a *râja-yogin.* This is entirely impossible.

"Tomorrow, at dawn, you will all go with Ânanda-Svâmi, who will show you a little known way, yet the shortest one, to my place. For certain reasons, you will go in the carriage of the Mahârâja to the nearest village only, whence it will be sent back. Do not worry about your baggage; it has been sent on from Bhurtpore. You will find another conveyance in the village, which will take you to Śrî-Muttra, the birthplace of Kṛishṇa. From there you will have to go by boat, on horseback, and even on foot through the forest. For the

---

*A secret temple into which only *initiated* individuals are admitted. Such temples existed formerly in all the *pagodas,* but now there remain only a few of them.

upâsikâ, a palanquin will be prepared but even she will have to go on foot for about fifteen *kos;** tell her she should not get discouraged: *our roads will prove to be much easier* than the Anglo-Indian or European means of communication; *I will see to that.* I advise you all to keep this visit to our Râjput jungles secret; it is none of the *baḍâ-Saabs'* business."

Then followed a few more lines of instructions and mention was made of the *śâlagrâma* he had sent the Colonel.

While our President, together with the Hindus, is examining with lively interest and reverence the treasure, I will describe this talisman and all we learned about its qualities that very evening from Ânanda-Svâmi.

A *śâlagrâma* is as famed in India as a *rudrâksha.* It is usually a round and sometimes an oval stone, black as tar and glossy; its size varies from that of the stone of a peach to that of a goose egg, yet on very rare occasions it may attain the size of a melon, in which case it becomes literally *priceless.* Its value, however, depends more on its various qualities than on its size or form. There exist very small *śâlagrâmas,* about the size of a pepper seed, which cost a fortune. As usually happens, there are to be found among them, as among the Egyptian *scarabs,* counterfeit stones of dishonest imitations; but an *initiated* Brâhmaṇa can never be fooled. This stone, by the way, is really no stone at all, but an ossified shell.

The real and most expensive *śâlagrâmas* are found only in one place, at the bottom of the Gaṇḍakî River, in Nepal, one of the main tributaries of the sacred Ganges. This place is protected from the seekers after *śâlagrâmas* by the soldiers of the Nepal ruler, who live on the banks in their barracks the year round; every *śâlagrâma* that is found is sent by them to the royal treasury. They are not to be bought from the Mahârâja for any price, but he occasionally makes presents of them to those Brâhmaṇa disciples to whose hands the stone will cling like a leech after being extended to them at a distance of several feet. This test is very seldom suc-

---

*A *kos* is about 1¼ English miles.

cessful; the English Resident, Hodson, however, was present at such a test and, according to witnesses, saw this experiment with his own eyes. *Sâlagrâmas* that are quite smooth, and have no other special qualities, are of little value. Some of them have been perforated by nature along their axis; others have all sorts of figures similar to carvings on them, such as a *Sudarśana* or *Chakra,* the Wheel of Vishṇu and his weapon. There exist *śâlagrâmas,* with and without holes in them, of such a nature that when carefully filed in two, they reveal on their smooth inside walls, pictures of the *Matsya* (fish), *Kûrma* (turtle) or some other *avatâras* (incarnations) of the god Vishṇu. Furthermore, if such a *śâlagrâma,* when placed in a container of milk, instead of dropping to the bottom (as an ordinary natural stone ought to do), begins to swim like a fish or a turtle, it is declared to be undoubtedly a genuine one; it is then rendered honors as though it were the god Vishṇu himself.

There exist *śâlagrâmas* (and to this latter kind belonged the specimen the Thâkur had sent to our President), on which the figures depict Krishṇa (the *avatâra* of Vishṇu) under the guise of a *gopâla* (shepherd) with his herd of cows. On it, the freakishness of nature attained its utmost skill: the picture looked as if it had been hollowed out by the most delicate of artist's chisels, even though it did require some imagination to detect the cows.*

The formation of such stones is attributed by students of natural science to some species of fish. The fish, it is said, selects, a small stone, nestles up to it closely, and then begins to spin a nest or a shell for itself, the material for which it emits, like the spider, out of its own organism. Having been immured in the shell for some time and feeling the tediousness of solitude, the fish breaks the shell and swims away; the stone and shell then turn into a *śâlagrâma.*

---

*We saw *śâlagrâmas* belonging to a Mahârâja, on which we found pictures of several avatâras, such as: *Ugra-Narasiṇha, i.e.,* Vishṇu, who under the guise of the lion *Hiraṇya-Kaśipu,* was tearing the tyrant of the *Râkshasas; Kalyâṇa-Narasiṇha*—Vishṇu smiling at *Prahlâda,* whom he had saved, etc. "This cannot be nature; it is the work of the devil," said a missionary.

This I read, however, in the native natural history of the *Dravidians*. To what extent this explanation is compatible with truth and Western science, I shall not venture to say.

The Colonel was unspeakably happy with such a rare gift. He examined the *śālagrāma* from all sides, admired it, and fussed over it. Having learned from Ânanda-Svâmi that he should wear it on his person for greater efficacy of its occult qualities, the Colonel started pestering me to sew it up immediately in a small leather bag with ribbon, to be tied around his waist. He fetched a needle, thread and scissors. Only by cutting up a pair of new kid gloves was I able to insure peace for the remainder of the evening.

Far past midnight, on my way to rest for a couple of hours before departure, I saw two figures on the steps of the terrace. One of them was seated with his head in his hands; the other stood facing him, with hands crossed on the chest. I recognized Nârâyaṇa and Ânanda-Svâmi . . . . .

———

— V —

[On the way to Mathurâ. — Râja-yoga and Haṭha-yoga. — Inner meaning of Hanuman. — Discussion on Śâlagrâmas and Daṇḍas with Ânanda Svâmi. — On Matter and Force. — Storing magnetic power.].

Next morning, everything was carried out according to the Ṭhâkur's program. At dawn, that is, half an hour before sunrise, since there is supposed to be no dawn in India, we departed in full starlight for some village and alighted from the carriage at the very minute the stars went out in unison, like gas burners under the hand of a theater usher, and the sun—the light of day, but the plague of tourists in India—glared at us, breathing fire and flame from the horizon.

It was six o'clock, and we still had some fifteen miles to go before nine o'clock in order to reach Mathurâ, a holy Hindu place of all sects, with the exception of the Śaivas. Only those firmly resolved to die can travel in Râjputâna after nine o'clock on a spring morning. Consequently, we stepped from our gilded carriage only to transfer to a covered gig dating from the time of the Portuguese dominion —and possibly that of Alexander of Macedonia—into which we had to climb by a ladder, as if onto an elephant. I sat with Nârâyaṇa and the Bâbû on one bench, and the Colonel sat between Ânanda-Svâmi and Mûljî on the other. This assignment of seats had its significance. The "silent general" was an ardent devotee of the mystic ways of the *hatha-yogins* and sympathized with Colonel O. in his fakir aspirations, but I rebelled against them, while the Bâbû simply laughed at "the Europeans who were in love with the dirty *bairâgins*."

The mysterious *śâlagrâma,* in spite of its thaumaturgic properties, must have caused the Colonel a certain awkwardness of movement. It was the size of a large orange. Its happy possessor, having fastened it around his waist with ribbons, could neither conceal its presence on his person nor keep it from moving from one place to another on his belt with every jolt of our antediluvian carriage. First the *śâlagrâma* stuck out on one side of him, then it peered out from under the thin duck coat on the other. Having to continually adjust it, O. kept rising from his seat and in general made himself a nuisance, driving me to nervous prostration.

Apparently Nârâyana's midnight conversation with the youthful Brother of the Grove had had its quieting effect. Even though the poor rejected candidate did not appear completely consoled, at least he seemed reconciled to his fate. While the *trio* of mystics solemnly discussed the wonder-working power of ashes from sacred cow dung, the Bâbû and I sought ways of breakfasting from the food hamper without jabbing our eyes or causing injury to others. We were hurled and thrown from one end of the gig to the other, in the most shameful manner, making me almost grumble at the Thâkur because of this carriage.

For the sake of the historical accuracy of this narrative, however, I hasten to censure myself: in using the word *trio,* I speak incorrectly. Only the "general" and the Colonel discussed the wonder-working power of the ashes with which the sect of Śiva daub themselves, whereas Ânanda-Svâmi corrected their numerous errors and wrong views. Nârâyana listened and learned.

Soon we hit a sandy stretch. Finally, the Bâbû and I had satisfied our hunger and settled down, after getting the food into our mouths, where it should have gone in the first place, were it not for the humps and bumps of the road, instead of into our eyes and noses. The Colonel, no longer an India rubber man on a string, also brightened up and the conversation became general and very edifying. Whatever ails a fellow, that's what he wants to talk about.

"It is not our fault, Colonel, that both you and I have been married," rationalized the distressed Mûljî. "You may have married owing to your own desire, but I was enslaved at the tender age of six . . . What was I to do? Kill my wife in order to become a *râja-yogin?* It wouldn't have helped, and would have been a still greater obstacle. What a choice! Not accepted as a *râja-yogin* and warned against *hatha-yogins!* Of course, it is a very dangerous system to practice, but what are we to do, Svâmi, when there is no other choice? Better *hatha* than nothing. After reaching a certain age, it is impossible to do without religion . . . absolutely impossible! . . ."

"It is possible to study philosophy without rushing to extremes," quietly commented Ânanda-Svâmi.

"It's easy for you to say. You weren't forced into marriage without being consulted, and all the paths to the secret sciences are open to you," replied Mûljî, angrily.

"It isn't, however, so much religion, but rather the attainment of the transcendental mysteries of *yoga,* that interests me in this science, somehow or other, and I must attain my goal. I *must* learn not only *prânâyâma,* but also everything that will contribute to the development of psychic powers," said O. heatedly.

"I trust that, first of all, you will learn how to wear your *śâlagrâma.* You almost bruised my elbows with it," I moaned, rubbing my arm after another jolt.

"Excuse me, and please bear with your companions. You must know I didn't do it purposely . . . . . Touch the bruised spot with the talisman, and I am sure the pain will disappear entirely! You don't want to? Well, do as you please. But do not forget that this *śâlagrâma* is the gift of our blessed Thâkur and that he, certainly, did not send it *without reason.*"

"Certainly *not without reason* but as a *test,* and not for you alone, as I now have learned to my sorrow! . . . ."

"In order for *śâlagrâmas, rudrâkshas,* and other similar *holy objects* to be effective, it is necessary, first of all, to believe in them," commented Nârâyana reproachfully. "And in order for them to benefit their owners, they must be treated every morning and evening according to the prescribed rules of the *śâstras,* otherwise they soon lose their properties and, consequently, bring only harm to him who wears them."

KíRAT KHAMB OR TOWER OF VICTORY AT CHITOR

VRIJI TEMPLE AT CHITOR

"The rules of which you speak, my dear Nârâyaṇa, are equal to *pûja*. Is this what you suggest to the Colonel?" I fired at him indignantly.

"Is that so?" expostulated O., somewhat agitated by what had been said, but not explaining what in particular, whether by the latest information from Nârâyaṇa or by my retort. "Is that true?" he again asked, turning to Ânanda-Svâmi.

The ascetic quietly nodded his head in assent but said nothing. There was silence.

Ever since his appearance among us, this youth had roused my curiosity. I definitely could not come to any positive conclusion about him and simply observed him from a distance. The Ṭhâkur's recommendation carried so much weight with me that, of course, I did not inquire whether this youth was a good, honest man, or a charlatan, of which there are many in India among those extolling themselves as *ascetics* and yogins. In this respect Ânanda-Svâmi was completely secure against suspicion. But I wanted very much to discover to what degree those astonishing psychic gifts, before which we all bowed in the person of the Ṭhâkur, were developed in the youth. Did he command the faculty, on a par with the Ṭhâkur's, of reading the thoughts of others, as if they were an open book before him? Could he not only read but also *direct* the thoughts of others, and produce at least some of those amazing manifestations which, apparently, came so easily to the Ṭhâkur? "Why had he sent him? For what purpose?"—I thought to myself.

I knew that the Colonel vainly hoped to attain, even in small measure, not only the heights of *râja-yoga*, but also those strange, inexplicable psycho-physiological faculties, in order to produce the so-called "miracles," for which certain *haṭha-yogins** are justly famous. As has been shown,

---

*Any one can dedicate himself to the study of *haṭha-yoga* according to the *dead* letter of the Patañjali system. To do this, it is not necessary either to be a philosopher or even to know how to read and write, but simply to possess the iron will and endurance of the Hindus, their indifference to physical suffering, their blind fanaticism, and their faith in a chosen *god*. Real *haṭha-yogins*, I would say, are much

râja-yoga requires training and an undeviating effort of a purely psychic nature in this direction from the earliest years; a comprehensive study and, especially, an understanding of the *secret* meaning of Patañjali's instructions instead of the dead letter of his system, as well as initiation into the mysteries which the initiated Brâhmaṇas will not disclose to anyone for any price. To become a *haṭha-yogin,* years of preternatural, superhuman effort and physical mortification are indispensable; one has to be born with such physiological *idiopathies,* otherwise nothing will come of it, except a fakir's repulsive exterior and pure charlatanry. Against the latter, the Thâkur thunders loudly; as to the former, he is in no position to offer it to the Colonel. Then why this useless comedy? Why allow our honest, trusting president to make a fool of himself in the eyes of the Hindus as well as his own? Should I, perhaps, ask Ânanda? Or should I keep my eye on him until he betrays in some way his mission? It did not seem probable, however, that he would betray himself! . . . I did not take my eyes off him last evening nor have I done so since five o'clock this morning, and yet I have not been able to detect even the hint of a smile or any definite expression on his youthful face. It has been impassive and absolutely impenetrable, behind the deathlike mask of utter serenity. His voice, soft and gentle, called to mind reading in a half-voiced monotone. It had not the least intonation, although flowers of Oriental eloquence were dropped now and then. His thoughts were forcefully and precisely expressed. Even in his eyes, there was a lack of expression, at times even of thought. His enormous pupils either contracted or dilated, either sparkled or were dimmed, as if the periodic movement of a clock

---

the same as mediums, but with *deliberation* and *volition,* which are lacking in the Western medium. They produce their phenomena *ad libitum,* making them dependent on their own wills and *control of the jinn,* whereas the spiritualists are themselves under the control of the jinn (spirits) that personify this as yet undiscovered power. *Haṭha-yogins* attain this also by terrible self-mortification, which they finally cease to feel like the *convulsionnaires* of St. Médard and certain Catholic saints. The method of the *râja-yogins,* however, is entirely different. Their motto is: *Mens sana in corpore sano.*

mechanism were at work behind them. I felt goose flesh all over my body when his radiant, peaceful eyes met my curious glance. But even then these eyes told me nothing. Without a doubt, he had even better command of himself than the Ṭhâkur.

In the meantime, the Colonel was still agitated. "But you see, I am not familiar with the ritual," he complained. "What am I to do? And what of the *sâlagrâma?*"

"Take it off and keep it in a jewel box," I suggested.

"Will you not teach me the necessary formulae when we get to Mathurâ, dear *guru?*" begged O. of the youthful sphinx, without paying any attention to my suggestion.

"Unfortunately, I must decline your request. Only *Brâhmaṇa-Vaishṇavas* (of the sect of Vishṇu, who are initiated into the *archana** (ritual) of the *sânkha,† padma,‡ tulsî,§* and *sâlagrâma* can in turn initiate others. I do not possess that right."

"Then, perhaps, you will have time to persuade one of these Brâhmaṇas? Please try, I beg you."

"I shall try, but my success is very doubtful," answered Ânanda looking at everyone and yet at no one. "However, this *sâlagrâma* is endowed with powerful properties even without superfluous *japas* (ceremonies), and I should warn you."

"You don't say! Tell me about it, please . . . . ."

"This stone represents Gopâla-Kṛishṇa.‖ He who wears it on his person must avoid meeting with cows. Otherwise the cows, a whole herd of them lowing joyfully, will rush after the possessor of such a *sâlagrâma.* It attracts them by its irresistible magnetic force . . ."

Archana—magical formula.
†*Sânkha*—shellfish.
‡*Padma*—sacred lotus.
§*Tulsî*—a plant; all these objects are dedicated to Vishṇu.
‖*Gopâla-Kṛishṇa* is Kṛishṇa the Shepherd. There are *sâlagrâmas* which represent *Sampat-Kṛishṇa,* "the squanderer of riches"; *Samtâna-Kṛishṇa,* "the bestower of children," etc., one for every occasion and need. If cows do not run after a man wearing a *Gopâla-Kṛishṇa,* the stone is said to be *counterfeit.*

I looked at Ânanda-Svâmi with amazement. Was he or was he not making fun of us? His face, however, remained, as usual, serious and calm.

The Colonel shuddered slightly.

"That's right," interposed Mûljî. "My grandfather had such a *śâlagrâma,* and once, when he was serving as *Divân* (prime minister) to the Thâkur of Wadhwân, the herd belonging to the latter almost gored my grandfather when showering affection upon him."

"And you see, Colonel, Mathurâ is brimful of cows, and of *sacred* ones at that," I threatened, barely refraining from laughter.

"And there are even more 'sacred monkeys'!" the Bâbû prodded.

"The reason for that, Bâbû, is that unnecessary photographs of you may not be taken," sarcastically remarked the pious Mûljî. "There is no need for you to help Maam-Sâhib. She is not bound to respect our beliefs, but you are a Hindu."

"As theosophists, we are obligated to respect *all* beliefs," said our president aphoristically. "But the point of the matter does not rest there, but rather in the question, how can I make use of the *śâlagrâma* with benefit. However, I shall consult the Thâkur about that," he added, noticeably calming down. "What is that bamboo you have, Ânanda-Svâmi?" he asked unexpectedly, showing interest in the new object and curiously examining the stick that hung on the arm of the ascetic.

"That's a *Hanumanta bera* . . . the magic wand of all the Madras ascetics," the Bâbû volunteered in answer.

"Is that so?" inquired the Colonel, doubting the reliability of the Bâbû's knowledge. "May I ask you, Ânanda-Svâmi, to give me some particulars about it? I have read about such a wand in the writings of Jacolliot. Does he describe it accurately?"

"No, because he gathered his information from those who themselves knew nothing about the *danda*—which is the name for such a wand—and who deceived him sinfully."

"Well," asked the Colonel, "Can you give us the history

of your bamboo wand and tell us why it is considered magical and called 'Hanuman's'?"

"To you I may speak. You are theosophists and have the right to our trust. I am at your service. Proceed with questions."

"Why, then, for instance, do you wear objects that are consecrated to *Śiva* and Hanuman, while denouncing the gods as fiction? What is the mystery?"

"There is not the slightest mystery. The whole problem lies in the fact that in our mythology there is no single fable that is not founded on a truth. I wear a *rudrâksha* and a *danda*, not because the Brâhmanas thought to surround this truth with the fog of one or another fable, but because the wood and fruit from which they are made have in themselves properties beneficial to a certain previously conceived purpose of mine."

"Well, that's a rather hazardous thing for you. Those to whom you do not explain the real meaning or the reason for such action will see no difference between you and the *hatha-yogins*."

"Having renounced the world," replied Ânanda, "we see no reason to concern ourselves with one or another opinion about us. People may think whatever they please."

"You have just spoken of the wood and fruit of which the *danda* and *rudrâksha* are made as having beneficial properties for your purpose. Can you tell us something about these properties?"

"I can tell you only the dead letter of the legend, and the rites that are based on it. The real meaning is not revealed to us until our third initiation."

Two deep sighs were heard simultaneously in the gig. Ânanda's face, however, remained impassive, though he did briefly glance at Nârâyana.

"*Hanumanta bera* (the tree of Hanuman) grows only in the Udayagiri Hills,* about a hundred miles from Nel-

---

Udayagiri comes from two words: *udaya*—sunrise and *giri*—hills. They are located east of the Coromandel (real pronunciation *Kuru Manal*, "black sands") Coast, while the *Astagiri* (Western Mountains) are on the Malabar Coast. Both chains are joined in the south by the *Nîlgiri* or "Light Blue" Hills.

lore, in the Madras Presidency," Ânanda began in his quiet, monotonous voice. *"Hanumanta bera* is the favorite tree of monkeys from the tribe of Hanuman and has, therefore, become sacred and been named in his honor. Only ignorant materialists are prone to seeing in Hanuman an actual monkey, the residence of—a god. In our mythology, Hanuman is called the *vâhana* of Râma, *i.e.*, the seat or physical prototype of the one who himself represents the personification of the qualities of the sun.* Hanuman is the forefather of the Dravidians, a race distinct in every way from the Brâhmaṇas of the North; he is called the *vâhana* of Râma because our ancestors were actually the Children of the Sun, *Sûryavaṇśa,* allies of the Sun in the South and in the Tropics, as well as allies of the great 'Sun-King,' metaphorically speaking. In short, Hanuman, if viewed symbolically, is the collective representation of the Southern peoples, even by the Occidentals. Historically, he is Bhîmasena, the son of Kuntî, the aunt of Krishṇa on the paternal side; mythologically, he is the son of Vâyu, god of the air, guardian and ferryman at the river *Virajâ,* the Hindu Styx, which every mortal has to cross into the world of *shades* and which *no one crosses without the aid of Hanuman.* The meaning of this is that before man can attain, in other and more evolved worlds, that stage of progress when he no longer needs the grossly objective form, he must begin at the point of inception of humanity under the guise of the monkey-like man, with all his animal passions and instincts. In order to become a *deva* one has to be born first as a man. One has, thereafter, to win each step, each rung that leads to the higher stage, *by personal effort* and merit. It is not difficult to understand why the Brâhmaṇas teach that this

---

*Râma, as king and hero, is a fully historical figure, as has been shown by many Orientalists. He is the representation of the Sun, *un dieu solaire.* A *vâhana* is merely the "bearer" of anything, the recipient, the objective form in which is enclosed, and through which is portrayed, something incorporeal, *i.e.*, the *essential nature* of substance. Thus the body is the *vâhana* of the soul, which in Brâhmanic philosophy and in the Sanskrit language is called the "rider" of the *vâhana,* as is the case with any other incorporeal essence manifested through matter.

river *Virajâ* which, according to their teachings, has such a tremendous symbolical significance in our spiritual evolution, is protected by Hanuman and, therefore, why the monkey-god himself is so honored.* In performing his ablutions at sunrise, every Brâhmana closes his nostrils, ears, eyes and mouth with the fingers of both hands and concentrates his whole attention on a sacred four-syllabled word which must be pronounced aloud three times. This daily ritual is particularly obligatory for the Brâhmana-brahmachârins."

"Is this not because in the *Ramâyana* Hanuman is also called a 'brahmachârin,' a 'virgin ascetic' profoundly versed in logic and the *navavyâkaranas,* or all the nine systems of grammar?" innocently asked the Bengalî.

"Do not interrupt, Bâbû! . . . . It is impolite and also interferes with our listening," angrily exclaimed Mûljî.

"Indeed, 'virgin ascetic' and 'brahmachârin' are epithets rightfully belonging to Hanuman," quietly confirmed the Madras brahmachârin as if not noticing the deliberate insult. "Hanuman is even considered as the founder of the Sanskrit grammar. Consequently, no poet or author fails to praise him—as he would Sarasvatî, the goddess of secret wisdom, in an encomium on the first page of his work."

"When shall we hear about 'the magic wand'?" complainingly asked the Colonel.

"I am again at your service," replied the French Brâhmana, bowing slightly. "On the day of *Hanumanta Jayantî,†* the devotees of the monkey-warrior spend the entire day fasting and performing *pûja.* Then exactly at the 'fortunate' hour, designated by the initiated astrologers, they depart for the Udayagiri Hills where, after performing the prescribed ceremonies, they cut slender branches from the sacred trees, *Hanumanta bera,* and carry them home."

Hanuman is the personified symbol of "the earthly man," who in spite of his animal nature, unfolds his spiritual nature by personal effort and, having overcome the former, emerges as the intellectual victor over all things earthly, finally becoming a god-like individual worthy to walk arm in arm with Râma, the embodiment of the highest divinity.

†Hanuman's birthday, in the month of April.

"Similar to your stick?"

"In appearance exactly the same. But as there are very few learned Brâhmaṇas who succeed in finishing the *preparation* of the stick — more than a year of daily care is required before it becomes a 'magic wand'—such a one as this is consequently extremely rare."

"And what are the properties of 'the wand' when it has been prepared in accordance with all the rules? . . . . ."

"That depends upon its owner, as is also the case with a *rudrâksha*, a *tulsî*, or any other similar object. The properties imparted to it are various. If you ask a sectarian Brâhmaṇa about them, he will tell you that by means of his *danḍa* he can summon forth the 'spirits' under his subjection and make *piśâchas* leave the human bodies they have taken possession of; that the *danḍa* helps one in acquiring and developing clairvoyance; that it protects the possessor from *jinn* (evil spirits), diseases and the evil eye; that it cures all illnesses; in short, that its properties are identical to those which the great 'monkey-god' himself possessed, and so forth."

"You are repeating to us merely that which a *sectarian* would have probably replied to our question. But you do not belong to that class. We would like to know what *you* could tell us."

"My answer is that the stick without the hand which imparts to it the power to perform one or another deed is useless; in the hand of a *râja-yogin, whose mind and will function with complete consciousness,* the stick becomes the conductor of that will, like a telegraph wire which conducts the thoughts of him who sends the dispatch, yet remains but a piece of ordinary metal in the absence of such an agent. In the hand of a *haṭha-yogin,* its operations are frequently amazing, but as the mind of the motivating agent functions *unconsciously,* the properties of the *danḍa* are variable and not always consistent with reason and strict morality."

"But does the *haṭha-yogin* act unconsciously like our mediums?"

"No, not altogether. In principle, it is his desires and even thoughts that act; therefore he *does* not act unconsciously. But, believing in his nonexistent gods and their help, he is not *aware of his own complete consciousness* and does not admit his own personal control. Separating his acts from their cause, *i.e.,* from his own conscious will, since most of such wonder-working *sannyâsins* are not philosophers but merely fanatics, he himself considers the phenomena performed by him as the work of Hanuman and leads others into error, spreading only superstition and, frequently, great evil as well, in place of knowledge and good."

"So then my own *sâlagrâma,*" asked the Colonel, "will not function without my will? How may I conjoin the two? Teach me, for the sake of truth and in the name of humanity! Can I, for instance, heal with it, performing mesmeric passes? . . . . ."

"If your will is strong, your desire to help humanity and your love for it unshaken, then with time you will probably produce a powerful effect on it. But, I repeat, your *sâlagrâma* possesses its own particular, intrinsic qualities. It is also a magnet of its own kind, with which you can perform various experiments, diversifying them without end, but its specific properties will always remain with it."

"*Gare aux vaches, mon Colonel,*" I laughed.

"Oh, stop, I ask you! Do not interfere!" replied the deeply interested Colonel, waving his hand in protest. "How about the *rudrâkshas* around your neck, the *tulsî* and the *tutti quanti* of articles used by the ascetics? What about them? Are they the same as the *danda?* Hm? As you know, they are all *holy relics* of Śiva and Vishnu, of various Rudras and *devatâs,* in which you do not believe, but the emblems of which you wear just the same, as if no other objects existed in the world with similar properties useful to you," commented the Colonel, winking at the ascetic who did not even turn a hair.

"You are mistaken. I merely do not believe in the actuality and personality of such gods. I reject the shadow but not the being itself. I believe in these cosmic forces clothed by popular fantasy in the shape of preserver and destroyer. Knowing something of the occult correlations of such forces with the forces of nature, and with her material manifestations, I cannot help but believe in them. Otherwise such

individuals as the Ṭhâkur, and even myself, would not devote ourselves completely and wholly to serving these forces."

"But why, in that case," I asked, for the first time turning to him directly, "do precisely 'such' as the Ṭhâkur sacrifice truth and spirit to mere form? . . . Look at our Mûljî,
who has smeared his forehead with white ashes, undoubtedly in honor of Mathurâ. What is the purpose of this daubing?"

"It is not 'daubing,' Maam-Sâhib," replied the "general"
somewhat offended, "but respect for age-old customs . . . . ."

"But you are not a Śaiva.* Why then do you follow the
custom of these sectarians? . . . . ."

"Because it is generally accepted."

"And of what does the philosophy of this generally accepted custom consist? On what is it based?"

"On a fable," replied the Bâbû, interrupting again. "Śiva,
you see, was also a *brahmachârin*, a 'virgin ascetic,' like
Hanuman. *Śmaśâna*† was his favorite abode. There, entirely besmeared with the ashes of the dead; with a human
skull, instead of a goblet, for water; with a thousand and
eight snakes instead of garlands of flowers completely covering him; and with a *Kadruśesha*† on his head, he had such
a horrible outward appearance that he earned the appella-
tion of *Ugra*.§ On the other hand, however, when his colleagues, the other gods, married him to Pârvâti (Kâlî, etc.)
to pacify his too ferocious character, *Ugra* became *Kshânta*,
the saint.‖ So in memory of his ascetic deeds, the Śaivas
rub their bodies and faces with white ashes. The twofold
morality of the fable is: do not become a *brahmachârin* and
an ascetic until you are sure of your temperament, and then
marry if you wish to become a holy martyr . . . . ."

---

*Śaiva is a devotee of Śiva; a *Vaishnava*, one of Vishṇu. *Rudra*
is a title of both gods and means "lord."

†*Śmaśâna*—the place of cremation of the Brâhmaṇas.

‡*Cobra de capello*. Many fakirs of the Śaiva sect wear a live snake
in place of a turban on their heads.

§*Ugra* means ferocious.

‖*Kshânta* means saint. A play on words: "from *ugra* he became
kshânta" means from the *ferocious* he was transformed into the *holy*
one.

"That's enough chatter from you! You can find something to ridicule in everything."

"By no means, my dear Mûljî. I am helping Maam-Sâhib to gather information and am showing her the complete logic and benefit of rubbing ashes on the body."

"This rubbing has its basis in hygiene," explained Ânanda. "The Śaiva ascetics avoid many epidemic diseases by means of the metod. You know, it isn't the ashes of cremated bodies, but of a certain medicinal root mixed with cow dung."

"But why don't the *râja-yogins* rub their bodies in this pleasant manner?"

"They have other means that are even better."

"That must be the reason why they do not age, at least outwardly," I thought, looking at Ânanda.

O. continued to squint at the *daṇḍa* and the necklace of his *guru* and again led the attack.

"All that may be so, and you have explained very well to us why you do *not* do this or the other. But I still cannot understand why the *râja-yogins,* the initiated as well as the candidates for initiation, perform, nevertheless, some of the practices of the *haṭha-yogins.* What difference is there, for example, between the use of the *daṇḍa* and the *rudrâksha* by the *râja-yogin* and their use by the *haṭha-yogin?*"

"This can be explained only to him who possesses a correct view of the difference between these two kinds of *yoga* and of the natural properties of the said objects. *Haṭha-yoga* is the latest and, in comparison with *râja-yoga,* a modern compromise of mysticism. It is the result of centuries of the slipshod practice of philosophy, the victory of the external form and ritual over the spirit of the teaching and, consequently, the gradual degeneration of *Brahma-vidyâ,* the divine wisdom. Having lost, as the result of personal ambition and earthly passions, the faculty for union with Brahman, that is, with Unconditioned Nature, the majority of the Brâhmaṇas, debarred from the final supreme initiation, the difficulties of which they could not surmount, substituted *haṭha-yoga* for *râja-yoga.* Believers in the reality of the former are convinced that *Śiva-Mâhâtmya* himself resides in each seed of *rudrâksha,* and that is why they attribute every manifestation, such as clairvoyance or the healing of sickness taking place with the aid of *rudrâksha,* for instance, not to their own power and will, but to the direct action and participation of Śiva. The *râja-yogin,* on the contrary, denies in principle such an intervention, as they do the personality of Śiva. For him there are no anthropomorphic gods, but only the unconditioned, double-edged power of creation and destruction, the one universal, primordial substance, of which he is an inalienable particle, even though, in the deceptive consciousness of his earthly senses, he appears to be a transient individual. Having verified its properties by years of methodical experiments and recognizing this power in himself, he endows the given object with it and concentrates it in the object, be the latter a *rudrâksha,* a *śâlagrâma* or a *danda.* Then, when occasion arises, using his own will and discretion, he aims, in one direction or another, this power, the twofold quality of which is attraction and repulsion. Śiva has nothing to do with it. By such means he transforms also the wand or *danda* into a *vâhana,* filling it with his own power and spirit and giving it for the time being his own properties. In the West, your magnetizers, impregnating with their life-current either paper or any other object to be used by the sick, do exactly the same, only to an incomparably lesser degree."

"Pardon me," interrupted the Colonel, "but you speak of power, spirit, properties and might as if all these were the same as the life-force, or the 'magnetic' current. I realize that the magnetizer can impregnate an inanimate object with the surplus of his own vitality for purposes of healing. I myself have done it. But how am I to understand your statement about a transference to such an object of will, thought, conscious action, etc., *i.e.,* of incorporeal, purely psychological qualities and properties . . . Is that really possible? . . ."

"For him who knows exactly nothing or very little about *râja-yogins* and the real *Brahma-vidyâ,* and for him who is unfamiliar with the psychology of the East, substance is the product of his own conceptions, or of deductions of Western science with its hypotheses: in other words, the result of *unquestionably relative ideas*. For the Westerner every substance, from the life-force current to the mineral, is matter. He is ignorant of the successive levels, from conditioned and limited substance, to primordial and unconditioned substance, *i.e.*, primordial matter—*mûlaprakriti*. Hence it is exceedingly difficult, if not impossible, to explain to him the nature of the actions of the *râja-yogin* and of the transference of the essence of his creative power to an inanimate object. For the Western scientist, whose ideas of substance are based on the correlation of his organism with the external world and are limited to this frame alone, *everything* that is not matter is either 'nothing,' or simply an incorporeal quality. He either does not believe in spirit or, if he does, is incapable of clearly comprehending the 'Spirit-*Sat*,' and the 'spirit-power.' According to his opinion, spirit is something non-substantial, consequently, not to be separated and not transferable. He is ignorant of the properties and of all the conditions of *force*. Ancient Western theurgy, however, brings to our attention in its own chronicles innumerable examples of inanimate objects endowed with temporary motion and, it would seem, with consciousness and even volition. The religious beliefs of contemporary Westerners testify to the same thing. What, on the whole, is known to the Western scientist about universal substance, about its essential nature and modifications? All that you know about matter and its properties, about the physical and spiritual senses, is but relative knowledge conditioned by the attributes of your terrestrial organism, your personal experience and the conclusions of science, and is founded on external senses, not on the real qualities of substance. Consequently, if I were to tell you that the time is not far off when your chemists, starting with preserves and beef extract, as well as those of milk and other animal products, will finally achieve an extract of the vital principle, something that has already been accomplished in days of old by the homeopaths and by such unconscious alchemists as a certain Professor Jäger—you would laugh. In spite of such unbelief, I shall allow myself to submit this information in the light of a prophecy."

"But what comparison is there here? . . . Is it possible to seal spirit in a bottle? That may be read about in a story like the one of 'The Fisherman and the Jinni'—the spirit imprisoned in a vessel under the Seal of Solomon—in *A Thousand and One Nights*."

"Then why did you select precisely this seal for the symbol of your Society?"

"Because it is the figure of *Śrî-Yantra*, the *Chakra* or 'Wheel of Vishṇu,' the most ancient symbol of India . . . . ."

" 'Solomon's Seal,' which is found among our people as well as among the Chaldeans, among the primitive people of Europe as well as the natives of both the Americas, Africa and Asia, proves only one thing: The story of 'The Fisherman and the Jinni' is based on fact. The jinni, an evil and, at the same time, a good, obliging spirit, is the personified symbol of that power in nature which I have been speaking about: the power that *creates* and *destroys*, that *attracts* and *repels*. Solomon, in popular legends, is a 'magician' and an adept. He is the patron of the Judaic as well as the European Kabalists, just as Hermes is the patron of the Egyptian Magi. This power concentrated on any object, whether by Solomon or Hermes, or a *râja-yogin* of India, in other words, an adept initiated into the secret sciences, is nothing else but spirit without attributes and qualitative matter. It is this very power that has created man, the *vâhana* of Parabrahman and Mûlaprakṛiti. In his turn, a human being who is aware in himself of this twofold power can transmit its surplus to other *vâhanas*. But in order to create and develop in himself such surplus, he must, first of all, renounce his own personality, devote himself completely to the service of mankind, forget his personal *I*, make himself at first worthy of being a collaborator with nature and only then—become an *adept*."

"But how, and in what way, does he help humanity or even its progress by the use of *daṇḍas* and *rudrâkshas?* I understand the desire to become an adept, to study the secrets of nature for a *personal*, so to say selfish purpose at first, and then to help others with one's knowledge; but I see no relation whatever between *rudrâkshas* and adepts as benefactors of mankind! . . ."

"I am sorry, but I shall not undertake to explain this to you in your present spiritual blindness. I repeat, in order to become a *râja-yogin*, it is necessary first of all to renounce *unconditionally* one's own personality and to have no *selfish* purposes, as only *hatha-yogins* are concerned with such purposes, as a result of which they have degraded the meaning of the secret sciences in the eyes of the uninitiated."

"Could you not," insisted the Colonel, somewhat embarrassed by this direct lesson, "help me by a simple example to understand why the *râja-yogins* particularly, as well as the *hatha-yogins* whom they scorn, carry wands, such as these *dandas*? . . ."

"So that the essence of the twofold power does not become dissipated under the pressure of the external eventualities of daily living and would be available in a reservoir, so to speak, always ready for use in case of possible emergencies . . ."

"What kind, for instance?"

"Imagine that you are walking down the street with a *râja-yogin* and carrying on a conversation on entirely commonplace subjects which, however, for one or another reason, interest him. In one hand he holds the *danda* which is always with him—like this one," said Ânanda, pointing to his own seven-knotted stick. "From behind a corner, a mad dog rushes at you. Danger is close, and the question of your safety depends on the speed of action, reckoned not by minutes or seconds, but by instants. Although thought acts with the speed of electricity, nevertheless the co-ordinating mind presently occupied with extraneous subjects, for the purpose of extracting from the perceptive apparatus those impulses of will that are necessary for repelling the dog, may take half a second longer than it is necessary for the dog to bite you. Without his *danda*, the *râja-yogin* would possibly have no time to help you. But the *danda*, which is imbued with the essence of the *râja-yogin's* power, acts with the speed of lightning: directed against the animal, it instantly paralyzes its impulse to jump on you; a repetition of the motion by the *râja-yogin* could even kill without touching the beast if that proved *necessary*. This is what the *danda* could do in *ordinary* circumstances. However, on this account to call it a *magic wand* is incorrect, as neither 'life' nor a *rudrâksha* can be isolated from our conscious will and thought, or act independently of us. To attribute to them such properties means to acknowledge in them the presence of a conscious apparatus, as in man, and amounts to a deliberate dissemination of superstition and a gross worship of matter."

"You have just said that a *râja-yogin* is never without a *danda* in his hand. However, I have never seen such a wand in the hands of the Thâkur....."

"The active power does not lie in the external form of the *vâhana,* and it is not a *danda* alone that is selected as a carrier or vehicle of the 'power'," was the evasive answer we received.

At that moment, the noisy, rattling gig, kicking up its rear and puffing through its linen top, with wheels squeaking, and making the most incredible sounds, roared down the pavement of Mathurâ, the promised land of the pious *Vaishnavas* (devotees of Vishnu).

"Śrî-Muttra!" exclaimed Mûljî, falling face down on the floor of the gig. "Śrî-Muttra!" repeated after him Nârâyana, thoughtfully looking into the distance as if expecting someone. Only Ânanda did not as much as turn his head as we drove in. While the rest of us crowded, shoved, and fell over one another in order to see from under the linen top the row of pink temples, festooned with monkeys, he did not bat an eye, even when I very nearly crushed his dainty bare foot. When I apologized, he merely looked *into me* (not at me) with his gentle, doe-like eyes, as if wishing to find in me just exactly what I was apologizing for....

I was awe-stricken by the glance. Forgetting Mathurâ, I turned my thoughts to the recollection of the "automaton-man" who lost his soul in the tale of some American Hoffmann.

— VI —

My reflections and cogitations about the absence of a
"personal" soul in Ânanda were suddenly interrupted in a
wholly unexpected manner. We were driving between two
rows of buildings with balconies hanging almost halfway
over the road, when over our very heads things suddenly
began to fall with thuds on the cloth top of the carriage,
racing around, fidgeting and chattering. With a shrieking noise which rose above the multitudinous sounds emanating from our own vehicle, we were attacked, or perhaps
only greeted in their own fashion, by an entire troop of
large and small monkeys. They clung to the sides of the
carriage, peeped into the openings, climbed over one another and over our heads and shoulders. Their appearance was so sudden that I hardly realized what was going
on. They all pounced on a little basket containing food
which unfortunately stood wide-open on a bench. In the
twinkling of an eye, the bottle with cold coffee was broken
and Mûljî bathed in the black liquid; the box of tea was
torn to shreds and the tea itself scattered all over the carriage and the pavement; while the Colonel sat crowned
with a nice patty, and my dress was smeared with jam.

There were some ten to fifteen of them and from the
very moment of their appearance such a typically pungent
smell pervaded the carriage that I almost suffocated. The

monkeys touched no one; evidently they were merely hunting for food; in any case, our driver had hardly time to stop his horses while turning a corner, before the whole troop had disappeared as fast as they had come . . . . . Two Brâhmaṇas with shaven heads, who had attempted to jump to the rescue of our carriage, on seeing their "gods" retreating, quietly returned to their respective places on the steps of the pagoda.

In order to reach the place of rest prepared for us, we had to drive almost the whole length of the town. Mathurâ, lit by the brilliant morning sun, the rays of which hid centuries of soot and the filth of old houses, appeared to us most picturesque. The town is situated fan-like on the western, steep shore of the Jumnâ and has spread over the high foothills receding into the distance like green waves. Śrî-Krishṇa,* Avatâra of Vishṇu, proved his artistic taste when he first chose Mathurâ as the place of his birth and later made this locality the arena of his mystically amorous adventures with the *gopîs*—shepherdesses, the overwhelming number of which being probably the case of his turning blue. To what extent this hypothesis is true, I am not prepared to say, but this was the spirit of the explanation given by the Bâbû upon witnessing the awe-inspired dread of Mûljî before the huge idol of the god-shepherd painted dark blue from head to foot, from his cheeks to his reed pipe. Later on we will look into the philosophical and ethnographical causes of his blue color.

We crossed the river on a bridge made of flat-bottomed barges, a construction which is for some reason or other especially praised when compared with others. The sacred river, competitor of the Ganges, was filled to the brim with Hindus of both sexes purifying themselves of their sins, as is their early morning custom. On the steep shore, marble steps lead to the water, each landing being ornamented by

---

*Śrî—literally "bliss"—one of the names of Lakshmî, the consort of Vishṇu. At present, however, this name has become an adjective, an epithet, and is synonymous with holiness. Thus we have Śrî-Muttra, Śrî Krishṇa, etc., *i.e.*, Blessed or Holy Muttra, Blessed Krishṇa.

a miniature temple in honor of one of the shepherdesses. The whole town is criss-crossed with narrow streets of uneven stone steps, ascending and descending like the streets of Malta, up and down which it is hardly possible to ride even on a mule. However, the elephants, also *sacred,* with their heavy pillar-like legs, move easily over them, going to visit each other from one pagoda to the next. It appears that meeting each other trunk to trunk and realizing the impossibility of continuing—one uphill and the other down —without one of them having to turn around, the elephants resort to the following trick: After exchanging a few words, accompanied by flapping of the ears and embraces with the trunk, and ascertaining their mutual friendship, the smaller of the two leans against the wall and the larger one lies down on the ground and tries to become as inconspicuous as possible. Then the first one lifts a leg and cautiously, without haste, climbs over his friend easily and gracefully. Sometimes this elephant stumbles and falls, though the trunk of the elephant lying down, raised in the form of a question mark throughout the entire hazardous operation, is always ready to help with all its might his smaller and weaker brother. The respect and helpfulness given to each other by the elephants have become proverbial and are a standing reproach to the people.*

---

*It is remarkable that the elephants, creatures with great ambition and easily offended, never fight each other when living in the towns, though they often destroy one another in their native habitat. It is also remarkable that while they show each other signs of mutual respect, they never become friends, but frequently choose as objects of their passionate and fiery attachment dogs, donkeys and other smaller animals. One such elephant becoming attached to a donkey took it under his protective care. The elephant was free and belonged to a pagoda, while the donkey was hired out for work. Once an English soldier, who had hired it, mounted it and began to hit its sides with his heavy boots. The elephant stood at the gate of the stable where his friend lived and, observing the abuse of his favorite, took hold of the British warrior with his trunk and gave him such a shaking that the latter, upon freeing himself, wanted, in his rage, to shoot the elephant on the spot. He was persuaded not to do it because the other elephants standing near would sooner or later *certainly kill him,* so astounding is the *esprit de corps* of the elephants. Interested by what he had heard,

Mathurâ is a regular zoo. There are more animals in it than men, though the population reaches 300,000 in the months of the pilgrimage. All the streets are literally clogged with "sacred" bulls and elephants. The roofs of the houses and the temples are covered with "sacred" monkeys, and over one's head soar, like clouds darkening God's light, "sacred" peacocks and parrots. All live in freedom, belong to no one, but on the contrary rule like masters, not only the property of the town, but the townsmen themselves. The ill-fated bazaar merchants are forced to carry their food in tightly closed baskets which they open halfway and with the greatest precaution for the benefit of the buyers; otherwise the monkeys, who are always hanging around the gates of the bazaar and are accustomed to levying an assessment on every carriage—which explains their attack on us— will carry off everything and, in addition, will tear out the hair of anyone who defends his wares too energetically. The elephants alone behave themselves with great dignity and honor. They never snatch anything and will modestly stand next to a stall with sweets, patiently waiting until they are treated. In Mathurâ in 1880 there were some 30,000 monkeys, some 5,000 bulls and several hundred elephants. The smell was such that all through my day's stay in the sacred town I did not once remove the perfumed handkerchief from my nose. Saintliness surrounded us on all sides, wafted at us from every corner, assaulting our noses so that by evening we "whites" had swollen noses from sneezing. *Holy sannyâsins* stood on their heads at every crossroad; *sacred* bulls spread a soft carpet of their own production over the unpaved streets; while from the roofs, *sacred* monkeys threw at us stolen fruits and vegetables now fully digested by their insatiable stomachs . . . . . By evening I ceased reproaching

---

he forgave the elephant and, as a peace offering, gave him a piece of sugar cane. The elephant stood over it for awhile, thought a bit and then, taking the luscious morsel, went straight to the donkey and, with his trunk, put it into the mouth of the abused creature, then turned around and went his way "without looking at me, like a man who had been offended," said the soldier who related the circumstance to us himself.

the Bâbû for his atheism. I fully understood his hatred of the "gods" and sympathized with him.

Apart from its saintliness, Mathurâ is one of the most interesting and ancient cities in India. In the days of the observant Megasthenes, the Greeks took home recollections of many sacred *Vaishnava* cities. Thus, quoting the ambassador of Seleucus, Arrianus mentions Mathurâ (Μέθορά, *Methora*) and Κλεισόβορα, Kleisobora (?), calling them the chief towns of the *Sûrasenas*. It is probable that Megasthenes meant by Kleisobora *Kailâspur*, as both Mathurâ and this town were built by the descendants of *Sûrasena*, the grandfather of Krishna. The Greek writer speaks also of *Bouduan* (Βούδυαν) and of *Kradeuan* (Κραδεύαν) as being the progenitors of this tribe of *Sûrasenas*, the foremost in the country at the time.* Megasthenes, following the Greek habit of distorting words, probably refers to the Buddha and Kroshtu-deva, the progenitors of the tribe of Yadu, the *Induvaṃśa* or "lunar" race. According to the genealogical tree officially examined, verified and certified by the administration of the Râjâ of Udaipur, these two names actually head the list of the descendants of Buddha† and Ella (the earth), one of whom was Krishna, and they are often mentioned in the *Purânas*. As far back as the time of the flowering of Krishna (according to the Brâhmanas some 5,000 years ago, and according to the Orientalists some 1200 years B.C.), Mathurâ was an ancient city.

Now, however, there remains of the erstwhile strongly fortified city merely three half-destroyed gates and some ruins of a former mighty fortress. The monkeys have completed the destruction begun by the Afghâns, and even the mosque of Aurangzîb, with its four towers of light blue tiles, has become crooked from neglect. At present there is no place for Moslems at Muttra. Even American missionaries, not

---

* [Arrian, *Anabasis of Alexander*, Book VIII (*Indica*), viii.]

†The adjective *Buddha* (all-wise) should not be confused with Gautama the Buddha, the well-known reformer and the founder of Buddhism, who acquired that title in his advanced age. There were in India many *Buddhas* before the time of Prince Gautama.

easily dislodged from the nests of idol-worshippers, dodged the monkeys and the bulls and took to their heels long ago. Dark azure Krishnas and their menagerie, with attendant Brâhmaṇas, remained all-powerful masters.

There was a time, however, when the birthplace of Krishṇa, the divine Don Juan of India, was famous for its luxury and wealth; it was this fame that attracted the first Afghân conquerors. At the time of his expedition against Kanauj in 1017, Mahmûd of Ghaznî, having heard of the treasures in the city of "Krishṇa Vâsudeva," marched there with his army and finding the town defenseless, because the Brâhmaṇas were performing their *pûja,* took possession of and sacked it. The army of Hanuman had evidently deteriorated; its descendants fled; "for ten years after the raid of the hated Moguls, the sacred city did not see within its walls any of its allies, beloved of the gods" (*i.e.,* the monkeys), say the chronicles of Mathurâ. Nice allies! There probably was nothing left to eat in the sacred city, and in consequence they took to their heels.

Mahmûd broke up and burned innumerable idols and collected many treasures of gold, silver and precious stones. He would have destroyed the numerous temples also, but decided that this would require many months; other chronicles say that he spared them on account of their wonderful beauty. One thing is sure—and this we can read in one of his letters to the governor of Ghaznî — Muhmûd was amazed at the beauty of the city and its wealth. Here is an excerpt from this letter, which I have copied from documents selected and published by the East India Company.

There are here 1,000 edifices, as firm as the faith of the faithful, most of them of marble; besides innumerable temples; nor is it likely this city has attained its present condition but at the expense of many millions of dinars; nor could such another be constructed under a period of two centuries.*

Further on, the author tells us that among the things found in the temples of Mathurâ were "five idols, made

---

*E. Thornton, *Gazetteer of India,* 1857, p. 656.

of pure gold, whose eyes were rubies each worth 50,000 dinars. On one of the idols was found a sapphire weighing 300 miskals.* Besides these, "there were found 100 idols made of silver, which were carried away on as many camels." Mahmûd remained at Mathurâ "twenty days during which the town suffered greatly from fire," not including the losses due to sacking.

After these events Mathurâ was left alone for many centuries, until it was sacked a second time by the Afghâns, namely by the army of Ahmad-Shâh-Durrânî, in 1757. Ahmad did not command this army in person, having given the control of these robbers to his Sardâr, Jahân-Khân, called by the Jesuits Zanus. Tieffentaller† writes that this army numbered 25,000 cavalry-men and then adds:

"Muttra is a populous city, abounding in wealthy inhabitants. In this city, and in another town, called Bendroban [Vrindâvana], very famous throughout India, on account of the incarnation of Krishna, the Afghâns practised great cruelties, and displayed their hatred of idols and idolaters, burning houses, together with their inmates; slaughtering others with the sword and lance; hauling off into captivity maidens and youths, men and women. In the temples of the idols they slaughtered kine, regarded as sacred by the superstitious people, and smeared the images and pavement with blood."‡

Finally, after the death of Najaf-Khân, the Marâthâ king, Sindhia, in his turn, took possession of Mathurâ and

---

*This measure is used even now for weighing pearls: in Turkey it is equivalent to 4.804 grams; in Egypt—4.663; and in Persia—4.536.

† [Joseph Tieffentaller was a Jesuit missionary and noted geographer in Hindostan. Born at Salurn (Bolzano, Italy), April 27, 1710; died at Lucknow, July 5, 1785. Went in 1743 to the East India mission, where he held various positions, particularly within the Empire of the Great Mogul. Fine scholar with an unusual talent for languages. First European to write an exact description of Hindostan; author of numerous studies on Hinduism, astronomy, natural sciences and history. The famous A. H. Anquetil-Duperron made part of these works accessible to the learned world in his Recherches . . . sur l'Inde (1786). —Compiler.]

‡E. Thornton, op. cit., p. 656.

then presented it to the French adventurer Perron "in *jaghire.*"* It was only in 1803 that the town was occupied by the English, *with no resistance whatever on the part of the inhabitants,* and secured the same year by a special treaty concluded by the East India Company. Thus the English became once more the "conquerors," as they like to call themselves in India.

With the exception of a few fortified towns, the whole country passed into the hands of the English, in much the same manner, by the way, without creating excitement anywhere . . . . The *most honorable* fathers of the Company never lost an opportunity. First they became protectors and custodians, fathers and benefactors of the persecuted rulers of India; then they tried to show the latter all the advantages to be derived from an alliance with them; finally the matter ended thus: Notwithstanding all the treaties and agreements, they told their ally one fine day *"ôtes toi de là, que je m'y mette,"* and added his domains to the other kingdoms which they had conquered in the same warrior-like fashion, taking permanent possession of them. Why waste one's precious strength, conquering *suo Marte,* when you can better attain it *per casum obliquum?*

In his political *Memoirs* the honest Colonel Tod tells us about the remarkable reply he got in 1817 from the old

---

*A grant made on condition of military service.

[Pierre Cuellier who adopted the name of Perron, was a French adventurer born at Château-de-Loir (Sarthe) around 1775. He engaged at first in various mercantile ventures and also learned how to make cannons. After many adventures, he sailed for India where, after reaching Poona, he enlisted in the army of Sindhia and built for him a formidable artillery. He rapidly advanced in rank and exhibited unusual courage at the taking of Delhi in 1788. He soon became the commander of the Marâthâ army and waged successful campaigns, acquiring great power over various Râjâs in the central part of India. When finally Gen. Lake entered the picture, Perron found no support for his plans and retired to Lucknow with his family and the riches he had acquired. He went back to France with ten million and bought the estate of Fresne (Loir-et-Cher) in 1806 where he lived until his death in 1843.—*Compiler.*]

and blind Nestor of India, Zalîm-Singh Jhâla,* the Thâkur of Kotah:

..... A smile would play over the features of the orbless politician when the envoy disclaimed all idea of its being a war of aggrandizement. To all such protestations he would say, "Mahârâja, I cannot doubt you believe what you say; but remember what old Zalim tells you; the day is not distant when one emblem of power (*eki sicca*) will be recognized throughout India.† You come to our country, Mahrâj, in a lucky time; *pfut*‡ is ripe and there remains for you to put it piecemeal into your mouths. Do not believe, that it is your power and bravery that makes you the masters of India. You are indebted for it only to our disunion and to the quarrels of our rulers."§

However strange it may seem, after quoting these words Tod adds to them his own, evidently quite sincere, thought; "These words are not without their deep meaning, *though I hope that the prophecy will never be realized.*" This nevertheless was realized in full. The English have swallowed all the pieces of *pfut,* one after the other, and even succeeded in snatching from the mouth of France the pieces she was about to swallow. John Bull has an excellent digestion.

Now, having finished with the English, let us examine the patron of Mathurâ. To ascertain whether definite data exists about Krishna, we must turn to the Orientalists. By listing their different opinions we get the following:

1. Krishna is one of the ten *avatâras* of Vishnu. The period of his birth is not yet determined. It varies between 1200 B.C. and 1200 A.D.

2. Krishna is an historical personage, because he is called the "Black Prince" (*kri*) of the tribe of Yadu, and everything points to his Ethiopian origin.

---

*Zalîm-Singh Jhâla, the potentate of Kotah, was a well-known hero in India. Even the English had to retire before this Râjput and his indomitable courage. He died in 1827.

† [Tod, *Annals*, etc., Vol. II, p. 531, ed. of 1894.—*Compiler.*]

‡*Pfut* is a sort of sweet melon or cantaloupe, which bursts asunder when ripe, breaking into pieces. Synonyms of the word *pfut* in the Hindî language are "disunion, quarrel, disagreement." Zalîm-Singh, who spoke, as do all Hindus, by using similes, compared the states and minor domains of India with this fruit.

§ [This passage has not been located in Col. Tod's work.—*Compiler.*]

3. Krishna is either a myth or a monkey, because he is represented as being blue, and blue men, as is well known, do not exist, whereas there are blue monkeys.

4. Krishna is the personification of all the virtues, and here follow some laudatory verses of the *Bhagavad-Gîtâ.*

5. Krishna is the personification of immorality; as proof of this the *Purânas* and the sect of the *Vallabhachâryas* are mentioned.

This is sufficient to convince one that the sum total of information concerning this hero-god is worthless. The Orientalists evolve their hypotheses because the Brâhmanas are silent; and the European public in general cares nothing for this particular one of the numerous Indian gods. It is certainly not the later deification of Krishna which is of interest, but the fact, that in his case, as well as in those of many other gods of the Brâhmanas, everything points to one of the ancient prehistoric heroes, more definite data about whom might lead to extremely important ethnological discoveries and might throw a brilliant light on the prehistoric, and later on the historic, races of both Europe and Asia. It has now become very clear to me that the Scandinavian, Egyptian, Greek, Central Asiatic, German and Slavonic gods were nearly all, at least the most important of them, once living heroes of antiquity, born in prehistoric India and generally in Asia. But it would have been well if this had become clear to those authorities who direct the minds of the profane or *non*-specialists, those who themselves do not study, and discovering nothing of their own, accept the word of their "authorities" literally. As a matter of fact, in all questions concerning the ancient and still existing religions founded on symbolism, as for instance the religion of the Brâhmanas, our best Orientalists are also *profanes* (*pro fanum*), as are their followers. They stand "*outside* the temple," just as the general public does, because the Brâhmanas do not allow our *Oriental* scholars into their pagodas —this inner world behind their public presentations. But many exceptions were made for us, as is well known in India, and, to the great irritation of the Anglo-Indians, we were admitted into places where no one of them had ever been.

This happened also at Mathurâ. Before Ânanda-Svâmi, *the envoy of the Thâkur,* the doors which were usually tightly locked to all except the officiating *Vaishnavas* were opened, and we were allowed to see places where no foot of a *feringhee* or *mlechchha* had entered since the time of the Afghâns. But here also, as in Jubbulpore, only two of us were admitted, Colonel O. and myself, whereas the Hindus who had lost their caste waited outside.

In Mathurâ, we became convinced of the fact that the inhabitants of the Greek Olympus were born nearer to the Himâlayas than to the country of Homer, that Parnassus must be sought near the Bâmiân, and that Apollo, Hercules, Bacchus and Orpheus are *avatâras* of Krishna, Baladeva, Vâgîsa* and Arjuna, the friend of Krishna, one of the

---

*Vâgîsa is the god of the Word; dressed in the skin of a leopard or a tiger, he is sitting with his feet under him like a *yogin.* Vâgîsa is one of the *aspects* of Śiva, as well as of Vishnu; such a role belongs to many gods, all of whom were at first *brahmachârins* or "celibate ascetics." The head of this god, as well as his neck, are covered with garlands of *bilva,* a plant similar to the grapevine from which a strongly intoxicating drink is made and the dry leaves of which are constantly chewed by the hatha-yogins. The fact that the Greek Bacchus was born as Śiva-Vâgîsa is proved by the following. The first appearance of Vâgîsa (dressed like Bacchus and crowned with a grapevine) occurred on Mount *Su-Meru* (*su,* saintly, and *meru,* mountain), near Bâmiân in the Paropamisos. "He there taught humanity the art of agriculture and civilization." The historians of Alexander called this mountain *Su-Meros,* with the usual ending, and insisted even in those days that it was the abode of Bacchus. According to the tradition of the Brâhmanas and on the word of Arrian, it was here that the Macedonian held a Bacchanalia with his generals; crowned with *bilva,* they drank heavily. This mountain, like many others, is covered with wild grapevines. According to the mythology of the Greeks, Bacchus was born from the thigh of Jupiter. In Greek *mêros* means *thigh.* Is it not evident that the Greeks either confused this word with *meru,* mountain in Sanskrit (pronounced by the Greeks as *mêros*), or simply forgot their place of origin, as the centuries and millennia passed between the autochthone of Attica and the Macedonian? Their mountain "Tomaros" must also have originated in the Paropamisos. As the letter *d* changes in Greek into *z, Deus, Zeus,* in the same way the letter *s* often becomes a *t. Sumeru* became first *Sumêros,* and later "Tomaros," in Greece.

Pâṇḍavas. It is not in vain that enthusiasts like Pococke,* the author of *India in Greece,* tried to prove, *not having seen what we saw in the inner sanctum of the temples of Mathurâ,* that all Greece with her gods, as well as Egypt with its *zoolatria,* came wholesale from India, not modern India of course, which is locked in by its Himâlayan frontier, but the prehistoric land.

In one of the temples,† we saw Kṛishṇa playing the pipe in company with other gods, on a mountain which the Brâhmaṇas who showed us around called "Parnassus." We were told that a part of the Paropamisos (Bâmiân) was called thus in ancient times. These mountains were generally called, and are so even today, Devanîka, because according to tradition they are inhabited by "earthly gods," *bhûdevas* (*bhûmi*—earth), *i.e.*, deified heroes.‡ In the *Purâṇas,* we read that the abode of the gods during the period of their religious retreat was always situated on mountains, where they built little huts out of bamboo which are called *parṇasi* even today; Râma and Kṛishṇa also lived on the mountain Parnassus, in "parṇasi."§

---

*[Edward Pococke (1604-1691) was an English Orientalist and Biblical scholar educated at Corpus Christi college, Oxford. After studying Arabic at Aleppo, he occupied the Arabic chair at Oxford, and later on the chair of Hebrew as well. Though his *magnum opus* is considered to be his complete edition of the Arabic history of Bar-Hebraeus (Abulfaragius), one of the most valuable studies issued from his pen is his *India in Greece; or, Truth in Mythology,* London, 1852, 8vo., the conclusions of which have been, for some reason or other, largely ignored by later scholars.—*Compiler.*]

†Up to this point I have tried in my story to point out accurately the different places and to call the temples by their names. I am very sorry that here I *cannot name* the temples of Mathurâ, because, having received permission to publish the facts, we were made to give *our word of honor* and to promise most solemnly *not to mention the names.*

‡*Vide* on the subject of Parnassus, etc., Capt. Francis Wilford's essay "On Mount Caucasus," in *Asiatick Researches,* Calcutta, 1801, Vol. VI, p. 497.

§In the *Ramâyaṇa* and the *Mahâbhârata* the word Parnassus occurs frequently. It is difficult to say, however, whether the mountains had been called after the huts, or *vice versa.*

Just as Bacchus is the *avatâra* of Vâgîśa, so is Apollo the Greek personification of Krishna. Everything tends to prove it. Krishna is called *Muralîdhara, i.e.,* "flute-bearer"; he is the god of music. The pipe was invented before the lyre, of which the primitive pastoral tribes were ignorant. The *Purânas* say that the *bânslî* (the pipe made of reeds, from the word *bâna* — reed) was the favorite instrument of Kanyâ (one of Krishna's names)* because his herds preferred the *bânslî* of their divine shepherd to the *chatâra* or *vînâ* (lyre).†

In Muttra alone, not counting other cities consecrated to his name (such as Dvârakâ and Nâthdvâra), Krishna appears in seven different personalities or *aspects,* each one of which ought to be the object of serious cogitation for the Orientalists. The similarity of these additional "personalities," or separate gods, so to say, with those of Western mythologies is quite striking!

Let us examine, for instance, Krishna-Kanyâ more closely. Here we find the god of Hindu music represented as looking for a place for his religious rituals and meditations on the Asiatic "Parnassus."‡ Compare him with Apollo as presented in the hymn in his honor,§ where the poet describes him as seeking a place for his altar on the borders of the Greek Parnassus. Hills, mountains, streams, rivers, all nature sing their praises to both of these gods in almost the same words. Near the stream, by the cave, Krishna-Kanyâ meets the snake Nâgaputra and overcomes it. Apollo finds the snake Python and kills it in the same way. Between

---

*"Krishna-Kanyâ" is the god of music and the inventor of the chromatic scale. In Greece this invention is ascribed to Timothy, a contemporary of Alexander of Macedonia, who could easily have brought it from India. One should compare the Greek hymns in Apollo's honor to the hymns of *Jayadeva,* composed 3,000 years ago in honor of Krishna. There is a collection of them at Mathurâ.

†The Greek *kithara,* taken probably from the six-stringed *chatâra* of the Hindus, produced in its turn the Anglo-Saxon and the German *zither,* and later the Spanish *guitarra. Chatâra* is a compound word, from *chah*—six [Skt. *shash*], and *târa*—string or wire.

‡On statues, bas-reliefs and in the hymns of Jayadeva.

§Hesiod, *The Homeric Hymns:* Hymn to Delian Apollo, lines 22-24.

the snakes *Putra* and *Python* there is more similarity
than in the sound alone.

In the muses of Apollo we recognize many of the *gopîs*
or shepherdesses beloved by Kṛishṇa. The chief ones among
them are aspects of the goddesses of science and art, Sarasvatî, the goddess of wisdom, Lakshmî, the goddess of poetry,
etc.

The statue of "Kṛishṇa on Parnassus" was first transferred
from the cave of the "Vihâra of Girdhana"* to Nâthdvâra,
and later to Mathurâ. Just as in the worship of Apollo, the
"mysteries" of Kṛishṇa were performed in caves. One can
recognize the Pythian Apollo in other statues also, for instance in the great statue of Kṛishṇa-Kanyâ killing the
black snake Kâlîya-Nâga which, according to the local and
Purâṇic tradition, was poisoning the waters of the Jumnâ
before it was killed by the hero. Kṛishṇa-Kanyâ is represented as dragging the many-headed Hydra out of the river
and then crushing its head under his foot.

Diodorus says that *Kan* was one of the titles of the Egyptian Apollo in his aspect of Sun God. It is not far from *Kan*
to *Kanyâ*. Kṛishṇa-Kanyâ is called *Nîlanâth* (the blue
god), due to his azure color. Then again *Nîlanâth* accom-
panies the dead souls into *Sûrya-Svarga* (the sun paradise),
and in this *aspect,* instead of a human head, he has an
eagle's head and holds in his hands a lotus. At all times the
eagle serves him as his *vâhana.* In Turin there are hieroglyphic inscriptions describing the Egyptian *Kan* as follows: The head of an eagle on a blue body, in the hands
a lotus, and lotuses before him on the altar. As *Nîlanâth,*
Kṛishṇa is also painted blue, because he is the symbol of
space—*Ouranos.* The same can be said of *Kan.* Both *Kanyâ*
and *Kan* are the so-called "gods of the mysteries"; it was
in their honor that the "mysteries" were performed in ancient Egypt, Greece and India; in the latter they are performed even today. Having seen Kṛishṇa-Nîlanâth with his
bird's head in the temple of Muttra, I almost mistook him
for Osiris with the *Ibis* head, the spouse and brother of Isis,
whom he resembles. Finally, one of the names of Apollo of

---
* [Colloquial for *Govardhana.*]

Delos is *Oulios;* he is also blue and has an eagle's head. Who borrowed from whom? Did the Egyptians borrow from the Hindus or the Brâhmaṇas from the Greeks and Egyptians? All these gods are so-called "solar" gods; they are all heroes, warriors and shepherds, having their herds of cows and bulls, like Hermes, Mercury and others. In every country where they are worshipped, we find them surrounded by bulls and cows—animals, which in mythology always have a mysterious connection with the sun (*Hari*). With the modern Pârsîs, who are degenerate worshippers of Zoroaster, the cow and all its products are held sacred; the same applies to the bull. At sunrise the Pârsî of Bombay stretches out his arms to Ormazd, the "fiery-eyed orb," and drinks without squirming a teaspoonful of *nirang.* This is his ambrosia, the cow's nectar. The cow and the bull were deified in Chaldaea and Scandinavia, in Egypt as much as in present-day India. We find cow's horns on the head of Isis; we see the bull killed by Ahriman; Hermes and Apollo are shepherds for the "herds of the luminary of days," and Krishṇa is likewise for the herd of Vishṇu (the same sun). The daughter of Brahmâ transforms herself into a cow to avoid the sinful passion of her father, but in spite of this metamorphosis Brahmâ still impregnates her. The bull Apis was held more sacred than the Pharaoh, and his life was more precious to the people than the whole kingdom. To this day, the Anglo-Indians, notwithstanding their despotism, have never yet dared to kill or even strike a "sacred bull" that may have wandered into their garden. With all ancient people the cow was the symbol of earth or nature, impregnated and vivified by its creator, the *unknowable* spirit. "The cow is the same as a Brâhmaṇa," we were told by a Śâstrin at Muttra, in answer to our inquiries. The cow is the *vâhana of purusha* (spirit).

"The *Ramâyaṇa* is a fairy tale! The *Mahâbhârata*—a collection of most grotesque superstitions and wild phantasies," we heard said many times. Let us see. Râma, the first incarnation of Vishṇu, goes to Lankâ, accompanied by *Hari, i.e.,* Krishṇa again but in his first aspect. Rameses-Sesostris, the personification of the same sun (Osiris, Vishṇu, Apollo and *tutti quanti*), sets out on an expedition to India.

In the army of Râma are his allies; monkeys, bears, eagles and the entire animal kingdom. In the army of Rameses are the cynocephali,* satyrs and other mythical creatures. We must also bear in mind the following: To this very day many of the Râjput tribes are named according to different animal species. For instance, the *Induvaṇśas* have a tribe of *Aśvas* (horses), of *Takshakas* (snakes), of *Śaśas* (hares), etc., while the *Sûryavaṇśas*, at the head of which stood Râma, have even now a tribe of *Mûshas* (mice), and, according to their genealogies, have had tribes of monkeys (*Bandars*) and *Garuḍas* (eagles). Bearing in mind these details, and noting which are of interest to an archaeologist or ethnologist, is it not a pity that, instead of trying to tear the veil hiding historical facts, the Orientalists do not try to lift it a little to find out if the *Ramâyaṇa* and the *Mahâbhârata* might be hiding something more important than tales about armies of animals and magicians? They should first try to disentangle this web of gods and goddesses with all their puzzling names and only then pass judgment. If one studies the "mythology" of the Brâhmaṇas *without prejudice,* one can easily find the guiding thread which will lead directly to the discovery of the origin of the different races—the thread now lost to the archaeologist and the historian in the impenetrable fog of confused facts and names which were distorted by the Greeks.

This is certainly not the place to prove these views. Many similar ideas have already been expressed, but all in vain; the efforts were shattered against the rock of prejudice, and no Orientalist would favor these ideas. However, even Plato said that the religion of Greece was taken wholesale from Egypt, and that its Gods, as well as those of Egypt, were all derived from the East. And not only the gods. We find in India the names of tribes, mountains, lakes and localities, and current legends about them, all of which clearly show the following: That either the Greeks and Romans, and before them the Egyptians, derived their Pantheon of gods from India, and that these people themselves, with their

---

*The *Cynocephalus* is the same species of monkeys as Hanuman; they are cousins, if not brothers.

PALACE OF THE MAHĀRĀŅA AT UDAIPUR

LAKE PICHOLA, UDAIPUR

ancestors, the *autochthones,* the Pelasgians and Etruscans, came from Asia; that the Brâhmaṇas "from the banks of the Oxus" first saw the light on the shores of the Nile, the Aegian Sea or the Tiber. It is impossible that such coincidences, such similarities in names, legends, and enduring customs, should be pure chance. Not a mountain, a river or a god in ancient Greece or Rome, but has a *prototype* in India, ancient or modern. We can recognize nearly every name, though as usual distorted by the Greeks. For instance, the "Sandrokottos" of Magasthenes suddenly turns out to be King Chandragupta, the grandfather of Aśoka. Let us take the Pelasgians as an example. They were, some time ago, the center of interest; but as their origin was about as difficult to discover as a buried treasure, the scientists gave it up as an unsolvable problem. But did anyone ever try to see if there were any connection between them and the ancient peoples of India, as in the case of the Greek autochthones? As far as I remember, people laughed at Pococke, the author of *India in Greece.* This, however, was 35 years ago, when people knew very little about the *Purânas.* If the question about the Pelasgians and the prehistoric Greeks were once more raised, the assertion of Pococke that "the primeval history of Greece and Rome is the ancient history of India," would be vindicated. But as long as the assertions of the Brahmanic literature are held to be mere fairy tales, the earliest history of the Central Asiatic people who settled in Europe will remain shrouded in impenetrable darkness. Most strange is it to observe the lack of attention paid to the Brâhmanic legends which still await their Champollion. Surely the *Mahâbhârata* deserves as much effort as was spent on the Rosetta Stone, and the day will certainly dawn when that which is called *fables and myths* in Greek will *prove to be facts and history* in Sanskrit.

Let us look squarely at the facts. They stare us "in the face," and should be judged, if not by the public, then at least by some experts in philology and archaeology. For instance, prior to the "Great War," the whole country now called Bengal belonged to the *Induvanśas,* the Sons of the Moon, Buddhists long *before* Gautama the Buddha and the epoch of the reformer; in other words, Jainam-Gayâ (the present *Buddha-Gayâ*) was the capital of Palâśa, the ancient name of the province of Bihâr.* Still earlier it was called *Pâlivarta* and *Pâliktana, i.e.,* the land where people spoke *Pâli,* now the religious language of the Buddhists. *Pâli,* as known to the Brâhmaṇas, preceded *Sanskrit,* which is shown by the names of these two languages. *Pâli* stands in the same relation to Sanskrit, as the Slavonic to the modern Russian. *Pâli* means primeval, coarse, and *Saṃskṛita*—polished, finished and perfected.

What does history know about the Pelasgians? Historians know nothing about their tongue, belief and origin, or at least so little that they have ceased discussing them. All our information is limited to a few verses of Asius, a poet who lived some 700 B.C., and some words of Aeschylus. The first tells us that King Pelasgus, the ancestor of the Pelasgians, *grew out of black soil* and calls him, probably on that account, "Godlike."

'Αντίθεον δὲ Πελασγὸν ἐν ὑφικόμοισιν ὄρεσσι
Γαῖα μέλαιν' ἀνέδωκεν, ἵνα θνητῶν γένος εἴη †

Aeschylus, on the other hand, makes Pelasgus the son of Palaichthôn (Παλαίχθων).‡ Would it not be more reasonable in view of what has been said above, to suppose, as some people have already done (Sir William Jones among others), that this mystical Pelasgus was born in *Gayâ,* the capital of Palâśa, or in Bihâr, instead of having grown out of *gaia* ("earth", in Greek)? Is not Pococke nearer the truth than the Orientalist authorities? He was ridiculed for supposing that King Pelasgus was actually the son of *Palaichthôn,* the "ancient fatherland" of the Greeks, *i.e., Pâliktana,* the country where *Pâli* was spoken in ancient Bengal. On the other hand, one philologist assures us that the

---

*Derived from the word *palâśa* (*Butea frondosa*), a plant which covers all the hills and valleys of that province.

†["The Godlike Pelasgus, on the wooded mountains, black earth gave up, that the race of mortals might exist." This statement by Asius may be found in Pausanias' *Itinerary* or *Description of Greece,* Book VIII (Arcadia), i, 4.]

‡[In his *Supplices,* 250-251.]

Pelasgians derived their name from the word *pelagos* (sea), because they came to Greece by way of the sea! Another authority, an etymologist, derives the name from πελαργός, stork, and a third party, Wachsmuth and Müller, derive it from the words πολέω, to till, and ἀγρός, field. In that case the English can also be called *Pelasgians* because they too must come and go only by way of the sea, their land being surrounded by the *pelagos*. Shall we also call them storks, or migratory birds, considering their habits? There never was an agricultural people, cultivating their land, that could not claim the name of *Pelagros*.

We may be told that even the first hypothesis *est un peu trop tirée par les cheveux!* I will not deny it. But King Pelasgus had to be born *somewhere* and of *someone*. In any case, the supposition that *Pelasgus,* the son of *Palaichthôn* was born in *Palâśa,* the province of *Pâliktana,* is far more reasonable than that he crawled out of the "black soil" like a worm after rain. Isn't it strange that notwithstanding their complete lack of knowledge about the *origin* of the people of Greece and Italy, the learned academies of Europe have always laughed at the attempts of some Orientalists* to prove that the cradle of all these mysterious prehistoric peoples, the primitive as well as the civilized, such as the Etruscans and Pelasgians, should be sought in India, among its numerous tribes. Nevertheless, after studying the genealogies of the Râjput tribal chiefs, their Râjâs and Thâkurs, and the ancient geographical names in their country, according to the *Purânas,* one is easily convinced that there is hardly a people in Greece, or a geographical name, that does not correspond, quite incomprehensibly so, if our hypothesis is rejected, to the names of the tribes and localities of India. Why not try then to verify our theory, which is at the same time a hypothesis upheld by some of our best known Orientalists in the world of scholarship? Especially so because in ancient Greece alone, there are many Greek names which *do not mean anything* in that language, a fact which never occurs in regard to indigenous

---

*Some of the best known, such as, Colebrooke, Sir William Jones, Wilson, Tod and others less known.

names of either people or localities. Pococke found in the geographical names of Greece a whole catalogue of such seemingly *meaningless* names unrelated to anything, if their roots are to be sought in Greek dialects; but as soon as they are compared with names in the Sanskrit language found in the *Purânas,* or with the genealogies of Râjasthân, they immediately acquire a meaning. Among such etymologically unexplainable words are the following: Stymphoea, Dodona, Chaonia, Crossaea, Ithaca, Locri, Corinthos, Ossa, Arcadia, Achaia, Boeotia, Elida, Larissa, Pharsalus, etc. Among the tribes of the *Sûryavanśas* and *Induvanśas,* the *Kurus* and *Pândavas* who, according to the *Mahâbhârata,* migrated after the "Great War" into the "Kukarmadeśa," the *Land of Sin,* (*i.e.,* the land of the West), we can trace nearly all the names of the ancient Greek tribes who fought on the fields of Troy. Vâlmîki and Vyâsa are the Hesiod and Homer of ancient India. Her *bhâts* (bards) were born before those of Scandinavia, before the Provençal troubadours or the minnesingers of ancient Germany; these *bhâts,* to whom people ascribed the faculty of prevision, as was the case with their European descendants, left us in their songs* the ancient as well as the more recent names of the compatriots who had left India and become their enemies and which later populated Europe, Asia Minor, and even a part of Africa. Thirty-six Râjput tribes, *Râjkula,* hold the key to the origin of the Greek tribes.†

Let us see if a couple of our examples will not make us wonder at certain "coincidences." Let us begin with the tribes of "Gokulas," from the land of Gokuladeśa‡ who lived from ancient times on the Jumnâ. They are spoken

---

*There are still extant 69 books of the *bhât* Chund, who was called *Trikula,* the "three-tribed one." We have seen them. They contain 100,000 stanzas consecrated to the description of three Râjput tribes. Chund lived in the 12th century A.D.

† [This subject is further elaborated in a serious article in *The Theosophist,* Vol. II, January and March, 1881, entitled "A Guide to Greek Nomenclature." It was written by Dayarama Varma, Secretary of the Ârya Samâja in Multan, Pañjâb. This article, however, was not concluded.—*Compiler.*]

‡*Go*—a cow; *kula*—a tribe; *deśa*—land; pronounced *Gokuladeśa.*

of in the *Purânas* as very brave warriors, skillful in the use of the bow and arrow, and living the life of shepherds between wars. The land of the Gokulas was the scene of Krishna's youthful love conquests over the *gopîs* (shepherd-nymphs) and the abode of Nanda, his tutor. Even in our day the Gokulas are renowned for their extremely solid, round, tower-like houses, built like those of the Pelasgians.

Several Orientalists are quite convinced that the Greek Cyclops *Kuklôpes,* (Κύκλωπες), are the Indian *Gokulas.* Ancient as well as modern etymologists speculated about them, but did not find much, though some of them came very near the truth. What wondrous things have been imagined about the Cyclops! First they appeared as "builders," age-old architects, then as the "archers," and finally as "miners." From Homer to the German philologists Kruse and Bauer, from Strabo to Major Jacob, one theory after another, each one more curious than the former, was put forward. The lamp, which they wore as miners on their foreheads, was supposed to be "the reason for the fable of the One-eyed Polyphemos." One writer asserted one thing, another something else. Kruse tells us that the Cyclops got their name from the circular (κύκλος) shape of Pelasgian buildings which looked like beehives and had a round opening similar to an eye (*ôps*).* This is more plausible than the hypothesis of another Orientalist who derives the term "one-eyed" from the "Greek idea of an Olympian god, supposedly closing one eye in taking aim," with his "thunderbolt-arrow."† But even the Kruse hypothesis is not worth much. However, if anyone wants to get additional evidence for the hypothesis of Pococke who asserts that the mythical Cyclops are the contemporary *Gokulas* of the Jumnâ, he should stay for a time at Muttra or Dvârakâ, and visit their annual shepherd-festival in honor of Krishna and his *gopîs.*

---

* [Friedrich Karl Hermann Kruse, *Hellas, oder geographisch-antiquarische Darstellung des alten Griechenlandes und seiner Colonien,* etc., Leipzig, 1825-27, Vol. I, p. 440.]

†G.A.F.Ast, *Grund. der Phil.* [It is uncertain whether the reference is to his *Grundlinien der Philosophie,* Landshut, 1807, or his *Grundriss der Philologie,* Landshut, 1808.]

If he succeeds, as we did, in being present at this solemn festivity, or at the birthday of Krishna, he will witness a spectacle in which everything but the actors—costumes, stage setting, the smallest details, including the barbarous native music—has remained the same as when these religious mystery-plays were witnessed by the *Hari-Kulas,* the *Agni-Kulas,* and the *Gohil-Kulas* of Râjasthân, in the beginning of the "Black Age" (Kali-yuga), 5,000 years ago, according to native chronologists.

I will try to describe this unique and allegorical spectacle in my next letter.

———

—VII—

Instead of a couple of hours, we stayed two days at
Mathurâ and vicinity. The Thâkur sent word telling us
to remain for the spring festival of the "Gokula Ashtama."*
The day of Krishna's birth comes in August, but it has a
prologue in the spring, at the same time as the festival of
Gaurî, the Râjput Ceres.

The similarity between Krishna and the Greek Apollo,
between the epithets given to the latter by the Greeks, the
Romans and other European people, and the corresponding Indian names for their favorite Avatâra is so striking
that it cannot fail to interest all who love ancient mythologies. I repeat, it cannot be a mere coincidence. Especially remarkable is the similarity in the names given to the
sun, which is personified by both of these *"gods."* *Hari-*
Krishna is the *scorching* (destructive) sun. *Ari*-Krishna, is

---

Gokula is the tribe of the cow (*go*); Krishna was raised by the
shepherd Nanda; the *prologue* of this holiday comes in spring at the
birthplace of Krishna. *Ashtama* is the first quarter of the moon.

621

simply the sun. Kṛishṇa, the "lord of rays" (Phoebus), and his celestial abode is called *Haripura* (Heliopolis?) or City of the Sun.*

"The *Dii Majores* of the Rājputs are the same in number and title as amongst the Greeks and Romans, being the deities who figuratively preside over the planetary system," rightly remarks Tod.† For that reason, all the religious rituals, the dances of the *nâchnîs* and the mysteries, *i.e.*, the performance of scenes taken from their mythology, always have as their basis an astronomical meaning. *Bhânu Saptamî*, "the seventh day of the sun," also called the "birth of the sun" or Vishṇu (the entrance of the sun into the sign of *Makara*, Capricorn, in the solar month of *Magha*, in January) is a great holiday at Udaipur. The chariot of the Sun, harnessed to eight horses, is taken out of the temple of Vishṇu and brought back again, in a ceremony similar to that used on the day of the accession to the throne of a new rânâ. The summer solstice is called by them the "Night of the Gods," because Vishṇu (like the Sun) is resting during the four rainy months on his couch, the snake Ananta.

A description of *all* the Hindu holidays, or even of the chief ones, would require the publication of a complete library. *Sât vâram aur nau tyauhâr*, "nine holidays in seven days," is a Rājput saying, which does not require any commentary. I will describe only the mystery-play we saw performed in the vicinity of Muttra.

The pastoral holiday of *Gaurî*, the local Ceres, is opened by the *gopîs* or shepherdesses. *Gaurî* is one of the forms of *Pârvatî*, or *Durgâ-mâtâ*, the "powerful mother," the Hindu goddess of harvest and plenty. *Durgâ-mâtâ* is similar to the *mater montana*, an epithet associated, according to Dio-

---

*Rājputs believe in two kinds of "Paradise," two localities or Elysian Fields: one, purely spiritual; the other of material quality. In their songs, the bards teach the warrior that the one killed on the battlefield "by steel," and "performing his duty of honor," will go to the "spiritual paradise" and never return to earth. The freed spark (*jyotis*) will unite itself with the parent fire, the Sun, Sûrya.

†*Annals*, etc., Vol. I, p. 513, ed. of 1894.

dorus, with Cybelê or Vesta, in her role of "guardian of the children"; *mater montana* is called in Râjasthân *Ambâ-mâtâ* (mother of the mountain) and appears here as the patroness and guardian of boys, the future warriors. The altars of *Gaurî-Pârvatî-Mâtâ*, "the powerful mother of the mountain," crown nearly every high hill in Mewâr, the heart of Râjasthân; it is to her that all the "temple-fortresses" of the country are consecrated. Her activities are more varied, and her duties more difficult and manifold than those of her equivalent worshipped in Rome, Greece and even Egypt, as everything tends to show that she is the prototype of Isis. Like Diana of Ephesus, *Gaurî-Durgâ* is crowned with a crescent; like Cybelê, she has on her head a crenellated tower;* and, under the name of *Devî-Durgâ* (force, power), is regarded as the patroness of all the fortified places. She is also *Mâtâ-Jananî*, "mother creatrix," *viz.*, is performing the duties of Juno, *Juno Lucina; as Padma*, "whose throne rests on a lotus," she is the Isis of the Nile; as *Gaurî-Tripura* (literally—three cities, Tripolis?), "governing three cities," and as *Âtma-devî*, "the goddess of souls," she is of course the *Hecata Triformis* of the Greeks. In other words, *Gaurî* synthesizes in herself all the goddesses of Greece and Egypt, beginning with Diana and Proserpine and ending with Isis and Astoreth. Chiefly, however, she is "Earth," the Hindu Ceres, who appears in the mysteries seated on sheaves of wheat in a chariot pulled by a cow,† and holding in her hands a *kâma-kumbha,* a vase looking like a horn of plenty, from which fruit and seed are falling.

After the procession there appears *Kâma-deva,* the God of love, the cupid of India, whose bow and arrow are replaced here by garlands of flowers and a pointed bamboo stick. He hits with the latter, one of the *gopîs*, the daughter of Nanda, who falls hopelessly in love with Krishṇa. The chorus bursts into song. This is the hymn to Kâma from the *Bhavishya-Purâṇa*:

---

*The whole province of Mewâr and the environs of Udaipur are strewn with such ancient towers, and they are all under the guardianship of *Ambâ* and *Guri-Durgâ*.

†Earth or *Pṛithivî* is symbolized by the Hindus as a *cow*.

"Hail, god of the flowery bow; hail, warrior with a fish on thy banner; hail, powerful divinity, who causeth the firmness of the sage to forsake him, and subduest the guardian deities of eight regions!....

"Glory be to Madana, to Kâma; to Him who is formed as the God of Gods; to Him, by whom Brahmâ, Vishnu, Śiva, Indra, are filled with emotions of rapture!"*

Then appears Guhânâtha (Krishna in his aspect of "Ruler of the Cave"—*Guhâ*—which must not be confused with *Gopînâtha*, the "Ruler of the Shepherdesses"). He is wrapped in an animal skin, crowned with *kuśa* grass, and playing on a bamboo pipe; attracted by his music, *gopîs* begin to gather round him. In the first act the *gopîs* are not shepherdesses, and the *Guhânâtha* himself is transformed from the "god of the cave" into the "god of the mountain," *Govardhananâtha* or *Nâthjî* (Ruler of all the Rulers). He is crowned with a brilliant crown of rays, like Phoebus, for he is the sun itself, like Vishnu, Apollo and Osiris. The modest pipe is replaced with the *chatâra,* the *six-stringed* lyre,† on which the blue god begins to play, not a melody, but, as I thought, a *scale,* and a very monotonous one at that. But, as I was told this was a musical tune as old as the "music of the spheres," I became resigned to it.

In front of the metamorphosed *god* appear the *gopîs,* who by this time have been transformed into *sounds.*

They are the nine *râginîs; râga* is the musical *scale,* and *râginîs* (the feminine plural) are the wives of the *râgas.*

I use the word "sounds" as there seems to be no other suitable expression. This is not my fault, but the fault of the sages who invented Sanskrit music, in which, in addition

---

Asiatick Researches, Vol. III, 1799, p. 278: "The Lunar Year of the Hindus," by Sir Wm. Jones.

[This passage is quoted by Col. Tod in his *Annals,* etc., Vol. I, p. 544, ed. of 1894.—*Compiler.*]

†Music which to the European ear is really without melody, yet possessing a *full seven-note scale.* Though the monk Guido Aretinus is generally believed to have been the first to use the *seventh* note (in the 13th century), and the Greeks actually knew but *six* notes, still a seven-note scale exists in the *Purânas.*

to its undeniable attraction, though unpleasant to my ear, a whole mythology is to be found.

Here are the proofs:

The Sanskrit inventors of music established six *râgas, i.e.,* scales, the names of which are, *Śrîrâga,* (*râga* means sir or lord), *Vasanta, Pañchama, Bhairava, Megha, Naṭa-nârâyaṇa.*

Each of these *râgas* has five wives, and each of these wives has eight children. Every *râga,* every *râgiṇî* and every *râga-child* has a name, attributes, personal biography, genealogy, and, if he had been born in Russia, probably would have had a special service record! However, having been born in India, each one of them received the title of a god, goddess, or godling. The philosophy of this is that every singer and musician in India who sings and plays has at his disposal 276 different *scales,* with seven notes in each; each note represents some special sound of the animal kingdom and must represent some emotion.

The animal sounds and their corresponding emotions are taken by me from an original work of the Sanskrit Musical Society,* because this will explain better than anything else *what it was* that Krishṇa *Nâthjî* and his *râginîs* represented:

Notes of the Scale		Sanskrit Names	Types of animal sounds	Representing various shades of:
सा Sâ	Do	Shaḍja	Peacock	Heroism, Wonder, Terror.
ऋ Ṛi	Re	Ṛishabha	Bull	
ग Ga	Mi	Gândhâra	Goat	Compassion.
म Ma	Fa	Madhyama	Crane	Humor, Love.
प Pa	Sol	Pañchama	Blackbird	Freedom from care.
ध Dha	La	Dhaivata	Frog	Disgust, Alarm.
नि Ni	Si	Nishâda	Elephant	Pity, Awareness of Strength.

* [Cf. *The Theosophist,* Vol. I, November, 1879, pp. 46-49: "Hindu Music," by Bulwant Trimbuk, Hon. Sec'y of the Poona "Gâyan Samâj." —*Compiler.*]

These "sounds" representing shades of emotion were personified by the *nau râginîs** dancing in front of Krishna. They were the personifications of the "nine passions," *nau râsas,* begotten by the melody of the god of music,† creations of his which sprang into being by the magical power of Vâch.‡ The performance, quite as much as the idea itself was charming. Holding each other's hands, the *nau râginîs* first dance before their creator; then another transformation takes place. The flaming god of the sun appears before the spectators, this time not *incognito,* and the *nau râginîs* become transformed into the signs of the Zodiac; this is the beginning of the astronomical mystery-play with the goddess-constellations forming a circle around the Sun-god and dancing the famous *Râsa-Maṇḍala,* the dance of the stars. The *nau râginîs* and the *nau râsas* disappear once more, and the signs of the Zodiac remain. The *Râsa-Maṇḍala* continues. The slow movements and the graceful mimicry become more lively and grow faster and faster.§ The mystical dance on the banks of the Jumnâ reminds one of the dance of the *almehs* in Egypt and transports one to the sandy banks of the Nile.

In the third act everything changes once more. Krishna once again appears as a shepherd, with his shepherd's hook, and around him play and sing again the gopîs-shepherdesses. The *nau râginîs* have once more been transformed into the *nau râsas,* the "nine passions," and try to lead the shepherd, a *brahmachârin,* away from the path of truth. They do not succeed, however. Krishna is victorious in his virtues, and the shepherdesses—*en sont pour leurs frais.*

Nau means "nine."

†"Nine passions," or the nine muses of Apollo.

‡The god of *sound,* in this case of mystical, *occult* sound.

§The cymbals, the *tabor* and the *muralî* (a kind of flute), nearly drove me mad; but I learned a great deal that evening. The *chobis* of Mathurâ have a widespread and well-deserved fame in India as singers and mimics, and the base voices of the Brâhmaṇas, together with the contraltos and tenors of the "celestial singers" of the pagoda, were full of harmony. That is the vocal music; as for the instrumental music, however, it eventually becomes unbearable to a European listener.

Krishna, without paying any attention to the flirtation of the shepherdesses, continues to play on his pipe which has now replaced the six-stringed *chatâra*. The cows of his sacred herd, however, being probably ashamed of the shepherdesses, scatter. The sun has set, and the stage grows dark. Then appear the ferocious Kâchhîs (another tribe of the Râjput) and take the cows away. The Gokulas or *Kuklôpes* pursue them and try to get the cows back. When they appear, the spectator is confronted with the ferocious Cyclop-shepherds of Homer, the hairy giants who knew neither law nor restraint . . . . . They creep out of caves and descend from trees; on the chest of each one of them *shines like a fiery eye an enormous firefly, pinned to the animal skin* . . . . .

These fireflies are the only light in the cave of the shepherd or in the round tower of a poor Gokula and are used even in our day by the tribe of Nanda, the educator of Krishna. Often at night, going out to look for a lost cow or bull, the Gokulas pin several such fireflies to their turbans to have some light. Is it not here in this tribe of Gokulas that one should seek the origin and explanation of the Greek *Kuklôpes?* The fireflies explain perfectly the "lantern on the forehead" of the Cyclop-*miners*, and also the fact that Homer knew them to be a tribe of shepherds, *Gokulas*, whose chief and only representative was the "one-eyed" Polyphemus.

The mystery-play ended very late. The Brâhmana-*Chobîs* (called thus on account of the *choba* or mace, which they carry during the performance) had besieged the tyrant Kansa in his palace, demolishing his fortress, and chasing him into the bushes,* long before we left the pagoda. The performance over, the "god Krishna" joined our party, and turned out to be a very young and tall Râjput who, to our astonishment, spoke English. It is to him that I owe most of the information which I obtained in Mathurâ. He ex-

---

*Kansa is the uncle of Krishna and the usurper of his throne. Every year the Brâhmana-*Chobîs* besiege his palace and allegedly kill him in the forest, whither he fled for refuge.

plained the meaning of many things which we did not understand in the performance, in which he played the leading role.

He thoroughly believed in Krishna, the hero, but disavowed, as we did, Krishna, the god. It is from him that we learned that the worship of the seventh aspect of Krishna—one of the seven most important ones under which he is deified in Râjasthân, *i.e., Madan-Mohan,* the "divinity which intoxicates you with love"—is exclusively in the hands of the *Brâhmana*-women. *Madan-Mohan* is the shepherd who enchants the shepherdesses, named the *gopîs*. At the present time, the high priestess of the blue god is very old and very strict with the temple *nâchnîs,* whose duty consists of playing the roles of the *gopîs* and courting the blue god. This severity has had its effect on her temple which suffers from a lack of "celestial musicians."* They have to borrow the little singers of *heaven* from other pagodas, outside of Râjasthân.

There exist, as we said, *seven* main statues or idols of Krishna in this country; these were described by Tod, the only Englishman, I think, who was allowed to approach the sanctuary, as we were ourselves fifty years later.

These seven "miracle-working" statues were brought centuries ago by a mysterious person, Balba, who later became the high priest of Râjasthân. When dying, he distributed them among his seven "grandsons," the progeny of his spiritual son (and adopted one), and now they are the source of enormous revenues to his descendants, the officiating Brâhmanas of the seven chief pagodas of the country.

The man who played the part of Krishna, and whose name I forget, obtained permission for us to go and see *Nonita,*† "Krishna, the child." *Nonita* sits on a lotus, which

---

*The celestial musicians or singers in the pagodas, as is well known, are always the sons of the *nâchnîs,* the dancing girls. This is nowhere censored, except in Râjasthân. In this country of knightly tradition, the *nâchnîs* are real vestals.

†It is written *nava* (new)-*nîta* (butter). During his childhood, *Nonita* had a great liking for fresh butter and often stole it from his neighbors. Hence his name.

looks like a cabbage, thoughtfully holding in his hand a small cake (*peḍa*) ; these cakes are made of dough mixed with the water of the Jumnâ exclusively. From the time of the Afghâns, who with their typical iconoclasm, threw *Nonita* into the Jumnâ, he rested until 1803 on the bottom of the river. When by chance he was fished out, he had still not eaten his cake and continued to examine it in the same attentive way, as though mistrusting it. I entirely sympathize with his reluctance. I will never forget the "sacred" cake which was brought to me as a token of most unusual kindness. Having eaten it, I felt sick to my stomach and a feeling of deep depression remained with me for the rest of the day.

There exists another idol of Krishṇa, *Gokuljî,* found in a miraculous way, which is also in the possession of a Brâhmaṇa-woman. We did not see either of them, however, though we wanted very much to visit the island on the Jumnâ, where both of them are. A large group of *yoginîs,* or female yogins, live there under the leadership of an old Brâhmaṇa-woman. We preferred, however, to visit two or three other temples and to see, and especially to *hear,* the famous *bhaṭṭas.*

Visiting the temples and their varied idols, I had quite forgotten the *śâlagrâma,* which was travelling on either the heart or the back of our president, Colonel O., who did not part with it for a second. My thoughts were so much occupied with mythological comparisons, that even had someone spoken of the stone, I probably would not have paid any attention. But the talisman forced itself upon us, and in circumstances which it would have been difficult to ignore.

Emerging on the last evening of our stay, from the dilapidated palace where Ânanda had put us on our arrival, we decided to walk over and visit the temple of Gopâla-Krishṇa. The pagoda was so near to our house that the ramshackle carriage which followed us seemed superfluous. We sent it back, as we really did not need it merely for crossing the square. I went ahead with Nârâyaṇa, the Bâbû and Ânanda-Svâmi; the Colonel followed us with a retinue of Brâhmaṇas, pundits, and śâstrîns. Mûljî was their interpreter.

In five minutes, notwithstanding the frequent stops and obstacles caused by the monkeys constantly jumping under our feet, and processions of donkeys and loaded carts, we reached the porch of the pagoda, where I sat on the step of the broad stairway awaiting the head of our party. Ânanda-Svâmi was standing about two paces from me talking quietly to Nârâyaṇa, with whom he had evidently become friendly; I had sent the Bâbû to buy some goodies for the "sacred" quadrupeds and especially the *quadromanes.*

The temple of Gopâla-Kṛishṇa stands at the end of a narrow lane, from where nothing could be seen but the corner of the big square we had just crossed. While waiting for the Colonel and the Bâbû to bring the nuts, I sat calmly, fairly successful in holding off the crowd of monkeys who were boldly attempting to empty my pockets. These animals were so accustomed to living among people, that even our appearance, so very different from that of the natives, did not excite in them any feeling other than that of the normal expectancy of a handout. A whole colony of them were around me, and it would have been difficult to ignore their sly little sparkling eyes, which attentively watched every motion of my hands. One of them, an old monkey missing several teeth, grabbed, unbeknownst to me, one of my gloves and began to chew on a corner of it.

Then the Bâbû arrived with the nuts and some raisins. He threw them to the monkeys and then the real fun began. The monkeys chattered and fought, while we looked on and laughed. Suddenly from the direction of the square we heard a most unexpected and awful howling, as if a whole pack of tigers were loose . . . the shrieks of the crowd, the bellowing of bulls, the trumpeting of elephants — all mingled in one long drawn-out roar. As it approached us, it became louder and louder. I was ready to follow the example of the monkeys who had immediately disappeared, when Ânanda-Svâmi distracted my attention from the unknown danger and focussed it on himself. Staring pop-eyed at him, I must have looked so frightened, that the Bâbû, not knowing the reason for it, jumped in front of me in order to protect me with his slim figure, while Nârâyaṇa seized a big stick and stood at my side like a gladiator. Thus we stood all three for a couple of seconds, not saying a word, as though petrified.

What had happened? To anyone who had had no chance to study the ascetic, as I had, from morning until night for three whole days, nothing unusual. Upon hearing the bellowing, Ânanda-Svâmi, who usually moved slowly and gracefully, was now suddenly transformed. In an instant, with a jump which would have done credit to an athlete, he was at the end of the lane. Then with the dexterity of an acrobat, he climbed up the corner of a house and hung by his right arm. It looked as though he were pointing with his left hand at something in the distance.

"What is he doing?" I cried, coming to.

"He is using his *daṇḍa*, Maam-Saab," laughed the Bâbû, who by now had calmed down.

Only then did I notice that the Svâmi, *his hand holding the magical staff, really was pointing toward the square.*

As though to prove the Bâbû right (although the sound of voices was nearing), the awful roaring ceased at once— only a couple of weak bellowings could still be heard. Then a whole crowd of Brâhmaṇas filled the lane, among them the Colonel . . . but my God, in what a state!

He had lost his hat and apparently his glasses also. His snow white coat and trousers were unspeakably dirty with manure and dust, and had been transformed into rags covered with spots and fragments the shade of rotten weeds beloved by London esthetes, and brown stains like chewing tobacco. His face was as red as a ripe cherry, his hair was dishevelled, and his beard was full of straw and hay. He appeared to be very embarrassed.

"I warned the Colonel not to go near the sacred cows, but he did not listen to my advice," shouted Mûljî.

"The devil take them, your sacred cows!" retorted our president, "I wanted to give them some bread and spiced cakes, and they started pushing me around, some ten of them. I tried to get away, but they followed me . . . they tossed their heads, threw up their tails and aimed for my pocket . . . bellowing terribly the whole time . . . I was deafened . . . Then I fell down . . .just slipped and fell!"

"Certainly, when you had the *śâlagrâma* under your shirt; Ânandajî* warned you to take care and not approach the cows!"

"It wasn't the *śâlagrâma,* but the bread; they didn't follow me before, but when I offered some bread . . ."

"You never were so near to them before," insisted Mûljî. "It's the *śâlagrâma* which attracted them."

"No, the bread! As soon as I took a piece into my hand and gave it to the first one, the others tried to get at my pockets . . ."

"At the *śâlagrâma* and not at the pocket," corrected the "general."

"They were all after me, squeezed me into a corner," the poor Colonel continued to explain, as if excusing himself to me, "and so I fell. The Brâhmaṇas, waving their arms *begged* the cows in Sanskrit to leave me alone; but none of them went after the cows with their sticks! And the onslaught of the cows grew steadily worse!"

At these words, an expression of devout fright appeared on Mûljî's face.

"To strike a cow of Gopâla-Kṛishṇa! . . ."

"Did they hurt you?" I asked, feeling still too frightened and shocked by the suddenness of it all to appreciate the comic situation.

"No, I think not," he answered, checking himself over, "but I did get dirty . . . the damned cows! Too bad I didn't have a stick with me! . . ."

"I beg of you, Colonel, not to speak that way," anxiously whispered Nârâyaṇa, fearfully looking around at the Brâhmaṇas. "It is lucky they do not understand you . . . They might kill all of us for the sake of their sacred cows!"

"It would have been even worse, Saab," said the Bâbû, "had it not been for Ânanda-Svâmi . . . It was he who saved you with his *daṇḍa.*"

Ji is a polite adjective, something like "Honorable," but used after the name.

"I didn't even see him there. He went ahead with you, didn't he?"

"He was acting on the 'sacred' herd from on high!" continued the Bâbû, laughing. "He stood like Indra with his arrows . . . . there, near that balcony . . ."

"Simply looking!" I interrupted. "All was over *before* his *daṇḍa* acted."

"You know, *Upâsikâ, that it isn't so,*" said Nârâyaṇa reproachfully, stepping aside to join the "Brother of the Grove." Ânanda had jumped down from his perch just at the moment when the first Brâhmaṇas appeared in the lane. Later we learned that, having let the men pass, he prevented some of the cows from following them into the narrow passage. The herd raced after the poor president, until he disappeared into the lane.

"What was he doing, and how did he prevent the cows from coming?" I questioned "Kṛishṇa," who had joined us some minutes later.

"He stood at the entrance and *waved his daṇḍa into them.*"

"Into them! Do you mean *towards* them? . . . He simply frightened them away."

"No, no, it was *into them. My* cows could not be frightened by mere waving."

He said "my" cows as though seriously thinking he was Kṛishṇa.

We had to leave without seeing the temple of Gopâla. The sun had set, and we went back under the cover of the fast approaching darkness, which very fortunately hid the sorry appearance of our president. We prepared to leave Mathurâ. To the great distress of the Colonel, all our baggage was sent from Bhurtpore direct to the interior of Râjasthân, so he could not even change his clothes. Our cool-headed chief, however, did not lose his initiative; he bought the white dress of a native and appeared before us in a costume which was a strange mixture of Râjput and European styles.

He seemingly understood that he had been taught a lesson. The *śâlagrâma* disappeared from his body and there was nothing any longer to remind us of its "magic" presence. Its possession, however, proved to be very useful to us. The Brâhmaṇas, having learned about it, envied the President and were surprised that the sacred object had not lost its power when worn by an impure *mlechchha*. They then showed us an even greater respect mingled with superstitious awe.

During the night we left Mathurâ in a large primitive boat and sailed down the river. It reminded us of a Venetian gondola; there was a table in it with benches around, and it even had room for a kitchen. The latter, however, proved useless, as we had to leave the boat at 2 A.M., and were taken to some "vassal" in the forest, to use Ânanda's expression, to spend the night there. To my great delight, I found an iron bed in the room prepared for me, which appeared to have been brought there from some first class hotel. It even had a mosquito net made of clean muslin to protect one against the mosquitoes. Our friends, the Ṭhâkur and Ânanda, were veritable miracle-workers: *un lit à sommier* in the midst of Râjput forests!

The next day we went to a small village of bards. The *bhâts* or *bhaṭṭas* and the *chârans* or *châraṇas, i.e.,* bards and chroniclers,* have been employed from olden days to haul things. Such a profession began as a courtesy, and ended by becoming a trade. In this country, inhabited by constantly warring tribes and the robber bands of Bhîls and Meras, there was no way in days of old to send either money or furniture from place to place on the main road. The bards were the only class respected by the robbers, and their curse was feared by them. Taking charge of a sum of money or an object of value, the *bhât* guaranteed its delivery with his life. If the robbers, regardless of his official standing, took that which had been confided to him, he at once committed suicide by plunging a knife into his heart, and, sprinkling his enemies with his blood, died cursing them. *This curse always took effect,* the Râjputs told us. Centuries have rolled by, and today the *bhâts*, though carrying millions, are never

---

*Bhât is a bard or genealogist, while châraṇ is a writer of chronicles, and both are poets and singers.

touched by the robbers, even if they are a hundred to one. The *bhâṭs* serve as transfer agents all over Râjasthân, and their standing makes them sacred in the eyes of even the fiercest robber.

> . . . . . even the savage Koli and Bhîl, and the plundering Sahrae [Saora] of the desert, dread the anathema of these singular races, who conduct the caravans through the wildest and most desolate regions. The traveler avails himself of such convoy who desires to proceed to the coast by Jalor, Bhinmahl, Sanchor, and Radhanpur, whence he may pursue his route to Surat, or Muscat-Mandavi [Maska Mânḍavî].*

Thus wrote a resident of Mewâr.

The *chârans* and *bhâṭs* are Râjputs; both assume the place of Brâhmaṇas among the inhabitants of Râjasthân since the office of chronicle-writers or genealogists gives them the right to perform religious rites. After the cow and the bull, the *bhâṭ* is the most sacred being with the Râjputs, and the entire family of a *bhâṭ* is equally sacred and inviolable.

When encountering robbers, the *bhâṭ* confronts them with a knife in his hand and utters the well-known warning. If the thieves do not pay attention to the first warning, the *bhâṭ* will inflict upon himself a slight wound and sprinkle the robbers with his blood. If that does not produce the desired effect, and the caravan is sacked, he will kill himself; his wife, children and relatives are also obligated to commit suicide, uttering the same curses. Contempt for life is the first lesson the *bhâṭs* and *chârans* learn in their childhood.

The next morning we rose after a good rest in the woods, and Ânanda took us to visit a *chârana*, with whose family we spent the rest of the day. The old man, in his long, wide, white dress, looked like Ossian emerged from the canvas of a picture. Sitting on the floor with his *chatâra* in his hands, he sang to us legends about the ancient valor of the sons of his country, about the fall of Chitor, the Chauhân heroes (the tribe of the Ṭhâkur), and about *the bliss of death in the performance of an honorable duty,* the keeping of one's word, or the saving of one's country . . . His two

---

*[Col. J. Tod, *Annals*, etc., "Personal Narrative." Vol. I, p. 661, ed. of 1894].

sons, tall and handsome Râjputs, took their turn singing;
their legends were all about the deeds of Krishna, Balarâma,
Arjuna and the *Harikula* tribes. Their wives and their old
mother waited upon us and served us food, quite at a loss
to know how to please the "Saabs," who were going to
visit the "Great Thâkur."

The costume of the *bhât-women* is very picturesque—a
dark woolen skirt with a snow-white *sârî* over it; and in their
black hair are flowers, corals and golden ornaments. The
women here remind one of the pretty women of Naples in
the olden days. In that blessed corner of India there is
neither caste nor fanaticism, as is the case with the Bombay
Brâhmanas. The *bhâts* and *chârans* form, so to say, an
imperium in imperio. They depend on no one and the
government wisely refrains from meddling in their affairs:
the whole of Râjasthân would rise in defence of their sacred
bhâts. They are the last link which connects the sad present
with the glory of their unforgettable past.

These singers, unknown in Europe and but little known
even in India itself, are probably in possession (we ourselves
have no doubt of it) of the first pages of the *history of
humanity as a whole,* and not of Âryâvarta alone. All that
remains of India's past are her heroic songs. But these songs
give the *bhâts* the right to be recognized as the primeval
historians of the whole of humanity. They lived long before
the Greek fables first attracted the attention of the poets,
including Herodotus, the father of history, some thousands
of years ago; the *bhâts* sing about *actual* events and *living*
people, not mere myths. According to the opinion of the
earlier Orientalists, like Sir William Jones, Wilson and
others, Calliope was deified in India from the time of Vyâsa,
the contemporary of Job. These Sanskritists, even though
mistaken at times in their conclusions, never sacrificed truth
and fact for a profitable position. Many thousands of scrolls
of historical genealogies and chronicles have been preserved
in verse; their poetical exaggerations would not deter a
historian from deriving from them facts and events, the
narrative of which in any European tongue would most
likely upset all the deductions of not only Macaulay and
Grote but even of our *Russian historians.* "Chand-bhu-

jamga"* and the worship of the muses, as we saw from the reading of hundreds of genealogies belonging to the Sûrya-vanśas, tribes now long vanished away, did not prevent the bards from telling the truth, unlike other poets; and mere praise of the "prehistoric" chieftains cannot prevent anyone from recognizing in these chronicles obvious historical events. The fact alone that the Râjput bards so often told their contemporary rulers the bitter truth is sufficient proof that they did not sacrifice the latter to worldly benefits. When hurt or grieved by the acts of their rulers, they condemned them openly, unmindful of consequences. Under the merciless whip of the bard's satire many a tyrant trembled, and much good resulted for the poor people, who looked upon the bards as their chief defenders. Even today the *visha* (poison of the word) of the bard is held to be more dangerous than the sword of the enemy, and more terrible even than the English themselves in the eyes of a Râjput prince.

The "initiated" bards (there are such among them) told us that the enormous collection of their chronicles — the most ancient scrolls of which were written down from oral tradition — fill all the gaps and explain all the errors in the history of the world; we were told that in them are to be found all the necessary proof that it was the tribes of Râjasthân that in prehistoric time had populated the shores of the northern seas, the Baltic, the Black, the Caspian and others; that all the Germanic and *especially the Slavonic peoples* of Europe are the descendants of tribes that had left Râjasthân (called in ancient days *Raethâna*). As a matter of fact, if the Finns and Magyars of Hungary have to look for their origin in Central Asia and Tibet, the Swedes — in Kashgar, the Germans (of Max Müller only, by the way) — on the Oxus, why then could we not look for the ancestors of the Variago-Russ in the forests and the "great desert" of Jaisalmer? Who knows but that the Slav forefathers of our "fellow-brothers," the most ancient† Bulgars, Serbs, Czechs

---

*Snake-stanza or verse.

†Namely the near-Danube Slavs, not the Chudes who came from Altai.

and us Russians, actually rest under the seven tiers of the prehistoric cities of Surâshṭra, Amber and Udaipur? Alaric and Chingîz-Khân certainly did not originate their strange burial ritual. When the majestic mound was erected over the bodies of these two heroes, Gibbon tells us, an enormous space all around it was planted with trees "in order forever to prevent any human foot from treading on the sacred remains."*

---

* [This quotation from Gibbon has not been verified, and no mention of such mounds has been found. In the case of Alaric, the Gothic conqueror of the late fourth and early fifth century, his body was buried under the riverbed of the Busento, the stream being temporarily turned aside from its course while the grave was dug; when the work was finished, the river was turned back into its usual channel, and the captives by whose hands the labor had been done were put to death that none could learn their secret.

As far as the facts are known in regard to Chingîz-Khân (*Vide* René Grousset, *Le Conquérant du monde*, Paris, 1944, concluding chapter) his body was entombed on the high slopes of the Burqan-Qaldun (now Kentei), a mountain or mountain-chain considered sacred among the Mongols. From it descend the rivers Tola, Kerulen and Onon in the N.E. of the present Mongolian Peoples Republic, about 120 miles N.E. of Ulan Bator. The tomb of Chingîz-Khân has never been definitely located by scholars, yet H.P.B. testifies to its actual existence (Cf. *Isis Unveiled*, Vol. I, pp. 598-99), but locates it "near Lake Tabasun Nor."

This statement is by no means as definite as might appear at first glance. The names of Tabasun, Dabusun, and other variants, occur in widely separate localities on the map of Mongolia. The *National Geographic Magazine* map of China (1945) shows *Dabusun* as a small settlement in Outer Mongolia, at about 44°30′ north latitude and 115° east longitude, very close to the Kerulen River which flows into the Hulun Nor, and not far below the Wall of Chingîz-Khân, about 500 miles east of Ulan Bator. No lake, however, is indicated in this region, and even the settlement itself does not appear on other maps of the area. The *Gazetteer No. 22, China*, of the U.S. Board on Geographic Names, lists a lake called *Tabun Nor*, also called *Ta-pu-su Hu*, whose geographic coordinates are 45°09′ north and 116°30′ east. This is in Inner Mongolia. This is supported by the map of "Mongolia and Adjacent Regions," Army Map Service, 1942, No. 5204, which shows a lake by the name of *Dabasu Nor* at approximately that location; and also by Herbert Mueller's "Map of All Mongolia," published by him at 53 Pei Ho Yen, Peking, 1939, wherein a lake called *Dabeson Nor* occurs in the same location.

The *National Geographic Magazine* map of China (1945) shows

Thus also were buried in ancient times the heroes of Râjasthân, as told in a song of the bard Chanda. Where today you find the "Valley of Death," the desert of India that leads to the valley of the Indus, there were formerly virgin forests. Bygone millenniums have reduced them to dust, and the country where such mounds are still to be found is now desert. In the Russian steppes there are many such "mounds"; and that which we call "baba"* is also called "bâbâ" in India, only here the word means "father." I saw several such stone bâbâs in Mewâr.

A whole cemetery of such round mounds with "bâbâs" on them was not far from the house of the bard. Here thousands of *Gosâîns* (monk-warriors,) called here *Kânphatâ-yogins* were killed. We were shown the place in the forest where their remains rest; the bards cover the mounds daily with branches of mountain ash which is consecrated to them, as was also the case with the *Celtic priests,* and then pour sacred water on them. The respect for the dead in general, and especially for warriors killed on the battlefield, is a trait of these heathen which might well be adopted by some of the Christian peoples. I know of some officers' tombs, and even one of a general, in the Caucasus and at Sebastopol, who were killed or died of wounds, which are quite neglected and forgotten, and even without a cross over them . . .

As late as the beginning of this century the *Kânphatâ-yogins* were still as famous in the military chronicles of

---

three other lakes of similar name, namely: 1) *Dabasun Nor* or Yenhai Tzu, practically at 40° north and 108° east. This is most likely the Yenhai Tze or the Tayenhai Tze listed in *Lippincott's Gazetteer of the World* as a salt lake in No. Ordos Desert, Suiyuan Province, China, 90 miles WSW of Paotow, across the Yellow River, 8 miles long and 2 miles wide, and from which natron is extracted. There can hardly be any doubt that this is Abbé Huc's *Dabsoun Nor* (Cf. *Travels,* etc., Vol. I, pp, 204 *et seq.*); 2) *Dabasu Nor,* just west of Koko Nor, about 37° north and 99° east. This is just east of the famous Tsaidam Marshes; and 3) *Dabasun Nor,* right in the Tsaidam Marshes, about 37° north and 95° east.

The problem, as is obvious, is rather complicated.—*Compiler.*]

*[A rough-hewn stone idol on burial mounds. The word itself means in Russian an old peasant-woman.—*Compiler.*]

Râjasthân as in past centuries. They lived (and live even today, though in smaller numbers since the arrival of the English) in "brotherhoods" numbering thousands. They are simple, uneducated *hatha-yogins,* yet brave warriors; the native rulers frequently concluded alliances with them, especially defensive ones. Their ferocious audacity has become proverbial. They were the bravest and most fearless warriors of the country, the priests of Bala (Balarâma), the god of power. Now the Râjâs have stopped fighting amongst themselves and the *Kânphatâ-yogins,* no longer finding an outlet for their warlike exploits have begun to kill each other; without enemies, they fight each other instead. A number of them sit under the trees on tiger and lion skins, covered from head to foot with white ashes and with disheveled and unkempt hair tied like a turban on their heads. Beside each of them burns an altar of live coals; they spread the latter from time to time upon their feet and knees, as if the coals were made of foil. The smell of burned human flesh that rose with the steam, and the sizzling of the fires, made me realize that these were really live coals . . .

"What a horror," I said to the Colonel and Ânanda in French. "Here Colonel, take a lesson in *hatha-yoga* from these . . . You can hardly find anything better!"

But the sight proved too disgusting even for the inquisitive Colonel. He could not stand it and turned away, saying that he preferred the tombs of the dead to the tortures of the living yogins.

Further on we saw a cemetery of ordinary warriors with "bâbâs" over the tombs of Râjputs killed in battle. The ashes of the burned bodies were brought home, and over the tombs of the "chieftains" there were, instead of mere "bâbâs," more elaborate tombstones. On some of them was moulded the figure of the warrior himself on horseback and in full accoutrements, with his shield, sword and lance; near him was his wife, a sure sign that she had burned herself on the tomb of her husband, *i.e.,* had performed *satî.* The thought of what had happened here at the time of the burning alive of the widow spoiled the pleasure of the walk for me.

In Râjasthân every locality made sacred by the *Mâhâ-Satî*, *i.e.*, great self-sacrifice (cremation), is at once transformed into an arena of "spirit" action, or an "unclean place." This, however, is not the case with the Râjputs only. The "spirits" of suicides in the Occident also, presumably repenting their act, return to live the remainder of their forcibly interrupted lives in bodies less comfortable, and hence more apt to be vicious. Even with us in Russia the suicides do not rest quietly in their tombs, if we are to believe popular tradition. Whatever may be the case, in India their "spirits" reach the highest point of troublesomeness. Spiritists would be overjoyed here, but the *non*-spiritists complain greatly. Where these ghostly suicides took place, among the funeral pyres where so often a young wife, full of beauty and earthly happiness, was burned pitilessly, and where a sobbing mother was at the same time blessing her daughter and urging her to commit the *deed of saintliness*, and the father, compelled to be present at the *Mâhâ-Satî* from beginning to end, sang hymns to perhaps his only daughter, whose young and palpitating body was tortured in the consuming flames, the "demons" were soon to appear, on the *night of the ninth day*. Here, free of charge, immediately appear the *Jigger-Khor*, the frightful *Harpy* of bygone days led by the *Dakinî*.* Both of these demons, as is well known, wander during the night, attacking the living; the *Jigger-Khor* eats their hearts, tearing them out of the living bodies. Some of the mausoleums, like the tombs of Pompeii, are built with an inner room, where yearly rituals are performed in honor of the dead. For a Râjput, this is the most frightful and awful day of the year, but one which, according to the general custom, he cannot avoid. He is obliged to visit the burial room quite alone, and there perform the ritual, sprinkling the room with water and making offerings of flowers and rice, and then to lie prone on the floor for two hours, muttering *mantras*.

"My own brother," an old bard told us, "one of the bravest warriors of Mewâr, coming home from *Pitri-îśvars*

---

*The *Dâkinî* is an evil spirit which acts as a guide for the *Jigger-Khor*, who is a blind Harpy.

(as this ritual is called) found that during these two hours
he had grown grey, like an old man . . . And he wasn't
even thirty."

"Why? Did he see anything?"

"No, but he felt . . . he felt all the time the contact of
the icy hands of *Jigger-Khor,* who looked for his heart. He
was saved by the *mantras.* Yes, the day of *Pitṛi-îśvars** is
a great day . . . but an awful one. At the cemetery we have
just now visited, *they* flit about every night."

"Whom do you mean by 'they'?"

"*Bhûtas* (spirits). Going out of the back door on the
verandah, one can see in the evening, even from here, how
they flicker like multi-colored lights over the tombs . . ."

"Light blue," corrected Ânanda, "you merely see the
shahâba, the fleeting lights you can find in all cemeteries,
and especially on the battlefields," he added thoughtfully.

"Yes, yes, on the battlefields of course. And where, if not
here, are there more bodies of brave warriors? These lights
are their souls."

"Not their souls, but simply phosphorescent lights produced by the putrefaction of so many bodies."

"Our *Mahârâja,* the *Ṭhâkur-Sâhib,* also told us this.
Neither he nor you believe in the *Ḍâkinî* and *Jigger-Khor,*
because they would not dare to touch you; they are not
afraid of us, however.†

Pitṛis are ancestors, the dead relatives and forebears. *Pitṛi* means
father, *îś* or *îśvara* is lord. Thus *Pitṛi-îśvars* means "dead ancestors."

†Nothing can dispel the superstition of a Râjput, not even such an
authority as the Ṭhâkur. Colonel Tod tells us in his *Memoirs* about
his friend, Captain Waugh who, having heard a lot about the "lights,"
the "devils" and the "witches," and suspecting that this time the
Ḍâkinî was a hyena he had noticed in the early morning, rode to the
cemetery on horseback and waited for the beast. He came upon and
killed "the horse of the Ḍâkinî," on which the witch (Harpy) *Jigger-
Khor* rode during the night. Hearing that the hyena was killed, the
Râjputs became frightened and predicted that a calamity would befall
the captain for the death of the "horse" of the witch. The following
day Waugh fell off his horse and broke his leg, thus justifying their
superstitious prediction.

[This is related by Col. Tod in his *Annals,* etc., Vol. I. p. 69. footnote, in the ed. of 1894.—*Compiler.*]

The contradiction and skepticism of Ânanda seemingly did not please the old man. He grew sullen and suddenly plucking the strings of his *chatâra* began to sing a song about the *jauhar*. *Jauhar* is the awful ritual, when the powerless warriors, convinced of their inability to overcome the enemy, gather together their wives, mothers and brides and kill them with their own hands, later burning their bodies on the pyre. The year 1275 will always be remembered in Râjasthân; the bards sing to this day about the "fall of the city of Chitor" and about "the death of *Rânî-Padminî*," the innocent cause of the battle and of the fall of the city, which was sacked three times in recorded history, and its entire tribe destroyed.* Chitor perished finally in 1676, but then it was defended not by its legal rulers but by its conquerors and destroyers. The legend refers to the year 1275 and is full of beauty and interest. Here is one of its episodes:

Bhim-Singh, the uncle of the child-râjan and his tutor, falls in love with and marries the daughter of Chauhân Hammir-Singh, King of Ceylon, the beautiful *Padminî,* a surname used only in reference to "a beauty among beauties." Her beauty, talents, nobility of soul, and self-denial, brought her to the pyre, and Chitor to its final fall, and provided favorite subjects for the popular legends in Râjwâra (Râjasthân).†

---

*The Râjput word *sâkâ* (which was probably borrowed from them by the Anglo-Saxons and the Gauls) corresponds to the modern *sack* or *sac,* as in "le sac d'une ville"—the looting of a conquered city. Here is what the author of *Annals and Antiquities of Râjasthân* writes about this word: "The besieged Râjputs, having lost all hope of a victory, at the last moment kill all their women; then the warriors, dressed in long yellow shirts, throw themselves in a last effort upon the enemy and inevitably die. This is called by them performing the *sâkâ,* when each *sâkhâ* or branch is cut off from the tree by the enemy. Chitor suffered complete *sâkâ* three times."

†[On the authority of Col. Tod, Padminî was the wife of Bhim-Singh, uncle of Rânâ Lakshman-Singh of Sisodia. But more modern texts give Ratna-Singh, son and successor of Rawal Samar Singh of Mewâr, as Padminî's husband. This is due to the fact that when Tod wrote his *Annals,* etc., the very name of Ratna-Singh had disappeared from the books of the Bhâts, and even from their memory, a century before Tod, leaving only Ratna's imaginary queen Padminî. It is to be

I will now quote, as far as I am able to do so, the lovely
ballad of the bards, which our old host sang for us. I will
give a literal translation, though condensing, of course, many
of the events in this historical and forever memorable battle.

> It is not the Chitor city that the heart of
>   'Alâ al-dîn yearns for,
> It is the lotus-eyed Padminî, the wife of
>   the brave Bhim-Singh.
> Pathân is eager.* Behold he sends a messenger
>   to the Durbâr of the Mahârâja.
> "Give me Rânî† for Delhi. Take all my
>   Kingdom and wealth.
> All I possess for *Rânî*, for this pearl of
>   the East:
> Otherwise you will perish! I will sack Chitor,
>   your city, forever,
> Will destroy *Agni-Kula*‡ and
>   tear out your heart!"
> Our King Bhim-Singh grew angry and glanced
>   with fiery eye.
> "I don't want your kingdom, Caliph, I
>   am not afraid of the Moguls!...
> You won't possess the Rânî-Queen, the
>   faithful Padminî.
> I spit into your beard, enemy! Come!
>   The Agni-Kulas are waiting for you!"
> The town is besieged, Padminî is starving, the
>   Mogul is victorious.
> Once more he sends a messenger: "Let me only
>   glance at Rânî-Padminî!

---

noted that this Padminî may not be the one in Malik Muḥammad's
poem entitled *Padmâvatî*, as the author speaks of her as being the
daughter of Gandharvasena of Siṃhala island, whereas Tod makes her,
evidently on the authority of the Bhâṭs, the daughter of Hammir-Singh
Chauhân of Ceylon.—*Compiler.*]

  *'Alâ al-dîn, a Pathân Emperor.

  †*Rânî* is the feminine form of *rânâ*. The wife of the *rânâ* of Udaipur
is called *rânî*.

  ‡"*Agni-kula*," the tribe of *Agni* (fire) which was wiped out with
Chitor.

I will come without armed escort . . . I will place my
   trust in you, Râjan,
The Râjput will keep his word!"
Being sorry for the beautiful Rânî, to avoid
   the *jauhar,*
Bhim-Singh gave his consent; he let in the Caliph
   through the gates of Chitor.
Alone and without an escort . . .
   The wicked Pathân saw the reflection
of Rânî the beautiful, in the mirrors of the wall
   of the Durbâr hall.*
'Alâ fell in love; for his trust, the Pathân prepared
   for the râjan a wicked treason . . .
"For your trust I pay by trusting you,"
   said Bhim-Singh to 'Alâ al-dîn, "I follow
   you, in parting,
To the gates of Chitor . . ." All at once
   'Alâ shouted for the armed escort
   and took Bhim-Singh as prisoner, and to the
   Pathân camp, treacherously,
He took him, saying: "Oh, Râjput! You are
   a hostage of 'Alâ al-dîn,
Give me Padminî, buy back your kingdom and
   freedom!" . . .†

The inhabitants of Chitor, besieged by 80,000 men of
the Pathân traitor's army, were in despair. The aldermen

---

*The historian Ferishta confirms this fact, telling that 'Alâ al-dîn
was allowed to look at Rânî-Padminî only by means of mirrors arranged in the Durbâr hall.

†This is an historical fact. 'Alâ al-dîn trusted Bhim-Singh, knowing
that a Râjput would prefer to die rather than not to keep his word,
and acted thus merely to lure him into a trap. On account of his
fanaticism and hypocrisy, this most successful and warlike of all the
rulers of India greatly resembles Aurangzîb, the last ruler of the
Tîmûr dynasty. The title of "Sikander-Sâni," the second Alexander
(of Macedonia), which he chose for himself, and had stamped on his
coins, was, according to the chroniclers well-deserved. In India he was
a regular Attila, the scourge of the râjans, and he almost entirely annihilated the tribe of *Agni* at Chitor.

held a council: should they relinquish Padminî in exchange
for the release of the Râjâ, or would that be dishonorable?
But the Rânî herself decided it was her duty to sacrifice
herself to save her beloved husband, and never allow herself to be taken alive by 'Alâ al-dîn. Having taken counsel
with his uncle Gaura and his son Badul,* it was decided to
try and free Bhim-Singh, without dishonoring the Rânî
or forfeiting her life. They sent a message telling the emperor
that they would give him Padminî if he would lift the
siege and withdraw; that they would deliver her into his
hands, but that she could not be sent without the ceremony
due her rank; she must go with a numerous escort of
courtiers, taking along her belongings and dowry; and finally that the women and girls of Chitor, with the exception of
those who would want to accompany her to Delhi, must
first say good-bye to her. The Caliph consented and prepared himself for the event, vowing to observe the Chitor
custom regarding the women's privilege of travelling in
tightly closed palanquins.

Then the women left the town, "the mothers and older
relatives of the Râjput warriors," in more than 700 palanquins; each carried by six disguised warriors. The king's
tents were surrounded, according to the Caliph's promise,
by kanâts, linen walls which were thickly lined. The palanquins with the escort entered between them. Bhim-Singh
was granted half an hour to take leave of his Rânî; but as
soon as he appeared he was placed in one of the empty
palanquins and quickly carried away. In the other palanquins were hidden arms and 700 warriors, the flower of
the youth of Chitor. The half hour's grace had not elapsed,
when 'Alâ al-dîn, jealous of the lengthy parting and suspecting treason, suddenly and in spite of his oath forced his
way through the kanâts. These facts are confirmed by the
historian Ferishta. Instead of the beautiful Padminî and her
suite of young girls, the Caliph found some 5,000 warriors
and hundreds of respectable but ugly women, who "tore
into the Moguls like wild cats." The Râjputs, having pre-

---

*Badul was one of the greatest heroes of Râjasthân in the Middle
Ages. He killed with his own hands a great number of Moguls.

viously decided to sacrifice their lives, sought only to cover the flight of Bhim-Singh, and, surrounded from all sides, under the pressure of 80,000 men, perished *to the last man.* Upon seeing their sons and relatives being killed the brave old Râjput women plunged daggers into their hearts, and as the ballad runs:

> "It was not a hill that grew up in the
>   valley of Chitor,
> It was the bodies of brave warriors, *they*
>   *should not be ashamed.**
> They all died for their king . . . And above
>   this hill, there is another hill,
> Made of the bodies of the mothers and
>   women of Râjwara . . ."

Râjâ Bhim-Singh was given a fast steed and thus succeeded in escaping from the Moguls chasing him. The deed of their fellow-warriors and of their old mothers inspired the inhabitants of Chitor to such a degree, that during the next few days they performed wonders of bravery. The besieged finally drove away the besieging force and 'Alâ al-dîn was forced to withdraw, having lost half of his army.

But alas! the flower of the youth of Chitor perished in the Pathân camp! Some months later the Pathân king, still in love, once more besieged the town and this time he was the conqueror. Led by Bhim-Singh, the whole town, with the exception of the women and children, came through the

---

*I draw the attention of the reader to this expression which is an oath of the Râjputs. The word *lajjâ* means literally "shame," a word used by them in the sense of dishonor. "Lâj-rakho," *let me not be ashamed,* means literally, "let me be free from shame," as the word *shame* is synonymous with *dishonor.* Is this not the same phrase as was used by the "warriors of Vladimir," and voiced, I believe, by "Dobrinya Nikitich"? Is this not what was meant by the words of Sviatoslav, when he told his staff: "Let us perish here—the dead know no shame!" The expression *lâj-rakho,* "let me be free from shame," can be found in the chronicles of Udaipur some 3,000 years ago, uttered by the Sûryavanśa Balarâma. It is certainly not the Râjputs who took it from the Variago-Russ!

city gates to give battle. These heroes, without a moment's hesitation, threw themselves on their enemies who outnumbered them ten to one, as history tells, and were "mowed down on the battlefield," in the words of the ballad, "like sheaves before the breath of the cyclone." The motto of the Râjputs was the same as that of the ancient, as well as the modern Russians: *let us perish, the dead know no shame.*

The young Badul was saved, though gravely wounded; he was the cousin of Padminî and only 12 years old at the time, but according to the Râjput ideas he was already expected to defend his country and to die for it.

The heroes of Chitor remind one of the heroes of the Black Mountain (Montenegro). The latter possess many traits of character similar to those of the Râjputs: the same fabulous bravery, the same disdain of physical suffering, and the same deep-rooted love of their country. The brave young men, only twelve and thirteen years old, about whom we read so much in the seventies and eighties, seem to be the very incarnation of Badul of Chitor.

This episode is described most tellingly in *Khumân-Râsa,* but in the warlike epic, sung by the old bard, it was even more striking. The distinguished old man seemed quite transformed: his black eyes sparkled, as if shining with warlike passion at the strains of his own song; his wrinkled face at times wore an expression of hatred for the enemy, at the thought of the "*sâkâ* of Chitor," at others it expressed the feeling of deep sorrow and grief for the suffering women and mothers imprisoned in the besieged town, at the thought of their preparation for the *jauhar* (self-immolation), in order not to fall into the hands of the Moguls and be dishonored by the enemy.

"*Myn bhûka ho!*—I am hungry! . . . I am hungry! . . ." shouted the goddess of death and destruction soaring over the battlefield; she was the patroness of the besieged town and her feelings were hurt by the act of the râjan. Implacable Kâlî bends over a warrior and the latter falls into the icy embrace of Yamî (the devî of death); she points her *chirâg* (lantern) towards another, and the sword falls from his hand and his shield drops, covering his face "like the shadow of the tomb, throwing its black pall over the remains of a buried warrior."

Badul, covered with blood, came back to Chitor alone. Then a monologue takes place between him and the wife of his uncle, the unhappy Padminî, she who caused the fall of the city. Before joining her husband, *i.e.*, performing *satî* and *jauhar*, she wished to hear from the young man of the last deeds of her "Ruler," «*son doux seigneur et maître.*»

Badul answers:

"He was the reaper of the battlefield; I only
    gathered the sheaves,
Step by step I followed, like the harvester
    after the sharp scythe,
I saw him, our father, prepare for himself
    a bed of honor;
And cover it with a bloody carpet; and he
    chose as pillow the prince
Of the Moguls—and he lay upon him. He now
    sleeps soundly and sweetly,
Guarded by the bodies of his enemies, who fell
    asleep by his hand."

Padminî, the widow, again asks her nephew:

"Tell me, Badul, how did my King, my dearest
    ruler fight?"
And Badul answers: "Oh, mother, how could
    I describe his bravery?
When no foe was left
    to dread or admire him?"
The *Rânî* smiles; she takes leave of the brave
    young man, and says: "My Ruler waits for me...
    the pyre is already burning."

She throws herself into the fire, and the women and young girls of Chitor follow her . . .

The official history of Udaipur, as well as its chronicles,

add that 22,000 girls and wives of Chitor followed Padminî "into the flames that spared their honor and name." They sacrificed their lives to their duty and were burned in a terrible conflagration like the women-folk of the underground city near Cawnpore (see Part I).

Ferishta (the historian) mentions only those *sâkâs* of 'Alâ al-dîn and Akbar, and thus is not fair to history. But even he tells us about the horrors of such mass-burning and about the cave of *Mahâ-Satî*.

In the *memoirs* of Tod we find the following description of "an author . . . the only Englishman," as he says, who was "admitted to Chitor," a place *sacred* in those days.

The Tatar conqueror took possession of an inanimate capital, strewed with brave defenders, the smoke yet issuing from the recesses where lay consumed the once fair object of his desire; and since this devoted day the cavern has been sacred: no eye has penetrated its gloom and superstition has placed as its guardian a huge serpent, whose "venomous breath" extinguishes the light which might guide intruders to "the place of sacrifice."*

The choking emanations, and the fear of live, not mythical, snakes forced Tod to turn back. *Khumân-Râsâ* asserts that this cave leads to a beautiful palace, and many Englishmen believe in its existence.

Tod speaks, however, as if there had been but one "mass burning," one *Mahâ-Satî* or *jauhar*, after the *sâkâ* of 'Alâ al-dîn. As a matter of fact, the words, "no eye has penetrated its gloom," refer to a later *satî*, because the terrible event of 1275 was but the forerunner of a still worse though less poetical one, and Tod himself describes this second mass-burning in the days of Akbar, the famous emperor, the son and heir of Humâyûn.

The campsite of this enlightened, but at times cruel ruler, is shown near Chitor even today; it has a pyramidal marble pillar erected over it, which is called by the people *Akbar-Kâ-Dewân*, the "Lamp of Akbar." His camp stretched from

---

* [Tod, *Annals*, etc., "Annals of Mewâr," Vol. I, p. 248 and footnote, ed. 1894.]

the village of Pandowly, some ten miles from the besieged fortress, and its advance tents were almost at the foot of the rock.

Chitor * is one of the most ancient cities of Udaipur or Mewâr and was always famous for its heroes. Here, in a few words, is its history from 1275 to 1803, omitting the prehistoric and ante-Moslem raids.

In 1303 'Alâ al-dîn once more appeared under the walls of Chitor, and having stormed it, destroyed all he could, sparing, strangely enough, the place once made sacred by the presence of the woman he so passionately loved. The palace of Bhim-Singh and of the "lovely Padminî" remained untouched; the high pillar, the obelisk of the *Jainas* and its Buddhist temple erected in 896 were also miraculously saved, as Padminî belonged to the religion of Ceylon . . . *Où la poésie de l'amour va-t-elle se nicher!* . . . 'Alâ al-dîn, the cruel tyrant and fanatic, playing the part of a gentle knight!

Chitor proper, namely the old town with its fortress, is built on an enormous rock, while the modern town, built since 1350, is situated at its foot. Below runs the river Gambheri over which there is a remarkable bridge of nine arches, the one in the middle being semicircular, and having Gothic arches at each side. The lower town is uninteresting. One must climb the rock to the old town and visit the ancient buildings, to get a good idea of its archaeological value. Inside the fortress, which according to legend has existed from the time of Krishna (who, by the way, has two temples here, the largest in the whole country), there still stands the *Nau Lakha Bhandar,* the inner citadel, built no doubt by *mythical* Cyclops, to judge by the massive nature of its walls and towers. Close to it is the palace of Padminî, whose crenelated walls have remained untouched by time, the destroyer. There you see her abode with its high rooms which have remained empty, while the poor unfortunate beauty, as well as her sisters, have acquired the unenviable *post-mortem* reputation of *bhûtas* or midnight demons. In

---

*Though our visit to this town was much later, I am describing it now, in order not to revert to the subject again.

the Durbâr or Throne Hall can still be seen the *mirror* walls. They received their name from the mosaic-like *scales* covering them; these are small pieces of polished steel, like those in Persian palaces.* Only the miracle of love could have made 'Alâ al-dîn see in these "mirrors" the beautiful figure of Padminî and fall in love with her. After looking at them and trying hard to catch the reflection of my own, rather well-known face, I finally discovered, after a long search, my right eye on my forehead, and my nose near my left ear. With such an *anamorphosis* of the beloved object before his eyes, the Caliph should not have been moved to commit such a sin! . . .

Near the temples of Krishṇa there are two reservoirs (*tanks*), each 125 feet long, 50 feet wide and 50 feet deep, made of enormous black marble slabs. The top of the rock is crowned by a temple consecrated to the "destructive forces," with the three-pronged symbol of Śiva at its entrance. The walls are incredibly massive, so that it would have taken a long time for the god, the patron of the temple, to prove his destructive power if he had chosen to destroy them. Scattered throughout the fortress there still remain some 80 *tanks,* many of them full of water. The most wonderful building, however, though not a very old one, is the *Kîrat Khambh,* "the Pillar of Victory," built by *Rânâ Khambh,*† after the brilliant victory of this Râjput over the allied forces of Mâlvâ and Gujarât. The obelisk stands on a terrace 42 feet square; it rises 122 feet above a quadrangular pedestal, each side of which is 35 feet long. This obelisk has nine floors, one room with a side corridor on each floor, and a spiral staircase passing through all of them. The tower is crowned with a cupola. The building is of white marble and is covered from top to bottom with carvings. A complete mythology is written on its walls. In addition, there exist in the town two or three ancient private palaces and seven equally ancient towers.

After 'Alâ al-dîn, Chitor was taken again by Bahâdur-Shah,

---

*The question is: did the Persians imitate the ancient Hindus in thus decorating their walls, or did the Râjputs imitate the Iranians?
†Who reigned at Mewâr from 1418 to 1468.

king of Gujarât, in 1533. Bahâdur in his turn was driven out by Humâyûn, the Delhi Padishâh, who returned the city to its former Râjput owners. Later, in 1567, Chitor was taken by the Emperor Akbar. In that year, the *sâkâ* was followed by a *jauhar*. The terrible fires of the cave of *Mahâ-Satî* were once more lit; once more the blood of women and children flowed, and the whole tribe of Râjputs, having reduced their women to ashes, rushed out of the city gates towards the Moguls and was annihilated, "for the dead know no shame."

What a terribly bloody dream is the history of Chitor! Upon its founding by a mythical hero, *"Râjâ Hûn"* in prehistoric ages, the goddess of "power and destruction" and the patroness of all the fortified places, *Durgâ*, promised the first kings of Chitor never to leave her beloved rock without protection. As long as the *Eklingji-Dewân** will remain faithful to her, she, Eklingji, "the one born of a lionesss," will not forsake them.† The first Râjâ of Chitor, the

---

*One of the titles of the Udaipur Mahârânâs.

†Rome had its Romulus; Chitor had a *second* founder, the nephew of Râjâ-Mori, whose origin is also buried in the myths of antiquity. *Bappa* (the infant), called *Sailâdhîsa*, "Ruler of the Rock," was, according to the *Purânas*, this nephew. Like all the early princes, he was also the shepherd of the "herd of the Sun" and once met on the mountain the hermit *Chiranjîva* (the ever-living), who slept soundly for more than three centuries in the bushes. In gratitude for being wakened, the latter initiates the prince into the "mysteries of Śiva" and thus makes of him the husband of Kâlî, in her *aspect* of Eklingji, born of the "goddess-lioness," the same Kâlî. All "initiated" men are called by the Śaivas *bridegrooms* or even *husbands* of Eklingji (Îśa, Pârvatî, Durgâ, Gaurî, the goddess of earth, *Ambâ-mâtâ*, the universal mother; these are all aspects of Kâlî). Eklingji is the goddess who under her name of *Gaurî-devî* is the guardian of mountains, rocks and fortified places. She is the same as Cibelê, and like the Greek goddess is represented as crowned with a headgear like a crenelated tower. After marrying Eklingji (*i.e.*, becoming "initiated"), *Bappa* gets from his spiritual spouse a complete accoutrement, a bow and arrows, a shield, a lance and a sword, which she gives him personally. After that, being unconquerable as Achilles, he drives away his uncle, and becomes with the aid of the goddess, King of Chitor, while Durgâ-Eklingji becomes the patroness of the city, as she is the goddess of the rock on which the city was built.

"initiated" *Bappa,* was the spiritual husband of the goddess. He took an oath at his consecration by *Chiranjîva,** and as long as the Râjâs kept this oath the goddess would not allow Chitor to fall. As long as its Râjâs bear the titles of *Râjâ-Guru,* "Râjâ-teacher," *Hindua Sûraj,* the "Sun of the Hindus," and *Chukwa,* "Ruler of the World," Chitor would not suffer.

But some later Râjâs—so says the same legend—in their pride, forgot the oath, and even failed to show due respect to the goddess. They began to include other gods, such as Kṛishṇa (hateful to Śiva) in their worship and the bright red color of the banner began to grow darker. Durgâ-Eklingji promised her protection to the descendants of *Bappa* so long as they remained faithful. At the first *sâkâ* of 'Alâ al-dîn, twelve râjâs, crowned rulers of Rajwâra, defended their banner, but it no longer possessed its power, and they were killed on the battlefield. At the time of the second *sâkâ,* started by Bahâdur Shâh, the Ṭhâkur of Delhi of the reigning house of Mewâr sacrificed himself to the goddess, by killing himself on her altar, and she saved the town. But the third time, during the terrible days of the siege by young Akbar, Durgâ-Ambâ, taking her original aspect of Kâlî, remained deaf to all the pleas. She turned away from her crenelated crown, and when she appeared to Samarśi (Râjâ of Chitor in 1412) to declare that "Hindu glory was fading," it was for the last time.† Udai-Singh, Râjâ of Mewâr was

---

*This oath of the *Kânphatâ-yogins* is even now taken yearly by the Udaipur Râjâs: "I swear by *Guru-Chiranjîva* and the goddess Eklingji; I swear by Takiak, the wise snake, and by Hari, the Wise One; I swear by Bhavânî (Pallas) to smite the enemy. Smite! Smite!" The arms which *Bappa* got from Eklingji, the bow and arrows, the lance, the shield and the sword, are kept in the treasury of the Râjâs of Udaipur. "Warrior-monks" take their oaths upon them.

†*Vide* the Chronicles of the Bard Chund, the last volume, p. 2.

[Col. James Tod, in his *Annals and Antiquities of Râjasthân* (Vol. I, p, 237, footnote, in the 1894 ed.), has the following to say concerning this Chronicle (we preserve his spelling of proper names):

"The work of Chund is a universal history of the period in which he wrote. In the sixty-nine books, comprising one hundred thousand stanzas, relating to the exploits of Prithwi Raj, every noble

the last of the kings who sinned against this goddess, having fled at the first appearance of Akbar and his army. Then the goddess turned away from Chitor forever. The famous city fell, notwithstanding its desperate defence. It was not Durgâ-Eklingji, but Kâlî who appeared in front of Udai-Singh's horse, shouting her usual war cry — "*Myn bhûka-ho!*" (I am hungry); she disappeared and satiated herself with the last of the famous tribe of *Agni-Kula.*

Thirty thousand men perished during the days when Akbar besieged Chitor. An awful *jauhar* was then prepared and the 8,000 Râjputs who were still alive, after eating together the last *bîḍa* * and donning saffron-yellow gowns (the emblem of the burning pyre), went to perform their terrible duty. Nine *Rânîs* (queens), and five princesses (their daughters), two infant sons of the Râjâ and all the women of various classes perished at the hands of husbands, sons, brothers and relatives; their bodies were cremated in the

---

family of Rajasthan will find some record of their ancestors. It is accordingly treasured among the archives of each race having any pretensions to the name of Rajpoot. From this he can trace his marital forefathers who 'drank of the wave of battle' in the passes of Kirman, when 'the clouds of war rolled from Himâchal' to the plains of Hindusthan. The wars of Prithwi Raj, his alliances, his numerous and powerful tributaries, their abodes and pedigrees, make the works of Chund invaluable as historic and geographical memoranda, besides being treasures in mythology, manners, and the annals of the mind. To read this poet well is a sure road to honour, and my own *Gooru* was allowed, even by the professional bards, to excel therein. As he read, I rapidly translated about thirty thousand stanzas. Familiar with the dialects in which it is written, I have fancied that I seized occasionally the poet's spirit; but it were presumption to suppose that I embodied all his brilliancy, or fully comprehended the depth of his allusions. But I knew for whom he wrote. The most familiar of his images and sentiments I heard daily from the mouths of those around me, the descendants of the men whose deeds he rehearses. I was enabled thus to seize his meaning, where one more skilled in poetic lore might have failed, and to make my prosaic version of some value."

—*Compiler.*]

*Bîḍa or *pân* is a strong-smelling leaf of betel, prepared with various spices, which is served by the Hindus at farewell meetings and eaten by all those present.

cave of *Mahâ-Satî.* Then this army, 8,000 men strong, opened wide the gates and rushed like an irresistible torrent upon the army of Akbar. Not one of them survived, and not one of the *yellow*-shirts was dishonored by surrender.

Yes, the Râjput divinity deserted them in this terrible, awful last day of Chitor. The rock of their independence and power was shattered; their temples and palaces were reduced to dust, and Akbar even carried away all the symbols of the reigning house: the *nagâḍâs* * whose sound used to proclaim to the population for miles around the arrival and departure of the râjâs and princes; the cande-labras from the altar of the "great mother," *Ambâ-Matâ,* who gave the sword to *Bappa,* and even the sword itself.† From that day on, the expression *Chitor sâkâ kâ pâp,* "I swear by the sin of the sâkâ of Chitor" has become a sacred and inviolable oath with the Râjputs.

"*Tîjo sâkâ Chitor ra* (the third sâkâ of Chitor) has brought Râjasthân to its present condition," said the bard, gloomily finishing his song, "The great mother has left us, and now for three centuries past Râjasthân has been slowly dying . . . The Sun has left us . . . Sûryavanśas are dete-riorating . . ."

Alas! This was but a metaphor. The sun was scorching us even in this impenetrable forest. I felt weary in this stifling atmosphere, lying on the carpets of the darkened verandah,

---

*A large drum, some eight or ten feet in diameter.

†Counting his victims, Akbar gauged his success by the golden *zinaras* (necklaces) which distinguished kingly or noble families. They weighed 74½ *mans* (one *man* = four pounds). From that day the figure 74½ is called *tilak,* "cursed." Placed on a letter of a Râjput, or on any document, this figure represents an inviolable oath, because it is synonymous with an oath by "the sin of the sâkâ of Chitor." The man who does not keep it is driven out of the tribe and town in which he lives, and is generally damned, and often even killed.

[The Hindustânî *man,* often referred to by the old English word *maund,* a basket, is a measure of weight containing 40 seers of vary-ing values. The Bengal man weighs 82-2/7 lbs.; that of Surat, 41 lbs.; of Bombay, 28 lbs.; of Madras, 25 lbs. In Arabia, it equals 2.98 lbs. (1350 grams). There is apparently a great deal of discrepancy as to its weight-value.—*Compiler.*]

and could hardly say a word. My curiosity and interest, however, overcame both laziness and heat, and I enquired about the present state of Chitor; what had become of it after the *sâkâ* of Akbar?

Ânanda answered for the bard.

"One of the Mewâr Râjâs took possession of the ruins soon after the raid, but in 1676 he opened its gates and surrendered to Aurangzîb, on his first demand and without a battle. Chitor was not returned to its Râjput rulers until the end of the last century."

"Did you visit it? . . . Did you see its ruins? . . ."

"Yes I did, all that remains of it. The once unconquerable Chitor has been deserted by its people, as well as by the government of the *Rânâ*. According to the former, the curse of the goddess is upon the town; as for the latter, it is quite useless. 'The residence of kings, which for 3,000 years lifted its crowned head high above all other Indian cities,' says the Chronicle, 'has now become the refuge of wild beasts, which have made their lairs in former temples . . .' The sacred capital is now defended only by *gosâîns* and *yogins,* and the *Rânâ,** and the princes of royal blood are denied access by special decree of the Mahant, the chief of the warrior-monks; neither the curse of the goddess, nor the wild animals, nor the *Jigger-khors* (demon-Harpies) dare touch the yogins; and that is the reason you are not afraid of them," added the bard, reproachfully.

The ascetic of Pondicherry did not react to this remark and the truth of the superstitious singer's view remained unsupported and unclarified for posterity. Nârâyana, however, turned to Ânanda asking him if it was all right to tell us about the rôle the ancestors of the Thâkur played during the last act of the bloody drama of Chitor.

The silent ascetic bowed in acquiescence. Nârâyana, stating that the episode he was about to narrate was officially entered in the Chronicles of the royal houses of Salûmbra

---

*Rânâ is today the title of the Râjâ of Udaipur alone. There is the same difference between a *Rânâ* and a *Râjan,* as between an Emperor and a King.

and Mertia, and is sung by all the bards, began his story.*
"The names of Jaimal and Pattâ are forever immortal
and inseparable in the history of Chitor," began Nârâyana,
whose eyes sparkled as he mentioned the ancestors of the
Thâkur who had rejected him, showing how much the poor
boy deified his hero. "They will always remain a symbol of
unparalled heroism and will live in the hearts of the Râjputs
and of all Hindus as sacred, as long as there remains in the
land the least spark of memory of our glorious past . . .
At the time when the defender of the 'Gates of the Sun,'
the leader of the Salûmbras, perished, the choice of a new
ruler fell upon Pattâ from Kailwârâ. He was only 16 years
old. His father, a warrior, was mortally wounded seven
years before, in one of the previous battles, and his mother
refused the honor of *satî* at the request of her husband who
was dying from wounds, sacrificing her glorious death to
her only son, whom she educated as the heir of a famed
family. In the Occident you glorify the mother of the Grac-
chi, and the Spartan and Roman matrons; but they are but
feeble examples compared to the great-grandmother of
Thâkur-Sâhib's father on his mother's side. In giving the
sword to her son, she told him to put on the 'yellow shirt'
and to die for Chitor. But as Colonel Tod rightly remarked,
she went further than the Roman mother, sustaining her son
by a personal example. She did more even than that. The
young Pattâ was engaged: being afraid that his love for his
betrothed might influence her son's conduct during the
battle, she gave the betrothed† a lance and a dagger and, taking her by the hand, led her down the rock towards the city
gates, where the defenders of Chitor witnessed the prowess

---

*"But the names which shine brightest in this gloomy page of the
annals of Mewâr, which are still held sacred by the bard and the true
Râjpoot and immortalized by Akbar's own pen, are Jaimal of Bednor
and Pattâ of Kailwârâ, both of the sixteen superior vassals of Mewâr.
The first was a Râthore of the Mertia house, the bravest of the brave
clans of Mârwâr; the other was head of the Jaggawuts, another grand
shoot from Chonda." [Tod, *Annals*, etc., "Annals of Mewâr," Vol. I, p.
302, ed. of 1894.]

†In India an "engagement" is tantamount to marriage and cannot
be dissolved. The betrothed, according to law, is already the wife.

of two women, one of them quite old and the other a mere child. 'Defending herself like a lioness and attacking like a tigress,' says the Chronicle, the young Amazon finally fell dead at the feet of the old heroine who had performed that day such miracles of bravery. Is it a wonder then, that such an example of fearless patriotism on the part of their mothers and daughters, transformed the Râjput warriors into veritable lions, fully deserving the name of *Singh* (lion)! The defence lasted from sunrise to late at night. Seeing his betrothed killed, Pattâ gave his mother a sign. In a loud voice he ordered a *jauhar,* requesting the women themselves to light the fires in the cave, and telling his warriors in the background to kill the women when all was ready. Pattâ and his mother at the head of an advanced detachment threw themselves upon the Moguls. Read what the Emperor himself says about this desperate attack, in which the *old woman-warrior,* as she is called by Akbar, 'with her own hands lopped off the heads of his bravest Sardârs.' *Shaiṭân* himself possessed that Râjput woman, he writes. Jaimal, the cousin of Pattâ, was performing similar deeds of prowess at the other gates and joined in the general attack on the enemy that evening. Finally, when Pattâ himself was killed, shot through and through, his mother, 'looking like a bloody Kâlî,' bravely picked up his body and carried it, under a rain of arrows and bullets, to the city gates, and leaving it to be burned, returned to the battlefield. Jaimal of Bednore was killed by the Emperor himself, who was very proud of it for the rest of his life. This fact is vouched for by the historian Abu-'l-Fazl and the Emperor Jahângîr, who calls the gun*

---

*A lock with a wick. "He [Akbar] named the matchlock with which he shot Jaimal *Saṅgrâm,* being one of great superiority and choice, and with which he had slain three or four thousand birds and beasts." (*Tûzuk-i-Jahângîrî*). Akbar accomplished even more. He was so struck with the heroism of Jaimal and Pattâ, that he ordered the erection of statues to both of them at the entrance to his palace at Delhi. This is what Bernier writes to London from Delhi on July 1st, 1663:

"I find nothing remarkable at the entrance but two large elephants of stone, which are on the two sides of one of the gates. Upon one of them is the statue of Jaimal, that famous Râjâ of Chitor, and upon the other Pattâ, his brother. These are two gallant men that, together with their mother, who was yet braver than they, cut out so much work

with which Akbar killed Jaimal, *Saṅgrâm.* Yes, great were the heroes that our India produced!"

A few more ballads, a few more heroic songs, and we heard Ânanda call us, reminding us that the sun had set, and it was time for us to start on our journey . . .

The Hindus mounted an elephant, while the Bâbû, the Colonel and I climbed into a covered cart drawn by oxen. We intended to visit the ruins of an ancient temple, in a section of which, preserved by time, lived a yogin and his disciples. We were to reach it towards morning, so had to drive slowly all night through the forest. We were not afraid, however, neither of the tigers nor of the robber-Bhîls. The Colonel had his *śâlagrâma,* and he was much more afraid now of the cows than of all the royal tigers of wild Râja-sthân. As for myself, I had an inexplicable feeling of security at the thought of the Ṭhâkur and even of Ânanda. Besides, the old bard and his two sons were also with us.

I fell asleep quite sure of my safety and that I would awake next morning hale and hearty, and dreamed of the Ṭhâkur's great-grandmother who, with a mere twig, was driving away from me a whole herd of tigers that were trying to get their paws into my pockets like the monkeys of Mathurâ.

(To be continued.)*

RADDA-BAI.

---

for Akbar; and who in the sieges of towns which they maintained against him, gave such extraordinary proofs of their generosity, that at length they would rather be killed in the sallies with their mother, than submit; and for this gallantry it is, that even their enemies thought them worthy to have these statues erected to them. These two large elephants, together with the two resolute men astride on them make an impression, at first entering into this fortress, of I know not what greatness and respectful awe."

[Translated from the original French of François Bernier, in his *Voyages,* etc., Amsterdam, 1710, Vol. II, pp. 33-34.—*Compiler.*]

* [No continuation of this story has ever been found, either in published form or in MSS. in spite of a far-reaching search. This last installment or Chapter VII of Part II of the story appeared in Vol. 184 of the *Russkiy Vestnik,* August, 1886, pp. 684-718. At that time, H.P.B. was progressively more and more occupied with writing *The Secret Doctrine,* and maybe found no time to continue writing her travel-stories.—*Compiler.*]

ADDENDUM

NOTE ON THE TRANSLITERATION OF
SANSKRIT AND OTHER TERMS

The system of diacritical marks used in the text of
this volume, and in the General Bibliography, as well as
the Index, does not strictly follow any one specific
scholar, to the exclusion of all others. In regard to Sanskrit, while adhering to a very large extent to Sir Monier-
Williams' *Sanskrit-English Dictionary*, as for instance in
the case of the *Anusvâra*, the transliteration includes
forms introduced by other Sanskrit scholars as well, being therefore of a selective nature.

The transliteration of other than Sanskrit terms has
been checked with a variety of sources, and a selection
has been made to conform with the standards adopted by
the best known scholars.

As in previous volumes of this series, we have continued the usage of a circumflex over a long vowel, rather
then using the "macron" or a line over them. This policy
avoided a great many alterations which might have resulted in confusion or uncertainty.

GENERAL BIBLIOGRAPHY

Arranged alphabetically according to Authors, except in cases when author is unknown; the work appears then in its own alphabetical sequence by title.

AESCHYLUS (525-456 B.C.). *Supplices* (Suppliants). Loeb Class. Libr.—*The Sphinx*. Fragment of a lost play.

Aitareya Brâhmaṇam of the Rigveda . . . . Edited, translated and explained by Martin Haug. Bombay, 1863, 2 vols. Reprint of translation in *Sacred Books of the Hindus*, extra Vol. 4.

ALTEKAR, DR. A. S. *The Position of Women in Hindu Civilization*, etc. Benares: The Culture Publication House, Hindu University, 1938.

ANQUETIL-DUPERRON, A. B. (1731-1805). *Recherches historiques et géographiques sur l'Inde*, Berlin, 1786-87, 2 vols.

ARRIANUS, FLAVIUS (2nd cent.). *Anabasis of Alexander*, to which is appended his *Indica* (Indian History). Loeb Class. Library.

Asiatick Researches; or, Transactions of the Society instituted in Bengal, for inquiring into the History and Antiquities, the Arts, Sciences, and Literature, of Asia. Calcutta, 1788-1839, 20 vols. 4to; another edition, printed verbatim from the Calcutta ed., London, J. Sewell, 1801-12, 11 vols., 8vo.—Index to first 18 vols. of the Calcutta ed., Calcutta, 1835, See WILFORD.

ASIUS (ca. 700 B.C.). Fragments in Pausanias' *Itinerary* or *Description of Greece*. Loeb Classical Series.

AST, G. A. F. (1778-1841). Uncertain ref. either to his *Grundlinien der Philosophie*, Landshut, 1807, or his *Grundriss der Philologie*, Landshut, 1808.

Atharva-Veda. The *Samhitâ* is ed. by R. Roth and W. D. Whitney, Berlin, 1855-56.—With the Comm. of Sâyaṇâchârya. Ed. by Shankar Pândurant Pandit, Bombay, 1895-98, 4 vols.—Transl. into English verse by Ralph T. H. Griffith, Benares, 1895-96, 2 vols. Transl. by

W. D. Whitney; rev. & ed. by C. R. Lanman, Cambridge, Mass., 1905.—Transl. into English prose by M. Bloomfield, Oxford, 1897, in *SBE*, Vol. XLII.

Avesta (or *Zend-Avesta*). Transl. by James Darmesteter (1849-1894). Part I. *The Vendidâd*. Part II. *The Sîrôzahs, Yashts, and Nyâyis*. Part III (Tr. by L. H. Mills). *Yasna, Visparad*, etc. Oxford: Clarendon Press, *SBE* IV, XXIII, XXXI. Original edition is of 1880; 2nd ed. of 1895, somewhat abbreviated as far as Introduction goes. His French translation is of 1892-93, in the *Annales du Musée Guimet*, Vols. 21, 22, 24.

BALDWIN, JOHN DENISON (1809-1883). *Pre-Historic Nations; or, inquiries concerning some of the great peoples and civilizations of antiquity, and their probable relation to a still older civilization of the Ethiopians or Cushites of Arabia*. London, 1869, 8vo.

BARROS, JOAO DE (1496-1570). *Décadas da Asia*, 1552, 1553, 1563, 1615. Continued by Diogo do Couto.

BARTHÉLEMY SAINT-HILAIRE, JULES (1805-1895). *Le Bouddha et sa religion*, Paris, 1860—*Du Bouddhisme*, etc., Paris, 1866.

BERNIER, DR. FRANÇOIS (1620-1688). *Voyages. Contenant la description des Etats du Grand Mogol*, etc. Amsterdam, 1699, 2 tomes, ill.; also 1710. Transl. as *Travels in the Mogul Empire A.D. 1656-1668*. Transl. on the basis of Irving Brock's version and annotated by Archibald Constable (1891). 3rd ed., rev. by Vincent A. Smith, London: Oxford Univ. Press, 1934.

Bhâgavatamâhâtmya. Edited with the *Bhâgavatapurâṇa* by Vâsudeva Lakshmaṇa Śarman Paṇśîkar, Bombay, Nirṇayasâgara Press, 1929.

Bhavishyapurâṇa. MS form, ff. 9, 556. Bombay: Venkateśvara Press, 1910.

Bibliotheca Indica; a collection of original works (in Sanskrit, Hindi, Persian, and Arabic) publ. by the Asiatic Society of Bengal. Calcutta, Benares, Tungoo, London & Hertford, 1845—. Old and New Series, 4to & 8vo.

BRASSEUR-DE-BOURBOURG, ABBÉ CHARLES ÉTIENNE. (1814-1874). *Monuments anciens du Mexique et du Yucatan*, etc. Ill. by de Waldeck. Paris, 1866, fol., xxiii, 83.

Bṛihaspati, Aphorisms of (sometimes as Bârhaspatya). Belongs to the Chârvâka School. Discussed in the *Sarvadarśanasaṃgraha* of Mâdhava Vidyâraṇya, transl. by E. B. Cowell and A. E. Gough. London: Trübner & Co., 1892; 2nd ed., 1894, in Trübner's Oriental Series.

BRUCE, JAMES (1730-1794). *Travels to Discover the Source of the Nile in the Years 1768-73*, published in 1790 in five octavo volumes, lavishly illustrated. Best ed. is the 3rd., 1813.

BRUGSCH-BEY, HEINRICH KARL (1827-94). *A History of Egypt under the Pharaohs.* Transl. from the German by Philip Smith; 2nd ed., London: J. Murray, 1881; 2 vols.

BÜCHNER, LUDWIG (1824-99). *Force and Matter.* Transl. and ed. from the last edition of *Kraft und Stoff* by J. F. Collingwood. London: Trübner & Co., 1864.

BURNOUF, EUGÈNE (1801-1852). *Introduction à l'histoire du Bouddhisme indien*, Paris, 1844; 2nd ed., 1876.

BUSHBY, H. J. (1820- ?). *Widow-Burning, A Narrative.* London, 1855.

CARPENTER, DR. WM. BENJAMIN (1813-1885). *The Principles of General and Comparative Physiology*, London, 1839.

CLARKE, EDWARD DANIEL (1769-1822). *Travels in Various Countries of Europe, Asia and Africa.* London, 1810-19; 2nd ed., 1811-23; 4th ed., 1816-24.

CLIFFORD, W. K. (1845-1879). "Body and Mind," in *Fortnightly Review*, Vol. XVI, December, 1874; in bookform, New York, 1891.— *Lectures and Essays*, 1879.

Concerning the Territories Acquired by the East India Company. Untraced.

COUTO, DIOGO DO (1542-1616). *Da Asia*, etc., Lisbon, 1780.

DALVI, DINANÂTH ATMARAM, "Âryan Trigonometry," *The Theosophist*, Vol. I, October, 1879.

DANTE, ALIGHIERI (1265-1321). *La Divina Commedia.*

DAYÂNANDA SARASVATÎ SVÂMI (1827-1883). *Ṛigvedâdi-Bhâshya-Bhû-mikâ*. Introduction to the Commentary on the Ṛig and other *Vedas*. In Sanskrit and Hindî. There is a transl. by Ghasi Ram, Merut, 1925, xii, 507 pp.

DESCARTES, RENÉ (1596-1650). *Les Méditations*.

DONIZETTI, GAETANO (1798-1848). *La Favorita*, 1840.

DU BOIS-REYMOND, EMIL (1818-1896). Address to the Congress of German Natuforschers, Leipzig, 1872.

DUFF, JAMES GRANT (1789-1858). *A History of the Mahrattas*. London, 1826, 3 vols.; 3rd ed., Bombay (pr.), London, 1873.

EASTWICK, EDWARD BACKHOUSE (1814-83). *A Handbook for India;* being an account of the three Presidencies, and of the Overland Route . . . With Vocabularies and Dialogues of the spoken languages of India . . . London: Hertford (pr.), 1859, 8vo. (One of John Murray's (1808-92) *Handbooks for Travellers in India*).

ELPHINSTONE, MOUNTSTUART (1779-1859). *History of India*, 1841.

ERSKINE, SIR WILLIAM (1773-1852). *History of India under Bâbar and Humâyûn*, edited by his son in London, 1854, 2 vols.

FAYRER, SIR JOSEPH (1824-1907). *The Thanatophidia of India*: being a description of venomous snakes of the Indian Peninsula, with an account of the influence of their poison on life; and a series of experiments. London, 1872, fol.; 2nd ed., rev. & enl., 1874.

FERGUSSON, JAMES (1808-1886). *Illustration of the Rock-Cut Temples of India*, 1845, fol. & 8vo. Text and Ill. in separate volumes.

FIRDAUZÎ, ABU'L KÂSIM MANSUR (941-1020). *Shâhnâmah*, or *Book of Kings*. A complete history of Persia in nearly 60,000 verses which has taken its place as the national epic of the people. English abridgment by J. Atkinson, London, 1832; repr. 1886, 1892. Complete transl. in Italian by I. Pizzi, Turin, 1886-88, 8 vols.

Fortnightly Review. Also known as *The Fortnightly*, published in London since 1865.

Gazetteer No. 22: China. U.S. Board on Geographic Names.

GOGOL', NIKOLAY VASSILYEVICH (1809-1852). "How Ivan Ivanovich and Ivan Nikiforovich quarrelled with each other," a story.

GROUSSET, RENÉ (1885-1952). *Le Conquérant du monde,* Paris, 1944.

Guide to the Curiosities of Âgra. Untraced.

HAECKEL, ERNST HEINRICH PHILIPP AUGUST (1834-1919). *Anthropogenie, oder Entwickelungsgeschichte des Menschen.* 2nd ed., Leipzig, 1874, 8vo.; 4th ed., 1891, 2 vols.—Transl. as *The Evolution of Man,* London, 1879, 8vo.

HAUG, MARTIN (1827-1876). *Essays on the Sacred Languages, Writings, and Religion of the Parsees,* Bombay, 1862; 2nd & 3rd ed., 1878.

HEBER, REGINALD (1783-1826). *Narrative of a Journey through the Upper Provinces of India, from Calcutta to Bombay, 1824-1825,* London, 1828.

HESIOD (ca. 850 B.C.). *The Homeric Hymns.* Loeb Classical Library.

HIOUEN-THSANG (ca. 605-664). Consult Stanislas A. Julien, *Voyages des pèlerins Bouddhistes.* Vol. I — *Historie de la vie de Hiouen-Thsang et de ses voyages dans l'Inde,* etc., by Hoeili and Yenthsong, Paris, 1853; Vol. II—*Si-yu-ki. Mémoires sur les contrées occidentales,* Paris, 1857-58.

HUC, ABBÉ É. R. (1813-1860). *Travels,* etc. English transl. by W. Hazlitt, 1852.

HUXLEY, THOMAS HENRY (1825-95). *Lay Sermons:* "The Scientific Aspects of Positivism," 1880.—*Protoplasm: The Physical Basis of Life,* Melbourne, 1869 (orig. as one of the "Lay Sermons," delivered in Edinburgh, Nov. 8, 1868, republ. in *The Fortnightly Review.*—"On the Hypothesis that Animals are Automata, and its History," in *The Fortnightly Review,* Vol. XVI, November, 1874.

JAHÂNGÎR (1569-1627). *Tûzuk-i-Jahângîrî* or Memoirs of the Mogul Emperor Jahângîr, which were either written by himself or dictated to a scribe. They appeared at Ghazipur in 1863 and at Aligarh in 1864; Engl. transl. by Alexander Rogers and ed. by Henry Beveridge, 1909-14, 2 vols., xv, 478. Oriental Translation Fund, Vol. 19.

Journal Asiatique, Paris, 1827. See under Tod.

Journal of the Asiatic Society of Bengal. See under Prinsep.

Journal of the Bombay Branch of the Royal Asiatic Society. See under Stevenson and Westergaard.

KANE, DR. P. V. *History of Dharmaśâstra,* Poona: Bhandarkar Oriental Research Institute, 1941.

KAYE, SIR JOHN WILLIAM (1814-1876). *The History of the Sepoy War in India: 1857-58,* etc. London, 1864-76, 3 vols.—*Lives of Indian Officers, Illustrative of the Civil and Military Services of India,* London: A. Strahan & Co., 1867, 2 vols.: "Life of Cornwallis." Kaye's work was later continued by G. B. Malleson.

KEENE, COL. HENRY GEORGE (1825-1915). *The Moghul Empire; from the death of Aurangzeb to the overthrow of the Mahratta Power.* London: Wm. H. Allen & Co., 1866.

KHANDALAVALA, NAVROJI DORABJI. "Primitive Mazdayasnyan Teachings," *The Theosophist,* Vol. VI, November and December, 1885.

KHUMÂN RÂSA (or Khummân Râso). A poetic Chronicle of the ruling family of Mewâr, dating from the 16th century, and said to be founded on a work of the 9th century, no fragment of which, however, has survived.

KHUNRATH, HENRY (b. ca. 1560). *Amphitheatrum sapientiae aeternae solius verae,* etc., an unfinished work which appeared after his death with preface and conclusion by Erasmus Wohlfahrt. Hanoviae: Giulielmus Antonius, 1609, fol. 2 pts.; also Magdeburg, 1608, and Hamburg, 1611. The 1619 ed. contains twelve plates. An early German ed. of 1602 is also known. French transl., Paris: Chacornac, 1898, 2 vols., 8vo., with the 12 plates.

KRUSE, FRIEDRICH KARL HERMANN (1790-1866). *Hellas,* etc., Leipzig, 1825-27, 2 pts.

KULLÛKA-BHAṬṬA. *History of India.* Untraced.

Legends of the Mogul Empire. A collection of traditions translated from the Urdu and Marâṭhâ tongues. *Untraced.*

LEGOUVÉ, ERNEST (1807-1903) and A. E. SCRIBE (1791-1861). *Adrienne Lecouvreur*, comedy-drama performed in the Théatre de la République, April 14, 1849.

LEWES, GEORGE HENRY (1817-1878). *Problems of Life and Mind*, London, 1874-79, 4 vols.

Lippincott's Gazetteer of the World, edited by Leon E. Seltzer. Columbia Univ. Press, 1962.

MÂDHAVA VIDYÂRAṆYA. *Śaṃkaradigvijaya* or *Saṃkshepaśaṃkarajaya*. Edited with Achyutarâya Moḍaka's commentary by pandits of the Ânandâśrama, Poona, 1891, 1915 & 1932.

Mahâbhârata (attributed to Vyâsa). Edited (with the *Harivaṇśa*) for the Asiatic Society of Bengal, Calcutta, 1834-39, 5 vols, 4to.—Ed. with comm. of Nîlakaṇṭha, by R. Kinjawadekar. Poona: Chitrachala Press, 1929-33, 6 vols.—Transl. by K. M. Ganguli and Pratap Chandra Roy. Calcutta: Bhârata Press, 1883-96, 12 vols.; 2nd ed., Calcutta: Datta N. Bose & Co., 1923, etc.—Transl. by M. N. Dutt. Calcutta: Elysium Press, 1895-1905, 18 vols.

Mahâvaṇśa. Edited by Wilhelm Geiger. London: for Pâli Text Society, Oxford Univ. Press, 1908 (Roman), *PTS* 63.—Transl. by G. Turnour (1799-1843) as *The Mahâwanso*, Ceylon, 1836, 1837. First Pâli text to be translated. Original in Roman characters.— Transl. by W. Geiger and Mabel Bode. London: Oxford Univ. Press, 1912. *PTS*., trans. ser. (3.).

MAJOR, R. H. (1818-1891), Editor, *India in the Fifteenth Century*, London, 1857. Includes Count Wielhorsky's English translation of Athanasius Nikitin's *Hozhdeniye* or Travelog.

MALALASEKERA, DR. GEORGE PEIRIS (1899-1973). *A Dictionary of Pâli Proper Names*. London: J. Murray, 1937-38, 2 vols.

MALIK MUḤAMMAD OF JÂ'ISI. Lived in the times of Jahângîr. Author of *Padmâvatî* written in Hindu verse.

MALTE-BRUN, CONRAD (1755-1826). *Précis de la géographie universelle*, 4th & rev. ed. by J. J. N. Huot, Paris, 1836-37.

MANRIQUE, FRAY SEBASTIAN (ca. 1590-1669). *Itinerario de las Misiones Orientales*, etc. (Rome, 1649, 4to.). Translated with introduction and Notes by C. Eckford Luard assisted by H. Hosten. London: Hakluyt Society, 1927, 2 vols.

Mānavadharmaśāstra or *Manusmriti.* Text critically ed. by J. Jolly. London: Trübner & Co., 1887. Trübner's Oriental Series.—Transl. by G. Bühler. Oxford: Clarendon Press, 1866, *SBE*, Vol. XXV.

MARTINEAU, JAMES (1805-1900). *Endeavours after the Christian Life,* 1843, 1847.—*Hours of Thought,* 1876, 1879.

MEYERBEER, GIACOMO (first known as Jakob Meyer Beer, 1791-1863). *Dinorah, oder die Wahlfahrt nach Plöermel.* Comic opera in three acts, played in Paris at the Opéra Comique, June 6, 1859.

MINAYEV, IVAN PAVLOVICH (1840-90). *Studies in the Phonetics and Morphology of the Pāli,* St. Petersburg, 1872.—*Journey to Ceylon and India,* St. Petersburg, 1878.—*Buddhism: Researches and Materials,* St. Petersburg, 1887. [Russian texts.]

MOLIÈRE, JEAN BAPTISTE POQUELIN (1622-1673). *Georges Dandin,* a farce, 1668.

MOREL, MAJOR. *A Few Days in 1857 in India.* Untraced.

Moskovskiya Vedomosty (Moscow Gazette). Newspaper published by the University of Moscow. Started April 26, 1756; daily since 1859. Edited since 1872 by M. N. Katkov, until his death in 1887.

MÜLLER, F. MAX (1823-1900). "Comparative Mythology," *in Chips from a German Workshop.* London: Longmans, Green & Co., 1867-75, 4 vols.; also New York, 1885.—"The Meaning of Nirvâna," in same work as above.—Lecture on Nirvâna in the *Trübner's American and Oriental Literary Record,* October 16, 1869.—*Sahitya Grantha.* Not definitely identified, but is likely to be some unpublished polemics between Müller and Swâmi Dayânanda Sarasvatî (cf. *The Secret Doctrine,* Vol. I, p. 360).

Mundakôpanishad. Transl. in *The Upanishads* by F. Max Müller. Part II, Oxford: Clarendon Press, *SBE,* Vol. XV.—Also in *The Twelve Principal Upanishads,* publ. by Tookaram Tatya, Bombay: Bombay Theos. Publ. Fund, 1891.

MURRAY, HUGH (1779-1846). *Historical Account of Discoveries and Travels in Asia, from the earliest ages to the present time,* Edinburgh, 1820, 8vo.

National Geographic Magazine. Map of China, 1945. Washington, D.C.

National Reformer. Edited by J. Barker and "Iconoclast" (C. Bradlaugh), London, 1860-64; new series, 1865-93.

NIKITIN, ATHANASIUS (d. 1472). *Hozhdeniye za tri morya* (Travel Beyond the Three Seas). See under Major, *Polnoye, Sofiyskiy* and Wielhorsky.

Our Conquerors, Who Are They? Pamphlet issued anonymously.

PAUL, DR. N. C. (in India as NAVÎNACHANDRA PÂLA). *A Treatise on the Yoga Philosophy,* 2nd ed., Calcutta: *Indian Echo* Press, 1883, ii, 52 pp. 8vo; 3rd ed. by T. Tatya, Bombay, 1888; *very scarce.*

PINKERTON, JOHN (1758-1826). *Modern Geography,* etc., London, 1802, 2 vols.; also ed. of 1804 and 1811.

Pioneer, The, "Official Report on the Hardvâr Mella," February 19, 1880.

POCOCKE, EDWARD (1604-1691). *India in Greece; or, Truth in Mythology,* London: J. J. Griffin, 1852.

Polnoye sobraniye russkih lyetopisey (Complete Collection of Russian Chronicles), publ. by the Archaeological Commission, St. Petersburg (pr. by Eduard Pratz), 1843, etc. Contains the original text of Athanasius Nikitin's *Hozhdeniye* or Travelog.

Preserver of the Five Chief Virtues, The. Untraced.

PRINSEP, JAMES (1799-1840). "Interpretation of the most ancient of the Inscriptions on the Pillar called the lât of Feroz Shâh, near Delhi, and of the Allâhâbâd, Radhia and Mattiah Pillar, or lât, inscriptions which agree therewith," in the *Journal of the Asiatic Society of Bengal,* Vol. VI, No. 67, July, 1837.

PUSHKIN, ALEXANDER SERGUEYEVICH (1799-1837). *Ruslan and Ludmila,* 1820.—*Zimniy vecher* (Winter Evening), 1825.

RAGHUNANDANA. *Śuddhitattva.* Untraced.

Râmâyana (attributed to Vâlmîki). Ed. by T. R. Krishnâchârya and and T. R. Vyâsâchârya. Bombay: Nirnaya-sâgara Press, 1911-13.— Transl. by Ralph T. H. Griffith. London: Trübner & Co., 1870-74, 5 vols.

RASPE, RUDOLF ERICH (1737-1794). *Adventures of Baron Munchausen.*
The original ed. of this shilling book of only 49 pages appeared in
London in 1875, entitled *Baron Munchausen's Narrative of his Mar-
vellous Travels and Campaigns in Russia.* Subsequent editions were
enlarged and expanded by various editors and publishers, the 7th
English edition of 1793 being the usual text.

Reading Library (in Russian: *Biblioteka dlya chteniya*), journal
founded by O. I. Senkovsky (1800-1858).

Ṛigveda-Saṃhitâ. Edited by F. Max Müller (Saṃhitâ and pada texts
in nâgari). 2nd ed., London: Trübner & Co., 1877, 2 vols. 8vo.—
—Transl. by H. H. Wilson. London: Trübner & Co., and Wm. H.
Allen & Co., 1850, 54, 57, 66, 88.—Transl. by R. T. H. Griffith.
Benares: E. J. Lazarus & Co., 1889-92.—Transl. by F. Max Müller
and Hermann Oldenberg. Oxford: Clarendon Press, 1891, 1897, *SBE*,
Vols. XXXII & XLVI.

Russkiy Vestnik (Russian Messenger). Monthly founded by M. N.
Katkov in 1856 and published at Moscow. Edited by other journalists after his death in 1887.

SCHÖPFFER, C. *Die Erde steht fest,* 5th ed., 1854.

Skandapurâṇa. Text in Roman in *Die Legende vom Devadâruvana* by
Wilhelm Jahn, *ZDMG* 69 (1915), and 70 (1916). No English translation.

Sofiyskiy Vremennik (Sophian Chronicle), edited by Paul Stroyev,
Moscow, 1820-21. Contains Athanasius Nikitin's *Hozhdeniye* or
Travelog.

STEVENSON, REV. JOHN, D.D. (1798-1858). Article in the *Journal of
the Bombay Branch of the Asiatic Society,* Vol. V, p. 322.

STRABO (63 B.C.—after 21 A.D.). *Geography.* Loeb Classical Series.

ŚUKADEVA. *Śukâshṭaka.*

TAGORE, RÂJÂ SURENDRONÂTH (or Sir Saurîndramohana Ṭhâkura). *On
the Music of the Âryans.* Not definitely identified under that title.

Taittirîya-Âraṇyaka. Of the Black *Yajurveda.* With the Comm. of
Sâyanâchârya. Edited by Râjendralâla Mitra. Calcutta, Asiatic So-

ciety of Bengal, 1872, in *Bibliotheca Indica.—Taittirîyasamhitâ*. Transl. by A. B. Keith. Cambridge, Mass.: Harvard Univ., 1914, *HSO*, 18, 19.

TAYLOR, DR. ALFRED SWAINE (1806-1880). *The Principles and Practice of Medical Jurisprudence*, London, 1865; also ed. of 1873, 1883, 1894 and 1928.

THORNTON, EDWARD (1799-1875). *A Gazetteer of the Territories under the Government of the East India Company, and of the Native States on the Continent of India*, 1854, 4 vols.; also 1857 and 1858; rev. & ed. by Sir R. Lethbridge, 1886, 8vo.

TOD, COL. JAMES (1782-1835). *Annals and Antiquities of Râjasthân*, etc. London: Smith, Elder & Co., 1829-32, two volumes; 2nd ed., Madras, 1873 rev. ed. in 2 vols., Calcutta: S. K. Lahiri & Co., 1894; London, Oxford Univ. Press, 1920, in 3 vols.—"De l'origine asiatique de quelques-unes des anciennes tribus de l'Europe, etc.," in *Journal Asiatique*, Paris, Vol. X, May, 1927.

TRAVANCORE, MAHÂRÂJA OF. "The Border Land between Matter and Spirit," in *The Theosophist*, Vol. VI, November, 1884.

TRIMBUK, BULWANT, "Hindu Music," *The Theosophist*, Vol. I, November, 1879.

Tripiṭaka (or *Tipiṭaka* in Pâli), meaning "Three Baskets." Chief Scripture of the Theravâda School of Buddhism. Issued by the Pâli Text Society. Consult also *SBE*, Vols. X, XI, XIII, XVII, XX.

Trübner's American and Oriental Literary Record, London, 1865, etc. See Müller, F. Max.

TURGENYEV, IVAN SERGUEYEVICH (1818-1883). *Fathers and Sons*, 1862.

TYNDALL, JOHN (1820-1893). "Scientific Use of the Imagination," "Scientific Materialism," "Belfast Address" (1874), all in *Fragments of Science*, 5th ed., New York: D. Appleton, 1884; 6th ed., 1891.

Vâstuśâstra. General title bearing on the subject of architecture and building. There is a work on the *Vâstuvidyâ* edited by T. Ganapati Sâstrî. Trivandrum: Travancore Government Press, 1913, in *TSS* 30.

Veda-Bhâshya. Monthly Journal published at Bombay by Svâmi Dayânanda Sarasvatî.

Vedântasâra (Sadânanda Yogîndra). Translated with copious annotations by Major G. A. Jacob. London: Trübner & Co., 1881. Trübner's Oriental Series; 2nd ed., 1888; 4th ed., 1904. Many other translations.

WESTERGAARD, NILS LUDWIG (1815-1878). Letter in the *Journal of the Bombay Branch of the Royal Asiatic Society*, Bombay, May, 1844.

WIELHORSKY, COUNT. His translation of Athanasius Nikitin's *Hozhdeniye za tri morya* (Travel beyond the Three Seas) is in R. H. Major's work, which see under MAJOR.

WILFORD, CAPT. FRANCIS (? -1822). "On Mount Caucasus," in *Asiatick Researches*, Calcutta, 1801, Vol. VI, pp. 455-539.

WILSON, REV. JOHN (1804-1875). Missionary of the Free Church of Scotland. *History of the Suppression of Infanticide in Western India under the Government of Bombay*, Bombay, 1855.

WILSON, HORACE H. (1786-1860). "On the Supposed Vaidik Authority for the Burning of Hindu Widows, and the Funeral Ceremonies of the Hindus" in the *Journal of the Asiatic Society of Great Britain and Ireland*, Vol. XVI, 1856, p. 201, and 1858-60, p. 209.

Yajurveda. See *Taittirîya-Âraṇyaka*.

YULE, SIR HENRY (1820-1889) and A. C. BURNELL (1840-1882). *A Dictionary of Anglo-Indian Colloquial Words and Phrases*, London, Murray, 1903.

Zend-Avesta. See under *Avesta*.

INDEX

INDEX

[In the alphabetical arrangement of sub-entries of various chief headings, the word "and" has been disregarded. References to definitions of terms are in italics.]

H

Hadês ("Ἀδης), and Pâtâla, 67.
Haeckel, E. H. P. A. (1834-1919):
363; and Virchow, 360.
—— Anthropogenesis, and Sham-
râo, 175 et seq.
Ḥâfiz (pseud. of Shams al-Dîn
Muḥammad, ca. 1300-1388), a
Sûfî, 419 fn.
Hahn, Yevgueniy Feodorovich, von
(1807-1874), xxiii.
Haidar (Arab.), lion, 213 fn.
Hair, various styles of, in India,
162 fn.
Ḥakîm (pl. ḥukamâ), native doctors, 452.
Hammamat, inscription on rock of,
130.
Hammir-Singh, King of Ceylon &
Padminî, 643, 643-44 fn.
Hanuman: 363, 364; "Abode of"
at Allâhâbâd, 345-46; as personified symbol of earthly man,
589 fn.; and Darwin, 39; monkey-god, 10; real meaning of,
& gods connected with it, 588;
and river Virajâ, 588; tail of, &
temple of Nâsik, 118-19; tail of,
as deus ex machina, 119; vâhana of Râma, 588; and Western
lands, 39.
Hanuman-Nâṭaka, drama of, 38.
Hanumanta bera, tree of Hanuman & its properties, 587-88,
589, 590-91.
Hanumanta Jayantî, birthday of
Hanuman, 589 & fn.
Hardvâr (or Hari-dvâra): cholera
at, 28; described, 261; Melâs at,
29 fn., 260.
Hardyman, General, takes Jubbulpore by cruel cunning, 302.
Hari: name of Śiva, 288; and
Râma, 613; the sun, 265; and
symbols of bull & cow, 613.
Hari-kâ-pairâ, stairs of Vishṇu at
Hardvâr, 263.

Hari-Krishṇa, scorching sun, 621.
Hari-Kulas, and origin of term
Hêrakleês, 265 & fn.; of Râjâ-
sthân, 620, 636.
Harimukh: Egyptian name for
Sphinx, & summit in Kashmîr,
265.
Haripura, City of the Sun, 622.
Hârîta, founder of Kauśika-gotra,
94 fn.
Harpy, Jigger-Khor as a, 641.
Hârûn al-Rashîd (766?-809), and
al-Maʿmûn, 511.
Hastings, Warren (1732-1818),
263 fn.
Hatha-Yoga: dangerous, 582;
dead-letter of, 583 fn.; as mod-
ern compromise of mysticism,
593.
Hatha-Yogins: 462, 580; as mediums with volition, 584 fn.;
and daṇḍas, 590; degrade meaning of sacred sciences, 596; indispensable conditions to become
an, 584; in error about real
cause of their powers, 591; of
Râjasthân, 640.
Hator, 131.
Haug, Martin (1827-76): biogr.
80 fn.; on antiquity of Aitareya-
Brâhmaṇa, 225.
He (or Nei), name for a deity,
419 & fn.
Headgears, of Indian crowd, 44-
45.
Healing, by herbs and tiger's claw,
348.
Heat: and heatstroke, 452; in Râjasthân, 443-44, 448, 547; and
a quarrel, 448 et seq.; relieved
by chewing certain leaves, 366-
67.
Heber , Reginald (1783-1826):
and Allâhâbâd, 330; biogr., 53
fn.; on Hindus as builders, 53,
512.
Hecata Triformis, and Gaurî, 623.

704   BLAVATSKY: COLLECTED WRITINGS

Newton, Sir Isaac (1642-1727), mistaken according to Dalvi, 164.

Niebuhr, B. G. (1776-1831), on Scythia, 224.

Night, moonlit, in India, 287-88.

Nikitin, Athanasius (d. 1472): biogr. 18 fn.; travels to India, 18-19 fn.

——*Hozhdeniye, etc.*, 18-19 fn.

Nîlanâth: blue god as name for Krishna & similarity with Osiris, 612.

Nirang, cow's urine, 613.

Nirvâna: *does not exist*, but *is*, 340; identical with Moksha, 336; is *nought* because it is *all*, 339; Müller confused on, 338; nature of, discussed, 336 *et seq.*; and paranirvâna, 566 fn.; synonymous to "name of God," 335 & fn.

Nishâda, note Ni on Hindu scale, 625.

Nizâm, 213.

Nizâm al-dîn Awliyâ' (1238-1325), Moslem saint, 405-06 & fn.

Nonita, statue of Krishna the child, 628-29.

Norendro-Das-Sen, Bâbû, 102.

Norma (Bellini), 90.

Norris, Judge, offends natives, 492-93.

North-West Provinces (now mostly Pakistan), *passim.*

Novoye Vremya (St. Petersburg), xxxvi *et seq.*

Nûr-Jahân (Mihr al-Nisâ, 1577-1645), 425 fn.

O

Objects, inanimate, moved by theurgic knowledge, 595.

Oboroten', Russian term for were-animals, 219 fn.

Observatory, of Jay-Singh II at Delhi, 408.

O'Connell, Daniel (1775-1847), leader of Irish Party, 491.

Oken, Lorenz (1779-1851), 364 & fn.

Olcott, Col. Henry S. (1832-1907): and Ânanda Svâmi, 570 *et seq.*; and durbâr painting, 500 *et seq.*; misadventure of, with cows, 630 *et seq.*; on H.P.B.'s Russian stories, xxxiii *et seq.*; and Râjput guards, 459-60; received medal for thesis on mechanics, 384; and śâlagrâma, 577-79, 585-86; and yoga practices, 461 *et seq.*

—— *Old Diary Leaves*: xxix, xxxvii, 29 fn.; on Dayânanda Sarasvatî, 29 fn.; on Sumangala, 334 fn.

Olla, palm leaf for writing, 526 & fn.

Olympus, gods of, originated in India, 609 *et seq.*

Omar II ('Umar bin-'Abdul Aziz, 8th cent.), ninth Umayyad caliph, conquers Sind, 510.

Oneness, of Parabrahman, 540.

Ôps, eye, 619.

Orchhâ, Râjâ of, 388.

Orientalists: at odds with each other, 248-49; confused on origin of Krishna, 607-08; not allowed into pagodas, 608; prejudiced, 614.

Orissa, 500.

Ormazd, Eye of, title of Sun, 3.

Orpheus: and Chinese Kui, 289; derived from *orphnos* (ὀρφνός), 298.

Oudh, nawâbs of, 404, 406.

Oulios, baneful, deadly, as name of Apollo of Delos, 612-13.

Our Conquerors, etc., on Sepoys' role in conquering India for the English, 489-90 fn.

Ouranos, as space, 612.

S

718 BLAVATSKY: COLLECTED WRITINGS